A BIRDER'S GUIDE TO BELIZE

by

Bert Frenz

American Birding

ASSOCIATION

Library of Congress Catalog Number: 2012955084
ISBN-13: 978-1-878788-45-0
First Edition
    1   2   3   4   5   6   7   8
Printed in the United States of America

Publisher
    American Birding Association, Inc.

Editor
    Paul E. Lehman

Associate Editors
    H. Lee Jones, Virginia Maynard

Maps
    Virginia Maynard and Cindy Lippincott

Cover Photograph
    FRONT COVER
    Keel-billed Toucan, the national bird of Belize
    © Bert Frenz, www.bafrenz.com

Other Photographs
    All black-and-white photos are by Bert Frenz.

Distributed by
    American Birding Association
    1618 W. Colorado Avenue
    Colorado Springs, Colorado 80904 USA
    phone: (800) 850-2473 or (719) 578-9703
    fax: (719) 578-1480
    www.aba.org

DEDICATION

I often wondered why books are repeatedly dedicated to spouses. I wonder no longer. Shari, my espoused non-birder, has put up with my keen—she uses the word fanatical—interest in birding for much of our married life and especially during the past decade when I have allocated most of my waking time to my avocation. She has accompanied me from Nome, Alaska, to Tikal, Guatemala, from the sandy beaches of tiny Half Moon Caye to the humid jungles of Cockscomb, from plush resorts to lodging without electricity and its toilets a seeming mile away in pitch darkness. And, recently she has endured my deaf ears while my eyes peer at a computer screen and my fingers transfer ten years of memories and notes into this book. So, without reservation, I dedicate this book to my wife, Shari.

ACKNOWLEDGMENTS

Although I toyed with the idea of writing this book years ago, it never would have come to fruition without the recommendation and support of Cindy Lippincott. She and her husband, Bob Berman, accompanied us on four of our Belize birding trips. Not only did their birding skills substantially contribute to finding many of the special birds and seeking out new birding sites, but also Cindy was the one to recognize that I had accumulated a lot of logistical knowledge that would be valuable to other birders as well.

Anyone who is familiar with birds and birding in Belize will recognize the name of H. Lee Jones. He is the author of the field guide, *Birds of Belize*, as well as many other relevant publications, and he continues as the regional editor for the Central America region in the journal *North American Birds*. Lee provided much of the supplementary background material and review for this book and was thereby essential to its completion. Personal correspondence and the opportunities to bird together at Cockscomb Basin Wildlife Sanctuary and Mayflower Bocawina National Park were both a thrill and a great source of information.

A third person I am pleased to acknowledge is Vladimir Rodriguez, formerly birding guide and now manager at La Milpa Ecolodge and Research Center. He has taught me many bird songs and important plants and habitats for finding birds, and he is an excellent model of what a first-rate birding guide should be.

A very thorough and helpful review of an earlier draft of the manuscript was provided by Michael A. Patten and Brenda D. Smith-Patten. I also thank Michael O'Brien for his insights and corrections. Barbara Ribble is duly acknowledged for her thorough review of the manuscript, correcting grammatical errors and making textual suggestions. Finally, I am indebted to Paul Lehman and Virginia Maynard for suggestions regarding earlier drafts, as well as seeing the book through to publication.

Compiling thousands of bird sightings certainly would not have been possible without a large number of contributors to whom I am indebted. Of special note are the detailed checklists from Israel Manzanero for Blue Hole National Park, Vladimir Rodriguez for Hill Bank and La Milpa, Steve N.G.

Howell for Monkey Bay, Roni Martinez for the Mountain Pine Ridge and Chiquibul areas, and Rick Romero for Hidden Valley, Mountain Pine Ridge, and Caracol. Many documents and bird accounts for northeast Belize were provided by Zoe Walker. The bird list for the Corozal area was reviewed and greatly supplemented by Graham Sampson, Germain Valladarez, and Jorge and Hugo Sanchez.

I thank the following individuals for field-trip reports and special sightings. These observers include the dozens of fellow birders who joined me on our lengthy birding trips: Doug Allen, Edward Allen, Taber Allison, Marge Anderson, Renner Anderson, John and Janice Armstrong, Neil Arnold, Christian Artuso, John and Pam Ash, Gustav Asplund, Mel and Beth Bailey, Philip Balderamos, Marygrace Barber, Olivier Barden, Sara Barker, Scott Barnes, Karen Barry, Millie Basden, Nick Bayly, Casey Beachell, Carol Beardmore, Raymond Belding, Bob Bell, Chris Benesh, Mike and Kay Berger, Bob Berman, Jason Berry, Jim and Dorothy Beveridge, Marguerite Bevis, Jessie Birckhead, Deb Bishop, Peter Blancher, Sid and Beryl Bloor, Bob and Heather Bobbitt, Peter Bono, Than Boves, Curtis Bradley, Bob and Pat Brandt, Donald Brightsmith, Charles Britt, Van and Karen Brown, Tim Brush, Robert Buchsbaum, Paul and Pat Buescher, Gene and Sandy Bullock, Rudi Burgos, Erneldo Bustamante, John Cahill, Peter Cahill, Rob Cahill, Bob and Juanita Candee, Mike and Jill Carle, Jay Carlisle, Duane Carmony, Mary Case, Neil and Mona Case, Karen Chiasson, Tom and Charlu Choate, Jim and Betty Church, Joyann Cirigliano, Darren Clark, Don and Helen Cline, Jim and Pat Coe, Teri Cohen, Steve Collins, Ron and Carol Conkey, Glenn Crawford, Robert Crawford, Doug Daniels, Forrest Davis, Richard Davis, Jorge de Leon, Ray and Nancy De Long, Martin Dellwo, Eric Demers, Jim Dennis, Jack Despres, Coen Dexter, Maggie Doster, Lily Douglas, Matt Dufort, Steve Dunbar, Jon Dunn, Stan and Darnelle Dunn, Kent and Linda Dunnam, Pete Dunne, Pete Dunten, Curtis Dykstra, Wayne Ealding, Roberto Echeverria, Tom Edell, Knut Eisermann, George Elford, Mike Ellis, Bob and Arlene Emrick, Marcus England, Bill Etter, Bob and Helen Ewald, Andrew Farnsworth, Todd Fellenbaum, Rob Fergus, Bert Filemyr, Ben Finegan, Robbie Fischer, John Fitch, Trina Fitzgerald, Dirk Francisco, Christian Friis, Ralph and Dorothy Fritzinger, Geraldo Garcia, Sandy Gennrich, Lenney Gentle, Jeff Gerbracht, Brian Gibbons, Lenard Gillett, Lori Gladulich, Jorge Gomez, May Gong, Leonard and Barbara Graf, Carl and Sandy Greenbaum, Alexander Grimwade, William Gruenbaum, Al Guarente, Seth Guikema, Mary Gustafson, Richard Guthrie, Mike Haldeman, Wayne Hall, John Hannan, Sam Harboldt, Jim Hardesty, Christopher Harris, Bill Hart, Michael Harvey, Chris Hatten, Charles Heese, Dave Herdegen, Armas Hill, Robert Hill, Ray Hillesheim, Rob Hirons, Stephen Hodgin, Jim and Ramona Hofmann, Clay and Joyce Holland, Edmond Holroyd, Jim Hoover, Adib Hoy, Rich Hoyer, Richard and June Hoyle, Dan Hubbard, Mark and Joanie Hubinger, Alison Huff, Pamela Hunt, Luz Hunter, Pablo Ical, Nelda and Gilford Ikenberry, Marshall Iliff, George Jett, Milo and Dee Johnson, Ron and Judy Johnson, Tom Johnson, Andy Jones, Ian Jones, Lee Jones, Paul Jones, James Kamstra, Adam Keats, Eugene Keferl, Jerry Kelly, Dave Klauber, Ed and Carlyn Kline, Oliver Komar, Bonnie Kot, Bruce Kronmiller, Wally and Virginia Landeck, David Larsen, Jim and Anne Lawrence, Russ and Margaret Lawson, Dan Leach, Jerry Ledbetter, Cindy Lippincott, James Lowther, Hilberto Lucero, Craig Lucker, Carl Lundblad, Eulene Lyttle, Steve and Cecile Magyar, Phillip Mai, Curtis and Michelle Manly, Glen Manzanero, Chris Marsh, Robert Martinez, Mike Matherly, Mike Mathews, Michael Mathieson, Sharon Matola, Audrey Mayer, Kent McFarland, Carol McKay, Alan and Donna McKenzie, Gordon and Maxine McLean, Joel McNeal, Mark McReynolds, Barbara Meding, Jan Meerman, Dusty Mellor, Carolyn Merchant, Alex Merritt, Basilio Mes, Orlando Meza, Bill Miller, Bruce Miller, Haynes Miller, Robert Miller, Steven Mlodinow, Don and Jean Molde, Joseph Morlan, Tom Morris, Brennan Mulrooney, Don and Gail Murphy, Lukas Musher, Wilfred Mutrie, Bruce Neville, Barbara Nevin, Andy Newman, Michael O'Brien, Chet Ogan, Luis Oliveros, Maynor Ovando, Ramon Pacheco, Donna Paino, Cindy and Dan Parliament, Michael Patten, Joanie Patterson, Joan Paulbeck, Guillaume Péron, Ryan Phillips, Sara Pike, Freddy Pineda, Bill and Ilse Plumley, Chester Pop, Joe Poston, John and Joanne Powles, Mark Pretti, Caleb Putnam, Judy Radocha, Frank Rider, Bob Ringler, Antonio Rodriguez, Stephen Rossiter, Daniel Roth, Jim Rowoth, Cliff Rummenie, Jeffrey Saffle, Alejandro Sagone, Anne Sammis, Graham Sampson, Larry Santos, David Sarkozi, Larry and Marlene Sazama, Tom and Edie Schall, Dan and Samantha Scheiman, John and Carol Schenck, Jill Schmidt, Daniel Schneider, Tom Schulenberg, Bob Schutsky, Glenn and Iris Scott, Ben and Willie Seibold, Charles Sellers, Yeray Seminario, Monica Setter, Don and Jodi Shannon, James Sipiora, Larry Sirvio, Jeff and Angela Skevington, Andrew Slater, Ken and Judy Smith, Brenda Smith-Patten, William Stein, Mike Stinson, Jessica Stokes, Chuck and Penny Suikki, Terry Swope, Lance Tanino, Mike Tanis, Bryan Tarbox, William Tarbox, Philip Taylor, Chris Tenney, Drew Thate, Peter and Millie Thomas, Jim Tietz, Sam Tillett, Fred and Cathy Tilly, Morgan Tingley, Francis Toldi, Ken and Jane Trease, Joel Trick, Jake Turin, Jerry and Doris Turner, Eric Tut, Jeronie Tut, Eddie Tzib, Jeronimo Tzib, Jonathan Urbina, Marvin Vasquez, Mark Vukovich, Christian Walker, Paul and Zoe Walker, Valerie Wallin, Nathaniel Wander, Heidi Ware, Linda Warschauer, Linda Widdop, Ralph and Dorothy Wiggers, James Williams, Sheri Williamson, Jan Wilson, Cole Wolf, Chris Wood, Doug Wood, Eric Wood, Paul Wood, Woody and Gwen Woodhouse, Brenda Wright, Lee and Pat Yoder, Larry and Carmen York, and Louise Zemaitis.

TABLE OF CONTENTS

INTRODUCTION 1
    Why Bird in Belize? 1
    Belize History 2
    Geography and Ecology 3
    Birding Suggestions 4
    Mammals, Reptiles, and Amphibians 12
    Getting There and Around 14
    Where to Stay 19
    Travel Tips 22
    How to Use This Guide 28
    Recommended Readings 30
    Supplemental Material 33

PHILIP GOLDSON HIGHWAY 35
    Corozal Area 38
    Sarteneja Road 41
    Cerros Maya Site and Copper Bank 45
    Shipstern Nature Reserve and Sarteneja National Tree Park . . 46
    San Victor Loop 50
    Gallon Jug Road, August Pine Ridge, and Blue Creek Village . . . 51
    La Milpa Ecolodge and Research Center 58
    Chan Chich Lodge 62
    Laguna Seca 67
    Honey Camp Road 67
    New River to Lamanai 68
    Lamanai Maya Site 73
    Hill Bank Field Station 78
    Crooked Tree Wildlife Sanctuary 81
    Altun Ha Maya Site and Old Northern Highway 87

GEORGE PRICE HIGHWAY 91
    Tropical Education Center, Belize Zoo Jungle Lodge,
      and Belize Zoo River Camp 93
    Belize Zoo 95
    Monkey Bay Wildlife Sanctuary 97
    Coastal Highway 100

Shrimp and Tilapia Farms 103
Fresh Catch Belize, Ltd. 104
Gales Point and Manatee Lagoons 105
Guanacaste National Park. 106
Pook's Hill 109
Maya Mountains. 111
Mountain Pine Ridge 115
Hidden Valley Inn 117
Thousand Foot Falls National Monument 119
Rio Frio Caves and Douglas Da Silva 120
Vaca Plateau 123
Chiquibul National Park and Las Cuevas Research Station . . . 123
Caracol Archaeological Reserve 125
Spanish Lookout and Aguacate Lagoon 127
San Ignacio Resort Hotel, Cahal Pech Maya Site, and
    Branchmouth Park 131
El Pilar Maya Site 133
George Price Highway Resorts 135
Macal River Resorts 138
Black Rock Lodge 139
The Lodge at Chaa Creek. 140
Belize Botanic Gardens and duPlooy's Jungle Lodge 141
Xunantunich Maya Site 143
Hydro Road and Arenal Road 144
Tikal National Park (Guatemala) 146

HUMMINGBIRD HIGHWAY 157
St. Herman's Blue Hole National Park 160
Five Blues Lake National Park 166
Dangriga 170
Gra Gra Lagoon National Park 173

SOUTHERN HIGHWAY 177
Mayflower Bocawina National Park 183
Hopkins Village Area 187
Cockscomb Basin Wildlife Sanctuary 190
Red Bank. 198
BFREE and Bladen River Nature Reserve 201
Nim Li Punit Maya Site 205
The Lodge at Big Falls 207
San Antonio Road and The Dump 208
Lubaantun Maya Site 211
Blue Creek and Blue Creek Cave 213
Río Blanco National Park 215
Pueblo Viejo Falls 215
Aguacaliente Wildlife Sanctuary 216

Jacinto Creek and Cuxlin Ha 219
Rio Grande, Belcampo Belize, and Wilson Landing 220
Cattle Landing 222
Joe Taylor Creek 223
Punta Gorda 225
Boom Creek Road and Hickatee Cottages 228
Santa Anna Road and Cotton Tree Lodge 230
Moho River, Boom Creek Village, and Santa Anna 231

THE CAYS 235
Ambergris Caye 237
Caye Caulker 240
Half Moon Caye Monument 245
Turneffe Atoll 247
Man-O'-War Caye and South Water Caye Marine Reserve . . 248

ANNOTATED CHECKLIST OF THE BIRDS OF BELIZE 251

SEASONAL ABUNDANCE OF THE BIRDS OF BELIZE
Bar Graphs by H. Lee Jones 308

APPENDIX A: Habitats and Ecoregions 336

APPENDIX B: Mammals, Reptiles, and Amphibians of Belize . . 348

APPENDIX C: References 352

APPENDIX D: Index of Birding Sites 357

INDEX 364

GAZETTEER 374

Gartered Trogon   Bert Frenz

INTRODUCTION

*I will proceed with firm resolution to attempt the being an author. It is a
terrible thing to me; far better am I fitted to study and delineate in the
forest, than to arrange phrases with suitable grammatical skill.*
John James Audubon, September 30, 1826, *The European Journals.*

WHY BIRD IN BELIZE?

Well, the birds of course. The spectacularly colorful are the first to grab
attention: aptly named Keel-billed Toucans, multi-colored fruit eaters
with oversized bills; noisy flocks of Red-lored and White-fronted Parrots in
flight and decorating tree canopies; petite buttery bundles of yellow-and-
white manakins snapping their wings as they cross a lek hidden on the jungle
floor; extravagant Blue-crowned Motmots with crafted long tails; sedate
Gartered and Slaty-tailed Trogons just waiting to be photographed. And it is
the appeal of finding another species at every turn in the trail, including dozens
of life birds in a few days, or 100+ in a week. Next it is the drab brown birds
that stimulate the challenge of birding in dark jungles for birds more easily
heard than seen. Finally, it is the nemesis birds, the ones we have missed on
prior trips and want one more crack at finding.

There are other reasons to choose Belize for your next birding trip. Its
scenic beauty is delightful, from 1,000-foot waterfalls, serpentine jungle rivers,
and transparent turquoise seas surrounding the longest barrier reef in the
northern hemisphere, with its brightly colored tropical fish, to the dark
tropical forests hiding monkeys, Kinkajous, coatis, and the more elusive
Jaguars and tapirs. Another appeal is the chance to explore the numerous and
impressive Maya sites, some carefully restored and others still enveloped in
deep jungles.

Between 65 and 70% of Belize is still covered by native forests and, in
contrast to the rest of Central America, much of the country is protected by
national parks and other conservation reserves. The United Nation's World

Database of Protected Areas for 2010 concluded that the protected area as a percent of total land area is about 28%. A conservation ethic is prevalent among the Belizeans, and it is noteworthy that two of the first five laws passed by the legislature upon the country's 1981 independence—the National Park System Act and the Wildlife Protection Act—were environmentally related.

One of the reasons Belize has been able to preserve its ecological resources is its relatively small human population (though currently at a high birth rate). Historically, upwards of a million Maya lived within the bounds of present-day Belize, but with the arrival of the Europeans came diseases that wiped out much of the native population. Considered more a source for extracting Logwood and mahogany than as a British colonial settlement, the area saw slow population growth. Even today, with just over 300,000 living in Belize, it is the least populated country in Central America. In fact, Belize has almost 10% more land than El Salvador, yet has only 4.3% the number of inhabitants. And, half the population is concentrated in Belize City and five other smaller towns, leaving the lush and relatively unscarred birding areas nearly vacant of people.

Lying just beyond Mexico, Belize City easily is accessed by a short flight from the southern US. Belize holds advantages for American birders over other tropical countries; for example, it is English-speaking, readily traveled and explored, its businesses accept US dollars, and it has a democratic government and friendly people. Compulsory education results in an adult literacy rate of 80 to 90%. Like Costa Rica, Belize receives substantial income from eco-tourism and has developed conservation attitudes that protect the environment. Birders are welcome!

BELIZE HISTORY

Once a land of raiding buccaneers and musket-carrying Spanish soldiers, of mahogany loggers and British colonialists, of ancient cities buried beneath dense jungles, Belize by a quirk of history has become the sparsely populated last frontier of Central America and a stronghold of tropical birds living in largely unspoiled habitats.

First explored 17 centuries ago by nomadic Paleo-Indians, its history is dominated by the Maya civilization at its peak from A.D. 300 to 900, the Classic Period. Large Maya cities, now popular birding sites, were once home to thousands: Cerros and Santa Rita in the north; Altun Ha, Lamanai, and La Milpa in central Belize; Xunantunich and El Pilar in the west; and Caracol, Nim Li Punit, and Lubaantun in the south. From a military tactical view, the dates A.D. 556 and 562 mark a high point when Lord Water of Caracol defeated Tikal.

By the time Columbus passed along the southern coast, the Maya had abandoned many of their great cities, yet some cities such as Lamanai remained inhabited still at the Spanish Conquest of 1546. Spanish missionaries constructed a church at Lamanai while soldiers continued to spread their control of the frontier. Meanwhile, the English started settlements as well, especially for the extraction of the dye-containing Logwood. In 1765 Captain James Cook visited Río Hondo and Four Mile Lagoon, which he called La Laguna de Cuatro Millas, and 33 years later the British defeated the Spanish for control of the region.

Disease imported by European colonists decimated the once-dominant Maya population, but many descendants of the survivors still live in what became a British colony (British Honduras) in 1840. Two decades earlier, the Garifuna—descendants of Carib Indians and Black African slaves—arrived from Honduras, and with the African slaves emancipated in 1838, they added another component to the population mix. Mennonite farmers from Mexico immigrated to northern Belize in 1958. British Honduras remained a crown colony until in 1964 self-government was granted, a name change was made to Belize a decade later, and complete independence was acquired on 21 September 1981. For more on Belize history, see the supplementary material entitled "Important Dates in Belize History" at www.bafrenz.com.

GEOGRAPHY AND ECOLOGY

Geography: Belize is slightly smaller than New Hampshire, slightly larger than El Salvador. Denali National Park and Preserve in Alaska is larger than the country of Belize. With a north-south length of 174 miles and a maximum width of 75 miles, it comprises 8,867 square miles (22,964 square kilometers). Wedged between Mexico on the north and Guatemala on the west and south, Belize includes a barrier reef about 15 miles offshore and stretching the length of the country. Its Mexican border is defined by the Hondo River and its southern border with Guatemala by the Sarstoon River, the western border being an arbitrary north-south line disputed between the governments of Belize and Guatemala. Although its population density is 34 people per square mile, most are concentrated in the coastal cities of Belize City, Dangriga, and San Pedro, and the inland towns of Orange Walk, San Ignacio, and its capital, Belmopan. Locations of cities and towns follow a pattern set down since the settlement of the Maya, who used the seacoast and rivers to transport trade goods, a tradition carried on by the British during the extraction of timber logs for export.

Northern Belize is the southern extension of Mexico's Yucatán Peninsula, and it shares the same properties of a flat lowland coastal plain, although with higher rainfall than its northern component. Along Philip Goldson Highway, elevation varies little within its extremes of 9 to 36 feet, and when heading westward along the Gallon Jug Road toward Mexico the elevation does not rise until the Rio Bravo Escarpment near the Guatemala border at 300 to 500 feet.

The coastal plain continues south to Punta Gorda and the southern border with Guatemala, but the southern half of Belize includes the Maya Mountains in the interior, rising to an elevation between 2,300 and 3,700 feet The highest peaks are Victoria Peak (a two-to-three-day hike south from Cockscomb Basin) and remote and nearly inaccessible Doyle's Delight.

Some 200 cays (pronunced *keys*) range from tiny to mid-sized, the largest being Caye Caulker at five miles by one-half mile. The much larger 25-mile-long Ambergris Caye is not a true cay but a long, narrow peninsula. It became a "cay" only when the ancient Maya dug a narrow canal across its northern end to connect Chetumal Bay with the sea. Ambergris Caye is the most commercialized, and the next being Caye Caulker—the only two cays with a population base. San Pedro on Ambergris Caye has an estimated population of over 10,000 people.

Climate: Belize weather is warm, moist, and tropical. Rain falls in Belize City about half of the days from June to October, but on average only four days in April and five in March. Rainfall varies by latitude, with annual rainfall of 51 inches (130 cm) in Corozal, 79 inches (201 cm) in Belize City, and 177 inches (450 cm) in Punta Gorda (Beletsky 2005).

Mean temperatures in Belize City are lows of 68°F (20°C) to highs of 82°F (28°C) during the winter months from December to February, and lows of 76°F (24°C) to highs of 89°F (32°C) during the summer months from May to August. By contrast, Mountain Pine Ridge has average lows of 63°F (17°C) in December and 71°F (22°C) in May.

Habitats: The type of forest found in a given area depends largely on soil and rainfall. Northern and coastal Belize has mainly pine or pine/oak broken-canopy forests and savanna, lying on dry sandy soils, whereas the karst foothills of central and eastern Belize support vastly different tree species. Belize lies within the subtropical belt, the northern component of the tropics, and as such, it experiences greater variation in temperature, humidity, and rainfall than does the equatorial tropics. A detailed discussion of habitats is included in Appendix A.

BIRDING SUGGESTIONS

When to visit: Most birding visits to Belize occur during February and March, the driest portion of the dry season. The wet season extends from June through November and sometimes into January. While the wet season starts dramatically with one to several days of heavy rain in spring, summer thundershowers gradually change in fall with cold fronts that bring lighter rain over longer periods, diminishing over a several-month period anywhere from November to February. Annual rainfall, most of which falls during July and August, ranges from 51 inches in the north to 177 inches in the south, although there is quite a bit of annual variation. During the wet season many of the roads leading to birding sites are too muddy for normal passenger vehicles. Temperatures are warmest along the coast and coolest in the hills—although not substantially so—with the coldest month being January and the warmest being May.

Travel Journals – Author's Note: In this book, I have included a number of excerpts from my daily journals written during our Belize visits. Primarily, their inclusion is intended to give the reader a feel for birding sites, including the habitats, logistical issues, species highlights, and bird stories that often do not come through as vividly in a traditional text description. They are meant to leave you with the feeling of "having been there."

Birders visiting from early December to mid-March will likely miss almost all passage migrants except Purple Martin. By mid- to late March nesting species such as Swallow-tailed and Plumbeous Kites, Streaked, Sulphur-bellied, and Piratic Flycatchers, and Yellow-green Vireos have returned from South America. The nesting season extends from March to the early rainy season in July. The spring movement of neotropical migrants, particularly shorebirds and passerines, extends from March to early June. Strategically, the suggestions included in this book are independent of season. Passage migrants move through all of Belize; however, for most species the cays see substantially more traffic than does the mainland. For example, during migration, Swainson's Thrush is relatively uncommon on the mainland but is common on the cays. Likewise, Bay-breasted Warbler is uncommon on the mainland but is a fairly common migrant on the cays. Birding during peak migration can be spectacular, as shown by several examples on the cays: 20 Yellow-billed Cuckoos on 28 April, 40 Ovenbirds on 29 September, 110 Common Yellowthroats on 18 October; or on the mainland with thousands

SEASONALITY FOR CHOOSING BEST BIRDING VISIT												
		Most Birding Visits										
	Coolest Month				Warmest Month							
			Spring Migration					Fall Migration				
		Driest Months				Wettest Months						
	Dry Season					Rainy Season						
			Nesting Season									
DEC	JAN	FEB	MAR	APR	MAY	JUN	JUL	AUG	SEP	OCT	NOV	

of Dickcissels at New River Lagoon on 22 April and 1,000–3,500 Eastern Kingbirds daily at Punta Gorda from mid- to late September. Use the Annotated Checklist and the Bar Graphs to find the best locations and timing for specific species.

Planning your itinerary: A frequent comment made by birders who plan their own itineraries is that they tried to cover too much territory in too short a time. The most relaxing one-week trip would be to stay at one hotel/resort and conduct day trips from that location. Splitting the week between two lodging sites would probably be satisfactory for most birders. A two-week trip could accommodate four lodging locations, or maybe five if they are relatively close together. Consider the following areas for lodging from which you can reach good birding sites:

- Orange Walk / Crooked Tree
- La Milpa / Chan Chich
- George Price Highway (eastern portion near Belize City)
- San Ignacio area
- Tikal
- Mountain Pine Ridge
- Dangriga area
- Punta Gorda area

This list by no means covers all good birding areas, so obviously it would take a longer stay or multiple visits to achieve a more thorough coverage of Belize's birding possibilities.

Christmas Bird Counts: Four Christmas Bird Counts (CBCs) are held in Belize and can be an excellent way to meet and bird with local and visiting birders. These one-day events canvass 15-mile diameter circles encompassing Gallon Jug, Belmopan, Punta Gorda, and an area northwest of Belize City. To participate, contact the CBC compiler for the particular count. Contacts can be found at www.audubon.org/bird/CBC/.

Best times for birding: Tropical birds are most active at sunrise and just before sunset. Getting out an hour or so before sunrise is good for hearing owls and nightjars and increases one's odds of seeing, not just hearing, tinamous, wood-quail, quail-doves, and mammals. As sunlight begins to illuminate and warm the crowns of trees, look for birds feeding on fruiting trees. By mid-morning, head into the shaded forest where it is cooler to watch for woodcreepers, antbirds, flycatchers, and others that rarely leave the deep shade. But be sure to find an opening to the sky starting about 9:30 AM, when rising air currents lift raptors upward. By late morning, most birds retire to hidden perches, and birding almost comes to a standstill. It's a good time to check out flowers and feeders for hummingbirds. After lunch, take a siesta. Alternatively, find a secluded deep-forest site, sit on your portable three-legged stool, and see what passes by. If you venture out again in mid-afternoon (around 2:30 PM), your best luck would be to go to the deep forest to find an ant swarm and its attendant parade of birds. You may spend a week or more of birding before you come upon a swarm, but it will be a highlight of your trip. From late afternoon until dusk, the birds will again become active and you quite likely will add a handful or two of species to your day list.

When darkness is complete, try owling, either on foot or from an open vehicle. In remote areas, night birding can be rewarding for owls, nightjars, and potoos, as well as for an appreciable number of mammals such as Kinkajous, various opossums, Northern Tamanduas, Pacas, Gray Foxes, and White-tailed Deer.

Daylight hours at Belize City are as follows:

Belize City:	Sunrise	Sunset
• January	6:23–6:25	17:30–17:47
• February	6:25–6:12	17:48–17:59
• March	6:11–5:50	17:59–18:05
• April	5:47–5:27	18:06–18:13
• May	5:27–5:17	18:13–18:23
• June	5:17–5:22	18:23–18:31
• July	5:22–5:32	18:31–18:27
• August	5:32–5:39	18:26–18:07
• September	5:39–5:43	18:07–17:43
• October	5:43–5:51	17:42–17:22
• November	5:52–6:07	17:21–17:16
• December	6:07–6:23	17:17–17:28

Habitats: As any experienced birder knows, the more habitats visited, the more species are found. Although a botanist undoubtedly would use a more complex system, for the birder's perspective the habitat types classified by Jones and Vallely (2001) are more useful. Here is their classification scheme, with some examples from in this book.

Forested Habitats	Examples
submontane broadleaf forest	Caracol, Las Cuevas Research Station
lowland broadleaf forest (includes high second growth)	La Milpa, Chan Chich, Blue Hole, Mayflower Bocawina, Red Bank
submontane pine forest	Mountain Pine Ridge, including Hidden Valley and Thousand Foot Falls
lowland pine forest	Crooked Tree, Old Northern Highway, August Pine Ridge, Southern Highway
mangrove and littoral forest	Gra Gra Lagoon National Park, Joe Taylor Creek, Caye Caulker, New River ferry

Transitional Habitats	*Examples*
scrub, low second growth	Copper Bank, Five Blues Lake road, Old Northern Highway
savanna (pine, oak, calabash, palmetto)	August Pine Ridge, Tropical Education Center, Coastal Highway

Unforested Habitats	*Examples*
cultivated land, pastureland, fallow fields, ornamental/ landscaped vegetation (parks, towns, villages)	Spanish Lookout, San Victor loop, Belize Botanic Gardens, San Ignacio, Pelican Beach Resort (Dangriga)
wetlands with emergent vegetation (sedge savannas, wet meadows, marshes, ricefields)	Blue Creek rice fields, Aguacaliente Wildlife Sanctuary, Edenthal-Neustadt, Sittee River loop, The Dump
lagoons, ponds, rivers, streams	Crooked Tree, New River, Laguna Seca, Four Mile Lagoon, Moho River
beaches, sandflats, mudflats, aquaculture farms	Corozal beach, Nova shrimp farms, Dangriga, Ambergris Caye, Caye Caulker
ocean	Inner Channel, Man-O'-War Caye, offshore reefs

Certainly, habitat determines what species might be present. Yet so does rainfall. Thus, a drier lowland broadleaf forest at La Milpa in Orange Walk District supports a somewhat different assemblage than does the wetter broadleaf forest of Cockscomb Basin in Stann Creek District or the still wetter forest of Lubaantun in Toledo District. Some species are common in northern Belize, rare in central Belize, and never found in southern Belize, and vice versa. Ecoregions, i.e., geographic regions containing similar habitat, are discussed more fully in Appendix A.

Using plants to find birds: If you closely watch a good birding guide, you will notice that he or she knows where flowers are blooming and trees are fruiting and heads the group in that direction. Probably the most productive flower for birdfinding in Belize is the prolific *Combretum fruticosum* (Combretacae), variously called Curassow Crest, Orange Flame Vine, or Chameleon Vine. It can host a dozen birds of many species on a single blanket of blooms.

Seen from miles away, the yellow blooms of the native tree Quamwood blanket the hillside canopies. Quamwood attracts pollinating hummingbirds and flower-eating Crested Guans, a species locally known as quam. Scarlet Macaws are canopy feeders, seeking out the fruit of Polewood (*Xylopia frutescens*). Watch the attractive red flowers of Tiger's Claw (*Erythrina indica*) for Long-billed Hermits, banana tree flowers for Violet Sabrewing, and ornamental *Heliconia* species for other hummingbirds. Bamboo thickets attract Yellow-billed Cacique, and if you find a patch of Spiny Bamboo growing in central Belize, you might chance upon Blue Seedeaters or Slate-colored Seedeaters.

Flycatchers, manakins, euphonias, tanagers, and especially hummingbirds are attracted to a very common shrub called Polly Red-Head, Scarlet Bush, or Firebush (*Hamelia patens*), which at all seasons displays small tubular flowers and dark purple fruit when ripe. The easily recognized paired fruits of Cojoton or Huevo de Caballo (*Stemmadenia donnell-smithii*) provide food for parrots, vireos, tanagers, and honeycreepers. Olive-throated Parakeets feed on the pink blossoms of Stinking Toe (*Cassia grandis*).

The tiny pinkish-red flowers of Moho or Mahowa (*Trichospermum grewiifolium*) trees readily attract hummingbirds and honeycreepers. As a pioneer tree, it grows along roadsides and in large clearings in the forest. Another bird attractant are the fruits of the strangler fig. These *Ficus* species have the curious cycle of starting life high in tree branches and extending roots around and fusing to the host tree before the roots reach the ground, and remaining long after the host tree has died and rotted away.

The Trumpet Tree, often called by its genus name *Cecropia*, offers fruit popular with many birds, Kinkajous, and other animals. Its big leaves and open canopy also make it a convenient marker for describing a bird location to accompanying birders. It is one of the first trees you will learn in the American tropics. For photos of Belize trees and flowers visit www.bafrenz.com.

Birding at resorts where you are not a guest: With very few exceptions, lodges, resorts, and hotels in Belize allow visitors to bird their properties, even if they are not guests of the establishment. These places often are the best birding opportunities locally available. Here's why: extensive plantings of flowers and fruiting trees are not only attractive, but they also draw and concentrate many birds that otherwise might require a longer search to find; resorts and lodges are situated on expansive acreage

Protocol: Even though most managers and owners ask nothing in return for the privilege of birding their properties, it is only proper not to abuse this generous offer. The easiest way to arrange and compensate a visit is as follows: (1) contact the establishment a day beforehand if you are an individual or small party, a month before if you are a larger group, and ask permission to bird, (2) ask where you can bird and what areas you should avoid early in the morning while guests are sleeping, (3) make reservations for lunch at their restaurant, and (4) book any tours or rentals that interest you. Lunch is typically about US$10 at most places—although it can be as high as US$30 at the most exclusive resorts—and it likely will be a delicious meal in the generous quantity that we normally expect for an evening dinner. The birding opportunity is well worth the price of a meal, and both parties are happy with the arrangement.

and often include groomed trails, creek and river frontage, primary forest, or well-established secondary forest; and they provide facilities such as bathrooms, restaurants, canoe rentals, and guided tours.

Ant swarms: Finding an ant swarm will make your day! Not only is it likely to include otherwise elusive bird species, but they are so engaged in frenzied feeding that you can watch them at your leisure. Here's an example:

Cockscomb Basin, 27 February journal entry: We have stumbled on an ant swarm, an event high on every tropical birder's wish list. The first bird I recognize is a Bright-rumped Attila, followed by a succession of other birds quickly hopping through the tangled underbrush. Each look is but a few seconds and in light dimmer than one candlepower. Even though we can see only about 20 feet into the snarled web of leaves, roots, vines, and branches obstructing the view, the ant swarm produces a constantly revolving scene of many male and female Red-throated and Red-crowned Ant-Tanagers, Ruddy and Tawny-winged Woodcreepers, two Melodious Blackbirds, and two Gray-headed Tanagers. Even better is a brown bird with a distinct dark mark running from its eye to the back of its head. . .Buff-throated Foliage-gleaner. Back to watching the show, we add both sexes of Barred Antshrike, Dot-winged Antwren, Dusky Antbird, Eye-ringed Flatbill, and a couple of Spot-breasted Wrens to the entertainment list. Also Hooded Warbler and a female White-collared Manakin, Black-and-white Warbler, and a Smoky-brown Woodpecker.

Forty-five minutes have passed when I notice spiders racing across the footpath. I think nothing of the first few, but when the spiders continue to escape I become aware that the ant swarm is headed my way and the spiders lead the panicky crowd. This is the reason birds follow ant swarms. The birds aren't after the ants, but rather the birds are after the other insects and spiders uprooted by the armies of ants marauding their home sites.

When the show finally plays out after an hour, we list the birds we've identified, including a large woodcreeper, probably Ivory-billed, and the species heard while we watched: Rufous-breasted Spinetail, Gray-chested Dove, Blue Ground-Dove, and Short-billed Pigeon. When I total the list, I've recorded 22 species at or near the ant swarm.

Mixed-species flocks: Another serendipity while birding in the tropics is to come upon a mixed-species flock. Birding can be transformed from a dull hour of finding almost nothing to a bonanza of dozens of birds simultaneously.

[Caracol, 22 February] When we see a Black-throated Shrike-Tanager in close proximity to an Olivaceous Woodcreeper, we know we might be on to something good. In quick succession we find Golden-crowned Warbler and Tawny-winged Woodcreeper. More birds are flitting through the understory, in and out of view. . . . Black-and-white Warbler, Worm-eating Warbler. . .We stand in a clearing of the dense forest that surrounds Caracol Maya ruins; the birds move along the periphery of the cleared path and now follow it as it turns along the entrance way. . . .Red-throated Ant-Tanagers, Ivory-billed Woodcreepers. . .We walk slowly, keeping pace with the feeding flock. . .Yellow-bellied Flycatcher, Lesser Greenlet. Each time I see the shrike-tanager, I know we are staying with the mixed flock, for it is the sentinel, the one keeping the flock oriented. The momentary flashes of

wings and bodies give us partial clues to identifying the birds: Eye-ringed Flatbill, Hooded Warbler, White-breasted Wood-Wren. Most move so quickly and so many different species are present that it takes us many minutes to put the pieces together and be sure what we are seeing: Sulphur-rumped Flycatcher, Plain Xenops, Wedge-billed Woodcreeper. . .Using our radios, we call again to the others who are exploring the ruins or resting at the picnic area. . .White-whiskered Puffbird, Dot-winged Antwren, Magnolia Warbler. . .Others join us. . . Olive-backed Euphonia, Chestnut-sided Warbler, Bright-rumped Attila. Now we get down to the hard species, the new ones, the ones we are slow at identifying: Buff-throated Foliage-gleaner, Dusky Antbird, Sepia-capped Flycatcher, and finally the one that thrills me the most, a pair of Plain Antvireos. When we gather for lunch at the picnic tables, with birders calling out names, I write down the list of birds in the mixed flock. It comes to 26 species observed during the one hour we watched them feeding together. The best I've ever seen!

Identifying birds by ear. A birder trying to find warblers on their nesting grounds in the US and Canada knows the advantage of recognizing their songs. Even more so, a birder in the tropics is immensely more successful if he or she has studied bird vocalizations. The showy birds that favor sunny exposed habitats are readily identified by sight, but the elusive drabber birds that hide in the dense jungles frequently go unseen and unidentified if you or your guide does not recognize bird songs. A source for world bird songs, including Belize, is the growing number of shared bird songs at www.xeno-canto.org.

Four excellent collections of bird vocalizations cover many of the species you are likely to encounter in Belize:

- *A Bird Walk at Chan Chich.* Recorded by John V. Moore, the jacket describes the cassette tape as "Vocalizations from 150 species of birds plus selected mammals recorded in northwestern Belize, Central America." A list of included species can be found on: http://johnvmoorenaturerecordings.com/pubs/ChanChich/main.htm. An updated version with four additional species and more vocalizations is now available on CD.

- *Bird Songs of Belize, Guatemala, and Mexico.* A cassette tape containing recordings of nearly 70 species made by Dale Delaney and produced by the Library of Natural Sounds, Cornell Laboratory of Ornithology.

- *Songs from a Belizean Rainforest.* A CD including 93 tracks of over 100 species recorded in the Columbia River Forest Reserve in southern Belize.

- Produced with a different intent—mainly as an introduction to the birds of Belize—a DVD by Wayne Hall entitled *The Birds of Belize* is a collection of video recordings with audio. Regularly updated, version 8.0 includes 277 species. In addition to a visual guide, the accompanying audio tracks provide a facile tool for learning the calls and songs at the same time as viewing the species. Videos can be viewed at www.youtube.com/user/BelizeBirds. Proceeds from DVD sales benefit Mayflower Bocawina National Park and the

DVDs are sold for US$10 at the park headquarters as well as at other Belize outlets such as Cockscomb Basin, Belize Zoo, and Hickatee Cottages. Contact Wayne Hall, 2411 Ingra Street, Anchorage, AK 99508; 907-278-2122; shadow@matnet.com.

Reporting rarities: The checklists included in the appendices can serve as a guide for the rarity of birds in Belize. In 2001, Lee Jones wrote, "Central America is a new frontier with every bit the sense of discovery and excitement as New York in Ludlow Griscom's day or California in the 1960s." Each year new species are added to the Belize list. If you encounter a rare or out-of-range species, please report it to the appropriate regional editor for *North American Birds*, a quarterly ABA publication. Include the date of sighting, number seen/heard, specific location, observers, and a detailed description of the bird. If possible, include a photograph or sound recording. For Belize and other Central American countries, contact H. Lee Jones, 901 East Washington Street, Suite 126, Colton, California 92324; lee_jones@att.net.

Consider submitting your trip lists to eBird. All species entries can further our understanding of geographic range. Consult the ecoregional checklists (see www.bafrenz.com), and for locally lesser-known species, keep or submit notes on your sighting, including specific location and not just district.

MAMMALS, REPTILES, AND AMPHIBIANS

Most wildlife is protected by Belize law. Habitats supporting non-avian wildlife are large, contiguous and well-preserved, and human pressures (hunting, poaching, collecting) are relatively low. As a result, the chances of seeing non-avian fauna are relatively high. In trips led by the author, a total of 30 mammal species were seen in Belize. With more time spent in Mexico, over a considerably larger area and a greater variety of habitats, the tour groups have seen only 20 mammal species.

Some mammals such as Yucatan Squirrels and White-nosed Coatis are conspicuous and not easily missed. Others are shy, such as Northern Tamanduas, and will seek cover if approached by a large group, so they are most often seen by single persons birding quietly. Many are nocturnal, such as Kinkajous and opossums, and are most often found while owling with bright flashlights. Jaguars are found by persistence and luck. Mammals, such as Baird's Tapir, that are rare, nocturnal, and shy are the hardest to find, but you can find their footprints.

Among the reptiles, the easiest to find are Morelet's Crocodiles on the rivers, American Crocodiles in coastal brackish water habitats, Green Iguanas sunning in riverside trees, Striped Basilisks racing across water, Festive Ameiva and various anoles seeking dense cover, spiny-tailed Brown

Green Iguana   Bert Frenz

Iguanas in drier habitats, and a small number of snakes most often encountered while driving the back roads. Occasionally, Boa Constrictors can be found lounging on riverside bushes or seeking prey in the denser forests. Central American River Turtles escape underwater from sunning spots on nearly submerged roots and branches when disturbed by a canoe or kayak. While hiking through tropical forests, one occasionally can find Rainforest Frogs in the leaf litter. When owling near ponds or streams, you can sometimes hear Marine Toads, also called Cane Toad but more commonly referred to by its pre-2006 scientific name *Bufo marinus*. Its vocalization is distinctly similar to Vermiculated Screech-Owl. Harmless geckos are often heard and seen in rooms and near buildings. Numerous anoles and lizards are commonplace, the most noteworthy being the Striped Basilisk, commonly called the Jesus Christ Lizard because of its ability to run so quickly across the surface of water to avoid sinking.

Several good reference books covering mammals, reptiles, and amphibians are listed later in this chapter in the Recommended Readings section. A checklist of species, including scientific names, is included in Appendix B. Photos are at www.bafrenz.com.

GETTING THERE AND AROUND

By *air:* Philip Goldson International Airport in Ladyville (a northern suburb of Belize City) is about a two-and-a-half-hour flight from the US. Direct flights leave from:

- Miami via American Airlines
- Dallas/Fort Worth via American Airlines
- Houston via United/Continental Airlines and TACA
- Atlanta via Delta Airlines
- Charlotte via US Airways (weekends or reduced schedule)

TACA flights from the West Coast stop at San Salvador. A less expensive alternative to flying into Belize is to fly to Cancun, Mexico, then take a first-class Mexican bus to Chetumal, and then a Belizean bus to Belize City or other destinations.

Domestic planes serve many locations. The predominant airlines are Maya Island Air (M) and Tropic Air (T) and they serve: Philip Goldson International (M,T), Belize City Municipal (M,T), Belmopan (T), Caye Caulker (M,T), Caye Chapel (M), Corozal (M,T), Dangriga (M,T), Flores in Guatemala (M,T), Hidden Valley (T), Kanantik (T), Placencia (M,T), Punta Gorda (M,T), Rio Dorado (T), San Pedro on Ambergris Caye (M,T), San Pedro Sula in Honduras (M), Sarteneja (T), and Savannah (M).

There are also direct flights from Corozal to Ambergris Caye and thence to Caye Caulker. Most hotels on Ambergris Caye will arrange air travel for you at no extra cost.

Each of the two Belize airlines offers flights from Philip Goldson International Airport and from Belize Municipal Airport in Belize City. Flights are cheaper from Municipal Airport, and for a party of four sharing a taxi between the two airports, the savings in airfare are enough that you should consider the alternatives. The airports are nine miles apart and taxi fare is about US$20. The many other private airstrips in Belize are accessible by chartered airplanes. Also available is charter helicopter service, for aerial sightseeing and access to remote locations. Contacts:

- Maya Island Air Regional, Municipal Airport, Building #1, 2nd Floor, Belize City; (011) 501-233-1140; fax (011) 501-223-1722; info@mayaislandair.com; www.mayaislandair.com.
- Tropic Air, P.O. Box 20, San Pedro, Belize; (011) 501-262-2012 or toll-free in US: 800-422-3435; fax (011) 501-226-2338; reservations@tropicair.com; www.tropicair.com.
- Astrum Helicopters; Cisco Base, Mi2le 3.5 Price (Western) Highway, Belize City; (011) 501-222-5100 or toll free in US: 888-278-7864; info@astrumhelicopters.com; www.astrumhelicopters.com.

By ship: As of 2011, six cruise-ship lines visit Belize: Carnival Cruise Lines, Celebrity Cruise Lines, Holland America Cruise Lines, Norwegian Cruise Lines, Princess Cruise Lines, and Royal Caribbean Cruise Lines. Each of the 20 different cruise ships carry 2,000 to as many as 4,300+ passengers. According to the Belize Tourism Board, annual passenger total peaked in 2004 at 851,436, but it was still over 750,000 in 2011. Cruises take place any month of the year and typically are between 7 and 11 days in length. The 2011 schedule showed 273 ship arrivals at Belize City, the majority in port on Wednesdays and Thursdays. However, all visits to Belize are one day only, from 7 or 8 AM to 4, 5, or 6 PM.

Few birds are seen from the larger ships, the most common being frigate-birds, pelicans, and cormorants. With only a few hours to see the country, birding opportunities are minimal. Of the shore excursions available, your best bets would be Lamanai or Altun Ha, although neither visit will do justice to the birding opportunities at these sites, as the trips are often rushed and the guides may have little interest in stopping for birds. Yet one birder reported seeing 75 species on a Lamanai trip in 2007. Sometimes a shore excursion to Crooked Tree is offered, but it may not meet the minimum number of participants required. Another option that has been tried successfully is to hire a local cab for a day trip to Crooked Tree Wildlife Sanctuary for about US$150. You could also rent a boat when you get there, but you would find more birds from land in the short time available.

By rental car: More than a dozen car-rental companies offer vehicles, and one of them allows you to take the vehicle to Tikal, Guatemala (see below). For a list and contacts, check out www.travelbelize.org, select "plan your visit," "getting around," "by road," and "vehicle rental" in that order. Almost all of these companies operate out of Belize City, although some also have offices in Dangriga, Placencia, and San Ignacio.

If you intend to stay only on the major highways—note, Coastal Highway is not a major highway—all of which are now paved, then you can rent a sedan. Because many models come with a paved-road-only restriction, this substantially limits where you can bird. You will be much better off if you rent a four-wheel drive high-clearance SUV or truck.

Belize law requires all vehicles to be covered by liability insurance, although collision insurance is optional. Car-rental companies charge a high premium for this insurance and it may add 20% to the rental cost. You may have a credit card or insurance policy that covers collision insurance on rental vehicles, but it might cover you only for "bound surfaces." You will find many unpaved roads in Belize, especially if you are a birder. It's a judgment call though, as traffic in Belize is limited except along George Price Highway. If you intend to cross into Guatemala for a visit to Tikal, be sure this trip is allowed by the rental-car company. Apparently, only Crystal Auto Rentals (www.crystal-belize.com) permits travel across the border, and vehicle insurance lapses once you cross. See the section on Tikal for alternative transportation.

If you are staying at a resort you can usually ask them to make transportation arrangements for you. If they are handling your birding activities as well, you probably will not need to rent a vehicle. Nonetheless, while your stay at one or more resorts may occupy the majority of your visit, you may still want to explore a few birding sites on your own in transit between the airport and resorts, for which the autonomy of a rental car would be advantageous.

By bus: Bus travel is a very common mode of transportation for Belizeans. Service along main highways is usually hourly, sometimes half-hourly during peak times. Regular buses (Bluebird school buses) have cheap fares and you can stop anywhere along the route. Express non-stop buses may be air-conditioned and serve only the main towns. Schedules and fares can change at any time. Details on bus transportation can be found at http://belizebus.wordpress.com/.

By RV or automobile from the US: Many travelers are surprised that you can drive by RV or automobile from the US to Belize. Nonetheless, an increasing number of birders have done just that. By car, traveling all daylight hours, it takes about three days from South Texas to Belize. A more leisurely trip, with a couple of stopover birding days, takes about one week. A typical route would start near McAllen, Texas, and make Mexico stops at Tampico, Poza Rica, Veracruz, Villahermosa, Palenque (optional), and Chetumal. The best road map for traveling through Mexico is entitled *Mexico Tourist Road Atlas*, published annually by Guia Roji. For details on campgrounds in Belize, see the supplementary material at www.bafrenz.com.

Belize roads

To the surprise of first-time visitors to Belize, the **major highways** are well paved, spaciously wide, and relatively free of traffic. With improving economic conditions, more citizens will own vehicles, but for now the main traffic is commercial trucks and buses. Philip Goldson Highway is most traveled by slow-moving overladen sugarcane trucks, and Hummingbird Highway has a few trucks carrying oranges from the orchards to the juice factories and, more recently, crude-oil trucks headed to coastal ships. George Price Highway is more heavily traveled from Belize City to Belmopan and less so from there to San Ignacio. Southern Highway is nearly devoid of vehicular traffic. Coastal Highway, undifferentiated from major highways on many commercial maps, is not a major highway and is unpaved.

Minor non-paved roads (e.g., Sarteneja, Gallon Jug, Coastal, Chiquibul, San Antonio, etc.) branch from the main highways. Some of these roads are perpetually dreadful, whereas most others are only seasonally dreadful. Even in the dry season, you will need a vehicle with high clearance and rugged suspension. Construction material, if any, for these side roads is hardpan caliche, limestone gravel, or rocks. They are frequently potholed and rutted. Some Belizeans travel these roads at a fast pace, others at a dangerously slow pace. When asking a native about travel times, your actual driving time can be anywhere from half to double the estimate given.

In addition to the minor roads, there are **poorly maintained roads**: dirt and gravel roads and two-track drivable trails leading to birding sites. During the rainy season—and sometimes during the dry season—many of these roads are impassable because ruts become too deep even for trucks and high-clearance SUVs. At the end of the rainy season, graders smooth the roads, once again allowing normal vehicular traffic.

Road names and signs: Note that while the main roads—Philip Goldson, George Price, Hummingbird, and Southern Highways—have designated names rather than numbers, the minor roads rarely are named. Thus Chiquibul and Coastal are locally known, whereas Sarteneja, Gallon Jug,

San Ignacio, Cayo District   Bert Frenz

and San Antonio are road names invented for purposes of this book, in each case attributed to a village near the end of the road. No roads in Belize have numbers and only in the past few years have signs been erected to identify village names and important turnoffs, many still lacking. There are very few directional signs —although this certainly is improving with the recent big green overhead signs at major intersections—and most of the original mileposts have disappeared or collapsed. Nonetheless, with the directions and maps included in this book, it is unlikely you will become lost.

Birding tour companies

Over a dozen companies offer packaged birding tours of Belize. Domestic companies arrange custom tours year-round. Non-domestic companies run their tours during the months of September to April, the majority choosing February and March. Tour length from arrival to departure ranges from 5 to 18 days, with an average stay of 11 days. Almost all of the tours concentrate on several of the best hotspots (e.g., Crooked Tree, Chan Chich, Hidden Valley) but miss many other excellent birding areas discussed in this book. Some companies include Tikal in their itineraries. The tour lengths and months, given below, are examples of past trips and are subject to change.

- Amazilia Tours, San José, Costa Rica; (506) 22 80 69 82; drazog@yahoo.com; www.amaziliatours.com. 12-day tours in March and September.
- Bird Belize, a division of Wildside Nature Tours, 888-875-9453; info@wildsidenaturetours.com; http://wildsidenaturetours.com/bird-belize. 10- to 14-day scheduled tours November to March and custom tours.
- Birdquest, Two Jays, Kemple End, Stonyhurst, Clitheroe, Lancashire BB7 9QY, England, UK; +44 1254 826317; birders@birdquest-tours.com; www.birdquest-tours.com. 16-day tours in March. Custom tours.
- Field Guides, 9433 Bee Cave Road, Building 1, Suite 150, Austin, TX 78733; 512-263-7295 or 800-728-4953; fieldguides@fieldguides.com; www.fieldguides.com. 7-day tours in April.
- Fun Birding Tours, 72 Avenida Pastor, Rio Rico, AZ 85648-8001; 520-281-0571; richard@funbirdingtours.com; www.funbirdingtours.com. 9- to 11-day custom tours.
- High Lonesome Birdtours, 570 S. Little Bear Trail, Sierra Vista, AZ 85635; 443-838-6589; hilone@hilonesome.com; www.hilonesome.com. 13-day tours in November.
- Mark Pretti Nature Tours, 2915 Keeling Rd., Hereford, AZ 85615; 520-803-6889; mpnaturetours@earthlink.net; www.markpretti naturetours.com. 11-day tours in February; custom trips can be arranged.

- Nature Treks & Passages, P.O. Box 542, Bryantville, MA 02327; 781-789-8127; info@naturetreks.net; www.naturetreks.net. 8-day tours in January.
- Paradise Expeditions, P.O. Box 106, San Ignacio, Cayo District, Belize; (011) 501-610-5593; info@ birdinginbelize.com; www.birdinginbelize.com. Custom tours year-round.
- Victor Emanuel Nature Tours (VENT), 2525 Wallingwood Drive, Suite 1003, Austin, TX 78746; 512-328-5221 or 800-328-8368; info@ventbird.com; www.ventbird.com. 5- to 18-day tours December to March.
- Wildside Nature Tours, 241 Emerald Drive, Yardley, PA 19067; 610-564-0941 or 888-875-9453; info@Wildside NatureTours.com; www.wildsidetoursinc.com. 10- to 14-day tours January to March; also Tikal trips.
- WINGS, 1643 N. Alvernon Way, Suite 109, Tucson, AZ 85712; 520-320-9868 or 866-547-9868; wings@wingsbirds.com; http://wingsbirds.com. 8-day tour in January.

WHERE TO STAY

Although hundreds of lodging choices are scattered throughout Belize—readily found in an Internet search—this book describes only a few places to stay, selected either because of their proximity to birding sites or because the lodge itself is a good birding site. Depending on the quality and size of the establishment, services offered typically include some or all of the following:

- Transportation to/from Philip Goldson International Airport
- Room, from basic to extravagant
- Meals, priced separately or as a package
- Activities such as caving, tubing, snorkeling, canoeing, horse riding
- Birding trails
- Local birding guides, naturalists, and tour guides
- Booked tours to local sites or as far away as Tikal

Resorts, eco-lodges, hotels, field stations, tropical education facilities: Many resorts are superb birding sites, and a birder could easily be satisfied with the opportunities on site and on nearby day trips arranged by the resort. Resorts, lodges, and hotels mentioned in this book are included in the chapters pertaining to the nearby birding locations. Contact information is also given. The resorts and eco-lodges range in capacity from a few rooms to facilities that can handle conferences for 100+ people. A few in the list are rather simple and quaint hotels that cater especially to birders. Some of the facilities do not fit the resort category, but rather are associated with tropical education. Nightly rates run the gamut from low double digits to US$1,000 and up suites and, as expected, the prices reflect the quality of the accommodations although not necessarily the quality of the birding experience. Use this book mostly as a pointer to what is available and then check the Internet sites to learn more about the offerings.

Lodging referenced in this book (arranged from north to south):

Corozal District	Area	Gazetteer #	Page #
Tony's Inn & Beach Resort	Corozal	2	40
Fernando's Seaside Guesthouse	Sarteneja	4	49
Fireburn Village	Sarteneja	10	49

Orange Walk District	Area	Gazetteer #	Page #
La Milpa Ecolodge	Rio Bravo Conservation and Management Area	20	58
Lamanai Outpost Lodge	New River	23	77
Blue Creek Hillside B&B	Blue Creek	18	56
Hill Bank Field Station	Rio Bravo Conservation and Management Area	28	78
Chan Chich Lodge	Gallon Jug	32	62

Belize District	Area	Gazetteer #	Page #
Best Western Belize Biltmore	Belize City	34	38
Caribbean Villas	Ambergris Caye	16	239
Seaside Cabanas	Caye Caulker	24	241
Maruba Resort Jungle Spa	Altun Ha	22	89
Silver Fox Guest House	Altun Ha	22	89
Crooked Tree Lodge	Crooked Tree	21	85
Bird's Eye View Lodge	Crooked Tree	21	85
Belize Zoo Jungle Lodge	George Price Hwy.	37	94
Cheers Restaurant and Cabanas	George Price Hwy.	40	99
Monkey Bay Wildlife Sanctuary	George Price Hwy.	40	97
Manatee Lodge	Coastal Hwy.	47	106

Cayo District	Area	Gazetteer #	Page #
Banana Bank Lodge	George Price Hwy.	42	108
Caesar's Place	George Price Hwy.	46	92
Pook's Hill Lodge	George Price Hwy.	48	109
Caves Branch Jungle Lodge	Hummingbird Hwy.	50	165
Jaguar Creek Ministries	Hummingbird Hwy.	50	164
San Ignacio Resort Hotel	San Ignacio	49	131

Cahal Pech Village Resort	San Ignacio	49	131
Windy Hill Resort	San Ignacio	53	136
Log Cab-Inn Resort	San Ignacio	53	136
Crystal Paradise Resort	San Ignacio	51	116
Mango Walk Inn	San Ignacio	51	116
Clarissa Falls Resort	San Ignacio	53	136
The Lodge at Chaa Creek	San Ignacio	55	140
duPlooy's Jungle Lodge	San Ignacio	55	141
Black Rock Lodge	San Ignacio	60	139
Hidden Valley Inn	Mountain Pine Ridge	59	117
Pine Ridge Lodge	Mountain Pine Ridge	58	116
Gaïa Riverlodge	Mountain Pine Ridge	58	116
Blancaneaux Lodge	Mountain Pine Ridge	58	116
Las Cuevas Research Station	Chiquibul Natl. Park	78	123

Stann Creek District	Area	Gazetteer #	Page #
Pelican Beach Resort	Dangriga	67	170
Jaguar Reef Lodge	Dangriga	72	189
Cockscomb Basin Wildlife Sanct.	Dangriga	75	194
Mama Noots Eco Resort	Dangriga	68	186
Coco Plum Island Resort	Inner Channel	69	250
Pelican Beach Resort	S. Water Caye, near Man-O'-War Caye	69	250

Toledo District	Area	Gazetteer #	Page #
BFREE Protected Area	Southern Hwy.	82	201
The Lodge at Big Falls	Punta Gorda	92	207
Belcampo Belize	Punta Gorda	99	220
Cuxlin Ha Resort	Punta Gorda	99	219
Sea Front Inn	Punta Gorda	101	225
Cotton Tree Lodge	Punta Gorda	102	230
Hickatee Cottages	Punta Gorda	102	228

Budget accommodations: A Homestay program allows visitors to stay in the homes of Belizean families, "cooking and eating together, helping with daily chores and talking, playing, and learning with and from host family members." In addition to the benefits of this intercultural exchange, the opportunity can be an economical way to visit birding sites. The daily rate is about US$40 per night per person, including three meals. Homestay families can accommodate one or two people per household and most guests stay one to three nights. Locations at Armenia, Crooked Tree, Gales Point, La Democracia, and St. Margaret's Village are close to the excellent birding areas of Blue Hole National Park, Crooked Tree Wildlife Sanctuary, Coastal

Highway, George Price Highway, and Five Blues Lake National Park. For details on the Homestay program, see www.monkeybaybelize.org/homestay.html or contact Monkey Bay Wildlife Sanctuary at mbay@btl.net. Also budget-priced and available through Monkey Bay Wildlife Sanctuary are field-station accommodations in Mountain Pine Ridge on Privassion Creek, near Blancaneaux, and on Tobacco Caye, with access to Man-O'-War Caye.

Campgrounds: Tent camping is perhaps the cheapest accommodation option for visitors birding Belize and it has the added advantage of your hearing owls and nightjars and being awakened with the dawn chorus. In 2001 Belize had only one "real" campground for RVs. Subsequently more have been built. All of the major highways now have at least one RV campground that has water, electric, and dump facilities. For complete details on RV and tent camping in Belize, see the supplementary material at www.bafrenz.com.

TRAVEL TIPS

Currency, economy, and expenses: The exchange rate for the Belize dollar is fixed to the US dollar at a ratio of 2:1. As US dollars are accepted everywhere, there is no need to exchange money, although those visitors with other currencies need to do so. US coins are generally not accepted in Belize. ATMs, available in all of the larger cities, dispense Belize dollars, and the change you receive from purchases will be Belize currency. Always use your Belize currency before using US currency because you will not get a

---

Useful facts for travelers . . .

* Language: English throughout; also Creole, Spanish, and three Maya languages.
* Currency: 1US$ = 2 BZ$; US dollars accepted throughout.
* Credit cards accepted at most mid- and all high-end establishments.
* ATMs in major cities, although typically only Belize Bank accepts international cards.
* Taxes (GST): 12.5% general sales tax on all services and most goods.
* Taxes (hotels): 9% tax on hotels and resorts, in addition to 12.5% sales tax.
* Service charges: Additional amount added to some hotel costs.
* Tipping: 10% sometimes added to restaurant bills; otherwise same custom as US.
* Time: same as Central Standard Time in the US; Daylight Savings Time is not observed.
* Electricity: 110 volts. No adapters necessary for US appliances. Remote sites are powered by solar energy and diesel generators.
* Entry requirements: A passport valid for more than six months beyond the date of departure. If arriving by car or RV, entry is more complicated; see "Border crossing" section below for details.

reasonable exchange rate in Belize or the US when you attempt to exchange Belize currency.

Although the Belize economy appears to be stable from year to year, the government borrows heavily and often teeters on the verge of bankruptcy. During a short birding trip, none of this is likely to affect your plans. However, prices rise each year, and as in the rest of the world, gasoline and diesel prices have risen sharply. Gasoline is high by Mexican and Central American standards and nearly double the price in the US. Diesel averages cheaper than gasoline.

Other than fuel costs, prices for most items likely to be purchased by a tourist are about the same as in the US. The same holds true for groceries and resort restaurants, which range widely in price as they do elsewhere. Locally grown food and Belizean menu choices are the most economical. Away from resorts, restaurants can be much cheaper than in the US, especially when one considers that a 10% tip or less is quite acceptable and most places do not add sales tax. Anything imported from another country, particularly the US, will be sold at premium prices. For example, DEET insect sprays are hard to find and expensive if you do find them. Very few items are a bargain. The one notable exception is rum, particularly 1 Barrel Rum.

Telephone system: Belize telephone numbers for accommodations, tours, guides, airlines, etc. are listed in this book in the form (011) 501-555-1234. This is the set of numbers you would dial to reach Belize when calling from the US or Canada. The first three digits indicate an international

* *Exit requirements: Exit fee must be paid; in 2011, departure and conservation fees totaled US$39.25 per person.*
* *Taxis: Available at international airport and most towns; fares are strictly regulated within Belize City, but many cabbies will take advantage of tourists' ignorance of the established rates.*
* *Buses: Scheduled bus service to and from all main towns as well as to Chetumal and Cancun, Mexico, and to the Guatemala border.*
* *Religions: Roman Catholic, Anglican, Protestant, Muslim, and regional ethnic religions.*
* *Government: Parliamentary democracy, two-party system, member of British Commonwealth, independent since 1981.*
* *Agriculture: Cane sugar (half of exports), citrus, bananas.*
* *Industries: Tourism, food processing, construction, garment production.*
* *Trade partners: US (#1), plus UK, European Union, Canada, Mexico, Caribbean Community.*

call, 501 is the area code for the entire country of Belize, and the last seven digits are the number for the local establishment. If you are calling from Europe, replace (011) with (00). If you are calling from within Belize from a phone booth or other local phone, dial only the last seven digits. If a listed number is in the US, it is identified as such, starting with the area code.

The Belize telephone system is a monopoly and the only company is BTL. Telephone rates are very high compared to those in other countries. Before the advent of Internet cafes, it was not unusual to pay US$30 to use a local merchant's telephone to dial the US to collect e-mail.

Although your cell phone may operate in Belize, you may not want to use it because of the high cost. Before you leave your country of origin, contact your cell-phone carrier and inquire about an International Plan and ask specifically what they will charge you when making calls from Belize, including the rates in-country and out-of-country.

A good alternative, if making only a few calls, is to buy a "calling card." In reality, this might look like a cash register receipt with an access number. For a quick local call, US$2 would give you a few minutes time. For more extensive out-of-country calling, it is simpler and cheaper to buy a cell phone in Belize and use prepaid "Digicell" phone cards. Dialing the prefix 10-10-199, the US area code (with the "1" prefix) and the phone number cuts the cost of calls at least by half, to about US$0.25 per minute. As a last resort, you might choose to charge your call to your credit card, but don't be surprised if the expense is exorbitant.

What to wear: While most tourists wear shorts, T-shirts, and sandals, you will need additional clothes for birding, particularly in the southern two-thirds of Belize. Mostly, you will want to be prepared against insects by wearing long-sleeve shirts, long pants, socks that you can roll up over your pants, and a hat that not only protects from insects but also from the sun. Get shirts and pants that are light-weight, quick-drying polyester or cotton, chiefly sold at outdoor-recreation stores. Tennis shoes will work for many birding areas, but waterproof boots are much better. At the higher elevations of Mountain Pine Ridge you will want a sweater, sweatshirt, or light jacket in winter. Also take along a light-weight raincoat or poncho, useful anywhere in the country for frequent, albeit short, rain showers. Many birders find a collapsible umbrella a better alternative to hot and sweaty raincoats, as you can still bird without getting your binoculars wet.

What to bring: In addition to the standard birding gear, consider bringing a handheld GPS, as this book provides hundreds of coordinates of birding sites, highway turns, and resort locations. Get rechargeable AA batteries for your equipment and bring along the recharger. Also bring insect repellent (best if it contains at least 25% DEET) and sunscreen. Women especially should consider bringing cranberry drinks or cranberry tablets to stave off urinary infections caused by not drinking enough water during hot birding days. Snack foods are expensive and not readily available in Belize, so consider bringing granola bars and other forms of between-meal snacks.

Food and water: Most locally grown vegetables from the Mennonite farms of Belize are of good quality. Restaurants range from acceptable to outstanding, and you are unlikely to find one where you need be concerned about getting sick on the food. However, do not buy prepared food from street vendors! Drinking water is generally safe, although buying readily available bottled water is a smart safeguard.

The most common Belizean meal is rice and beans, often served with chicken, pork, or beef. It is delicious, readily available, and the cheapest menu item in dining establishments. Most restaurants prepare it in bulk in the morning, which makes it an excellent lunchtime menu item, but not necessarily a wise dinner choice. Another advantage of ordering rice and beans for lunch is that it can be served immediately. Be aware that "rice and beans" and "beans and rice" are not the same thing! The former is rice with cooked (and drained) red and/or black beans mixed in. The latter is a stewed-bean "soup" and white rice served separately. Seafood is widely served. Cuisines include Creole, Central American, Mexican, American, and Chinese.

Medical care: Hospitals and clinics are located in all of the larger cities and towns and are well-equipped to handle the infections, insect bites, and common ailments that are the most likely reason a tourist might choose to use their services. However, most hospitals in Belize are ill-equipped to handle more severe medical problems—Belize Medical Associates, a private hospital in Belize City, being perhaps the one exception. For anything other than routine medical needs, you would be wise to consider one of two alternatives. Just north of the Belize border is Chetumal, Mexico, which has major hospitals and clinics for its quarter-million city population. For medical emergencies, consider being airlifted to the US, Mexico City, or Guatemala City. Insurance, such as Medex, can be purchased for such airlift situations.

Immunization: Remember to get any prescription drugs you might need before you cross the border. There are no required immunization shots for entry into Belize, but there are recommendations. The best advice is to check with your doctor. In the past, most visitors have been told to get the Hepatitis A vaccine if they have not already done so, to make sure tetanus immunization is up to date (i.e., within 10 years), and to get a prescription and purchase the malaria prophylaxis. Confirm when to start and end the malaria prophylaxis, which might begin before you leave home and extend after you leave Belize.

In prior years the prophylaxis was strongly recommended by the CDC for people who are in rural areas of Belize, particularly the farther south you travel. Although consulting with a physician is certainly recommended, many

US physicians know little about the latest advances in malaria treatment and prevention. A travel-medicine clinic may be a good choice. The CDC is your best source of information. Recommendations change from year to year.

Insect bites: Unlike in the US and Canada where it is obvious when you are being bitten by mosquitoes and flies, the insects of Belize are more subtle and you often do not know of their presence until after you see bumps, red marks, or painful swelling on your skin. Most insect bites are harmless, albeit irritating, especially if you are unfortunate enough to brush against vegetation harboring hundreds, if not thousands, of near microscopic mites, in which case, the itching that follows can be almost unbearable.

The one insect you particularly want to avoid is the **botfly**, most commonly encountered at Cockscomb Basin Wildlife Sanctuary, but also Chan Chich, San Ignacio, and several other birding areas. In its cycle, the victim receives the fly eggs transferred in a mosquito bite. The warmth of the host induces the egg to hatch, the larva burrows under the skin, and grows, eventually producing a bump on the skin. The body or head, the size of a rice grain, usually is not obvious until after you have returned from your trip. The living larva causes sensations varying from itching to pain—one victim described it as "broken glass turning under the skin"—over a period of weeks. In the US, the symptoms are most often misdiagnosed, but, when recognized, the most common remedy is for a doctor to incise the skin and release the larva, which may have grown to over an inch long. In Belize, various home remedies include smothering the bump with Vaseline or axle grease, perhaps covering that with a cap, and waiting for the suffocating larvae to evacuate. You do not want to pull out only part of the larva's body. If you do nothing about the larva, it will come out on its own, fall to the ground, and pupate into an adult fly.

Getting caught in the botfly cycle is quite common—ask most Belize birding guides—but it can be avoided, as can other insect bites. Wear long pants, a long-sleeved shirt, and a hat, and pull your socks over your pant legs. Spray any exposed skin with repellent, preferably containing DEET. Also, stick to the cleared trails and avoid bushwhacking through tall grass. Although some people highly discourage its use under the mistaken impression that it can be extremely harmful, others strongly recommend using a Permethrin spray on clothing before going in the field. You even can spray it on your clothes before leaving home. It lasts through several wash cycles and it deters almost all mites and other biting insects, even the near-microscopic ones that can easily pass through even tightly woven cloth.

Snakes: Snakes are most often encountered on the roads and rarely on the trails. A good identification guide is mentioned in the Recommended Readings section of this chapter. From a safety point of view, the one snake with which you do not want to come in close contact with is the Fer-de-lance, called locally the Tommygoff. It resembles a rattlesnake with its spear-shaped head and patterned series of beige, brown, and black triangles on its back, but without the rattlesnake's rattles. Its venom may be deadly, and a snake bite requires immediate attention. Being primarily a nocturnal snake, Fer-de-lance is not often seen—there is one on view at the Belize Zoo, however. Wearing high rubber boots or thick leather shoes, rather than low-cut tennis shoes, is a safeguard. The best way to avoid close contact with snakes is to stay on groomed paths, removed of leaf litter.

Trees to avoid: Many trees encountered in the jungle are covered with sharp spines, such as Give-and-take Palm and Warree (*Astrocaryum mexicanum*), and a few are poisonous, e.g., Black Poisonwood (*Metopium brownei*), which causes itching and blistering and is more toxic than the Poison Ivy of North America. Warree Palm or Warree Cohune takes its name from the White-lipped Peccary, called Warree in Belize because the tree's spines resemble those of the peccary. Bullhorn Acacia (*Acacia cookii*) not only has painful spines but also protective ants that secrete formic acid on the tips. When hiking, avoid touching trees you do not recognize. If you should lose your balance hiking a steep slope, you would be better off to fall on the ground than to grab a spiny tree. For photos of Belize trees, see www.bafrenz.com.

Cautions and safety: Warnings for travelers to Belize City are often cited by the US Embassy, with a recommendation to maintain a high level of situational awareness (http://belize.usembassy.gov). In general, it is safe to take a taxi into Belize City to catch a water taxi to the cays or to the nicer hotels. However, as is also the case for many US cities, don't wander the streets at night. Fortunately, the city is easy to avoid and the good birding sites are not there. Elsewhere in the country, safety is rarely of concern. As in any country, use common sense and avoid situations and areas that give the appearance of being unsafe, particularly at night. A realistic threat, although statistically remote, is from Guatemalan thieves crossing into Belize illegally and entering a tourist destination area or birding area (e.g., Caracol and El Pilar) and demanding money and valued possessions. Such activity receives swift action from the Belize security forces. The threat is serious enough that visits to remote Caracol now require military escort. Fortunately these incidents have been rare.

As a tourist your most likely exposure is from petty theft intended to support a drug habit and committed by someone simply picking up an item left unattended. Incidents are more likely to occur near cities and towns, rather than in birding areas. The best safeguard is to keep your valuables hidden in your vehicle (and avoid waiting to put them in the trunk until after you arrive at a site, when you can be seen doing so); also keep vehicle doors locked.

Border crossing: For visitors arriving by air or water, the border crossing is straightforward and quick. A passport valid for more than six months after entry is required. Residents of the US, Canada, the UK, and Caribbean countries do not need a visa prior to entering the country. Passports are automatically stamped with a 30-day visa upon entry that must be renewed if you plan on staying more than 30 days.

For those arriving by car or RV, the procedure is more complicated and time-consuming. For details on border procedures when entering by highway, see the supplementary material at www.bafrenz.com.

HOW TO USE THIS GUIDE

Chapter arrangement: Chapters 2 through 5 are arranged in geographic order, following the Belize highway system from north to south. Each chapter follows a principal paved highway, and includes a road log highlighting the birding stops and mileages. Chapter 6 describes birding sites on the cays.

Birding site descriptions: Approximately 90 birding sites are described in detail and another 55 are mentioned in passing. With a few exceptions, all have been visited by the author. Some site descriptions include a selected journal entry from a visit to the site, describing settings, birds, and experiences. Most are outlined as follows:

- description, including trails, conditions, vendors, and facilities such as toilets, accommodations, and exhibits;
- birding strategy for arranging the visit, finding birds, and optimizing time;
- pointer to appropriate ecoregion in Appendix A;
- habitat, including reference to descriptions in Appendix A;
- concerns, such as safety, difficulty, and access;
- fees, subject to change, for entrance, tours, or services;
- contacts, including name, address, phone and fax numbers, e-mail, web site;
- GPS coordinates to aid in locating sites;
- location and directions;
- map(s), illustrating the directions or the site layout; and
- list of key species found at the site.

Within the key species list, those marked as [R] are rare, have occurred at the site before and could be expected to occur again, though the chances of seeing any one of them are slim. Species marked [S] are present at the site only during the summer season, which for some species may be as early as February. Transitory migrants are marked [T] and are expected in fall and/or spring migration, but not in summer or winter. Finally, those species in boldface can be considered target species, ones easier to find at the site than most other sites or otherwise of special interest to most birders. The key

Boat-billed Heron   Bert Frenz

species list is only a fraction of the birds reported for the site. For a complete list of those that have occurred or might occur, refer to the particular ecoregion list (see www.bafrenz.com).

Belize maps, GPS coordinates, and elevations: Apparently, no truly accurate or complete map of Belize exists. Some prominent roads traveled daily by dozens of vehicles are not on any map. Villages exist whose names do not grace a map. Roads twist and turn in directions not illustrated on a map. The most accurate view of the country is the satellite images readily available through *Google Earth*, yet the country's boundaries, placement of villages, and names of objects are often off by miles.

Backed by the most popular Belize map, a larger wall-map purchased from the government office in Belmopan, a collection of 133 page-sized topographic maps spanning the country, dozens of local maps, hundreds of handwritten directions with mileage markers, at least 500 personally measured GPS coordinates— and much of this crosschecked with the Google Earth satellite photos—this book probably now has better maps and directional guides for Belize than any other source!

GPS coordinates presented in this book are almost always those measured using a handheld GPS, supplemented occasionally by *Google Earth* coordinates where measured values were not taken. The measured values and the *Google Earth* values agree to within about the width of the highways. Elevations were also measured with a handheld GPS, but in this case it seems that the *Google Earth* values are more accurate and consistent, so these are the ones used in the text. The measured values and the *Google Earth* values differ by plus-or-minus 20 feet (seven meters).

The maps and directions in this book should be sufficient to find any of the birding sites described. Nonetheless, you may also wish to purchase a country map of Belize. A good inexpensive one is entitled *An International Travel Map of Belize*, on a scale of 1:350,000, and is available in most US and Canada map stores, at www.itmb.com, or by phone at 604-273-1400. An interesting collection of Belize maps can be viewed at http://ambergris caye.com/maps/.

Recommended Readings

Field guides

Jones, H.L. 2003. *Birds of Belize*. University of Texas Press, Austin. Also published in London by Christopher Helm, 2004. This is the recommended field guide for all the birds of Belize. It contains the most specific commentary on each species by H. Lee Jones, and all species are illustrated by Dana Gardner. 317 pp.

Howell, S.N.G., and S. Webb. 1995. *A Guide to the Birds of Mexico and Northern Central America*. Oxford University Press, New York. The best book for Mexico, it also contains excellent information on Belize species and is a great companion book to Jones (2003). Howell and Webb is a large book, not easy to carry in the field. Some birders have split this paperbound book, taken it to a copy shop to have it rebound in spiral or other flat-laying format, then opted to carry just the artwork in the field. 1,010 pp.

Van Perlo, B. 2006. *Birds of Mexico and Central America*. Princeton University Press, Princeton, NJ. Its chief advantage is its compact size that neatly fits in a pocket. Its disadvantages are it covers too many species that do not occur in Belize, its drawings are too small, and descriptions too brief. 336pp.

You might want to take along your favorite North American guide as well.

Bird checklists

Jones, H.L., and A.C. Vallely. 2001. *Annotated Checklist of the Birds of Belize*. Lynx Edicions, Barcelona, Spain. Annotated country list with information on habitat and distribution and abundance by district. 72pp.

Mammals, amphibians, reptiles, fish

Beletsky, L. 2010. *Belize & Northern Guatemala (Travellers' Wildlife Guides)*. Interlink Books, Northampton, MA. Extensive coverage of geography, ecology, conservation, and natural history of Belize, with well-illustrated guide to the most often found amphibians, reptiles, birds, mammals, and marine life. 477pp.

Garel, T., and S. Matola. 1996. *A Field Guide to the Snakes of Belize.* The Belize Zoo and Tropical Education Center, Belize City. Photographs, descriptions, habitats, and natural history of Belize snakes. 147pp.

Lee, J.C. 2000. *Field Guide to the Amphibians and Reptiles of the Maya World: The Lowlands of Mexico, Northern Guatemala, and Belize.* Cornell University Press, Ithaca, NY. 448pp.

Reid, F.A. 2009. *A Field Guide to the Mammals of Central America and Southeast Mexico.* Second Edition. Oxford University Press, New York. Excellent and comprehensive book covering the mammals of Belize. 384pp

Smith, C.L. 1997. *National Audubon Society Field Guide to Tropical Marine Fishes: Caribbean, Gulf of Mexico, Florida, Bahamas, Bermuda.* Knopf, New York. 720 pp.

Stafford, P.J., and J.R. Meyer. 1999. *A Guide to the Reptiles of Belize.* Academic Press, San Diego. 356 pp.

Butterflies

Garwood, K., and R. Lehman. 2011. *Butterflies of Central America Vol. 1.* Self-published, McAllen, TX. www.neotropicalbutterflies.com. 304 pp.

Glassberg, J. 2007. *A Swift Guide to the Butterflies of Mexico and Central America.* Sunstreak Books, Morristown, NJ. 272 pp.

Meerman, J.C. 2001. *Lepidoptera of Belize.* Association of Tropical Lepidoptera, Gainesville, FL. This is an annotated checklist of the "more conspicuous" butterflies and moths of Belize. It does not include skippers or hairstreaks, which together comprise well over half of all Belize butterflies; however, it does include minimal distributional information, which cannot be found elsewhere. The list includes 454 species and some information on seasonality and caterpillar food plants. An abbreviated checklist of 221 species of *Nymphalidae* and their geographic distribution by district is at http://biological-diversity.info/nymphal.htm.

Plants

Smith, N., S.A. Mori, A. Henderson, D.W. Stevenson, and S.V. Heald, eds. 2003. *Flowering Plants of the Neotropics.* Princeton University Press, Princeton, NJ. Comparatively expensive, yet more complete in examining 280 families of plants of the Neotropics, it is beautifully illustrated. No one book can cover flowers, but this one is a start toward narrowing identification to family. 616 pp.

Zuchowski, W. 2006. *A Guide to Tropical Plants of Costa Rica.* Zona Tropical, Miami. Although not specific to Belize, this well-written and lavishly illustrated book can provide an excellent background for understanding tropical plants. 529 pp.

Other books

Awe, J. 2006. *Maya Cities and Sacred Caves – A Guide to the Maya Sites of Belize.* Cubola Productions, Benque Viejo del Carmen, Belize. Excellent archeological guide to the most visited Maya sites, which are also good birding sites. 103 pp.

Barcott, B. 2008. *The Last Flight of the Scarlet Macaw: One Woman's Fight to Save the World's Most Beautiful Bird*. Random House, New York. Dramatic narrative of Sharon Matola's fight to stop construction of a dam flooding a macaw nesting area in the Maya Mountains. 313 pp.

Bridgewater, S. 2012. *A Natural History of Belize – Inside the Maya Forest*. University of Texas Press, Austin. Comprehensive natural history of the Chiquibul Forest based on research findings of scientists studying at Las Cuevas Research Station. 390 pp.

Coe, W.R. 1988. *Tikal – A Handbook of the Ancient Maya Ruins: With a Guide Map*. The University Museum, University of Pennsylvania, Philadelphia. One of many Tikal archaeology guidebooks, this one is well illustrated and narrated, featuring a detailed map. 129 pp.

Kricher, J. 1999. *A Neotropical Companion*. Princeton University Press, Princeton, NJ. Considered by many the best introduction to the natural history of the New World tropics. 451pp.

Morris, D. 1883. *The Colony of British Honduras*. Edward Stanford, London. Includes early history and subtitled "Its resources and prospects; with particular reference to its indigenous plants and economic productions." 152 pp.

Rabinowitz, A. 2000. *Jaguar: One Man's Struggle to Establish the World's First Jaguar Preserve*. Island Press, Washington, D.C. An excellent commentary by biologist Alan Rabinowitz on his struggles to study Jaguars at what eventually became Cockscomb Basin Wildlife Sanctuary and the world's first Jaguar preserve. 416pp.

Journals

North American Birds. Published by the American Birding Association. www.aba.org/nab. A quarterly journal that reports bird sightings on a seasonal basis in regions throughout North and Middle America, including one covering Belize and the rest of Central America.

Web sites

www.biodiversity.bz. Biodiversity & Environmental Resource Data System of Belize (BERDS). An incredible resource for information on protected areas, habitats, and the flora and fauna of Belize, this site was used as an invaluable source for biological details in preparing this book. See also http://biological-diversity.info/species-list.htm for a good variety of check-lists, with many photographed species of flora and fauna.

www.belizenet.com/history. *A History of Belize*. A 14-chapter online book of the detailed history of Belize, edited by Robert Leslie.

www.belizeaudubon.org. Belize Audubon Society. Details about the many national parks and other reserves managed by this non-governmental membership organization.

http://ambergriscaye.com/index.php. Welcome to Ambergris Caye, Belize. Although the web site provides plenty of information about Ambergris Caye, it also is a potpourri of numerous other details about the country. The site is also a hub connecting to many other Belize web sites.

SUPPLEMENTAL MATERIAL

Descriptions of additional birding sites, hundreds of photos of birds and site habitats, bird identification comparison charts, expanded travel journals, *Google Earth* markers and tracks, detailed location checklists, Belize birding guide contacts, recent updates, a timeline history of Belize, information on campgrounds and border crossings, and other birding information that could not be included in this book are available at:

www.bafrenz.com
To access the information,
enter USERNAME – BelizeBirder
PASSWORD – Touc@n
(the fifth character is the "at" sign)

Any updates or corrections can be submitted at this site. They would be greatly appreciated.

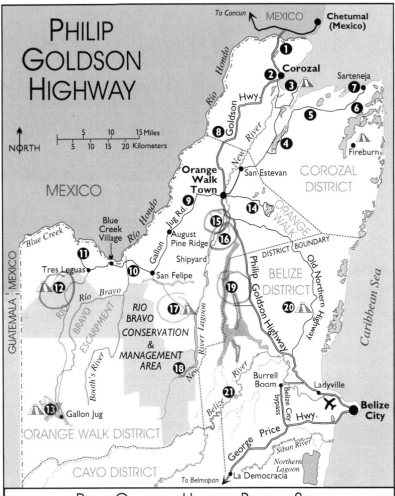

PHILIP GOLDSON HIGHWAY

To Cancun — MEXICO — Chetumal (Mexico)

NORTH

5 10 15 Miles
5 10 15 20 Kilometers

MEXICO

Rio Hondo

Rio Hondo

Goldson Hwy.

New River

Corozal

Sarteneja

Fireburn

COROZAL DISTRICT

San Estevan

Orange Walk Town

Blue Creek Village

Tres Leguas

Rio Bravo

RIO BRAVO ESCARPMENT

Booth's River

Blue Creek

Jug Rd.

Gallon

August Pine Ridge

Shipyard

San Felipe

RIO BRAVO CONSERVATION & MANAGEMENT AREA

New River Lagoon

ORANGE WALK

DISTRICT BOUNDARY

BELIZE DISTRICT

Old Northern Highway

Philip Goldson Highway

Caribbean Sea

Gallon Jug

ORANGE WALK DISTRICT

Belize River

Burrell Boom

Ladyville

Belize City bypass

George Price Highway

Sibun River

Northern Lagoon

La Democracia

To Belmopan

Belize City Hwy.

Belize City

CAYO DISTRICT

PHILIP GOLDSON HIGHWAY BIRDING SITES

1. Four Mile Lagoon
2. Corozal
3. Cerros Maya Site, Copper Bank
4. Progresso Lagoon
5. Sarteneja Road
6. Shipstern Nature Reserve
7. Sarteneja National Tree Park
8. San Victor
9. Gallon Jug Road
10. Blue Creek rice fields
11. Edenthal-Neustadt marshes
12. La Milpa Ecolodge
13. Chan Chich Lodge
14. Honey Camp Road and Lagoon
15. Shipyard Road
16. New River
17. Lamanai Maya Site
18. Hill Bank Field Station
19. Crooked Tree Wildlife Sanctuary
20. Altun Ha Maya Site, Old Northern Highway
21. Community Baboon Sanctuary

CHAPTER 2
PHILIP GOLDSON HIGHWAY

If you reach Belize by driving through Mexico, two pleasant surprises greet you soon after crossing the border: the common language is English and the main highways are smooth and wide. Philip Goldson Highway permits driving at 55 to 65 mph (90 to 105 kph) with ease as you gently curve through flat countryside. (Until September 2012 Philip Goldson Highway was called Northern Highway, and undoubtedly local people will continue using the old name for some time.) Northernmost of the six districts of Belize, Corozal District is an agricultural area where sugarcane is the main crop. Part of the Yucatán Peninsula, its birdlife resembles that of southeastern Mexico along the Caribbean Sea. Many of the birding sites—boldfaced in the next paragraphs and described in detail in subsequent pages—might be considered of less importance when compared to southern and western locations, yet they can offer pleasant birding days that include species rare or absent farther south.

Goldson Highway runs from the border with Mexico to Belize City. Zero your odometer at the Mexico border. After running the gauntlet of immigration buildings, the first birding spot is on the left at **Four Mile Lagoon** in two miles. At 3.7 miles, the old highway bypasses Corozal, but the paved road runs through the town and is the major route. Corozal Town is the principal city of northern Belize and the starting point for most local birding. Once a major Maya trading area, the first archaeological site you pass is **Santa Rita** on the right at 7.8 miles. It is a good birding stop as well. Note the bus station on the left at 8.4, a principal transportation mode to move between cities and villages of Belize as well as connections to Cancun, Mexico. The only gas station in Corozal is at 8.8 and soon thereafter is your first good view of Corozal Bay and the Caribbean Sea. At 9.2, full hook-ups make Caribbean Village Campground and RV Park a favorite for RVers.

At 9.6 is the main access road to many good birding areas. Dubbed the **Sarteneja Road** because its terminus meets the sea at Sarteneja, the route includes **Four Mile Lagoon** (another), **Pueblo Nuevo Ferry, Copper Bank, Cerros Maya site, Progresso Lagoon, Shipstern Nature Reserve,** and **Sarteneja National Tree Park**.

The airport entrance road at 10.1 leads to small commercial planes that provide easy and quick transport to Ambergris Caye, Belize City, and other locations. The highway threads through sleepy little villages— Concepcion, San Jose, Buena Vista, and others—with buildings that reflect a British colonial architecture.

Entering at 19.5 and exiting at 23.5 is the **San Victor loop,** which runs along cane fields and offers an excellent representation of northern Belize bird life. At 27 the highway crosses into Orange Walk District. Like its northern neighbor, the district is characterized by sugarcane fields, but agriculturally also boasts sorghum, rice, and vegetables. Pine/palmetto savanna stretches across untilled acreage, shifting to remnant secondary lowland broadleaf forests along the lagoons and rivers. Substantial protected forests are mostly in the westerly Bravo Hills beyond the Rio Bravo Escarpment.

In the northern half of Belize and lying west of Philip Goldson Highway, Orange Walk District includes such famous birding sites as **Lamanai** and **Chan Chich**, as well as many lesser-known sites that can be very rewarding. Access to all of these sites starts from Goldson Highway, and principally from Orange Walk Town.

Several side roads, e.g., at mile 28 to Douglas and at 32 to San Ramon Río Hondo on the Mexico border, can offer interesting birding if you have time and have exhausted the better sites. At 35, Goldson Highway leads directly to Orange Walk, the second largest city in Belize and a 10-minute drive from end to end, with streets closely lined with shops and houses and milling with people. From the fire station starts **Gallon Jug Road**, which leads to Mennonite rice fields near **Blue Creek Village**, the **La**

**Road Log for
Philip Goldson Highway**

*The road can be traveled at moderate to fast speeds, slowed by villages and by sugarcane trucks that move slowly. Birding sites are in **bold**.*

Miles Heading South (North)
Mile S (Mile N)

0.0 (83.1) Mexico/Belize border at bridge over Río Hondo. Free Zone, Immigration and Customs buildings. Customs checkpoint.

1.1 (82.0) T-intersection; turn left (right goes to insurance office).

1.4 (81.7) Curve right to Corozal.

1.6 (81.5) Police checkpoint for Belize vehicle liability insurance.

2.1 (81.0) **Four Mile Lagoon.**

3.7 (79.5) Old Northern Highway exits to the right. Continue left.

7.5 (75.6) "Corozal Welcomes You."

7.8 (75.3) **Santa Rita Maya site** (2 blocks to the right).

7.9 (75.2) Curve left and merge with traffic from right.

8.4 (74.7) Bus station on left.

8.8 (74.3) Texaco station on right. Road then curves right.

9.2 (73.9) Caribbean Village Campground and RV Park on right.

9.6 (73.5) **Sarteneja Road** on left to ferry. Continue straight.

10.1 (73.0) Airport entrance road on right.

15.1 (68.0) Turn right at San Francisco T-intersection.

17.7 (65.4) Old Northern Highway intersects from right.

18.8 (64.3) Curve left in Louisville.

19.5 (63.6) Road on right heads to start of **San Victor Loop**.

23.5 (59.6) Road on right is other end of **San Victor Loop**.

27.1 (56.0) Border of Corozal and Orange Walk Districts.

27.9 (55.2) Road on right (in San Pablo) leads to Douglas (3 miles).

28.4 (54.7) Road on right leads to Noh Mul Maya site.

28.9 (54.2) San Jose Shell station.

31.6 (51.5) Road to right leads to San Ramon Rio Hondo.
35.3 (47.8) Continue left at fork; right goes to Orange Walk Town.
35.8 (47.3) Bridge over New River.
*37.4 (45.7) Continue straight at roundabout. Left goes to **Honey Camp Lagoon**. Right goes to **Gallon Jug Road**.*
38.8 (44.3) Bridge over New River.
39.7 (43.4) Speed bumps.
40.0 (43.1) Exit left; right goes to Orange Walk Town.
40.8 (42.3) Sugarcane factory on left.
*41.7 (41.4) Road on right leads to **Shipyard, Lamanai, and Hill Bank**.*
42.0 (41.1) Driveway on left goes to Reyes & Sons River Tours.
*42.2 (40.9) Tower Hill Bridge over **New River**.*
42.4 (40.7) Pac Te-Ha Tours and Lamanai EcoAdventures on right.
*43.1 (40.0) Continue straight through Carmelita. **Old Northern Highway** on left.*
Border of Orange Walk and Belize Districts.
59.9 (23.2) BTL tower on left.
*61.1 (22.0) Continue straight. Road to **Crooked Tree Wildlife Sanctuary** on right.*
*69.3 (13.8) Side road on right, leading to **Jabiru nest** in 0.2 mile.*
71.1 (12.0) Marsh beside highway can be good birding.
*73.0 (10.1) Continue straight. Road on left is **Old Northern Highway**, leads to Altun Ha.*
*73.7 (9.4) **Salt Creek Estates Road** on left.*
*75.1 (8.8) **Double Run Road** to Belize River on right.*
75.4 (7.7) Texaco station.
78.1 (5.0) Continue straight. Road to left is Belize City Bypass.
78.3 (4.8) "Welcome to Ladyville."
82.7 (0.4) Marage Road to shrimp farms.
83.1 (0.0) Entrance road on right leads to airport. Belize City is straight ahead.

Milpa Ecolodge and Research Center of Rio Bravo Conservation and Management Area, and ultimately to Gallon Jug and adjacent **Chan Chich**.

Alternatively, Goldson Highway, starting at 35, has a newly constructed bypass of Orange Walk Town and at the roundabout at mile 37 is the road to **Honey Camp Lagoon**. The highway crosses the **New River** several times, the intersection at 41.7 on the road log followed by Tower Hill Bridge at 42.2 being the main access points for birders. The road leads to the Mennonite farm community of **Shipyard** and ultimately **Lamanai** and **Hill Bank**, both built along the New River. Easier access is by boat, chartered from several establishments at Tower Hill Bridge. While driving the highway, scan wet ditches for Gray-necked Wood-Rails. **Old Northern Highway** intersects at 43 and again at 73, its northern portion offering excellent birding, including the oft-visited Maya site at **Altun Ha**. Between the two intersections is an imperceptible, heretofore unmarked, change from Orange Walk District to Belize District.

South of the New River, the countryside reverts to pine/palmetto savanna, a thinned pine forest with myriad palmettos poking out of flat, wet land. Watch for Laughing Falcons and Yellow-headed Parrots along this stretch. After crossing into Belize District, watch for the tall BTL microwave tower on the left at 60. Almost immediately after the tower is the turnoff to **Crooked Tree Wildlife Sanctuary**, one of the best-known and most-visited birding sites in Belize. At 69 is a side road heading west, where you can find a Jabiru nest and, in March, you may find the adults tending one or two chicks. At 71 the highway adjoins a marsh worth a search for Muscovy Duck, Black-collared Hawk, and

Ruddy Crake. At 74 is **Salt Creek Estates Road** on the left. Along this stretch of road, censused on the Belize City Christmas Bird Count, almost 200 bird species have been recorded, including Thicket Tinamou, Bicolored Hawk, Vermiculated Screech-Owl, Yucatan Poorwill, and Yucatan Jay. Recently the estate has been sold and birders now can visit a 1,000-acre portion of the original estate by contacting Smuggler's Run Plantation at their website: www.smugglersrunplantation.com; or by email at info@ smugglersrunplantation.com. Tours must be booked in advance. At 75, just north of the Texaco station by a quarter-mile, **Double Run Road** is to the right, along the Belize River. This is one of the few sites where Grassland Yellow-Finch has been found.

At 78 is the T-intersection with the Belize City Bypass. Use this road to get to birding sites at **Community Baboon Sanctuary** and to connect to George Price Highway. Heading straight, though, enter Ladyville and pass the entrance to the former Nova Ladyville shrimp farms at 79 (see page 103 for information on birding shrimp farms). A new access point is **Captain Hook's Restaurant and Shrimp Farm** on Marage Road, just 0.4 mile before the airport turnoff. The site is at N 17° 34.02' W 88° 18.00' about 1.5 miles north of Goldson Highway. Stop for a meal or drink and view several shrimp ponds from an observation tower. The Philip Goldson International Airport access road is at 83. Goldson Highway extends into the city, but for birding purposes the highway log stops at the airport in Ladyville, a northern suburb of Belize City.

At the heart of Belize and the population hub from which radiate the Goldson and Price Highways, Belize District includes Belize City, its international airport, the point of entry for cruise ships, and the portion of the country most often seen by tourists. Birders are likely to forego visiting the city. Lonely Planet warns, "While most visits to Belize are trouble-free, violent crime can be a problem . . .confined mainly to Belize City." Given that the city offers little of interest in bird life that cannot be found elsewhere, it can and probably should be avoided. For those who seek accommodations in Belize City, Best Western Biltmore has been recommended. You can bird the grounds and the waterfront. This is a reliable site to see Eurasian Collared-Dove. Contact: Best Western Belize Biltmore Plaza Hotel, P.O. Box 959, 3-1/2 Miles Philip Goldson Highway, Belize City, Belize District; (011) 501-223-2302 or toll-free in US: 888-790-5264; fax (011) 501-223-2301; reservations@belizebiltmore.com; www.belizebiltmore.com.

COROZAL AREA

Description: The largest town with the most facilities, **Corozal Town** is the hub for northern Belize birding, offering a city market, an RV park, several hotels, and Tony's, a small resort with a favorite restaurant. Check

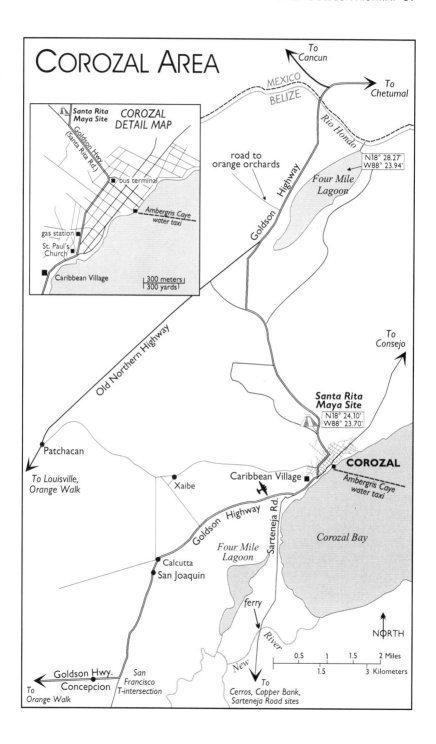

COROZAL AREA

To Cancun

MEXICO
BELIZE

To Chetumal

Río Hondo

COROZAL DETAIL MAP

Santa Rita Maya Site

Goldson Hwy. (Santa Rita Rd)

bus terminal

Ambergris Caye water taxi

gas station

St. Paul's Church

Caribbean Village

300 meters
300 yards

road to orange orchards

Goldson Highway

Four Mile Lagoon

N18° 28.27'
W88° 23.94'

To Consejo

Old Northern Highway

Santa Rita Maya Site

N18° 24.10'
W88° 23.70'

COROZAL

Ambergris Caye water taxi

Patchacan

To Louisville, Orange Walk

Xaibe

Caribbean Village

Sarteneja Rd.

Corozal Bay

Goldson Highway

Four Mile Lagoon

Calcutta

San Joaquin

ferry

River

New

NORTH

Goldson Hwy.

San Francisco T-intersection

Concepcion

To Orange Walk

To Cerros, Copper Bank, Sarteneja Road sites

0.5   1   1.5   2 Miles
1.5   3 Kilometers

the road log for the locations of the gas station, bus station, and airport. The boat dock also offers transport to Ambergris Caye.

Birding strategy: Perhaps your most interesting sighting from the shores of the Caribbean at Corozal will be the Magnificent Frigatebirds that soar high above you. Surprisingly, in March 2011, from the beach at the resort, a guest photographed a Brown Noddy flying low over Corozal Bay. Scan the bay for floating birds and you likely will find American Coots and maybe ducks. Except for Blue-winged Teal, ducks are rather hard to come by in Belize, though small flocks of Ring-necked Ducks and Lesser Scaup have been seen in Chetumal Bay. Look for patches of undisturbed woods, such as that behind Caribbean Village, where you can find Ferruginous Pygmy-Owl, Collared Aracari, Keel-billed Toucan, and, best of all, Black Catbird, a species found at only a few mainland sites. Barn Owl has been seen often in Corozal Town near St. Paul's by the Sea Church.

Several birding sites—Rio Hondo, Four Mile Lagoon (north), orange orchards, and Santa Rita—are within five miles of the city center. Each might be best visited for an hour or so in the early morning or could be combined in a full morning's birding, although birding slows considerably at these sites after about 10 AM, unless skies are overcast. For more, and usually better, birding head out along the Sarteneja Road or make a half-day trip of the San Victor loop.

Key species of the Corozal Bay perimeter: [boldface = target species, R = rare, S = summer, T = transitory migrant] Lesser Scaup, Double-crested Cormorant, Hook-billed Kite, **Ornate Hawk-Eagle**, Peregrine Falcon, Ruddy Crake, American Coot, **Wilson's Plover**, Western and Least Sandpipers, Herring Gull, Sandwich Tern, Eurasian Collared-Dove, White-winged Dove, Common Ground-Dove, Yellow-lored Parrot, Barn Owl, Ferruginous Pygmy-Owl, Green-breasted Mango, Cinnamon

Ecoregion and habitats: Appendix A, Ecoregion 1, Corozal coastal savannas. Habitats include remnant secondary lowland broadleaf forest and scrub (BFL3), agricultural (AG1, AG4), coastal bays, lagoons, and rivers (BFL1, BFL2), and population center (PC).

Contact: Tony's Inn & Beach Resort, South End, Corozal Town, P.O. Box 12, Corozal District; (011) 501-422-2055/422-3555 or toll-free in US: 800-447-2931 or 633-4734; tonys@btl.net; www.tonysinn.com.

Location: Four Mile Lagoon is at N 18° 28.27' W 88° 23.94' and is 6.7 miles north of the Texaco station in Corozal Town. Easily overlooked, Santa Rita Maya site is at N 18° 24.10' W 88° 23.70', with an entrance road from Goldson Highway one mile north of the Texaco station in town. At the curve on the north side of Corozal Town, continue north for just 0.1 mile and look for the Super Santa Rita grocery on your left. Take the dirt road west for 0.2 mile and you will see the site on your right.

Hummingbird, Yucatan Woodpecker, **Yucatan Flycatcher**, Scissor-tailed and Fork-tailed Flycatchers, Rufous-browed Peppershrike, Yucatan Jay, Bank Swallow [T], **Black Catbird**, Gray-crowned Yellowthroat, **Olive Sparrow**, Green-backed Sparrow, Northern Cardinal, Blue Grosbeak, Eastern Meadowlark, Hooded Oriole, **Orange** and **Altamira Orioles**, **Lesser Goldfinch**, Tricolored Munia (non-native).

Sarteneja Road

[25 January]   Our early-morning birding starts just a couple of miles from Corozal at a canal leading to Four Mile Lagoon. When we reach the lagoon I see a Pale-vented Pigeon across the water, conveniently perched in the open. Driving a road I've not found on any of a dozen Belize maps I've examined, we move on to the New River. While we wait for the ferry to reach our side a very vocal Red-billed Pigeon curiously circles over me when I imitate its call. Onboard, the experience certainly makes us recognize, "Toto, I've a feeling we're not in Kansas anymore." Two strong-armed dark men take turns cranking a wheel and pulley that slowly transports the rickety wooden ferry across the water on taut cables. A kingfisher crisscrosses the narrow tree-lined New River while a Morelet's Crocodile lurks in the shadows of overhanging palmettos.

We head east, then south, then north, as we drive around Progresso Lagoon, since there is no road over its connection to the sea. Secondary broadleaf forest surrounds us, frequently interspersed with sugarcane fields and, later, corn, bean, and other vegetable fields, tended by Mennonites. The road—if you can call this a road—is a broad white limestone base seriously potholed. About 2-1/2 hours after departure, we arrive at Shipstern and are greeted by the reserve warden.

Description: The road to Sarteneja passes some remarkable birding sites, culminating in Shipstern Nature Reserve. Only 39 miles from Corozal Town, it doesn't seem far away until you drive the dusty roads you take to get there.

The first part of the road—an easy morning or late afternoon trip from Corozal—includes many good birding stops and opportunities to see northern species that do not extend into central or southern Belize. Following the Sarteneja route, the gravel and hardpan road sees limited traffic and birding is good throughout. To reach Shipstern for a day trip requires a very early morning start from Corozal or Orange Walk. Alternatively, consider staying in Sarteneja.

Birding strategy: If one of your goals is a comprehensive Belize life list, you need to concentrate on a few species that are most readily found at birding sites along Sarteneja Road, including Shipstern Nature Reserve, and that become increasingly difficult to find as you travel south. Also, this area of Belize is little explored by birders, so the opportunity of adding to our ornithological knowledge is greatest.   Two species have Belize ranges restricted to the northeast corner: Caribbean Dove, which favors littoral forest, and Orange Oriole, which inhabits forest edge and open areas with scattered trees. Other species with restricted ranges are: Thicket Tinamou, Wilson's Plover, Yellow-lored Parrot, Buff-bellied Hummingbird, Cinnamon Hummingbird, Yucatan Woodpecker, Yucatan Jay, Black Catbird, Rose-throated Tanager, Altamira Oriole, and Lesser Goldfinch. In appropriate habitat, these could be found throughout this portion of northeastern Corozal District. Also, check Shipstern for the breeding colonies of Reddish Egrets and Roseate Spoonbills. See the Key Species lists on pages 40 and 49 as well for other species in the area.

Along Sarteneja Road the first stop, **Four Mile Lagoon**, is reached in a bit over one mile. Not to be confused with the Four Mile Lagoon near Rio Hondo, this distinctly separate water body carries the same name on maps. A narrow canal connects from the road to the lagoon on the south, with a small cleared section of forest on the west. In early morning, between here and the **Pueblo Nuevo Ferry**, this two-mile stretch could easily produce 50 species in a couple of hours, including Lesser Yellow-headed Vulture, Pale-vented and Red-billed Pigeons, Plain-breasted Ground-Dove, Yucatan Woodpecker, Gray-breasted Martin, Mangrove Swallow, and Yellow-tailed Oriole.

After Four Mile Lagoon, stop at the failed **Corozal beach property** site (mile 1.5), a cleared area extending from the road to Corozal Bay, and look for shorebirds, notably Wilson's Plovers, which sometimes occur here in flocks. The empty lots separated by narrow canals favor Little Blue Herons and Fork-tailed Flycatchers. Next stop, at 3, is a wetlands reaching to the forest on both sides of the road. Ruddy Crakes are reliable at this spot, especially at dawn and dusk when they are easily heard, if not seen.

Road Log for Sarteneja Road:

Start from Goldson Highway, 9.6 miles south of the Mexico border and at the southern end of Corozal Town. This intersection is marked with a sign for the ferry.

0.0 Intersection with Goldson Highway. Pass through residential area, making several turns (left, right, right, left), but staying on main road.

1.3 **Four Mile Lagoon** on right.

1.5 Corozal beach (failed development). Road is pot-holed hard-pan when dry.

3.2 Wetlands for Ruddy Crake.

3.6 **Pueblo Nuevo Ferry** (operates 24 hours/day, no fee).

6.1 Pass turnoff on left to **Cerros Maya site** and **Copper Bank**. Turn right (south) toward Progresso. N 18° 18.72' W 88° 23.62'. Roads can be muddy. Progresso Lagoon is out of sight to the east.

11.3 Progresso (north side).

13.0 **Progresso Lagoon** on left.

14.7 Large pond on right. Approaching "T" for San Estevan and Shipstern. N 18° 11.68' W 88° 26.02'.

14.9 Turn left, heading east.

16.7 Turn left.

17.9 Passing beside Mennonite farmland and secondary forest. Lagoon on left.

21.4 Road marker 19. Subsequent markers increase numerically to 34 at Shipstern.

25.2 Village of Chunox.

31.0 Pass spur on right.

33.3 Waree Bight, an Eco Resort Community.

36.1 "Welcome to Shipstern" sign.

36.3 Road marker 34.

38.9 **Shipstern Nature Reserve** headquarters and butterfly center on right.

39.5 End of Shipstern Reserve.

41.1 **Sarteneja Natl. Tree Park**, including museum and trails.

41.9 Fishing village of **Sarteneja** on Caribbean coast.

43.1 Continue through village to point, birding along the way.

44.5 Exit Sarteneja; pass Shipstern, heading south.

67.3 Access to Progresso Lagoon.

71.3 South side of Progresso Lagoon (equivalent to 14.9).

Turn left at "T" (instead of right, which heads back the way you came).

77.4 San Estevan (north side). Curve left in village.

78.4 San Estevan (south side). Broken pavement, potholes.

83.0 Turn right at intersection.

83.3 San Estevan roundabout (on Orange Walk bypass). Turn right toward Corozal (or straight if returning to Orange Walk Town).

85.4 Orange Walk split. Continue north to Corozal.

111.5 Back at starting point in Corozal Town.

The hand-crank ferry over New River provides a good viewpoint from which to watch the river. Although the trip is short, you may wait a half-hour for your turn to drive aboard. Birds of this part of New River include Boat-billed Heron, Limpkin, Sungrebe, and American Pygmy Kingfisher. Continue birding along the roadsides, until you reach the T-intersection at 6.1 miles. Turning left would take you to **Cerros Maya site** and **Copper Bank**, treated below in a separate section.

Turn right to continue on Sarteneja Road toward Shipstern Nature Reserve. After various directional changes you will come to **Progresso Lagoon** and the small village of Progresso. You can access the lagoon through the village and various housing developments. Be sure to stop at a large pond on the right at mile 15, looking for Black-bellied Whistling-Ducks, Muscovy Ducks, and long-legged waders.

Immediately thereafter you will come to a T-intersection. Remember this intersection as it provides an alternate return route to Corozal or Orange Walk, via San Estevan. Turn left for Shipstern.

The Mennonite community will become more apparent now as you may encounter horse-drawn carriages and families dressed in traditional clothing, as well as countryside of farmlands with vegetables and other crops. The fenced edges and the remnant forest patches, particularly along Progresso Lagoon, are good birding habitat for dozens of Indigo Buntings, mixed with Blue Grosbeaks, White-collared Seedeaters, and a few Blue-black Grassquits.

The boundary of **Shipstern Nature Reserve** is at 36 miles and the headquarters is at 39. This birding site, as well as **Sarteneja National Tree Park** at 41, is treated in a separate section. The road terminates at the Caribbean coast in **Sarteneja**, about 42 miles from Corozal. Along the shore you can find Magnificent Frigatebirds, Black-bellied Plovers, and Royal Terns, and other birds by wandering through the village side streets and in wetlands and littoral forests near the airport. A two-day visit at Fireburn Nature Reserve on Shipstern Lagoon produced 85 species, including Great Tinamou, Great Curassow, Yellow-lored Parrot, Buff-bellied Hummingbird, and Yucatan Jay. Habitat at Fireburn is unusual for northeast Belize, and its high forest and broken ridge more closely resemble the Gallon Jug area. See the Key Species list on page 49.

On the return trip you might consider turning left at the T-intersection described earlier and driving through San Estevan. The condition of the road depends on rainfall and the season, and you may find it severely potholed and muddied by cane trucks, which line the road during harvest. Once you reach the San Estevan roundabout near Orange Walk Town, you will be back on excellent highway.

Ecoregion and habitats: Appendix A, Ecoregion 1, Corozal coastal savannas. Habitats include: lowland broadleaf forest (BFL2, BFL3), mangrove and littoral forest (LF2), fresh and brackish water, coastal seafront, savanna and agricultural areas (AG1, AG3), and small villages (PC).

Concerns: This road is often rough, although scenic, and drive time is long for a day trip. If the goal is to bird Shipstern, plan on spending a night or more there or in Sarteneja (see page 49). Get fuel before leaving, as there are no stations en route.

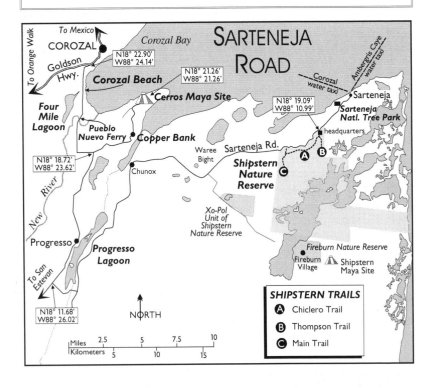

Cerros Maya Site
and Copper Bank

[26 January] We traverse the quiet streets of Copper Bank, studying the overgrown lots which attract species that prefer semi-open and edge habitat. The scattered fruiting trees adorning the yards of humble dwellings attract Cinnamon Hummingbirds and Yucatan Woodpeckers, specialties of the north. The best prize awaits us. I see the oriole's orange head and black wings, then concentrate on its back because that will distinguish it from the more common Hooded Oriole. It's orange! I've located an Orange Oriole, a tough find in Belize.

We drive a few miles in the direction of Cerros Maya site, but stop where others last year found a nesting Ornate Hawk-Eagle family. Being a resident of primary broadleaf forest, this raptor is hard to find and most of us have not seen one before. Here we are in the midst of a densely wooded forest, cut through by a wide red dirt road, giving us a vantage point for seeing the canopy of tall trees. We hear an adult calling just as we arrive and relocate the nest high in a tree. After a long wait we see the hawk-eagle with a kingly top feather so deserving to be called ornate. What a way to top off an incredible morning of birding!

Description: Oft times the birding en route to Cerros is so good that the Maya site is almost an afterthought. The small but historically important Maya site dates to the Late Pre-classic period (400 B.C. to A.D. 100) and includes a 4,000-foot canal system and raised-field agriculture as well as astronomical achievements significant so early in the Maya culture. One of the temples displays colorful replicas of 6- to 13-foot-high masks, overlaying and pro-tecting the originals discovered during excavations in the 1970s.

Birding strategy: Bird Sarteneja Road from Corozal to mile 6.1, especially Four Mile Lagoon, Corozal beach and wetlands, and Pueblo Nuevo Ferry. At the T-intersection, jog left (northeast) toward Copper Bank on hardpan road in poor condition. Look for Common Ground-Dove, Yellow-lored Parrot, and Black Catbird. At 8.6 you will be at the southwest edge of **Copper Bank**. Drive and bird through six blocks of village, each about 0.1 mile on edge, watching for parrots and orioles, especially Orange Oriole. If you find fruiting and flowering trees, stop for what is bound to be a good show of hummingbirds, flycatchers, and warblers. Look especially for Buff-bellied and Cinnamon Hummingbirds, which are similar to the more common Rufous-tailed Hummingbird. The edge habitat northeast of the village is the most productive. Yucatan Woodpecker can be found here, but it

---

Concerns: *Bring mosquito repellent for Cerros.*
Fees and facilities: *Entrance US$10 for non-residents, BZ$10 for residents. Archeological exhibits and toilets at Cerros.*
Location and directions: *N 18° 21.26' W 88° 21.26' at Cerros. The site is about 12 miles from Corozal Town, passing through Copper Bank en route. Start from Corozal Town, following the Sarteneja travel log. Also, a boat can be chartered from Corozal Town (e.g., at Tony's Inn & Beach Resort) for a 20-minute ride to Cerros.*

is often misidentified because of its close similarity to the more common Golden-fronted Woodpecker. Look for a bird that is smaller bodied, shorter tailed, smaller billed, with a more rounded head and yellow-white (not red) nasal tufts. The differentiation is a bit like separating Downy and Hairy Woodpeckers. See the Key Species list on page 49.

A ssuming your odometer reads approximately 9.1, continue on the dirt road out of town and at 10.7 you will reach where the Ornate Hawk-Eagle nest was hidden in 2005–2007 in tall trees on your left (north). This is shortly before a fork in the road (left to Cerros Maya site, right to Cerros Sands). The tree was shortened, perhaps by a hurricane, destroying the nest, yet the hawk-eagle was still in the same area in 2011. To continue toward Cerros, turn left at the fork and reach the parking lot for the Maya site at 11.5. An attendant will collect an entrance fee. Cerros borders the sea and is wooded with a cleared understory. Several trails extend through the site, some with a view of the sea and others passing through deeper forest, especially the one leading to the ball court.

Shipstern Nature Reserve and Sarteneja National Tree Park

Description: Established as a nature reserve in 1981 and expanded thereafter, Shipstern Nature Reserve encompasses 26,000 acres of pristine waterlogged jungle, savanna, and mangrove swamp, the largest such tract in Belize. The reserve juts out into Chetumal Bay in northeastern Belize and from the air the terrain looks totally inaccessible by land. However, Shipstern offers several good hiking trails leading through the hardwood forest and to the savanna, as well as boat trips through the swamps to Wood Stork and heron rookeries. Treetop blinds, positioned in the canopy, offer good opportunities to see wild cats and other nocturnal wildlife for overnight or early-morning stays.

Birding strategy: Like most tropical sites, birding is best in the early morning, and the long drive to Shipstern brings you too late in the morning, so it would be best to plan on spending the night at Shipstern or nearby Sarteneja. Once there, the nature reserve administration requires you to be accompanied by a guide. A self-guided hike along the Chiclero Botanical Trail is offered at no extra charge. While beneficial for botanical pursuits, having many well-marked native species, it offers fewer desired bird species. The Thompson Trail will provide better birding.

In Belize, Caribbean Dove is localized only to Ambergris Caye and the Sarteneja region. It can be heard during the summer months but is usually silent at other seasons. It is a common resident north of Shipstern Lagoon and is less often found at Xo-Pol and south of the lagoon.

At night from the headquarters area, Yucatan Poorwill, Yucatan Nightjar, and Northern Potoo have been heard. In 2003 at the headquarters a female potoo successfully raised a chick. Buff-bellied Hummingbirds are fairly common at the vegetation bordering the road to Sarteneja and to Cowpen, especially from May to November. Here Buff-bellieds are more common than Rufous-tailed Hummingbirds. Another specialty of Corozal District is Yucatan Woodpecker. In a year-long study, out of 135 encounters, Laesser (2003) found 39% were Yucatans while 61% were Golden-fronteds.

Yucatan Flycatcher is more readily found here than in other parts of Belize. All four *Myiarchus* flycatchers are fairly common, although their seasons differ. Yucatan Flycatcher favors rather dry forest, but can be found in nearly every type of forest. It follows ant swarms. Black Catbirds prefer littoral forest habitat (Robin's Land) and, secondarily, mixed mangroves and shrubs (Cowpen) or forest edge. Eastern Kingbirds are not found outside the migration window, but at peak migration they are a sight to behold. In 15 minutes, 5:45 to 6:00 PM, an amazing 1,050 flew over Thompson Trail on 9 April 2003.

Migration in Belize is more prominent along the coast, with Shipstern well-positioned to catch the transitory wave. Expected passage migrants include: Swallow-tailed Kite, Least Sandpiper, Chimney Swift, Eastern Wood-Pewee, Acadian, Alder, Willow, Least, and Great Crested Flycatchers, White-eyed, Yellow-throated, and Red-eyed Vireos, Purple Martin, Tree, Northern Rough-winged, Bank, Cliff, and Barn Swallows, Veery, Swainson's Thrush, Ovenbird, Worm-eating Warbler, Louisiana and Northern Waterthrushes, Black-and-white, Prothonotary, Tennessee, and Kentucky Warblers, Common Yellowthroat, Hooded Warbler, American Redstart, Northern Parula, Bay-breasted, Blackburnian, Yellow, Chestnut-sided, Yellow-rumped, and Black-throated Green Warblers, Yellow-breasted Chat, Summer and Scarlet Tanagers, Rose-breasted Grosbeak, Indigo Bunting, and Dickcissel. A few of these remain in the area during the winter.

Less-often seen migrants include: Broad-winged Hawk, Western Sandpiper, Black Tern, Yellow-billed Cuckoo, Common Nighthawk, Chuck-will's-widow, Gray-cheeked Thrush, Golden-winged, Swainson's, Mourning, Cerulean, Yellow-throated, Canada, and Wilson's Warblers, Painted Bunting, and Baltimore Oriole.

Both transient Yellow Warbler and resident Mangrove Yellow Warbler are common. The Mangrove Yellow Warbler favors dwarf mangroves and sparsely wooded herbaceous wetlands north of the lagoon, but also areas near Shipstern Landing, at Iguana Camp, and Cowpen. Unlike other parts of Belize, at Shipstern Nature Reserve, including Xo-Pol and Fireburn, Rose-throated Tanagers are common and can be found in all types of forests.

White-necked Puffbird   Bert Frenz

Both the common Olive Sparrow and look-alike fairly common Green-backed Sparrow occur. Both stay to forest edges, not interior, the Olive Sparrow in open landscapes north and south of the lagoon, including dwarf mangroves and sparsely wooded herbaceous wetlands, while the Green-backed Sparrow uses all types of forest but mostly occurs to the south of the lagoon, including Fireburn. Blue Buntings are more common in moist forests, especially near the beginning of the Main Trail. At its southern limit in the Yucatán Peninsula, Orange Oriole is difficult to find. The headquarters area, where it attempted nest building in 2003, is a likely spot.

A guided trip can be arranged to Xo-Pol, a 1,500-acre parcel west of the reserve where the forest is taller and older and there is a crocodile pond with a treetop blind over a Jaguar trail. Birds of Xo-Pol include Muscovy Duck, Snail Kite, Ruddy Quail-Dove, Wedge-tailed Sabrewing, White-necked Puffbird, Red-capped Manakin, and Gray-headed Tanager. A one-day lagoon rookery tour by boat to see Reddish Egrets, Roseate Spoonbills, and Wood Storks could prove worthwhile, especially because Reddish Egret is difficult to find on mainland Belize. Also available is a visit to the Shipstern Maya archaeological site near Sarteneja.

This northeastern corner of Belize was nearly flattened by 1955 Hurricane *Janet*, so the secondary forests here have grown up since that time, except for one original mahogany nicknamed Big George. The **Sarteneja National Tree Park** includes the best accessible stand of mahogany trees left in the country, just 2.2 miles beyond Shipstern headquarters (N 18° 20.46' W 88° 9.62' at museum). Entrance is included in the Shipstern Nature Reserve fee. Tours are available from staff at Shipstern. Facilities include hiking trails and a good museum covering the history of mahogany in Belize. After birding here, you can continue another mile to the coastal village of Sarteneja.

Key species of Shipstern Nature Reserve and other northeast Belize sites: Thicket Tinamou, Black-bellied Whistling-Duck, Lesser Scaup, Lesser Yellow-headed Vulture, Common Black-Hawk, Broad-winged Hawk [T], **Clapper Rail**, Black-bellied Plover, **Wilson's Plover**, Black-necked Stilt, Short-billed Dowitcher, **Long-billed Dowitcher**, Wilson's Snipe, Forster's Tern, **White-crowned Pigeon**, White-winged Dove, Common Ground-Dove, **Caribbean Dove**, Yellow-lored Parrot, Mangrove Cuckoo, Vermiculated Screech-Owl, Great Horned [R] and Mottled Owls, Lesser and Common [S] Nighthawks, Yucatan Nightjar, Chimney [T] and Vaux's Swifts, Canivet's Emerald, **Buff-bellied Hummingbird**, Cinnamon Hummingbird, **Yucatan Woodpecker**, **Northern Beardless-Tyrannulet**, Alder and Willow Flycatchers, **Yucatan Flycatcher**, **Yucatan Vireo**, Rufous-browed Peppershrike, Yucatan Jay, Bank [T] and Cliff [T] Swallows, White-bellied Wren, Veery [T], **Black Catbird**, Mangrove Yellow Warbler, **Olive Sparrow**, Green-backed Sparrow, **Rose-throated Tanager**, Northern Cardinal, **Gray-throated Chat**, **Dickcissel**, **Orange Oriole**, Altamira Oriole.

> **Ecoregion and habitats:** Appendix A, Ecoregion 2, Shipstern lowlands and wetlands. Habitats include: lowland broadleaf forest (BFL3), bajo (BFL2), coastal savanna, mangrove, and littoral forest (LF2), fresh and brackish water, and saline coastal lagoon.
>
> **Fees and contact:** Entrance US$7.50 per person. Accessing better birding trails, e.g., the Thompson Trail, requires use of a local guide at a group rate of US$6.25 for non-residents, BZ$6.25 for residents. A guided trip to Xo-Pol is about US$30 for fuel and US$10 per hour. A one-day lagoon rookery tour is about US$150 per group. Contact: Shipsternbelize@ yahoo.com.
>
> **Facilities:** Pit toilets, museum of sorts, butterfly enclosure. A house with two rooms and bunk beds (looks Spartan) is available and would facilitate stays to see nocturnal animals. For the Shipstern Lagoon crossing and overnight stay at Fireburn Village, contact Paul and Zoe Walker at Wildtracks, a manatee rehabilitation center, P.O. Box 278, Belize City; (011) 501-650-6578; office@wildtracksbelize.org; www.wildtracksbelize.org. For overnighting in Sarteneja Village, Fernando's Seaside Guesthouse, (011) 501-423-2085; sartenejabelize@hotmail.com; http://cybercayecaulker.com/sarteneja.html.
>
> **Location:** N 18° 19.09' W 88° 10.99' at headquarters. Starting from Corozal Town, take the Sarteneja Road route to mile 38.9. Alternatively, starting from Orange Walk Town, read the directions in reverse from 83.3 to 71.3 and then forward from 14.9 to 38.9. Estimated drive time, with occasional brief stops for birding, is three hours. Fuel up before leaving, as there are no gas stations en route.
>
> **Alternative transportation:** The Ambergris Caye ferry between Corozal Town and San Pedro stops at Sarteneja. Also, a bus travels between Belize City and Sarteneja, a three-hour trip. Using the bus would require an overnight stay in Sarteneja to allow time for birding.

Important habitat: large rookeries for Wood Stork (200 pairs), Great Egret, **Reddish Egret** (largest colony in Belize), White Ibis, Roseate Spoonbill; major migration route for a wide variety of species.

In addition to birds, the reserve holds Nine-banded Armadillo, Paca, White-nosed Coati, Ocelot, Margay, Jaguarundi, Puma, Jaguar, West Indian Manatee, Baird's Tapir, peccaries, deer (but no monkeys), as well as American and Morelet's Crocodiles and 60 species of amphibians and reptiles. The site also protects a rare Kuka Palm forest.

San Victor Loop

[30 January] I'm particularly keen on finding Lesser Goldfinch, a species infrequently reported in Belize but known to occur in this quadrant. The rural road takes us alongside cane fields interspersed with fallow cornfields, clumps of trees, and wide weedy patches. Each copse is an oasis in a desert of monoculture sugarcane. Our first stop brings us a pair of Ferruginous Pygmy-Owls cuddled side by side. . .At another stop at a tree thicket, we are amazed at the variety of species represented, from Green-breasted Mango to Grayish Saltator. In fact, we tally up 32 species while standing in one spot. Later, while walking along a farm road adjacent to an abandoned field, I identify another Philadelphia Vireo—first none for six years, now two within three days. At yet another stop in trees above a cow pen, we watch a secretive vireo that eventually gives us enough clues to piece it together as a Yucatan Vireo, a surprise miles from the coast. Best of all, we get marvelous looks at Lesser Goldfinch.

Description: A rural road that might otherwise be dismissed as un-interesting turns out to be a great birding spot for northern Belize specialties. This route is drive-and-stop birding, with the best sites near copses of trees or long-abandoned fields.

Birding strategy: Assuming you are starting from the northern end of the loop, zero your odometer at the Goldson Highway intersection near San Narciso. Tricolored Munia was discovered on the outskirts of the village in February 2009 and 15–20 were seen at the same location the next month. Continue 1.4 miles to the west side of the village. Here you will find cane fields

Ecoregion and habitats: Appendix A, Ecoregion 1, Corozal coastal savannas. Habitats include: agricultural fields (AG1), scrub, wooded edges (BFL3).

Concerns: Pull to the side of the road to allow traffic to pass, although it should be minimal. After heavy rainfall, the road can be very muddy with deep ruts, a problem for low-clearance, non-four-wheel-drive vehicles.

Location: N 18° 18.61' W 88° 30.67' at east side of San Narciso. The start is 11 miles (20 minutes) from Corozal or about 20 miles (35 minutes) from Orange Walk. If approaching from Corozal Town, start from San Narciso at mile 19.5 on the Goldson Highway log. If coming from Orange Walk Town, you could enter the loop at mile 59.6 following in reverse of the directions above, although the birding might be better starting from San Narciso at mile 63.6.

surrounding a wooded oasis (N 18° 17.98' W 88° 31.67'). At 3.1 miles, another small wooded area with a short path is good birding habitat. Farm roads abutting at 3.5 and 4.7 are more birding stops, as are the brushy edges of the cane fields for Gray-crowned Yellowthroat and Green-backed Sparrow; from farther in the fields you should hear Eastern Meadowlarks, a species that finds more suitable habitat in northern Belize than farther south. Other species you can find here include Aplomado Falcon, Mourning Dove (fall migration), Striped Cuckoo, Cinnamon Hummingbird, Common Tody-Flycatcher, and Bronzed Cowbird. Throughout, be on the lookout for Lesser Goldfinch feeding in the fallow fields. If you miss them in the fields, you could find them in San Victor, which starts at 5.3.

Turn left in the village at 5.6 miles. If it is still early in the day you may find additional species along the cane fields before you reach the T-intersection at 9.2 miles (N 18° 15.09' W 88° 31.20'). To complete the loop, heading toward Corozal, continue north (left) through the village of Santa Clara to San Narciso at 13.3 miles.

GALLON JUG ROAD, AUGUST PINE RIDGE, AND BLUE CREEK VILLAGE

[23 February] To reach the area by dawn, five of us leave Corozal at 4:30 AM. Under a clear starlit sky and with little traffic, our transit is easy. Illuminated only by my headlights, the rows of white spots on a reddish pig-shaped Paca are clearly visible as the strictly nocturnal mammal wanders about the road ahead of me. Surprising to me, many workers already are awake and standing in groups in the little towns we pass, waiting for the bus. As we head west and then south, Yo Creek and the even smaller villages have paved roads, but the five-mile stretches between population centers are hard packed, liberally sprinkled with potholes. A Gray Fox crosses our path at first light.

At dawn we stop at a small wooded area and pond surrounded by vast open fields of sorghum, ripe for harvest. The birding is remarkably good and we remain at this small oasis for a couple of hours, adding new birds; Plain-breasted Ground-Dove, Common Tody-Flycatcher, and Fork-tailed Flycatcher lead the list. We continue to travel through Mennonite farmlands—flat, moist, and well-maintained. We stop at a sorghum field to walk along a farm path and hear a raucous chorus coming from the forested edge a half-mile away. Even from this distance we can see the large flock and soon they wing in our direction, a boisterous, rowdy flock of about 500 White-fronted Parrots.

Description: An excellent road for birding, Gallon Jug Road also leads to the best northwestern Belize sites, boldfaced below and described in detail in subsequent sections. The road is pot-holed hardpan, except for short paved sections through villages. SUVs with good suspension can travel these roads surprisingly quickly; however, riders in heavy-duty pickups with multi-ply tires endure a painful ride unless they drive slowly. Mennonite farms line the road from Trinidad to Tres Leguas, roughly miles 10 to 38 on the Gallon Jug Road log.

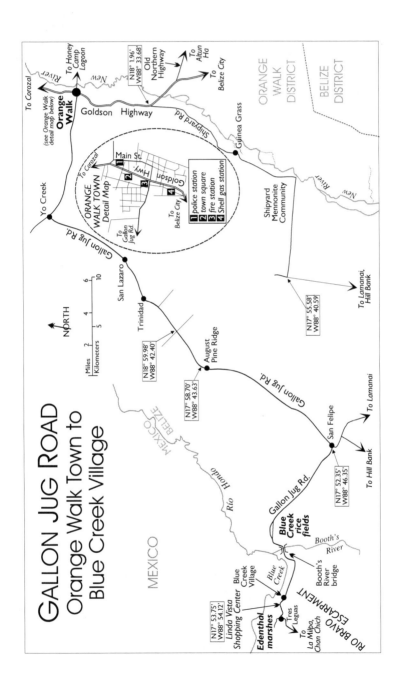

GALLON JUG ROAD
Orange Walk Town to
Blue Creek Village

NORTH

Miles
Kilometers

ORANGE
WALK
DISTRICT

BELIZE
DISTRICT

To Corozal

New River

To Honey Camp Lagoon

Orange Walk
(see Orange Walk detail map below)

N18° 1.96'
W88° 33.68'

Old Northern Highway

To Altun Ha

To Belize City

Goldson Highway

Shipyard Rd.

Guinea Grass

New River

Yo Creek

ORANGE WALK TOWN
Detail Map

To Corozal

Main St.

Goldson Hwy.

1 police station
2 town square
3 fire station
4 Shell gas station

To Belize City

To Gallon Jug Rd.

Shipyard Mennonite Community

To Lamanai, Hill Bank

Gallon Jug Rd.

San Lazaro

Trinidad

N18° 59.98'
W88° 42.40'

August Pine Ridge

N17° 58.70'
W88° 43.63'

N17° 55.58'
W88° 40.59

Gallon Jug Rd.

San Felipe

To Lamanai

To Hill Bank

N17° 52.35'
W88° 46.35'

MEXICO

BELIZE

Rio Hondo

Gallon Jug Rd.

Blue Creek rice fields

Booth's River

Booth's River bridge

Blue Creek Village

Linda Vista Shopping Center

N17° 53.75'
W88° 54.12'

Edenthal marshes

Blue Creek

Tres Leguas

To La Milpa, Chan Chich

RIO BRAVO ESCARPMENT

MEXICO

B irds seem to be everywhere along this road with more birding opportunities than can fit in a day's excursion, so you would do well to plan ahead, reducing your stops to those that best fit the birds you most want to find. Alternatively, stay at a local B&B at mile 33 (see box on page 56). Even after many trips, you are likely to find new birding stops and species not found previously along the route. Most roadside birding is best done in the early morning, shortly after sunrise, which in most cases necessitates a predawn drive (watch out for workers heading to the cane fields in the Orange Walk area). Midday birding can be good in the rice fields and in the more heavily wooded areas near the escarpment. With a couple of rest breaks, travel time from Orange Walk to La Milpa (44 miles) is about two hours, although with birding it could easily be eight hours.

Birding strategy: To hear nocturnal species and the dawn chorus, plan on starting from Orange Walk Town an hour before sunrise. From central Orange Walk Town, Gallon Jug Road heads west out of town. Reset your odometer at the Fire Station. If you are traveling pre-dawn you likely will find little of interest along the country road or at the villages of Yo Creek at 5 miles, San Lazaro at 9, or Trinidad at 10. After the Trinidad water tower at 11, start looking for likely birding spots. You could make your first stop near mile 12. If you arrive early enough, you should hear forest-falcons, owls, and pauraques. For species of the agricultural fields, pine savanna, and brushlands, concentrate on miles 12 through 25. To get the largest variety of birds, check all of the habitats—shrubby fence lines, wooded patches often near farmhouses, sorghum fields, disturbed pine savanna, and utility poles and wires. Plain-breasted Ground-Dove can be found along the road, but it is easily confused with the commonly occurring female Ruddy Ground-Dove and the rarely found Common Ground-Dove.

A t 12 on the right side of the road, a woodlot of fruiting trees is a productive spot. From here to San Felipe is good birding habitat along the road, although you will often be interrupted by farm trucks, tractors, and rural buses. Take advantage of abutting farm roads, mostly on the right side of the main road, thus avoiding the Belizeans' friendly greeting of honking horns as you stand beside the road. A particularly good side road intersects at mile 13.4; it is worth birding for a quarter-mile as it transitions from open fields with brushy fencerows to wetlands and brushlands, followed by pine savanna and palmettos. The fallow fields are a good bet for Fork-tailed Flycatcher. Green-breasted Mango is common here. In scrubby spots, listen for Striped Cuckoo. Check puddles of water under shading trees or shrubs for the more elusive species such as American Pygmy Kingfisher, Stub-tailed Spadebill, and Gray-throated Chat. You probably won't want to drive the whole road as it continues to Mexico—you can see the hills of Mexico to the west. Elsewhere along the main road, look for sorghum fields that attract Red-billed Pigeons and White-fronted Parrots, sometimes in the hundreds. Productive stopping points might be at miles 13.8 (about 1.4 miles before reaching the north side of August Pine Ridge), 18.4, and 21.4.

At 22.9 you enter the north side of San Felipe. The key T-intersection is at 23.3, marked by a Roman Catholic school at the corner. From here you can reach birding sites at **Lamanai** and **Hill Bank**, although these roads are not the easiest way to get to either place. Turn right to continue on Gallon Jug Road.

Once it gets too hot (at about 10 AM), move on to the rice fields and marshes, at 27–31 miles and the Edenthal area beyond 37.7 on the road log. The vast rice fields in the Blue Creek Village Mennonite community are noted for long-legged waders, particularly Jabiru, especially at harvest time. Eight martin and swallow species fly over these fields and waterways. Adjacent to the fields are small wooded areas, canals, and riparian habitat along Booth's River. There are multiple ways of crisscrossing along the perimeter roads of the rice fields. Try the side road at 27.7 that leads through rice fields to a wooded ridge and eventually loops back to Gallon Jug Road at 28.6. Some of these perimeter roads are probably private property, so avoid them if unsure or look for a rice farmer and ask permission.

Stop at Booth's River bridge, mile 29, for kingfishers and swallows. Park after the bridge and walk the area, seeking herons, Ruddy Crakes, kingfishers, and swallows. All three bitterns—Pinnated, American, and Least—are possible though difficult. Recent sightings of Red-tailed Hawks suggest a breeding group disjunct from the better known population in Mountain Pine Ridge. A

Road Log for Gallon Jug Road

The starting point is the Fire Station in central Orange Walk Town, about an hour's drive time (27 miles) from Corozal Town or one-and-a-half hours (54 miles) from Belize City. You can exit Goldson Highway from three different intersections to reach central Orange Walk Town, but the simplest directions are from the east bypass. On the Goldson Highway log, exit at mile 37.4 (45.7 if heading north), N 18° 5.06' W 88° 32.95'.

Location: The 71-mile road starts in Orange Walk Town, reaches Gallon Jug and ends at Chan Chich, all within the Orange Walk District. From N 18° 1.61' W 88° 41.10' (at Trinidad) to N 17° 54.09' W 88° 58.51' (at Tres Leguas), road elevation ranges from 20 to 467 feet.

0.0 Intersection with Goldson Highway. Turn west toward Orange Walk Town.

0.6 Bridge.

0.7 Curve right, then turn left.

0.8 Stoplight. Pass police station.

1.0 Orange Walk Town Center Square. Clock tower. Fruit and vegetable stands.

1.1 Stoplight. TURN RIGHT just after fire station, N 18° 4.75' W 88° 33.73'. A Shell gas station is one block south of the fire station. If you do not have a full tank of gas, refuel there before continuing. It is a convenient bathroom break as well.

11.0 Trinidad water tower.

12.1 Birding stop at woodlot of fruiting trees.

13.4 Birding stop. N 18° 59.98' W 88° 42.40'.

15.2 **August Pine Ridge** (north side). N 17° 58.70' W 88° 43.63'. Elevation 47 feet.

17.0 August Pine Ridge (water tower). Hills of Mexico to the west.

23.3 San Felipe T-intersection. N 17° 52.35' W 88° 46.35'. Roman Catholic school on corner;

TURN RIGHT to continue on the **Gallon Jug Road.**
27.7 Side road eventually looping to mile 28.6.
28.6 Side road through **rice fields** to T-intersection (straight for loop to 27.7 or right to explore more of rice fields and to return the way you came in).
29.1 Bridge over Booth's River.
31.0 Blue Creek Village. Paved road through town.
32.2 Base of Rio Bravo Escarpment.
33.3 Blue Creek Hillside B&B.
33.3 Linda Vista Shopping Center: gas, grocery, and hardware store (closed on Sundays). N 17° 53.75' W 88° 54.12'.
34.6 Road on left (to Blumenfeld).
35.5 Road on left leads into deep woods with good birding.
36.9 Road on left leads uphill; birding on forest edges.
37.7 T-intersection near Tres Leguas. TURN LEFT for La Milpa and Chan Chich.
38.0 Sign for Programme for Belize. Forest soon starts.
40.4 Drawbridge gate with guard. Permission required to pass.
43.8 Programme for Belize: **La Milpa Ecolodge and Research Center.** N 17° 50.48' W 89° 1.14'.
56.6 Gate for Gallon Jug with guard (open 5:30 AM to 8:30 PM).
60.8 To **Laguna Seca** (on right).
64.6 Forest opens on right. Farmlands follow.
65.6 Gallon Jug to the right. Continue straight.
66.0 Pass farm road on right. Curve right.
66.9 Fork left toward Chan Chich Lodge, entering forest again.
67.9 Bridge.
70.0 Fork right.
71.0 Suspension bridge (Chan Chich Creek) and manicured lawns.
71.5 **Chan Chich Lodge.** N 17° 32.34' W 89° 6.72'.

remarkable 18 White-tailed Hawks were observed in 2005, with fewer numbers other dates. A Belize rarity, Crested Caracara, has been seen in recent years in fields between San Felipe and Blue Creek Village. Another rarity is Grassland Yellow-Finch, which has been found sparingly in this area since 1994.

A paved road leads through Blue Creek Village starting at mile 31. After the low-elevation, flat cattle fields, the landscape abruptly changes at the Rio Bravo Escarpment, rising over 400 feet in just over a mile of roadway. Elevation increases to 447 feet and reaches 518 feet in the surrounding hills to the northwest and a peak of 679 feet to the south. Much of the steep area has not been cleared of trees, so the birding habitat is quite different. Stop at the Linda Vista Shopping Center, a Mennonite store—closed on Sundays—for clean bathrooms, soft drinks, excellent ice cream, a well-stocked hardware supply for any mechanical problems you might have had, and refueling if needed.

The landscape near Tres Leguas becomes more wooded, and two side roads to the left at 35.5 and 36.9 can be productive for forest-edge birds, including Great Curassow, Smoky-brown Woodpecker, Green-backed Sparrow, and Black-cowled Oriole. At the T-intersection at 37.7 you need to check your watch and decide whether to visit the Edenthal-Neustadt marshes or head on to La Milpa or Chan Chich.

Alternatively, continue straight ahead at the T-intersection through Tres Leguas, drop slightly in elevation to 350 feet and check out the extensive marshes and rice fields beyond. This is another great location for ducks, herons, rails, and some shorebirds, such as Least Sandpiper and Long-billed Dowitcher, as well as nesting Jabiru and hunting

White-tailed Hawks. Alongside the road a Spotted Rail, hardly ever seen in Belize, was photographed in 2011. Soras are common. From the T-intersection to the marshes is about 1.5 miles. Continue birding at least to the next T-intersection at 2.2 miles and, if you have time and inclination, continue birding the rice fields in the Neustadt area beyond.

Return to the T-intersection at 37.7 and turn right if continuing to La Milpa. The road soon narrows and deteriorates. Check the roadsides for Black-throated Bobwhite and Fork-tailed Flycatcher.

At 38 the forest starts again at the sign for Programme for Belize and 2.4 miles farther you will be stopped by a drawbridge gate with a resident guard. Property beyond is private and you will need previously secured reservations at La Milpa or Chan Chich to continue. After the guard has taken down your name and license plate number, he will release the gate and you can continue to 44, the driveway for La Milpa. Details on Programme for Belize and the **La Milpa Ecolodge and Research Center** are provided in a separate section. If you are just passing through to Gallon Jug, you might want to stop here briefly to scan the lawns, scrub, and trees. Tropical Pewee, Blue Bunting, Montezuma Oropendola, and, if trees are fruiting, a host of other species can be seen from the road. Continuing briefly uphill, on the left is a gravel pit and an opening in the forest from which you can scan for parrots, aracaris, and other canopy birds. At 50 is a prior breeding location of a pair of Ornate Hawk-Eagles that relocated in 2007 but may still be nesting nearby.

The gated entrance to Gallon Jug is at 57 and a resident guard is working 5:30 AM to 8:30 PM. Again, you will need Chan Chich reservations to gain admission past this point. Almost immediately after the gate is the Cedar Crossing bridge where Amazon Kingfisher can be seen. If you haven't already seen Great Curassows and Ocellated Turkeys and you are driving in early

Ecoregion and habitats: Appendix A, Ecoregion 3, Orange Walk agricultural lowlands. Habitats include: agricultural (particularly rice and sorghum, AG2, AG3) and pine savanna (PFL), with lowland broadleaf forest (BFL3, BFL5) beyond the escarpment; small villages and widely separated farm houses (PC).

Concerns: The main gas station en route is closed on Sundays. It is best to start with a full tank. The farmlands are privately owned. Trespassing is not advised, although if you find a farmer and ask permission, you will probably be invited. There is plenty of good birding from the main road and side roads; with a spotting scope you can see the more-distant birds. If your goal is to reach Chan Chich by mid-afternoon, allow four hours for driving, leaving the remainder for birding. Note: you cannot proceed beyond mile 40 without reservations at either La Milpa or Chan Chich.

Contact: If you want more time to bird the Blue Creek rice field areas, consider staying in Blue Creek Village. Blue Creek Hillside B&B; P.O. Box 2, Blue Creek, Orange Walk District; (011) 501-323-0155; bchillsideb_b@yahoo.com; www.belizeexplorer. com and select Destination Guide, then Orange Walk District, then Blue Creek Village.

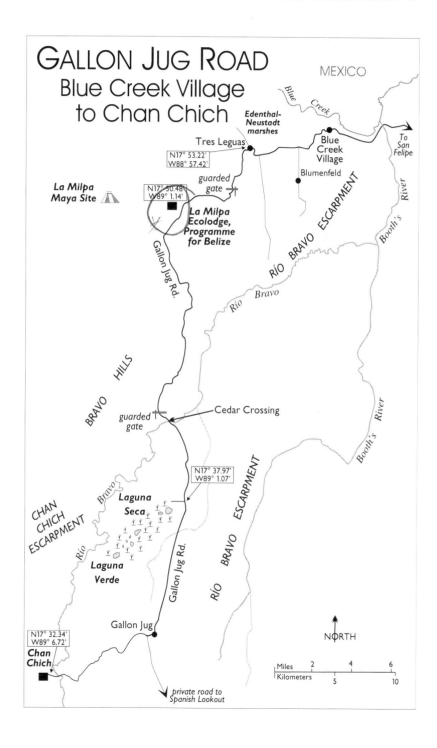

GALLON JUG ROAD
Blue Creek Village to Chan Chich

MEXICO

Blue Creek

Edenthal-Neustadt marshes

Tres Leguas

Blue Creek Village

To San Felipe

N17° 53.22'
W88° 57.42'

Blumenfeld

guarded gate

Booth's River

La Milpa Maya Site

N17° 50.48'
W89° 1.14'

La Milpa Ecolodge, Programme for Belize

RÍO BRAVO ESCARPMENT

Gallon Jug Rd.

Río Bravo

BRAVO HILLS

guarded gate — Cedar Crossing

Booth's River

N17° 37.97'
W89° 1.07'

CHAN CHICH ESCARPMENT

Bravo

Laguna Seca

Laguna Verde

Río

Gallon Jug Rd.

RÍO BRAVO ESCARPMENT

Gallon Jug

N17° 32.34'
W89° 6.72'

Chan Chich

NORTH

| Miles | 2 | 4 | 6 |
| Kilometers | | 5 | 10 |

private road to Spanish Lookout

morning, you are bound to see them between here and Gallon Jug; in fact you could see dozens. At 61 is the turnoff for **Laguna Seca** on the right, described separately below. Another 4 miles farther on, the forest opens on the right and farmlands follow. The turnoff to Gallon Jug is on the right at 66, but continue straight if your goal is Chan Chich. Signs will lead the way to the suspension bridge crossing Chan Chich Creek at 71 and you will start to notice the manicured lawns, cultured flowers, and beautiful cabanas of Chan Chich before you reach the terminus at 71.5. Details on **Chan Chich** are treated in a subsequent section.

Key species of the **August Pine Ridge/San Felipe area**: **Black-throated Bobwhite**, White-tailed Kite, **Northern Harrier**, Crane Hawk, American Kestrel, Crested Caracara [R], Red-billed Pigeon, White-winged Dove, **Plain-breasted Ground-Dove**, Ferruginous Pygmy-Owl, Green-breasted Mango, **Acorn Woodpecker**, Yucatan Woodpecker, Common Tody-Flycatcher, Vermilion, Scissor-tailed, and Fork-tailed Flycatchers, Gray-crowned Yellowthroat, **Grassland Yellow-Finch**, Blue Grosbeak, Eastern Meadowlark, Altamira Oriole, **Lesser Goldfinch**.

Key species of **Blue Creek rice fields and Edenthal marshes**: Black-bellied Whistling-Duck, Blue-winged Teal, **Cinnamon Teal**, Jabiru, Wood Stork, Pinnated [R], American [R], and Least Bitterns, Roseate Spoonbill, Lesser Yellow-headed Vulture, White-tailed and Snail Kites, Swainson's Hawk [R], **White-tailed Hawk**, Red-tailed Hawk, American Kestrel, **Aplomado** and **Peregrine Falcons**, Ruddy Crake, **Sora**, **Spotted Rail** [R], Purple and Common Gallinules, **American Golden-Plover** [T], Black-necked Stilt, Greater and Lesser Yellowlegs, White-rumped [T] and Pectoral [T] Sandpipers, Long-billed Dowitcher, Wilson's Snipe, Red-winged Blackbird, Tricolored Munia (non-native).

LA MILPA ECOLODGE AND RESEARCH CENTER
Rio Bravo Conservation and Management Area

[15 February] Excellent birding before breakfast and just outside our sleeping accommodations is a luxury. The fruiting trees are where dozens of colorful tropical birds dine for their breakfast. We enjoy a three-ring circus of performers highlighted by Red-lored Parrots, Keel-billed Toucans, and Red-legged Honeycreepers. More new species include White-necked Jacobin (a large hummingbird), Collared Aracari (a saw-toothed painted toucan), and Black-crowned Tityra (a tropical flycatcher). Before our 7:30 breakfast we see almost three dozen species, most of them in one cluster of flowering trees.

After a scrumptious meal, we drive a short distance to the La Milpa Maya ruins. Birds are a bit sparse in the deep forest, but they usually are among the "best" birds because they are rarely seen. My best today is a Stub-tailed Spadebill, an aptly named feather ball with a wide bill, abbreviated tail, and obvious eye ring.

Well under four inches from bill tip to tail tip, a brown object hiding in dense underbrush in a dark forest is not easy to see.

In the afternoon we again stick to the deep forest paths, characterized by long lulls in bird activity, but punctuated with some exciting finds. Best are Ruddy Quail-Dove, Ochre-bellied and Sulphur-rumped Flycatchers, Bright-rumped Attila, and Black-throated Shrike-Tanager. Vladimir frequently whistles a forlorn "Hey Ricky" call and has a Northern Schiffornis answer back, but usually from a distant point far beyond the 20 or so feet we can see into the forest. His efforts are rewarded toward the end of our hike when one appears on a tree in the middle of the path.

This evening we sit on the back of a pickup truck and drive the entrance road, using a high-beam flashlight to search the trees. Our first bird is an Ocellated Turkey precariously balanced on a too-thin branch high in the tree. Strongly locked claws must keep this top-heavy ball of feathers from tottering over while asleep. Next we see a Crested Guan in much the same type of perch, but even higher. We have three other sightings this evening, all of individual Mottled Owls.

Description: The La Milpa Ecolodge and Research Center is located in the northwest section of the Rio Bravo Conservation and Management Area, privately owned and managed by Programme for Belize, a non-profit Belizean conservation organization. The protected area is 260,000 acres, over 4 % of the country's land area. Nearly 300 species of birds have been found at the La Milpa portion of this protected area. Included in the preserve are the La Milpa Maya ruins, third-largest archaeological site in Belize. Unlike many others elsewhere in Mexico and Central America, these ruins are unaltered since their discovery. The main plaza, flat but for the substantial trees growing through the once-plastered surface, is surrounded by tree-covered hills. These hills are not natural, but instead they are the blocked-limestone temples covered by a thin ground layer accumulated through 1,150 years of forest takeover. This Maya site probably maintained a peak population of 46,000 inhabitants and was continuously used for over 1,200 years, beginning around 400 B.C. The rainforest in this part of Belize is a lowland broadleaf forest, a dry rainforest with about 60 inches annual rainfall, contrasting to rainforests farther south that receive twice that amount.

The diversity of birds within the Bravo Hills—including La Milpa, Chan Chich, Aguacate Lagoon, and El Pilar—is truly amazing and includes 14 dove species, 9 parrots, 13 hummingbirds, all 4 trogons, all 5 kingfishers, 8 woodpeckers, 8 woodcreepers, 48 flycatchers, 32 warblers, 14 tanagers, and 17 in the oriole family. Many rarities have been found here once or twice and only seldom elsewhere in Belize (see list below).

Birding strategy: First, contact Programme for Belize to arrange a visit for one or more nights. There are enough good birding opportunities in the area to stay three nights or more, but even one night will be an exciting side-trip. You can rely on the local guide(s) to help you design your daily itinerary. A typical day would include a sunrise short walk around the open areas and perhaps the access road, concentrating on birds attracted to the fruiting trees. Ocellated Turkeys routinely walk about the clearing. Breakfast would be followed by a morning walk, usually along a forest trail, making sure you find an opening to the sky around 10 AM to watch rising raptors. Look especially for King Vulture, Double-toothed Kite, White Hawk, and Black and Ornate Hawk-Eagles. A mid-afternoon jungle hike will find birds sparse, but you might get lucky and find an ant swarm. Late afternoon will bring better chances again for soaring raptors and nectar-seeking hummingbirds. Also check out the feeders at the palapa for consistent Rufous-tailed Hummingbirds and White-bellied Emeralds, regular Green-breasted Mango, and occasional Ruby-throated and Scaly-breasted Hummingbirds. After a leisurely break under the palapa, followed by dinner, you can gather again around 7 PM for a nocturnal ride seeking Crested Guan, Great Curassow, Mottled Owl, Yucatan Nightjar, and Northern Potoo, as well as a good chance at seeing mammals such as Kinkajous, opossums, deer, cats, and foxes. A nocturnal walk toward the Maya site can produce the same species, plus Yucatan Poorwill. The ruins are a reliable spot for Central American Pygmy-Owl.

Another birding spot not to miss is the carefully hidden garbage dump. If you like sedentary birding, bring your three-legged stool and spend a morning or early evening sitting about 30

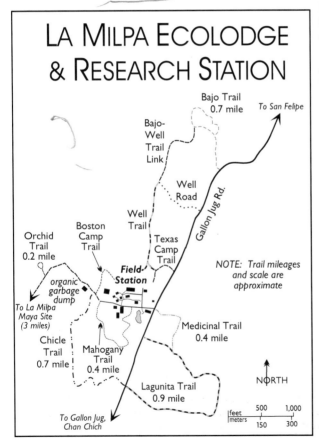

LA MILPA ECOLODGE & RESEARCH STATION

Bajo Trail
0.7 mile

To San Felipe

Bajo-Well Trail Link

Well Road

Gallon Jug Rd.

Well Trail

Boston Camp Trail

Orchid Trail
0.2 mile

Texas Camp Trail

Field Station

NOTE: Trail mileages and scale are approximate

organic garbage dump

To La Milpa Maya Site
(3 miles)

Chicle Trail
0.7 mile

Mahogany Trail
0.4 mile

Medicinal Trail
0.4 mile

Lagunita Trail
0.9 mile

NORTH

To Gallon Jug,
Chan Chich

feet   500   1,000
meters   150   300

feet from the edge of the pit. You should find 20+ species, including Gray-headed Dove, Northern Schiffornis, Tawny-winged Woodcreeper, Kentucky Warbler, Gray-headed Tanager, and Green-backed Sparrow, in addition to Central American Agouti and White-nosed Coati. The guides can help you find special birds. Here are some suggestions: For Great Tinamou, Barred Forest-Falcon, Mottled Owl, Black-and-white Owl, and others, get out before first light and you are likely to hear them calling from the forest surrounding the cabanas or near the driveway entrance. For Tody Motmot, go to the La Milpa Maya site and especially the dense cohune ridge, as well as the terminal end of the Mahogany Trail. Although quite rare, a Crested Eagle has been seen at the Maya site several times recently. For Rose-throated Tanager and Gray-throated Chat, take the Bajo Trail in early morning.

Key species of La Milpa and Chan Chich: **Great Tinamou**, Thicket and Slaty-breasted Tinamous, **Crested Guan**, **Great Curassow**, **Spotted Wood-Quail**, **Ocellated Turkey**, **Pinnated Bittern**, **Agami Heron**, King Vulture, Double-toothed Kite, Bicolored, Crane, and White Hawks, Black Hawk-Eagle, **Ornate** and **Black-and-white Hawk-Eagles**, Barred Forest-Falcon, Scaled Pigeon, Ruddy Quail-Dove, Brown-hooded and Mealy Parrots, Vermiculated Screech-Owl, Mottled Owl, **Black-and-white Owl**, **Yucatan Nightjar**, Northern Potoo, Lesser Swallow-tailed Swift, **Scaly-breasted Hummingbird**, Wedge-tailed Sabrewing, White-necked Jacobin, Purple-crowned Fairy, **Tody Motmot**, White-whiskered Puffbird,

Ecoregion and habitats: Appendix A, Ecoregion 6, Bravo Hills northern hardwood forests. Habitats include: dense tropical moist lowland broadleaf forest (BFL2, BFL3, BFL4, BFL5) with a broad opening near the guest facilities (PC).

Concerns: Bring bug repellent, a flashlight, and perhaps a small fan. Solar power runs out around 10 PM and the generator is not turned on until 5 AM.

Fees and contact: A complete La Milpa package is available through Programme for Belize, and arrangements can be made for day visits. Guests at Chan Chich can also arrange a day visit. Programme for Belize, P.O. Box 749, #1 Eyre Street, Belize City, Belize District; (011) 501-227-5616 or 227-5617 or 227-1020; fax (011) 501-227-5635; pfbel@btl.net; www.pfbelize.org.

Facilities and tours: Private cabanas with hot showers and bathrooms, shared dormitories with communal bathrooms, dining room serving excellent Belizean meals, nature library, gift shop. Various walks are included in the package, utilizing excellent birding guides (particularly Vladimir Rodriguez) and which can be tailored to your interests, including birding, medicinal plants, Maya ruins. Night drives are also available. There is also a camp where college students study tropical ecology.

Location: N 17° 50.47' W 89° 1.14'; elevation 468 feet. Use the Gallon Jug Road log to reach La Milpa. The entrance gate is at mile 40.4 and the facilities are at mile 43.8. Starting in early morning and birding en route can bring you to La Milpa in time for lunch if you don't stop repeatedly, or by mid-afternoon if you bird more intensely. Driving straight through from Orange Walk will take about two hours.

Emerald Toucanet, Chestnut-colored Woodpecker, **Plain Antvireo**, Black-faced Antthrush, **Scaly-throated Leaftosser**, Buff-throated Foliage-gleaner, **Strong-billed Woodcreeper**, Northern Barred-Woodcreeper, Yellow-bellied Tyrannulet, Sepia-capped Flycatcher, Eye-ringed Flatbill, **Ruddy-tailed Flycatcher**, Rufous Mourner, Yucatan Flycatcher, Northern Schiffornis, **Speckled Mourner** [R], Cinnamon Becard, **Lovely Cotinga**, **Rufous Piha**, Green Shrike-Vireo, White-throated Thrush, Swainson's and Golden-crowned Warblers, Gray-headed Tanager, Black-throated Shrike-Tanager, Green Honeycreeper, **Rose-throated Tanager**, **Gray-throated Chat**, **Blue Bunting**, Giant Cowbird, Elegant Euphonia [R].

CHAN CHICH LODGE

[5 February] A broad parkway forms from a narrow, well-graded gravel road shouldered on each side by a wide short-grass border, terminated by the tall forest edge. This is the road from La Milpa to Gallon Jug and prime habitat for browsing Great Curassows and Ocellated Turkeys. Amazingly, in the dim morning light we count 14 curassows and 87 turkeys en route. At the bridge just beyond the gatekeeper, we see our first Amazon Kingfisher resting on the railing. Entering Chan Chich, we are awed by the beauty of this forested resort, the quaintly attractive cabanas, the manicured grounds, and the first-class amenities. We have great success on the wooded and streamside trails. Most impressive is the good look we get at a Rufous Mourner, followed shortly by the larger but nearly identical Rufous Piha. A Northern Schiffornis comes within close view, another brown bird to add to the mourner, piha, Chestnut-colored Woodpecker, woodcreepers, and Wood Thrush—a morning of rufous birds.

Description: One of the best-known birding sites in Belize because of its excellent accommodations, Chan Chich Lodge is visited by many bird tour companies. The surrounding jungle, accessed by carefully tended trails, and the beautiful grounds attract a spectacular list of over 350 bird species. The Gallon Jug Christmas Bird Count has been conducted since 1991, typically identifying some 200 species each year. Almost all of the birders who visit Chan Chich stay at the lodge because of its isolation on 130,000 acres, reached only by air or a long road trip blocked by two security gates. The property includes 12 individual cabanas and a two-bedroom villa, restaurant, pool, nine miles of hiking trails, nature guides, and more. The lodge is built atop the plaza of an unexcavated Maya site.

Birding strategy: Gallon Jug, Chan Chich, and La Milpa share much of the same habitat; for a combined list of key birds and other specialties, see the preceding La Milpa section. Depend on the staff of Chan Chich Lodge to offer you the best alternatives and to know of recent sightings. Some species change locations, such as nesting hawk-eagles. Others are consistent for several years, such as Lovely Cotinga, and then move on to other territories.

On a pre-breakfast stroll along the paved entrance road, looking up you could see Red-lored Parrots feeding in the exposed canopy, catching the soft

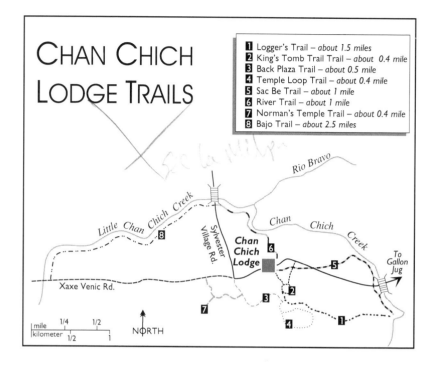

CHAN CHICH
LODGE TRAILS

1 Logger's Trail – about 1.5 miles
2 King's Tomb Trail Trail – about 0.4 mile
3 Back Plaza Trail – about 0.5 mile
4 Temple Loop Trail – about 0.4 mile
5 Sac Be Trail – about 1 mile
6 River Trail – about 1 mile
7 Norman's Temple Trail – about 0.4 mile
8 Bajo Trail – about 2.5 miles

Ecoregion and habitats: Appendix A, Ecoregion 6, Bravo Hills northern hardwood forests. Habitats include: dense tropical moist lowland broadleaf forest, wetter than La Milpa (whose forest it shares) and therefore taller (BFL1, BFL2, BFL3, BFL4, BFL5). Also some agricultural land (AG3) at Gallon Jug, and supplemental plantings at the resort (PC).

Laguna Seca (see next site) habitats include: lagoon, partially overgrown into marshlands and partially open water, adjacent to cohune forest cleared of understory (BFL1, BFL2, BFL4).

Contact: Chan Chich Lodge, P.O. Box 37, Belize City, Belize; (011) 501-223-4419; info@chanchich.com; www.chanchich.com.

Chan Chich Location: N 17° 32.34' W 89° 6.72'; elevation 466 feet at lodge. A private airstrip allows guests to arrive by a 30-minute charter flight. By land, follow the Gallon Jug Road log to the end, 71 miles (3.5 hours) from Orange Walk Town.

Laguna Seca Location: N 17° 38.16' W 89° 2.14' at cohune forest. About 12 miles (1/2 hour) from Chan Chich, the access road is at mile 60.8 on the Gallon Jug road log, N 17° 37.97' W 89° 1.07'. Turn west and continue for 1.2 miles. Park at the end of the road and walk through the wooded area, following the perimeter of water and marsh.

Concerns at Laguna Seca: Watch out for fire ants and chiggers in the tall grass; use insect repellent.

hues of morning light. You may hear Gray-headed Doves and looking to the ground you might see one or two feed in the leaf litter.

Your birding could continue from the breakfast table with good views of a Stripe-throated Hermit feeding on flowers, White-collared and Red-capped Manakins at the bushes, or Collared Aracaris coming to the *Psychotria* flowers. Also attracted to the *Psychotria* is Ochre-bellied Flycatcher. In the Main Plaza look for Wedge-tailed Sabrewing and Chestnut-colored Woodpecker visiting the Tulip Tree for nectar or see a small flock of Green Honeycreepers or perhaps a Scrub Euphonia high in the canopy. Bicolored Hawk has been observed hunting high in the trees, although chances of sighting this reclusive hawk are slim.

Behind the lodge in an enormous tree you will see the elongated oriole nests of Montezuma Oropendola and here is your chance to watch brood parasitic Giant Cowbirds. An Ornate Hawk-Eagle sometimes perches on another tall tree. Most recently its nest has been on Sylvester Road. Nearby the lodge is the start of Upper Plaza trail, a good site to find a generous variety of woodcreepers, including one of the hardest to find elsewhere, the Strong-billed Woodcreeper. Here also is a good area for Royal Flycatcher and Tody Motmot, another specialty of Chan Chich.

Continue walking among the tall trees along King's Tomb Trail. The darkened forest is habitat for the shy, drab birds: Rufous Mourner, Northern Schiffornis, and Rufous Piha. The Rufous Mourner can also be found on the Sac Be Trail. Ruddy-tailed Flycatcher could be found here as well as on other darkened trails such as Logger's Trail. Also found on Logger's Trail are Great Tinamou, Spotted Wood-Quail, Tody Motmot, and Barred Forest-Falcon, seen as well as heard. If you hear shuffling dry leaves along this trail, trace the sound for it may well be a Scaly-throated Leaftosser.

The edge habitat where Sac Be Trail and Logger's Trail abut the grassy area at the suspension bridge is excellent birding. Here is a reliable spot to find perching White-whiskered Puffbird and Yellow-bellied Flycatcher. A bit into the canopied shadows of the paved road is a favorite nesting spot for Scaly-breasted Hummingbird. At Chan Chich Creek, which flows under the suspension bridge, you can find Green Heron, Wilson's Snipe, and Amazon Kingfisher. You may hear a calling Black Hawk-Eagle in flight overhead; it has a favorite perch nearby.

Beyond the suspension bridge and up a small incline is the trail to Trish's Hill, a sublime view of the Chan Chich Creek valley. Once it provided a view of an Ornate Hawk-Eagle nest, since abandoned, but other treats may yet be in store, such as a Black-throated Shrike-Tanager.

B ack at the lodge, you can continue westward and then north along Sylvester Village Road where the canopy shades the gravel road. Here is where White-throated Flycatcher has been found in the xibal or low-lying swampy area. Buff-bellied Hummingbird occurs here, too. Ahead and to the west is Bajo Trail for hearing Carolina (White-browed) Wren and finding Rose-throated Tanager and Gray-throated Chat. Or, to the east is River Trail, a favorite for Ruddy Quail-Dove and antbirds, especially as you get nearer to the lodge. Above, foraging in the canopy are Central American Spider Monkeys. At the convergence of Chan Chich Creek and Little Chan Chich Creek look for Agami Heron, Sun-

Rufous-tailed Jacamar   Bert Frenz

grebe, and American Pygmy Kingfisher. In dull green bamboo slivers you might find the glossy blue light bulbs of feeding male Blue Buntings.

Also visit Chan Chich escarpment, about 6 miles north-northeast of the lodge, an hour's drive from Chan Chich. Here, in a couple of hours 10+ raptor species can often be observed, including King Vulture, Double-toothed Kite, White and Short-tailed Hawks, and Black and Black-and-white Hawk-Eagles. Emerald Toucanet and Lovely Cotinga have also been spotted from this vantage point.

Other sites to visit are Laguna Verde for Pinnated Bittern, Ruddy Crake, and Gray-necked Wood-Rail, and the farmlands of Gallon Jug for species not found elsewhere in forested areas such as Lesser Yellow-headed Vulture,

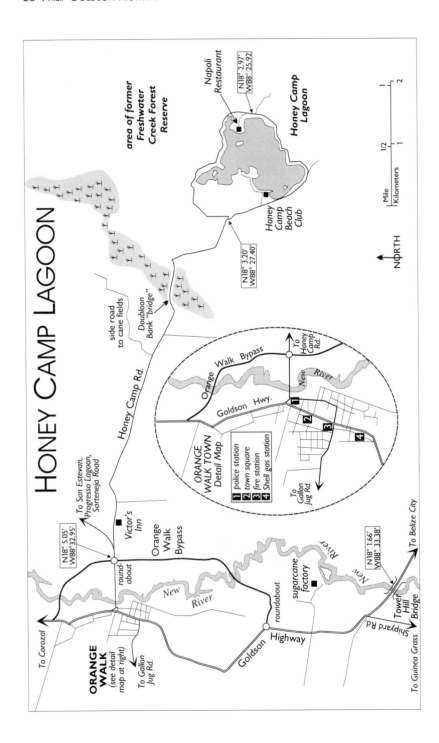

HONEY CAMP LAGOON

area of former
Freshwater
Creek Forest
Reserve

Napoli
Restaurant

N18° 2.97'
W88° 25.92'

Honey Camp
Lagoon

Honey Camp
Beach Club

N18° 3.20'
W88° 27.40'

side road
to cane fields

Doubloon
Bank "bridge"

Honey Camp Rd.

Orange Walk Bypass

Goldson Hwy.

New River

To Honey
Camp Rd.

ORANGE WALK TOWN
Detail Map

1 police station
2 town square
3 fire station
4 Shell gas station

To
Gallon
Jug Rd.

To San Estevan,
Progresso Lagoon,
Sarteneja Road

N18° 5.05'
W88° 32.95'

Victor's
Inn

Orange
Walk
Bypass

round-
about

New River

ORANGE
WALK
(see detail
map at right)

To Corozal

To Gallon
Jug Rd.

sugarcane
factory

New River

roundabout

Goldson Highway

N18° 1.66'
W88° 33.38'

To Belize City

Shipyard Rd.

Tower
Hill
Bridge

To Guinea Grass

NORTH

Mile
Kilometers

1/2 1

1 2

White-tailed Kite, Vermilion and Fork-tailed Flycatchers, and Eastern Meadowlark. Check the next section for good birding at nearby Laguna Seca.

Chan Chich offers night drives, as does La Milpa, and in addition to the species seen at the latter you may find a Barn Owl at Gallon Jug.

Laguna Seca

Description: An easy stop—worth at least an hour's time while visiting Chan Chich or about one hour from La Milpa—this location is one of the easier spots to seek waterbirds in what otherwise is dense forest. Here the palms in the cohune forest have tall trunks, unlike the nearly trunkless ones at the La Milpa ruins. A trail leads to a fairly large Maya ruin. Surrounded by forest on three sides is a lagoon where Morelet's Crocodiles occur, and you may find Least Grebe, Anhinga, **Pinnated Bittern**, Bare-throated Tiger-Heron, Agami Heron, Black-collared Hawk, Ruddy Crake, Purple Gallinule, Sungrebe, Limpkin, American Pygmy Kingfisher, and Mangrove Swallow. Other species such as Plumbeous Kite, Ornate Hawk-Eagle, Tody Motmot, Strong-billed Woodcreeper, Yucatan Flycatcher, Lovely Cotinga, Golden-crowned Warbler, and Giant Cowbird have been recorded. A Barn Owl can usually be found roosting in the palms.

HONEY CAMP ROAD AND HONEY CAMP LAGOON

Birding strategy: The best birding is along the roadsides from miles 2 to 6 on Honey Camp Road. If the roads are good, you can continue birding around the lagoon perimeter, although access is somewhat limited because lake frontage is private property. The swamp and lagoon reserve boast an impressive bird checklist, including a number of species that are recorded for Corozal District only at this location.

From the intersection with Goldson Highway, exit the roundabout at the sign for San Estevan, heading east. In 0.2 mile you will come to a Y-intersection. Choosing the left fork will take you to San Estevan and thence to Progresso Lagoon and birding sites at Shipstern Nature Reserve and Sarteneja. Note: the San Estevan Road can be torn up as a result of heavy sugarcane truck use. For details on those birding sites, see the section on Sarteneja Road (page 41). San Estevan is 4.6 miles from the Y-intersection, extends for one mile, and then it is another 6.1 miles to the T-intersection south of Progresso Lagoon. From here you can pick up the Sarteneja Road log at mile 14.9. For Honey Camp Road, stay right and at 0.5 pass Victor's Inn and Foodery on the right. Victor's offers Belizean food, rudimentary rooms for rent, and RV hook-ups. If you stay there, ask Victor or Tony for suggestions on private places with access to Honey Camp Lagoon.

At 2.8 miles is a general area where Gray-throated Chats have been found consistently. In Belize this species can be hard to find, so knowing a few reliable spots will help in your search. A T-intersection near here is a side road leading to cane fields. Species found in the first quarter-mile include Squirrel Cuckoo, Lineated Woodpecker, Yellow-olive Flycatcher, Bright-rumped Attila, and Mangrove Vireo. Back on the main road, walking or drive-and-stop birding along the roadsides for the next three miles or so is worthwhile in the early morning and late afternoon. Starting around 4.1 you can see marshlands and overflying Wood Storks, Snail Kites, and Common Black-Hawks, as well as nesting Green-breasted Mangos. At 5.3 is Doubloon Bank Bridge, a narrow land-bridge with lagoons on both sides. Look for Purple Gallinule, Limpkin, Greater and Lesser Yellowlegs, Mangrove Swallow, and other marsh birds.

Ecoregion and habitats: Appendix A, Ecoregion 4, New River riparian watershed. Habitats include: secondary forest (BFL3), scrub, marshes, lagoons (BFL2), and cane fields (AG1). The reserve features rainforest, pine savanna (PFL), and a large population of logwood.

Concerns: Honey Camp Road can be deeply rutted after heavy rains, sometimes making the road impassable.

Location: N 18° 2.97' W 88° 25.92' at east end of lagoon. Starting with directions from Goldson Highway, turn off at the Orange Walk Town bypass at the roundabout at 37.4 heading south or at 45.7 heading north on the highway, N 18° 5.06' W 88° 32.95'.

Key species of Freshwater Creek Forest Reserve, Honey Camp Road and Lagoon: Black-throated Bobwhite, Lesser Yellow-headed Vulture, Gray-headed, Swallow-tailed [T], White-tailed, and Snail Kites, Common Black-Hawk, Collared Forest-Falcon, Purple Gallinule, Limpkin, Yellow-lored Parrot, Ferruginous Pygmy-Owl, Green-breasted Mango, Cinnamon Hummingbird, American Pygmy Kingfisher, White-necked Puffbird, Yucatan Flycatcher, Black-crowned Tityra, Yucatan Vireo, Rufous-browed Peppershrike, Rose-throated Tanager, Gray-throated Chat, Yellow-tailed and Altamira Orioles.

NEW RIVER TO LAMANAI

[Morning, 23 February] The boat moves quickly toward the opening of a narrow side channel, Orlando cuts the engine, and we glide noiselessly between the mangroves. Seeking Sungrebe, which we've seen in prior years, and Agami Heron, not seen previously, we look in every direction and especially into the narrow tunnel separating the overhanging mangrove branches from the surface of the New River. In the midst of a dark tangle, Bob and I see a dark heron with a wide slash of chestnut across its belly. Bob exclaims, "Agami Heron," and all eyes

turn. The excitement pushes the heron deeper into the mangroves. Most herons are show-offs, large waders proudly displaying their fanciful feathers. Not so for the rare and reticent Agami. But we are persistent and look into the snarl, heavily shaded by the leaf canopy. Roots and branches are more numerous than the gaps of open space separating them. . .Orlando moves the boat around to the other side of the thin peninsula. . .This time the lanky bird is wading at the edge, bent over as it ducks under the protruding roots, and we all get a full view of the mosaic of green, pale blue, and chestnut with offsetting yellow face and bill and blue plume.

[Evening, 28 January] We return to our boat as the sun sets orangely over the lagoon. Announcing the end of day, a Collared Forest-Falcon moans its repeated plea of "Help" and we have the unusually good fortune of seeing it perched atop a leafless tree on the horizon. We see Limpkins finding roosting sites, and as darkness falls, out come Lesser Nighthawks. Bats stay closer to the river's surface—small Proboscis Bats and large Greater Fishing Bats. Pauraques call from the marsh, still in dim light. We bring out the high-powered flashlights and illuminate a dark shadow poking above the shoreline canopy, revealing a Laughing Falcon at rest.

But the real show does not begin until darkness tightens its chokehold on the jungle. Now the stars come out; legions brighten the sky. For a couple of hours we follow glowing eyes with our flashlights. Those at the water's surface are crocodiles, surprisingly common given that we only saw one on our daylight trip. The pairs of eyes above the water's surface extinguish quickly as the reptiles slip below. Lee finds two red-orange eyes blazing back at us from the top of a dead limb. Like the anatomical trees in Tolkien's Lord of the Rings, the large fiery eyes of a Northern Potoo glare menacingly at us; closer approach shows a body color and shape that could easily substitute for an extension of the dead tree trunk on which it rests. . . We come upon a Yucatan Poorwill, then a Yucatan Nightjar..

Description: Combined with a visit to Lamanai, this is easily in the Top 10 Belize birding sites. Once a prominent trade and commerce route for the Maya and later the European colonists, New River now transports tourists to the famous ruins. The river widens to New River Lagoon, the largest lake in Belize. Along the shore the epiphyte-covered trees block the view of marshes and agricultural lands beyond, water lilies float on shallow waterways, and a confusing maze of side-channels hold lurking wildlife. The river stretches from Corozal Bay to Hill Bank, with Orange Walk Town its more convenient launching point and Lamanai its most popular destination.

Boats typically head upstream and directly to Lamanai; however good birding is also found downstream, north from Tower Hill Bridge, toward the rum factory and sugarcane factory. Here, the waterways are devoid of the tourist boats common upstream. Boating at trolling speed, with frequent reversals, you can ply the sometimes narrow, sometimes wide, river ways, searching the jungle-like shoreline for a host of herons and egrets, including Yellow-crowned Night-Heron and Boat-billed Heron. You may find a secluded marsh, and if you can disembark you will step ashore into a surreal

Jurassic scene of Muscovy Ducks in flight, Black-bellied Whistling-Ducks feeding, Spotted and Solitary Sandpipers poking in the mud, a Gray-necked Wood-Rail skirting the edge of a small pond, several Bare-throated Tiger-Herons perched high in an old gnarled tree, a flock of Black-necked Stilts flashing black and white across the marsh, where below several White Ibises probe. Elsewhere, trees overhang the river and in the shadows lurk Least Grebe and Sungrebe. In the sunnier, more open marshes, Green Herons, Purple Gallinules, and Northern Jacanas are readily found.

Heading upstream toward Lamanai, habitat is similar, with dozens of feeder creeks to investigate. Kingfishers are in abundance, and it would not be unusual to count two dozen Ringed, a dozen Belted, another dozen Green, and one or two Amazon and American Pygmy Kingfishers. You will readily find Snail Kites. Harder to find, but still likely to be seen is Black-collared Hawk. A popular haunt is a noticeably wider portion of the river where the water is spread with floating lily pads and Northern Jacanas are common. When you find black-hawks, be careful in your identification as Great Black-Hawks are expected but Commons are not.

Not long before you reach Lamanai you will encounter Belize's best known Jabiru nesting site. Just as the river opens into the New River Lagoon, look to the right over the low swamp, past the rising shoreline, to an enormous ceiba tree—the national tree of Guatemala—silhouetted against the horizon. On a broad horizontal branch rests a huge nest, and if your visit is in February, you likely will see one or two juveniles and one or both adults. At a height of 52 inches and a wingspan of 7-1/2 feet, an adult Jabiru standing beside the nest is clearly recognizable even at this half-mile distance.

Birding strategy: Boats normally transit New River in an hour, with limited interest in stopping for wildlife. If you are traveling alone and this is your only choice, your best birding will be when you arrive at Lamanai. To make the most of birding along the river, you or your group will need to monopolize the boat. Make arrangements for boat travel at least a few days before departure, being specific on the length of time you want the boat and driver and whether you want them to prepare and bring lunch for you. If you are including a night cruise, make sure the driver has a high-powered flashlight connected to his boat battery. Ask if they will bring water or drinks for you.

To optimize birding opportunities, arrive at the boat dock shortly after sunrise. Ask the driver to head north of Tower Hill Bridge toward the sugar-cane factory (barges still transport sugar along this section of the New River). Bird the waterways in this area for an hour or so before heading south toward Lamanai. If your driver is a knowledgeable birding guide, ask him to show you sites where he has found the specialties: Agami Heron, nesting Jabiru, Sungrebe, and roosting Lesser Nighthawk and Northern Potoo. Normally the object is to travel slowly, but if nothing much is being seen ask your driver to speed up. Tell your driver that you would like to arrive at Lamanai by 11 AM; but take your time if the birding is good.

After birding at Lamanai (see next section), you'll probably head back to the boat docks quickly. But if you have made arrangements for a night cruise, negotiate the time of departure, which probably will be about 5 PM, or you might spend a half-hour or so at Dawson Creek (see below) before leaving the lagoon at 5:30. Travel the first half of the return distance at faster speeds, stopping for anything interesting. Once you have reached the Mennonite community at Shipyard, now in evening darkness, slow down and search the trees at water's edge for reflected eyes of birds, mammals, reptiles,

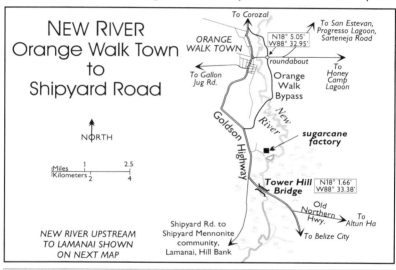

Ecoregion and habitats: *Appendix A, Ecoregion 4, New River riparian watershed. Habitats include: riparian lowland broadleaf forest (BFL1, BFL2, BFL3) and lowland pine forest (PFL).*

Concerns: *The incredible number of cruise-ship passengers visiting Belize has put undue pressure on day-excursions on the New River to Lamanai. Speedboats carrying tourists typically jet at top speeds, trailing a wake and sometimes disrupting birding activities. To avoid this disruption, schedule your visit for Saturday, Sunday, or Monday, or perhaps Friday. You can also check www.cruisecal.com for cruise ships in port on any particular day. Use insect repellent for Lamanai. Bring rain jackets and umbrellas. You will also need a light jacket for warmth if traveling the river at night. If you are spending an extended time on the water, the lack of a toilet may be of concern, so be sure to take advantage of the ones at the dock and at Lamanai.*

Location: *N 18° 1.66' W 88° 33.38' at New River boat docks, which are south of Orange Walk Town at Tower Hill Bridge, mile 42.2 heading south or 40.9 heading north on the Goldson Highway log.*

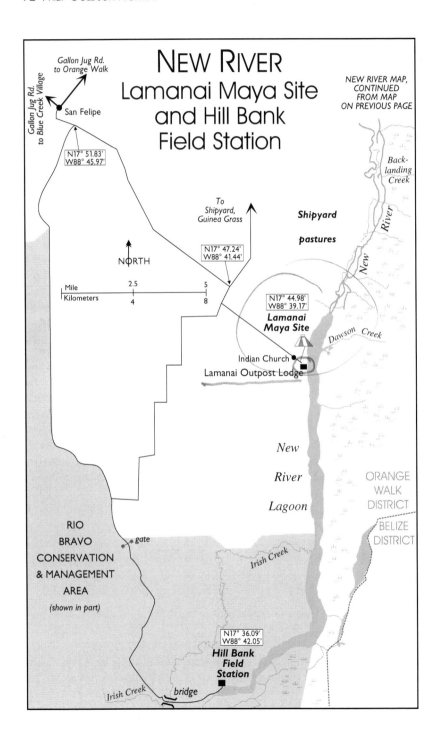

and insects. After you have had your fill of nocturnal birding, ask the driver to head to the dock at high speed. In a carefully arranged trip you should reach the dock by about 8 PM.

An alternative to the above is to stay at Lamanai Outpost Lodge (see section on Lamanai below). The lodge can provide a sunset cruise, starting around 4:30, and a spotlight safari, starting around 7:30 PM. During spring migration you might see thousands of Tree Swallows, mixed with Purple Martins, Northern Rough-Swinged Swallow, and Barn Swallows moving northward along the New River.

The lodge can also ferry you across New River Lagoon to Dawson Creek and a pine savanna that abounds in parrots, including Yellow-lored and Yellow-headed, the best location to find Black Catbirds, as well as a good chance to find Botteri's Sparrow. Flocks of up to 30 Yellow-headed Parrots have been reported in pine savanna along the river, especially in early morning and late evening. Least Bittern has been found regularly and probably breeds. Carolina (White-browed) Wren has been heard singing along the creek. Black-throated Bobwhite, Agami Heron, and Lesser Goldfinch also occur here. Thousands of migrating Dickcissels were observed on one day in April.

Key species of New River: Black-bellied Whistling-Duck, Muscovy Duck, Least and Pied-billed Grebes, **Jabiru**, **Least Bittern**, Bare-throated Tiger-Heron, **Agami Heron**, Black-crowned Night-Heron, **Boat-billed Heron**, Roseate Spoonbill, Lesser Yellow-headed Vulture, Snail Kite, **Black-collared Hawk**, Great Black-Hawk, Short-tailed Hawk, Collared Forest-Falcon, Gray-necked Wood-Rail, Sora, **Purple Gallinule**, **Sungrebe**, **Limpkin**, Black-necked Stilt, Yellow-lored and Yellow-headed Parrots, Mangrove Cuckoo [R], Mottled Owl, Lesser Nighthawk, **Yucatan Poorwill**, Chuck-will's-widow [R,T], **Yucatan Nightjar**, **Northern Potoo**, **American Pygmy Kingfisher**, Northern Beardless-Tyrannulet, Yucatan Flycatcher, Carolina Wren, Black Catbird, **Botteri's Sparrow**, Grasshopper Sparrow, Dickcissel, Lesser Goldfinch.

LAMANAI MAYA SITE

[23 February] Although we've been traveling through jungles earlier in the trip, this is the first time the forest deserves the name we usually imagine as jungle: steamy, tall, and lush, with vines, palms, and mahogany, echoing with parrots, tropical songsters, and the screams of Yucatan Black Howlers. We see the howlers lumbering through the forest canopy. Careful not to stand directly beneath them—defecating is a defense—we watch them eating, playing, and caring for their young, and of course roaring like a drunken sailor using a bullhorn.

The birders seek the surrounding jungles and the tunneled paths connecting sites. Our group gets separated and four of us slowly walk one of the narrowest and most canopied when we see something stirring up the leaf litter on the forest floor. I soon discover multiple birds tossing leaves and eventually recognize we've stumbled on an ant swarm. A half-hour of watching gives us excellent views of Tawny-winged, Ruddy, and Ivory-billed Woodcreepers, Wood Thrush, Ovenbird, Kentucky Warbler, Gray-headed Tanager, Red-crowned Ant-Tanager and, most amazingly, our second sighting of a Black-faced Antthrush. Watching over this procession is a Blue-crowned Motmot, silently perched low on a fallen branch. When the group gathers again at the dock, we compare stories about what we've seen. We hear of Plain Xenops hanging from a vine, 12 woodcreepers of 5 species, a quietly perched White-whiskered Puffbird, and calling Stub-tailed Spadebills, and a single-person sighting of a Pheasant Cuckoo, an extremely elusive species.

Description: Located on New River Lagoon, the 950-acre archeological site of Lamanai—Maya for "Submerged Crocodile"—is one of the longest occupied areas in Belize, extending to after the arrival of the Spanish around 1544 and therefore one of the very few Maya sites retaining its original name. Between 1974 and 1986, Dr. David Pendergast and his team of archaeologists mapped 940 structures, including 85 that were sampled or intensively excavated. More have been uncovered since then and many others lie buried beneath rubble hills hidden in the jungle, some dating to 900 B.C., hundreds of years before most other Maya sites, and some temples still occupied to at least A.D. 1200 when most other sites had been abandoned. Maya were still residing at Lamanai in 1640 when they rebelled against the Spanish and burned the Spanish church. Now we come to Lamanai to see the birds, the monkeys, and The Mask, where construction began in 200 B.C. and temples were modified several times to A.D. 1300. The Mask, a 10-foot square stone face of an undocumented Maya ruler, remained hidden from view by successive temple renovations by succeeding rulers and when unmasked, it showed brilliant color until a rainstorm washed away the paint and the artistic details. Most of the Lamanai restorations have occurred in the past decade. An excellent review of Lamanai Maya and archeological history can be found at:
   - www.beyondtouring.com/Lamanai/lamanai_intro.htm, and
   - http://people.uncw.edu/simmonss/Lamanai%20overview%20of
      %20LAP.htm.

In addition to the ruins, visitors can see the historic remains of two Christian churches erected over Maya temples during Spanish occupation, and a sugar mill built during the British colonial period.

Birding strategy: Lamanai can be accessed by a difficult road or a beautiful river, the latter being the most popular route. Arriving in midday means the jungle will be steamy hot, yet birds in the shaded areas are likely to be active enough to give you a good list of exciting sightings. For better timing, consider staying overnight at Lamanai Outpost Lodge.

Almost anywhere along the trails and amongst the ruins is productive birding. Study the map to get your bearings. From the boat landing dock, walk left (south) toward the covered picnic tables and vendors selling souvenirs; just a bit uphill are modern toilets and the museum housing Lamanai artifacts. Here are a few suggestions for hiking routes:

Jaguar Temple N10-9 to High Temple N10-43: From the picnic area head north on the stone walkway. Just before the tall steps on your left is a good spot to find trogons and Keel-billed Toucans. A bit forward of this spot and slightly to the right is a giant Strangler Fig whose high canopy is easily seen and which is a favorite spot for Scrub, Yellow-throated, and Olive-backed Euphonias, and assorted migrant warblers. Continue left, up the stone stairs to

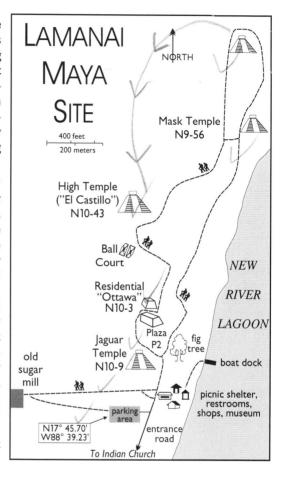

the expansive plaza. On your left is the impressive and recently renovated Jaguar Temple N10-9. The 65-foot temple rises in nine tiers; at the base on both sides of the stairway are masks of a Jaguar with a protruding nose. The temple continued to be modified until at least A.D. 1200. Bird the periphery, crossing Plaza 2 to the southwest corner of Plaza N10-3, also known as "Ottawa," an administrative and elite residential area. From here, running along the western edge of the N10-3 is one of the most productive forest trails for Collared Forest-Falcon, Slaty-tailed Trogon, Rufous-tailed Jacamar, Chestnut-colored Woodpecker, and various woodcreepers. The narrow trail opens up to the Ball Court—constructed in the ninth century— followed by the spectacular High Temple N10-43, the largest known Pre-classic structure in the entire Maya world. This is another reliable spot for Slaty-tailed Trogon. If you are energetic, you can climb the steep 108-foot

Lamanai High Temple   Bert Frenz

temple to its top, using a tethered rope for balance. The temple rises above the canopy, so from the lofty apex you have a grand view of the dense forest canopy and New River Lagoon, and an eye-to-eye view of soaring vultures.

Mask Temple N9-56: You can reach this landmark temple—built about 200 B.C. and modified up to A.D. 800—from two routes, either the trail starting from the giant fig tree and paralleling New River, or from a trail extending from the High Temple. Both trails pass through closed-canopy jungle with dense understory. Look for Plain Xenops and Long-billed Gnatwren in hanging vine tangles. Listen for the clear whistle of a Tawny-crowned Greenlet high in the canopy or the emphatic *TEACH-cher* or staccato fussing of Black-throated Shrike-Tanager signaling a mixed-species flock. Also listen for rustling leaves on the forest floor, a possible indicator of birds following an ant swarm. Rustling might also indicate a troop of Collared Peccaries or White-nosed Coatis moving through the jungle, just barely in sight. Yucatan Black Howlers are likely in the canopy and, if so, you will hear roaring long before you close in on the source. When you reach the Mask Temple, see if you can find Red-capped Manakins just north of the temple. Continue north beyond the Mask Temple to complete the loop through the jungle and back to the High Temple.

Old Sugar Mill: A productive trail leads from the restrooms and museum to the historic sugar mill, started by the British in the 1850s and abandoned in the early 1880s. From the back side of the restroom building there are two trailheads that soon converge on the main trail through the jungle. White-whiskered Puffbird frequents these trails, sometimes very close to the south trailhead and sometimes farther along after the trails converge. The bird is usually silent and sedentary, so unless you are observant you could easily walk past the perched bird at eye level and only a dozen feet away. Also found here is Buff-bellied Hummingbird, about as far south as you are likely to find one. Just inside the north trailhead, there is a poorly groomed spur threading northward. You need not walk far along this spur to start finding the more elusive forest species such as Dusky Antbird, Northern Bentbill, Eye-ringed Flatbill, and Northern Schiffornis. On the main trail to the sugar mill, look for Green-backed Sparrow and listen for calling wrens. An alternative trail returning from the sugar mill leads to the parking lot. If you have more time to explore, continue past the parking lot and along the nicely wooded entrance road, where, among other species, you may find Worm-eating, Kentucky, and Hooded Warblers, perhaps simultaneously.

Key species of Lamanai: Collared Forest-Falcon, White-crowned Parrot, Pheasant Cuckoo [R], Mottled Owl, Lesser Swallow-tailed Swift, **Purple-crowned Fairy**, **Slaty-tailed Trogon**, Collared Trogon, Tody Motmot, **White-whiskered Puffbird**, Rufous-tailed Jacamar, Smoky-brown, Golden-olive, and Chestnut-colored Woodpeckers, Dusky Antbird, **Black-faced Antthrush**, Plain Xenops, Olivaceous and Streak-headed

---

Ecoregion and habitats: *Appendix A, Ecoregion 4, New River riparian watershed. Habitats include: lowland broadleaf forest (BFL1, BFL4) with open areas at Maya temples.*

Concerns: *Use insect spray and wear long pants and long-sleeved shirts. Use a guide or a trail map to avoid getting lost on the trails. If your boat has a scheduled departure time, be aware of where you are and the distance to the dock, as it is easy to underestimate the time it takes to return.*

Fees and contact: *Entrance US$10 for non-residents, BZ$10 for residents, is usually included in the price of tours and boat trips. If you travel to Lamanai by road, you will be charged the fee. Modern bathrooms, souvenir shops, and a museum are adjacent to the ruins. Lunch is available at Lamanai Outpost Lodge, an outstanding resort about a mile from the ruins.*

Lamanai Outpost Lodge, P.O. Box 63, Orange Walk Town; (011) 501-672-2000; outpost @lamanai.com; www.lamanai.com. From US: Booking Office, 103 First Street East, Suite 201, Tierra Verde, FL 33715; 888-733-7864 or 727-867-4481; fax 727-864-4062; reefsruins@aol.com.

Location: *N 17° 45.70' W 88° 39.23' at parking lot. For travel by boat, see the section on New River. By road, two routes lead to Lamanai from Orange Walk Town (each 32–36 miles one-way).*

Woodcreepers, Ochre-bellied Flycatcher, Northern Bentbill, Stub-tailed
Spadebill, Royal Flycatcher, Bright-rumped Attila, White-collared and
Red-capped Manakins, Tawny-crowned Greenlet, Long-billed Gnatwren,
Gray-headed Tanager, **Black-throated Shrike-Tanager**, Black-faced and
Blue-black Grosbeaks, Blue Bunting.

Tours and contacts: *If you are staying at Lamanai Outpost Lodge, boat arrangements will be made for you. Many other resorts and tour companies schedule trips on
the New River to Lamanai. Three companies that charter boats are:*
*Reyes & Sons River Tours, Tower Hill Bridgefoot Embankment, Orange Walk District;
(011) 501-322-3342 or 322-3327 or cellular (011) 610-1548 or 914-9835; fax (011)
501-322-3327; reyesandsons@hotmail.com. Ask for Aldofo Reyes. The best driver and
birding guide is his son Amir Reyes.*
*Lamanai Eco Tours, 49-1/2 miles Goldson (Northern) Highway, Carmelita Village, Orange
Walk District; (011) 501-610-1753; errolcadell@yahoo.com. Ask for Errol Cadel.*
*Jungle River Tours, 20 Lovers' Lane, Orange Walk Town; (011) 501-670-3035;
lamanaimayatour@btl.net or novedcris@yahoo.com. Ask for Antonio.*
*Lamanai River Tours; (011) 501-670-0700. Tours can also be arranged through Hotel
de la Fuente, 14 Main St., Orange Walk Town; (011) 501-322-2290; fax (011)
501-322-3651; info@hoteldelafuente.com; www.hoteldelafuente.com.*
*For those staying on Ambergris Caye, it is possible to charter a boat from the island to
the mainland, then along the New River to Orange Walk and thence to Lamanai. See
www.ambergriscaye.com for suggestions. These trips are often arranged through Reyes
& Sons, listed above.*

HILL BANK FIELD STATION
Rio Bravo Conservation and Management Area

[By boat, 27 January] In mid-afternoon we continue upriver to Hill Bank...After
settling into our rooms, we begin a late afternoon bird walk. Vladimir zeroes in on
four Yellow-headed Parrots. The endangered parrots—with only partially yellow
heads—are the endemic belizensis subspecies. After dinner our plans for a
nocturnal drive through the forests are threatened by a tropical downpour, yet as
quickly as the rain begins, it ends. We board the beds and cabs of two pickup
trucks for a starlit ride on narrow two-rut roads, each vehicle heading in different
directions and scanning for wildlife with high-intensity spotlights. Our group finds
little at first, but then, excitedly, Linda cries out, "Pig," the first word coming to
mind when she sees a Baird's Tapir feeding beside the road. We see the
unusually large black mammal hustle deeper into the forest just as my spotlight
finds a second one with head and shoulders protruding from the dense foliage.
It's my first sighting of this mammal in the wild and a species I would not have
expected to find. When we return to the research station, I hear from Bob that
their truckload found a Boat-billed Heron, a Kinkajou—a monkey-like relative of
the raccoon—and a Mottled Owl.

[By car, 22 February] We are on the Hill Bank road, a narrow one-lane,
two-track farm road bumping through Mennonite territory. We don't look
forward to the rugged ride back, but are soon rewarded with a sighting that
would have made worthwhile a trip ten times longer. Shari is driving—so she

can't complain about my speed or the many bumps—and she stops suddenly, exclaiming, "There's something big in the road ahead." I put up my binoculars and shout, "Jaguar." I crack open my door to photograph the rear end of a Jaguar slowly lumbering along the two-track heading away from us. Shari drives farther and I again photograph the Jaguar's rear end; it still hasn't detected our presence a quarter-mile behind. A third stop and we see the Jaguar turn its head to watch us. We slowly gain ground on the giant cat and get even better views. More photos, another cat march and car roll, and the Jaguar stops again and turns for another photo opportunity. One more approach and still closer, but this time the Jaguar turns and walks into the jungle. I check the car clock; we've watched the Jaguar for an amazing five full minutes. Top that!

Description: Hill Bank Field Station is on the banks of New River Lagoon, within the Rio Bravo Conservation and Management Area, which extends to La Milpa Ecolodge and Research Center. Operated by Programme for Belize, the station serves both as a research base and a site for specialized tourism. The Hill Bank area featured in colonial history as a logging camp for over 150 years and even today poachers sometimes take mahogany from the dense forest stands. Up until the 1960s, Belize Estate and Produce Company cut mahogany, cedar, and Santa Maria at Gallon Jug; transported logs via railroad —no longer in existence—to New River Lagoon at Hill Bank; from there the logs floated the New River past Orange Walk Town to Chetumal Bay and thence to Belize City. Nowadays, its remoteness and lack of easy accessibility renders it a great place to find native mammals and birds.

Researchers have compiled an impressive bird checklist and continued birding has resulted in a 2012 total of 356 species, including a good number of rarities for the region (see sample list below).

Birding strategy: Hill Bank Field Station requires at least a one-night stay, given the time to reach the site. Combining it with a New River boat tour and a visit at Lamanai allows for an afternoon Hill Bank visit, an overnight stay, a day of birding, and a nocturnal return to Orange Walk Town. An alternative is to combine Hill Bank with birding the Mennonite areas from Yo Creek to San Felipe and continuing the drive to the field station. For a longer stay, consider taking a canoe ride from Hill Bank to the mouth of Irish Creek and then paddling a mile or so along the creek. One such trip scored a vocalizing Pheasant Cuckoo, 4 Jabirus (including 2 nestlings), 5 Sungrebes, 15 Limpkins, Mottled Owl, 15 Ringed Kingfishers, 8 Belted Kingfishers, 25 Green Kingfishers, and 2 American Pygmy Kingfishers.

A local bird guide can be contracted through Programme for Belize. Because all birding is within walking distance of the cabanas and dormitories, the day and night can easily be divided into four or more brief hikes. A short drive to Irish Creek and birding along the road is a worthwhile trip. Very rarely reported in Belize, one male Slate-colored Seedeater was observed and recorded singing at a bamboo patch west of the road at Irish Creek 23

February 2009. A night drive on the narrow dark roads through the jungle can be highly rewarding for finding nocturnal mammals and birds. From the deck of the cabanas, Limpkins can be heard calling from the marsh at night.

Directions: For travel by car or truck, be advised that the roads are narrow, pot-holed, rough, and overgrown with plant life, and when wet, the deep ruts are nearly impassable. To reach Hill Bank by road from Orange Walk Town, two routes are available. One route is via Shipyard Road (see details at www.bafrenz.com).

From San Felipe (see map on page 52): For the second land route, follow the Gallon Jug Road log until San Felipe at mile 23.3, N 17° 52.35' W 88° 46.35'. A Roman Catholic school is at this intersection and there may be a sign pointing to Lamanai. Beyond here, there are no signs. Drive time for this section of road is about 1-1/4 hours. Without stops, total drive time from Orange Walk Town is about 2-1/2 hours. Zero your odometer at the Catholic school in San Felipe. After passing the road on your right that heads to La Milpa and Gallon Jug, continue heading south. At 0.3, curve left and wind out of town and into the countryside. At 0.9 is a T-intersection (see map on page 72) at N 17° 51.83' W 88° 45.97'. Straight ahead would lead to Lamanai. Turn right for Hill Bank. Continue straight at a minor crossroads at 1.8, pass through farmlands on one or both sides for nearly 5 miles and then a forested area at 6.7. More farmlands follow, with farm roads abutting on the left at 7.7 and 9.5. A Uniform Crake was found at 9 miles and the Jaguar sighting described in the journal entry was at 10.8.

At 14.6 the farm road connecting to Indian Church and Lamanai intersects from the left. Continue straight ahead to 16.0, the gate to Programme for Belize. At 21.3 the road crosses Irish Creek on a wooden bridge, an excellent birding area. Turn left at 22.5 and reach Hill Bank Field Station at 22.8.

Ecoregion and habitats: Appendix A, Ecoregion 4, New River riparian watershed. Habitats include: lowland broadleaf forest (BFL1, BFL2, BFL3) and a small research station (PC).

Concerns: *Logistically, this trip takes more planning than others, requiring more attention to details for transportation, gasoline, lodging, meals, and guides. Make arrangements with Programme for Belize well ahead of your planned arrival.*

Facilities and contact: *The Hill Bank Field Station is well kept, more rugged than a resort, but comfortably adequate for most birders. Six dormitory rooms each have three beds and a sitting room overlooking the river. They share two large bathroom facilities. In addition, two large cabanas have multiple beds and private showers. The dining room serves tasty Belizean meals in buffet style. Programme for Belize, P.O. Box 749, #1 Eyre Street, Belize City, Belize District; (011) 501-227-5616 or 227-5617 or 227-1020; fax (011) 501-227-5635; pfbel@btl.net; www.pfbelize.org.*

Location: *N 17° 36.09' W 88° 42.05' at facilities. For travel by water, see the section for New River. For travel by car or truck, see the section above, "Directions."*

Key **species of Hill Bank**: Great and Thicket Tinamous, Great Curassow, Jabiru, Hook-billed Kite, Ornate Hawk-Eagle, Barred Forest-Falcon, Ruddy and Uniform [R] Crakes, **Limpkin**, Scaled Pigeon, **Yellow-headed Parrot**, Pheasant Cuckoo, Mottled and Stygian Owls, Common Nighthawk [S], **Yucatan Poorwill, Yucatan Nightjar**, Northern Potoo, Azure-crowned Hummingbird, Collared Trogon, American Pygmy Kingfisher, White-necked Puffbird, Rufous-tailed Jacamar, Dusky Antbird, Black-faced Antthrush, Scaly-throated Leaftosser, Plain Xenops, Ruddy and Olivaceous Woodcreepers, Yellow-bellied Tyrannulet, Ochre-bellied Flycatcher, Slate-headed Tody-Flycatcher, Stub-tailed, Royal, and White-throated [R] Flycatchers, Black-crowned Tityra, **Gray-collared Becard**, White-bellied Wren, **Slate-colored Seedeater** [R], Gray-throated Chat, **Blue Seedeater** [R], Blue Bunting.

CROOKED TREE WILDLIFE SANCTUARY

[13 February] Along the shore of the lagoon our small boat putters slowly, then stops and glides. Perched in Logwood trees are herons and egrets and ibis, including a Glossy Ibis, which is rare for Belize but regularly found here. Jacanas and Blue-winged Teal occupy the shoreline; Limpkins hide farther into the crooked wood. Snail Kites perch higher and near the tops of the trees bask colorful Green Iguanas. We get our first view of a Black-collared Hawk, content to perch before us. Nearby, but at shore level, is a pair of Gray-necked Wood-Rails feathered in soft tones of black, gray, and rufous, set off by a big yellow bill and bright red legs. A Mangrove Cuckoo, a rarity for this area, makes a quick appearance. "Mangrove" plays highly as an adjective today as we also see Mangrove Swallows and hear Mangrove Vireos.

The water channel narrows into a creek and the parade of birds continues as we sit in the canopied shade, leisurely birding. Robert, our guide and navigator, makes special effort to find an Agami Heron, checking all of its usual haunts, but perhaps it is still too early in the season to find them, for his efforts go unrewarded. Instead we find many Black-crowned Night-Herons, Boat-billed Herons, and a single Bare-throated Tiger-Heron. Perhaps the real show belongs to the kingfishers. In a few hours' time we see a dozen Ringed Kingfishers, nearly as many Belted Kingfishers, and three Green Kingfishers. Nearing lunchtime, Robert leaves Spanish Creek and heads back to the lodge, where we enjoy a delicious Belizean-style meal, including my favorite fried plantains.

Description: This small birding-haven community, where many residents are named Gillett, Tillett, or Tillette, originated around 1750 when their ancestor moved here in search of the Logwood tree. Now the village is laid out with birding trails, lodges cater to birders, and boats can be chartered to explore the lagoons, Black Creek, and Spanish Creek. Crooked Tree Wildlife Sanctuary was founded by Belize Audubon Society in 1984 and now comprises over 41,000 acres of protected habitat. In spite of the influence of birding tourism, the place has a laid-back, casual native-village feel to it.

Phenomenal numbers of birds appear at the Crooked Tree lagoons in springtime. Among the best days were 22–23 March 2010 with the following one-day counts: 5,000 Black-bellied Whistling-Ducks, 200 Fulvous Whistling-Ducks, 3,000 Blue-winged Teal, 1,500 Neotropic Cormorants, 200 Great Blue Herons, 3,000 Great Egrets, 250 Little Blue Herons, 70 Tricolored Herons, 50 Green Herons, 2,000 White Ibis, 300 Roseate Spoonbills, 45 Jabirus, 2,000 Wood Storks, 60 Snail Kites, 1,500 American Coots, 1,200 Limpkins, 60 Black-bellied Plovers, 1,500 Black-necked Stilts, 500 Northern Jacanas, 100 Greater Yellowlegs, 800 Lesser Yellowlegs, 250 Pectoral Sandpipers, 50 Stilt Sandpipers, 20 Long-billed Dowitchers, 100 Caspian Terns, 20 Prothonotary Warblers. Scan Black-bellied Plovers carefully during migration; you might be lucky to find Belize-rare American Golden-Plovers, as did one birding group on 14 March 2011 when they saw five golden-plovers.

Birding strategy by boat: Crooked Tree is a birding area that takes at least two days to explore properly: one morning by boat and another by land. A popular place for boat rentals, birding guides, lodging, and meals is Bird's Eye View Lodge & Tours. Boats and canoes can be rented for individuals as well as groups of 20–30. Operated by Lenard (Lenny) Gillett, the three-hour boat ride typically takes the Spanish Creek route going south along Northern Lagoon, stopping before Southern Lagoon, then heading west along Spanish Creek to the boardwalk, and follows Spanish Creek a bit farther south before returning. An alternative route takes you along Black Creek. You'll definitely need the birding guides to steer through the maze of water passages and to show you the favorite hideouts of the many bird specialties. One of these is Agami Heron, an elusive bird that is more often missed than seen because the water levels must be just right to provide enough float for the boat, but not too high to push the herons deep into the overhanging mangroves. Although water recession is not consistent each year, April is perhaps the best month. The herons hang out along Spanish Creek, not far from the Spanish Creek boardwalk. Just south of Spanish Creek's confluence with Northern Lagoon is the site where Yellow-breasted Crake was observed many times from December 1998–March 1999. Commonly seen animals include Morelet's Crocodile, Brown Iguana, Green Iguana, Yucatan Black Howler, Neotropical River Otter, and freshwater turtles. If you aren't already staying at Bird's Eye View, be sure to prearrange finishing up your morning boat ride with a Creole-style lunch at the lodge.

Birding strategy by land: Quite a different set of birds awaits you when you explore Crooked Tree by land. Undoubtedly, your first stop will be along the causeway, with its strategic view of Northern Lagoon. Birds are seen at any time, however at low water levels the expansive mudflats entice an amazing number and diversity of birds: 10+ Jabirus (one of the most sought-after birds of the refuge, with counts as high as 59 individuals on 28

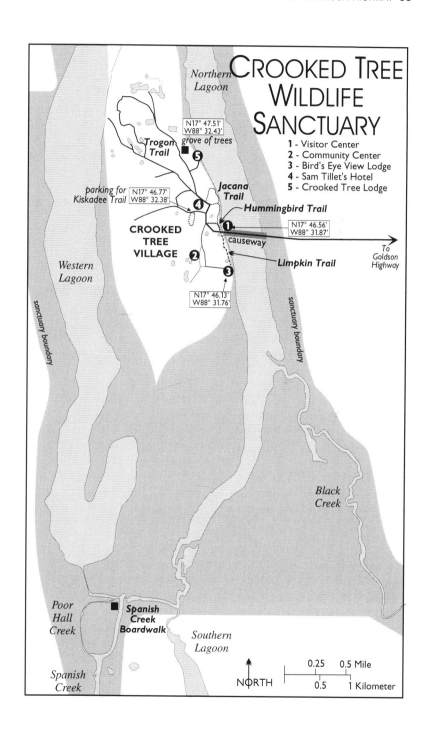

CROOKED TREE
WILDLIFE
SANCTUARY

Northern Lagoon

N17° 47.51'
W88° 32.43'
grove of trees

Trogon Trail

5

1 - Visitor Center
2 - Community Center
3 - Bird's Eye View Lodge
4 - Sam Tillet's Hotel
5 - Crooked Tree Lodge

parking for Kiskadee Trail
N17° 46.77'
W88° 32.38'

4

Jacana Trail

Hummingbird Trail

1
N17° 46.56'
W88° 31.87'

causeway

CROOKED
TREE
VILLAGE

2

Western Lagoon

Limpkin Trail

3

N17° 46.13'
W88° 31.76'

To Goldson Highway

sanctuary boundary

sanctuary boundary

Black Creek

Poor Hall Creek

Spanish Creek Boardwalk

Southern Lagoon

Spanish Creek

NORTH

0.25   0.5 Mile

0.5   1 Kilometer

Bare-throated Tiger-Heron (juvenile)   Bert Frenz

February 2003), dozens of Wood Storks, thousands of egrets and herons of at least 9 species (14 species are on the Crooked Tree checklist), hundreds of Neotropic Cormorants (and perhaps one or two Double-cresteds), dozens of Snail Kites, and hundreds of Caspian Terns. A Southern Lapwing—an accidental visitor from South America and the rarest bird to show up at Crooked Tree—first arrived in spring of 2004 and remained until spring 2008, most often encountered at the shallow pond behind Bird's Eye View Lodge.

The causeway itself is a good place to find kingfishers, Common Tody-Flycatcher, Fork-tailed Flycatcher, Mangrove Vireo, and warblers. At the end of the causeway, pay the entrance fee at the Belize Audubon building on the right. You can explore the village and outlying areas. Zero your odometer at the visitor center and continue into the village 0.2 mile to the T-intersection. For Bird's Eye View Lodge, turn left and then left again, following signs to the lodge and lagoon front, one mile from the T-intersection. However, for Crooked Tree Lodge and to bird the trails, turn right at the T-intersection, passing Sam Tillett's Place at 0.6 mile and a split in the road at 0.7. Dirt streets in the village are labeled as trails with bird names and several of them extend out into the surrounding refuge. To take Kiskadee Trail, fork left for another 0.2 mile and reach a grassy parking space at N 17° 46.77' W 88° 32.38'. From the parking spot, a wooded trail leads under a tall canopy, open enough to see the top for Collared Aracaris and, slightly above eye level, nesting Rufous-tailed Hummingbirds. Even in the heat of the day, this wooded area can be quite productive for finding elusive species such as Northern Bentbill. This is a particularly good site to bring a three-legged stool and bird patiently in the shade for an hour or two. You might be amazed by the diversity of birds that will feed in the surrounding trees.

A productive route is Trogon Trail through secondary broadleaf forest in the village and then pine/palmetto savanna beyond the last houses. Near the transition at N 17° 47.51' W 88° 32.43' is a grove of trees without under-brush, which is favored by dozens of species including Yucatan Jay and Northern Cardinal. In the pine/palmetto savanna, look for Acorn and Ladder-backed Woodpeckers, Grace's Warbler, and Chipping Sparrow. Earlier along

Ecoregion and habitats: Appendix A, Ecoregion 5, Crooked Tree and Altun Ha coastal savannas and forests. Habitats include: the village of Crooked Tree (PC), large lagoons and narrow river ways surrounded by swamps and low-elevation secondary broadleaf forest (BFL1, BFL2, BFL3) and, at slightly higher elevation, pine/palmetto savanna (PFL).

Concerns: In the rainy season, Crooked Tree may not be accessible when the lagoon floods the causeway. In addition, mudflats will be covered and largely devoid of birds. Later, in winter, brief, warm tropical rains often interrupt birding by boat, so wear drip-dry clothes, bring a raincoat, or carry an umbrella. Use sun-block lotion. For the village trails, ask at the visitor center about flooding conditions. Sometimes Jacana Trail is too flooded to walk and the back half of Trogon Trail is too muddy to drive.

Location and directions: Start from mile 61.1 heading south or 22.0 heading north on the Goldson Highway log, N 17° 46.50' W 88° 28.83', which is 24 miles (36 minutes) south of Orange Walk Town or 23 miles northwest of Philip Goldson International Airport. Turn west from the intersection and follow the potholed gravel road through scrub and wetlands for 2.7 miles to the beginning of the causeway across the lagoon. On the opposite end of the causeway at 3.3 miles is the Crooked Tree Wildlife Sanctuary Visitor Center.

Fees, facilities, and contacts: Entrance US$4 for non-residents, BZ$2 for residents, and is paid at Belize Audubon Society's Visitor Center on the right side of the road just after exiting the causeway. Toilets and a small gift shop are at the visitor center. A larger gift and bird book shop is at Bird's Eye View Lodge. For boat rentals, lodging, meals, guides, and tours check the Internet, particularly for Bird's Eye View Lodge and Crooked Tree Lodge. In the past, many birders explored Crooked Tree with Sam Tillett, a well-known birding guide and operator of Sam Tillett's Hotel & Tours. Sadly, Mr. Tillett died in 2008.

Bird's Eye View Lodge, manager Verna Gillett-Samuels, reservations Kira Samuels, P.O. Box 1976, Belize City; (011) 501-203-2040; fax (011) 501-222-4869; birdseye@btl.net; www.birdseyeviewbelize.com.

Crooked Tree Lodge, owners Mick and Angie Webb; Crooked Tree Village, Belize District; (011) 501-626-3820 or 501-623-5035 or from US: 207-404-9066; contact@crookedtreelodgebelize.com or michaelcjwebb@hotmail.com; www.crookedtreelodgebelize.com.

Trogon Trail, an unnamed trail leads to the lagoon. Follow signs for Crooked Tree Lodge to reach this backside view of the shoreline and water.

The trailhead for Woodcreeper Trail (N 17° 46.02' W 88° 31.79') begins at the edge of the woods, about 250 yards south of Bird's Eye View Lodge. Appropriately named, it is a good site to find woodcreepers following an ant swarm. On a recent visit the ant-swarm attendants included Tawny-winged, Ruddy, and Ivory-billed Woodcreepers, as well as Yucatan Jay, Hooded Warbler, Gray-headed Tanager, and Gray-throated Chat.

Jacana Trail follows the lagoon shoreline, which at rainy times is flooded, but otherwise is good for shorebirds, including the vagrant Southern Lapwing and, at Crooked Tree Lodge, Belize's only record of Canada Goose.

If you explore the meandering roads far beyond the village, be sure to take along a map or GPS, as it is easy to get hopelessly lost. When you leave the Crooked Tree area, heading back to Goldson Highway, look for Yellow-headed Parrots in the pine savanna.

Key species of Crooked Tree (creeks and lagoon): Black-bellied Whistling-Duck, **Fulvous Whistling-Duck, Muscovy Duck**, **American Wigeon**, Northern Shoveler [R], Northern Pintail [R], **Ring-necked Duck, Lesser Scaup**, Masked Duck [R], **Least Grebe, Jabiru**, Wood Stork, American White Pelican, Least Bittern, Bare-throated Tiger-Heron, **Agami Heron**, Black-crowned Night-Heron, **Boat-billed Heron**, White Ibis, **Glossy Ibis**, Roseate Spoonbill, **Lesser Yellow-headed Vulture, Snail Kite, Black-collared Hawk**, Great Black-Hawk, Gray-necked Wood-Rail, Purple and Common Gallinules, American Coot, **Sun-grebe, Limpkin**, Semipalmated Plover, Black-necked Stilt, Solitary Sandpiper, **White-rumped Sandpiper** [T], Pectoral [T] and Stilt Sand-pipers, Wilson's Phalarope [R,T], Gull-billed and Caspian Terns, Mangrove Cuckoo [R], American Pygmy Kingfisher, Rufous-breasted Spinetail, Fork-tailed Flycatcher, Tree, Mangrove, Bank [T], and Cliff [T] Swallows.

Key species of Crooked Tree (inland trails and savanna): Black-throated Bobwhite, Aplomado Falcon, Yellow-lored Parrot, **Yellow-headed Parrot**, Striped Cuckoo, Lesser Nighthawk, Canivet's Emerald, Buff-bellied Hummingbird, **Acorn** and **Yucatan Woodpeckers**, Ladder-backed Woodpecker, Northern Beardless-Tyrannulet, Slate-headed Tody-Flycatcher, Eastern Wood-Pewee [T], Vermilion and Yucatan Flycatchers, Rufous-browed Peppershrike, **Yucatan Jay, Grace's War-bler**, Grayish Saltator, Olive and Green-backed Sparrows, **Chipping Sparrow**, Northern Cardinal.

ALTUN HA MAYA SITE AND OLD NORTHERN HIGHWAY

[8 February] This morning we reach Altun Ha by the less traveled, more rural Old Northern Highway route. At our first stop at a creek overflowing from yesterday's rain, we hear a Thicket Tinamou, a northern Belize specialty, and are searching for a Green Kingfisher when Pat exclaims, "King Vulture". Walking to where she stands we see the vulture perched prominently on a high tree and can clearly make out the bright white eye and multicolored naked head with its strange yellow-orange wattles on the bill. A short while later we see a couple of Lesser Yellow-headed Vultures and, of course, the omnipresent Turkey and Black Vultures, completing the quartet of Belizean vulture species in a couple of hours.

We arrive at Altun Ha and encounter eight busloads of lightly and brightly clad tourists, fresh off the cruise ships docked at Belize City. Partly to avoid the tourist chatter and partly to find birds, we walk down a tightly forested path toward the lagoon at its terminus. Trogons flourish at Altun Ha, mostly Black-headed, but here I see a well-hidden Gartered. The lagoon is within sight, but the waterlogged trail reaches a depth of six inches. . .

I hear on the two-way radio that Judy has found a fruiting tree abounding in birds. We make our way to her location and spend the next hour seeing dozens of birds of 19 species, all feeding in the same Strangler Fig encircling a tall Cohune Palm. It seems every Yellow-throated Euphonia has a red berry pinched in its bill. The best bird, however, is a flycatcher that I am convinced is Caribbean Elaenia, uncommon on the cays and hardly ever reported on the mainland, and I collect enough details and photos to report this for inclusion in North American Birds.

Description: The Maya ruins at Altun Ha are the most famous in northern Belize, with two main plazas and 13 temples at the site. The city of 3,000 population was important as a trading post and ceremonial center between 600 B.C. and A.D. 900, when the Classic Maya civilization collapsed.

Birding strategy from south to north: If you are coming from Belize City or Crooked Tree, start on the south end of Old Northern Highway and plan to reach Altun Ha by 9 AM when the gates open. The start of the old highway is 20 miles north of Belize City. Turn east, zero your odometer, and continue northeast on Old Northern Highway. Almost the entire road to Altun Ha is paved, although its condition quickly deteriorates. At 2.8 follow signs to Altun Ha, passing pine savanna and lowland broadleaf forest, and the crocodile sanctuary at 6.9. Wet lowlands, marshes, and ponds along the road are worth checking. Least Bittern and roosting Northern Potoo have been seen from the road. Veer left at the Y-intersection at 11.3 toward Altun Ha, continuing west on unpaved Rockstone Pond No. 1 Road. If you reach the village of Lucky Strike, you missed the turn and need to double back. Mayan Wells restaurant is at 12.0, Belize Jungle Gardens (butterfly gardens) is at 12.6, and the turnoff for Toucan Alley B&B is at 12.8. The roadsides and gardens in this area can be quite productive for birding, with Great Tinamou, Black-throated Bobwhite, Crane Hawk, and Piratic Flycatcher possible. The Altun Ha parking lot at 13.4.

Birding strategy from north to south: If you are originating from Corozal or Orange Walk, start the circuit from the north end of Old Northern Highway. The best birding is at the north end. However, this is the longer and more time-consuming route to Altun Ha, and you most likely will not arrive at the Maya site until late morning when the bird activity is slowest.

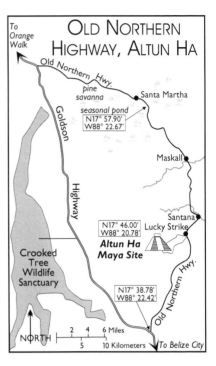

OLD NORTHERN HIGHWAY, ALTUN HA

From Goldson Highway turn east onto Old Northern Highway, zero your odometer, and bird leisurely beside the road until you reach Altun Ha, 32 miles distant. Cross a small bridge over a creek at 0.5, and for the next four miles make repeated stops, choosing different habitats. The road is mostly rough gravel, with huge potholes and broken pavement. At 7.0 is pine savanna with palmetto, introduced Australian Pines, and perhaps a temporary lake on the right. Yellow-headed Parrot, Gray-crowned Yellowthroat, and Gray-throated Chat are found in this area. The Santa Martha water tower, surrounded by lowland broadleaf forest, is at 10.8. A good birding stop is across the road from the Government School. Bird the next mile thoroughly, especially at 12.7 if the pond and wetlands have flooded from recent rains. The pond (N 17° 57.90' W 88° 22.67') easily could hold a dozen species you haven't seen earlier in the day. After the pond, speed up as fast as the road will allow, stopping infrequently, as the birding is likely to be better at Altun Ha than anywhere in the next 17 miles. En route you will encounter sugarcane fields at 14, marshes and palms and then taller trees at 15. Lodging landmarks are: Maruba Resort Jungle Spa at 19, Altun Ha Jungle Resort at 20.5, and Silver Fox Guest House at 22. Maskall Village spans a mile starting at 21 and centered on Northern River. In small ponds here Fulvous Whistling-Duck has been found. Dawson's Vista in St. Anne's Village is at 25 and Santana Community is at 27. Just past Lucky Strike Community Center, veer right at the Y-intersection toward Altun Ha. Bird the roadsides from Mayan Wells restaurant at 30 to the Altun Ha parking lot at 32. After you have birded the archaeology site, you can complete the Old Northern Highway route heading south, as it will be faster than returning the way you came. The round trip is 75 miles.

Birding strategy at Altun Ha: The best birding is at the edges of the excavated archaeological site where cruise-ship tourists spend little or no time. Talk to some of the local archaeology guides and they may be able to point out where they recently have seen the larger and more colorful birds such as toucans and trogons. The west and south boundaries of the site seem the most productive. Be sure to visit the wooded trail starting from the south end and leading to Rockstone Pond, as the more elusive birds are found here. In open areas near the ruins, scan the skies for Black and Ornate Hawk-Eagles, and, in fall migration, Swallow-tailed Kites.

Ecoregion and habitats: Appendix A, Ecoregion 5, Crooked Tree and Altun Ha coastal savannas and forests. Habitats include: alongside the highway are disturbed lowland broadleaf forest (BFL3), pine savanna (PFL), and some sugarcane fields (AG1), interspersed with small villages (PC). At Altun Ha grass lawns connect the excavated ruins, but the surrounding areas are thickly forested and a wide jungle path through tall trees leads to a lagoon (BFL2).

Concerns: The northern end of the highway is potholed, rough, and typically traveled only by locals. There was a report of a delivery truck being held up by robbers and sometimes the locals tell other stories of mischief. Traveling with a larger group or a local guide may improve safety, and in most ways the route seems little different from other rural areas. The southern end (south of Altun Ha) was newly repaved in 2006—but by 2007 was severely potholed—and it is the route that the tour buses take. The Maya site is often crowded with tourists from the cruise ships. To avoid most of the crowds, schedule your visit for Saturday, Sunday, or Monday, or perhaps Friday. You can also check www.cruisecal.com for cruise ships in port on any particular day. Best birding at the ruins is during the early morning and late afternoon (toucans are regular then), but travel time makes this difficult unless staying at one of the many nearby resorts. Use insect repellent—and high-topped boots if recent rains—for birding the trail to the lagoon.

Fees and facilities: Altun Ha entrance US$10 for non-residents, BZ$10 for residents. Guides can identify the common birds but are better at explaining the Maya history and archeological ruins. Few facilities are along the highway, but near Altun Ha there are a number of lodges and restaurants. One recommended is Mayan Wells Restaurant, where after a traditional Belizean meal you can bird the restaurant site. Altun Ha has modern bathrooms and local vendors selling souvenirs.

Maruba Resort Jungle Spa; (011) 501-225-5555; maruba@maruba-spa.com; www.maruba-spa.com. From the US: P.O. Box 300703, Houston, TX 77230; 800-627-8227 or 713-799-2031; fax 713-795-8573.

Silver Fox Guest House; Mile 38 Old Northern Highway, Maskall Village, Belize District; (011) 501-205-5541 or 205-5522; contact-us@silverfoxinbelize.com; www.silverfoxinbelize.com

Location: N 17° 46.00' W 88° 20.78' at Altun Ha entrance. Altun Ha is on Old Northern Highway which heads east from Goldson Highway. The old and new highways intersect at two locations. The northern one is less than a mile south of Orange Walk Town, which is mile 43.1 heading south (or 40.0 heading north) and intersects at N 18° 1.22' W 88° 32.63'. Alternatively, the southern intersection is 20 miles north of Belize City or 12 miles south of Crooked Tree or 34 miles south of Orange Walk. This intersection is at mile 73.0 (10.1), N 17° 38.78' W 88° 22.42'.

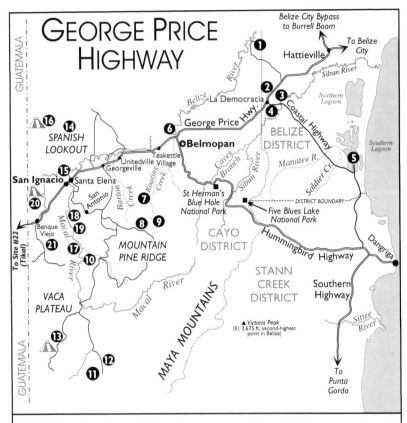

GEORGE PRICE HIGHWAY

Belize City Bypass to Burrell Boom

To Belize City

Hattieville

Sibun River

Northern Lagoon

GUATEMALA

Belize River

La Democracia

George Price Hwy.

❶

❷
❸
❹

Coastal Highway

BELIZE DISTRICT

Southern Lagoon

❻
Belmopan

❶❻ **❶❹**

SPANISH LOOKOUT

Teakettle
Unitedville Village
Georgeville

Caves Branch

Sibun River

Manatee R.

❺

San Ignacio Santa Elena

❶❺

San Antonio

Burton Creek

Roaring Creek

❼

St Herman's
Blue Hole
National Park

DISTRICT BOUNDARY

Soldier Ck.

❷❶

Benque Viejo

❶❽ **❶❾**

❽ **❾**

Five Blues Lake
National Park

*To Site #22
(Tikal)*

❷❶

❶❼ **❿**

MOUNTAIN
PINE RIDGE

CAYO DISTRICT

Hummingbird Highway

Dangriga

VACA
PLATEAU

Macal River

River

Macal River

MAYA MOUNTAINS

STANN
CREEK
DISTRICT

Southern
Highway

GUATEMALA

❶❸

❶❷

❶❶

▲ *Victoria Peak*
(El. 3,675 ft, second-highest point in Belize)

Sittee River

*To
Punta
Gorda*

GEORGE PRICE HIGHWAY BIRDING SITES

❶ Big Falls Farm, Cox Lagoon
❷ Belize Zoo
❸ Tropical Education Center
❹ Monkey Bay Wildlife Sanctuary
❺ Coastal Highway, Gales Point
❻ Guanacaste National Park
❼ Pook's Hill
❽ Hidden Valley Inn
❾ Thousand Foot Falls
❿ Rio Frio Caves and
   Douglas Da Silva
⓫ Chiquibul National Park
⓬ Las Cuevas Research Station
⓭ 🏛Caracol

⓮ Spanish Lookout and
   Aguacate Lagoon
⓯ San Ignacio Sites
⓰ 🏛 El Pilar Maya Site
3 Macal River Resorts:
⓱ Black Rock Lodge
⓲ Lodge at Chaa Creek
⓳ du Plooy's Lodge
⓴ 🏛 Xunantunich Maya Site
㉑ Hydro Road
㉒ 🏛Tikal, Guatemala
   (not shown on map)

| | 5 | 10 | 15 Miles |
NORTH | 5 | 10 | 15 | 20 Kilometers |

CHAPTER 3
GEORGE PRICE HIGHWAY

Gone are the cane fields and little villages of Goldson Highway as you turn westward from the Belize City Bypass for the long, fast stretch on George Price Highway, Belize's speedway to Belmopan. (Similar to the name change for the Northern Highway, Western Highway was changed in September 2012 to the George Price Highway.) Sprinkled with a few sparse pines, the palmetto savanna passes by quickly. Beyond the flat, dry grasslands, strange limestone hills pop up on the horizon, sticking up abruptly with rough, unnaturally sharp vertical lines. Progress slows once you reach the outskirts of Belmopan and is slower yet after you pass the Hummingbird Highway turnoff at **Guanacaste National Park**. Now it is one village followed by the next, each bordered by speed bumps. The terrain has changed too: more wooded, more streams. Approaching the San Ignacio area, signs advertise resorts, many of which cater to birders. Penetrating the twin villages of Santa Elena and San Ignacio is like driving a maze of left and right turns, one-way streets, and one-way bridges. Eventually you escape out the other side and the country opens up a bit, until Price Highway finally terminates at the Guatemala border.

The first birding sites are concentrated between miles 9 and 16 of Price Highway. Additional sites are nearby on the **Coastal Highway** intersecting at 14. The birding here can be incredibly good, easily worth more than a day or two. This area can be reached from accommodations near Belize City or Belmopan. Alternatively, consider staying at Cheers, **Monkey Bay**, or the **Belize Zoo Jungle Lodge**. The latter two cater to students and researchers, but they usually have rooms and meals available for tourists as well. The properties along the south side of Price Highway, including Amigo's, a popular restaurant and bar at mile 16, border the Sibun River. Attempts at cattle raising proved unsuccessful and the land is now predominantly orange groves or has reverted to savanna and secondary lowland broadleaf forest. There is excellent birding in riparian forests along the Sibun and near **Fresh Catch** fish farm. Canoe and kayak trips down the river can be arranged locally.

At 23 the Price Highway crosses Beaver Dam Creek just past St. Mathews Village. This area has one of only three Belize records for Blue-throated Goldentail, the first of six Belize records for Long-billed Starthroat, and one of the southernmost records for Rose-throated Tanager in Belize. In April 2009, two Ocellated Turkeys crossed the road near here.

Price Highway crosses into Cayo District, curiously named after the Spanish word for island or cay. So why is the landlocked district on the Guatemala border called Cayo? Before roads, all commerce in British Honduras traveled by boat, and Cayo boats carried chicle and other goods from San Ignacio to Belize City on the Belize River. Until the 1960s, "El Cayo" was the name for San Ignacio, which has the appearance of being an island between the Mopan and Macal Rivers.

The Cayo District of western Belize—especially miles 32 to 62 on Price Highway—incorporates more birding sites than any other. Many popular resorts lie in the coolest part of the country, some positioned in lowland broadleaf forests and riparian forests along the Macal and Mopan Rivers or along creeks flowing from the highlands. There are also lowland and submontane pine forests on the slopes and plateau of the Maya Mountains, as well as agricultural lands in the broad valley of **Spanish Lookout** between Maya Mountains and Yalbac Hills. All lower-elevation sites are within an hour's drive of San Ignacio, the hub of commercial activity. Maya Mountain sites, accessed from Price Highway at mile 47.3 or 53.2 on the log, are best visited by staying at lodges in the **Mountain Pine Ridge**.

Road Log for George Price Highway

Although Price Highway originates in Belize City, this road log begins at its intersection with the Belize City Bypass.

Birding sites in **boldface**
Heading West (East)

0.0 (63.1) Belize City Bypass at Hattieville.

0.2 (62.9) Hector Creek bridge.

0.8 (62.3) Gas station, followed by speed bumps.

8.9 (54.2) Road to **Big Falls Farm** and **Cox Lagoon**.

9.8 (53.3) Taiwan shopping center.

13.5 (49.6) **Tropical Education Center / Belize Zoo Jungle Lodge**.

13.7 (49.4) **Belize Zoo** on right. Parking for large vehicles on left.

14.3 (48.8) **Coastal Highway** on left, with Mile 31 gas station at intersection.

14.8 (48.3) La Democracia water tower.

15.8 (47.3) Cheers Restaurant and Cabanas.

16.0 (47.1) **Monkey Bay Wildlife Sanctuary**.

16.1 (47.0) Amigo's Restaurant. Unmarked border of Cayo and Belize districts.

23.3 (39.8) Beaver Dam Creek.

31.3 (31.8) Banana Bank Lodge on right. Texaco station on left.

32.3 (30.8) **Guanacaste National Park** on right. Hummingbird Highway on left.

32.4 (30.7) Roaring Creek bridge.

32.6 (30.5) Texaco station. Village of Roaring Creek.

37.5 (25.6) Road to **Pook's Hill** on left. Teakettle Village.

42.3 (20.8) Road to **Spanish Lookout** and **Aguacate Lagoon**. Eastern route.

45.2 (17.9) Caesar's Place. Unitedville.

45.3 (17.8) Barton Creek bridge, Village of Georgeville.

47.3 (15.8) Chiquibul Road to **Mountain Pine Ridge** on left.

Price Highway (con't.)

48.6 (14.5) Ministry of Agriculture, Central Farm, Running W Farm.

*49.0 (14.1) Road to **Spanish Lookout** and **Aguacate Lagoon**. Western route.*

52.5 (10.6) Hospital on left. To Aguada Hotel on right.

*53.2 (9.9) San Antonio Road to **Mountain Pine Ridge** on left. Enter Santa Elena.*

53.3 (9.8) Veer right, with Social Security office on left.

53.4 (9.7) Turn left.

53.5 (9.6) Turn right, heading downhill toward bridge.

53.6 (9.5) Macal River bridge. Enter San Ignacio. Open-air market.

53.7 (9.4) Veer right. Savannah Sports Park on left.

*53.9 (9.2) Turn left. Road to **Branchmouth Park** on right.*

54.1 (9.0) Curve left; cemetery on left. Sacred Heart school on right.

*54.6 (8.5) Bullet Tree Road to **El Pilar** on right.*

54.8 (8.3) Veer right, with small red-and-white statue on left.

*55.0 (8.1) Turn right. Straight ahead is **Cahal Pech** Maya site.*

55.1 (8.0) Texaco station on left. Sign on right "Benque Viejo 8 miles."

55.6 (7.5) Another Texaco station on left.

*55.9 (7.2) **Log Cab-Inn Resort** on left. **Windy Hill Resort** on right.*

56.1 (7.0) Inglewood Camping Ground on left.

*58.7 (4.4) **Clarissa Falls Resort** on right.*

*59.0 (4.1) **Macal River Resorts Road** on right.*

*60.5 (2.6) Ferry to **Xunantunich** Maya site on right.*

61.4 (1.7) Turn left. Benque Viejo.

*62.1 (1.0) **Arenal/Hydro Road** on left.*

62.2 (0.9) Cemetery on right.

*63.1 (0.0) Guatemala border. Road to **Tikal National Park**.*

BELIZE ZOO AREA

Tropical Education Center, Belize Zoo Jungle Lodge, and Belize Zoo River Camp

Description: Much of the savanna along the eastern part of Price Highway is sparse, with scattered palmetto and even fewer pines. In the area of Tropical Education Center and Belize Zoo, however, the dense pines grow tall and bird diversity and density increases. Formerly known only as Tropical Education Center (TEC), it is now also known as Belize Zoo Jungle Lodge. The 84-acre site is across the highway from Belize Zoo. The two organizations function as one unit. Students, researchers, and other interested individuals and groups have available to them dormitories, a guest house, cabana, toilets, outdoor showers, classroom, library, kitchen, and dining area. The lodging facilities are also open to the general public. The offerings include dormitory-style accommodations as well as private, nicely equipped cabanas.

Birding strategy: The educational center, open to the public, includes Savannah Nature Trail, a boardwalk, and viewing platforms. The center includes a small pond and, when it is not totally dry, birders may see Gray-necked Wood-Rail, Solitary Sandpiper, Louisiana Waterthrush, and other birds attracted to the water. In the trees surrounding the pond, Yellow-lored Parrot can be found. The pines attract Acorn Woodpecker.

In addition to the zoo property and the TEC/Belize Zoo Jungle Lodge parcel, a third non-contiguous parcel of 110 acres, named Belize Zoo River Camp, fronts along the Sibun River and is just ten minutes away. Blue Seedeaters have been found along the Sibun River. The forested river camp abuts a protected area and is an important biological corridor. Check out the web site for offerings of birding tours, canoe trips, natural-history lectures, and nocturnal visits to the zoo. Of special interest is a two-hour or more kayak trip that puts in at Monkey Bay Wildlife Sanctuary, follows the Sibun River to just beyond the Coastal Highway bridge, and puts out at Belize Zoo River Camp. Although the tilapia farm is not directly in line of sight from the river,

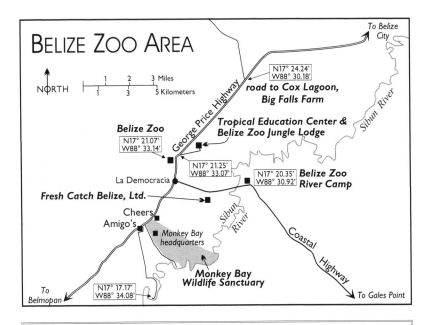

Ecoregion and habitats: Appendix A, Ecoregion 8, Belize and Sibun Rivers riparian forests and coastal savannas. Habitats include: savanna (PFL), secondary lowland broadleaf forest (BFL3), swamp forest around lagoon (BFL2), and riparian along Belize River (BFL1), as well as agricultural lands (AG) and building complex (PC).

Location: N 17° 29.53' W 88° 35.37' for Big Falls Farm at Belize River. N 17° 27.17' W 88° 32.55' at Cox Lagoon. Heading west on Price Highway, the dirt road to Big Falls Farm intersects at mile 8.9, N 17° 24.24' W 88° 30.18'.

TEC/Belize Zoo Jungle Lodge: N 17° 21.25' W 88° 33.07' at highway entrance. Located at mile 13.5 when heading west on the Price Highway, it is across the highway from Belize Zoo. Travel time is less than an hour from Philip Goldson International Airport. Belize Zoo River Camp: N 17° 20.35' W 88° 30.92', 2.5 miles south of the intersection of Price and Coastal Highways, just 0.3 mile south of the Sibun River bridge. Contact Belize Zoo for permission to enter the camp.

Fees and contact: Day visitors have not been charged an entrance fee in past years. Check the web site for prices on lodging, meals, and tours. TEC / Belize Zoo Jungle Lodge, P.O. Box 1787, Belize City, Belize District; (011) 501-220-8003; fax (011) 501-220-8010; tec@belizezoo.org; www.belizezoo.org.

the congregations of birds indicate it is close by. As manager Sharon Matola states, "You are guaranteed to see colonies of Wood Storks." The colony is one of three places in Belize where the storks nest, and from the kayaks you can see the adults and young and hear their vocalizations. Other frequently seen species are Bare-throated Tiger-Heron, King Vulture, Black-headed Trogon, and Passerini's Tanager. Jabirus are usually present. Boat-billed Herons have been seen.

Key Species: For TEC, see the list for Belize Zoo on page 97. For Belize Zoo River Camp, consult the list for Monkey Bay Wildlife Sanctuary (see pages 99–100).

Belize Zoo

Description: In addition to being a must-see for anyone unfamiliar with neotropical fauna, Belize Zoo is a good birding stop on the way to other sites and is definitely worth two or three hours of exploration, particularly just after its 8:30 AM opening. The tall and thick jungle on 29 acres lies like an island in a flat sea of dry savanna. The zoo specializes in the animals of Belize, and visitors can see Baird's Tapir, Paca, Jaguar, Ocelot, and the other mammals that are difficult to find in the wild. Unobtrusive areas are carved out of a jungle of trees; black wire screening separates visitors from the wildlife, but melds into the dark shadows to all but disappear. Foliage is so thick that finding the wild cats is often a challenge, and coming upon them is like discovering them in the wild. Bird life is abundant, both in and out of the cages. Although a few birds are deliberately caged—including "Bert," the Jabiru—most are wild birds that wander about. Birds pass freely through the screening, delight in the free lunch and ample water, and have grown accustomed to humans, thus allowing close approach.

Created in 1983 through the efforts of Sharon Matola, the zoo began as a way to save the animals used in filming a documentary on tropical forests. It now serves as an important education facility for over 10,000 school children per year. Facilities include toilets and a shop for gifts and snacks. Restaurants are within a few miles on Price Highway.

Birding strategy: Pick up a zoo map when you pay admission. The wild birds have remarkably consistent territories in the zoo. A female Red-capped Manakin hasn't strayed more than 50 feet from the spider monkey area in seven years, Gray Catbirds are in greatest numbers at the tapir enclosure, and the Melodious Blackbirds hang out with the peccaries. A Gray-necked Wood-Rail has nested at the pond, at eye level but well hidden in the dense foliage. Hepatic Tanagers, a bit unusual for this area, are invariably at the tall pines near the pond; Summer Tanagers occur as well. If you step off the main zoo circuit, you can find a trail through the surrounding pine forest. Here it is

Wood Stork   Bert Frenz

Ecoregion and habitats: *Appendix A, Ecoregion 8, Belize and Sibun Rivers riparian forests and coastal savannas. Habitats include: lowland broadleaf forest (BFL3) and pine savanna (PFL) amongst supplemental plantings and water sources (PC).*

Fees and contact: *Entrance US$10 for adults, US$5 for children, BZ$5 for residents. Belize Zoo, P.O. Box 1787, Belize City, Belize District; (011) 501-220-8004; fax (011) 501-220-8010; info@belizezoo.org; www.belizezoo.org.*

Location: *N 17° 21.07' W 88° 33.14'. Located at mile 13.7 heading west on the Price Highway log, it is across the highway from TEC/Belize Zoo Jungle Lodge.*

easier to keep an eye to the sky and find soaring Great Black-Hawk and Roadside and Short-tailed Hawks. Both Olive and Green-backed Sparrows occur here, proffering an identification challenge. The zoo and TEC are good places to study kingbird vocalizations, as they are among the few sites where Couch's is nearly as common as Tropical.

Key species of Belize Zoo and TEC/Belize Zoo Jungle Lodge: [boldface = target species, R = rare, S = summer, T = transitory migrant] Great and Little Tinamous, Jabiru, Common and Great Black-Hawks, **White-tailed Hawk**, Gray-necked Wood-Rail, Stygian Owl [R], Lesser and Common [S] Nighthawks, Stripe-throated Hermit, White-necked Jacobin, Canivet's Emerald, Azure-crowned and Cinnamon Hummingbirds, **Acorn Woodpecker**, Yellow-bellied Sapsucker, Northern Beardless-Tyrannulet, Common Tody-Flycatcher, Yellow-olive Flycatcher, Tropical Pewee, Fork-tailed Flycatcher, **Red-capped Manakin**, Red-eyed [T] and Yellow-green [S] Vireos, Rufous-browed Peppershrike, White-bellied Wren, Gray-crowned Yellowthroat, **Grace's Warbler**, Yellow-breasted Chat, **Slate-colored Seedeater** [R], Thick-billed Seed-Finch, **Olive Sparrow**, Green-backed, Chipping, and Grasshopper Sparrows, **Hepatic Tanager**, Yellow-backed and Yellow-tailed Orioles, Scrub Euphonia.

Monkey Bay Wildlife Sanctuary

[12 February] "This place has more birds per erg of energy expended than any other," remarks Bob, as he leisurely sits in a chair and watches the birds pass by. We had driven our cars down the dirt road 1.75 miles from Price Highway to the Sibun (pronounced "say-boon") River and then walked back a hundred yards to a fruiting fig tree, the spot where we spent so much time last year. A profusion of birds feed on the tree, from Streak-headed Woodcreeper to Ochre-bellied Flycatcher to Yellow-billed Cacique, and we see species after species moving quickly through the leaves. Lower to the ground, Rufous-breasted Spinetails call constantly. We carefully study a becard and get a good close-up look at its head, confirming White-winged Becard, a southern Belize species that is expanding its range northward. Most of us return to our nearby campsite for lunch. Some return to the river for a Big Sit, lounging on lawn chairs and stools along the gravel river banks, watching the crystal clear water flow swiftly past. Remarkably, from 2:30 to 5:30, barely moving from one spot, they record 50–60 species. Their total includes 18 warbler species playing in a puddle. In the evening, we enjoy a delicious, healthy meal at the dining hall of Monkey Bay Wildlife Sanctuary. The day's total at the sanctuary reaches an incredible 135 species. Today we've added Crested Guan, White-necked Puffbird, White-winged Becard, and Cedar Waxwing, bringing the checklist for the 1,000-acre sanctuary to 273 species.

Description: Former Peace Corps worker Mathew Miller and his wife Marga worked with the owner to convert the property, originally a cattle ranch of limited success, into a wildlife preserve and an environmental-education site. The access road to the Sibun River is open to birders, as is the river itself. Complete accommodations include tent camping, bunkhouses, private rooms, meals, museum, and library. Although primarily intended for students taking courses on tropical ecology, the accommodations are available for tourists as well. The property is adjacent to the 2,250-acre Monkey Bay National Park, which is the release site for Yucatan Black Howlers and other rehabilitated animals cared for at the Wildlife Care Center.

Birding strategy: This site is such easy birding it doesn't require much preparation beyond bringing binoculars and, perhaps, a three-legged stool to enjoy hours of delightful birding. From the Monkey Bay entrance road off Price Highway, you will soon come to the headquarters on your left. Continue down the dirt road for about 1.5 miles to the Sibun River. Most of the property within the sanctuary is off-limits and too difficult to traverse. Although birds can be found throughout the length of the access road, they concentrate along the last quarter-mile. Best spots are the bamboo patch, the fig tree, and the river. The key spot where you can easily spend a couple of hours is along the access road at the large fruiting fig tree, which stands nearly alone in an area where other canopy trees are not present. Dozens of species of flycatchers, warblers, and others visit the tree, often simultaneously. In the dense shrubs beneath the large tree, low to the ground, you can hear Rufous-breasted Spinetails constantly calling. This is undoubtedly the easiest location in Belize to see these shy spinetails that hide so successfully elsewhere, but here they can be approached to within a few feet. Also hiding at the base of the tree are Green-backed Sparrows. The same dense shrubs are an excellent place to see both Great and Barred Antshrikes.

From the tree you have a clear view to distant tall trees and are likely to see flocks of White-fronted and Red-lored Parrots, and small numbers of Keel-billed Toucans. Check for perched Plumbeous and Gray-headed Kites, Bat Falcon, and soaring Black Hawk-Eagle. Listen for doves and you should hear Scaled and Short-billed Pigeons, Ruddy and Blue Ground-Doves, and White-tipped Doves.

At the end of the road by the river is a pleasantly shaded spot where you can hear and see Yellow-tailed Orioles singing and should see a few dozen species visiting the fresh water and feeding along the riversides. It is also a delightful swimming spot, especially on hot afternoons.

The most sought-after bird at Monkey Bay is Blue Seedeater, which occupies a tiny range in Belize. From the large tree move slowly north along the access road back toward Price Highway, paying particular attention to the spiny bamboo thickets. This is the habitat for this rare species, but it may take patience to see one. Don't think the first seedeater you see is the elusive Blue Seedeater. Male Blue-black Grassquit and female Variable Seedeater, White-collared Seedeater, and Thick-billed Seed-Finch are all Blue

Seedeater look-alikes and they all are regular here. An even more elusive seedeater, Slate-colored Seedeater, also adopts spiny bamboo habitat and has been reported at Monkey Bay about a quarter-mile from Sibun River. Another reported site is at Sibun River, 0.6 mile downstream from its confluence with Caves Branch at Hellgate. The two locations are about three miles apart. Kayak or canoe trips along the Sibun River would be your best method of reaching appropriate habitat.

Continue northward along the access road; as the forested edges become denser you may find Gray-chested Dove. The thicker sections are good areas in which to listen for Black-faced Antthrush; perhaps you will be lucky enough to see one gingerly walking the forest floor. This is also the area to find Black-headed and Gartered Trogons and Blue-crowned Motmot. Surrounding Monkey Bay Wildlife Sanctuary are more open lands where Black-throated Bobwhites scurry through brambles. Lesser Yellow-headed Vultures stay low, while King Vultures soar high. White-tailed Hawks regularly hunt over the savanna. Aplomado Falcons often perch here on dead snags, and flocks of Yellow-headed Parrots can be heard approaching before they fly over.

Key species of Monkey Bay Wildlife Sanctuary: Great and Little Tinamous, Black-throated Bobwhite, King Vulture, Plumbeous Kite [S], Short-tailed Hawk, **White-tailed Hawk**, **Aplomado Falcon**, Ruddy and Gray-breasted [R] Crakes, Sungrebe, Scaled and Short-billed Pigeons, Blue Ground-Dove, Gray-headed Dove, **Yellow-headed Parrot**, Common Nighthawk [S], White-collared and Lesser Swallow-tailed Swifts, **Azure-**

Ecoregion and habitats: Appendix A, Ecoregion 8, Belize and Sibun Rivers riparian forests and coastal savannas. Habitats include: educational facilities and lodging (PC); secondary lowland fig-dominated broadleaf forest adjoining Sibun River (BFL1); small parcel of bamboo (BFL2). Sanctuary also has pine/oak–palm savanna (PFL), transitional stunted forest vegetation (BFL3), and cohune ridge (BFL4).

Fees and contacts: No fees for birding, but contact Monkey Bay beforehand for advice. Inquire at Monkey Bay for canoe rentals and guided hiking/canoeing at Big Falls Farm, Cox Lagoon, Sibun River, and Indian Creek Trail. RV parking (no hookups) can be arranged next door at Amigo's. Also consider Cheers Restaurant and Cabanas, adjacent to Monkey Bay.

Mathew Miller, Monkey Bay Wildlife Sanctuary, P.O. Box 187, Belmopan; (011) 501-820-3032; fax (011) 501-822-3361; mbay@btl.net; www.monkeybaybelize.org.

Cheers Restaurant and Cabanas, P.O. Box 346, Belmopan; (011) 501-822-8014; fax (011) 501-820-2062; info@cheersrestaurant.bz; www.cheersrestaurant.bz.

Sue Hufford, Amigo's Restaurant, Mile 31-2/3, Price Highway; (011) 501-802-8000; fax (011) 501-820-2015; hriex@hughes.net.

Location: N 17° 19.26' W 88° 34.16'; elevation 191 feet at entrance road off Price Highway. N 17° 18.00' W 88° 33.26'; elevation 90 feet at Sibun River. Within three miles are multiple birding sites and accommodations.

crowned **Hummingbird**, Amazon and American Pygmy Kingfishers, **Acorn Woodpecker**, **Great Antshrike**, Dusky Antbird, Black-faced Antthrush, **Rufous-breasted Spinetail**, Buff-throated Foliage-gleaner, Streak-headed Woodcreeper, Yellow-bellied Tyrannulet, Slate-headed Tody-Flycatcher, Stub-tailed Spadebill, Black Phoebe, Yucatan Flycatcher, Cinnamon and White-winged Becards, Red-capped Manakin, Philadelphia and Yellow-green [S] Vireos, Tawny-crowned Greenlet, Rufous-browed Pepper-shrike, Band-backed and White-bellied Wrens, **Grace's Warbler**, Yellow-breasted Chat, Gray-headed, Crimson-collared, Passerini's, and Golden-hooded Tanagers, Grayish and Buff-throated Saltators, **Slate-colored Seedeater** [R], Thick-billed Seed-Finch, Yellow-faced Grassquit, Hepatic Tanager, **Blue Seedeater** [R], Yellow-billed Cacique, Scrub Euphonia.

COASTAL HIGHWAY

[12 February] From our first trip to Belize in 2001, I remember the Coastal Highway as an ungraded, pot-holed, washboard gravel road. Getting lost on Coastal Highway is nearly impossible, however, because no roads intersect it, and virtually no driveways meet it because almost no one lives along the road. But we still wonder where we are, so we use a GPS and the detailed topological maps to trace our progress and identify the rivers and creeks we cross. The first is Sibun River. We study a small patch of Curassow Crest because of the birds it attracts. Flitting in and out of view is a Yellow-tailed Oriole, more easily identified by its yellow wing patch than the thin yellow edge to its tail. The black bird with a vivid red rump is Passerini's Tanager. From the bridge over Soldier Creek we look down at a fast-moving stream snaking around a limestone boulder and see a Black Phoebe leapfrogging from rock to rock. Amongst bamboos growing streamside I find an Olive-backed Euphonia. If I spent more time among the bamboo, I wonder if I could find the elusive Blue Seedeater. We continue on the gravel road, now passing through a vast pine savanna with ragged limestone foothills in the distance. At one stop I hear Yellow-headed Parrots approach and we have the good fortune of seeing them passing directly overhead.

Description: Unpopulated, off the beaten path, and through some habitats not visited at other birding spots, this route can produce species you might otherwise miss in Belize. En route, there are no facilities until you reach Gales Point, and very few there. The unpaved Coastal Highway is also known as Manatee Highway, Manatee Road, or the "Shortcut".

Birding strategy: Birding sites described more fully in subsequent sections are in boldface. Here is a general outline for birding along Coastal Highway. Get an early start in the morning and plan on spending most of the day traversing the highway and back. Alternatively, book reservations at **Manatee Lodge**. When birding the highway, stop frequently and at varying habitats, sampling rivers, orchards, and the savanna. In addition to off-highway sites, the best spots are Sibun River (mile 2.2), the pine savanna (6 to 8), the orange grove at the residence (13.8), and Soldier/Plantation Creek (17.2).

Starting with its intersection with Price Highway, the first half-mile is paved and then turns to dirt. At 0.6 mile is the entrance on the right to **Fresh Catch Belize, Ltd.**, a tilapia fish-farm operation that supports an impressive array of waterbirds. Stop at 2.2 miles at the bridge over the Sibun River, a very productive birding area. The surrounding area includes orange groves and secondary broadleaf forest of *Cecropia* and palms. Species expected here

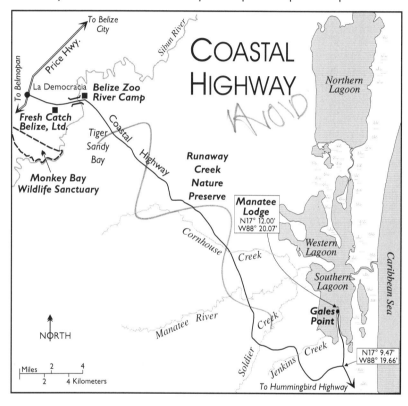

Ecoregion and habitats: *Appendix A, Ecoregion 8, Belize and Sibun Rivers riparian forests and coastal savannas. Habitats include: riparian lowland broadleaf forest (BFL1), broken ridge (BFL3), pine-palmetto savanna (PFL), and orange groves (AG4).*

Concerns: *Check your gas tank level the night before you leave as there are no facilities along the way. The wide road is red gravel, potholed, and washboard, typically traveled at 25 mph when not birding.*

Location: *The 35-mile Coastal Highway intersects Price Highway on the log at mile 14.3 at the Mile 31 gas station near La Democracia, N 17° 20.55' W 88° 33.29'. This intersection is marked with a sign for Coastal Highway. The opposite end of Coastal Highway intersects with Hummingbird Highway at mile 46.3 on that log (N 16° 59.89' W 88° 18.90'), about eight miles from Dangriga.*

include Ruddy Crake, Rufous-breasted Spinetail, Common Tody-Flycatcher, and Thick-billed Seed-Finch. Ferruginous Pygmy-Owl is not to be found in the coastal lowlands of central Belize and this location along the river is about as close to the coast as it resides. Likewise, Golden-hooded Tanager is at the edge of its range here.

Continuing on Coastal Highway, on the left at 2.5 is the entrance to **Belize Zoo River Camp**. Within this property is the pickup point for kayak trips on Sibun River. Contact **Tropical Education Center** for permission to enter. Many signs from 5.2 to 7.8 mark the vast 6,137-acre extent of Runaway Creek Nature Preserve. This private preserve is owned and managed by the Foundation for Wildlife Conservation, Inc. of Milwaukee, Wisconsin. Their web site is www.zoosociety.org/Conservation/BWB-ASF. A published report lists 297 species recorded on the preserve. Where the preserve borders Sibun River an Orange-crowned Warbler was mist-netted 16 December 2001, the first documented Belize record. Also banded on the south bank of the river and within the preserve was Blue Seedeater, found in spiny bamboo where it transitions into secondary broadleaf riparian forest, a microhabitat that can be found at several locations along Coastal Highway.

At mile 6 you will see the first of the tall rounded hills and will be entering Tiger Sandy Bay and its broadleaf forest. The habitat switches to pine savanna, surrounded by hills with broadleaf forest, which become closer by 7.5. An old lumber camp, shown on some maps, is at 7.8. Some species often missed in other parts of Belize are easier to find here. Search particularly for Yellow-headed Parrot (mile 9), Grace's Warbler (similar Yellow-throated also occurs), and Olive, Chipping, and Grasshopper Sparrows. Other species favoring pine savanna and found here are Black-throated Bobwhite, Aplomado Falcon, Red-lored Parrot, Acorn Woodpecker, and Fork-tailed Flycatcher. Creeks en route are worth checking, including Cornhouse Creek at 12.5, which includes a trail of sorts along the creek through woods (protect against mosquitoes). In another mile you will be passing a tall broadleaf forest of Cohune Palm, Coconut Palm, and *Cecropia*. A very productive stop is at 14, a residence in tall trees owned by Egbert and his brother. He may offer to sell you mosquito fans fashioned from trees and will welcome you into his orchard to look at birds, which are most active at dawn and dusk.

Check out Manatee River, about a quarter-mile farther, and Jenkins Creek at mile 19, separated by Marian Neal Farm. At 17 is another creek variously called Soldier Creek or Plantation Creek on maps. Tall bamboo grows along the creek. Nearby in a very tall canopy tree an Olive-sided Flycatcher —typically a migrant through Belize—was observed in winter during successive years. Extensive orange groves on both sides of the road at 20 can add a few species to your day list. Where the groves abut elevation rises, White-collared Swifts can be observed hawking insects above the citrus trees.

At 23 you come to a T-intersection, N 17° 9.47' W 88° 19.66'. At this intersection Belize's only record for Yellow-winged Cacique was observed 6 October 2003. For birding, you probably will want to turn left and head to **Gales Point** and **Manatee Lagoons**. Check the section describing Gales Point for further directions.

If you want to continue on Coastal Highway toward Dangriga, turn right at the T-intersection. The road has several twists and curves, but no turns until you reach its end at Hummingbird Highway at 35 miles. At address "Mile 30 Coastal Highway" is Paradise Shrimp Farms, just off the Caribbean coast.

Key species of Coastal Highway, including Runaway Creek: Black-throated Bobwhite, Lesser Yellow-headed Vulture, Osprey, **Plumbeous Kite** [S], Common and Great Black-Hawks, Short-tailed Hawk, **White-tailed Hawk**, Zone-tailed Hawk [R], Collared Forest-Falcon, Laughing Falcon, **Aplomado Falcon**, Limpkin, Plain-breasted and Blue Ground-Doves, Gray-headed and Gray-chested Doves, **Yellow-headed Parrot**, Striped Cuckoo, Spectacled [R] and Striped [R] Owls, White-necked Jacobin, **Acorn** and **Ladder-backed Woodpeckers**, Great Antshrike, Black-faced Antthrush, Rufous-breasted Spinetail, **Streak-headed Wood-creeper**, Northern Beardless-Tyrannulet, Olive-sided and White-throated [R] Flycatchers, Black Phoebe, Fork-tailed Flycatcher, White-winged Becard, Swainson's Warbler, Gray-crowned Yellowthroat, **Grace's Warbler**, Yellow-breasted Chat, Passerini's Tanager, Grayish and Buff-throated Saltators, Thick-billed Seed-Finch, Yellow-faced Grassquit, Grassland Yellow-Finch [R], **Olive** and **Botteri's** [R] **Sparrows**, Chipping Sparrow, **Savannah** [R] and **Grasshopper Sparrows**, Hepatic Tanager, Northern Cardinal, **Blue Seedeater** [R], **Dickcissel** [T].

Shrimp and Tilapia Farms

Shrimp and tilapia farms often host large numbers of birds, and in many cases they are the only places you likely will find certain species. Covering thousands of acres, divided into individual earthen ponds averaging 25 acres each, these shrimp-farm enterprises are where the bulk of long-legged waders, including Jabiru, and shorebirds are found. Birding strategy is to inquire locally, trying to find "someone who knows someone" or at least knows the location of a shrimp farm. One suggestion off Goldson Highway is Captain Hook's Restaurant and Shrimp Farm near Philip Goldson International Airport (see page 38). Two possibilities along the Coastal Highway are Fresh Catch Belize, Ltd. with tilapia fish ponds near La Democracia on Price Highway, 0.6 mile south on the Coastal Highway, and Paradise Shrimp Farms, about 15 miles from Dangriga. Fresh Catch Belize is described in detail below. Also try the Department of Agriculture rice fields at Spanish Lookout. Other shrimp farms are located primarily in the Belize and Stann Creek districts, near Dangriga, All Pines, Placencia, and Independence, three of which are identified on the Southern Highway log. *Note: It has become increasingly difficult to gain access to these private properties. You need advance permission from the manager at most places. If you are not given access at the gate, ask the gate keeper to call the manager for permission.*

Key species of coastal shrimp and tilapia farms: Black-bellied Whistling-Duck, American Wigeon, Blue-winged Teal, **Cinnamon Teal** [R], **Northern Shoveler, Northern Pintail, Green-winged Teal**, Ring-necked Duck [R], Lesser Scaup, **Jabiru**, Wood Stork, American White Pelican, Bare-throated Tiger-Heron, **Reddish Egret**, Black-crowned Night-Heron, Glossy Ibis [R], Roseate Spoonbill, Lesser Yellow-headed Vulture, Osprey, Common Black-Hawk, Peregrine Falcon, **Clapper Rail**, **Sora**, Common Gallinule, American Coot, Limpkin, Black-bellied Plover, **Collared Plover**, Snowy Plover [R,T], **Wilson's Plover**, Semipalmated Plover, Killdeer, Black-necked Stilt, **American Avocet**, Solitary Sandpiper, Greater Yellowlegs, Willet, Lesser Yellowlegs, Whimbrel, Long-billed Curlew [R], Hudsonian [R,T] and Marbled [R] Godwits, Ruddy Turnstone, **Red Knot** [R], Sanderling, Semipalmated [T], Western, and Least Sandpipers, **White-rumped Sandpiper** [T], Pectoral Sandpiper [T], **Stilt Sandpiper**, Short-billed and Long-billed Dowitchers, Wilson's Phalarope [R,T], Laughing and Ring-billed [R] Gulls, Least, Gull-billed, Caspian, Black [T], Forster's [R], Royal, and Sandwich Terns, Ringed, Belted, and Green Kingfishers, Fork-tailed Fly-catcher, Mangrove and Yucatan Vireos, Tree, Mangrove, and Bank [T] Swallows.

Fresh Catch Belize, Ltd.

[21 February] We are immediately struck by the sheer number of birds we can see: hundreds of Blue-winged Teal, dozens of Wood Storks and Neotropic Cormorants, 18 Great Blue Herons standing on a few dredge mounds and many more elsewhere, flocks of Least Sandpipers and 10–15 Spotted Sandpipers. Overhead fly Gray-breasted Martins, Tree Swallows, Mangrove Swallows, and Northern Rough-winged Swallows. An Osprey flies past us with a fish in its talons. A large flock of dowitchers circles the ponds several times, coming in for a landing, but soon taking off again. From their soft "tu tu tu" calls given in flight I note that they are Short-billed, a surprise so far inland. A real prize is an American Avocet, a species I have not seen in Belize before. After careful inspection of the huge teal flock, I pick out one male and three female Ring-necked Ducks. We head toward the more active tilapia ponds and a worker tells us Jabirus are on the opposite end. In a mixed flock we see hundreds of Great Egrets and Snowy Egrets, as well as a flock of Black-necked Stilts. And there stands a Jabiru, a giant amongst its peers.

Description: Fresh Catch Belize, Ltd. is a tilapia fish farm opened in December 2002, and in 2004 it produced 850,000 pounds of tilapia. The facility includes 36 production ponds, with plans for expansion to a total of 150 acres of ponds. Private property and only accessible by permission, this commercial enterprise hosts long-legged waders, shorebirds, and other water-seeking birds that can be hard to find elsewhere. Although 18 miles from the Caribbean coast, the site has attracted several species not expected inland, such as Black-bellied Plover, American Avocet, and Short-billed Dowitcher.

Birding strategy: Stop at the gate and ask the attendant or the manager for permission to bird. Individuals and small groups have gained access in the past, but there is no guarantee this will continue in the future. As you pass the administration buildings, the ponds on the right seem to harbor the most species, however the long-legged waders congregate at the opposite end. Perhaps the best spots change with water levels and timing of the fish operation. The largest concentration of Jabirus can be found here, and on one date (27 January) an amazing 120 Jabirus and 300 Wood Storks were reported. For bird specialties, see the list on the previous page.

Ecoregion and habitats: Appendix A, Ecoregion 9, Central coastal savannas, littoral forests and Caribbean coast. Although not along the coast, the artificially created brackish ponds (LF3) produce the same species collection.

Concerns: Fresh Catch Belize is an industrial site, not set up for birding tourism, and does not carry insurance for mishaps to visitors. Although a great birding spot, birders could wear out their welcome, so exercise care and sensitivity.

Contact: Make contact at the entrance gate. A web search will produce more information about the fish operation. A site with photographs is at www.aquaculture.co.il/projects/Belize.html.

Location: N 17° 19.83' W 88° 32.62' at gate. Start from the intersection of Price Highway, follow Coastal Highway south, passing La Democracia Community Center on the left, and at 0.6 mile turn right, N 17° 20.36' W 88° 32.73'. The 0.8-mile gravel entrance road includes an S-curve and a left turn before the guarded gate.

Gales Point and Manatee Lagoons

Description: Gales Point is a narrow peninsula extending two miles into Southern Lagoon. Southern Lagoon and Northern Lagoon, also known as Manatee Lagoons, are part of the proposed Manatee Reserve for the endangered West Indian Manatees and the Hawksbill Sea Turtles, as well as breeding grounds for herons and ibises. The eastern part of the reserve is covered by mangrove forests and the western portion is swamp forests and savanna. Boats from Gales Point can also explore Manatee River, Western Lagoon, Bird's Isle, and Northern Lagoon. The underwater springs where the manatees congregate are almost within eyesight from the pier at Manatee Lodge, so surfacing manatees can sometimes be seen from land. Manatee

Lodge offers lodging, meals, and tours, including boating trips to the manatees and throughout Manatee Lagoons.

Birding strategy: Numerous buildings line the shore at Gales Point, limiting land access to good habitat. Combine this site with a trip along Coastal Highway or, for better water access, book reservations at Manatee Lodge. If you are not staying at the lodge and would like to stay for lunch, reserve beforehand.

Ecoregion and habitats: Appendix A, Ecoregion 9, Central coastal savannas, littoral forests, and Caribbean coast. Habitats include: mangrove forests and brackish coastal lagoons (LF3); village (PC).

Fees and contact: Boat tours of varied destinations and durations can be arranged at Manatee Lodge. Birding tours along Coastal Highway can also be booked. Manatee Lodge, Gales Point Manatee Village, Belize District; (011) 501-220-8040 or toll-free in US: 877-462-6283; manateelodge@yahoo.com; www.manateelodge.com.

Location: N 17° 12.00' W 88° 20.07' at Manatee Lodge. Starting either from Price Highway or Hummingbird Highway, follow Coastal Highway to N 17° 9.47' W 88° 19.66' (see page 103). At the T-intersection head north to Gales Point, starting at 1.1 miles, and follow Main Street through town. Bee Hive Inn is on the lagoon at right at 1.7 and Gales Point Wildlife Sanctuary is at 2.2. Manatee Lodge is at the end of the peninsula at 3.0 miles from the T-intersection. See the section on Coastal Highway for additional information.

Key species of Gales Point and Manatee Lagoons: Lesser Scaup, Jabiru, Wood Stork, Magnificent Frigatebird, Brown Booby, Neotropic and Double-crested Cormorants, Anhinga, American White Pelican, Black-crowned Night-Heron, Boat-billed Heron, White Ibis, Roseate Spoonbill, Osprey, Swallow-tailed Kite [T], Common and Great Black-Hawks, Ruddy Crake, Rufous-necked Wood-Rail, Limpkin, Wilson's and Semipalmated Plovers, Willet, Wilson's Snipe, Herring Gull, Gull-billed Tern, **Black Tern** [T], Sandwich Tern, Pale-vented Pigeon, Mangrove Cuckoo [R], Green-breasted Mango, **Cinnamon Hummingbird**, **Yucatan Vireo**, **Mangrove Yellow Warbler**.

BELMOPAN TO SAN IGNACIO
Guanacaste National Park

[24 February] In prior years, we never gave justice to Guanacaste National Park, the birds being mostly sedentary during our early afternoon visits. This year's schedule allows us to be at the park at 6:45 AM. We arrive in a thin fog that stretches spider-web wisps across the massive branches of Guanacaste, Strangler Fig, Neotropic Cedar, and Stinking Toe. Light rain falls on the big-leafed canopy, catching the drops before they reach us 75 feet below. The rain irrigates the dense growths of epiphytes clinging to the supporting tree branches,

eventually trickling to the understory of plants we often see in our northern homes, chosen because they adapt equally well to the limited light of jungles and living rooms. We break free of darkness at a limestone out-cropping and then reenter the dark forest, passing a well-marked Black Poisonwood Tree, an under-stated reminder not to grab just any tree for balance when de-scending a steep slope. Most times I've hiked this trail, birds have been sparse, but the beauty of nature's flora compensates, and for fauna we have an Agouti staring back at us from 50 feet up trail and a pair of Yucatan Squirrels chasing across the labyrinth above us.

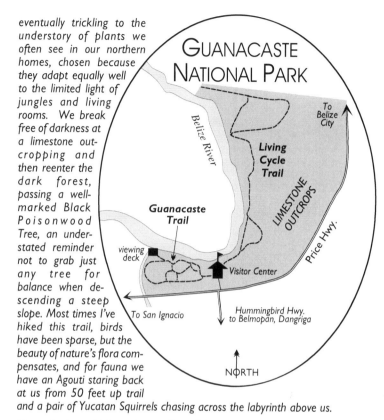

Description: Relatively small at 50 acres, this national park protects some remarkable trees, including the giant Guanacaste tree, which can stretch over 130 feet. Visits in five different years met with varying birding success, but they always yielded a few surprises. Facilities include toilets and a small museum with a few nature books for sale. There are two miles of well-groomed trails. For lodging and meals, the park is closest to Belmopan, but it is also within easy reach of the San Ignacio resorts.

Birding strategy: Birding is best in early morning, even before the gate opens. Park outside the gate, walk inside, and bird the grassy forest opening near the administration building. This area is especially productive when sunlight first hits the canopy. To avoid theft or mischief, move your vehicle inside to the parking lot once the attendant arrives.

Two primary trails make loops, the shorter one follows Roaring Creek and then Belize River, beginning to the left from the parking lot; the longer one penetrates the jungle, beginning behind the building. If your visit will be brief, take the trail to the river. If you can spend a few hours, take both trails. The shorter loop trail starts parallel and relatively close to Price Highway, yet the tree density blocks the traffic noise and makes you feel as if in a remote tall forest. A good photo op is in front of the giant Guanacaste tree; even with a large group you are unlikely to block its broad trunk. White-breasted Wood-Wren is common along the trail, easily heard and with much patience can be seen as well. Wood Thrush and Ovenbird are much easier to see and may be hopping along the path in front of you. As you hike, listen for the shrill calls of a Rufous-tailed Jacamar. If you hear it, look for thick vines that descend from the tree, forming a U-shaped swing; here is where you likely will see the sedentary bird waiting for a meal to fly within an easy leap from the vine.

Soon you will reach some rapids in the Belize River where, from within the forest, it may seem odd to see Snowy Egret, Little Blue and Green Herons, Mangrove Swallow, and the kingfishers: Belted, Amazon, and Green. As the trail loops back, following the river, there is a spot where a deck overlooks the water. Near here Dot-winged Antwrens are often found.

One of the prettiest hiking trails in Belize is the Living Cycle Trail, about a two-hour walk. Replete with narrow bridges crossing rivulets flowing with recent rains, footpaths climbing and descending over uneven terrain, the loop trail meanders under a tall and shading broadleaf canopy. You are bound to encounter a woodcreeper or two, most likely Ivory-billed, though perhaps Ruddy, Wedge-billed, or Streak-headed. The shaded forest is also good for flycatchers such as Greenish Elaenia, and Ochre-bellied, Sepia-capped, and Yellow-olive Flycatchers. There is a portion of the trail where it opens up at a limestone outcropping. If you arrive at that spot between 9 AM and 11 AM scan the skies for raptors; Black Hawk-Eagle is regular (and frequently heard

Ecoregion and habitats: Appendix A, Ecoregion 11, Cayo central lowlands and foothills. Habitats include: riparian lowland broadleaf forest at the confluence of Roaring Creek and Belize River (BFL1).

Fees: Entrance US$5 for non-residents, BZ$2 for residents. The attendant—who changes from year to year—might be knowledgeable about the animal and plant life, and may be willing to guide for an appropriate tip.

Contacts: Guanacaste National Park; (011) 501-223-5004; www.belizeaudubon. org. Only a mile east of Guanacaste National Park is Banana Bank Lodge, a popular place where birders stay. Banana Bank has about 8 miles of river front, 1,500 acres of jungle, lagoons, pastureland, and old-growth trees. Its bird list includes over 240 species recorded on the 4,000+ acres of Banana Bank Ranch. After exiting Price Highway at the Banana Bank sign, take the dirt road for a quarter-mile, fork right, and continue until you reach the river and road's end. Park here and pound a small gong to summon the boat. Detailed and alternative directions are on their website. Banana Bank Lodge, John and Carolyn Carr, P.O. Box 48, Belmopan; (011) 501-832-2020; bbl@bananabank.com; www.bananabank.com.

Location: N 17° 15.68' W 88° 47.27' at parking lot. Easy to find, the park lies at the intersection of Price Highway, mile 32.3 on the log, and Hummingbird Highway (mile 0).

before seen), often soaring high above the canopy. Its distinctive profile cuts the sky, showing the paddle-shaped wings arching forward, much like Hook-billed Kite but more subtle.

Key species of Guanacaste National Park: Black Hawk-Eagle, Sungrebe, Blue Ground-Dove, Long-billed and Stripe-throated Hermits, Green-breasted Mango, Canivet's Emerald, Blue-crowned Motmot, **Amazon Kingfisher**, Rufous-tailed Jacamar, Collared Aracari, Smoky-brown and Golden-olive Woodpeckers, Dusky Antbird, **Black-faced Ant-thrush**, Plain Xenops, Tawny-winged Woodcreeper, **Ruddy Woodcreeper**, Wedge-billed and Streak-headed Woodcreepers, Dot-winged Antwren, **Yellow-bellied Tyrannulet**, Sepia-capped Flycatcher, Stub-tailed Spadebill, **Black Phoebe**, Bright-rumped Attila, Black-crowned Tityra, **White-winged Becard**, Gray-collared Becard, Red-capped Manakin, White-bellied Wren, Long-billed Gnatwren, Swainson's Warbler, Buff-throated Saltator, Blue Bunting.

Pook's Hill

Description: Tapir Mountain Nature Reserve is a protected area of 6,741 acres, available to researchers but closed to tourism. However, adjacent to Tapir Mountain is the 300-acre Pook's Hill private reserve along Roaring Creek. The lodge accommodates guests in an excellent natural setting. With advance permission, individuals or small groups can also bird the reserve for a morning and arrange for a fixed-menu lunch. Like many of the resort lodges of Cayo District, a field naturalist is in residence. The Pook's Hill checklist includes an impressive 315 species; however, the list includes many entries that stretch the imagination.

On the same entrance road leading from Teakettle Village is **Actun Tunichil Muknal**, a well-known archaeological site within a cave, protected by Belize Audubon Society. Entrance fee is US$15. The water-filled cave can be visited with licensed tour guides through trips arranged at most local resorts. As part of Tapir Mountain Nature Reserve, the site enjoys excellent birding along the 1.2-mile hike to the cave entrance. On one such tour a birder reported 31 species, including Bare-throated Tiger-Heron, Ornate Hawk-Eagle, and Dusky Antbird. A nesting pair of Orange-breasted Falcons resides near Roaring Creek, upriver from the cave.

Birding strategy: Pook's Hill can be visited as a day trip from San Ignacio or Belmopan. You can get a good taste of the birdlife here at the base of the Tapir Mountains in a morning or full day, but to explore all of the birding trails, staying at the resort is recommended. Whether you choose the Top Trails or the River Trails, you are bound to find a good list of species that could reach 75+ in a morning. Birding is excellent from the veranda, where flowers attract hummingbirds such as Long-billed Hermit, White-necked Jacobin, and Purple-crowned Fairy. A large lawn plot gives a clear view of the sky, and foothill locations such as this are a good place to study swifts overhead. Five species have been reported here, including about 35 Chestnut-collared Swifts mixed with about 15 Vaux's in 2011. The perimeter of the lawn plot is good edge habitat. Here White-winged Becard can be found at the northern edge of its range. Easy, flat trails extend through forest and along Roaring Creek and provide good cover

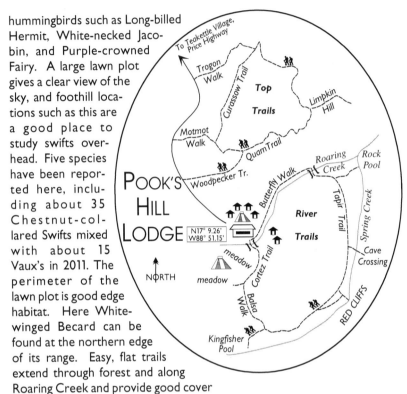

for the more elusive interior-forest lurkers such as Stub-tailed Spadebill and Sulphur-rumped Flycatcher as well as White-collared Manakin. Agami Heron has consistently been found on the small streams that drain into Roaring Creek, including the spot near the suspension bridge. Other trails extend above the lodge, offering such diverse species as Hook-billed Kite, White-whiskered Puffbird, Bananaquit, and Gray-headed Tanager. In the cohune forest at the upper trails, Ruddy-tailed Flycatcher and Pheasant Cuckoo have been consistent. The biggest surprise is the first Belize record for Black-headed Grosbeak, found 23 January 2003 along Tapir Trail. At the northeast corner of the trail, near the river, Uniform Crake has been observed. At night listen for Spectacled Owl; both adults and immatures have been seen or heard consistently for at least ten years. They have been found in *Cecropia* trees right outside the lodge and a few times from the bridge to the newer cabanas, and also at a day roost on a trail adjacent to the lower meadow.

Key species of Pook's Hill: Great, Little, and Slaty-breasted Tinamous, **Agami Heron**, King Vulture, Hook-billed Kite, White Hawk, Black Hawk-Eagle, Barred Forest-Falcon, **Uniform Crake** [R], Scaled Pigeon, Gray-

Ecoregion and habitats: Appendix A, Ecoregion 11, Cayo central lowlands and foothills. Habitats include: lowland broadleaf forest on foothills of Maya Mountains (BFF1 bordering on BFM1); resort with supplemental plantings (PC).

Contact: Ray and Vicki Snaddon, Pook's Hill Ltd., P.O. Box 14, Belmopan, Belize; (011) 501-832-2017; pookshill@hughes.net or pookshill@yahoo.com; www.pookshilllodge.com.

Location: N 17° 9.26' W 88° 51.15' at reception area. Guests of the lodge can arrange pickup from Philip Goldson International Airport and other locations.

Directions: Start from mile 37.5 heading west on the Price Highway, in Teakettle Village, which is about 17 miles east of San Ignacio or 6 miles west of Belmopan. Zero your odometer at this intersection, N 17° 13.54' W 88° 51.17', which is marked with a sign for Pook's Hill. Turn south on a gravel road and in 0.2 mile curve right. At 0.4 turn left (often unsigned), while still in Teakettle Village. At 4.0 turn right on to a track signed for Pook's Hill; left leads to Actun Tunichil Muknal. Enter a narrow road through forest with an enclosed canopy, and drive uphill until you reach the Pook's Hill parking lot at 5.6. The lodge facilities are another 0.1 mile.

headed and Gray-chested Doves, Mealy Parrot, **Pheasant Cuckoo**, Vermiculated Screech-Owl, **Spectacled Owl**, Central American Pygmy-Owl, Chestnut-collared [R], White-collared, Vaux's, and Lesser Swallow-tailed Swifts, Scaly-breasted Hummingbird, **Wedge-tailed Sabrewing**, White-necked Jacobin, Purple-crowned Fairy, **Tody Motmot**, White-whiskered Puffbird, Rufous-tailed Jacamar, **Emerald Toucanet**, Great Antshrike, Plain Antvireo [R], Dusky Antbird, Black-faced Antthrush, Buff-throated Foliage-gleaner, Plain Xenops, Tawny-winged and Olivaceous Woodcreepers, Northern Barred-Woodcreeper, Yellow-bellied Tyrannulet, Sepia-capped Flycatcher, Slate-headed Tody-Flycatcher, Eye-ringed Flatbill, Stub-tailed Spadebill, Royal Flycatcher, **Ruddy-tailed Flycatcher**, Sulphur-rumped Flycatcher, Black Phoebe, Rufous Mourner, White-winged Becard, Tawny-crowned Greenlet, Band-backed Wren, Crimson-collared Tanager, Black-faced Grosbeak, Yellow-backed Oriole.

MAYA MOUNTAINS

Quite distinctive from other parts of Belize, the Maya Mountains are at a higher elevation, support a somewhat cooler climate, and contain much more pine forest habitat and, thus, a good number of bird species not seen at lower elevation. The next pages first give directions to and through the Maya Mountains and then elaborate on lodges and birding sites within the mountains.

Concerns: There are no gas stations in Mountain Pine Ridge and surrounding Maya Mountain areas, so fill your fuel tank beforehand. Depending on rainfall and the last time roads were graded, the red clay and rock roads can be difficult, sometimes painfully so if driving a pickup truck on hard tires. The road to Thousand Foot Falls and a few other roads can be so rutted as to do damage to cars with low clearance. In the rainy season (July to February, peaking in September and October), four-wheel-drive is recommended to navigate the slippery clay, and there can be bad spots here and there in the dry season, too.

Directions: Two roads lead up into the Maya Mountains and its Mountain Pine Ridge and thence to Vaca Plateau, both originating from Price Highway. If you are starting from San Ignacio, take the route via Cristo Rey and San Antonio until it joins with Chiquibul Road. Starting from Belize City and other points east, take Chiquibul Road from its intersection with Price Highway.

Route via Cristo Rey and San Antonio Road: From Hawksworth Bridge over the Macal River in San Ignacio, it is 0.4 mile east to the turnoff for Mountain Pine Ridge. This is mile 9.4 heading east on the Price Highway log, N 17° 9.64' W 89° 3.73'.

Mile

0.0 Intersection of Price Highway and Cristo Rey Road. Elevation 283 feet. Signed for Mountain Pine Ridge. TURN RIGHT onto road heading uphill.

0.8 Maya Mountain Lodge on right. Road becomes dirt.

3.2 Village of Cristo Rey. Four speed bumps.

3.8 **Crystal Paradise Resort**. Birding trails and boat rentals on Macal River.

6.4 Sac Tunich.

5.1 Mango Walk Inn.

6.0 Entrance on right to Mystic River Resort, Macaw Bank, and In the Bush Resort. Excellent birding along the road and trails around river. Canoe rentals and excellent food at Mystic River Road Resort.

8.1 Garcia Sisters.

8.6 Start of San Antonio. Elevation 690 feet.

9.2 Turn left to Mountain Pine Ridge. Right leads to emergency gas barrel.

12.2 Intersection with Chiquibul Road. TURN RIGHT at T-intersection. Travel time from San Ignacio to this point is 1/2 to 3/4 hour.

Skip to "Continuation of Chiquibul Road" (below), joining at mile 8.5.

Route via Chiquibul Road: Near Georgeville on Price Highway, a well marked sign marks the start of Chiquibul Road leading to Mountain Pine Ridge. This is mile 47.3 heading west on the Price Highway log, N 17° 11.54' W 88° 58.93'. Travel time to Caracol is at least two hours. A number of stops along the road, e.g., Barton Creek Cave and Green Hills Butterfly Ranch, are worthwhile in their own regard and can be productive birding areas.

0.0 Intersection of Price Highway and Chiquibul Road. Elevation 274 feet. Signed for Mountain Pine Ridge. TURN LEFT (south) on to road heading uphill.

0.2 Pavement ends at bump at edge of Georgeville.

1.4 Limestone quarry (on left).

3.1 Barton Creek Farms (on left).

4.6 Maya Ranch (on right).

4.8 Road to **Barton Creek Archaeological Reserve** (on left). Entrance fee US$10. Also Barton Creek Outpost for tent camping.

6.8 Sign "El Progresso 7 miles" on road to left.

7.6 **Green Hills Butterfly Ranch** (on right). Entrance fee US$12.50. 230 bird species recorded on their 100 acres, and they offer the best hummingbird feeders in Belize. The gardens attract 200–300 hummingbirds of 7–10 hummingbird species daily. Contact is: Jan Meerman, Mile 8 Pine Ridge Road, Cayo District. (011) 501-834-4017; meerman@biological-diversity.info; http://green-hills.net.

7.9 Mountain Equestrian Trails (on left).

7.9 Slate Creek Canyon Eco Park (on left), part of **Slate Creek Preserve.**

8.5 T-intersection. Road from San Antonio on right. Continue south.

Continuation of Chiquibul Road: Both routes from Price Highway join at the T-intersection and Chiquibul Road continues upward to Mountain Pine Ridge and eventually Caracol.

8.9 Bols Cave (on right).

9.0 Misty Mountain (on left).

9.8 Forest Reserve Boundary. Forestry gate. Bark-beetle damage. An attendant will record your vehicle license-plate number and open the gate. This is a convenient bathroom break (ask the attendant for directions) and could be a birding stop at the forested area just beyond the gate.

10.9 Old Mai Gate Village (tent camping). Start of pines. Elevation 1,300 feet.

13.4 T-intersection with Cooma Cairn Road. Left goes to **Hidden Valley** and **Thousand Foot Falls,** described in another section. Continue on Chiquibul Road for Caracol.

13.5 Pine Ridge Lodge road at bridge.

14.1 Access road to Blancaneaux Lodge and Gaïa Riverlodge.

16.9 First of several bridges. Elevation dropping to Vaca Plateau.

20.9 Side road to Rio On Pool. Nesting pair of Orange-breasted Falcons in area.

23.3 Side road to **Rio Frio Caves**. N 16° 58.39' W 88° 59.51'. Shortly after the turnoff to the cave, a military guard may stop traffic. See the Caracol section on page 126 for details on the possibility of escorted vehicles.

23.5 Village of **Douglas Da Silva** (named Augustine on older maps).

30.2 Continue right. Chalillo Road to dam goes left. Dam covers former nesting grounds of Belize's Scarlet Macaws.

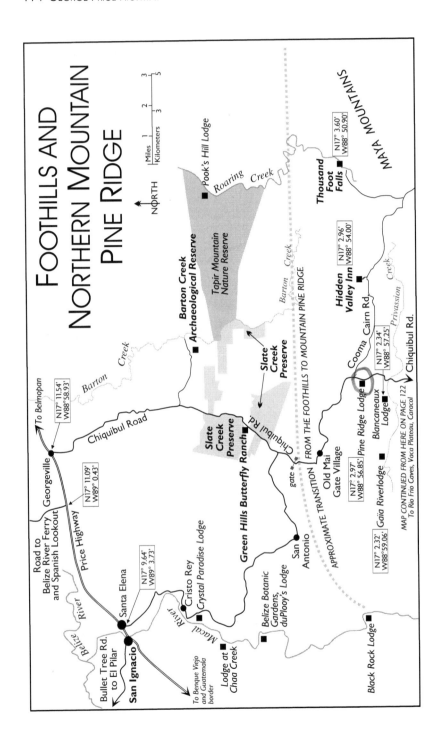

FOOTHILLS AND NORTHERN MOUNTAIN PINE RIDGE

MAYA MOUNTAINS

NORTH

Miles
Kilometers

To Belmopan

N17° 11.54'
W88° 58.93'

Roaring Creek

Pook's Hill Lodge

Thousand Foot Falls
N17° 3.60'
W88° 50.90'

Barton Creek Archaeological Reserve

Tapir Mountain Nature Reserve

Barton Creek

Hidden Valley Inn
N17° 2.96'
W88° 54.00'

Slate Creek Preserve

FROM THE FOOTHILLS TO MOUNTAIN PINE RIDGE

Cooma Cairn Rd.

Privassion Creek

Barton Creek

Georgeville
N17° 11.09'
W89° 0.43'

Chiquibul Road

Chiquibul Rd.

N17° 2.34'
W88° 57.25'

Road to Belize River Ferry and Spanish Lookout

Slate Creek Preserve

Chiquibul Rd.

Pine Ridge Lodge
N17° 2.97'
W88° 56.85'

Blancaneaux Lodge

Chiquibul Rd.

To Río Frío Caves, Vaca Plateau, Caracol

MAP CONTINUED FROM HERE ON PAGE 122

Green Hills Butterfly Ranch

gate

Old Mai Gate Village

Price Highway

Santa Elena
N17° 9.64'
W89° 3.73'

Cristo Rey

Crystal Paradise Lodge

San Antonio

Gaïa Riverlodge
N17° 2.32'
W88° 59.06'

APPROXIMATE TRANSITION

Belize River

Macal River

Bullet Tree Rd. to El Pilar

San Ignacio

Lodge at Chaa Creek

Belize Botanic Gardens, duPlooy's Lodge

To Benque Viejo and Guatemala border

Black Rock Lodge

33.3 Guacamallo Bridge over Macal River, a worthwhile birding stop.

34.9 Millionario Road on left leads into **Chiquibul National Park** and Chiquibul Forest Reserve to **Las Cuevas Research Station**.

35.4 Pavement starts on hill climb and can be slippery. Tall forest begins.

44.8 End of pavement. Welcome to Caracol sign.

45.0 **Caracol parking lot**.

Mountain Pine Ridge

Description: "Ridge" refers to a forest type, not topography. Mountain Pine Ridge, a forest reserve 300 square miles in area, occupies a portion of Maya Mountains at its northern end. Elevation is 1,300–3,300 feet and drops to 600 feet on the plateau. To the east, Baldy Beacon rises to 3,346 feet. Temperatures are quite pleasant year round, with average lows 17°C (63°F) in December and 22°C (71°F) in May. Few people live in this area, although there are several upscale lodges and resorts. From these, birders can easily reach Thousand Foot Falls, Rio Frio Caves, and—in the Vaca Plateau and Chiquibul forests—Caracol, Las Cuevas, and Macal River.

The avifauna has changed a great deal since the completion of Chalillo Dam in September 2005 and the subsequent filling of the reservoir. Species rare or not previously recorded in Mountain Pine Ridge have been observed with increasing frequency at the reservoir, including Blue-winged Teal, Pied-billed Grebe, Magnificent Frigatebird, Anhinga, Brown Pelican, herons and egrets, Spotted Sandpiper, and even a pair of Laughing Gulls. Access to Chalillo Lake is restricted to those accompanied by rangers for Friends for Conservation and Development (FCD), co-managers of Chiquibul; (011) 501-823-2657; info@fcdbelize.org; www.fcdbelize.org.

Birding strategy: To do this area justice, it would be best to book accommodations at one of the lodges catering to birders and eco-tourists, planning on a minimum two- or three-night stay. Some of the lodges offer

Ecoregion and habitats: Appendix A, Ecoregion 13, Mountain Pine Ridge submontane forests. Habitats include: mostly submontane pine forest (PFM) bordered on the north by Cayo broadleaf forest foothills (BFF1) and on the east by submontane broadleaf forest (BFM1). Following a severe drought in 2000, much of the forest has been devastated by Southern Pine Beetles, reducing the habitat to shrubland, but a few untouched dense stands exist. Open areas are dominated by Tiger Fern.

Contacts: Several excellent lodges cater to birders. Most are expensive, but they offer amenities that justify their prices. A stay at one of the lodges is included in many Belize birding tours. Of course, you can also book these on your own and take advantage of the many local tours arranged by the lodges, accompanied by bird guides. The location of each lodge is identified in the road log on the preceding pages.

Note: **Hidden Valley Inn** is included in its own section, owing to its extensive private birding areas.

spectacular birding on their spacious premises. A day trip, starting before dawn, to Caracol should be included in your stay. The area can be visited also as a day trip from San Ignacio, although it would be a very long day.

Crystal Paradise Resort in Cristo Rey offers birding tours led by resident bird guides, the Tut brothers. They have a checklist of neighborhood birds that includes 220 species. The lodge and attractive cabanas are in a jungle setting beside the Macal River. The resort includes nature trails and an observation tower. It is located at mile 3.8 on the route via Cristo Rey and San Antonio Road. Contact: Crystal Paradise Resort, P. O. Box 126, Cristo Rey Village, San Ignacio, Cayo District; (011) 501-834-4016 or 610-5593; fax (011) 501-834-4016; info@crystalparadise.com, www.crystalparadise.com.

Mango Walk Inn in Cristo Rey offers rustic cabins, lit by kerosene lamps, with outdoor showers, at a fraction of the cost of Mountain Pine Ridge resorts. Excellent and extensive birding habitat along the Macal River has included Vermiculated Screech-Owl and Mottled Owl. The 3/4-mile access road is at mile 5.1 on the route via San Antonio Road. Contact: Mango Walk Inn, P.O. Box 204, San Ignacio, Cayo District; (011) 501-609-8892 or 628-6670; deirdre@mangowalkinnbz.com.

Pine Ridge Lodge is located on 103 acres, including fruit orchards and vegetable gardens, and has six cottages overlooking Little Vaqueros Creek. Relatively inexpensive; no electricity but charming and comfortable. At N 17° 2.97' W 88° 56.85', the lodge is at mile 13.5 on the Chiquibul Road log. Contact: Pine Ridge Lodge, P.O. Box 128, San Ignacio, Cayo District; (011) 501-661-8264 or toll-free in US: 800-316-0706, fax in US: 216-781-1273; pineridgelodge@lycos.com; www.pineridgelodge.com.

Gaïa Riverlodge (formerly Five Sisters Lodge) stands beside five waterfalls where the gushing water empties into the Privassion River. Stygian Owl regularly appears at the lodge. The turnoff for the lodge is mile 14.1 on the Chiquibul Road log. Gaïa Riverlodge is 2.3 miles from the turnoff; the parking lot is at N 17° 2.32' W 88° 59.06'. Contact: Gaïa Riverlodge, P.O. Box 173, San Ignacio, Cayo District; (011) 501-834-4024; fax (011) 223-0002; info@gaiariverlodge.com; www.gaiariverlodge.com..

Blancaneaux Lodge was created by Francis Ford Coppola; seven luxury villas and 14 cabanas are laid out on a hillside above the Privassion River. The turnoff for the lodge is mile 14.1 on the Chiquibul Road log. A half-mile from the turnoff, Blancaneaux Lodge is on the left and a private airstrip on the right, at N 17° 2.34' W 88° 57.25'. Contact: Blancaneaux Lodge, P. O. Box B, Central Farm, Cayo District; (011) 501-824-4912 or 824-3878 or toll-free in US: 800-746-3743; info@blancaneaux.com; www.coppolaresorts.com/blancaneaux.

Key species of Mountain Pine Ridge: Great, Little, and Slaty-breasted Tinamous, Crested Guan, Ocellated Turkey, **King Vulture**, **Swallow-tailed** [S], **Double-toothed**, and **Plumbeous** [S] **Kites**, Sharp-shinned [R], Cooper's [R], and White Hawks, **Solitary Eagle** [R], Broad-winged Hawk, **Red-tailed Hawk**, **Black-and-white Hawk-Eagle**, Merlin, **Orange-breasted Falcon**, Scaled Pigeon, Scarlet Macaw, Vermiculated Screech-Owl, Ferruginous Pygmy-Owl, **Stygian Owl**, Lesser Nighthawk, **Common Nighthawk** [S], **Chestnut-collared Swift** [R], White-collared and Lesser Swallow-tailed Swifts, **Azure-crowned Hummingbird**, Purple-crowned Fairy, Collared Trogon, **Tody** and **Keel-billed Motmots**, Acorn Wood-pecker, Yellow-bellied Sapsucker, **Greater Pewee**, Lovely Cotinga, **Plumbeous Vireo**, Blue-headed Vireo [R], Green Jay, Ridgway's Rough-winged, Cliff [T], and Cave [R,T] Swallows, **Plain** and **Sedge Wrens**, Slate-colored Solitaire, **White-throated Thrush**, Gray-crowned Yellowthroat, **Grace's** and **Rufous-capped Warblers**, Golden-crowned Warbler, Golden-hooded Tanager, Yellow-faced Grassquit, **Rusty Sparrow**, Chipping and Grasshopper Sparrows, **Lincoln's Sparrow**, Hepatic and White-winged Tanagers, **Red-crowned Ant-Tanager**, Red-throated Ant-Tanager, Dickcissel, **Yellow-backed Oriole**, Yellow-tailed Oriole, **Red Crossbill**, **Black-headed Siskin**.

Hidden Valley Inn

[1 March] Today is a symphony with a slow andante, a dramatic finale, and a surprising encore. The mountains of Belize are much lower than those we visited in Mexico a month ago. Yet the change in elevation is enough to put us into pine forests once we reach 1,300 feet elevation. We head to Thousand Foot Falls and can see the broad tree-filled canyon and the plunging waterfall. After several minutes search, we locate the pair of Orange-breasted Falcons that claim this canyon as theirs. They are perched on the other side, identifiable as raptors with binoculars, and color-marked to Orange-breasted through a scope at 60X.

We head to another canyon and its falls aptly named King Vulture Falls. When we arrive we quickly spot a few King Vultures on the opposite canyon wall... Another raptor is below us on our side of the canyon; through binoculars, its gray-black color makes us suspect we're seeing a Plumbeous Kite. But the large bill with an extensive bright yellow cere, thin yellow orbital ring, tail length, and overall size and color all match Solitary Eagle. We recognize we are focusing on two separate birds. Suddenly one takes flight, moves to the second and copulates. We've never had a confirmed sighting of the rare Solitary Eagle on any of our Mexico and Belize trips.

Darkness sets in and we return to the inn, bubbling with excitement over our good fortune. But the concert is not over yet. In the midst of our pre-dinner gathering, Craig suddenly bursts into the room exclaiming, "Stygian Owl." We race out to the front lawn to see him spotlighting the owl atop a pine tree. Everyone gets a good look. What an encore to a marvelous day!

Description: Only guests of the inn—and only 12 rooms are available—may explore the 90 miles of roads and trails through 7,200 acres of Hidden Valley. Pine forests, including some untouched by bark beetles, spectacular waterfalls, and fern-tree forests offer excellent birding. The property extends to the edge of the mountains, and from Bull's Point, named after the original land owner, the 1,880-foot promontory offers a view of Belmopan to the east, Spanish Lookout to the north, Guatemala on the horizon, and a good spot to see soaring White Hawks. Scan the foothills and you may find Orange-breasted Falcon as well. Specialty birds of Hidden Valley

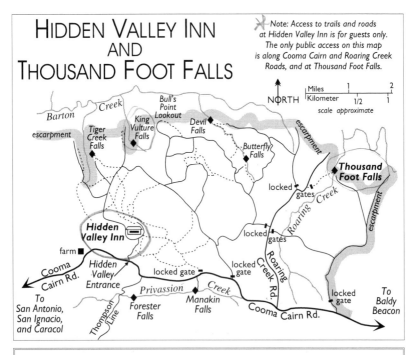

HIDDEN VALLEY INN
AND
THOUSAND FOOT FALLS

Note: Access to trails and roads at Hidden Valley Inn is for guests only. The only public access on this map is along Cooma Cairn and Roaring Creek Roads, and at Thousand Foot Falls.

Ecoregion and habitats: Appendix A, Ecoregion 13, Mountain Pine Ridge submontane forests. Habitats include: submontane pine forest (PFM) with submontane broadleaf forest (BFM1) on the slopes. Shrubland characterizes the forests reduced by the bark beetles, but some dense pine forest stands are on the property. Also a resort complex with supplemental plantings and bird feeders (PC).

Contact: Hidden Valley Inn, P.O. Box 170, Belmopan, Cayo District; (011) 501-822-3320 or toll-free in US: 866-443-3364; fax (011) 501-822-3334; reservations@hiddenvalleyinn.com; www.hiddenvalleyinn.com.

Location: N 17° 2.96' W 88° 54.00'; elevation 1,971 feet at lodge parking lot. See the directions for Thousand Foot Falls and the entrance to Hidden Valley Inn at mile 3.3 on the Cooma Cairn Road. The resort can also arrange transportation from Philip Goldson International Airport.

are King Vulture, Broad-winged Hawk, Black-and-white Hawk-Eagle, Stygian Owl, Lovely Cotinga, and Plain Wren. A pair of Keel-billed Motmots nested and raised a chick in 2009. A pair of Orange-breasted Falcons nests at King Vulture Falls, a must-visit birding stop. In addition to the King Vultures invariably found here, you may also see Double-toothed Kite, Solitary Eagle, and Black-and-white Hawk-Eagle from this viewpoint. Other specialties are listed in the Mountain Pine Ridge section above, including rarities found only at Hidden Valley. Rick Romero, the on-site birding guide, keeps on top of the birds' whereabouts and is invaluable for keying into the right habitat for each species. The guide can also arrange a day tour at Caracol. Excellent rooms and meals, sauna, and swimming pool and pleasant manicured surroundings make this an inviting place to stay.

Thousand Foot Falls National Monument

Description: Also called Hidden Valley Falls, this dramatic waterfall surrounded by submontane pine forest is actually 1,600 feet high—probably the highest in Central America—and was designated a national monument in 2004. For birders it is well known for the pair of Orange-breasted Falcons that nest beside the waterfall. Swallow-tailed Kites and White-collared Swifts often soar in the updrafts. The flowers and fruiting trees at the grounds bordering the viewpoint attract many birds, including Plumbeous Vireo, Grace's and Rufous-capped Warblers, Golden-hooded Tanager, Yellow-faced Grassquit, Hepatic Tanager, Black-headed Siskin, and, for at least two years, wintering Hermit Warbler. Plain Wren has occurred. Rusty Sparrows are easily found along the entrance road. Other specialties are listed in the Mountain Pine Ridge section on page 117

Birding strategy: The best time to visit the falls is at or before 9:30 AM, when King Vultures fly over the gorge. Naturalist/caretaker Pedro Mai can assist in pointing out the Orange-breasted Falcons' nest or favorite perches. Sometimes it can take an hour or more to locate a falcon, best found by scanning the horizon, waterfall, and highest perches with a spotting scope at high power. Pedro says Slate-colored Solitaire nests here, arriving in April.

Ecoregion and habitats: Appendix A, Ecoregion 13, Mountain Pine Ridge submontane forests. Habitat is submontane broadleaf forest (BFM1).

Concerns: The entrance road is steep and can contain deep ruts that might cause damage to cars with low clearance. If it is foggy, do not bother driving to the falls, as you will not see them.

Fees and contact: Entrance is US$1. Hours are 7 AM to 5 PM. (011) 501-609-6749 or attendant Pedro Mai's cell phone 600-1374. Facilities at the national monument include an observation platform, toilets, picnic tables, and a gift shop featuring local crafts.

Location: N 17° 3.60' W 88° 50.90'; elevation 2,050 feet at viewing platform.

A dawn departure from San Ignacio or Belmopan would allow sufficient time to bird en route, and especially along Cooma Cairn Road, where one can find the non-migratory local Red-tailed Hawk, Rufous-capped Warbler, Rusty Sparrow, and Hepatic Tanager. As you near the falls area watch the sky for Swallow-tailed Kites.

Directions: In the section on Maya Mountains, start from mile 13.4 on the Chiquibul Road log, N 17° 3.08' W 88° 56.86'. The T-intersection is marked by many signs, including Hidden Valley Inn. Zero your odometer and head east on Cooma Cairn Road. At 1.9 you pass the Forest Reserve Boundary, elevation 1,077 feet, where there is extensive bark-beetle damage. Mt. Pleasant Farm is at 2.8 and the entrance road to **Hidden Valley Inn** is on the left at 3.3 miles. At 6.5 on Cooma Cairn, turn left on the entrance road to Thousand Foot Falls, N 17° 1.69' W 88° 51.82'; the elevation has climbed to 2,564 feet. Typically, this is where the red dirt and rock road is at its worst, as you descend toward the national monument. On the left at 7.6 is the locked gate leading into Hidden Valley property. The Thousand Foot Falls parking lot is at 9.2. An alternative route to Thousand Foot Falls is through the Hidden Valley property. This route is the same distance but on a much better road, available only to guests of the inn.

Cooma Cairn Road connects to other winding mountain roads, eventually reaching the Bald Hills with the highest peak **Baldy Beacon** (3,346 feet), eight miles beyond the turnoff for Thousand Foot Falls.

Rio Frio Caves and Douglas Da Silva

Description: Rio Frio Caves are karst formations and a large cave system surrounded by semi-deciduous broadleaf forest. A worthwhile stop en route to or from Caracol, the limestone cave is open at both ends and arches to 65 feet at its center. A stream runs throughout its half-mile length and enough sunlight filters through so that flashlights are not needed. Ridgway's Rough-winged Swallows fly at the cave's entrance. Depending on the time of day, the surrounding forest could offer good birding.

Over 140 species have been reported from here, including Crested Owl, Lesser Swallow-tailed Swift, Purple-crowned Fairy, Acorn Woodpecker,

Ecoregion and habitats: Appendix A, Ecoregion 13, Mountain Pine Ridge submontane forests. Habitat is submontane broadleaf forest (BFM2).
Location: N 16° 58.75' W 89° 0.34'; elevation 1,495 feet at parking lot. Follow the Chiquibul Road log to mile 23.3 in the section on Maya Mountains. From the main road at Douglas Da Silva, turn down the side-road marked for the caves, and 0.2 mile farther turn right at another sign. The parking lot is at another mile. In rainy weather the last part of the road may be too muddy to drive, so just park and walk.

King Vulture   Bert Frenz

Dot-winged Antwren, Buff-throated Foliage-gleaner, Ruddy Woodcreeper, Eye-ringed Flatbill, Yellow-olive, Royal, Sulphur-rumped, and Olive-sided Flycatchers, Greater Pewee, Green Shrike-Vireo, Plain and Sedge Wrens, White-throated Thrush, Rufous-capped Warbler, Green Honeycreeper, Orange-billed and Chipping Sparrows, Hepatic Tanager, both ant-tanagers, Blue-black Grosbeak, Yellow-throated Euphonia, and Black-headed Siskin. One of the Belize rarities, Violet-crowned Woodnymph, was recorded here once. In 2009 one and then two Shiny Cowbirds were documented on two dates in June.

A lookout tower at Douglas Da Silva is great for raptor-watching. Species reported include Hook-billed, Swallow-tailed, Double-toothed, and Plumbeous Kites, White Hawk, Great Black-Hawk, Gray and Short-tailed Hawks, Barred Forest-Falcon, and Merlin. Solitary Eagle has been reported regularly since 2004. Even if you visit midday and do not find many birds, you will be impressed with the cave. The only facility at the cave is a pit toilet. Cave entrance is free.

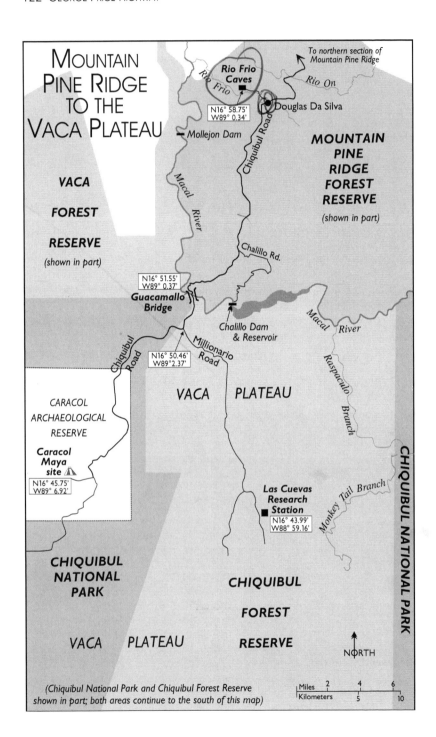

MOUNTAIN
PINE RIDGE
TO THE
VACA PLATEAU

To northern section of
Mountain Pine Ridge

Rio Frio
Caves

Rio Frio

Rio On

N16° 58.75'
W89° 0.34'

Douglas Da Silva

Mollejon Dam

Chiquibul Road

MOUNTAIN
PINE
RIDGE
FOREST
RESERVE
(shown in part)

VACA

FOREST

RESERVE
(shown in part)

Macal River

Chalillo Rd.

N16° 51.55'
W89° 0.37'

Guacamallo
Bridge

Chalillo Dam
& Reservoir

Macal River

Millionario Road

N16° 50.46'
W89°2.37'

Chiquibul Road

VACA PLATEAU

Raspaculo Branch

CARACOL
ARCHAEOLOGICAL
RESERVE

Caracol
Maya
site

N16° 45.75'
W89° 6.92'

Las Cuevas
Research
Station
N16° 43.99'
W88° 59.16'

Monkey Tail Branch

CHIQUIBUL NATIONAL PARK

CHIQUIBUL
NATIONAL
PARK

CHIQUIBUL

FOREST

VACA PLATEAU

RESERVE

NORTH

(Chiquibul National Park and Chiquibul Forest Reserve
shown in part; both areas continue to the south of this map)

Miles   2   4   6
Kilometers   5   10

VACA PLATEAU

While Mountain Pine Ridge is dominated by pine forest, farther south and west (along the Guatemala border) the elevation drops to the Vaca Plateau and the habitat changes. At the edge of the plateau are **Rio Frio Caves** and **Caracol** and the vast **Chiquibul National Park** and Chiquibul Forest Reserve. At the northern border of Vaca Plateau is Vaca Falls and **Black Rock Lodge**, treated in the section on Macal River resorts. **Hydro Road** penetrates the northwestern foothills of Vaca Plateau near the Guatemala border.

Ecoregion and habitats: Appendix A, Ecoregion 14, Southern submontane hardwood forests. Habitats include: semi-deciduous broadleaf forests (BFM2) with isolated pockets of pine and shrubland (PFM), including karst formations, large cave systems, and many waterfalls.

Directions: Follow the Chiquibul Road log. Vaca Plateau starts around mile 17 and continues to Caracol at mile 45. Hydro Road is accessed from Price Highway at Benque Viejo del Carmen, one mile east of the Guatemala border.

Chiquibul National Park and Las Cuevas Research Station

Description: The national park encompasses over 264,000 acres and is contiguous with Caracol Archaeological Reserve and Chiquibul Forest Reserve for a combined protected area of over 683 square miles. It is well known to birders for its Scarlet Macaws. Even if you do not make a visit farther into the park, stop at mile 33.3 on the Chiquibul Road log and bird at Guacamallo Bridge over the Macal River.

Birding Strategy: At Guacamallo Bridge, there is good birding in the open area around the river and bridge as well as in the forest before and after the bridge. Just beyond the bridge is a gravel road leading toward a British military training camp, and this road is worth birding as well. You are sure to find a Black Phoebe at the bridge, and in early morning and late afternoon Scarlet Macaws sometimes fly over the river, which seems to serve as a highway on the edge of their normal habitat. From a Royal Air Force Ornithological Society expedition in the mid-1980s, supplemented by more recent visits by birding groups, 190 species have been found at Guacamallo. The list includes: Spotted Wood-Quail, Ocellated Turkey, King Vulture, Swallow-tailed and White-tailed Kites, Sharp-shinned Hawk, Orange-breasted Falcon, Uniform Crake, Sungrebe, Wedge-tailed Sabrewing, Tody Motmot, Emerald Toucanet, Scaly-throated Leaftosser, Streaked Flycatcher, Grace's and Rufous-capped Warblers, Rusty Sparrow, Hepatic Tanager, Black-headed Siskin.

Ecoregion and habitats: Appendix A, Ecoregion 14, Southern submontane forests. Habitats include: submontane pine forest (PFM) and submontane broadleaf moist forest (BFM2). The park includes Doyle's Delight—the highest point in Belize, supporting cloud forest habitat inaccessible but for a few scientific explorations with helicopter transportation. This and Victoria Peak are the only zones of montane broad-leaved wet forest (BFM3) in Belize.

Contact*: Las Cuevas Research Station, San Jose Succotz, Cayo District; (011) 501-812-2657; fcd.lcrs@gmail.com; www.lascuevas.org.*

Location*: N 16° 43.99' W 88° 59.16'; elevation 1,919 feet at Las Cuevas. Shortly beyond Guacamallo Bridge on Chiquibul Road is the turnoff for Millionario Road, mile 34.9 on the log. Take Millionario Road for 8 miles, curve left at Millionario, and continue another 2.5 miles to Las Cuevas Research Station.*

Las Cuevas can be explored more thoroughly, particularly if you are camping there or staying overnight at the station. Scarlet Macaws are common at the station and you are much more likely to find them there than at Guacamallo Bridge. They can be found any month of the year, but especially in May and June. Along the roadside, look and listen for Great Antshrike, Plain Antvireo, Slaty and Dot-winged Antwrens, Dusky Antbird, Paltry Tyrannulet, Slate-headed Tody-Flycatcher, Green-backed Sparrow, and Blue Bunting. Chestnut-headed Oropendolas nest along the road. Barred Forest-Falcon and Green Shrike-Vireo call regularly near the station. Along the Monkeytail River trail and camp you can find Little Tinamou, Collared Forest-Falcon, Great Curassow, Central American Pygmy-Owl, Green Jay, and Band-backed and Nightingale Wrens. At the Bird Tower you can watch Swallow-tailed and Plumbeous Kites, Great Black-Hawk, Black and Ornate Hawk-Eagles, and you may be lucky enough to see a Lovely Cotinga. Near the Bird Tower trails Spotted Wood-Quail is seen frequently, Slate-colored Solitaire sings, and Scaly-throated Leaftosser has been found. A Tody Motmot and Rufous-tailed Jacamar reside near the Bird Tower trail cave, and Ridgway's Rough-winged Swallows nest in the cave. White-throated Thrush frequents Elegant Pond, as do Ochre-bellied and Sepia-capped Flycatchers and Prothonotary Warbler. (These birding suggestions were extracted from a pre-publication copy of the *Annotated checklist of birds for the vicinity of Las Cuevas Research Station, Chiquibul Forest Reserve, Belize* by Ian Jones, T. Fitzgerald, and P. Taylor).

Key Species of Chiquibul National Park: In addition to the species listed above for Guacamallo Bridge and Las Cuevas, consider those listed for Caracol in the next section.

Caracol Archaeological Reserve

[2 March] We drive through the remains of a pine forest mostly denuded by a bark-beetle infestation. The land is rough and red, and the contours are rolling, dipping low to a half-dozen narrow streams of clear rushing water. We watch two Plumbeous Kites bathed in early-morning light and see the male take flight, revealing his pretty rust-colored wing linings, fly to his mate, and copulate with her. We stop also for an Ocellated Turkey and a Red-tailed Hawk, the latter a non-migratory specialty of this locale. At the Caracol parking lot we begin hiking through the jungle toward the Maya ruins. We see so many birds, we barely walk a quarter-mile in two hours. We also watch a Deppe's Squirrel nimbly feeding in the tree branches. We get remarkably good views of an Ornate Hawk-Eagle, so close that its colorful head and raised crest fill the field of view.

Description: Caracol may well be the best location in the world to find Keel-billed Motmot. A recent study over a four-year period found a population of 20–25 at ruins sites where the birds utilize steep-sided unexcavated Maya structures as nest burrow sites.

Apparently the largest known city in the Maya world—at least in land area—Caracol stretches six to nine miles from its central plaza. Only a small portion of its 65 square miles has been excavated. The city supported an estimated population of 100,000–140,000 people. Most daunting is the 143-foot-high pyramid, highest in Belize and a good vantage point for viewing canopy birds such as Lovely Cotinga. Some habitation of the site was as early as 1200 B.C. and permanent structures were built by 900–600 B.C. Caracol played a major role in Maya history, dominating the region for a century after defeating Tikal in war in A.D 562. For more information on Caracol archaeology see www.caracol.org.

Birding strategy: Leave in darkness (5 AM from Mountain Pine Ridge lodges or 4 AM from San Ignacio) so that you can arrive at the ruins near dawn. You will be tempted to stop along the way for birding but don't linger too long, as the more elusive birds are at Caracol. Do pause, though, at Guaca-mallo Bridge over Macal River to look for an early-morning flight of Scarlet Macaws overhead. While walking the many trails that wander through dense jungle on the periphery of Caracol, look for Keel-billed Motmot, Collared Trogon, and various antbirds and drab tropical flycatchers. The motmots are more readily found January through March when the males are stridently vocalizing on territory. When located, the species is readily observed.

Move into the open areas adjacent to the excavated temples by 9:30 or 10 AM to look for soaring raptors. Better yet, climb the highest temple and be at eye level with the canopy. If you are lucky—and many birders have been—you might see a Lovely Cotinga feeding in the canopy. Unless you are proficient at recognizing bird songs, Caracol is one of the places where you can benefit greatly from an experienced local birding guide. Facilities include modern bathrooms, nicely sheltered picnic areas, and a good museum.

Key species of Caracol and Chiquibul National Park: Great, Little, and Slaty-breasted Tinamous, **Great Curassow, Spotted Wood-Quail**, Ocellated Turkey, King Vulture, Swallow-tailed [S], Double-toothed, and Plumbeous [S] Kites, Bicolored and White Hawks, Solitary [R] and Harpy [R] Eagles, Ornate Hawk-Eagle, **Black-and-white Hawk-Eagle**, Barred Forest-Falcon, Gray-chested Dove, Ruddy Quail-Dove, **Scarlet Macaw**, Mealy Parrot, Vermiculated Screech-Owl, Crested Owl [R], **Spectacled Owl**, Black-and-white Owl, Wedge-tailed Sabrewing, **Violet Sabrewing**, Purple-crowned Fairy, **Collared Trogon, Tody** and **Keel-billed Motmots**, White-whiskered Puffbird, **Emerald Toucanet**, Chestnut-colored Woodpecker, Russet Antshrike [R], **Plain Antvireo**, Dusky Antbird, Black-faced Antthrush, **Scaly-throated Leaftosser**, Buff-throated Foliage-gleaner, Tawny-winged, Ruddy, and Wedge-billed Woodcreepers, **Strong-billed Woodcreeper**, Northern Barred-Woodcreeper, Streak-headed Woodcreeper, Yellow-bellied Tyrannulet, Sepia-capped Flycatcher, Eye-ringed Flatbill, Black Phoebe, **Rufous Mourner**, Cinnamon Becard, **Lovely Cotinga**, Rufous Piha, Green Jay, **Ridgway's Rough-winged Swallow**, **Band-backed Wren**, White-bellied Wren, **Slate-colored Solitaire**, **Gray-cheeked Thrush** [T], Swainson's Thrush, **White-throated Thrush**, Rufous-capped and Golden-crowned Warblers, Bananaquit, Black-throated Shrike-Tanager, Crimson-collared and Golden-hooded Tanagers, Green Honeycreeper, Orange-billed and Rusty Sparrows, **White-winged Tanager**, Yellow-backed Oriole, **Chestnut-headed Oropendola**.

Ecoregion and habitats: *Appendix A, Ecoregion 14, Southern submontane hardwood forests. Habitats include: primary submontane broadleaf forest (BFM2). Caracol itself is on the extensive Vaca Plateau on the western edge of Maya Mountains, and the archaeological reserve is nearly 40 square miles in size, separated from the surrounding 412 square miles of Chiquibul National Park.*

Concerns: *Bring along lunch and drinks, as there is no food available at the site. In 2006 bandits crossing over from Guatemala robbed tourists at Caracol (and were arrested shortly thereafter). Subsequently, the Belize government established a military presence at Douglas Da Silva and required visitors to be escorted from there to Caracol on a prescribed schedule. The morning departure is not as early as most birders would like, and sometimes the military escorts are slow to get started, but if you make special arrangements, you can be escorted earlier. Inquire at the resort where you are staying for more details on the current situation.*

Fees: *Entrance US$15 for non-residents, BZ$15 for residents. Tours can be arranged from most lodges in the area.*

Location: *N 16° 45.75' W 89° 6.92'; elevation 1,737 feet at entrance. In the section on Maya Mountains, use the Chiquibul Road log, following it to the end of the road, 45 miles from Price Highway.*

SAN IGNACIO AND VICINITY

Spanish Lookout and Aguacate Lagoon

[15 February] Not far from the lagoon the forested road runs mid-level against Yalbac Hills so we can look down to a narrow creek in dense undergrowth, a cleared understory closer to us, a canopy above us, and see part way through the forest farther uphill: a good viewpoint at multiple levels. We locate a flock and it entertains us for an hour. We tally 22 species, all in a 100-yard strip. Clearly, some birds belong to a mixed-species flock moving and feeding together. These include two Plain Xenops, Sepia-capped Flycatcher, two Eye-ringed Flatbills, Sulphur-rumped Flycatcher, Tawny-crowned and Lesser Greenlets, Black-and-white and Golden-crowned Warblers.

Leaving the park and traveling through Mennonite farmlands, we stop to look for Plain-breasted Ground-Doves and find a few that are noticeably smaller, quite plain, and singing a slightly different rendition of the song that Ruddy sings. . . A hawk springs airborne and I notice something odd about the tail. It flies like a Turkey Vulture, with characteristic high dihedral and rocking instability. I record all the details of our observation, because Zone-tailed Hawk is a very uncommon winter visitor to Belize.

Description: An area not often visited by birders, Spanish Lookout can offer so many good birds as to deserve an allotment of two or more days of birding time. More traditional Mennonites live in other parts of Belize, whereas the Spanish Lookout settlement uses mechanized technology. Surprisingly modern, the village of Spanish Lookout is the hub of a Mennonite farming area. If you ever are looking for a mechanical part in Belize, this is the place to get it. And they serve excellent ice cream at a nice shop midtown on the main street. Take advantage of village facilities, including bathrooms, before you venture out into the farmlands and to Aguacate Lagoon.

Birding strategy and directions: The main target is Aguacate Lagoon and the forest patch three miles beyond the lake. You need to drive through a lot of farmland to get there, so choose where to spend your birding time. Hawks and doves are active in the middle of the day, so you can find them in the farmlands whether coming or going. Fortunately, the deep-forest birds can be active midday as well. Study the travel log below for the best birding stops, and you may want to visit over a two-day period to take it all in.

Starting from San Ignacio, follow Price Highway heading east 4.6 miles from the steel Hawksworth Bridge. The turnoff to Spanish Lookout is also marked on the Price Highway log heading west at 49.0 (14.1). Reset your odometer to zero at the Price Highway intersection (N 17° 11.09' W 89° 0.43'). Head north, and at 1.2 curve right and then at 1.3 curve left. At 1.5 is the Baking Pot ferry (hand-crank car ferry). Warning! After very heavy rains the river is too high for the ferry to operate, so you will need to take the alternate route to Spanish Lookout (see page 130). While you wait to load your vehicles onto the ferry you may find good birding along the Belize River.

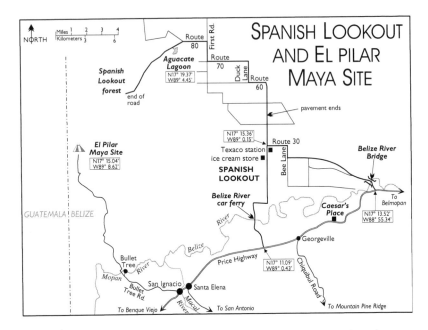

Birding is better after you cross the river. Look for grassquits and seedeaters, Painted Bunting, Bronzed Cowbird, and Belize-rare Crested Caracaras (see below for more details on the caracaras). At 2.3 turn right at a T-intersection, then left at an intersection at 2.9. Pull to the side to bird here briefly for parrots, pigeons, and grassland birds. Red-tailed Hawk has been found at this intersection. At 3.6 you will enter Spanish Lookout, and the road is hard-surfaced, with a commercial area lined with gas stations, farm stores, etc. Always worthwhile is the stop at 5.3 at Western Dairies (for ice cream). At 5.6 is a Texaco on the right (N 17° 15.36' W 89° 0.15').

Continue straight ahead at the T-intersection at 5.6 (Route 30 goes right). After the Shell gas station and store at 5.9 on the left, you will pass through farmland, now with road names and signs. At 6.5 there is a school on the left, and at 7.2 pavement ends. Continue through the crossroads. At 8.4 curve left onto Route 60, passing a road to the right. At 9.4 turn right at the T-intersection onto Duck Lane.

Look for Plain-breasted Ground-Doves on fence wires and posts. This species can be easily confused with Common Ground-Doves, which are not expected in Cayo District, and with female Ruddy Ground-Doves, which do occur here. The Plain-breasted is smaller and grayer, shorter tailed, and has less rufous in the wings in flight. It also has dark violet spots (as opposed to black spots and bars of Ruddy) on the wings, but that field mark is often difficult to discern.

At 10.2 pass a gravel pit on the left, and at 10.4 turn left on to Route 70. Pass a road on the right at 11.4; continue straight. At 12.4 turn right onto First Road, at 13.4 turn left onto Route 80, and at 14.6 curve left at the Y-intersection. At 14.9 you will see a wooden sign, "Aguacate Lake Established 1987." From the entrance sign to the lagoon is excellent birding. Like most tropical-forest birding, long lulls in activity can be followed by sessions of overwhelming bird movement. Patience is a virtue. Best birding is along the road, looking toward the creek and then the lagoon, but several trails lead uphill, offering other opportunities. Where the road borders the creek is the location described in the journal entry above. Also seen at this spot were Agami Heron and Bicolored Hawk.

At 15.1 take the short two-track to the lake, reaching a wood map sign at 15.4, a Y-intersection; take the two-track left to the lake, only a few hundred feet distant, and bird from the picnic area. You may be tempted to swim; but remember, crocodiles use the lake, too! For most visitors the trip ends with the lake. However, farmlands now extend for another mile-and-a-half, and excellent birding habitat exists in primary forest beyond, although you might need four-wheel drive to reach it.

At 15.5 is the end of the forest. A rough road continues southwest to secondary forest at 17.1. At 18.4 is primary forest, and at 18.7 you can park and bird along the road (N 17° 17.61' W 89° 6.51'). Another good spot for birding is farther along at 20.2.

The road dead-ends in another few tenths of a mile, but you are in good birding territory now, so start walking. This was once dense forest and now is selectively cleared of the biggest trees for timber, providing an advantage for peering through gaps in the canopy to see birds—such as Green Shrike-Vireo—that otherwise are hidden by the understory. Extensive changes, with major logging trails, may eliminate some species; yet a 2009 visit produced species such as Dot-winged Antwren, Yellow-bellied Tyrannulet, Rufous Piha, and the shrike-vireo.

On the return trip through the farmlands, search again for doves and hawks. When you reach the Texaco gas station at the edge of Spanish Lookout, consider taking the alternate route (described below), turning left instead of continuing straight ahead. In either case, you can try again to see Crested Caracaras if you missed them earlier. In 2007 and 2008 Crested Caracaras—very rare in Belize—were repeatedly being seen in the area of Central Farm, Running W Farm, and near Baking Pot ferry. In spring 2008 and 2009 the pair successfully nested in a Cohune Palm on Running W Farm near the ferry and sometimes could be observed from Price Highway at mile 48.8 on the log, very close to one turnoff for Spanish Lookout at mile 49.0 and not far from the alternative turnoff at mile 42.3.

Alternative route to Spanish Lookout. A bridge over the Belize River avoids the ferry crossing on the route described above. Start at mile 42.3 on the Price Highway log heading west and turn northwest (N 17° 13.52' W 88° 55.34'). Zero your odometer, and at 0.4 cross the bridge over the Belize River, a possible birding stop. At 4.7 turn right onto Bee Lane, at 5.3 bear left onto Route 30, and at 6.2 turn right at the T-intersection. The Texaco station is on the left; this corresponds to mile 5.6 on the other route. Use those directions to continue to the birding sites.

Key species of Spanish Lookout, Yalbac Hills, and Aguacate Lagoon: Great and Thicket Tinamous, Black-bellied Whistling-Duck, Pinnated Bittern [R], Bare-throated Tiger-Heron, Agami Heron, Hook-billed and White-tailed Kites, White Hawk, **White-tailed Hawk**, Red-tailed Hawk, **Crested Caracara**, American Kestrel, Purple Gallinule, Limpkin, Eurasian Collared-Dove, **Plain-breasted Ground-Dove**, Blue Ground-Dove, Mealy Parrot, Canivet's Emerald, **Purple-crowned Fairy**, **Slaty-tailed Trogon**, Rufous-tailed Jacamar, Chestnut-colored Woodpecker, Olivaceous Woodcreeper, Yellow-bellied Tyrannulet, Ochre-bellied Flycatcher, **Sepia-capped Flycatcher**, Eye-ringed Flatbill, **Rufous Mourner**, Scissor-tailed and Fork-tailed Flycatchers, Northern Schiffornis, Black-crowned Tityra, **Rufous Piha**, **Green Shrike-Vireo**, Gray-crowned Yellowthroat, Yellow-faced Grassquit, Eastern Meadowlark, Bronzed Cowbird.

Ecoregion and habitats: Appendix A, Ecoregion 6, Bravo Hills northern hardwood forests. Habitats include: the sprawling town of Spanish Lookout (PC), broad farmlands spanning rolling countryside (AG3, BFL3), with small isolated patches of primary lowland broadleaf forest (BFL5), a recreational lake (BFL2), and picnic area.
Location: N 17° 19.37' W 89° 4.45'; elevation 385 feet at Aguacate Lagoon. Spanish Lookout can be approached from four roads, two of which are too rough or remote to warrant description here. Of the remaining two, one is in the Belmopan direction and the other is closer to San Ignacio, although you might want to drive both for more birding opportunities.
Concerns: The main concern is that the local farmers will clear the forest lands for the excellent timber they contain and this wonderful birding spot will disappear. Refuel in Spanish Lookout and try not to get lost. After a while all the farm roads look the same, so if you make a wrong turn you may lose track of where you are.
Gas stations and Western Dairies are closed on Sundays. It would be best to schedule your visit during weekdays, as the lake is popular on weekends for picnickers and boaters. Roads are good until you pass Aguacate Lagoon; thereafter you may need a high-clearance vehicle.

San Ignacio Resort Hotel, Cahal Pech Maya site, and Branchmouth Park

Description: San Ignacio is the hub from which you can reach many birding sites on day trips. Sites within walking distance of the twin towns of San Ignacio and Santa Elena include Branchmouth Park (sometimes spelled as Branch Mouth Park) and Cahal Pech Maya site.

Advertised as "the only jungle in town" **San Ignacio Resort Hotel** is a complete service hotel, including a good restaurant. A surprisingly good birding site right inside a bustling town, a trail is easily accessed a few steps away from the hotel. For those not staying at the hotel, go to the front desk and ask to use the trail. There is no charge for this, but for a small fee you can also visit the iguana reserve at the end of the trail. The trail is well kept and includes self-guided signposts describing the medicinal plants and local animals. The bird list for the 17-acre site reportedly includes 175 species. Most are common species such as Plain Chachalaca, Gray Hawk, White-tipped Dove, Blue-crowned Motmot, and Collared Aracari. Look for Gray-necked Wood-Rail, Sungrebe, and Black Phoebe at the Macal River.

Cahal Pech Maya site is included here because of its easy access from San Ignacio Town. The Maya ruins are less than a mile walk from downtown and are adjacent to Cahal Pech Village Resort, described as "within a stone's throw." The site, dating to A.D. 400, is said to have been the home of an elite Maya family. The ruins are on a hill overlooking San Ignacio and consist of 34 structures abandoned by A.D 800. Typical birds seen at the Maya site are Plain Chachalaca, Ruddy Ground-Dove, Olive-throated Parakeet, White-fronted Parrot, Wedge-tailed Sabrewing, Blue-crowned Motmot, Collared Aracari, Lineated Woodpecker, Ivory-billed Woodcreeper, Masked Tityra, Yellow-green Vireo, Lesser Greenlet, and Wood Thrush. Interestingly, the first record in Belize for Chuck-will's-widow was a tower-killed bird at Cahal Pech 13 October 1991.

Also known as S.P.E.C.T.E. Green Iguana Park, **Branchmouth Park's** half-acre offers a pretty view of the confluence of the Macal and Mopan Rivers, where they form the Belize River. Secondary lowland broadleaf forest borders disturbed farmlands. A pair of Orange-breasted Falcons nests on private property at Santa Familia Sinkhole, about a mile from the park. Also on Branchmouth Road is Cosmos Camping and Cabanas, situated on 30 acres of land bordering the Macal River.

Location: N 17° 9.18' W 89° 4.08'. San Ignacio is about a 90-minute drive from Philip Goldson International Airport. If heading east, using the Price

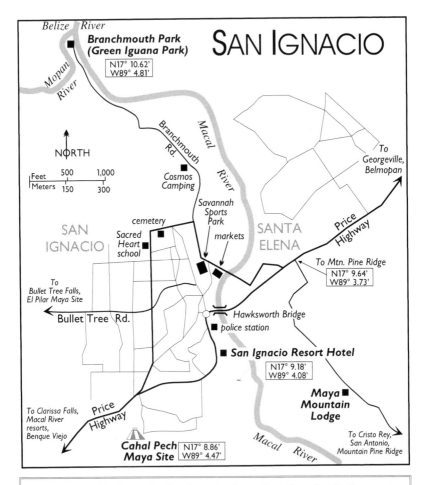

Ecoregion and habitats for San Ignacio: Appendix A, Ecoregion 10, Cayo western foothills. Habitats include: a few acres of disturbed lowland broadleaf forest (BFL3), dense, wet, lowland broadleaf forest (BFL1) downhill from the city (PC) to Macal River.
Contacts:
The San Ignacio Resort Hotel, P.O. Box 33, San Ignacio, Cayo District; (011) 501-824-2034/2125 or toll-free in US: 855-488-2624; fax (011) 501-824-2134; reservations@sanignaciobelize.com; www.sanignaciobelize.com.
Cahal Pech: US$5 for non-residents, BZ$5 for residents. Hours 8-5 daily. Institute of Archaeology, (011) 501-822-2107/2227; www.nichbelize.org/ia-maya-sites/ cahal-pech.html. Cahal Pech Village Resort, P.O. Box 1, San Ignacio, Cayo District; (011) 501-824-3740; fax (011) 501-824-2225; cahalpechresort@gmail.com or info@cahalpech.com; www.cahalpech.com.
Cosmos Camping and Cabanas, #15 Branchmouth Road, P.O. Box 117, San Ignacio, Cayo District; (011) 501-824-2116; cosmoscamping@btl.net; www.belizeexplorer.com/Cosmos-Camping-Cabanas.html.

Highway log, the hotel is at mile 8.7, i.e. 8.7 miles from the Guatemala border. If heading west, the directions are a bit more complicated. Just after crossing the Macal River, turn left at mile 53.7 on the Price Highway log and continue a block or two to the roundabout on the western side of the river. The large, steel Hawksworth Bridge is on your left, but don't go over it. Continue on Buena Vista Street up a steep hill, past the Town Hall and Police Station. Two-thirds of the way up the hill the fire station is on your left, followed by the parking lot for the hotel, 14 Buena Vista Street.

To reach Cahal Pech, start from the intersection of five roads at mile 55.0 heading west on the Price Highway log or 8.1 heading east, N 17° 9.05' W 89° 4.49'. Turn south, uphill on a road signed for Cahal Pech. Park near the top of the hill at the entrance to the museum (N 17° 8.86' W 89° 4.47'; elevation 545 feet).

Branchmouth Park is a 30-minute (1.3 mile) walk from downtown San Ignacio and therefore might be of interest to someone without a vehicle. The road can also be driven, although it is narrow and sometimes muddy in wet weather. The nature park is at the end of the road, which terminates in a parking lot under large fig trees. From there you can cross the Mopan River on a long, swinging footbridge leading to the San Jorge area. Just past a giant Guanacaste Tree, a farm driveway meets a town road that heads to Spanish Lookout (8 miles to the right) or back to San Ignacio (5 miles to the left). The park (N 17° 10.62' W 89° 4.81') is north of San Ignacio, accessed by a road branching from Price Highway at mile 53.9 on the log, heading west. Coming from the other direction, turn left at mile 8.1 and continue for 1.1 miles. This intersection is marked with a sign for S.P.E.C.T.E. Park and Cosmos Camping. Head north on the dirt road, passing Cosmos Camping on the left as well as a bit later on the right. The road dead-ends at the nature area, one mile from the Price Highway.

El Pilar Maya site

[17 February] At the edge of the ancient city, the sign proclaims, "Welcome to El Pilar — Occupation Period 250 BC–1000 AD." Plaza Copal stretches like a football stadium planted with tall trees, but cleared of the understory and carpeted in neatly clipped grass. The glory of the ancient city lies buried beneath the jungle; gray roots of giant trees ensnarl the limestone bricks like elephant trunks. Only the angular shape of the landscape reveals the secrets lying below: the flatness of the plaza, the paired slopes of a ball field, the tall squared peaks of a temple in a city whose occupation predates Tikal.

We hike into the Maya ruins and up crude stairs until we reach Alta Vista, a high point above a temple capped with even taller trees, but completely open on its western half. We are high above the tree canopy and our breathtaking view encompasses the skyline of broad jungles stretching to the hills of Guatemala. In fact, a buried causeway connects these temples to others submerged in Guatemala jungles. Sunlight pierces through the gray clouds, stirring the first *honeycreepers and tanagers to tree blossoms above us and in our canopy purview. We pick out a Green Honeycreeper; the rest are Red-legged. Dusky-capped Flycatchers call from many places today. Flocks of mostly green White-fronted Parrots wing across the green sea of treetops and Olive-throated Parakeets feed within closer view.*

Along the El Pilar Creek Water Trail, cleared of major debris, but narrow, leaf-strewn, and sometimes obscured by fallen trees and slipped vines, the trail is rigorously up and down. Partially hidden in the canopy, a half-dozen warbler species feed, but the late-morning heat has already quieted others.

Description: A 100-acre site protects Maya ruins which remain virtually the same as when they were discovered. Not fully investigated until 1993, the site includes 25 plazas and more than 70 major structures. It straddles the Belize/Guatemala border, and Tikal is only 30 miles west of El Pilar. Archaeologists excavated a tunnel beneath the grand stairway of the Winged Temple in Plaza Copal to bedrock and discovered an extensive construction history while passing through eight major plaza floors. El Pilar is listed as one of the 100 Most Endangered Sites by the World Monument Fund. Five trail systems, with lengths varying from 0.1 mile to 1.5 miles, offer extensive birding opportunities. Two are considered nature trails, as opposed to archae-ological, and extend to Chorro and El Pilar Creek. Local resorts, e.g., du-Plooy's, offer tours to El Pilar and consider it "one of the finest birdwatching sites in Western Belize." Facilities include a picnic area and pit toilets. An excellent article about El Pilar by archeologist D. Clark Wernecke, can be downloaded from www.belizefirst.com/bfjan/pilarhome.html.

Birding strategy: Flowering trees at the entrance gate attract hummingbirds. Bird both sides of the road to the parking area and pit toilets. From here, a nature trail on the left is completely arched by dense foliage, a treed tunnel opening on Plaza Copal. Use the ruins map to bird the area and head to Alta Vista for a topside canopy view. Outside the ruins runs a narrow road bordering dense dark snarls of twisted vines and branches where Slate-headed Tody-Flycatchers can be seen. A clear view to the sky can offer Hook-billed Kite and Black Hawk-Eagle, as well as flocks of Olive-throated Parakeets. Walking back to the parking lot, look for Tropical Gnatcatchers and Yellow-faced Grassquits. From the lot you can hike El Pilar Creek Water Trail, but leave some time to bird Bullet Tree Road on your return trip. Two-and-a-half miles south of the El Pilar Archaeological Reserve boundary a Keel-billed Motmot was found in a sinkhole in 1998 and three miles south of the boundary two Plain Wrens were found. At Bullet Tree Falls Boat-billed Heron, Gray-necked Wood-Rail, Vermiculated Screech-Owl, Amazon Kingfisher, and Yellow-green Vireo have been found.

Directions: Start from mile 54.6 heading west on the Price Highway log, N 17° 9.42' W 89° 4.43'. Alternatively, if you are using the log heading east, turn left at mile 8.1 and continue 0.4 mile to reach Bullet Tree Road. Zero

Ecoregion and habitats: Appendix A, Ecoregion 6, Bravo Hills northern hardwood forests. Habitats include: lowland broadleaf forest (BFL3, BFL5).

Concerns: Although a rare occurrence, tourists have been the target of thieves at this remote site. As a precaution, do not bring jewelry, valuables, and excess cash. Bird as a group. Park caretakers are at the entrance and military personnel may be present. If you are making a full day trip, bring water and lunch as no concessions are at or near the site.

Fees: Entrance US$10 non-residents, BZ$10 for non-residents. Ask for a map.

Location: N 17° 15.04' W 89° 8.62'; elevation 791 feet at parking lot. Located 10 miles northwest of San Ignacio on the Guatemala border, drive time from the city is about one hour on a narrow stony road that can be rough in spots, but free of mud.

your odometer at the start of Bullet Tree Road and head west, out of San Ignacio. You should see a sign "El Pilar 10 mi." Just outside of San Ignacio the road turns to dirt and you pass the last gas station on your left. As you approach Bullet Tree at 2.3 miles the road becomes hardtop again. Continue to a major fork in the road, with a bus shelter and community-center building in the middle. Veer left at this Y-intersection, cross the Mopan River, and then bend right. At 3.1 turn left onto Pilar Road, signed for El Pilar just as you are leaving Bullet Tree. At 7.3 you should find another sign "El Pilar 3 mi." The park boundary is at 9.3 and the gate where you pay the entrance fee is at 9.8. Continue to the parking area at 10.1.

Key species of El Pilar area: Little Tinamou, Crested Guan, Great Curassow, King Vulture, Hook-billed Kite, White Hawk, Black Hawk-Eagle, **Orange-breasted Falcon**, Mealy Parrot, Stripe-throated Hermit, Wedge-tailed Sabrewing, Canivet's Emerald, **Tody Motmot**, Blue-crowned Motmot, White-necked and White-whiskered Puffbirds, Dusky Antbird, Black-faced Antthrush, Buff-throated Foliage-gleaner, Plain Xenops, Olivaceous Woodcreeper, Northern Beardless-Tyrannulet, Ochre-bellied Flycatcher, Slate-headed Tody-Flycatcher, Sulphur-bellied Flycatcher [S], Tawny-crowned Greenlet, Green Jay, Band-backed Wren, **Plain Wren**, Golden-crowned Warbler, Yellow-faced Grassquit, Scrub Euphonia.

GEORGE PRICE HIGHWAY RESORTS

The highest concentration of resorts catering to birders is in the San Ignacio area of western Belize. All allow visitors to bird their grounds even if they are not staying at the resort (for details, see the section on birding for non-guests in Chapter 1, Where to Stay). The resorts can arrange round-trip transportation for guests from Philip Goldson International Airport and offer a variety of popular tour packages that include birding sites. This section describes the resorts along Price Highway just west of San Ignacio.

The **Log Cab-Inn Resort** is located on 25 acres of agricultural land, including citrus groves and grasslands. The resort grounds have lush ornamentals, vines, shrubs, and trees. The 100-acre **Windy Hill Resort** rests atop a hill with an impressive view of the heavily planted grounds and palm trees, a horse pasture, and the Mopan River. Trails include a U-shaped trail under a mile long, and longer trails, some along the river. The resort has access to the adjacent property with more hiking along the Mopan River. The gift shop offers a resort bird checklist with noteworthy sightings, although the Paltry Tyrannulet seems implausible. Several birding walks are offered, including morning and night walks.

Five generations of the Gálvez family have lived on 900-acre La Clarissa Ranch, which includes the **Clarissa Falls Resort**. Bordering the Mopan River and near a small waterfall, the resort offers more birding opportunities than others along this section of Price Highway, with a three- to five-hour hiking trail through jungles and one-hour hiking trails both directions along the river. Crested Caracara has been spotted on the trail to Calla Creek, as well as White-tailed Kite, Ferruginous Pygmy-Owl, and Northern Potoo. See the Macal River resorts area list for expected species. For visitors not staying at the resort, a minimal entrance fee of US$1 supports their Wildlife Sanctuary.

Ecoregion and habitats: Appendix A, Ecoregion 10, Cayo western foothills. Habitats include: broadleaf forest adjoining Macal and Mopan Rivers (BFF1), orange groves (AG4), supplemental plantings around resorts (PC).
Contacts:
Carla and Iris Mahmud, Log Cab-Inn Resort, Mile 68 Price Highway, San Ignacio, Cayo District; (011) 501-824-3367; fax (011) 501-824-2289; logcabins@btl.net; www.logcabinns-belize.com.
Bob and Lourdes Hales, Windy Hill Resort, Graceland Ranch, San Ignacio, Cayo District; (011) 501-824-2017 or toll-free in US: 800-946-3995; fax (011) 501-824-3080; windyhill@hughes.net; www.windyhillresort.com.
The Gálvez family, Clarissa Falls Resort, P.O. Box 44, Mile 70 Price Highway, San Ignacio, Cayo District; (011) 501-824-3916 or 625-6443 (fax is the same); clarifalls@btl.net; www.clarissafalls.com.
Locations: Heading west from San Ignacio, the entrance road for Log Cab-Inn Resort is at mile 55.9 on the Price Highway (N 17° 8.34' W 89° 5.09'). Windy Hill Resort is across the highway from Log Cab-Inn Resort. The entrance road to Clarissa Falls Resort is at mile 58.7 on the Price Highway log. After turning from the highway, continue through pastureland for 0.7 mile, turn left, and continue a few hundred feet farther to the parking lot, N 17° 6.67' W 89° 7.62'.

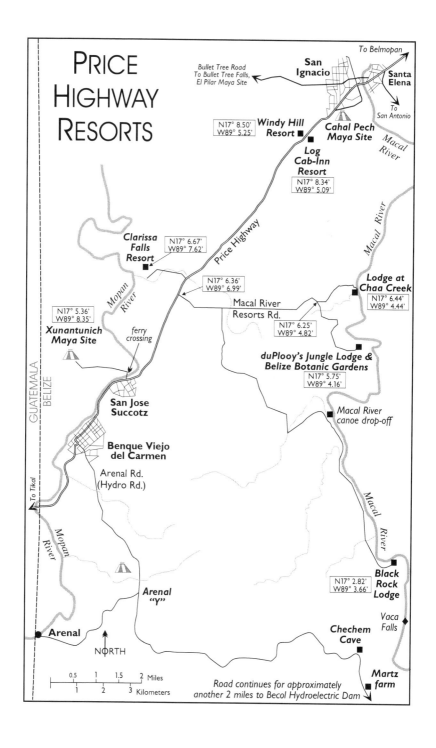

PRICE HIGHWAY RESORTS

To Belmopan

San Ignacio

Santa Elena

To San Antonio

Bullet Tree Road
To Bullet Tree Falls,
El Pilar Maya Site

N17° 8.50'
W89° 5.25' — Windy Hill Resort

Cahal Pech Maya Site

Macal River

Log Cab-Inn Resort
N17° 8.34'
W89° 5.09'

Price Highway

Macal River

Clarissa Falls Resort

N17° 6.67'
W89° 7.62'

N17° 6.36'
W89° 6.99'

Lodge at Chaa Creek
N17° 6.44'
W89° 4.44'

Macal River Resorts Rd.

N17° 5.36'
W89° 8.35'

Xunantunich Maya Site

Mopan River

ferry crossing

N17° 6.25'
W89° 4.82'

duPlooy's Jungle Lodge & Belize Botanic Gardens
N17° 5.75'
W89° 4.16'

San Jose Succotz

Macal River canoe drop-off

GUATEMALA

BELIZE

Benque Viejo del Carmen

Arenal Rd. (Hydro Rd.)

To Tikal

Mopan River

Macal River

N17° 2.82'
W89° 3.66'

Black Rock Lodge

Arenal "Y"

Vaca Falls

Arenal

NORTH

Chechem Cave

Martz farm

0.5   1   1.5   2 Miles
1   2   3 Kilometers

Road continues for approximately another 2 miles to Becol Hydroelectric Dam

MACAL RIVER RESORTS

Very popular as vacation retreats, these resorts offer excellent accommodations and many amenities in groomed subtropical environments. Each borders the Macal River in the foothills of the Maya Mountains and has hiking trails throughout their extensive land holdings. Although primarily intended for their guests, the resort properties are open to the public, as are their dining rooms. Each of the resorts can arrange canoeing trips on the Macal River, giving you another birding perspective. Also inquire about night birding with a local guide. Collectively, the resorts report a combined total of 349 species. These include all 4 tinamous, 6 kites, all 3 hawk-eagles, 7 owls, 15 hummingbirds, all 4 trogons, 8 woodpeckers, 7 woodcreepers, 6 antbirds, 46 flycatchers, 8 vireos, 8 swallows, 30 warblers, and 16 tanagers.

Key species of Macal River resorts area: Spotted Wood-Quail, Singing Quail, Least Grebe, King Vulture, Gray-headed and White-tailed Kites, Plumbeous Kite [S], White Hawk, Black Hawk-Eagle, Orange-breasted Falcon, Sungrebe, Striped Cuckoo, Pheasant Cuckoo, Barn Owl, Vermiculated Screech-Owl, Spectacled Owl, Black-and-white Owl, Yucatan Poorwill, Northern Potoo, Wedge-tailed Sabrewing, Black-crested Coquette [R], Canivet's Emerald, Tody Motmot, American Pygmy Kingfisher, White-whiskered Puffbird, Emerald Toucanet, Olivaceous Woodcreeper, Sepia-capped and White-throated Flycatchers, Black Phoebe, Streaked Flycatcher [S], Sulphur-bellied Flycatcher [S], Band-backed and Carolina Wrens, Rufous-capped Warbler, Crimson-collared Tanager, Yellow-faced Grassquit, Green-backed Sparrow, Blue Bunting.

Macal River Resorts Road

[15 February] My photos of Olive-throated Parakeets feeding in legume crops are ghostly pea soup: a concoction of bright greens, olives, and yellows stirred in the tendril wisps of gray fog. The cricket call of Yellow-faced Grassquits reaches our ears, but it is Blue-black Grassquits and White-collared Seedeaters we see mostly. Another mile, another half-hour, the fog lifts. A Bat Falcon perches on a lofty limb, and in the opposite direction two Collared Forest-Falcons call hauntingly. The last section of rocky road is steeply uphill, causing tires to spin in the loose gravel on the upside and brakes to pump on the downside. We reach the Belize Botanic Gardens, park, and walk.

Birding strategy: Don't be in a rush to reach the resorts, as the access road is great birding in itself. The wetlands and ponds offer Least Grebe, Gray-necked Wood-Rail, Common Gallinule, Killdeer, Northern Jacana, Solitary Sandpiper, Wilson's Snipe, and an assortment of egrets. In the fields you can find White-tailed Kite, White-fronted Parrot, Red-billed Pigeon, Groove-billed Ani, Vermilion and Fork-tailed Flycatchers, and Gray-crowned Yellowthroat. Scattered trees can yield Masked Tityra, Rose-throated Becard, Yellow-throated Vireo, Orchard Oriole, and Scrub Euphonia. As the roadsides change to the forest edge in the foothills, look for Plain Chachalaca, Plumbeous Kite, Roadside and Gray Hawks, Collared Forest-Falcon, and Bat Falcon. The first Cayo District record for Rose-throated Tanager, and the southernmost for Belize, was south of the road, just before the Y-intersection.

Directions: Drive west of San Ignacio on the Price Highway extension (called Benque Viejo Road) to a T-intersection marking the start of the gravel road to all three Macal River resorts. This intersection is only four miles from the Guatemala border and the same distance from San Ignacio. Drive time from San Ignacio to Chaa Creek and duPlooy's is 20–30 minutes and somewhat longer to Black Rock Lodge. The turnoff is at mile 59.0 on the Price Highway heading west, a T-intersection marked with signs for the resorts. Zero your odometer at the intersection, N 17° 6.36' W 89° 6.99'. Birding can be quite good along the entire road. At 0.8 mile the turnoff on the right heads to Black Rock Lodge. At 2.5 is a Y-intersection, N 17° 6.25' W 89° 4.82'. Left goes to The Lodge at Chaa Creek, while right heads to duPlooy's Jungle Lodge and the Belize Botanic Gardens.

> *Ecoregion and habitats for the road and the three resorts:* Appendix A, *Ecoregion 10, Cayo western foothills. Habitats include: agricultural lands (AG3, AG4) leading to lowland broadleaf forest and riparian forests bordering Macal River (BFF1); floral gardens at resorts (PC).*

Black Rock Lodge

[18 February] The road to Black Rock Lodge passes through spacious cow pastures and orange groves and then, as we enter dense secondary forest, it narrows to a single lane path with concrete supports for the wheels to keep from slipping down the steep embankment into the ravine. When our view opens again it is to a rock-faced canyon, the escarpment of Vaca Plateau, and a less steep forested hillside on our side of the rushing mountain stream, the Macal River. A pair of White Hawks circle above us, and later we see King Vultures and two Black Hawk-Eagles. On our walk to Vaca Falls, we see a pair of Rufous-capped Warblers, one carrying nesting material. Although I've observed these warblers high up in Mountain Pine Ridge, this pair is beyond the range map shown in Jones. We are three-fourths of the way to the falls when we learn that a flying Orange-breasted Falcon has been seen against the cliffs behind the lodge. Lunch is under an open-air A-frame with a dramatic view of the river and ravine.

Description: A private 250-acre jungle reserve in Black Rock Canyon, the lodge is surrounded by national parks and reserves. The entrance road passes through farms and citrus groves and then follows the Macal River higher into the foothills. The resort is down-mountain about 1,500 feet from the Vaca Plateau, described in the Maya Mountains section. Although the bird list for each Macal River resort is quite similar, Black Rock is the best place to find a resident pair of Orange-breasted Falcons, plus Spectacled Owl, Pheasant Cuckoo, Tody Motmot, and Rufous-capped Warbler.

Birding strategy: There are multiple places to bird, the best being the hike to Vaca Falls, the climb into the foothills, and around the ornamentally planted resort grounds. The comfortable deck at the open-air dining area is a convenient vantage point for studying the river and foothills of the Vaca Plateau and for searching for flying raptors and canopy species. One spot you might not think of visiting, but should, is the vegetable garbage dump where you can find Eye-ringed Flatbill, Stub-tailed Spadebill, and Yellow-billed Cacique. If you are staying at the resort, morning birding walks led by a local guide will help you find the key species. If you are visiting just for a day, ask for directions to where Pheasant Cuckoo has been heard recently. An evening visit, led by a guide, is the best chance of finding owls.

Contact: *Black Rock Lodge, P.O. Box 121, San Ignacio, Cayo District; (011) 501-834-4038 or 834-4039; blackrock@blackrocklodge.com; www.blackrocklodge.com.*

Location: *N 17° 2.82' W 89° 3.66'; elevation 410 feet at parking lot. At the T-intersection, mile 0.8 on Macal River Resorts Road, turn right. A sign marks the intersection. At mile 2.6 the road climbs to its highest point, 528 feet. At 4.4, after following a narrow path through the orchard, is the canoe launching point on Macal River. Cross a cattle guard at 4.8 and one mile farther the road becomes narrow one-lane with sharp drop-offs, water crossings, steep hills, and slippery spots. At 6.8 you will see the welcome sign for Black Rock Lodge and the parking lot is just ahead.*

The Lodge at Chaa Creek

Description: Offering thatched-roof cottages, family villas, a conference center for up to 100 people, and dining facilities, as well as numerous outdoor activities, the resort can easily please tourists for a week-long stay. The nature reserve features 7.5 miles of hiking trails and 6.5 miles of biking trails. Also on the 365-acre resort grounds is the Butterfly Farm, which provides an excellent presentation on the breeding and growth cycle of butterflies. For guests, the lodge offers a 6:30 AM nature walk led by staff naturalists Geovanni Guerra and Miguel Choco.

Birding Strategy: A morning walk through the immaculate grounds pleases birders, and the combination of open areas and remnant forest creates many edge areas popular with birds. Be sure to walk the trail beside the Macal River, passing through Giant Bamboo high enough to produce a canopy. Listen for Yellow-billed Caciques calling, and you could get a close-up look at this grackle-like bird with the straw-yellow bill. Crimson-collared Tanagers adopt this bamboo habitat as well. In the shadows of tall trees not far from the restaurant look for Blue-crowned Motmot and trogons. Here it is sometimes possible to see Black-headed and Gartered Trogons perched side-by-side. In trees just a few steps from the restaurant, Band-backed Wrens are active, especially in the morning.

Entrance fees: None, but contact the office upon arrival (or the day before if a large group) for permission to bird the grounds and ask about any restrictions, e.g., avoiding the lodging areas in early morning. Ask for their "Map and Bird List," a nicely produced map with trail numbers, showing the reserve and facilities. The Butterfly Farm entrance fee is US$5.50. You can also make reservations for lunch or dinner.

Contact: The Lodge at Chaa Creek, P.O. Box 53, San Ignacio, Cayo District; (011) 501-824-2037 or toll-free in US: 877-709-8708; fax (011) 501-824-2501 or toll-free in US: 800-861-1519; reservations@chaacreek.com; www.chaacreek.com.

Location: N 17° 6.44' W 89° 4.44' at parking lot. At the Y-intersection, mile 2.5 on Macal River Resorts Road, take the left fork. Climb the hill and enter the gate at 2.7. Then fork right toward the lodge; left goes to the Butterfly Reserve. The parking lot is at 3.0.

Belize Botanic Gardens and duPlooy's Jungle Lodge

[15 February] Through the delightful gardens, replete with hundreds of trees and shrubs all meticulously identified by label, we walk on the soft yellow-orange woodchip-strewn paths. At the pond darkened by overhanging trees, Blue-winged Teal feed in the shadowed shallows and a Least Grebe silently slips below the surface. A Gray-headed Dove calls softly from the trees beyond the pond. At the far end of the gardens, we climb single file up a steep trail into the rainforest, heading toward the fire tower. Briefly and repeatedly, birds pop into view and I struggle on the narrow path to let those behind me see the show, too. Fortunately, the parade moves along our column of observers, showing us Barred Antshrike, Yellow-olive Flycatcher, Lesser Greenlet, and Spot-breasted Wren feeding together in the understory.

From the tall fire tower we can see over the forest, extending from hillside through the valley to the distant horizon. We search for raptors, first seeing a large swift that transforms into a Bat Falcon on closer examination. . .We hike the Macal River trail and end up at the resort in time for lunch. While waiting for its preparation, we sit on the lofty deck overlooking forest dropping toward the river and are entertained by the close and repeated approach of a Rose-throated Becard, an exceedingly dark subspecies almost devoid of rosy throat.

Description: Like the other Macal River lodges, duPlooy's offers excellent facilities in a delightful setting. The small and intimate resort is surrounded by broadleaf forest. In addition, the property includes the Belize Botanic Gardens, including hundreds of native orchids, dozens of *heliconia*, and gingers.

Spectacled Owl   Bert Frenz

Birding strategy: Good birding starts along the entrance road. Near the highest point along the road is a good place to hear, if not see, the Yucatan subspecies of Carolina Wren, sometimes considered a separate species, the White-browed Wren. This high point is also a good spot to listen for owls after dark. Within duPlooy's, hiking trails cover a variety of habitats, including a hillside rainforest, canopy viewpoint, river walks, and floral gardens. In the botanic gardens the multitude of flowering plants attracts many birds. A pond in the gardens includes a blind for watching waterbirds. From the gardens a trail leads up into the rainforest, reaching a lofty lookout. Paralleling the Macal River, a jungle trail adds another habitat for bird finding and has the added attraction of a swinging footbridge across a small ravine. The trail includes one steep dip, but it is otherwise quite manageable. At one point the trail reaches a sandy beach along the river. Finally, a visit to duPlooy's would not be complete without the close-up birding opportunities afforded from the

Fees: *Entrance is US$5 plus tax for the botanic gardens, including access to the hiking trails. Detailed signs identify the plants and a 32-page booklet describes the Belize Botanic Gardens and some of its plants. The adjoining restaurant offers lunch and dinner, preferably by reservation.*

Contact: *Judy duPlooy, duPlooy's Jungle Lodge, P.O. Box 180, San Ignacio, Cayo District; (011) 501-824-3101 or in US: 512-707-1863; fax (011) 501-824-3301; info@duplooys.com www.duplooys.com.*

Location: *N 17° 5.75' W 89° 4.16' at parking lot. At the Y-intersection, mile 2.5 on Macal River Resorts Road, take the right fork. The gravel road climbs a steep hill and then descends. Belize Botanic Gardens are at 3.7, and the duPlooy's Lodge parking lot is at 4.0.*

wooden walkway and deck at canopy level in the restaurant and bar area. The river running 300 feet below the walkway can be seen through a thick jungle understory. Feeders lure the birds into excellent photographic position. Ridgway's Rough-winged Swallows nest in the river bank below the lodge.

Many activities are offered to guests of duPlooy's, and some of these are also available for other individuals and groups. Notably, a down-river canoeing trip from duPlooy's to San Ignacio or, starting from farther upriver, a trip back to duPlooy's can be arranged. In addition, a two-mile, two-hour, guided night-walk can be booked for Barn Owl, Vermiculated Screech-Owl, Mottled Owl, Ferruginous Pygmy-Owl, Black-and-white Owl, Northern Potoo, Kinkajou, and other nocturnal animals. Philip Mai is the local guide.

Xunantunich Maya Site

[20 February] It is said that the Maya built Xunantunich to protect access to the Belize River. We wait on the San Jose Succotz side of the Mopan River, a tributary of the Belize River, for the ferry to begin operation. A pair of Amazon Kingfishers meet on a branch overhanging the river and mate quickly. In a high bare-branched tree two parrots stop briefly and I notice the yellowish tail feathers as they land. I photograph the pair of White-fronted Parrots. At 7:30 the ferry operator motions to me to bring ahead my SUV. Down the steep embankment and onto the rickety planks I stop half-aboard to keep the ferry tilted toward shore and wait for Don's car to reach the lowered planks before moving to the other side of the ferry. Two vehicles and its passengers fill the ferry, so the operator turns the crank to move us across on the cable system. We then drive the mile to Xunantunich, pausing for a flock of Green Jays and several Keel-billed Toucans.

When we finally reach the flat main plaza of Xunantunich we are over 300 feet above the river, and rising another 130 feet—13 stories above us—is the monumental El Castillo temple. With a series of tall steps wrapping around all four sides of the tower, we cannot resist climbing to the top. Near the precipice, a 9-foot X 30-foot stucco frieze depicts Maya history between A.D. 800 and 900. The stonework is sharp and undamaged and quite realistic here atop the temple, adding grandeur to the place. (The original artifact was removed to a museum and we viewed a replica.) From the top, our unobstructed view extends to Guatemala in the west and Belize elsewhere, unbroken jungles but for the village nestled in the Belize River valley to the south and the thin line of a gravel road threading to the northwest. We walk through the forest surrounding the excavation and find others watching two Golden-crowned Warblers.

Description: Only a few miles from the Guatemala border, this impressive Maya site stands high above the surrounding jungle. A museum on the grounds features a three-dimensional model of the site and traces the history of Maya civilization. Most of the buildings date to A.D. 200–900, during the Maya Classic Era. This Maya site lies on the eastern part of the Petén district of Guatemala, which also includes Tikal. Xunantunich—variously pronounced as *shoo-NAHN-too-nich* or *zoo-nan-too-NICH* and originally split into two words Xunan Tunich, meaning stone woman—is certainly worth the visit as an historic site, but it also offers good birding in and under the tall canopy of surrounding forest and along the Mopan River. Facilities include a museum, modern toilets, gift shop, and a food concession.

Birding strategy: The ferry does not operate until 8 AM, but arriving early will give you time to bird along the river, and sometimes the ferry starts at 7:30. Here you may find Least Grebe, Neotropic Cormorant, Red-billed Pigeon, Amazon and American Pygmy Kingfishers, Black Phoebe, Yellow-throated Vireo, Mangrove Swallow, Louisiana Waterthrush, and Yellow Warbler.

After crossing, bird 0.7 mile along the entrance road until you reach the parking lot at the ruins headquarters. The entrance road is a particularly good place to find Green Jays, a species not nearly as easy to find in Belize as in Mexico. After parking, an uphill walk reaches the ruins in 0.3 mile. Birding at Xunantunich is in park-like open habitats with scattered trees and forest edge. Pheasant Cuckoo has been heard. Other good finds are: Hook-billed Kite, Black and Ornate Hawk-Eagles, Wedge-tailed Sabrewing, Canivet's Emerald, Collared Aracari, Olivaceous Woodcreeper, Royal Flycatcher, Green-backed Sparrow, and Scrub Euphonia.

Ecoregion and habitats: Appendix A, Ecoregion 10, Cayo western foothills. Habitats include lowland broadleaf forest (BFL3, BFF1). See also the species listed in the section for Macal River resorts, as that habitat is quite similar to Xunantunich.

Fees: Entrance US$10 for non-residents, BZ$10 for residents. Ferry is free.

Location: N 17° 5.36' W 89° 8.35', elevation 558 feet, at parking lot. Xunantunich is located about 6 miles southwest of San Ignacio and less than a mile from Benque Viejo on the Guatemala border. Start from mile 60.5 on the Price Highway log, N 17° 5.23' W 89° 7.74', where the Mopan River almost reaches the edge of the highway.

HYDRO ROAD AND ARENAL ROAD

[17 February] We are gradually climbing in elevation, now 275 feet higher than San Ignacio, on a well-maintained gravel road. Near the top of one rise a rail crosses the road in front of the car, perhaps 30 feet from us…Remarkably, the rail raises its wings as it scurries across—bright rufous wings set against a darker and grayer rufous back and crown—Uniform Crake! According to Lee Jones, Uniform Crake is an uncommon and rarely seen resident on the Belize mainland in the southern half. Our location is at the northern edge of the crake's range.

The road continues to climb and the habitat is dense secondary forest and perhaps primary forest at the hilltops. A profusion of pink flowering trees attracts a flock of Red-legged Honeycreepers, Canivet's Emerald, and a Ruby-throated Hummingbird. At 1,245 feet and after eleven miles of excellent habitat we come to a halt at a locked chain link fence with a guard posted at the entrance to the Becol Hydro Electric Power Generation plant and dam. Our mention of birds turns the guard to personal stories of hunting curassows, even though it is illegal in Belize. Birds are in profusion here, and as he talks we are interrupted by Black-faced Grosbeaks feeding on the tree branches in front of us.

Description: Not shown on most maps, this well-maintained road is known locally as Mollejon Dam Road, Hydro Road, or Arenal Road, a route that splits at a Y-intersection with the right leading to the border village of Arenal and the left leading to Mollejon Hydro Plant operated by Becol Hydro Electric Power Generation, about ten miles south of Benque Viejo del Carmen. As the road climbs in elevation, the heavily forested terrain is excellent bird habitat and is almost devoid of human habitation. The road is largely unknown to birders, so few reports have come from the area. Taking Hydro Road you will pass Chechem Ha, a cave discovered recently on the small farm of the Moralez family. Over 60 Maya jars, perhaps dating to 200 B.C., were found in the undisturbed cave occupied as early as 1300 B.C. to as late as A.D. 960. A hike to the cave entrance (admission US$20) passes the Macal River and Vaca Falls. Also on Hydro Road is Martz Farm, which offers hiking tours in the remote Vaca forest, as well as cabanas and tent camping.

Directions: Zero your odometer at the T-intersection at Price Highway in Benque Viejo and turn south on Arenal Road (Hydro Road). At 1.5 miles the elevation has climbed to 568 feet and you have a view of Guatemala to the right. An unexcavated Maya temple is visible on the right at 2.2. A Y-intersection is at 2.7. A right turn would lead to Arenal through citrus groves, papaya plantations, ravaged hillsides, and remnant secondary forest. The small village is another three miles and is on the Guatemala border. Better birding is likely in the other direction. Turn left at the "Y" and continue toward the dam and power plant. The Uniform Crake sighting described above was at 3.3 miles, elevation 616 feet. At 8.1 you will see a sign for Chechem Ha Cave and the elevation has climbed to 953 feet. Martz Farm is at 8.7, elevation 1,008 feet, and the highest point—1,251 feet—is at 10.6. The end of the public road is the guarded gate to Becol Hydro Electric Power Generation at 10.8. The dam is beyond the closed gate.

Key species of **Arenal Road and Hydro Road**: Thicket Tinamou, **Singing Quail**, White-tailed Kite, Black Hawk-Eagle, Barred Forest-

---

Ecoregion and habitats: Appendix A, Ecoregion 10, Cayo western foothills. Habitats include: lowland transitional broadleaf forest (BFL3) and citrus groves (AG4), rising to broadleaf forest foothills (BFF1) at elevations not often reached in Belize except at Mountain Pine Ridge. These foothills border Vaca Plateau, which is covered in Ecoregion 14 for southern submontane forests.

Contacts: *Antonio and William Moralez, Chechem Ha Cave; (011) 501-820-4063. Archeology report at www.famsi.org/reports/02086.*

Martz Farm Treehouses and Cabañas, P.O. Box 161, San Ignacio, Cayo District; (011) 501-501-834-4646 or 651-5953; info@martzfarm.com; www.martz-farm.com.

Falcon, **Uniform Crake** [R], Mealy Parrot, **Yucatan Poorwill**, Northern Potoo, Wedge-tailed Sabrewing, Canivet's Emerald, **Emerald Toucanet**, Rufous-breasted Spinetail, Dot-winged Antwren, Dusky Antbird, Black-faced Antthrush, Northern Schiffornis, **Carolina Wren**, Crimson-collared Tanager, Red-crowned Ant-Tanager, Black-faced and Blue-black Grosbeaks, Yellow-tailed Oriole, **Chestnut-headed Oropendola**.

TIKAL NATIONAL PARK, GUATEMALA

[27 January] We meet our guide Luis at 6:15 AM and head down the old airport runway, our main target being Pheasant Cuckoo. The first good bird of the morning, and rarely seen at Tikal, is Rose-throated Tanager. A few of us see it before it hides again. Such is the story of most birds we find this languid and darkly overcast morning. The birds sing and call profusely, yet they do not come out of hiding. A few dozen feet from the tanager, Chris hears a Gray-throated Chat, and again only a few get a glimpse. One that never comes out of hiding is Carolina (White-browed) Wren. Although it sings continuously, even the inducement of a recording will not get the wren to move from its hiding place more than 30 feet into the brush. So what happened to the Pheasant Cuckoo? Twice we hear a distant cuckoo—a "half-lifer" for me—but nothing better.

After a long midday break we resume birding at 4 PM, this time entering the Tikal ruins. Birding is much better this afternoon, with many highlights. I am delighted to get a good photo of an Eye-ringed Flatbill, not an easy bird to coax out of dark shadows. We make numerous attempts at seeing a Tody Motmot at Complex Q and again at Complex R, but have to settle for "heard-only." At Temple IV, Luis leads us to a Mottled Owl that he found a few weeks ago nesting nearby. On the opposite side of the temple, Luis finds us a Rufous Mourner.

We climb the steps up to the top of Temple IV. The sunset view is exquisite, highlighting the temples that protrude above the canopy. Brown Jays, Mealy Parrots, and Keel-billed Toucans wing above the canopy, and the best is an Orange-breasted Falcon in flight. As we descend the staircase and walk the trail, darkness is closing in and we can barely see the pair of Great Curassows that prowl a grassy edge of the forest. We hear a pair of Barred Forest-Falcons serenading nightfall and have the good fortune of seeing one of them. When we reach Acropolis Central we see one of the Orange-breasted Falcons fly to Temple I and disappear into a hole in the stonework. Now it is almost pitch black in the forest and we use our flashlights to navigate, finding spider monkeys, some scrabbling coatis, and a jumping spider. When we reach the cenote near the vendor booths, we hear the chorus of Bufo marinus and, with our lights, see two of the giant toads close up.

Description: Probably better known than any other birding site described in this book, especially among non-birders, Tikal National Park is a dream destination for anyone visiting Central America. Established in 1956, the national park is the first in all of Middle America and covers an area of 222 square miles, only a portion of which is the sprawling ancient city of Tikal abandoned over 1,000 years ago. Multiple pathways and trails crisscross the archaeological site under a tall canopy and often through dense understory, thus preserving excellent birding habitat and at the same time offering selective openings to see and photograph wildlife, which in addition to birds, includes easily seen Yucatan Black Howler, Central American Spider Monkey, White-nosed Coati, Gray Fox, Central American Agouti, Yucatan Squirrel, and White-tailed Deer, as well as more elusive mammals such as Northern Tamandua and the five cats.

Tikal reached its apogee in the Classic Period, although some monuments date to the 4th century B.C., and it is contemporary with Caracol in Belize, Copán in Honduras, and Palenque in Mexico. Most impressive at Tikal is the size and number of monuments among the thousands of structures spread over the 23 square miles of Maya residential area. Tikal is estimated to have supported 100,000–200,000 people, the largest population of any Classic Maya city. Key among the grandiose monuments are the tall step pyramids, Temples I–VI, built A.D. 695–766. At the heart of Tikal is the Great Plaza. Displaying beautiful examples of architecture topped by roof combs that tower above the canopy, Temple I (the Temple of the Giant Jaguar) faces Temple II (the Temple of the Masks). Spanning the south side of the Great Plaza is Central Acropolis, an immense structural complex almost 700 feet long and covering four acres.

Tikal National Park, Guatemala: View from Temple IV   Bert Frenz

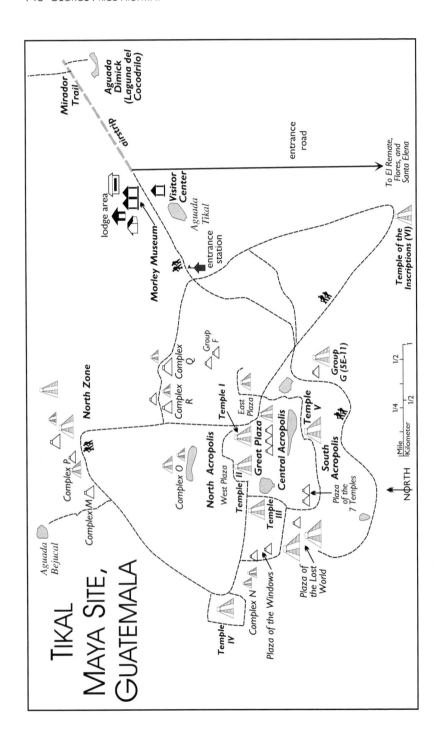

TIKAL
MAYA SITE,
GUATEMALA

Aguada
Bejucal

Complex M

Complex P

North Zone

Complex O

Complex R

Complex Q

Group F

Temple I

East Plaza

Temple II

West Plaza

North Acropolis

Great Plaza

Central Acropolis

Group G (5E-11)

Temple V

South Acropolis

Plaza of the 7 Temples

Temple III

Plaza of the Lost World

Complex N

Plaza of the Windows

Temple IV

NORTH

Mile
Kilometer

1/4   1/2   1

1/2   1

Temple of the Inscriptions (VI)

To El Remate, Flores, and Santa Elena

entrance road

entrance station

Aguada Tikal

Visitor Center

Morley Museum

lodge area

airstrip

Mirador Trail

Aguada Dimick (Laguna del Cocodrilo)

Temple IV, built in A.D. 741, is best known among birders as a viewpoint for watching canopy birds, sighting the resident pair of Orange-breasted Falcons, and excellent hawkwatching in general. Higher than any other building known in Pre-Columbian America and standing 212 feet from its base, Temple IV has newly constructed stairs that make the climb easier. From the top, one has a panoramic view across the dense rainforest and the tops of other distant temples poking above the canopy.

The Great Plaza is about a mile hike from the park entrance near Morley Museum; guidebooks and a colorful billboard map on the Tikal premises mark the leisurely walking time as 20 minutes. Birding pace is more typically one mile per hour. Since Tikal is so big, it is worthwhile to consider how much you can see in a day or part-day. Here are some sample times:

Leisurely pace	Birding pace	Route
10 min	30 min	Museum to Complex Q and R
20 min	60 min	Museum to Great Plaza
25 min	75 min	Museum to Temple of Inscriptions (VI)
15 min	45 min	Great Plaza to Temple IV
35 min	105 min	Complex R to Temple IV via North Zone
15 min	45 min	Great Plaza to Plaza of Seven Temples

In addition to the main walkways, dozens of trails meander throughout the park. Some, such as the well-marked Pisote Trail, are relatively close to the entrance. Although most tourists visit only the archaeological areas, birders definitely should explore the overgrown 1.5-mile airstrip and the trails that lead from it. The poorly drained bajos are low forest where the canopy is less than 50 feet and habitat supports bird species quite different from the tall forests surrounding the archaeological sites. Two types of forest are found here: the escobal forest dominated by palms and the tintal forest dominated by Logwood trees. Look for Ruddy Quail-Dove, Pheasant Cuckoo, Buff-bellied Hummingbird, Buff-throated Foliage-gleaner, Mangrove Vireo, Rose-throated Tanager, and Gray-throated Chat. Extending from the airstrip and main walking path are several trails. One trail is marked for the Mirador, a forest path that soon reaches a treehouse structure where you can climb steep wooden steps to a platform above the canopy. While youthful adventurers will not hesitate at the ascent, older folks may find risky the unlevel platform and unknown strength of the tree. The reward, however, is a view across Tikal and four temples rising above the continuous green canopy with, perhaps, a Gray-headed Kite perched at eye-level or Keel-billed Toucans feeding in the treetops.

Another trail leads a short distance to Aguada Dimick, marked by a sign warning "¡PELIGRO! COCODRILO." And, in fact, you are quite likely to find the Morelet's Crocodile in the pond. Look for American Pygmy Kingfisher as well. Open water is quite limited at Tikal, so also check out Aguada Tikal, which is next to the museum and shops. This is an easy spot to find relatively tame Gray-necked Wood-Rail, Limpkin, and Northern Jacana. Near the pond is a large tree where Montezuma Oropendolas nest; check for Giant Cowbirds inspecting the nests.

The open area around the hotels, restaurants, shops, and lawns is where the world's tamest Ocellated Turkeys parade. Look for parrots, woodpeckers, and orioles foraging in the trees. At night you can hear a Mottled Owl. Night birding can be excellent around the airstrip, a good place to see Yucatan Poorwill and, less frequently, Chuck-will's-widow.

In addition to birding within Tikal National Park, you can greatly expand your bird list by birding en route from Belize. The Guatemalan countryside is quite different from much of Belize. The rolling hills are similar to the Belize side near San Ignacio, but the forests have been cleared and only remnant secondary forest and wooded edges of fields are attractive for birding. If you cross the border in the morning, you may be ready for a lunch break at mile 13.2 (bring your own lunch as there is no place to buy it here). The spot is Vuelta Grande marsh, and standing beside the elevated road will give you a good viewpoint across the extensive wetlands. During one recent break, 32 species were seen, including six heron species, Limpkin, Northern Jacana, Common Tody-Flycatcher, Tropical Pewee, Bright-rumped Attila, House Wren, Blue-gray and Yellow-winged Tanagers, Black-cowled and Yellow-tailed Orioles, and Yellow-throated Euphonia. Just beyond Vuelta Grande, near San Luis, Crested Caracara was observed in 2010.

Another stop is in the village of El Remate, an artisan area along pretty Lago Petén Itzá. Lots of gift shops with local crafts will keep the shoppers happy, and birders can scan the lake for Brown Pelicans, Laughing Gulls, and Sandwich and Royal Terns—all surprises this far inland. At two to three miles wide and 16 miles long, this is the largest body of water in Petén.

Birding strategy: Although birders easily can explore Tikal on their own, a local birding guide might offer distinct advantages. A good guide should recognize the bird calls and help zero in on hard-to-see birds and is likely to know the current whereabouts of specialty birds. Many guides gather near the entrance to the archaeological sites and you will likely be solicited for their services. These guides are very knowledgeable of Maya history and archaeology and definitely add to the enjoyment of your visit. Many of the guides also know the most obvious birds, especially Keel-billed Toucans, and some of them can identify less obvious ones such as Bright-rumped Attila, but very few specialize in birding per se. One highly recommended guide, fluent in English and Spanish, knowledgeable in archaeology and birds, is Luis Oliveros

Figueroa, who lives on the outskirts of Tikal National Park at El Remate. In addition to morning visits inside the park that can combine birding and archaeology, Luis offers late afternoon and early evening visits when the park is closed except by special arrangement. Also, Luis can guide outside the ruins, typically the airport strip, in which case the daily entrance fee is not required.

The birding possibilities, the number of trails and overall area that can be covered, and the extensive bird list would suggest that a lengthy stay might be warranted. A day visit just doesn't leave enough time for birding. One overnight, starting from the Belize border in early morning would allow afternoon or evening birding along the airport strip, a morning visit of the archaeological sites while birding, and a return to Belize the same day. A two-night stay would give a fairly complete survey of the birding area, though the ruins are so majestic that most birders might wish to stay longer.

Concerns: Guatemalans are justly proud of this excellently preserved archaeological site surrounded by pristine rain forest, and the government rigorously protects tourists from threats that sometimes deter travelers to their country. Nonetheless, tourists visiting Tikal are a ripe opportunity for bandits who, typically, are armed and travel in groups. The bandits are interested only in your money and possessions; bodily harm is unlikely to occur if victims offer no defense. Incidents are infrequent, often separated by many years, and government military response is swift.

Dogs are not allowed in Tikal National Park. Lights are turned out at 9:30 PM; bring a flashlight. Food preparation in Guatemala is not as careful as it is in Belize. Drink only bottled water and beverages. Unless you are assured of preparation methods, avoid fresh fruits and raw vegetables that cannot be peeled, and anything that is not well cooked.

Fees and contacts: Daily entrance is US$20. This fee includes entrance to Sylvannus Morley Museum. To save money, upon arrival bird the airstrip and other areas outside the ruins gate until 4 PM and then purchase a ticket that will be good for late afternoon birding as well as for the next day.

An alternative to staying at the hotels inside Tikal National Park is to stay in El Remate, which is 15 minutes from the park entrance, with bus service readily available and starting early enough for sunrise birding at Tikal. A web search will bring up several alternatives. One owned by a former Floridian and his Guatemalan wife is often recommended: La Casa de Don David, El Remate, Flores, Petén, Guatemala; (011) 502-5306-2190 or 7928-8469; info@ lacasadedondavid.com; www.lacasadedondavid.com. The web site provides much area information as well.

Tikal National Park, 4 Avenida 21-43 Zona 14 2nd level, Guatemala City 01014, Guatemala; (011) 502-2367-2837 or 2366-5568 or toll-free in US 800-297-1880, ecoadventure@ tikalpark.com, www.tikalpark.com. This web site offers comprehensive information useful in planning a trip, including information about flying to Guatemala and ground transportation to/from Flores Airport. It also details ground transportation to/from Belize City and San Ignacio. At www. tikalpark.com/tikalhotels.htm, the Tikal web site provides up-to-date pricing and information on the three hotels within the National Park:

• Tikal Inn, tikalinn@tikalpark.com
• Jaguar Lodge, jaguarinn@tikalpark.com
• Jungle Lodge, junglelodge@tikalpark.com

As an alternative to making all of your own arrangements, many Belizean hotels and resorts, particularly those in the San Ignacio area, offer complete tour packages to Tikal. Most are one-day trips, but overnight trips also can be arranged. Use the contact information provided elsewhere in this book for the major hotels and resorts.

Described at www.tikalpark.com/birdingtour.htm are birding tours at Tikal, including prices. Arrangements must be made before arriving at Tikal. The web site does not mention the birding guide by name, but does offer an e-mail address for more information: ecoadventure@tikalpark.com. A recommended birding guide is Luis Oliveros Figueroa, El Remate, Flores, Petén, Guatemala; (011) 502-5581-2441; luistours_65@yahoo.com.

Location: In the Department of Petén, Guatemala, at N 17° 13.47' W 89° 36.72'; elevation 751 feet; 61 miles from the Belize border at Benque Viejo del Carmen.

Guatemala border crossing: If you are crossing the Belize/Guatemala border while traveling with an organized tour, your hosts will handle all the details. You will need your passport and cash for the Belize exit fees (US$39.25 in 2011) if these are not already included in your tour package.

An alternative is to drive your vehicle, park at the border, perhaps paying someone ~$10 to watch it. Then have a Guatemalan driver take you from the border to Tikal. The driver can also help with the border crossing and you can arrange for pickup at Tikal for the return.

If you are crossing the border in your own or a rental vehicle, the crossing is much more complicated. See the supplementary material at www.bafrenz.com for details.

Directions: From the Belize border the first 15 miles of road often are extremely rough and can become impassable in heavy rains. Yet in winter months all types of vehicles, including large trucks and motorhomes, navigate

White Hawk

Bert Frenz

Ecoregion and habitats: *Appendix A, Ecoregion 7, Tikal northern hardwood forests. Habitats include: lowland broadleaf forest, mostly high ridge (BFL5), but some swamp forest (BFL2) and broken ridge (BFL3) especially along the old airport runway. Supplemental plantings in the open areas of shops, restaurants, and hotels (PC). Sometimes referred to as a quasi-rainforest, rainfall is 40–95 inches, much drier than in equatorial rainforests. The porous underlying limestone limits the amount of permanent surface water, and only a few streams exist.*

this road. Thereafter the highway is paved and in good condition, as are most Guatemalan roads elsewhere in the country. The way to Tikal is well signed, with only one major turn.

Zero your odometer after passing the last border check and proceed downhill a few hundred feet to a bridge for which a toll will be collected (50 quetzales in 2008). You will immediately notice the poor condition of the road. Continue uphill to a Texaco station on the right at 0.3 mile. Fuel prices are less in Guatemala than in Belize, so you might want to refuel here.

Continue through a few villages, slowing for *tumolos*, called *topes* in Mexico, speed ramps in Belize, and speed bumps in the US. The poor road continues for 15 miles, often slick mud with broad water puddles, sometimes deep ruts, but usually wide enough for you to choose the best route through the mess. Continue straight at 7.5 miles, passing the turnoff to Mopan. Slow for *tumolos* at the military training facility at 10.3 and again for major *tumolos* at 12.8 when passing through a town.

At mile 13 is Vuelta Grande marsh (N 17° 0.36' W 89° 19.34'), a birding stop described above. You will be relieved to find paved highway beginning at 15, but keep your eyes peeled for potholes. Pass through Aldea La Maquna at 19.5; continue straight at turnoffs at miles 19.8 and 22.0.

At mile 40 veer right toward Tikal and Highway CA13 (N 16° 58.59' W 89° 41.11'). Just one mile farther you will see artisan stands beside the highway in El Remate. Stop here for birding along the shore of **Lago Petén Itzá** (N 16° 59.13' W 89° 41.52'). The border of Tikal National Park is at mile 51 from the border crossing, at a guarded gate. The entrance fee might be collected at this gate or it might be included in a package deal that includes lodging, guides, etc. The park is open every day from 6 AM to 6 PM. The speed limit of 25 mph along the lengthy entrance road is strictly enforced. Unusual yellow traffic signs mark the way, depicting regional animals such as Jaguar, anteater, crocodile, tapir, turkey, parrot, toucan, and monkey. At mile 61 the jungle opens up to the shops, hotels, and restaurants.

Key species of **Lago Petén Itzá**: Blue-winged Teal, Ring-necked Duck [R], Least Grebe, **Least Bittern**, Tricolored Heron, Lesser Yellow-headed Vulture, Osprey, White-tailed and Snail Kites, **Sora**, Purple Gallinule, Ruddy Crake, American Coot, Killdeer, Solitary and Least Sandpipers, Forster's Tern [R], **Royal Tern**, Sandwich Tern, White-winged Dove, **Striped Cuckoo**, Vermilion Flycatcher, Gray-collared Becard [R], Gray-crowned Yellowthroat, Blue-black Grassquit, Red-winged Blackbird, Yellow-billed Cacique, Tricolored Munia (non-native).

Key species of **Tikal National Park**: Great and Thicket Tinamous, **Crested Guan**, **Great Curassow**, **Ocellated Turkey**, King Vulture,

Gray-headed, Swallow-tailed [T], Double-toothed, Mississippi [R,T], and Plumbeous [T] Kites, White Hawk [R], Crested Eagle [R], Ornate and Black-and-white Hawk-Eagles, **Barred Forest-Falcon**, **Orange-breasted Falcon**, Limpkin, Northern Jacana, Scaled Pigeon, Gray-headed Dove, Ruddy Quail-Dove, Brown-hooded and Mealy Parrots, Black-and-white Owl, **Yucatan Poorwill**, **Chuck-will's-widow** [R], **Pheasant Cuckoo**, Lesser Swallow-tailed Swift, Scaly-breasted Hummingbird, **Wedge-tailed Sabrewing**, White-necked Jacobin, Black-crested Coquette [R], Canivet's Emerald, Buff-bellied Hummingbird, **Purple-crowned Fairy**, **Collared Trogon**, **Tody Motmot**, White-whiskered Puffbird, American Pygmy Kingfisher, Emerald Toucanet, **Chestnut-colored Woodpecker**, Russet Antshrike [R], **Plain Antvireo**, Black-faced Antthrush, **Scaly-throated Leaftosser**, Buff-throated Foliage-gleaner, Ruddy, Olivaceous, and Wedge-billed Woodcreepers, **Strong-billed Woodcreeper**, Northern Barred-Woodcreeper, Yellow-bellied Tyrannulet, **Sepia-capped Flycatcher**, Slate-headed Tody-Flycatcher, Eye-ringed Flatbill, **Royal** and **Ruddy-tailed Flycatchers**, Sulphur-rumped, Alder [T], and Willow [T] Flycatchers, Rufous Mourner, Yucatan, Streaked [S], and Piratic [S] Flycatchers, Black-crowned Tityra, Gray-collared Becard, Warbling Vireo [R], Tawny-crowned Greenlet, Northern Rough-winged Swallow, **Ridgway's Rough-winged Swallow**, **Carolina (White-browed) Wren**, White-bellied Wren, Swainson's and Golden-crowned Warblers, Gray-headed Tanager, Black-throated Shrike-Tanager, **Rose-throated Tanager**, **Gray-throated Chat**, **Blue Bunting**, **Giant Cowbird**.

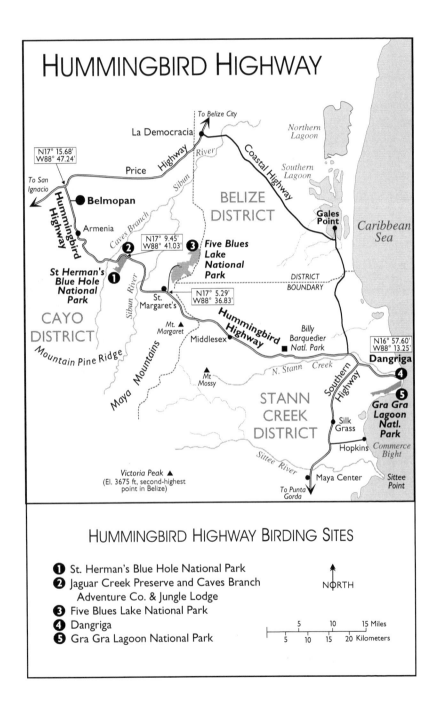

HUMMINGBIRD HIGHWAY

To Belize City

La Democracia

Northern Lagoon

N17° 15.68'
W88° 47.24'

Price Highway

River

Coastal Highway

Southern Lagoon

To San Ignacio

Hummingbird Highway

● Belmopan

Sibun

BELIZE DISTRICT

Caves Branch

Gales Point

Caribbean Sea

Armenia

N17° 9.45'
W88° 41.03'

❸ **Five Blues Lake National Park**

St Herman's Blue Hole National Park ❶

❷

Sibun River

St. Margaret's

N17° 5.29'
W88° 36.83'

DISTRICT BOUNDARY

CAYO DISTRICT

Mt. ▲ Margaret

Middlesex ●

Hummingbird Highway

Billy Barquedier ■ Natl. Park

N16° 57.60'
W88° 13.25'

Dangriga

Mountain Pine Ridge

Maya Mountains

▲ Mt Mossy

N. Stann Creek

Southern Highway

❹

❺

STANN CREEK DISTRICT

Silk ● Grass

Gra Gra Lagoon Natl. Park

Hopkins ●

Commerce Bight

Sittee River

Victoria Peak ▲
(El. 3675 ft, second-highest point in Belize)

● Maya Center

Sittee Point

To Punta Gorda

HUMMINGBIRD HIGHWAY BIRDING SITES

❶ St. Herman's Blue Hole National Park
❷ Jaguar Creek Preserve and Caves Branch
   Adventure Co. & Jungle Lodge
❸ Five Blues Lake National Park
❹ Dangriga
❺ Gra Gra Lagoon National Park

NORTH

5	10		15 Miles
5	10	15	20 Kilometers

CHAPTER 4
HUMMINGBIRD HIGHWAY

The evocative name of this highway is what first attracts your attention. No more likely to produce hummingbirds than other areas, perhaps it could have been called Beautiful Highway. Certainly it is the most scenic route in Belize and an exhilarating change from the monotonous agricultural lowlands and coastal pine savannas so prominent in the north. The smoothly paved highway snakes through the Maya Mountain foothills: steeply inclined, densely forested hills composed of ancient limestone—a karst landscape protruding from a flat plain. Below the surface lie limestone caves and subterranean streams that sometimes break to the surface to form swimming holes and lakes.

The bustle of Hummingbird Highway's intersection with Price Highway (mile 0.0 if you reset your trip odometer) increases as you soon pass a Texaco station on the outskirts of Belmopan, a city created from scratch in 1966–1970 after Hurricane *Hattie* flattened 75% of the former capital of Belize City in 1961. Fill your fuel tank here or at the Shell station a few blocks from the roundabout. A bureaucratic city lacking the charm of older villages, it provides an open-air market and a few inexpensive Belizean-fare restaurants, but little else to attract birders.

With the city left behind, the wild hill country is interrupted only briefly by such villages as Las Flores and Armenia, and their attendant speed bumps. The highway climbs to dramatic views of the jungle canopy dotted with palms, and it dips to clear shallow streams crossed by one-lane bridges, which year-by-year are being replaced by wider ones.

In the following travelogue **bold-faced locations** are described in greater detail in this chapter. From Belmopan to Dangriga, traffic moves at moderate speed, slowed by curves, hills, and one-way bridges. The bridge over Caves Branch at 11.3 could be a worthwhile stop for Mealy Parrot,

Yellow-bellied Tyrannulet, and Black Phoebe, and an opportunity to scan the skies for White Hawk.

At 12.4 miles is the first of two entrances—the second a mile farther—to **St. Herman's Blue Hole National Park**, the best birding site along Hummingbird Highway. Beyond the park, the lush, dense, and vibrantly green native vegetation intermixes with orange groves, especially in the flatter valleys.

At 23 miles, near St. Margaret's Village, is the gateway to **Five Blues Lake National Park**, an entrance road through orange groves that also become more common as you cross into Stann Creek District and continue southeast along the main highway. Trucks piled high with fresh oranges head toward the juice processing-plants at miles 25 and 40. Three-fourths of the farmers in Stann Creek District cultivate oranges, and the citrus industry is the second-largest agro-industry in Belize (sugar cane is the largest agroindustry), earning US$45 million (2007–2008) as an export crop, although agriculture pales in comparison to Belize's tourist industry (US$295 million in 2007).

On Cisco Wood's property, a bit over one mile southwest of Hummingbird Highway, stands 3,084-foot **Mt. Margaret**. For most good hikers it would be a two-day round-trip to the top, but an ambitious and energetic birder could be rewarded with Belize rarities such as Violet-crowned Wood-nymph, Tawny-throated Leaftosser, and Flame-colored Tanager. In Belize this is one of only three locations for the leaftosser and the only known location for the tanager. Peruse the key species list in the Mountain Pine Ridge section for other possibilities. An experienced mountain climber made the hike on 4 August 2008, using a local villager (Will Santos) as a guide. They started at Hummingbird Community (26.6) and ended at Over-the-top Camp (24.3), accomplishing the task in eight hours. At 32 miles is the village of Middlesex. Near here, on government land, many historical bird records

Road Log for Hummingbird Highway

Birding sites in **boldface**
Heading Southeast (Northwest)

0.0 (54.5) Intersection with Price Highway. **Guanacaste National Park**
0.8 (53.7) Texaco station on left.
1.4 (53.1) Roundabout. Belmopan on left. Continue straight.
1.6 (52.9) Village of Las Flores.
8.4 (46.1) Bridge and speed bump at village of Armenia.
11.3 (43.2) Bridge over Caves Branch River.
12.4 (42.1) Headquarters entrance to **Blue Hole National Park**
13.5 (41.0) Alternative entrance to Blue Hole National Park on right. **Jaguar Creek** and **Caves Branch** on left.
18.5 (36.0) Bridge over Sibun River.
19.6 (34.9) Bridge over Silver Creek.
22.6 (31.9) One-lane bridge. St. Margaret's Village on left.
23.1 (31.4) Access road to **Five Blues National Park** on left.
24.3 (30.2) Crossing from Cayo District into Stann Creek District at Over-the-Top Camp. To the south lies **Mt. Margaret**.
26.6 (27.9) One-lane bridge. Hummingbird Community follows.
31.9 (22.6) Speed bump in village of Middlesex.
33.7 (20.8) One-lane bridge. Valley Community follows.

Hummingbird Highway (continued)

34.8 (19.7) One-lane bridge with two more at 36.8 and 37.3.

37.5 (17.0) Entrance to Billy Barquedier National Park.

38.5 (16.0) One-lane bridge. Alternative entrance to Billy Barquedier.

38.7 (15.8) One-lane bridge. Alta Vista Village follows.

40.4 (14.1) Access road to Davis Falls on right, just past CPBL orange-juice factory.

40.5 (14.0) One-lane bridge.

42.4 (12.1) Pomona. Orange-juice factory on left. Tours can be arranged.

46.2 (8.3) ITVET campus. RV parking available.

*46.3 (8.2) Intersection with **Coastal Highway** on left.*

47.4 (7.1) Access road to Marie Sharp factory on left, followed by bridge.

48.6 (5.9) Esso station on right.

*48.9 (5.6) Intersection with **Southern Highway** on right.*

53.2 (1.3) Gulisi Garifuna Museum on right.

*53.3 (1.2) Speed bump entering **Dangriga**. Hospital on right.*

53.5 (1.0) Texaco station on right.

*54.2 (0.3) Street on left leads to **Dangriga Airport** and birding sites.*

*54.5 (0.0) Roundabout in Dangriga. Right leads to **Gra Gra Lagoon National Park**.*

were established, including those of Gray-breasted Crake, Black Rail, and Speckled Mourner.

Signposts at miles 37.5 and 38.5 point north toward 1,639-acre **Billy Barquedier National Park**, a work in progress. A 20-minute walk leads to waterfalls, and the quartzite hillside habitat is worth investigating if you have extra time to hike the difficult trails. A report (Miller and Miller 1994) detailing May and February surveys listed 151 species, most notably nesting Keel-billed Motmots. Other highlights are Great Curassow, Black-and-white Hawk-Eagle, Crested and Black-and-white Owls, Tody Motmot, Plain Antvireo, and Chestnut-headed Oropendola. Entrance fee is US$4. Contact is Hyacinth Ysaguirre, (011) 501-603-9936; hya172003@yahoo.com.

At 39 is Alta Vista Village, and between here and Pomona, House Sparrows were discovered in the mid-1990s. Now they can be found between here and mile 46 and then again in downtown Dangriga. Stop at the orange-juice factory at 42—you are likely to see the sparrows on the ground or near the factory buildings.

At 40, a signpost advertises Davis Falls. The dirt road is not for the faint-of-heart or those driving a low-clearance two-wheel-drive rental car. The road fords creeks a half-dozen times or more, some crossings over 100 feet long depending on water levels, though you won't sink in the rock-bottomed creek beds. Although this is a beautiful side trip, the habitat is all disturbed agricultural land and orange groves unless you can go far enough to get to higher elevation.

At 46 miles, on the right, is the modern campus of ITVET, the Institute for Technical, Vocational, and Educational Training. Common Pauraques forage here at dusk, hawking for insects attracted to the security lights and resting on the dirt road long enough to give you excellent looks. A hundred yards to the south, birding along North Stann Creek can be particularly productive.

Across the intersection from ITVET is the unpaved **Coastal Highway** leading to Gales Point and Price Highway. See pages 100–106 for birding and route information.

Just before the North Stann Creek bridge at 47 is a dirt road leading two miles north to the Marie Sharp factory, a locally-owned business offering a tasty cornucopia of spicy sauces and fruit preserves made from locally grown peppers and fruit. Factory tours can be arranged and birding in the adjacent orchards can be interesting.

Fuel, pay phone, snacks, and toilets are at the Esso Station at 49, followed by the hazardous intersection with **Southern Highway**, the route to fabulous birding sites described in the next chapter, many of which are easily reachable on day trips from Dangriga. At 53 a large outdoor sculpture marks the location of Gulisi Garifuna Museum.

Hummingbird Highway nearly reaches the Caribbean Sea, ending at a roundabout in **Dangriga**, mile 54.5. Turn left to go into town; a right turn leads to a fairly new and mostly undeveloped birding site, **Gra Gra Lagoon National Park**.

ST. HERMAN'S BLUE HOLE NATIONAL PARK

[2 March] Dense jungle grows over limestone mountains and an underground river. We see a part of this river where a karst cavern has collapsed to form a deep hole, the Blue Hole, and a 150-foot length of the river. Panning the horizon, we find a pair of distant Emerald Toucanets in the process of nest building. Hiking along the trail to the entrance to St. Herman's Cave, we alternate between concentrated sunlight beating down on us and intensely high humidity when the jungle wraps us in vibrant foliage. In the densest areas, the sounds of birds are everywhere but finding them is another matter. We glimpse Plain Xenops, Dot-winged Antwren, Dusky Antbird, and Cinnamon Becard, but only hear the calls of Slate-headed Tody-Flycatcher and Tawny-crowned Greenlet and the sweet song of Nightingale Wren.

Like peering through the glassed windows of a zoo-sized terrarium, we stand patiently in the narrow path, studying the dark jungle through a dense understory. Sometimes the jungle is so quiet the sound of footsteps and whispers of other birders seem overwhelming. Other times, the White-collared Manakins are firecrackers, jet planes, and bullets in the fast action of a computer game on steroids. I don't see the lek, but from the noise it must be somewhere near the intersection of the two paths at St. Herman's Cave. Sex is on the minds of birds today. While manakins are working at attracting mates, a pair of Blue-black Grosbeaks is breeding. I photograph nests of White-breasted Wood-Wren and Crimson-collared Tanager. At a stringy nest 20 feet above me, I can see an Eye-ringed Flatbill fly in, add a strand, and exit quickly. From the parking lot we get a broad view of the open sky. In the excitement of watching an immature Black Hawk-Eagle soaring low at the horizon, we almost overlook the White Hawk soaring in another patch of sky. But later we get an even better look at one perched 25 feet above us on an exposed branch.

Description: Were it transported 2,000 miles northward, St. Herman's Blue Hole would be a crown jewel in the US National Park system, rivaling the best in natural beauty and preservation of the environment. The park is signed and commonly known by its shortened name Blue Hole National Park. It gains fame from two easily visited geologic features: the deep blue cenote called the Blue Hole, an opening to a subterranean stream formed by collapsed karst, and St. Herman's Cave, a passageway through the limestone mountains that can be explored without a guide. Considered by many as one of the top three publicly accessible Belize birding sites, Blue Hole is not to be missed. With over 575 acres and five miles of trails there is plenty to explore at this national park.

Much of the park is easily accessible from the two parking lots. The east entrance includes a picnic area, toilets, and the start of three trails. One short walk leads sharply down 100 feet, following concrete steps with sturdy pipe

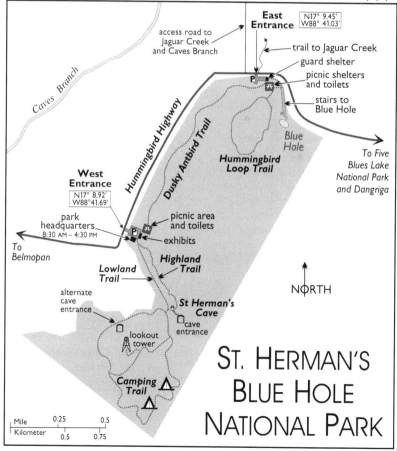

access road to
Jaguar Creek
and Caves Branch

East Entrance N17° 9.45' W88° 41.03'

trail to Jaguar Creek
guard shelter
picnic shelters and toilets
stairs to Blue Hole

Caves Branch

Hummingbird Highway

Dusky Antbird Trail

Blue Hole

Hummingbird Loop Trail

West Entrance N17° 8.92' W88°41.69'

park headquarters
8:30 AM – 4:30 PM

picnic area and toilets
exhibits

To Belmopan

To Five Blues Lake National Park and Dangriga

Lowland Trail

Highland Trail

↑ NORTH

alternate cave entrance

St Herman's Cave
cave entrance

lookout tower

Camping Trail △
△

| Mile | 0.25 | 0.5 |
| Kilometer | 0.5 | 0.75 |

ST. HERMAN'S
BLUE HOLE
NATIONAL PARK

railing to the Blue Hole. The steep and heavily vegetated sides of the hole—300 feet across—harbor many birds, noticed mostly by song. The closed-canopy picnic area, with its understory cleared, is excellent birding in early morning. From here you can take Hummingbird Loop Trail, sometimes fairly strenuous uphill hiking, or the flat Dusky Antbird Trail leading to the other parking lot. Both trails are most productive near their starts.

The west parking lot is at the main headquarters offices, which combine the fee desk, small gift store, and exhibits. Adjacent to this lot are a small picnic area, pit toilets, and the other end of the Dusky Antbird Trail. Leading from headquarters are Lowland and Highland Trails, which form a loop. Highland Trail is often steep, slippery when wet, and has fewer birds. Lowland Trail is flat and easy walking, though very sunny, hot, and humid when in unshaded areas. This trail borders orchards on one side and dense forests on the other, providing excellent edge habitat.

At St. Herman's Cave, Lowland Trail meets Highland Trail. The cave entrance can be accessed over a short steep rocky path. To the right, a loop trail heads uphill or, in the reverse direction, heads first along flatter areas. The uphill direction is steep and can be slippery. The lower direction is over tree roots and can be muddy, but is not otherwise difficult. Unless you are visiting multiple days or are immune to hot and humid conditions, you will not have time to explore the additional trails toward the lookout tower and camping trail.

Birding strategy: A birding guide who can identify birds by ear would be beneficial. The park manager, Israel Manzanero, is sometimes available for guiding, but he is often difficult to contact ahead of your arrival. Make next-day arrangements for a guide at the park office, open 8:30 AM–4:30 PM, or try to reach them by phone once you are in Belize (see next page).

At sunrise, start at an open area, e.g., the east parking lot, and study feeding birds on the fruiting trees just as sunlight warms the tops. You will also hear many birds calling, such as Little Tinamou and Black-faced Ant-thrush. Move into the picnic area beside the east parking lot, good for a dozen species such as White-whiskered Puffbird and Purple-crowned Fairy. Consistently, Red-throated Ant-Tanagers here are unusually tame and easily photographed close up. If you are the first visitor of the day to climb the stairs down to the Blue Hole, you might surprise a Rufous-tailed Jacamar or an Orange-billed Sparrow. Because the dense foliage makes seeing birds difficult, knowledge of bird songs will be invaluable, particularly for the local doves: Pale-vented, Scaled, Red-billed, and Short-billed Pigeons, White-tipped, Gray-headed, and Gray-chested Doves, Ruddy and Blue Ground Doves, and Ruddy Quail-Dove, all of which can be heard in a single morning. See Chapter 7 for help on identifying doves by call.

Dusky Antbird Trail is probably the easiest place in Belize to see Dusky Antbirds. You won't need to walk very far before you hear their calls and see them. Hummingbird Loop trail starts from the back of the picnic area and the first hundred yards of the uphill section might have a perched Tody Motmot. Farther along this steep trail you lose the edge habitat and birding slows dramatically. Instead, drive to the west parking lot and take the Lowland Trail to St. Herman's Cave. Birds are abundant here, attracted to the fruiting trees. Although often difficult to see, Slate-headed Tody-Flycatcher is almost always present in the dense underbrush near the beginning of the trail, and Cinnamon Becard sings from higher perches farther on. By mid-morning, several openings to the sky provide vantage points to scan for raptors, most noticeably King Vulture, hawk-eagles, and White Hawk.

As you approach St. Herman's Cave, the canopy closes above and you have better opportunities for Orange-billed Sparrow and elusive tyrant fly-catchers such as Northern Bentbill, Royal Flycatcher, and Eye-ringed Flatbill, particularly to the left of the cave and before the steep uphill Highland Trail. That trail eventually loops back to the headquarters, but it offers far fewer birds, so you will probably want to double back to the cave. An active White-collared Manakin lek is near the cave picnic area. Check out the cave entrance for Ridgway's Rough-winged Swallows, which nest in the cave and often perch conveniently for you to see the white loral spots and blackish-tipped undertail coverts. A Spectacled Owl has been observed perched above the cave entrance.

Ecoregion and habitats: Appendix A, Ecoregion 11, Cayo central lowlands and foothills. Habitats include: jungle-like humid broadleaf forest (BFF1) at the foothills of Maya Mountains.

Concerns: Arrive early (dawn) as the midday heat and humidity, even in winter, can be oppressive. You will be lucky if a cold front comes in, or else you probably will need to find a place in the shade to rest during midday while you wait for the late-afternoon pickup in activity. Otherwise, this will most likely be a half-day birding trip. Bring lunch and plenty of water. You will attract clouds of insects on most of the forest trails; the more-open trails (Lowland, Blue Hole) and the parking lots are less buggy. Trails are slippery when wet. Vehicle break-ins formerly were a problem before the parking lots were staffed; take extra care before the park managers arrive on duty at 8:30 AM.

Fees and contact: Entrance is US$4 for non-residents, BZ$2 for residents. The park is operated by Belize Audubon Society, 12 Fort Street, Belize City or P.O. Box 1001, Belize City; (011) 501-223-5004, (011) 501-223-4987, (011) 501-223-4988; fax (011) 501-223-4985; base@btl.net; www.belizeaudubon.org.

Location: West entrance – N 17° 8.92' W 88° 41.69'; 12.4 miles from Price Highway junction and 42.1 miles from the roundabout in Dangriga; park headquarters is here. East entrance – N 17° 9.45' W 88° 41.03'; 13.5 miles from Price Highway, 41.0 miles from Dangriga.

One of the most reliable sites in Belize to find Nightingale Wren is the uphill trail to the right of the cave. In early morning and at dusk its series of whistles of varying pitch can be heard emanating from the hillsides. The wren can also be heard calling from the slopes of the Blue Hole. Taking the trail in the opposite direction you will hear, and perhaps see, a few doves in the edge habitat.

Key species of St. Herman's Blue Hole National Park: [boldface = target species, R = rare, S = summer, T = transitory migrant] **Little Tinamou**, King Vulture, Swallow-tailed Kite [S], **White Hawk**, Black Hawk-Eagle, Barred Forest-Falcon, Orange-breasted Falcon [R], Short-billed Pigeon, Gray-chested Dove, Ruddy Quail-Dove, Brown-hooded Parrot, **Mealy Parrot**, Pheasant Cuckoo, **Spectacled Owl**, Black-and-white Owl, White-collared Swift, Stripe-throated Hermit, Wedge-tailed and Violet Sabrewings, **White-necked Jacobin**, Slaty-tailed Trogon, **Tody Motmot**, **White-whiskered Puffbird**, Rufous-tailed Jacamar, Emerald Toucanet, Black-cheeked Woodpecker, Great Antshrike, Dot-winged Antwren, **Dusky Antbird**, Black-faced Antthrush, **Scaly-throated Leaftosser**, Buff-throated Foliage-gleaner, **Olivaceous** and **Wedge-billed Woodcreepers**, Northern Barred-Woodcreeper, **Streak-headed Woodcreeper**, Yellow-bellied Tyrannulet, **Slate-headed Tody-Flycatcher**, Eye-ringed Flatbill, Stub-tailed Spadebill, **Royal Flycatcher**, Eastern Wood-Pewee [T], Willow Flycatcher [T], Rufous Mourner, Sulphur-bellied [S] and Piratic [S] Flycatchers, Northern Schiffornis, **Cinnamon Becard**, White-winged Becard, **White-collared Manakin**, Red-capped Manakin, Tawny-crowned Greenlet, Green Shrike-Vireo, **Green Jay**, **Ridgway's Rough-winged Swallow**, Band-backed Wren, **Nightingale Wren**, Gray-headed and Crimson-collared Tanagers, **Passerini's Tanager**, Golden-hooded Tanager, Green Honeycreeper, Buff-throated Saltator, Orange-billed Sparrow, Black-faced and Blue-black Grosbeaks, **Scrub Euphonia**.

Across Hummingbird Highway from Blue Hole National Park is **Jaguar Creek**, a private reserve protecting 712 acres of habitat similar to Blue Hole. Opposite Blue Hole's east parking lot you'll find a trail that leads northward to Jaguar Creek headquarters. The unpaved access road is also located across the highway, signed for Jaguar Creek as well as Caves Branch. Birding along this road—much easier walking than the ungroomed trail—can be good, especially at the adjacent wetlands and small ponds. The reserve includes frontage on Caves Branch River. It has private guest cottages, volunteer bunkhouses, a dining hall, and seminar/office complex. Jaguar Creek Ministries is an educational retreat center founded to serve children at risk. Although its primary use is for volunteer teams, guests are welcome and can book accommodations. Field trips, including overnight trips involving food and lodging, can be arranged for guests of Jaguar Creek. Between the national park and Sibun Forest Reserve (in the direction of Monkey Bay Wildlife Sanctuary) is Eden Conservancy, which protects an additional 1,200 acres.

Sharing the same entrance road is Ian Anderson's **Caves Branch Adventure Co. and Jungle Lodge**, with a range of accommodations. Even the rustic cabins with outdoor showers and kerosene lamps are nice. Birders can share the 58,000-acre Caves Branch Estate, birding along Caves Branch River and in the surrounding forest.

For the most part, the birds at Jaguar Creek and Caves Branch are the same as Blue Hole National Park. Good finds here include: Hook-billed Kite, Orange-breasted Falcon, Emerald Toucanet, Band-backed Wren, Mourning and Golden-cheeked Warblers, and Scarlet Tanager. Remarkably, a Brown

Black-cheeked Woodpecker   Bert Frenz

Violetear was photographed here 30 January 2010, a species usually found only at higher elevations. Caves Branch's terrain is different enough that Northern Harrier and Black Phoebe are found there.

> **Contact:** In Belize, **Jaguar Creek**, P.O. Box 446, Belmopan; (011) 501-820-2034; info@jaguarcreek.org; http://pathlight.org/jaguarcreek. In the US, Jaguar Creek Ministries, 3037-T Hopyard Rd., Pleasanton, CA 94588; 925-426-7284.
>
> **Caves Branch Adventure Co. and Jungle Lodge**, Mile 41-1/2 Hummingbird Hwy., P.O. Box 356, Belmopan; (011) 501-610-3451 or toll-free in US: (866) 357-2698; fax in US: 888-810-1333; info@cavesbranch.com; www.cavesbranch.com.

FIVE BLUES LAKE NATIONAL PARK

[2 March] We continue driving to Five Blues Lake National Park on a shake-rattle-and-roll road where top speed doesn't reach double digits. After parking at the entrance lot, we walk to the lake along a grassy path surrounded by tall jungle. White-collared and Red-capped Manakins sing and whistle from within its depths. At the lake we soak up the pretty scene of a paisley blue surface reflecting tree leaf patterns in the shadows, transitioning to a reed-choked shallow lake basking in the bright sunlight. In the distance I hear a Ruddy Crake trilling up and down scale.

Description: Five Blues Lake National Park derives its name from its lake, a 200-foot deep cenote of constantly changing colors. The cenote was formed by the collapse of an underground limestone cavern. In 2006 a hole opened in the bottom of the karstic lake, which drained almost completely within the next several weeks, a puzzling first for at least two generations of local residents and a bonanza for fish gatherers. In June 2007 the lake filled to above its previous water level and remained full thereafter.

This infrequently visited 4,000-acre park is accessed by a rough gravel-and-stone road running through St. Margaret's Village and extensive orange groves. A picnic shelter and outhouse are adjacent to the grassy parking area. The park's trail system (see this guide's map as well as a map on the wall of the picnic shelter) offers forest and lakeside options, as well as visits to small caves. Visitation—and funding!—is so limited that the trails might not be well groomed when you visit. A swim area, changing rooms, and a diving platform are located on Lake Trail beyond the canoe launch. Typically, a single canoe and crude board paddle are left unattended for anyone's use. The park can be used for secluded tent camping, thereby providing an excellent opportunity to see and hear Crested and Mottled Owls, Vermiculated Screech-Owl, and Northern Potoo.

Birding strategy: Some of the best birding is along the orchard road, where the orange trees as well as other fruiting trees attract a multitude of birds. You will want to stop repeatedly along the road and especially at those

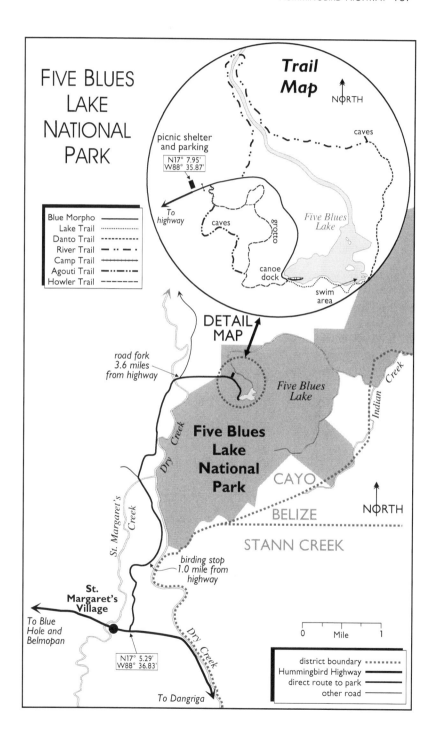

FIVE BLUES LAKE NATIONAL PARK

Trail Map

NORTH

picnic shelter and parking
N17° 7.95'
W88° 35.87'

caves

To highway

caves

grotto

Five Blues Lake

canoe dock

swim area

Blue Morpho
Lake Trail
Danto Trail
River Trail
Camp Trail
Agouti Trail
Howler Trail

DETAIL MAP

road fork
3.6 miles
from highway

Five Blues Lake

Indian Creek

Dry Creek

Five Blues Lake National Park

CAYO

BELIZE

NORTH

St. Margaret's Creek

STANN CREEK

birding stop
1.0 mile from
highway

St. Margaret's Village

To Blue Hole and Belmopan

N17° 5.29'
W88° 36.83'

Dry Creek

To Dangriga

0   Mile   1

district boundary
Hummingbird Highway
direct route to park
other road

spots where you can walk to the shallow Dry Creek through grassy wastelands that attract seedeaters.

At 4.4 miles from the highway you arrive at a grassy parking lot with picnic shelter and toilets. If you have been traveling at birding speed, however, those few miles might have taken you several hours. Walk past the gate and follow the road—impassable in a vehicle when wet—a quarter-mile or so to the canoe landing at the lake. In 2007 a pair of Lovely Cotingas was atop a dead tree near the lake entry point. A trail continues around the back of the lake to the swimming pier. A loop begins with Camp Trail, turns into Agouti Trail, and then loops back past the Grotto. This beautiful trail runs from the campsite at the picnic shelter through mature forest and limestone topo-graphy, including caves. You can also hike from Five Blues to Manatee Reserve, a three-day hike passing three or four cave systems.

Directions: The GPS reading at the access road's junction in St. Margaret's Village with Hummingbird Highway is N 17° 5.29' W 88° 36.83'. The 4.4-mile access road to the parking lot takes 25 bumpy minutes if you do not stop for birding. At 0.5 mile from the highway you will be reassured to see the sign "5 Blues 4 miles." A worthwhile birding stop is located at 1.0 mile near two short roads leading to Dry Creek. Turn left at the fork at 1.1 miles, pass another Five Blues sign at 3.0 miles, and cross a dry streambed at 3.5

Entrance road, Five Blues Lake National Park   Bert Frenz

miles. At 3.6 miles take the uphill road fork to the right; don't be fooled by the more-traveled road and its "Now entering National Park" sign on the left. This left road plunges into more citrus groves and can be impassable in wet weather, though it appears to be the better road when dry. Nonetheless, it does not lead to the lake and trails. This intersection (N 17° 7.91' W 88° 36.38') can be confusing. In less than a mile you reach the parking lot at the end of the drivable road. Five Blues Lake is a 15-minute walk past the gate.

Key species of **Five Blues Lake National Park**: King Vulture, White Hawk, Black Hawk-Eagle, Collared Forest-Falcon, Ruddy Crake, Short-billed Pigeon, Blue Ground-Dove, Brown-hooded Parrot, **Vermiculated Screech-Owl**, **Crested Owl** [R], Mottled Owl, Northern Potoo, Lesser Swallow-tailed Swift, Stripe-throated Hermit, **White-necked Jacobin**, Slaty-tailed Trogon, Tody Motmot, **Amazon Kingfisher**, White-whiskered Puffbird, Rufous-tailed Jacamar, Smoky-brown Woodpecker, Dot-winged Antwren, Dusky Antbird, Plain Xenops, Ruddy, Olivaceous, and Wedge-billed Woodcreepers, **Yellow-bellied Tyrannulet**, Sepia-capped Fly-catcher, Eye-ringed Flatbill, Royal Flycatcher, Black Phoebe, Fork-tailed Fly-catcher, Lovely Cotinga [R], Gray-crowned Yellowthroat, Black-throated Shrike-Tanager, Crimson-collared and Passerini's Tanagers, Grayish Saltator, Orange-billed and Green-backed Sparrows, Gray-throated Chat, Blue-black Grosbeak.

Ecoregion and habitats: Appendix A, Ecoregion 11, Cayo central lowlands and foothills. Habitats include: limestone karsts, cenote surrounded by broadleaf forest, steep limestone foothills (BFF1) of Maya Mountains, and an entrance road through orange groves (BFL3, AG4).

Concerns: The entrance road is tough going, but it can be navigated by an ordinary vehicle. Don't miss the turn at mile 3.6 (see above). Although vehicular break-ins have not been a problem in the past, the parking lot at the end of the road is remote and some people might be concerned about leaving valuables there while at the lake.

Fees and contacts: An unattended pay station is located in St. Margaret's Village, near the turnoff from Hummingbird Highway. Look for it and be sure to contribute your modest fee toward the park's upkeep and trail maintenance. The park was developed as a community initiative of St. Margaret's, managed by Friends of Five Blues Lake. A trail pamphlet is available for US$5. Mountain bikes and kayaks can be rented. If a guide is desired, try inquiring in the village.

Location: N 17° 7.95' W 88° 35.87' at parking lot and shelter. The access road is 23.1 miles from Price Highway and 31.4 miles (a 50-minute drive) from Dangriga.

DANGRIGA

[1 March] We head to the coastal mangroves north of Dangriga and just as we start our walk, I lose most of the group. Looking back, I see binoculars aimed at a tree and rejoining them I see they discovered a Prairie Warbler, considered "scarce on mainland" by Jones and the first I've seen in the country away from the cays. Continuing along the sandy coast, we hike past mangroves painted bright orange by lichen. Deep in the mangrove forest, skylight reflects off dark pools of brackish water forming mirror images that confuse the eye in separating reality from reflection. Out on the blue Caribbean, a mixed flock of pelicans, cormorants, and terns rests on a row of posts. We pick out a Caspian Tern and three Sandwich Terns among the many Royals.

Description: A coastal town of 11,000 residents, with lodging, restaurants, and supplies, Dangriga is a convenient location from which to explore a number of birding sites. Dangriga was formerly known as Stann Creek Town, where "Stann" referred to a safe haven or trading post for colonists coming from the Old World. Now most of the population is Garifuna, descendants of African slaves intermarried with Caribs of South America and arriving from Honduras in 1823. For Garifuna history and culture, visit the Gulisi Garifuna Museum (entrance US$5) at the western edge of town, next to the hospital. Just south of Dangriga, Gra Gra Lagoon National Park offers mangrove specialties not easily seen elsewhere in the country. Other popular sites for day trips, in order of increasing distance, include: Mayflower Bocawina National Park, Commerce Bight Forest Reserve, Sittee River and Hopkins, Cockscomb Basin Wildlife Sanctuary, Five Blues Lake National Park, and Red Bank. Local birding is described below.

Birding strategy: If you're staying in Dangriga and find yourself with time to spare, several places within walking distance may be worth exploring. Within the village itself, fruiting trees, the harbor, and canals can be productive for birds. It is also one of the few places you can add House Sparrow to your Belize list. Shorebirds found on the beach include Black-bellied and Semipalmated Plovers, Spotted Sandpiper, Greater Yellowlegs, Willet, Whimbrel, Ruddy Turnstone, Sanderling, and Western and Least Sandpipers. Dangriga is the only place where American Oystercatcher is seen regularly. Red Knot is another Belize rarity that has been found on the Dangriga beach. In 1990, the beached carcass of a Manx Shearwater was found, the only Belize record for this species.

The best birding is at and near the Pelican Beach Resort grounds where flowering trees and shrubs attract many species, including the occasional rarity such as Mangrove Cuckoo or Prairie Warbler. From there, walk north along the coastline looking for shorebirds. Eventually you'll reach a colorful contorted mangrove forest, after which point the vegetation may become impenetrable, but if you can forge ahead you'll likely see a variety of shorebirds and larids in the littoral zone. When you reach a narrow canal meeting the sea, you can turn inland toward an abandoned shrimp farm and Dangriga Airport. The path may be too overgrown to get through, but if you do make it, you'll find canals and impoundments gradually being choked with emergent vegetation that can harbor Black-bellied Whistling-Duck, Bare-throated Tiger-Heron, Sora, Northern Jacana, kingfishers, and sometimes Glossy Ibis. Keep an eye out for raptors, such as Osprey, White-tailed Kite, Common Black-Hawk, and Bat Falcon. A spotting scope is useful here.

Another local walk heads west along the road on the south side of Pelican Beach Resort , passes Dangriga Airport, and in a half-mile or so intersects a disused road that leads north beyond the airport runway to the same

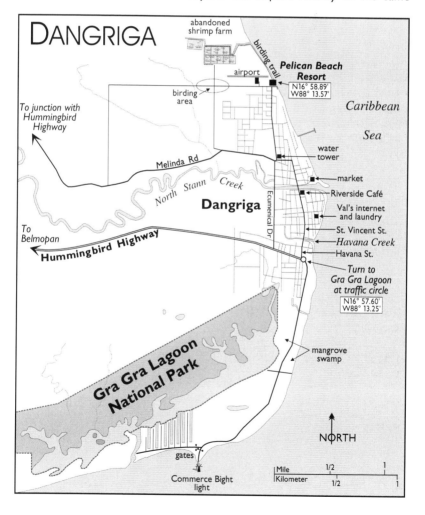

abandoned shrimp farm reached so laboriously from the sea (see map). The scrubby remnant of secondary forest at this junction and beyond can host a multitude of feeding birds. Over 30 species were tallied here once in an hour. Typical species are Yellow-bellied Elaenia, Dusky-capped and Boat-billed Flycatchers, Masked Tityra, Rose-throated Becard, Spot-breasted Wren, Northern Parula, Blue-gray Tanager, Blue-black Grassquit, Variable Seed-eater, Thick-billed Seed-Finch, Grayish Saltator, Rose-breasted Grosbeak, Melodious Blackbird, and Hooded Oriole.

Ecoregion and habitats: Appendix A, Ecoregion 9, Central coastal savannas, littoral forests, and Caribbean coast. Habitats include: Caribbean Sea, mangrove forest (LF3), canals, abandoned shrimp farm (AG5), and major population center (PC).

Concerns: Like all of the towns in Belize, Dangriga mills with people, a few of whom might appear to you to be untrustworthy because of drunken or drugged and solicitous behavior. Be on your guard and avoid taking unnecessary risks, particularly at night.

Facilities: Among the several restaurants, a favorite is Riverside Cafe with delicious Belizean food and lots of local color. A number of hotels in Dangriga offer clean, if unglamorous, accommodations. At the northern edge of town (see map) is Pelican Beach Resort, the most popular though most expensive place to stay, with gift shop, bar, restaurant, and an attractive beach-front setting. Local tours can be arranged through the resort. Outside of town and not within walking distance, you will find a wide variety of accommodations, the closest in Hopkins Village (accessed from Southern Highway), some of which are mentioned in that chapter.
Pelican Beach Resorts, P.O. Box 2, Dangriga; (011) 501-522-2044; fax (011) 501-522-2570; sales@pelicanbeachbelize.com; www.pelicanbeachbelize.com.

Location: N 16° 57.96' W 88° 13.33' in downtown Dangriga, a coastal town in Stann Creek District.

Directions: Dangriga can be reached by a 20-minute flight from Philip Goldson International Airport. By car, take Hummingbird Highway to its terminus at the sea. The easiest route to Dangriga Airport and Pelican Beach Resort is:

Mile

0.0 Roundabout at east end of Hummingbird Highway. Head west.

0.3 Turn right (north) onto Ecumenical Drive. Cross bridge over North Stann Creek.

1.7 T-intersection. Turn left for Dangriga Airport or right for Pelican Beach Resort.

An alternate route passes through town and the main business establishments:

Mile

0.0 Roundabout at east end of Hummingbird Highway. Right (south) heads to Gra Gra Lagoon National Park. Exit left (north) for Dangriga Town.

0.2 Havana Street to Pal's Hotel on right. Name changes to St. Victoria Street north of Havana Creek bridge.

0.4 Val's Internet (and laundry) one block away on right.

0.6 Riverside Cafe to right on south side of North Stann Creek. Cross bridge over Stann Creek; street becomes Commerce Street.

0.9 Curve left and then turn right so that water tower appears on the right.

1.0 Turn right at stop sign onto Ecumenical Drive. See Pelican Beach sign.

1.7 T-intersection. Turn left for Dangriga Airport or right for Pelican Beach Resort.

GRA GRA LAGOON NATIONAL PARK

[25 February] We head to the littoral zone near Dangriga where the mangroves are dense, but also support a high canopy of other trees. Appropriately, the first bird of the morning is a Mangrove Yellow Warbler and a bit later we hear the low-pitched call of the Mangrove Vireo. Judy finds a Sedge Wren—a rare bird—followed by a Plumbeous Kite and a Crane Hawk as well. Previously, we've not seen many shorebirds, but today at the mangrove swamp, the lagoon, and the seashore we find Black-bellied and Wilson's Plovers, Killdeer, Spotted and Solitary Sandpipers, Greater Yellowlegs, and Sanderling. Tom notices that the frigatebirds have gathered into an aerial mass. Intrigued, I count 81 frigatebirds in one group, with a half-dozen more stragglers in the opposite direction, all suspended in the uplifting air like kites on strings.

Description: This recently established 1,319-acre national park protects a remnant patch of mangroves surrounding a lagoon, an important nursery area for spiny lobster, brown shrimp, and fish. West Indian Manatees are seen along the estuary during mating season. In spite of its small size and limited accessibility, this site is worth coming back to more than once, as it protects species hard to find easily elsewhere. Its close proximity to Dangriga makes it convenient for travelers staying at the area's hotels and resorts.

Birding strategy: Be sure to check out all of the accessible area. Start with the sand flats and canals near the (unsigned) entrance, bird the wooded area from the road, and don't neglect the little roadside ditches, especially if they are water-filled. American Pygmy Kingfishers feel safe here behind a thick curtain of vegetation and often you can get close looks. Ten heron and egret species occur here regularly. Bird the crossroad in both directions— left to the Caribbean, right to the lagoon. Scanning the shoreline with a spotting scope could produce American Oystercatcher or even Collared Plover. Wetlands near the beach harbor Ruddy Crake and Sora. The short crossroad toward the lagoon borders wet habitat that attracts Solitary Sandpiper, Wilson's Snipe, and sometimes Rufous-necked Wood-Rail.

Continue down the main beach road. Turn right just before the first locked and guarded gate. You will come immediately to another gate that may be closed. Ask for permission to enter and continue birding along the vacant canal channels. Honk your car horn if necessary to get the attention of the guard. Sometimes on weekends or evenings a US$2.50 admission charge applies, mainly to local fishermen and it may be waived for birders. The road terminates at the sea and a wider canal where you can bird among the mangroves or view them across the canal. Mangrove Cuckoo and Mangrove Yellow Warbler occur here. In trees near the bay, Palm Warblers can be found, and Atlantic Bottlenose Dolphins frolic offshore. In 2009, gate attendant and 24-hour guard Danny mentioned that nightly he sees Barn Owls fishing and hears Vermiculated Screech-Owls calling.

Directions: Start at the roundabout at the end of Hummingbird Highway in Dangriga, mile 54.5 from Price Highway, N 16° 57.60' W 88° 13.25'. One year, but not the next year, a Gra Gra Lagoon sign at the circle pointed right (south) in the direction of the park. Zero your odometer at the traffic circle and continue south along the access road as it passes along a beach area and cleared forest land, presumably planned for resort development. At 0.7 you will notice the start of mangroves, the first good spot to look for Mangrove Yellow Warbler. At 1.0 the road to the right leads 0.1 mile to the lagoon. This is the main part of the national park. The road to the left leads 0.1 mile to the Caribbean. After checking out these areas, continue straight ahead and past a few houses, and at 2.1 the regular road ends at a locked gate. Don't enter this gate; instead turn right and drive 140 yards to the gate for Commerce Bight Development, probably unsigned. Ask for permission to enter and continue to 2.7, past seven water inlets, to the end of the road at a canal and the sea.

Key species of Dangriga and Gra Gra Lagoon National Park: Blue-winged Teal, Magnificent Frigatebird, Black-crowned Night-Heron, Lesser Yellow-headed Vulture, Osprey, Common Black-Hawk, American Kestrel, **Rufous-necked Wood-Rail**, **Sora**, Sungrebe, Limpkin, Black-bellied Plover, **Collared Plover** [R], Wilson's and Semipalmated Plovers, **American Oystercatcher**, Black-necked Stilt, Greater Yellowlegs, Willet, **Whimbrel**, **Long-billed Curlew** [R], Ruddy Turnstone, Red Knot [R], Sanderling, Western and Pectoral Sandpipers, Short-billed Dowitcher, Herring Gull, **Caspian Tern**, Common, Royal, and Sandwich Terns, **Black Skimmer**, Pomarine Jaeger [R], White-crowned Pigeon [R], **Mangrove Cuckoo**, Cinnamon Hummingbird, American Pygmy Kingfisher, Acadian [T] and Scissor-tailed Flycatchers, **Yucatan Vireo**, Prothonotary Warbler, **Mangrove Yellow Warbler**, Palm and Prairie [R] Warblers, House Sparrow.

American Pygmy Kingfisher

Bert Frenz

Ecoregion and habitats: Appendix A, Ecoregion 9, Central coastal savannas, littoral forests, and Caribbean coast. Habitats include: mangrove swamp, open beach, and lagoon (LF3).

Concerns: Bring bug repellent. As of 2009, the boundaries of the national park were not obvious, and good birding areas include adjacent private lands. An organizational structure is in development, and in time there may be an office, a method of paying admission, and a better definition of what areas are off-limits. Plans for offering canoe trips into the lagoon have also been discussed. Meanwhile, the coastal areas are continuously being cleared of native habitat and are perhaps destined to become seaside homes and resorts.

Location: N 16° 56.77' W 88° 13.49' where the crossroad meets the lagoon.

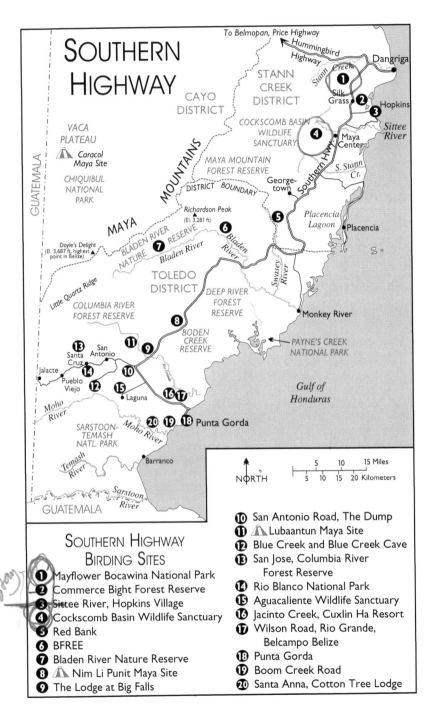

SOUTHERN HIGHWAY

To Belmopan, Price Highway

Hummingbird Highway

Dangriga

CAYO DISTRICT

STANN CREEK DISTRICT

Stann Creek

Silk Grass

1

2

3 Hopkins

Sittee River

VACA PLATEAU

△ Caracol Maya Site

CHIQUIBUL NATIONAL PARK

GUATEMALA

COCKSCOMB BASIN WILDLIFE SANCTUARY

4

Maya Center

S. Stann Cr.

MAYA MOUNTAIN FOREST RESERVE

Georgetown

DISTRICT BOUNDARY

MAYA MOUNTAINS

▲ Richardson Peak (El. 3,281 ft)

6

Bladen River

Bladen River

5

Placencia Lagoon

Placencia

Doyle's Delight (El. 3,687 ft, highest point in Belize) ▲

BLADEN RIVER NATURE RESERVE

7

Swasey River

Little Quartz Ridge

TOLEDO DISTRICT

COLUMBIA RIVER FOREST RESERVE

DEEP RIVER FOREST RESERVE

8

BODEN CREEK RESERVE

Monkey River

PAYNE'S CREEK NATIONAL PARK

13 Santa Cruz

San Antonio

11

9

14

Jalacte

Pueblo Viejo

10

12

15

Laguna

16 **17**

Gulf of Honduras

Moho River

SARSTOON-TEMASH NATL. PARK

Moho River

20 **19** **18** Punta Gorda

Temash River

Barranco

Sarstoon River

GUATEMALA

NORTH

	5	10	15 Miles
5	10	15	20 Kilometers

SOUTHERN HIGHWAY BIRDING SITES

1 Mayflower Bocawina National Park
2 Commerce Bight Forest Reserve
3 Sittee River, Hopkins Village
4 Cockscomb Basin Wildlife Sanctuary
5 Red Bank
6 BFREE
7 Bladen River Nature Reserve
8 △ Nim Li Punit Maya Site
9 The Lodge at Big Falls

10 San Antonio Road, The Dump
11 △ Lubaantun Maya Site
12 Blue Creek and Blue Creek Cave
13 San Jose, Columbia River Forest Reserve
14 Rio Blanco National Park
15 Aguacaliente Wildlife Sanctuary
16 Jacinto Creek, Cuxlin Ha Resort
17 Wilson Road, Rio Grande, Belcampo Belize
18 Punta Gorda
19 Boom Creek Road
20 Santa Anna, Cotton Tree Lodge

CHAPTER 5
SOUTHERN HIGHWAY

The coastal area of Stann Creek District, especially as it rises to the lush tropical foothills of the Maya Mountains, provides excellent birding. From the north, at least the first 35 miles of Southern Highway are easily reached as day trips from a base at Dangriga. If your intent is to drive the highway to its terminus in Punta Gorda, be sure you have enough fuel in your tank before leaving Dangriga, as there are no obvious stations for over 80 miles.

In the following travelogue **bold-faced locations** are described in greater detail subsequently in this chapter. Recently paved from Dangriga to Punta Gorda, straight and wide, Southern Highway is fast driving, with very little traffic. Watch out for speed bumps in the villages.

Zero your odometer at the Southern Highway intersection with Hummingbird Highway. The first birding site along Southern Highway is a brief 5.4 miles to an access road where Striped Cuckoo has been heard and seen. The species is more numerous than most birders recognize, yet because of its shy nature, your being acquainted with its distinctive two- to five-note whistle is the key to finding the bird. In the foothills to the west, **Mayflower Bocawina National Park** is a relative newcomer to birding sites, but it already boasts an impressive list of 262 species. Extensive citrus groves border the park's entrance road and most of the surrounding area along the first part of Southern Highway.

At 7.6 miles is the water tower and pedestrian ramp—a wide speed bump—of Silk Grass Village. Most of the villages for the next 20 miles have one or more of these well-marked ramps, forcing traffic to slow to a crawl. Just before the water tower is a dirt road leading to Commerce Bight Forest Reserve and the former establishment of Croc O'dile Isle, about two miles in the direction of the sea. Just south of the village you cross Freshwater Creek, which is the same creek running through Commerce Bight.

At mile 9.9 the access road to **Hopkins Village** forms part of a loop drive that can be good birding. The loop reaches the sea, then heads south to **Sittee River**, follows the river, and comes out again to Southern Highway. Hopkins has several appealing resorts that can be your home base for exploring this part of Belize.

The Sittee River crosses under the highway at 13.5 at Kendal Bridge, which was destroyed when the river overflowed during a severe 2008 tropical storm. If you have time, check out the bridge area for birds, or perhaps head to Sittee River Village and arrange a boat trip along the river.

Just beyond the village of Kendal is a road heading east and passing through farmlands. This is a reliable area to find Aplomado Falcon, which preys on Fork-tailed Flycatchers. Over 250 of these flycatchers were reported there on 2 February 2011, along with White-tailed Kite, White-tailed Hawk, American Kestrel, Aplomado and Peregrine Falcons.

A t 14.6 the Maya Center marks the entrance road to **Cockscomb Basin Wildlife Sanctuary**, arguably the premier Belize birding site. Local crafts are sold at the corner-lot building—toilets available as well—and this is the usual place to pay entrance fees.

Continuing south on Southern Highway, the roadside habitat returns to its more natural state of lowland pine/palmetto savanna. Just past the bridge over South Stann Creek is the turnoff at mile 21.9 for Placencia (alternatively spelled Placentia), a popular tourist site for beach-goers. Twenty-three

Road Log for Southern Highway

Birding sites in **boldface**
Heading South (North)

0.0 (94.9) Intersection with Hummingbird Highway.
5.4 (89.5) **Mayflower Bocawina National Park** on right.
7.6 (87.3) Entering Silk Grass Village. Access road to Commerce Bight Forest Reserve on left.
9.4 (85.5) Freshwater Creek bridge.
9.9 (85.0) Road to **Hopkins Village** on left.
12.1 (82.8) Road to Sittee River Village on left.
13.5 (81.4) Bridge over Sittee River, followed by speed bump entering Kendal.
14.6 (80.3) Maya Center on right.
14.7 (80.2) Entrance road to **Cockscomb Basin Wildlife Sanctuary** on right.
16.8 (78.1) Turnoff to All Pines on left (3 miles to shrimp pond).
21.9 (73.0) Turnoff to Placencia (23 miles).
22.3 (72.6) Santa Cruz water tower.
25.5 (69.4) Village of Santa Rosa.
26.7 (68.2) Village of San Roman.
28.4 (66.5) Access road to Georgetown and foothills on right.
31.4 (63.5) Access road to **Red Bank** on right.
37.8 (57.1) Border between Stann Creek District and Toledo District. Turn right toward Punta Gorda. Continuing straight takes you to Independence and Big Creek.
39.4 (55.5) Access road to Aqua Mar Shrimp Farm and Nova Toledo on left.
40.7 (54.2) Road to Monkey River and Monkey Bay Village on left.
43.3 (51.6) Bella Vista Village.
45.1 (49.8) Swasey River bridge.
52.3 (42.6) Bladen River bridge.

53.2 (41.7) Deep River Forest Reserve on left, continuing for about five miles.

55.8 (39.1) **BFREE Protected Area** and **Bladen River Nature Reserve.**

60.5 (34.4) Medina Bank and bridge over Deep River.

65.1 (29.8) Start of Golden Stream Corridor Preserve.

66.1 (29.8) Ya ax che'.

67.1 (27.8) Golden Stream bridge.

69.5 (25.4) Boden Creek bridge.

70.9 (24.0) Access road to **Nim Li Punit** *on right.* **Boden Creek Reserve** *on left.*

71.1 (23.8) Belize Lodge & Excursions on left. Indian Creek Village on both sides.

71.8 (23.1) Bridge.

75.6 (19.3) Alternate road to **Lubaantun Maya site** *on right.*

76.7 (18.2) Access road to **The Lodge at Big Falls** *on right.*

76.9 (18.0) Johnson's One Stop gas in Big Falls on right.

77.2 (17.7) Rio Grande bridge.

80.6 (14.3) Texaco station.

81.2 (13.7) Shell station on right, followed by T-intersection. Turn left. Right is **San Antonio Road.**

83.1 (11.8) Machaca Forest Reserve on right.

84.5 (10.4) Road to Laguna and **Aguacaliente Wildlife Sanctuary** *on right.*

87.0 (7.9) Road to **Santa Anna, Cotton Tree Lodge,** *Crique Sarco, Barranco, Sarstoon-Temash National Park, etc. on right.*

90.3 (4.6) Road to **Cuxlin Ha Resort** *on left. Eldridge at intersection.*

92.0 (2.9) Golden Motel on left.

92.2 (2.7) **Wilson Road** *to* **Belcampo Belize** *and* **Wilson Landing** *on left.*

93.8 (1.1) Soccer field on left. Curve sharply right. Village of **Cattle Landing.**

94.6 (0.3) **Joe Taylor Creek.**

94.8 (0.1) "Welcome to Punta Gorda" sign at Y-intersection.

miles from the turnoff, the site can offer a variety of coastal and open-habitat birds. A few birding tours visit Placencia, yet trip lists there typically involve common and widespread species. However, one rarity that turned up in July 2007 was a Wilson's Storm-Petrel, "dancing" at the surface of the water just beyond the surf, a first record for Belize. In December 2005 a Red-breasted Merganser was in Placencia Lagoon for three days. Rufous-necked Wood-Rail was found in December 2010 foraging at the edge of mangroves across the road from Turtle Inn. Other notables from the Placencia Peninsula are White-crowned Pigeon, Mangrove Cuckoo, Black-crested Coquette (recorded twice), Grassland Yellow-Finch, and a rather large concentration of Tropical Mockingbirds.

After passing through the villages of Santa Cruz, Santa Rosa, and San Roman, you find the turnoff to Georgetown at mile 28. The dirt access road passes through the village, then through citrus groves, and soon reaches the foothills. A Gray-breasted Crake was found here in August 2007. A few years ago this was a productive birding spot, but 2007 construction eliminated the best habitats. Perhaps, in time, it will revert back to its native state.

At 31 is the red sandy road to **Red Bank** and the foothills beyond, an excellent birding site best known for its flock of wintering Scarlet Macaws. You will need an early-morning start from the Dangriga area to reach Red Bank by sunrise to ensure your best chance of seeing the macaws as they fly between roosting sites and feeding sites. If you find them in a feeding area, they may remain active for two to three hours after sunrise.

It's a long way to the next birding site, so this usually marks the endpoint of day trips from Dangriga. At mile 38 is the turnoff for Independence and Big Creek, the latter a major shipping port for the country, particularly now that oil was discovered in Spanish Lookout and is transported daily by tanker trucks to this port. This intersection also marks the northern border of Toledo District. For the next 18 miles the landscape continues to be pine savanna, which soon becomes monotonous and is thus little visited by birders.

The turnoff for Monkey River, a coastal birding site, is at 41. Boat tours can be arranged through Ralph Zuniga, Monkey River EcoTours, (011) 501-720-2029, monkeyriverecotours@gmail.com; and through Clive Garbutt, Natural Adventure Tours, (011) 501-720-2028, sunsetinn@btl.net. Inquiries can also be made at monkeyriverguides@gmail.com.

At 43 is Bella Vista Village, a good rest stop where you can find food, drinks, and a toilet at the side-by-side stores left of the highway.

If your destination is BFREE (Belize Foundation for Research and Environmental Education), check your odometer here as it is easy to miss the turnoff at mile 55.8 on the road log below. Before the turnoff you pass the bridges over the Swasey River at 45.1 and over the Bladen River at 52.3. **BFREE** and **Bladen River Nature Reserve** are not places you can visit without prior arrangements. They offer some of the most secluded primary forests in the country. As you pass the reserve sign on the right and the lumber yard on the left, look toward the Maya Mountains. The tallest is 3,166-foot Richardson Peak, which lies just to the north of the reserve. Just before the turnoff to BFREE is a large meadow where Sedge Wrens and Grasshopper Sparrows are common—easy to find in spring when they are singing, but hard to find at other times of the year.

After passing Medina Bank the landscape transitions to lowland broadleaf forest, all of it second growth along the highway. You will see a few more villages now, populated with people living in plank houses with thatched roofs. Pass through Deep River Forest Reserve and then Golden Stream Corridor Preserve. This nine-mile stretch through the native community was finally paved in late 2009, completing the entire Southern Highway.

At about 71 miles you encounter the edge of foothills on the right and lush lowlands on the left. Here is the uphill road leading to **Nim Li Punit** Maya site, a worthwhile visit both for birds and archeology. Opposite the turnoff are **Boden Creek Reserve** and the site for Belize Lodge and Excursions.

At 76 is a marked turnoff for **Lubaantun**, another Maya site 6.7 miles distant. An easier route to the site starts from the Punta Gorda area. Next is the village of Big Falls, an odd name since there is no "big" falls here. Best known to birders for **The Lodge at Big Falls**, the turnoff is at 77, which also is the location of Coleman Cafe, a convenient lunch stop serving Belizean cuisine. In a few tenths of a mile you cross the **Rio Grande**, a river that features prominently in several birding sites.

At mile 81 you come to two gas stations, Texaco followed by Shell a half-mile farther, and these are your best opportunities to refuel for birding trips you will take from a Punta Gorda base. Shortly after passing the Texaco station the road climbs slightly and you have a broad view of the palm-tree studded forest pushing to the edge of the Gulf of Honduras, a scene reminiscent of Hawaii or Acapulco. The Shell station is at an important T-intersection when following directions to birding sites. The road to the right is referred to as **San Antonio Road** for want of a local name. Turn left for **Punta Gorda**.

About 0.2 mile after the T-intersection is a small round pond named Piedra Lagoon. In January 2010 the trees surrounding the pond held more than 300 Snowy Egrets and a Roseate Spoonbill.

Mile 84.5 marks the turnoff to the village of Laguna and adjacent **Aguacaliente Wildlife Sanctuary,** and 87 is the intersection with the road to **Santa Anna**, Barranco, and **Cotton Tree Lodge**. Barranco, Midway, Sunday Wood, Conejo, and Crique Sarco are on the outskirts of Sarstoon-Temash National Park, in which more than 200 bird species have been identified; entrance fee is US$5 and visits can be arranged through park rangers; call (011) 501-722-0103 or 722-0124 or inquire at Cotton Tree Lodge. More lodging is at 90 for **Cuxlin Ha Resort**, followed by Golden Motel and **Belcampo Belize**.

The soccer field at 94 lies in **Cattle Landing** and is the terminus of the designated Southern Highway. The road log continues farther, passing **Joe Taylor Creek**, an excellent kayak route for birding, and at 95 a large colorful sign welcomes you to **Punta Gorda**.

Key Species of Southern Highway coastal pine/palmetto savanna: Black-throated Bobwhite, White-tailed Hawk, Laughing, Aplomado, and Peregrine Falcons, Plain-breasted Ground-Dove, Yellow-headed Parrot, Striped Cuckoo, Acorn and Ladder-backed Woodpeckers, Fork-tailed Flycatcher, Sedge Wren, Gray-crowned Yellowthroat, Grace's Warbler, Rusty, Chipping, and Grasshopper Sparrows, Hepatic Tanager, Eastern Meadowlark, Yellow-backed Oriole.

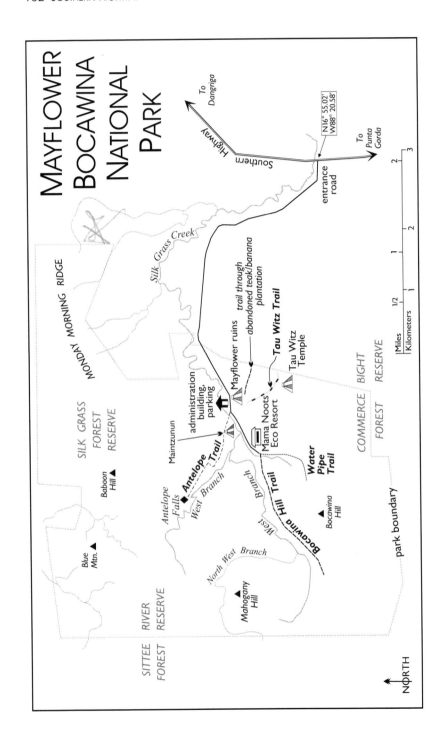

MAYFLOWER BOCAWINA NATIONAL PARK

[10 March] Lee is already at the edge of the Maya ruins when I park my car in the darkness. He tells me he has heard Spectacled and Black-and-white Owls. We walk quickly to the opposite side of the ruins and play a recording of Black-and-white Owl. Almost immediately an owl responds. A second owl calls from the tree just behind where we stand, and our high-intensity beams quickly find the bird. Having never seen one before, I'm surprised how big the owl is. Except for its ominously dark facial disks, it reminds me of a Barred Owl, and its deep bass voice resonates similarly as well.

A fruiting tree growing out of the ruins attracts two Violet Sabrewings. Soon we see a Stripe-throated Hummingbird and then three White-necked Jacobins in the same tree. And then the menagerie of hummingbirds includes a Green-breasted Mango. How impressive! We are distracted by a raucous flock of Brown Jays, clearly excited about something. We think "owl" and move to the base of a covered temple, looking up at the zone of riotous commotion. The jays seem to be circling a spot at the top. John sees the snake lying just at the edge of the temple top. It's a long Boa Constrictor seemingly climbing into a hole. It raises its head and looks back at those of us that climbed halfway up the ruins.

Description: Established in 2001, this national park preserves unexcavated Maya sites. Temple construction began before the 8th century and the site was occupied in the Post-Classic period of late 9th and early 10th centuries. The park has quickly gained a reputation for excellent birding. Although it is close to Cockscomb, its avifauna is surprisingly different. The park preserves 7,107 acres of wild forests, creeks, and waterfalls. Hiking trails run in multiple directions, some steeply uphill toward waterfalls. Along the entrance road is parking space beside the administration building, where you can pay your entrance fee, view exhibits, and use toilets. With permission of the warden, camping is allowed for a small fee.

Birding strategy: With many areas to bird, you will not have enough time in one day to visit all of them. If traveling the entrance road through the orchards at night, your vehicle lights could illuminate dozens of Common Pauraques. Schedule your arrival at the Mayflower Maya ruins site at or before 5:30 AM, at least a half-hour before first light. The area including the Maya site and nearby Mama Noots probably is the most reliable place in Belize to find Spectacled and Black-and-white Owls. Central American Pygmy-Owl is another species that favors the ruins area. If you miss the pre-dawn opportunity, come back after dinner, say 9 PM, and try again. Hiring a bird guide—inquire at Jaguar Reef Lodge (page 189)—who knows the most recent locations and recognizes the calls could prove advantageous.

After sunrise, stay at the **Mayflower Maya site**, only a small portion of which is cleared of its understory. Two tall pyramid-shaped mounds are buried beneath foliage. Easy walking, the open area is surrounded by tall fruiting trees that attract hummingbirds, toucans, and trogons. The

Mayflower area forms a cluster of eleven structures and two water reservoirs (aguadas). At the south end of the open area two trails start. On your right, the Tau Witz Trail leads toward Maya ruins of the same name. On the far left, the plantation trail passes among banana trees and subsequently a former teak plantation, providing a habitat different from most other places you are likely to visit; it could give you a rare opportunity of seeing, rather than only hearing, Little Tinamou and Black-faced Antthrush.

Across the entrance road from the Mayflower ruins is another open area with forest edge and Silk Grass Creek, a clear-running stream. Cinnamon Becard, Blue-black Grosbeak, and various tanagers and orioles favor this area. Prothonotary Warbler has been seen feeding along the creek edge, and Yellow-bellied Flycatcher often perches nearby at eye level.

Now decide how to spend the balance of the morning's birding. Choose between Antelope Trail and Bocawina Trail. Alternatively, walk or drive the entrance road toward Mama Noots Eco Resort, seeking fruiting trees. Carefully watching flowering trees can bring you 50+ species in a couple of hours.

A cross the footbridge behind the administration building is **Antelope Trail** leading into the forest and eventually to the falls. The first part is easy going, although it can be oppressively warm and humid as the day advances. Small openings to the sky and the canopy of fruiting vines and trees can reveal feeding hummingbirds and honeycreepers. All three species of honeycreepers—including Shining, which is very rare in the lowlands—have been seen on the same fruiting tree. Unobtrusive White-whiskered Puffbirds perch where, on your left, the forest transitions into a Cohune Palm plantation atop the Maintzunun Terrace Temple mound. The acropolis center rises 50 feet above Silk Grass Creek and is an active area for birds, including Cinnamon and White-winged Becards. Rose-throated also occurs here, and the rare Gray-collared has been seen as well, making it possible to see all four becards in a day. Another specialty of this trail is Slaty-tailed Trogon. Both Long-billed and Stripe-throated Hermits trap-line at flowers near the trail, and Violet Sabrewings can be heard, if not seen, in the dense forest. Orange-billed Sparrows also favor these denser areas. Learn to recognize their subtle call—like clicking your tongue on the roof of your mouth—or else you will pass dozens before you ever chance to see one. When the trail starts climbing, it is the first indicator of a much tougher hike ahead. Emerald Toucanet has been found here. Rainwater plunging down the once nicely constructed trail has eroded the way so severely that climbing is extremely strenuous, but the reward of a beautiful, cool waterfall at Antelope Falls may be worth the effort for some.

Gray-chested Dove   Bert Frenz

An easier hike to a waterfall is the **Bocawina Trail**. To reach the trailhead, continue on the entrance road, pass Mama Noots, and park in an open area just before the trail narrows at the end of the two-track road. Begin your hike here through a darkly forested area. This is another spot for Little Tinamou. Keel-billed Motmot has been heard and seen here on the uphill slope. Eventually the trail opens to a broad valley along a meandering creek and flanked by a good view of the steep foothills where soaring Swallow-tailed Kites and White Hawks might be seen. The edge habitat increases the bird count and gives you a chance to see canopy-feeding birds such as White-crowned Parrots, as well as offering grassy habitats for seedeaters and buntings. After the open area the forest again closes in and soon the trail climbs toward Bocawina Falls, but in this case the falls can be reached without undue effort. This tall broadleaf forest and cohune ridge can be particularly productive, especially if you have the patience to wait for the birds to come to you. Typical residents are Dot-winged Antwren, Sepia-capped Flycatcher, Rufous Mourner, Green Shrike-Vireo, Red-crowned Ant-Tanager, and Black-faced and Blue-black Grosbeaks. Stick to the trail, as Fer-de-lance occurs in the leaf litter of the undisturbed forest floor.

Key species of Mayflower Bocawina National Park: [boldface = target species, R = rare, S = summer, T = transitory migrant] Great Tinamou, **Little Tinamou**, Crested Guan, Gray-headed, Swallow-tailed [S], Double-toothed, and Plumbeous [S] Kites, Bicolored and White Hawks, Barred and Collared Forest-Falcons, Scaled and Short-billed Pigeons, Blue Ground-Dove, Gray-headed and Gray-chested Doves, Ruddy Quail-Dove, Brown-hooded Parrot, **Spectacled Owl**, **Central American Pygmy-Owl**, **Black-and-white Owl**, White-collared and Lesser Swallow-tailed Swifts, Long-billed and Stripe-throated Hermits, **Scaly-breasted Hummingbird**, **Violet Sabrewing**, White-necked Jacobin, Slaty-tailed and Collared Trogons, Tody Motmot, **Keel-billed Motmot**, White-whiskered Puffbird, Emerald Toucanet, Black-cheeked Woodpecker, Yellow-bellied Sapsucker, Dot-winged Antwren, **Dusky Antbird**, **Black-faced Antthrush**, **Buff-throated Foliage-gleaner**, Wedge-billed Woodcreeper, Yellow-bellied Tyrannulet, Northern Bentbill, Stub-tailed Spadebill, Sulphur-rumped Flycatcher, Bright-rumped Attila, Rufous Mourner, Sulphur-bellied [S] and Piratic [S] Flycatchers, Northern Schiffornis, **Cinnamon** and **White-winged Becards**, Gray-collared Becard, Tawny-crowned Greenlet, Green Shrike-Vireo, **Tropical Gnatcatcher**, Black-throated Shrike-Tanager, Crimson-collared and Golden-hooded Tanagers, Green and Shining [R] Honeycreepers, **Orange-billed Sparrow**.

Ecoregion and habitats: Appendix A, Ecoregion 12, Stann Creek eastern foothills. Habitats include: humid lowland broadleaf rainforest at the foothills of Maya Mountains (BFF2), former banana and teak plantation (AG4).

Concerns: The entrance road from Southern Highway to the Maya site and beyond can be very slippery after rains and it is difficult to stay on the muddy road. Bring insect repellent and plenty of water if you are hiking long distances.

Fees and contact: Entrance is US$5 for non-residents, BZ$2 for residents. The park is co-managed by local stakeholders, Friends of Mayflower, the Conservation Division of Forestry Department, and assisted by the Archaeology Department, P.O. Box 240, Dangriga, Stann Creek District; (011) 501-522-3641.

Mama Noots Eco Resort, Mayflower National Park, Stann Creek District, Belize, Central America; 813-784-0540 (from the US and Canada); reservations@mamanootsbelize.com

Location: N 16° 55.93' W 88° 23.00' at parking lot. The well-signed turnoff (N 16° 55.02' W 88° 20.58') from Southern Highway is 5.4 miles south of Hummingbird Highway. Continue west on the gravel entrance road through orange groves for 3.6 miles to the administrative building. Straight ahead another 0.4 mile is Mama Noots. Another 0.2 mile farther, the road ends at the start of Bocawina Trail.

HOPKINS VILLAGE AREA

Sittee River loop and Hopkins Village

[28 February] The upper part of Sittee River is edged by tall trees, attractive to many of the same species that inhabit Cockscomb. In fact, the river flows from Cockscomb Basin. Birding from a slow-moving boat is a comfortable way to see wildlife. Two Red-lored Parrots peek cutely from a hole in a dead palm tree, a beautiful blue honeycreeper dazzles us with its iridescent colors, and Keel-billed Toucans fly overhead. Other specialties today are Lesser Swallow-tailed Swift, Sulphur-rumped Flycatcher, and Passerini's Tanager. Equally fascinating are the many Green Iguanas sprawled across high tree limbs, Brown Iguana, Basilisk lizard, and the many flowering and fruiting trees that adorn the riverside.

[8 March] The road runs beside open marshland and I am tempted to stop and find out what birds prefer this habitat, but I'm anxious to reach the beachside Hopkins Village. At the sandy beach I find Black-bellied Plovers and Sanderlings. The sleepy native village has become the hub of many new resorts and seaside housing developments. New roads extend into the mangrove swamp and grand homes—the best I've seen in Belize—have stunning views of the Caribbean from their beach property. I continue on to Sittee River where we docked for several river cruises five and six years ago. Not much has changed here. I complete the 17-mile loop and am back on Southern Highway.

Description: This loop can provide a good list of new birds for the first-time visitor to Belize and is a likely route for those vacationing at Jaguar Reef Lodge or other Hopkins Village resorts and houses. The forest at the mouth of the Sittee River features Red, White, and Black Mangroves that are the tallest reported for the Caribbean region (see mile marker 7.4 below).

Birding strategy: A key species to seek is White-crowned Pigeon, as several recent sightings suggest there might be a breeding site in the Sittee River area. The road along the start of the loop is a good place to see Aplomado Falcon, Fork-tailed Flycatcher, Gray-crowned Yellowthroat, and Eastern Meadowlark. It passes through a natural sedge marsh and is excellent birding; rarely reported Pinnated Bittern, Black Rail, and Mangrove Cuckoo have been found here. The brushy habitat along the west edge of the marsh is good for Rufous-breasted Spinetail. Land trips can be done on your own or arranged through Jaguar Reef Lodge. The lodge offers the loop birding trip and includes a stop at Toucan Sittee, a small guest house on the Sittee River. They can also arrange Sittee River kayak trips. The charter speedboat service offered locally in earlier years is no longer in business and replacements pop up from time to time. Inquire locally or try the Internet for alternatives if you want to visit Sittee River by power boat. The marina is also one of the mainland points for boats heading to the cays. See, for example, Glover's Atoll Resort, www.glovers.com.bz.

Directions: From Southern Highway, the 17-mile loop begins at the turnoff for Hopkins Village.

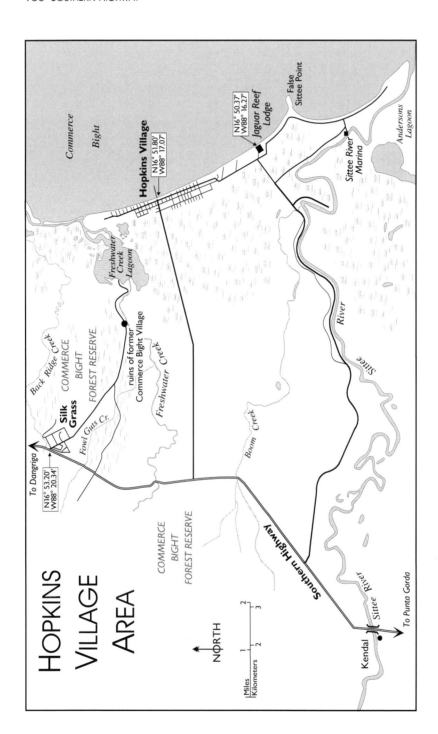

0.0 Turn east. Red gravel road passes through grassy wetlands.

4.1 Hopkins Village at Caribbean Sea. Turn right.

5.8 T-intersection. Continue straight, paralleling the coastline.

5.9 Belizean Dreams.

6.0 Jaguar Reef Lodge. N 16° 50.37' W 88° 16.27'.

7.4 T-intersection. Turn right, heading west. Straight ahead is Sittee Point, a gated community. The property extends through a mangrove forest at the mouth of the river.

7.5 Sittee River Marina on left. This is the launching point for boat trips. Turn right, heading north and northwest.

8.9 T-intersection. Turn left (southwest). Road follows Sittee River.

15.1 Southern Highway at sign for Sittee River Village. Another viewpoint for the Sittee River is from Kendal Bridge, 1.4 miles south (left) of this intersection. To complete the loop, turn right.

17.3 Back to start of loop.

> *Ecoregion and habitats:* Appendix A, Ecoregion 9, Central coastal savannas, littoral forests, and Caribbean coast. Habitats include: coastal marshes, sandy beaches, remnant mangrove forest (LF3), riparian along Sittee River (BFL1, BFL2, BFL3), houses and resorts (PC).
>
> *Contact:* Jaguar Reef Lodge; (011) 501-533-7040 or toll-free in US: 888-575-6778; fax (011) 501-523-7210; reservations@jaguar.com; www.jaguarreef.com.
>
> *Location:* N 16° 51.28' W 88° 20.76' at start of loop from Southern Highway, 9.9 miles south of Hummingbird Highway. Elevation drops to eight feet in Hopkins Village.

Key species of Sittee River and Hopkins Village area: **Pinnated Bittern**, Bare-throated Tiger-Heron, Lesser Yellow-headed and King Vultures, Osprey, Hook-billed, Swallow-tailed [T], White-tailed, and Plumbeous [S] Kites, Common and Great Black-Hawks, Short-tailed and White-tailed Hawks, Aplomado Falcon, Ruddy Crake, **Black** [R] and **Clapper Rails**, Sungrebe, Limpkin, Black-bellied Plover, Solitary Sandpiper, Sanderling, Pectoral Sandpiper [T], Caspian and Sandwich Terns, **White-crowned Pigeon**, White-winged Dove, Common Ground-Dove, Yellow-headed Parrot, **Mangrove Cuckoo** [R], Vermiculated Screech-Owl, Cinnamon Hummingbird, Amazon and American Pygmy Kingfishers, Collared Aracari, **Rufous-breasted Spinetail**, Fork-tailed Flycatcher, Gray-crowned Yellowthroat, Palm Warbler, **Mangrove Yellow Warbler**, Crimson-collared and Passerini's [S] Tanagers, Buff-throated Saltator, Variable Seedeater, Yellow-backed Oriole.

COCKSCOMB BASIN WILDLIFE SANCTUARY

[27 February] Cockscomb, named for the mountain range's resemblance to a rooster's comb, is unlike other areas we have visited so far: this 128,000-acre area is very nearly virgin jungle. Although the British removed trees here, the logging was selective for cedar and mahogany, the other tall trees were left standing, and in the intervening years the gaps have long since grown shut. Were it not for the paths cut through the jungle, it would be almost impenetrable. The variety of birds is most appealing. Almost every bird we see is different from any others we have seen earlier in the day; only a few appear in quantities greater than one to three. Even the road into the park offers many birds, and our bus stops frequently for us to get out and see Keel-billed Toucans, Barred Forest-Falcon, and a colony of Chestnut-headed Oropendolas building their three-foot-long oriole nests. We reach the visitor center and the small grassy area, positioned like a reverse oasis in the midst of thick jungle.

Our guides, Claude and Theodore, are excellent birders and their exuberance is contagious. Unlike other birding guides, when these two see a neat bird they whoop and holler, rush to the site, point enthusiastically, and continue to shout out the bird's identity. Rarely do all these antics scare away the birds. From our position in the small plot of lawn we jump from one species to another, rattling off Piratic Flycatcher, White-collared Manakin, and Passerini's and Golden-hooded Tanagers. Each bird is a splash of different colors, so dramatically bright that they seem unreal compared to the species of more temperate climates. We start our walk along one of the jungle paths and come to another clearing. Here we add Long-billed Hermit, Bananaquit, and Buff-throated Saltator. Along the trails we record Plumbeous Kite, Stripe-throated Hermit, Rufous-tailed Jacamar, and Smoky-brown Woodpecker. Other birds, largely unseen, are identified by song. Claude has cute phrases for some of them. The Short-billed Pigeon says, "Who cooked the food?" and the Pale-vented Pigeon chimes in with, "You cook good." During a lull in birds, Claude and Theodore tell us about the diverse plant life surrounding us. I notice the many pharmaceutical properties that the native Maya knew about these bushes and trees. Palm trees are abundant, but not the conventional kinds we see lining streets in Florida, Texas, and California. Most impressive is the Cohune Palm, typically without a trunk in juvenile years, with 30-foot fronds emitting from a grounded hub. It looks like a fern from the Jurassic Period.

Description: Cockscomb is a birding place that you can keep coming back to and always find new trails, birds, plants, and animals that you missed on previous visits. An impressive 337 bird species have been recorded at Cockscomb. Bird species are consistently found on certain trails and not on others, so it takes repeated visits to find most of them. For the birder not up to hiking, the ample open areas surrounding the headquarters and lodging can provide hours of entertainment and an impressive bird list.

The wildlife sanctuary has a fascinating history, largely told in Alan Rabinowitz's excellent book entitled *Jaguar*. In 1983, as a young zoologist he set about studying Jaguars in the wild, something that had not previously been undertaken. In the process he battled impossibly dense jungles, venomous snakes, obnoxious insects, drug traffickers, poachers, and a local mindset that saw the beautiful cats as a threatening menace and not a wonder of nature. He even survived a plane crash at a jungle site you can visit yet today. Rabinowitz succeeded in his scientific study and also in untangling bureaucratic red tape to establish *The Jaguar Preserve* as a protected sanctuary.

Most trails radiate from the headquarters hub, although a few less traveled trails branch from the park access road that starts at Maya Center on Southern Highway. The most productive trail is the first part of Victoria Peak Path and then branching left on River Overlook Trail and continuing on Wari Loop to tubing put-in (see map). Birded intensely, this route could easily take several hours. The second-best birding trail is River Path and, if time permits, the next best are Rubber Tree and Curassow Loop. Each of these trails is easy hiking, nicely groomed, and mostly shaded. A much more challenging trail is Ben's Bluff, which starts out at a comfortable incline, then becomes moderately steep to a waterfall, and eventually becomes taxing in the switchbacks climbing to the bluff itself, a gain of approximately 500 feet elevation. The reward is several species you are unlikely to find elsewhere on other trails in the preserve.

Trails that are less birdy, yet productive, include Wari Loop (beyond River Overlook), BYCC (Belize Youth Conservation Corps) Express, and Victoria Peak Path. The latter continues to the mountain peak, and unless you are a serious backpacker equipped with overnight camping gear you likely will explore only the first few miles. The Gibnut and Green Knowledge trails have less to offer the birder and typically involve more hiking and less birding. Because they are less traveled though they sometimes harbor the shy birds you could have missed earlier.

Birding strategy: You can buy a map at the office, look at a large billboard map posted outside, or use the one included here. In addition, trails are well marked with names and arrows.

The best strategy depends on how much time you have available to explore Cockscomb. Many less-intense birders find the heat and humidity limit their birding interest to half-days. Others, during midday, are willing to continue birding at a slower pace or take a break and then resume in mid-afternoon as it cools and birding activity increases. The following strategy divides the effort into several days or half-days, starting with the most productive routes and continuing with other suggestions to fill in the gaps.

On your first day, forego the many birding temptations along the nearly six-mile entrance road. Instead, start birding shortly after dawn at the open areas around the sanctuary headquarters. The birding becomes particularly good as the rising sun illuminates the treetops. Listen for Piratic

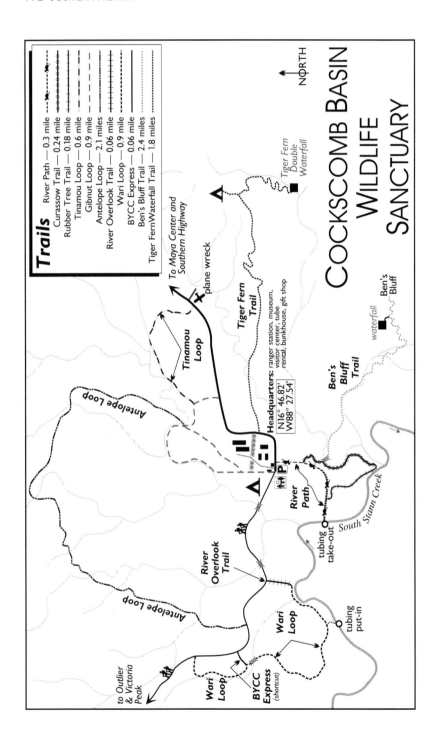

COCKSCOMB BASIN
WILDLIFE
SANCTUARY

NORTH

Trails

River Path — 0.3 mile
Curassow Trail — 0.24 mile
Rubber Tree Trail — 0.18 mile
Tinamou Loop — 0.6 mile
Gibnut Loop — 0.9 mile
Antelope Loop — 2.1 miles
River Overlook Trail — 0.06 mile
Wari Loop — 0.9 mile
BYCC Express — 0.06 mile
Ben's Bluff Trail — 2.4 miles
Tiger Fern/Waterfall Trail — 1.8 miles

Tiger Fern
Double
Waterfall

To Maya Center and
Southern Highway

plane wreck

Tiger Fern
Trail

Headquarters: ranger station, museum,
visitor center, tube
rental, bunkhouse, gift shop

N16° 46.82'
W88° 27.54

Ben's
Bluff

waterfall

Ben's
Bluff
Trail

Tinamou
Loop

Antelope Loop

Antelope Loop

River
Overlook
Trail

River Path

South Stann Creek

tubing
take-out

Wari
Loop

to Outlier
& Victoria
Peak

Wari
Loop

BYCC
Express
(shortcut)

tubing
put-in

Flycatchers from March to August, as this is probably the most consistent place in Belize to find them. Crested Guans often feed in the treetops here.

When you have completed the circuit of the open areas, take the **Victoria Peak Path** heading west (with the headquarters on your right and the parking lot on your left, it is straight ahead). Within a few hundred feet you will come to an open tenting area on your right. Overnight campers have heard and photographed Spectacled Owl here. This is a good birding spot for Yellow-faced Grassquit and other seedeaters, Barred Antshrike, Rufous-tailed Jacamar, various flycatchers and tanagers, and, at the red-flowered Tiger's Claw in the west corner, Long-billed Hermit. Following the trail, you can usually hear White-collared Manakins in the closed-canopy portion (if not, try similar habitat a quarter-mile farther down the path). When you have an open view to the sky, look for Golden-hooded Tanagers perched on the exposed tree limbs and listen for Scaled Pigeon and Blue Ground-Dove, usually cooing from a distance, but if you can see their perches you can align a spotting scope on them. In the dense brush on both sides of the path, Dusky Antbirds call and seedeaters sing. The trail curves slightly right, then left, passing over a footbridge. In winter Chestnut-sided Warblers usually reside here.

At one of the tiny bridges crossing flowing water you can see farther into the dense grasses, and here a Uniform Crake was sighted in March 2007. When you reach the fork at Wari Loop, listen for Great Antshrike and Rufous-breasted Spinetail. Turn left onto **River Overlook Trail** heading to South Stann Creek. Stripe-throated Hermits have a lek near this intersection and Scaly-breasted Hummingbirds nest between here and the river. The park bench at the creek is a good spot to watch a constant parade of birds feeding along the waterway and perhaps see a Neotropical River Otter swim by. Agami Heron has been seen from this spot. Look for it in stagnant backwater areas, preferably around dawn.

Continue west along **Wari Loop** trail. The denser forest here hosts the more elusive birds, particularly if you have the good fortune to come upon an ant swarm. You will come to a downhill path on the left, leading to the launch point for swimmers using rubber tubes to drift downstream. On 25 February 2009, while floating downstream on a tube, one swimmer saw a flock of 20–25 Scarlet Macaws flying overhead. It was a lucky sighting, as a better chance would be at mid- and upper elevations after a long hike from the headquarters. Better yet would be to visit Red Bank (see page 198).

The launch point is another good area for Dusky Antbird and Rufous-breasted Spinetail. Back on Wari Loop, another downhill spur, recently marked, is where a few Boat-billed Herons hang out above a mud hole where a Morelet's Crocodile lives. About 10 yards farther west on Wari Loop is where a Uniform Crake was sighted twice, 14 months apart, in 2007 and 2008.

After this stop, and assuming you are on a one-day agenda, double back to the headquarters area. You may get back to the picnic shelter next to the parking lot about time for an early lunch.

After lunch, the next route can be **River Path**. Look particularly for Scaly-breasted Hummingbird, Gray-headed Tanager, and Black-faced Grosbeak. At the river you can find kingfishers and, sometimes, Prothonotary Warbler. In the grassy area are Thick-billed Seed-Finches, and you might hear Yellow-tailed Orioles singing. Retreat a bit along River Path and take **Rubber Tree** followed by **Curassow Trail**. Antbirds, wrens, and especially the three forest doves—Gray-headed and Gray-chested Doves and Ruddy Quail-Dove—can be heard and usually seen here, the doves most often walking the forest floor, including on the path. You must keep quiet, however, to get and keep the doves in sight. If you head back to the parking lot now you will probably have used up most of one day. You may wish to explore Curassow Trail again on another day.

With a second day of birding, you can afford time to explore the entrance road. Pre-dawn birding could bring some exciting finds. If you drive the road in darkness, you may notice an occasional flash of light from

Ecoregion and habitats: Appendix A, Ecoregion 12, Stann Creek eastern foothills. Habitats include: on the eastern slope of Maya Mountains, primary and secondary tropical moist broadleaf forest in the lower foothills (BFF2) to pine forests (PFM) and elfin scrub at the highest elevations (BFM3), culminating in the second-highest point in Belize, Victoria Peak, at 3,675 feet (1,120 meters). Also riparian habitat along South Stann Creek watershed. Open area near headquarters and accommodations (PC).

Fees and contacts: Entrance US$5 for non-residents, BZ$2.50 for residents. The park is operated by Belize Audubon Society, 12 Fort Street, Belize City or P.O. Box 1001, Belize City; (011) 501-223-5004 or 223-4984 or 223-4988; fax (011) 501-223-4985; base@btl.net; www.belizeaudubon.org. The Cockscomb contact information is (011) 501-223-5004; www.belizeaudubon.org/protected_areas/ cockscomb-basin-wildlife-sanctuary.html.

The park offers basic accommodations including cabins, dormitories, and a communal kitchen. Tent camping has a designated area, and RV camping for small rigs is accommodated at the parking lot. Toilets are at two locations. The headquarters building sells a variety of natural history books and booklets.

Location: N 16° 46.82' W 88° 27.54' at park headquarters. Drive time from Dangriga to the park headquarters is approximately one hour. Off Southern Highway, the entrance road is at Maya Center (N 16° 47.80' W 88° 22.82'), 15 miles south of Hummingbird Highway. Pay the entrance fee at the Maya Center building at the turnoff. If you arrive before the center opens, you can pay at the Visitor Center of Cockscomb Basin Wildlife Sanctuary. The park itself starts four miles along the entrance road when you pass a gate and cattle guard, with a building in a clearing on the left. The total distance to the park headquarters is about six miles.

the roadside. These are trip cameras used to document Jaguars which wander up and down this road. Great Black-Hawk, nesting Keel-billed Toucans, Vermilion Flycatcher, and other open-area or disturbed-forest species are found on the less interesting first part of the road. However, a Black-and-white Owl was seen a half-mile from Southern Highway. When the forest closes in around the road, the birding gets better, particularly if you stop at forest openings. Soaring Swallow-tailed Kites, hiding Barred Forest-Falcons, and Chestnut-headed Oropendolas have been found here.

When you cross an open gate—the true entrance to Cockscomb—with a house on the left, the grassy open area is worth exploring. Black-and-white Owl, Yellow-bellied Sapsucker, and Lovely Cotinga have been recorded here. It's probably time now to head to the parking lot and hiking trails. Check out the open areas again briefly and then take Victoria Peak Path, turning left onto **Wari Loop**. However, this time keep on the loop trail past River Overlook, stopping at a wet area on the left with a short spur to a thin creek where Green Kingfisher and American Pygmy Kingfisher reside. As you continue on Wari Loop, listen for Orange-billed Sparrow. Also, be cognizant of collective squabbling calls that may signal a flock following an ant swarm. If found, your prospects are good for seeing Barred Antshrike, Buff-throated Foliage-gleaner, Dusky Antbird, Tawny-winged and Ruddy Woodcreepers, Northern Barred-Woodcreeper, Gray-headed Tanager, Red-crowned and Red-throated Ant-Tanagers, and up to a dozen other species. At BYCC Express check out a lowland, slightly more open area there and then either take the cutoff or continue all the way on the loop until you meet Victoria Peak Path again. The bird density may be less here than in some previously visited sections, but the rewards are ample. Expected birds include woodcreepers, flycatchers, and wintering warblers. At **Victoria Peak Path**, turn left (northwest) in the direction of the peak. The only hikers you are likely to see this far from headquarters are backpackers on a multiple-day hike. Great Curassow has been seen crossing the path here, and in openings to the sky Double-toothed and, seasonally, Plumbeous Kites can be seen soaring above. The two look-alikes—Rufous Mourner and Rufous Piha—as well as Northern Schiffornis, can be heard and, with patience, seen in the denser areas. You can hike this trail for three days, so check your watch and decide when it is time to return. Near the headquarters, the first part of **Gibnut Trail** is worth exploring. Gray-chested Dove and Slate-headed Tody-Flycatcher may be seen here.

A third day can be reserved for **Ben's Bluff**. For several reasons, suggested below, it would be beneficial to start this day by first light or earlier. This area is worth visiting for those not timid about hiking uphill in hot and humid weather. If you stop only briefly along the trail, plan on at least an hour's hike one-way. Soon after you switch from the River Path Trail to the

Curassow Trail you come to a short footbridge over a shallow slough. If you are here at dawn you have a chance of finding Agami Heron. The first part of the nearly two-mile **Waterfall Trail** (also labeled Ben's Bluff Trail) is easy walking and is reliable for seeing, as opposed to only hearing, Slaty-breasted Tinamou. Taking Waterfall Trail and then another 0.6 mile up a steep hill to Ben's Bluff—and not quitting before you reach the high elevation—will reward you with species you cannot find at lower elevations, most notably Olive-sided Flycatcher, Gray-crowned Yellowthroat, Grace's and Rufous-capped Warblers, Hepatic Tanager, and perhaps an eye-to-eye view of a perched Gray-headed Kite. In addition, from the bluff you will have a panoramic view of the entire basin, including Outlier Peak and, on a clear day, Victoria Peak.

One of the longer trails at 2.1 miles is **Antelope Loop**, where Barred Forest-Falcon, Tody Motmot, and Black-throated Shrike-Tanager have been found. A six- to seven-hour round-trip hike is required to reach Outlier Peak, elevation 1,920 feet. This is the only place in Belize where Gray-breasted Wood-Wren has been recorded.

In Belize, the only reliable spot—behind the waterfall and, with other swifts, above the ridgeline on the trail—to see Chestnut-collared Swift is at Upper Tiger Fern Falls, reached from **Tiger Fern Trail**, which spurs from the park entrance road. The swift is suspected, although not confirmed, to be nesting on the cliffs. The best time to visit is late March or early April. Coordinates of a 2008 sighting are N 16° 47.04' W 88° 26.51'. Also found along the upper reaches of Tiger Fern Trail is singing Nightingale Wren.

To give you an idea of the birding potential at Cockscomb, a group of about 20 birders with skills ranging from novice to professional divided into two competing teams, birded from 6:15 to 11:15 AM. Each team subdivided into multiple groups of two-to-four birders and spread out into most of the areas described above, thereby covering a diversity of habitats. The winning team found 160 species. The two teams tallied a combined total of 176 species. Two of the most experienced birders recorded 126 species, covering about six miles of trails. The key to their success was being able to identify birds by voice, as 37% of the species listed were heard only.

Mammals: Probably more species of mammals, including all five cats, reside at Cockscomb than at any other easily accessible park in Belize. As most of these species are nocturnal, your chance of seeing them is slim. They are most often encountered by lone, quiet birders who move slowly or are stationary for long periods of time. Mammals seen, cumulatively, by the author's tour groups in eleven visits are: Northern Tamandua, Nine-banded Armadillo, Yucatan Black Howler, Jaguar, Jaguarundi, White-nosed Coati,

Barred Antshrike   Bert Frenz

Neotropical River Otter, Gray Fox, Deppe's Squirrel, Yucatan Squirrel, and White-tailed Deer.

Key species of **Cockscomb Basin Wildlife Sanctuary**: A mixture of low- and high-elevation species, *M* marks mid- to high elevation exclusively or nearly so. Great, Little, and Slaty-breasted Tinamous, **Crested Guan**, **Spotted Wood-Quail**, **Agami Heron**, Boat-billed Heron, King Vulture, Gray-headed and Swallow-tailed [S] Kites, **Double-toothed Kite**, Plumbeous Kite [S], Bicolored and White Hawks, Black Hawk-Eagle, Barred Forest-Falcon, **Uniform Crake** [R], Scaled Pigeon, Gray-headed, and Gray-chested Doves, Ruddy Quail-Dove, Scarlet Macaw [M], Brown-hooded Parrot, Vermiculated Screech-Owl, **Spectacled Owl**, Black-and-white and Striped Owls, **Chestnut-collared Swift** [M,R], White-collared and Lesser Swallow-tailed Swifts, Band-tailed Barbthroat [R], **Scaly-breasted Hummingbird**, **Violet Sabrewing**, White-necked Jacobin, Brown Violetear [M], **Stripe-tailed Hummingbird** [M], Slaty-tailed and Collared Trogons, Tody and Keel-billed [M] Motmots, Rufous-tailed Jacamar, Emerald Toucanet,

Chestnut-colored Woodpecker, Great Antshrike, Plain Antvireo [M], **Dusky Antbird**, Black-faced Antthrush, Rufous-breasted Spinetail, **Buff-throated Foliage-gleaner**, Plain Xenops, Yellow-bellied Tyrannulet, Sepia-capped Flycatcher, Northern Bentbill, Stub-tailed Spadebill, Royal Flycatcher, **Rufous Mourner**, Streaked [S] and Sulphur-bellied [S] Flycatchers, **Piratic Flycatcher** [S], Cinnamon and White-winged Becards, Lovely Cotinga [R], Rufous Piha, Plumbeous Vireo [M], **Tawny-crowned Greenlet**, **Green Shrike-Vireo**, **Gray-breasted Wood-Wren** [M,R], **Slate-colored Solitaire** [M], White-throated Thrush, Rufous-capped Warbler [M], **Bananaquit**, Crimson-collared, Passerini's, and Golden-hooded Tanagers, Green and Shining [M] Honeycreepers, **Orange-billed Sparrow**, **Common Bush-Tanager** [M], White-winged Tanager [M], Black-faced and Blue-black Grosbeaks, **Chestnut-headed Oropendola**, White-vented Euphonia [M].

RED BANK

[26 February] "The macaws left the area about two weeks ago," Pablo tells us. They arrive in December to feed on the red fruit of Polewood, but when it is depleted the Scarlet Macaws leave the area to feed elsewhere. Since the forest fire that burned the hillside behind Red Bank a couple of years ago–apparently started by mischievous youths–less fruit has been available. In spite of the sad news, we decide to hike a forest trail a couple of miles from the village.

We move to the end of the road, park our cars, and begin hiking. Not 15 minutes along the trail, Pablo excitedly exclaims, "I hear a macaw!" and rushes up the hillside path toward a cliff viewpoint over the forest. Like flaming red and yellow arrows, three Scarlet Macaws wing across the green jungle. They alight on a huge tree. . .We continue the morning hike, birding in small groups. Climbing up to the cliff side where we were earlier, we scope a perched hawk.

Just then the three macaws return, flying above the canopy with kite tails flowing behind, amazingly graceful for such large birds. They choose a different, more distant, tree for perching. For nearly an hour the macaws stay in clear view browsing the treetops: spectacular splashes of rainbow colors on a bed of green foliage. The macaws swing their grandiose tails in the air, curve their heads and necks around the branches, hang upside down, and twist in all sorts of postures as they feed.

Description: The forested slopes of the foothills outside the Maya village of Red Bank are home to Belize's flock of wintering Scarlet Macaws. More than 150 birds feed on fruit trees such as Polewood *(Xylopia frutescens),* Annatto *(Bixa orellana),* Mountain Trumpet *(Pourouma aspera),* and Quamwood *(Schizolobium parahybum).* A few scouting macaws visit as early as late November to check the condition of the fruiting trees, bring back others about mid-December, peaking in February, and then stay to the end of March (latest is 4 April) as long as the food holds out. The fruiting trees have a four- to five-year production cycle, highest in the last year and then plummeting to the point of very little to no production and the concomitant absence of macaws.

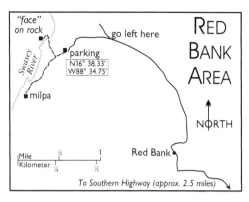

According to Sharon Matola, manager of the Belize Zoo, the macaws resided and have nested in the Upper Raspacula Valley between the Macal and Raspacula Rivers and commute to Red Bank over the divide at a 2,400-foot gap due west of Red Bank. Subsequently, late 2005 brought the completion of the controversial Chalillo Dam, which inundated the macaw nesting area, the only such area in Belize. Scarlet Macaws were still being seen at Red Bank in 2011, but their future is certainly precarious. An excellent book on Sharon Matola's crusade to save the macaws is entitled *The Last Flight of the Scarlet Macaw* by Bruce Barcott (2008).

Promoting the area for national park status might help protect these threatened birds as well as preserve an unusual and unexplained ancient (Maya?) artifact—a human face—carved into a boulder in the midst of the Swasey River. Because this is not a park or reserve, there are no planned and groomed trails. Instead, you can follow the trails used by the villagers to reach their milpas (farms), as shown on the map here. In the village a small shop offers soft drinks and a few food items. Other than a few small thatched shelters, no facilities lie beyond the village.

Birding strategy: Although you could make this trip on your own, it would be best if you hired a guide in Red Bank village. Arrive at the village at sunrise, drive to the back side, and park in the grassy clearing. You can begin to look for the macaws that might fly across the hillside, but also watch for other birds as they awaken. Sooner or later the village children will find you and offer to sell you handicrafts that their mothers have made (an opportunity to provide modest support to the village economy and potentially the macaw habitat). Ask them for Pablo Ical or have them point to his house. Pablo will collect the entrance fee and you can ask to hire him as your guide. He is particularly adept at locating the macaws by vocalization and he is improving his birding skills for other species, but mostly you need him to show you the way. Your business will promote birding tourism and habitat conservation for the village.

After you are done scanning the hillside for macaws and other birds feeding atop the canopy, here is the route that Pablo will probably take: From the side of the village closest to the hillside, curve to the right around the hills for 2.4 miles or farther if road conditions permit. Park here and continue on foot to a tiny creek, a 30-minute walk. You can bird along the way, but it would probably be best to move quickly to the creek and continue on an uphill trail to a cliff with a fabulous overview of the valley. From here you often can see the macaws flying over the jungle or perched, feeding at the top of the canopy. If they don't show up, you can continue downhill on the trail through the jungle, birding along the way. In the densest parts, Gray-chested Dove and Ruddy Quail-Dove are regular. Keep your ears tuned for the calling macaws; they always can be heard before they are seen. You can rest in the shade of a thatched palapa in the middle of a corn field (30 minutes from the tiny creek), then return the way you came. When you get to the cliff, scan for raptors. This is an excellent viewpoint, and you may see four kite species, White Hawk, black-hawks, and Black Hawk-Eagle, among others.

Head back to the tiny creek. Ask your guide if the river level is low enough and there is a way to get across it. If so, turn away from the hill, heading left after you re-cross the tiny stream and hike through the corn fields until you reach Swasey River. Check out the mud along the river and rivulets for footprints, as Baird's Tapir is common here. You may also find Jaguar scat on the trails. On the opposite side of Swasey River you can hike and bird along the river, keeping one eye cocked to the sky in search of soaring hawks and

Ecoregion and habitats: *Appendix A, Ecoregion 12, Stann Creek eastern foothills. Habitats include: lowland broadleaf forest (BFL1) along Swasey River and milpa-style agriculture (BFL3, AG3) at foothills of Maya Mountains (BFF2), small native village (PC).*

Concerns: *If you are starting from Dangriga, leave around 5 or 5:15 AM so that you arrive early enough to see the macaws. Plan on hiking and birding for three or four hours, and expect warm weather. If some members in your group do not want to hike, they can stay near the cars and bird there.*

Fees and contact: *Entrance is US$5, a contribution to the Mo'H Group which is proposing the national park status. (Mo'H is the K'ekchi and Mopan Maya word for Scarlet Macaw.) Pablo Ical, Mo'H Group, Red Bank Village, Stann Creek District; (011) 501-609-4826.*

Location: *N 16° 37.34' W 88° 33.60' at back side of Red Bank village and start of birding. The side road to Red Bank is well marked on Southern Highway, 31.4 miles south of the intersection at Hummingbird Highway. This is an hour (37 miles) from Dangriga.*

Directions: *Zero your odometer at the Red Bank turnoff (N 16° 36.28' W 88° 30.77') and head west on the red dirt road for 3.2 miles to the start of the village. At 3.5, turn right on a street heading toward the hills. At 3.7, park and wait at the back side of the village. Make arrangements for the guide and continue straight toward the hillside, curving right and then left on a narrow dirt road. At 5.5, turn left at the fork, and at 6.1 stop and park in a widening of the red road. This spot is N 16° 38.33' W 88° 34.75'.*

the other eye focused on the river for Amazon Kingfisher. Eventually you will get to the strange face carved in the rock in the river, but you will probably need to have the guide point it out to you. Backtrack to the tiny creek and then to the cars. Total walking time is about three hours, but it can take twice that if you get distracted by all the birds. The total walking distance is probably less than two miles.

Birding along the entrance road to Red Bank, near Southern Highway, could produce additional species. See the list on page 181 for species of the coastal pine savanna.

K**ey species of Red Bank**: Great and Little Tinamous, Crested Guan, Bare-throated Tiger-Heron, King Vulture, Swallow-tailed [S], Double-toothed, and Plumbeous [S] Kites, White Hawk, Black Hawk-Eagle, Collared Forest-Falcon, Scaled and Short-billed Pigeons, **Gray-chested Dove**, Ruddy Quail-Dove, **Scarlet Macaw**, Brown-hooded Parrot, Long-billed and Stripe-throated Hermits, **Scaly-breasted Hummingbird**, Blue-crowned Motmot, **Amazon Kingfisher**, Black-cheeked Woodpecker, Great Antshrike, Dusky Antbird, Rufous-breasted Spinetail, Black Phoebe, Piratic Flycatcher [S], Crimson-collared, Passerini's, and Golden-hooded Tanagers, Buff-throated Saltator, Orange-billed Sparrow, Blue-black Grosbeak, Yellow-backed Oriole.

BFREE AND BLADEN RIVER RESERVE

[6 March] At the entrance to the access road we park our cars and wait for a rugged truck with a shark's teeth jaw painted across the front. It takes a truck with this ferocity to tackle the deeply rutted, muddy, and waterlogged two-track that masquerades for a road. Three in the cab with driver Don and the rest of us hanging on to the metal barred cage built atop the pickup bed, we ride the bucking bronco like a kid's thrill ride at Disneyworld's outdoor adventure park. First we pass through a palmetto savanna and then through dense woods and cross Bladen River without a bridge. The forest surrounds the bunkhouse where we will sleep tonight, women in one room, men in the other, one couple to share the small center room. The outhouse is not a house, but rather a thatched roof supported by four posts and a wooden hutch with a hole cut in for the toilet seat. We quickly settle in to our accommodations, get a quick orientation from hostess Judy, and begin birding, hiking first through the forest to the lagoon where Boat-billed and Agami Herons occur. Mark sees an Agami just as it flies away and all of us see and hear the Boat-billeds. In fact, Jon and Joanie report two dozen Boat-billeds seen from the canoe when they paddle the length of the small lagoon.

After dinner in a darkened kitchen and dining area, illuminated by two fluorescent light fixtures powered by batteries charged during the day from solar panels, we go on a night walk, stumbling over the rocky debris of Maya ruins, heading to Bladen River. We use flashlights to scan the path ahead for

Fer-de-lances, happily finding none. We hear a Mottled Owl and find it perched above us a bit farther along the path. Other than the owl, the only other sounds are the Bufo marinus toads which I later record so that I can practice distinguishing them from Vermiculated Screech-Owls. At the Bladen the river moves swiftly and our lights find small fishes swimming in the clear water. Lights catch wings of small bats seeking insects above the surface, and after a long wait we see a Greater Fishing Bat fly over the water, as large as a nighthawk.

Description: Bladen River Nature Reserve, at 97,000 acres, is the largest protected reserve in Belize and is completely surrounded by additional preserves, a section even larger than the largest contiguous protected reserve in Costa Rica. Most of the area is either closed to everyone except scientists or is so remote that it cannot be accessed except by several days' travel by foot through the jungle. It is considered the most pristine habitat in the country.

Researchers usually stay at BFREE, which adjoins Bladen and shares the same lowland portions of the larger reserve. BFREE, an acronym for Belize Foundation for Research and Environmental Education, is focused on research and education, not tourism. Yet, they welcome birders and offer accommodations. The privilege to bird this remote and pristine environment and the impressive selection of bird species easily compensates for the lack of luxury resort accommodations illustrated in the above journal entry. In addition to the bunkhouse, cabins with somewhat better facilities may be available, if no researchers are in residence. A communal kitchen/dining/meeting building is at the hub of the small research facility, which includes a high tower and dish for satellite communication to the outside world, as well as a heliport. From the hub radiate several birding and nature trails. Almost all of the trails are through jungle, with canopy openings at the lagoon, river, and roadways. Walking is easy, generally, although Blue Pool Trail traverses tree roots and rock rubble. This place is not for everyone, but those who visit will certainly consider it one of the highlights of Belize.

Birding strategy: Because of its remote location, BFREE cannot be visited as a day trip. If you are approaching from the north, you could bird Red Bank in the morning and arrive at BFREE in the afternoon. An alternative route from the south might involve a visit to Nim Li Punit in the morning. It would be best if you spent two or more nights. Be sure to work out the details of your visit well ahead of time.

With a longer stay you should have time to explore all the trails. In a shorter visit, concentrate on the Lagoon Trail, an excellent path for deep-forest species. Northern Bentbills are quite numerous, as well as at least six species of woodcreepers, a dozen flycatchers, and five species of vireos. Duetting Gray-chested Dove and Ruddy Quail-Dove are easily heard here, and Gray-headed Doves are present also. The trail leads to a shallow

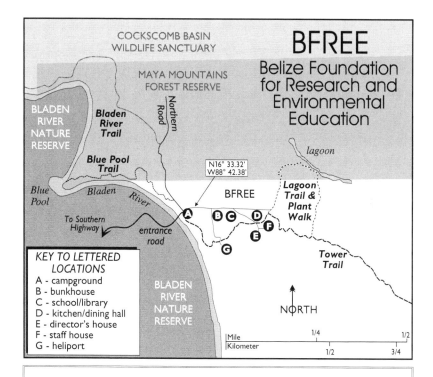

COCKSCOMB BASIN
WILDLIFE SANCTUARY

BFREE
Belize Foundation
for Research and
Environmental
Education

MAYA MOUNTAINS
FOREST RESERVE

BLADEN
RIVER
NATURE
RESERVE

*Bladen
River
Trail*

Northern Road

*Blue Pool
Trail*

lagoon

N16° 33.32'
W88° 42.38'

*Blue
Pool*

Bladen

River

BFREE

**Lagoon
Trail &
Plant
Walk**

To Southern
Highway

entrance
road

Ⓐ ⒷⒸ Ⓓ
Ⓕ
Ⓔ
Ⓖ

**Tower
Trail**

KEY TO LETTERED
LOCATIONS
A - campground
B - bunkhouse
C - school/library
D - kitchen/dining hall
E - director's house
F - staff house
G - heliport

BLADEN
RIVER
NATURE
RESERVE

N↑RTH

Mile   1/4   1/2
Kilometer
                          1/2   3/4

Ecoregion checklist and habitats: *Appendix A, Ecoregion 15, Toledo eastern foothills and submontane forests. Habitats include: old-growth lowland pine (PFL) and broadleaf forest (BFM) on the southeastern slope of Maya Mountains, riparian along Bladen River, and forested wetlands (BFL6); a small encampment (PC).*

Concerns: *Read the above journal to understand the accommodations. The entrance road is formidable and during much of the year—especially June through January—it is impassable by ordinary vehicles. Arrange with BFREE for transportation (at a cost to you) from Southern Highway. Bring insect repellent and a flashlight.*

Contact: *Jacob Marlin, Executive Director, BFREE, P.O. Box 129, Punta Gorda, Toledo District; in US: 4320 W. University Ave., Gainsville, FL 32607; 352-224-5669; jmarlin@bfreebz.org; www.bfreebz.org.*

Bladen is co-managed by Ya'axché Conservation Trust, a community-oriented non-profit organization. Visitors to Bladen must apply for research or education permits by contacting Ya'axché at (011) 501-722-0108 or yaaxche.info@gmail.com.

Location: *N 16° 33.32' W 88° 42.38' at headquarters. Drive time is a bit shorter from Punta Gorda than Dangriga. The entrance road to BFREE is off Southern Highway, 56 miles south of Hummingbird Highway or 39 miles north of Punta Gorda. The entrance is signed, but easy to miss. A sawmill is approximately across the highway. Coming from Dangriga, take a rest break at Turcio's Store and Tommy's Super Store in Bella Vista Village. The BFREE turnoff is then 12.5 miles farther south. From the highway you can see Richardson Peak, the highest point in view. BFREE is at the base of the mountains, about five miles distant.*

Harpy Eagle   Bert Frenz

lagoon choked on all sides by overhanging trees. Approach quietly to avoid spooking secretive Agami and Boat-billed Herons. Take the canoe that is stored on the shore and explore the lagoon. You will certainly find the Boat-billeds again, if not the Agami.

Take advantage of early-morning birding around the encampment, as the dawn chorus is amazing. You should be able to hear the duetting forest doves, Blue-crowned Motmot, Rufous-tailed Jacamar, Ruddy Woodcreeper, Northern Barred-Woodcreeper, Bright-rumped Attila, Lesser Greenlet, White-breasted Wood-Wren, Clay-colored Thrush, and many others. White-whiskered Puffbird can be found at eye level in the forest edge near the kitchen, and Yellow-bellied Tyrannulets sing constantly from the canopy. A walk along the entrance road from the bunkhouse to Bladen River and beyond can be productive. Look and listen for Long-billed Hermit, Tody Motmot, and Orange-billed Sparrow. In the savanna beyond, you can find Black-throated Bobwhite, Plumbeous Kite, Sedge Wren, and Grasshopper Sparrow. Blue Pool Trail is the one described in the journal entry, and although Vermiculated Screech-Owl was not found that evening, it is expected. Of Belize sites, BFREE and Bladen River Nature Reserve hold perhaps the largest diversity of birds, and one is almost never out of earshot of many. It also holds some of the rarest, including Harpy Eagle, first confirmed photographically in 2005. A pair built a nest in 2008, a pair was seen mating in December 2009, and a five-week-old chick was observed in November 2010. Violet-crowned Woodnymph, a hummingbird of high-elevation tropical moist broadleaf forest, is uncommon and local. Bladen is perhaps the best place in Belize to see it.

Key species of BFREE and Bladen River Nature Reserve: [A mixture of low- and high-elevation species, M marks mid- to high elevation exclusively or nearly so.] Great and Little Tinamous, Crested Guan, King Vulture, **Agami Heron**, Boat-billed Heron, Double-toothed and Plumbeous [S] Kites, Solitary Eagle [M,R], **Harpy Eagle** [R], Black Hawk-Eagle, **Black-and-white Hawk-Eagle**, Barred Forest-Falcon, Gray-headed Dove, **Gray-chested Dove**, **Ruddy Quail-Dove**, Scarlet Macaw, **Brown-hooded Parrot**, Vermiculated Screech-Owl, Crested [M, R] and Spectacled Owls, Central American Pygmy-Owl, Mottled and Black-and-white Owls, **Great Potoo**, Scaly-breasted Hummingbird, **Wedge-tailed Sabrewing**, White-necked Jacobin, **Violet-crowned Woodnymph** [M], Purple-crowned Fairy, **Collared Trogon**, Tody Motmot, **Keel-billed Motmot** [M], White-necked and White-whiskered Puffbirds, **Emerald Toucanet**, Chestnut-colored Woodpecker, **Russet Antshrike** [M], **Plain Antvireo** [M], **Slaty Antwren** [M], Dusky Antbird, Black-faced Antthrush, **Scaly-throated Leaftosser**, **Buff-throated Foliage-gleaner**, Tawny-winged, Ruddy, Olivaceous, and Wedge-billed Woodcreepers, Northern Barred-Woodcreeper, **Yellow-bellied Tyrannulet**, Sepia-capped Flycatcher, Paltry Tyrannulet, Ruddy-tailed Flycatcher, **Rufous Mourner**, Streaked [S], Sulphur-bellied [S], and Piratic [S] Flycatchers, Cinnamon Becard, Rufous Piha, Green Shrike-Vireo, Golden-crowned Warbler, Black-throated Shrike-Tanager, Passerini's and Golden-hooded Tanagers, Green Honeycreeper, **Shining Honeycreeper** [M], Orange-billed Sparrow, Hepatic and Scarlet [T] Tanagers, Black-faced Grosbeak, Chestnut-headed Oropendola.

SOUTHERN BELIZE

In the remainder of this chapter, all birding sites are accessible from Punta Gorda as a base of operations. For orientation, you may want to jump ahead to page 225 and read that section first. Otherwise, the chapter arrangement follows the same sequence as the rest of the book: starting from the north and moving south.

Nim Li Punit Maya Site

[8 March] The floral garden beauty of Nim Li Punit resembles Lubaantun, and like the other Maya site the birds are attracted to the fruiting trees, especially in early morning. A flycatcher easily dismissed as just another kiskadee by most, makes a noisy fussing call, and when it turns, its brown back and oversized bill mark it as a Boat-billed Flycatcher. The calls from a pair of loud Myiarchus *flycatchers are different from the other three species we've seen so far on this trip. These are Brown-crested Flycatchers, newly arrived for their summer residency. Blue Ground-Doves are more often seen than heard this morning, a turnabout from most days. Masked Tityras are abundant. We see Giant Cowbirds perched in the highest of bare trees, and even at a great distance their red eyes reflect sunrise. When we leave Nim Li Punit we stop at a small lake in Boden Creek Reserve, finding American Coots, which we have not seen for some time, and a single Ring-necked Duck.*

Description: A well-maintained and florally attractive Maya site with good birding habitat, the ruins date from the Maya Classic period. Rediscovered in 1976, the city flourished from the 5th to 8th centuries. Perched on high land, the ruins overlook the flat jungles below, with views of the Rio Grande. The site includes toilets, museum, and craft vendors.

Birding strategy: Bird amid the Maya temples, especially the forested edges. Although birds are everywhere, they certainly are most plentiful wherever there are flowers and fruiting trees.

The few species reports from this location have kept the list short, undoubtedly incomplete. Some sample species are: Little Tinamou, Swallow-tailed and Plumbeous Kites, Ruby-throated Hummingbird, Great Antshrike, Wedge-billed Woodcreeper, Ochre-bellied Flycatcher, Northern Bentbill, Streaked Flycatcher, Black-crowned Tityra, Philadelphia Vireo, Painted Bunting, and Giant Cowbird.

Don't miss the excellent museum. Although small, it has a good collection of artifacts that are well described; especially note the carved monuments, which include the second largest found in the Maya world. The nine-meter Big Hat stele is depicted on the $2 Belize note. When you leave, be sure to stop below the hill. There is one vantage point along the highway where you can scope out the birds on part of the lake at Boden Creek Reserve. In April 1998 a Burrowing Owl was discovered at a quarry just behind Belize Lodge and Excursions, one of only two records for Belize.

Ecoregion and habitats: Appendix A, Ecoregion 16, Toledo southern lowlands and foothills. Habitats include: lowland broadleaf forest foothills (BFF3) at the Maya site. Lowland broadleaf forests, lagoon, and creeks at Boden Creek Reserve (BFL6).

Fees and contact: Entrance US$10 for non-residents, BZ$10 for residents. Guided tours can be arranged through many of Punta Gorda area hotels and resorts. Nim Li Punit is across Southern Highway from Belize Lodge & Excursions' Indian Creek Lodge, which lies on the private 12,766-acre Boden Creek Reserve and offers complete birding tourist packages.

Location: N 16° 19.28' W 88° 49.43' at parking area. The turnoff from Southern Highway is at N 16° 19.02' W 88° 49.34', 24 miles north of Punta Gorda. After making the turn at the sign, continue 0.4 mile to the parking lot, gaining 190 feet in elevation.

The Lodge at Big Falls

Description: This attractive resort has nearly a mile of riverfront at a bend of the Rio Grande as well as an impressive bird list of about 180 species and over 350 species within five miles in the Big Falls area, including several specialties—such as Great Antshrike—that are harder to find farther north. It is best noted for brief occurrences of Wedge-tailed Sabrewing, Black-crested Coquette, Blue-throated Goldentail, and nesting Black-and-white Owl. A walk through dark woods along the turquoise Rio Grande, then among trees of the orange grove, can be productive. If you aren't staying at the lodge, contact them ahead of time to arrange to take their morning nature walk and stay for lunch. One birder reported seeing about 10 raptor species, mostly while he was enjoying breakfast.

Key species of The Lodge at Big Falls and nearby Big Falls area: Little Tinamou, Black-bellied Whistling-Duck, Bare-throated Tiger-Heron, Black-crowned Night-Heron, Boat-billed Heron, Gray-headed, Hook-billed, and Plumbeous [S] Kites, Common Black-Hawk, Swainson's Hawk [R], Black and Ornate Hawk-Eagles, Collared Forest-Falcon, Ruddy Crake, Sungrebe, Scaled Pigeon, White-winged and Gray-chested Doves, Brown-hooded Parrot, Barn and Mottled Owls, **Black-and-white Owl**, Lesser Swallow-tailed Swift, Scaly-breasted Hummingbird, White-necked Jacobin, Black-crested Coquette [R], Amazon Kingfisher, Great Antshrike, Dusky Antbird, Bare-crowned Antbird [R], Rufous-breasted Spinetail, Wedge-billed Wood-creeper, Stub-tailed Spadebill, Bright-rumped Attila, Sulphur-bellied Fly-catcher [S], White-winged Becard, Bananaquit, Crimson-collared and Passerini's Tanagers, Buff-throated Saltator, Thick-billed Seed-Finch, Green-backed Sparrow, Bronzed Cowbird.

Ecoregion and habitats: Appendix A, Ecoregion 16, Toledo southern lowlands and foothills. Habitats include: riparian lowland broadleaf forest (BFL6), citrus groves (AG4), resort community (PC).

Fees and contact: No entrance fee, but stop at the resort to ask for permission to bird. Guided nature and butterfly walks are US$12.50. The full-service resort has a birding guide, early-morning and night guided nature walks, and a variety of local birding tours by arrangement. They also offer kayaking trips on the Rio Grande and a mid-morning butterfly walk. Rob and Marta Hirons, The Lodge at Big Falls, P.O. Box 103, Punta Gorda, Toledo District; (011) 501-732-4444; info@thelodgeatbigfalls. com; www.thelodgeatbigfalls.com.

Location: N 16° 15.64' W 88° 53.44' at parking lot. In Big Falls, the Southern Highway turnoff is at N 16° 15.78' W 88° 52.92', 18.2 miles north of Punta Gorda. Follow signs to The Lodge at Big Falls. The parking lot is 0.7 mile from the highway.

San Antonio Road and The Dump

[10 March] We stop at a marshy area with a small open pond. Playing a series of crake and rail calls, I soon have three Ruddy Crakes calling from different directions. One calling Sora gets to within four feet of me, but we cannot see it in a 10-minute effort. Finally, it moves away, sight unseen, and calls again from 20 feet out. Just as I retreat toward the car, intent on leaving, another skulker lets out a burst of clicks. I return again, but the sounds do not repeat.

Description: Although labeled here for convenience as San Antonio Road, it could as well be named after Pueblo Viejo or a half-dozen other destinations reached from this westbound road toward the hills. The road is being paved in 2012, all the way to Jalacte on the Guatemala border.

The Dump is a marshy area of former rice fields, fallow for a decade and perhaps the most reliable place in Belize to find rails, although these elusive birds are much more likely to be heard than seen. Gray-breasted Crake is often counted here (four in 2010) on the Punta Gorda Christmas Bird Count, Spotted Rail was found once, and Black Rail (probably only one individual) a few times. Striped Owl can be found here, perhaps more easily than in other parts of Belize. A small population of one to three Willow Flycatchers has wintered since the mid-1990s. One or two White-throated Flycatchers have been found almost every winter from 2004 to 2011. According to Lee Jones, this flycatcher "is relatively quiet in winter and typically perches low in tall grasses, where it can be missed by those unfamiliar with its distinctive call." Flocks of up to 100 Grassland Yellow-Finches have been seen sporadically since 2006. Dickcissels are here in winter, as well as during migration. The Dump and any of the creek crossings are good places to seek kingfishers. White-necked Puffbirds can reliably be seen perched on power lines about a mile east of Mafredi. Farther along the road, the marshlands abut the distant foothills; at mid-morning, when the thermals form, watch for soaring raptors, including King Vulture and White Hawk.

From the main road, several side roads extend to other birding sites, most of which can be a day's activity each. These are boldfaced in the directional guide below and are described in subsequent sections. **Lubaantun** is a pleasant, easily accessible spot, as is **Blue Creek**. After the curve past Mafredi the paved road continues to **Rio Blanco National Park** and **Pueblo Viejo Falls** and, although not a difficult drive, requires an early-morning start so as to reach these sites while the birding is still good. Note that the side road to **Jimmy Cut** and **San Jose Village** is not paved. Much of this habitat was better before 2001's Hurricane *Iris* clipped many of the large trees. In an attempt to find forested areas at higher elevations, you can continue on this road toward Jalacte and Guatemala or else pursue the forests on the Jimmy Cut side road. In Jalacte you can ask for Martin Sho to be a trail

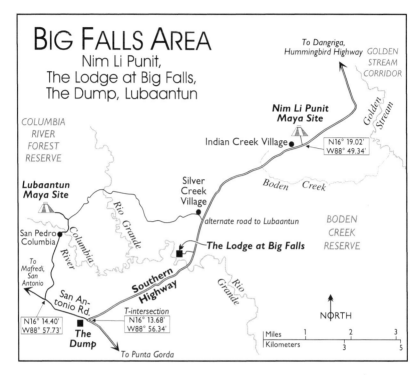

guide. He can take you to potentially good habitat, but the terrain is difficult to traverse and you will need him to show you the way.

Directions: At N 16° 13.68' W 88° 56.34', the San Antonio Road branches from Southern Highway 14 miles north of Punta Gorda:

Mile
0.0 T-intersection with Southern Highway. Turn west onto a paved road.
0.2 **The Dump**. N 16° 13.78', W 88° 56.57'; elevation 60 feet. Stop here for rails.
1.7 Road on right leads to San Pedro Columbia and **Lubaantun**.
3.2 Enter Mafredi (signed).
4.0 T-intersection. Road to left heads to **Blue Creek Village**. Curve right toward San Antonio.
4.9 Wooden bridge.
5.4 Y-intersection. Veer left. Right heads to **Jimmy Cut** and **San Jose**.
5.9 "Welcome to San Antonio" sign.
6.6 Veer left at Y-intersection.
10.2 "Welcome to Santa Cruz" sign.
10.7 Road on right leads to San Jose, a difficult road at best. N 16° 14.11' W 89° 4.52'; elevation 696 feet.
10.8 Bridge in Santa Cruz.
11.2 Western edge of Santa Cruz.
11.9 Boundary of Rio Blanco National Park.

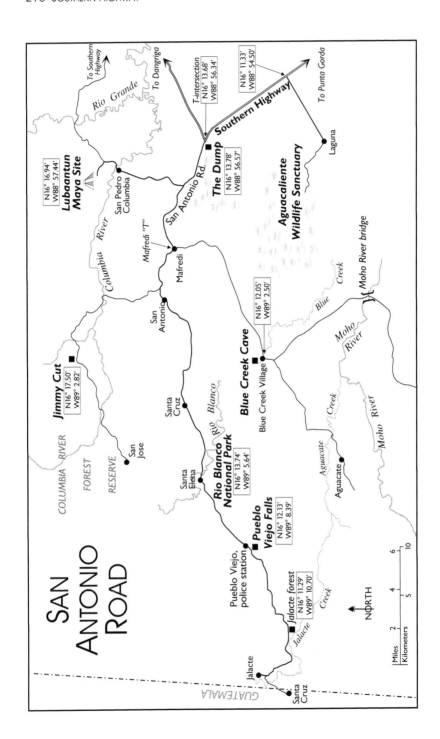

SAN
ANTONIO
ROAD

Rio Grande

To Southern Highway

To Dangriga

T-intersection
N16° 13.68'
W88° 56.34'

N16° 11.33'
W88° 54.50'

To Punta Gorda

Southern Highway

N16° 16.94'
W88° 57.44'
Lubaantun
Maya Site

San Pedro
Columbia

San Antonio Rd.

The Dump
N16° 13.78'
W88° 56.57'

Laguna

Aguacaliente
Wildlife Sanctuary

Columbia River

Mafredi "T"

Mafredi

Moho River bridge

San
Antonio

Blue
Creek

Moho
River

Jimmy Cut
N16° 17.50'
W89° 2.82'

Santa
Cruz

Rio Blanco

Blue Creek Cave
N16° 12.05'
W89° 2.50'

Blue Creek Village

COLUMBIA RIVER

FOREST

RESERVE

San
Jose

Santa
Elena

Rio Blanco
National Park
N16° 13.74'
W89° 5.64'

Aguacate
Creek

Aguacate

Moho River

Pueblo
Viejo Falls
N16° 12.13'
W89° 8.39'

Pueblo Viejo,
police station

Jalacte forest
N16° 11.29'
W89° 0.70'

NORTH

Miles
Kilometers

Jalacte

Jalacte

Santa
Cruz

GUATEMALA

12.2 Headquarters and parking for **Rio Blanco National Park**.
13.0 Village of Santa Elena (formerly Rio Blanco). N 16° 13.84'
      W 89° 6.34'; elevation 787 feet.
15.4 Village of Pueblo Viejo.
16.0 Police station and the way to Upper and Lower **Pueblo Viejo Falls**.
16.3 Wooden bridge.
18.4 Concrete bridge.
19.3 Birding spot in wooded area on left. N 16° 11.29' W 89° 10.70';
      elevation 924 feet.
19.7 Wooden bridge.
20.2 Trail on left leads to Santa Cruz, Guatemala.
21.6 Village of Jalacte.

Ecoregion and habitats: Appendix A, Ecoregion 16, Toledo southern lowlands and foothills. Habitats include: varied, from remnant rice fields (AG2) and marshes to riparian to lowland broadleaf forests (BFL6) to foothills of Maya Mountains (BFF3); a few small villages (PC).

Key species of The Dump: Black-bellied Whistling-Duck, Muscovy Duck, Pinnated [R] and American [R] Bitterns, **Least Bittern**, Bare-throated Tiger-Heron, Black-crowned Night-Heron, Lesser Yellow-headed Vulture, White-tailed Kite, Northern Harrier, White-tailed Hawk [R], Ruddy Crake, **Gray-breasted Crake**, Black Rail [R], **Clapper Rail**, Gray-necked Wood-Rail, **Sora**, Spotted Rail [R], Purple and Common Gallinules, Wilson's Snipe, Mourning Dove, Plain-breasted Dove, Striped Cuckoo, **Striped Owl**, American Pygmy Kingfisher, Great Antshrike, Rufous-breasted Spinetail, **Willow** and **White-throated Flycatchers**, Scissor-tailed Flycatcher, Tree, Bank, and Cliff Swallows, Gray-crowned Yellowthroat, Grayish Saltator, **Grassland Yellow-Finch**, Green-backed Sparrow, **Dickcissel**.

Lubaantun Maya Site

[6 March] The beauty of Lubaantun is what strikes us first. We stand at the entrance looking up to hills of disordered building blocks, some now randomly oriented, but many still forming the steps and walls of Maya temples. Trees tower above rubble heaps and flowering shrubs decorate edges. When we reach the main plaza we stand on a broad-leafed grass carpet, carefully trimmed to a few inches and spreading uniformly to the foot of temples. From various viewpoints we have long vistas across the tops of dense jungle. Tall trees provide us shade from the rising sun, and fruiting trees attract the birds. We stand at one spot for a couple of hours, barely moving 20 feet in any direction, for the puzzling birds continuously move in and out of the floral display. Some we identify quickly—Bright-rumped Attila, Blue-gray Tanager, Black-headed Saltator—but the flycatchers puzzle us, and speculation abounds. We sort through Myiarchus and feel confident we are watching both Dusky-capped and Great Crested. A drab tyrant with a light-colored bill becomes an Ochre-bellied Flycatcher.

Description: An easy-to-reach birding site, Lubaantun—pronounced "lew ba TOON" or "lew ban toon" without accent, meaning "place of fallen stones"—is a very pleasant place to bird and can offer a good variety of passerines. The Maya city dates to the Classic era (A.D. 730–890) and features unusual architecture, mostly of large stone blocks without mortar. It is said that the famous Crystal Skull, a quartz crystal rock claimed to be a pre-Columbian Mesoamerican artifact, was discovered here in 1926 by the Mitchell-Hedges party, the premise for the 2008 movie *Indiana Jones and the Kingdom of the Crystal Skull.* There is a trail through the jungle to Columbia Branch, starting near the Plaza of the Sacred Altar. Another trail through the woods links Butterfly Plaza to the river trail. Facilities include toilets and museum. Local vendors sell crafts.

Location: N 16° 16.94' W 88° 57.44' at parking lot. Lubaantun is 21 miles from Punta Gorda, about a half-hour drive. See San Antonio Road for details. Zero your odometer at the T-intersection of Southern Highway and San Antonio Road. At 1.7 miles turn right toward San Pedro Columbia. The intersection (N 16° 14.40' W 88° 57.73') is signed "Lubaantun 3.4 miles." At 2.8, cross a wooden bridge and a half-mile farther you will enter the village of San Pedro Columbia. Belize Agroforestry Research Center (BARC) is upriver less than a mile from San Pedro Columbia and shares the same habitat as nearby Lubaantun. At 4.0, turn left around a picturesque church and immediately turn right (no sign). At 4.7, turn left, guided by a sign to Lubaantun. Park at 5.3 and enter the Maya site.

Key species of Lubaantun, San Pedro Columbia, and BARC: Little Tinamou, King Vulture, Gray-headed and Plumbeous [S] Kites, **Crane Hawk** [R], **Gray-chested Dove**, Long-billed Hermit, Scaly-breasted Hummingbird, **White-necked Jacobin**, White-necked Puffbird, Black-cheeked Woodpecker, Dusky Antbird, Bare-crowned Antbird [R], Bright-rumped Attila, Sulphur-bellied Flycatcher [S], Black-crowned Tityra, Philadelphia Vireo, **Swainson's Warbler**, Crimson-collared and Passerini's Tanagers, Buff-throated Saltator, Blue-black Grosbeak, Painted Bunting.

Ecoregion and habitats: Appendix A, Ecoregion 16, Toledo southern lowlands and foothills. Habitats include: openings in lowland broadleaf forest (BFL6) in a park-like setting (PC).

Fees and resources: Entrance US$10 for non-residents, BZ$10 for residents. Guided tours can be arranged through many Punta Gorda area hotels and resorts. To learn more about Lubaantun as well as other Belize Maya sites, a good Internet resource is Wikipedia. See for example, http://en.wikipedia.org/wiki/Lubaantun.

Stripe-throated Hermit

Bert Frenz

Blue Creek and Blue Creek Cave

[10 March] My attention is diverted when I hear a familiar song coming from the hills. I cannot place the singer and ask George. When he says Nightingale Wren I immediately recall hearing this strange song elsewhere, like a young boy first learning to whistle and having no sense of music, each note random and off-key. We continue hiking toward Blue Creek Cave, the boulders and incline becoming too challenging for some, but the reward great for those who complete the trip. The cave mouth opens wide and tall, floored by pools of clear water wiggling with small fish and strewn with huge boulders and smaller rocks, making the approach tricky. Two White Hawks and a King Vulture soar above us, high up against the cliffs, riding the first thermals of the morning.

Birding strategy: Start your birding at the rice fields before and, more importantly, one mile west of Blue Creek Village. Look and listen for rails and crakes in the wet fields. Gray-breasted Crake occurs here, but is nearly impossible to see. Spotted Rail has been reported once. Scan the skies near the distant steep hills for raptors. In the village the attractive Blue Creek is surrounded by dense rainforest. The best birding often is the first 200 yards from the road bridge along the right side of the shallow creek before you reach the forest. Here the fruiting trees attract dozens of hummingbirds, honeycreepers, and orioles. For more birding, follow the obvious trail along the right side of the creek for about a mile to the cave, where the Río Blanco emerges from the mountains as Blue Creek. The last part of the river trail toward Blue Creek Cave is steep and rocky. However, you will find plenty of good birding before that part. The creek and cave are popular swimming spots, and the cave, also known as Hokeb Ha, can be explored—with local guides—for at least part of the five miles to where it comes out at Santa Cruz. Although not open year round, the guesthouse has toilets, food, and souvenirs. If you bird long near the start of the trail at the road, local vendors will soon spread their crafts on blankets in front of you. Much of their work is nicely made and inexpensive.

Although it is a tedious drive through countryside ravaged by Hurriane *Iris* in 2001, there has been substantial recovery since then. You can continue on the road beyond Blue Creek Village, passing through the villages of Santa Teresa, San Lucas, Corazon, Sunday Wood Creek Village, and Conejo until you reach the Moho River bridge near Santa Anna. This is the terminus of the Santa Anna route described on page 230 and at www.bafrenz.com for Sarstoon-Temash National Park.

Key species of Blue Creek: Little Tinamou, Muscovy Duck, Lesser Yellow-headed and King Vultures, Double-toothed Kite, **White Hawk**, Common and Great Black-Hawks, Short-tailed Hawk, Black Hawk-Eagle, **Gray-breasted Crake**, Gray-chested Dove, Brown-hooded Parrot, White-collared Swift, **Scaly-breasted Hummingbird**, White-necked Jacobin, Amazon and American Pygmy Kingfishers, **Great Antshrike**, Russet Ant-shrike [R], Bare-crowned Antbird [R], Black-faced Antthrush, Wedge-billed

Ecoregion and habitats: Appendix A, Ecoregion 16, Toledo southern lowlands and foothills. Habitats include: riparian lowland broadleaf forest at base of foothills of Maya Mountains (BFL6, BFF3).

Fees and contacts: No fee for the first part of the walk, but once you reach the site of a dilapidated canopy walkway, admission is US$2.50 to continue past the guesthouse and to the cave. Guided tours can be arranged through many Punta Gorda area hotels and resorts.

Location: N 16° 12.05' W 89° 2.75' at Blue Creek and the road. The creek is 23 miles from Punta Gorda, a 35- to 45-minute drive. Follow directions given for San Antonio Road. Zero your odometer at the Southern Highway T-intersection and continue on the gravel road for four miles to another T-intersection in Mafredi. Turn left, reaching the rice fields shortly after the right curve at mile 6. At 9 you will have a good view of the foothills on your right. Continue to Blue Creek Village at mile 12. The river and the start of birding on foot are at mile 13.

Woodcreeper, **Paltry Tyrannulet**, Royal Flycatcher, Black Phoebe, Bright-rumped Attila, Rufous Mourner, Northern Schiffornis, Cinnamon and White-winged Becards, Rufous Piha, Band-backed Wren, **Nightingale Wren**, Tropical Gnatcatcher, Black-throated Shrike-Tanager, Crimson-collared, Passerini's, and Golden-hooded Tanagers, Green Honeycreeper, **Orange-billed Sparrow**, Black-faced Grosbeak.

Río Blanco National Park

Description: This 105-acre national park—also reported as a 500-acre Indigenous Peoples Park—is within the Maya Mountain Forest Reserve and protects the high biodiversity of flora and fauna, which includes Jaguar, Ocelot, Margay, and Neotropical River Otter. Toilets, snacks, and local crafts are at park headquarters adjacent to the main road. Located about a quarter-mile hike from the road, the main attraction to tourism is the 20-foot waterfall on the Río Blanco, popular for swimming and quite pleasant after a hot morning of birding. Brave swimmers jump from a 25-foot-high rock into a deep pool below. The walk to the falls is easy. Beyond, the trails along the river and up the hillsides are often steep and not cleared of encroaching branches and stumble-inducing roots.

> *Ecoregion and habitats:* Appendix A, Ecoregion 16, Toledo southern lowlands and foothills. Habitats include: secondary broadleaf forest and disturbed shrubland in the foothills of Maya Mountains (BFF3).
>
> *Location:* N 16° 13.74' W 89° 5.64'; elevation 823 feet at parking lot and headquarters. The park is 26 miles from Punta Gorda, about an hour's drive. Follow directions to mile 12.2 on San Antonio Road.
>
> *Fees and contacts:* Entrance fee US$2.50. Camping and furnished dorms are available for an overnight stay. There is also a guesthouse in Santa Elena Village. Some Toledo-area hotels offer tours to Río Blanco National Park. They might also take you two miles farther to the Uxbenka Maya site, perched on a ridge overlooking the foothills and valleys of Maya Mountains.

Pueblo Viejo Falls

Description: "Old Town," as it is translated from the Spanish, is the oldest Maya village in southern Belize and lies only seven miles from the Guatemala border. Although the area once boasted the best preserved rainforest in this part of Belize, a 2001 hurricane leveled much of the forest. Still, it offers crystal-clear streams and in a series of falls a river that drops 80 feet into a deep limestone gorge. A hiking trail from Pueblo Viejo starts at the police station and leads to taller bush where you are more likely to find the higher-elevation birds.

Birding strategy: Considering the drive time, get an early predawn start from Punta Gorda. The first falls can be visited easily on your own. To take the trail into the forested hills, consider hiring a guide once you reach the village. The police station would be one place to ask for a guide.

A key species is Keel-billed Motmot, and the hills south of Pueblo Viejo are one of the best accessible areas in Belize to find this species. This is a good site to look for Band-tailed Barbthroat, Stripe-tailed Hummingbird, and Nightingale Wren. With a little effort, perhaps you will find Black-crested Coquette, Paltry Tyrannulet, and White-vented Euphonia. A rarity observed 8 April 1995 was Crested Eagle. A sampling of other species expected here are: Little Tinamou, King Vulture, Plumbeous Kite, Violet Sabrewing, Green-breasted Mango, Amazon Kingfisher, White-whiskered Puffbird, Chestnut-colored Woodpecker, Black-faced Antthrush, Slate-headed Tody-Flycatcher, Stub-tailed Spadebill, Cinnamon and White-winged Becards, Red-capped Manakin, Green Shrike-Vireo, Long-billed Gnatwren, Crimson-collared Tanager, Green Honeycreeper, Yellow-faced Grassquit, Green-backed Sparrow, Black-faced and Blue-black Grosbeaks.

Ecoregion and habitats: *Appendix A, Ecoregion 16, Toledo southern lowlands and foothills. Habitats include: picturesque series of waterfalls on Pueblo Creek through the foothills of Maya Mountains (BFF3).*

Fees and contacts: *No fees. Guided tours can be arranged through some of Punta Gorda area hotels and resorts.*

Location: *N 16° 12.13' W 89° 8.39'; elevation 904 feet at Upper Falls. Pueblo Viejo is about 30 miles from Punta Gorda, about 75 minutes drive time. Follow directions given for San Antonio Road, stopping at mile 16. Across from the police station take a grassy road downhill for a quarter-mile.*

AGUACALIENTE WILDLIFE SANCTUARY

[11 March] In first morning light, our guide Roberto and six of us start down a lane between fenced cow pastures. At the edge of the dark forest we continue on a wooden-slat boardwalk raised four feet above the ground. We reach the headquarters building and a scattered tent camp and makeshift kitchen where a group of young Brits are preparing for another day of boardwalk construction from the building to the river. An hour into our hike, we reach the river and stop to see a constant procession of Wood Storks fly over our heads, following the waterway and heading to lofty tree perches. Roberto points out an American Pygmy Kingfisher lurking low in a riverside bush.

Now, we begin the more arduous hiking along the river, poking our way along a sometimes muddy, sometimes brambled, sometimes low-ceilinged trail. Fortunately, this time the wetlands are mostly dry. We pass grassy mudflats, stopping occasionally to observe the many waterbirds, and are three hours into our hike when we first see Aguacaliente Swamp, not at all the way I pictured it.

Stretching more than a half-mile is a flat and solid golf green, bright yellow-green grass only a fraction of an inch high, flat and hard enough to lawn bowl and terminated by a shallow lagoon replete with hundreds of Neotropic Cormorants, Great Egrets, and Wood Storks, mixed with smaller numbers of six more heron species. Two White Ibis are in the mix and dozens of Killdeer and 10+ Northern Waterthrushes feed in the grassy field and along the bramble edges. Lesser Yellow-headed Vultures soar overhead and a pair of Roadside Hawks mate on a dead tree limb. We walk the putting green until tangled thorns prevent continuation, then we double back. We could circle around the lagoon in the opposite direction, but checking our water supply most of us have finished one bottle and are into our second, so we decide we don't have enough for the additional hours the hike would take. With only rest stops, the hike back takes us two hours and we reach our cars by noon. The hike and the terrain were much better than anticipated, and the scenery and birds were well worth the effort.

Description: At one time the elevated boardwalk, connecting the edge of Laguna Village to the lagoon, provided easy access through the stunted trees rising from wet forest. The lack of a view-blocking understory offers an opportunity to see, rather than only hear, species such as Gray-chested Dove, Western Slaty-Antshrike, Black-faced Antthrush, Northern Bentbill, and Orange-billed Sparrow. Unfortunately, the boardwalk has fallen into disrepair, necessitating walking beside the boardwalk instead of on top. The walking is rougher alongside the lagoon to the swamp, but the chief concern is actually the oppressive heat and humidity. Facilities are limited to a pit toilet at the ranger station and the long boardwalk.

Birding strategy: Get a local guide to show you this route, as it may change depending on weather conditions. In addition, a guide may be useful in securing permission to enter the reserve. Start hiking at dawn or earlier. Here is a distance guide, in miles, to the hiking trail: 0.0 at Laguna road and start of boardwalk, 0.8 at administration building and worker's camp, 1.2 at end of boardwalk and beginning of lagoon. Now follow the edge of the lagoon toward the swamp, which starts at 2.0 in the dry season and reaches brambles at 2.4 miles. The abundance of birds in the water areas can be impressive, with a few Jabirus, hundreds of Black-bellied Whistling-Ducks, Muscovy Ducks, Blue-winged Teal, Neotropic Cormorants, egrets, and Wood Storks, as many as 10 Plumbeous Kites in the air at one time, and 10 calling Striped Cuckoos. The number of reported species at Aguacaliente Wildlife Sanctuary is a remarkable 251. It is also a site where oddities seem to turn up, the strangest being two American Flamingos that circled the swamp one day in 2001.

Key species of Aguacaliente Wildlife Sanctuary: Little Tinamou, Black-bellied Whistling-Duck, **Muscovy Duck**, American Wigeon [R], Northern Shoveler [R], Blue-winged Teal, **Jabiru**, Wood Stork, American Bittern [R], Bare-throated Tiger-Heron, Black-crowned Night-Heron, Roseate Spoonbill, **Lesser Yellow-headed Vulture**, **Plumbeous Kite** [S],

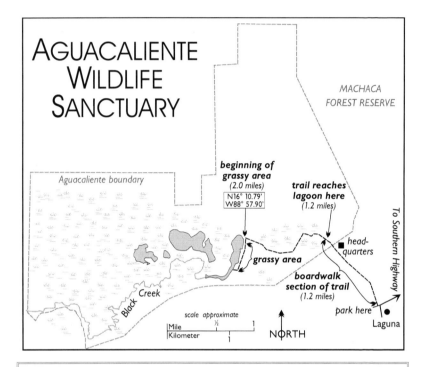

Ecoregion and habitats: *Appendix A, Ecoregion 16, Toledo southern lowlands and foothills. Habitats include: secondary lowland broadleaf forest leading to marshlands and open swamp (BFL6). The wildlife sanctuary protects 6,000 acres of lagoon and surrounding swamp and forest.*

Concerns: *This area can be a real adventure and a memorable experience, but some might bow out given that it can be difficult. The round-trip hike is 4.8 miles, half of which is over uneven and wet terrain. Weather undoubtedly will be warm to hot, so bring plenty of water. If you want dry feet, wear waterproof shoes, preferably rubber boots. During rainy periods, some parts of the hike could be through knee-high water. Bring bug spray. Caution: the thin wooden slats on the boardwalk are slippery and easily broken through, especially on the older section between Laguna and the administration building. Therefore, walk on either edge of the boardwalk where the upright posts support your weight or, better yet, next to the boardwalk.*

Fees and contacts: *In 2007 there was an entrance fee, with funds for Aguacaliente Management Team, but subsequently the group appears to have disbanded. With an unusable boardwalk the only access is through the bush and that would be impossible during the rainy season. In the past, The Lodge at Big Falls has offered tours for guests, but you should contact the lodge for updated information.*

Location: *N 16° 10.79' W 88° 57.90' in swamp. The turnoff to Laguna is 10 miles north of Punta Gorda at N 16° 11.33' W 88° 54.50'. Turn west on a gravel road and continue for another 2.3 miles to the village. Bear right along the edge of the village for 0.3 mile. Near here, park on the side of the road and you will see a sign marking the start of the path to the swamp.*

Zone-tailed Hawk [R], Black Hawk-Eagle, Crested Caracara [R], Ruddy Crake, Gray-necked Wood-Rail, Sungrebe, Killdeer, **Black-necked Stilt**, Solitary Sandpiper, Greater and Lesser Yellowlegs, Semipalmated [T], Western, Least, **Pectoral** [T], Stilt, and Buff-breasted [R,T] Sandpipers, Wilson's Snipe, Plain-breasted Ground-Dove, Gray-headed and Gray-chested Doves, Ruddy Quail-Dove, Brown-hooded Parrot, **Striped Cuckoo**, Amazon Kingfisher, **American Pygmy Kingfisher**, Great Antshrike, **Western Slaty-Antshrike**, Dusky and Bare-crowned [R] Antbirds, Black-faced Antthrush, Rufous-breasted Spinetail, Wedge-billed Woodcreeper, Yellow-bellied Tyrannulet, Northern Beardless-Tyrannulet, Northern Bentbill, Slate-headed Tody-Flycatcher, Stub-tailed Spadebill, Royal Flycatcher, Tawny-crowned Greenlet, Prothonotary Warbler, Orange-billed Sparrow, Blue-black Grosbeak, Painted Bunting, Bronzed and Giant Cowbirds.

Jacinto Creek and Cuxlin Ha

Description: Set in 300 acres of rainforest bordering Jacinto Creek, Cuxlin Ha is a combination resort, time-share, retirement village, youth hostel, and education center, with room rentals and RV space, and a major focus on community outreach toward helping native Belizeans develop employable skills. At Cuxlin Ha you live in the midst of a Maya village, yet have the luxury of a swimming pool with a refreshing waterfall.

Birding strategy: Starting from Eldridgeville, formerly known as Toledo Settlement and shown as such on most maps, the two-mile entrance road to Cuxlin Ha passes through wetlands where Rufous-breasted Spinetails call incessantly. The open areas at the resort and Maya housing favor passerines. From the main building you are always within earshot of Striped Cuckoo calling from the grassy areas near the river. Fruiting trees attract Yellow-bellied Elaenia, Great Crested Flycatcher, White-collared Manakin, Yellow-breasted Chat, Red-legged Honeycreeper, Buff-throated Saltator, Summer and Yellow-winged Tanagers, Black-faced Grosbeak, Baltimore Oriole, and Yellow-billed Cacique.

Ecoregion and habitats: Appendix A, Ecoregion 16, Toledo southern lowlands and foothills. Habitats include: primary lowland broadleaf forest, secondary forest, and open lands; riparian along Jacinto Creek (BFL6), a tributary of the Rio Grande. The entrance road is edged by scrubland (BFL3), often wet, leading to an ornamentally planted resort and village (PC).

Contact: Dona Scafe, Cuxlin Ha; (011) 501-732-4747 or 630-7673; cuxlinha@live.com; www.cuxlinha.com.

Location: Cuxlin Ha; N 16° 9.97' W 88° 50.59' at lodge. The access road to Cuxlin Ha starts from Southern Highway 4.6 miles north of Punta Gorda and continues eastward for 2.2 miles toward Jacinto Creek, a tributary of the Rio Grande.

Shrubs and wet areas along the entrance road, and skies overhead, offer Plain Chachalaca, Bare-throated Tiger-Heron, Wood Stork, Swallow-tailed and White-tailed Kites, Common Pauraque, Yellow-bellied Tyrannulet, Northern Bentbill, Mangrove Vireo, Tropical Gnatcatcher, Blue-black Grassquit, Variable Seedeater, Yellow-faced Grassquit, Black-headed Saltator, and Bronzed Cowbird. For species to be expected in the more deeply forested areas along Jacinto Creek, use the list of birds in the Rio Grande, Belcampo Belize, and Wilson Landing section below.

Rio Grande, Belcampo Belize, and Wilson Landing

[2 March] We hike Tapir Trail through the tall forest, following a tributary leading to the Rio Grande and again hear Western Slaty-Antshrikes. We are walking along the base of a steep limestone hill, capped by the lodge at 330 feet, although we cannot see it through the canopy. On the opposite side of the valley Big Hill reaches over 400 feet, strange peaks in the midst of otherwise flat coastal lands. Where we walk, though, it is dark jungle. A Yellow-olive Flycatcher comes close enough for me to take a rare flash photo. When I catch up to the group, they are watching a Rufous Mourner and this one selects a number of close perches so that we can study it, although the mourner isn't much to look at, being a uniformly brown bird. We reach the Rio Grande and complete our loop after a tedious climb up 340 steps—they are constructing a chair lift to a fancy resort lodge, which is positioned in Laughing Falcon Reserve along the Rio Grande and Caribbean. The view from the lodge extends a great distance over an untouched green forest canopy.

Description: The excellent habitats along the Rio Grande can be accessed from Wilson Road to Wilson Landing and from the enormous Laughing Falcon Reserve and Belcampo Belize, a luxury resort with concomitant amenities, not the least of which is the immense 12,000-acre expanse of old second-growth forest. The property borders the Rio Grande and Caribbean Sea. For guests, Belcampo Belize offers eco-tours, including a night cruise on the Rio Grande equipped with night-vision goggles and spotlights with red filters to avoid disturbing animals seen along the river.

Birding strategy: Take Wilson Road for 1.6 miles. One end of the Tapir Trail starts here and tunnels through the forest to the base of the chairlift at Belcampo Belize. This is excellent habitat for those birds that seek secluded dark forests, notably antbirds and tyrant flycatchers. The trail continues around the base of the hill and along the Rio Grande and comes out at Wilson Landing. At the split in the road, you can continue straight up the paved driveway to Belcampo Belize if you have reservations at the resort. Birding is also good near the resort where the flowering plants and trees and the concomitant insects attract vireos, warblers, tanagers, and euphonias. When trees are fruiting, over 20 Keel-billed Toucans have been seen. In February 2011 a Great Potoo was observed near the lodge. Next morning, starting at 5 AM, several Great Potoos could be heard along the river. In March, two were perched next to a hollowed-out tree limb stub, which has been described as a typical nesting site. One of the most impressive sights was on 14 October 2007 when an estimated 300 Hook-billed Kites moved southward overhead. Birding areas can also be reached from the end of Wilson Road. Park there and work back toward the resort.

Location: Belcampo Belize; N 16° 9.97' W 88° 48.70' at lodge. A spur from Southern Highway 2.7 miles north of Punta Gorda, Wilson Road accesses Belcampo Belize. The directions below are the shortest route to Belcampo Belize and Wilson Landing, but note several alternatives at T-intersections.

Mile

0.0 Intersection with Southern Highway. N 16° 8.05' W 88° 48.79'.

0.5 Continue straight. Right goes 3.2 miles to Rio Grande and Esso Landing.

0.9 Continue straight, following utility poles. Right goes to a quarry.

1.6 Split in road. A primitive but drivable road goes off to the right, leading to Wilson Landing on the Rio Grande in 0.6 mile, where there is parking for four to five vehicles (N 16° 9.92' W 88° 48.48'). This can be muddy in the rainy season, requiring four-wheel drive. A few hundred feet before the river is one end of Tapir Trail.

Alternatively, continuing straight at the 1.6 split takes you through orchards until you soon come to the base of Belcampo Belize, where there are two choices. Straight ahead is the other end of Tapir Trail, leading into the forest. Sharply right the road continues steeply uphill on a paved driveway to the lodge.

Key species of Belcampo Belize and Wilson Landing: Great Tinamou, Muscovy Duck, Bare-throated Tiger-Heron, Hook-billed Kite, Laughing Falcon, Ruddy Crake, **Sungrebe**, Short-billed Pigeon, Gray-headed Dove, **Gray-chested Dove**, Brown-hooded and Mealy Parrots, **Vermiculated Screech-Owl**, Spectacled [R], Mottled, and Black-and-white Owls, **Striped Owl**, **Great Potoo**, White-necked Jacobin, **Tody Motmot**, American Pygmy Kingfisher, Emerald Toucanet, **Great Antshrike**,

Ecoregion and habitats: Appendix A, Ecoregion 16, Toledo southern lowlands and foothills. Habitats include: primary lowland broadleaf forest, secondary forest, and open lands; riparian along Jacinto Creek and Rio Grande (BFL6); resort community (PC).

Contact: *Belcampo Belize, P.O. Box 135, Punta Gorda, Toledo District; (011) 501-722-0050; fax (011) 501-722-0051; info@belcampobz.com; www.belcampoinc.com/bz.*

Western Slaty-Antshrike, Dusky Antbird, Black-faced Antthrush, Tawny-winged, Ruddy, and Wedge-billed Woodcreepers, Northern Barred-Woodcreeper, Yellow-bellied Tyrannulet, Northern Bentbill, Royal Flycatcher, Rufous Mourner, Northern Schiffornis, Lovely Cotinga [R], **Philadelphia Vireo,** Tawny-crowned Greenlet, Prothonotary Warbler, Gray-headed, Crimson-collared, Passerini's, and Golden-hooded Tanagers, Buff-throated Saltator, Orange-billed Sparrow, Giant Cowbird.

Cattle Landing

Description: The Cattle Landing soccer field could easily be dismissed as uninteresting by most birders if it were not for the incredible sightings reported there by Lee Jones. The site holds the distinct advantage as a wide-open grassy field with an unobstructed view of the sky and positioned next to the sea; in other words, a great place to study migrating birds. A few of Belize's rarest birds have passed through and over Cattle Landing. In October 2007, the first Belize records for Shiny Cowbird and Spot-breasted Oriole were added. Other exciting discoveries include Crested Caracara 7 October, Zone-tailed Hawk 23 October and 5 November, Aplomado Falcon 18 October, and Orange-breasted Falcon 8 October.

Birding strategy: Starting with Purple Martins in early July, then Barn, Cliff, and Bank Swallows—in that order—from late July to September, the swallow parade ends in early November with many Tree Swallows. Rarely, a few Cave Swallows have been noted in flocks of migrating Cliff. Eastern Kingbirds migrate mid-August to early November, peaking in the third week of September, sometimes in numbers as high as 1,000 per hour. Dickcissels pass through Belize in September and October. On 15 September 2000, their peak was 700 counted in about 90 minutes.

Several thousand Hook-billed Kites migrate over Cattle Landing between mid-October and mid-November. From mid-September to late October, small numbers of Mississippi Kites have been seen passing through, as well as a very few rarities such as Sharp-shinned, Cooper's, Broad-winged, and Swainson's Hawks. Noteworthy finds include five Sharp-shinned Hawks 18–24 October 2001 and seven Cooper's Hawks 20 October–3 November 2001.

Ecoregion and habitats: Appendix A, Ecoregion 16, Toledo southern lowlands and foothills. Habitats include: Caribbean coast (LF4), soccer field with clear view of sky, and remnant patches of secondary lowland broadleaf forest (BFL3, BFL6).
Location: N 16° 7.25' W 88° 47.66', the southern end of the Southern Highway. The soccer field is one mile north of the Punta Gorda welcome sign.

Joe Taylor Creek

[28 February] The first American Pygmy Kingfisher flies by as we are climbing into kayaks. We see two more shortly thereafter. Joe Taylor Creek is the place to find these tiny, brightly orange kingfishers. The creek is narrow and deep, often the same in each dimension, about 20 feet. Smooth like mirrored glass, it takes no effort to paddle a few strokes and then drift silently while we search for birds in the mangroves. George is our guide. We pass his house, built on stilts and perched in the swamp at the edge of the creek. We scan his small yard for Rufous-necked Wood-Rails and Clapper Rails, species he says he sees there almost every dawn and dusk. This time they are hidden. The single monotone whistle of a Northern Beardless-Tyrannulet rings from high in the trees. As we drift silently along the creek, beneath the overarching canopy, we hear Ivory-billed Woodcreeper, Bright-rumped Attila, and Northern Schiffornis.

Birding strategy: Joe Taylor Creek is best explored by kayak in early morning or after 4 PM, if the tide is low and falling. Go to TIDE Tours, a subsidiary of Toledo Institute for Development and Environment, to rent kayaks and ask for George Elford to be your guide, best arranged a day or two beforehand. George is a bird guide and a champion kayaker, and the creek runs beside his house so he has an intimate knowledge of the rails and creekside birds, such as Yellow-crowned Night-Heron, Common Black-Hawk, Ruddy Crake, Sora, and Rufous-breasted Spinetail. In addition to exploring from kayak, you can disembark at a level and partially open side of the creek, pull the kayaks ashore, and hike slowly through the forest. Western Slaty-Antshrikes are here and you should get a close view of both the black male and chocolate female sporting white spots on their wings, perhaps reminiscent of Dot-winged Antwrens, but these birds are much larger. Northern Bentbill and Northern Schiffornis call often, and the habitat lends itself to getting good looks as well. The trail varies between a narrow path through dense jungle and more open areas, offering species such as Gray-chested Dove, Stripe-throated Hermit, Black-faced Antthrush, Tawny-winged Woodcreeper, Yellow-bellied Tyrannulet, Tawny-crowned Greenlet, Long-billed Gnatwren, and Thick-billed Seed-Finch.

Ecoregion and habitats: Appendix A, Ecoregion 16, Toledo southern lowlands and foothills. Habitats include: riparian forest and wetlands along a narrow freshwater creek running to the sea, densely forested often with a closed canopy over the creek (BFL6).

Fees and contact: Entrance is about US$1 usually charged with rentals. Kayaks rent by the hour, half-day, or full-day. A half-day rental is US$7.50 (singles or doubles same price). Guide fee is extra. TIDE Tours, 41 Front Street, P.O. Box 150, Punta Gorda, Toledo District; (011) 501-722-2129; fax (011) 501-722-2655; info@tidetours.org; www.tidetours.org.

Location: N 16° 6.59' W 88° 47.94' at bridge under highway. The creek enters the sea just 0.2 mile north of the Punta Gorda welcome sign. A short distance north of this crossing, look inland on a driveway for TIDE Tours.

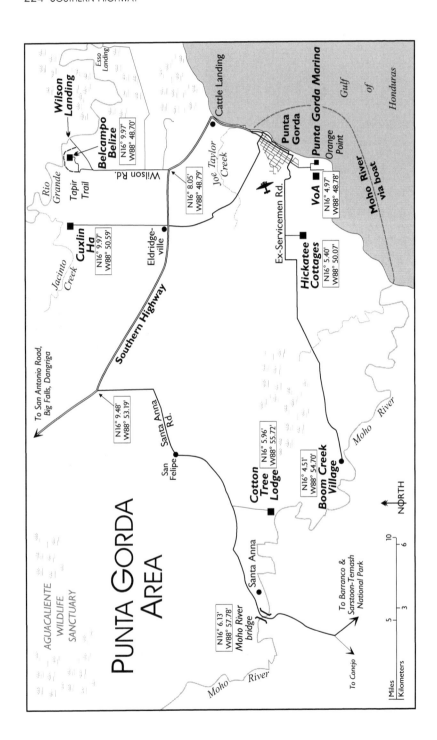

Esso Landing

Cattle Landing

Gulf

of

Honduras

Wilson Landing

Belcampo Belize

N16° 9.97'
W88° 48.70'

Punta Gorda

Punta Gorda Marina

Orange Point

Rio Grande

Tapir Trail

Wilson Rd.

Joe Taylor Creek

N16° 8.05'
W88° 48.79'

Ex-Servicemen Rd.

VoA

N16° 4.97'
W88° 48.78'

Moho River via boat

Cuxlin Ha

N16° 9.97'
W88° 50.59'

Eldridge-ville

Jacinto Creek

Hickatee Cottages

N16° 5.40'
W88° 50.07'

Southern Highway

To San Antonio Road,
Big Falls, Dangriga

N16° 9.48'
W88° 53.19'

Santa Anna Rd.

San Felipe

N16° 5.96'
W88° 55.72'

Cotton Tree Lodge

N16° 4.51'
W88° 54.70'

Boom Creek Village

Moho River

NORTH

PUNTA GORDA
AREA

AGUACALIENTE
WILDLIFE
SANCTUARY

Santa Anna

N16° 6.13'
W88° 57.78'
Moho River bridge

To Barranco &
Sarstoon-Temash National Park

To Conejo

Miles
Kilometers

10
6

5
3

Moho River

PUNTA GORDA

Description: Less visited by birders than most other districts, the southern part of Belize in Toledo District nonetheless holds an excellent storehouse of good birds and good birding in the forested foothills and lowland wetlands. Most commonly referred to as P.G., Punta Gorda is a laid-back town on the Bay of Honduras, not far from the border with Guatemala. The town is not necessarily the best habitat for birding; nonetheless some of the village and adjacent areas are worth investigating, especially if you are walking. One of the best finds is Western Slaty-Antshrike. On the other extreme, Punta Gorda is one of the few places you can find House Sparrow in Belize; look for them at the police station.

Punta Gorda is the base of operations, offering many resorts and hotels as well as restaurants, supplies, airport, boat dock, hospital, groceries, and an open-air market. Nine flights daily arrive from Belize City, Dangriga, and Placencia. Punta Gorda also can be reached by James Bus Line from Belize City, five hours by express bus, 6.5 hours by regular bus. Boats travel to Puerto Barrios and Livingston, Guatemala. In addition to the resorts outside of town, Punta Gorda has offerings of its own. Charlton Inn and St. Charles Inn are comfortable, modestly priced hotels in town. Nature's Way, where many backpackers stay, is lacking in facilities but inexpensive. Local lodging is also available at Coral House Inn, Beya Suites, and Sea Front Inn. The latter is located adjacent to the Punta Gorda welcome sign and is operated by Larry and Carol Smith; P.O. Box 20, Punta Gorda Town, Toledo District; (011) 501-722-2300; office@seafrontinn.com; www.seafrontinn.com.

In addition to town birding, day trips from P.G. are easy except, perhaps, those farthest into the foothills. In order of increasing travel time from town, the sites described in this chapter are: Joe Taylor Creek, Cattle Landing soccer field, Boom Creek Road and Hickatee Cottages, Jacinto Creek and Cuxlin Ha, Rio Grande, Belcampo Belize and Wilson Landing, Moho River, Boom Creek Village and Santa Anna, Aguacaliente Wildlife Sanctuary, Santa Anna Road and Cotton Tree Lodge, San Antonio Road, Lubaantun, Blue Creek and Blue Creek Cave, The Lodge at Big Falls, Nim Li Punit, Rio Blanco National Park, Pueblo Viejo Falls, San Jose, and Jimmy Cut.

Birding strategy: Sites described here are within walking distance of town. A few herons and terns and typically not much else wander the coastline, but rarities and amazing sightings sometimes occur. Ten days after Hurricane *Iris* hit in October 2001, an amazing 80 Keel-billed Toucans were observed in a two-hour period. The next month the first documented Belize records for American Pipit occurred. Early one December, 60 Roseate Terns showed up at the customs dock and some were still there at the end of the month. The only jaeger species recorded for the southern half of Belize is

Pomarine, and one was flying close to shore at Punta Gorda on 4 January 2002. More typically, they are seen from boats at sea, including up to a dozen from the ferry to Livingston, Guatemala.

To reach a few of the Punta Gorda coastal sites from the north end, where the Southern Highway log ends (see page 179), take Front Street south:

Mile
0.0   Southern Highway at Punta Gorda sign. Continue on Front Street (one-way).
0.1   Sea Front Inn on right.
0.3   Texaco gas station.
0.4   A cluster of buildings and structures, including James Bus Line, Police Station, Post Office, ferry dock to Guatemala, Customs and Immigration office, and shortly thereafter, Toledo Ecotourism Association.

Heading north from Punta Gorda, the first birding site is **Joe Taylor Creek,** which is described in more detail in the previous section. The creek is best viewed by kayak, yet sometimes you can check out the shore from **Cattle Landing** residential areas.

There are multiple ways to get to birding sites south of town, but the two main routes are West Street and Far West Street. If your goal is to reach **Hickatee Cottages** and **Boom Creek Road**, starting from the Punta Gorda sign on the north end of town, work your way south and west to Far West Street (see map). Take it past the tall telecommunications tower to a fork in the road and curve right. Here is an example route:

Mile
0.0   Southern Highway at Punta Gorda sign. Continue on Main Middle Street.
0.3   Turn right onto King Street.
0.5   Turn left onto Far West Street.
1.2   Pass telecommunications tower on right.
1.3   Turn right on Ex-Servicemen Road.

Alternatively, to reach the former VoA—now called Toledo Freezone—and other south Punta Gorda birding sites,

Mile
0.0   Southern Highway at Punta Gorda sign. Continue on Main Middle Street.
0.3   Turn right onto King Street.
0.4   Turn left onto West Street.
1.4   Jog left and enter a forested area.
1.5   Cross a small bridge.
1.7   T-intersection.

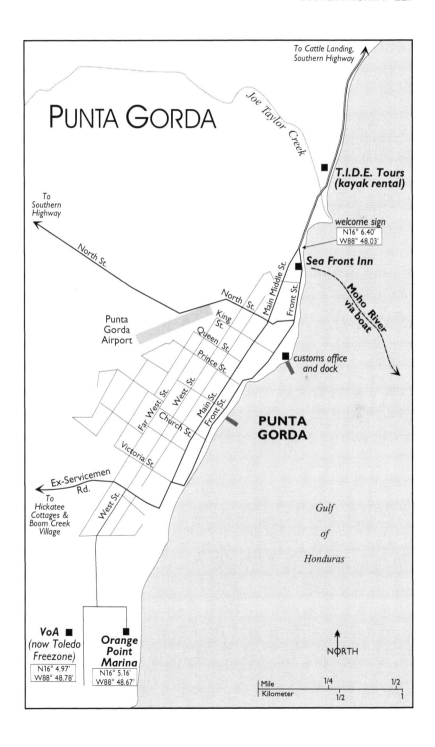

PUNTA GORDA

To Cattle Landing,
Southern Highway

Joe Taylor Creek

T.I.D.E. Tours
(kayak rental)

To
Southern
Highway

North St.

welcome sign
N16° 6.40'
W88° 48.03'

Sea Front Inn

North St.

Main Middle St.

Front St.

Moho River
via boat

Punta
Gorda
Airport

King
St.

Queen St.

Prince St.

customs office
and dock

Far West St.

West St.

Church St.

Main St.

Front St.

PUNTA
GORDA

Victoria St.

Ex-Servicemen
Rd.

To
Hickatee
Cottages &
Boom Creek
Village

West St.

Gulf

of

Honduras

VoA
(now Toledo
Freezone)
N16° 4.97'
W88° 48.78'

Orange
Point
Marina
N16° 5.16'
W88° 48.67'

NORTH

Mile   1/4   1/2
Kilometer   1/2   1

The wooded strip from 1.4 to 1.7 is good for birding. Left at the T-intersection leads to Punta Gorda (Orange Point) Marina (N 16° 5.16' W 88° 48.67'). Housing and commercial developments keep eroding the good habitat and limiting access to what remains. Much of this area is private property, so you will need to ask permission unless you limit yourself to the access roads. The marina area perpetually is scheduled for development so you might need permission to bird this area as well. If you visit the marina, exit the way you came in and after reaching the T-intersection continue around to the other side of the wooded area toward the old **VoA** (N 16° 4.97' W 88° 48.78'). The towers are no longer in operation and the property has been sold to private entities. Bird along the fenced peripheral, wooded edge, and near the sign marking "Falcon Forest" (private). Western Slaty-Antshrike occurs here within the broadleaf forest interior and forest edge.

Striped Owl occurs at VoA and is more easily found in the Punta Gorda area than elsewhere in Belize; it has been tallied on eight of ten CBCs, with a high count of three. Other local sites for this species include The Dump, Blue Creek Village rice fields, Belcampo Belize, Wilson Landing, and probably Sarstoon Delta. The open area surrounding VoA is a good place to observe all nine species of swallows, including Cave on rare occasions, as they migrate south between August and November. Rare fall migrants worth pursuing at VoA are Mississippi Kite and Broad-winged and Swainson's Hawks. More numerous migrants are Hook-billed, Swallow-tailed, and Plumbeous Kites, Mourning Dove, and Chimney Swift. VoA is the best place to find Scissor-tailed Flycatcher, rivaled only by the Corozal area on the opposite end of the country. Before cattle were released on the land, Glossy Ibis was reported and Gray-breasted Crake was found on a third of 39 visits 1997–2006.

Ecoregion and habitats: Appendix A, Ecoregion 16, Toledo southern lowlands and foothills. Habitats include: Caribbean coast (LF4), urban scrub, vacant lots (PC), and remnant patches of secondary lowland broadleaf forest (BFL3, BFL6).
Location: N 16° 6.40' W 88° 48.03' at "Welcome to Punta Gorda" sign. Southern Highway officially extends to Cattle Landing, 93.8 miles south of Hummingbird Highway, but the road continues in the same condition for another mile to Punta Gorda's welcome sign.

Boom Creek Road and Hickatee Cottages

Description: Ex-Servicemen Road leads west from Punta Gorda about 1.5 miles to Hickatee Cottages. In the 1990s the road was extended to Boom Creek Village, a small K'ekchi and Mestizo community on the banks of the Moho River. Boom Creek Road adds almost six miles of road through lowland broadleaf forest. Lee Jones compiled a list of 219 species at the cottages and along the Boom Creek Road, and more have been added since. Hickatee Cottages is a bed-and-breakfast of four cottages and Charlie's Bar, a building including bar, restaurant, reception, and information center. A relatively inexpensive place to stay, it has the added benefit for birders in that it is surrounded by rainforest. The property includes a mile of jungle trails. Hickatee Cottages offers a variety of day tours.

Birding strategy: Bird along the road. Make reservations for lunch at Hickatee Cottages or stop there for Charlie's Bar, from which 53 bird species have been recorded.

Key species of Boom Creek Road and Boom Creek Village: [See also the section on Moho River, page 231, and its species list]. Great and Little Tinamous, King Vulture, Gray-headed Kite, Bicolored Hawk [R], Gray-headed Dove, **Gray-chested Dove**, Brown-hooded Parrot, Mottled Owl, White-collared and Lesser Swallow-tailed Swifts, Band-tailed Barbthroat [R], Scaly-breasted Hummingbird, White-necked Jacobin, Brown Violetear [R], Slaty-tailed Trogon, Great Antshrike, **Western Slaty-Antshrike**, Dusky Antbird, **Black-faced Antthrush**, Tawny-winged, Ruddy, and Wedge-billed Woodcreepers, Yellow-bellied and Paltry [R] Tyrannulets, Sepia-capped Flycatcher, Northern Bentbill, Royal Flycatcher, Bright-rumped Attila, Northern Schiffornis, **White-winged Becard**, Tawny-crowned Greenlet, **Bananaquit**, Gray-headed, Crimson-collared, Passerini's, and Golden-hooded Tanagers, Buff-throated Saltator, Slate-colored Seedeater [R], Orange-billed and Green-backed Sparrows, Giant Cowbird, Scrub and White-vented [R] Euphonias.

Ecoregion and habitats: Appendix A, Ecoregion 16, Toledo southern lowlands and foothills. Habitats include: lowland broadleaf forest (BFL6) and lodge (PC).

Contacts: Hickatee Cottages, Kate and Ian Morton, P.O. Box 148, Ex-Servicemen Road, Punta Gorda Town, Toledo District; (011) 501-662-4475; cottages@hickatee.com; www.hickatee.com.

Location and directions: N 16° 5.65' W 88° 48.67' at intersection of Far West Street near Cemetery Road in Punta Gorda. See the section on Punta Gorda for directions through town to this intersection. Head west on Ex-servicemen Road. At 0.7 you will pass the western edge of Punta Gorda. Hickatee Cottages road is at 1.7, on the left (N 16° 5.40' W 88° 50.07'). Continue birding along Boom Creek Road. Your first approach to the Moho River will be at about 7 miles in Boom Creek Village (N 16° 4.51' W 88° 54.70').

Santa Anna Road
and Cotton Tree Lodge

Description: The previous section describes the Boom Creek Road approach to Moho River. There are two other approaches. The next section describes an approach by boat from the Bay of Honduras. This section describes the entrance by Santa Anna Road, the farthest north access, branching from Southern Highway. Not shown on Belize maps, the gravel road winds to the Maya village of Santa Anna and soon thereafter crosses the Moho River. The road passes through agricultural fields and pastures.

Birding strategy: For a list of bird specialties near the lodge see those for Boom Creek Road and for Moho River, which share similar habitat. Guests of Cotton Tree Lodge arrive via the river. However, if you are not staying at the lodge and do not want to charter a boat, you can drive Santa Anna Road. Using this route, the best spots to visit are Cotton Tree Lodge—stop for toilets, drinks, and lunch at the restaurant—and the bridge over Moho River. Sungrebe has been spotted from the bridge. After Moho River, consider birding Barranco and Sarstoon-Temash National Park. Cotton Tree Lodge offers day trips to Barranco.

Cotton Tree Lodge was built on an old farm and orchard that had quite an impressive number of fruiting and flowering trees and shrubs that attract birds. With a shaded lawn under mango and cacao trees and an elevated boardwalk, Cotton Tree Lodge offers one of the best places in southern Belize to see hummingbirds, thrushes, tanagers, honeycreepers, saltators, orioles, euphonias, and good views of normally secretive warblers such as Ovenbird, Kentucky, and Hooded.

Directions: Signs at Southern Highway (N 16° 9.48' W 88° 53.19') point to Santa Anna, Barranco, Cotton Tree Lodge, and Tranquility Lodge. Zero your odometer at this intersection and turn west on a gravel road. At 1.3 miles turn right to San Felipe at 2.8. At 4.7 miles is the entrance road, about one mile long, to Cotton Tree Resort. At 6.6 is the Santa Anna school and at 7.5 is the bridge over Moho River, (N 16° 6.13' W 88° 57.78').

Ecoregion and habitats: Appendix A, Ecoregion 16, Toledo southern lowlands and foothills. Habitats include: lowland scrublands and riparian along Moho River (BFL6); a few small villages (PC).

Contact: Cotton Tree Lodge, P.O. Box 104, Punta Gorda, Toledo District; (011) 501-670-0557; info@cottontreelodge.com; www.cottontreelodge.com. US office: Cotton Tree Lodge, 440 E. 117th St., Suite 4B, New York, NY 10035; 212-529-8622 or toll-free 866-480-4534; fax 917-591-3082.

Location: N 16° 5.96' W 88° 55.72' at lodge. Santa Anna Road turns off from Southern Highway eight miles north of Punta Gorda.

Moho River, Boom Creek Village, and Santa Anna

[7 March] The loud hissing of the boa constrictor surprises me and I jump back a foot. "Did you get a good picture?" someone on the boat asks me. "A little too good," I reply. The boa is not the only wildlife we see today. Yucatan Black Howlers complain from the tall trees and we see two of them high in the canopy. A Neotropical River Otter swims in front of the boat and dives out of sight. Sleeping Proboscis Bats cling to the side of a tree stump pushing from the river bottom. And then there are the birds. Roberto is good at identifying bird calls and he points out Bright-rumped Attila. I'm impressed with the cheerful quail-like melody of the brightly colored Yellow-tailed Orioles, a song I more easily remember. We pass along Red Mangroves, tallest here in Toledo District and densely lining the river shore. Seeing birds in thick leaf cover is hard, so our attention is drawn mostly to birds in flight—Osprey, Swallow-tailed and Plumbeous Kites, Mangrove Swallows—or perched prominently: Bare-throated Tiger-Heron, Boat-billed Herons, Hook-billed Kite, Common Black-Hawks.

We stop at Santa Anna and disembark for a break that soon becomes lunch and a siesta under shade trees. Local women wash clothes in the river, attended by toddlers playing beside them. The women stand waist deep in the water, vigorously pounding the clothes on flat rocks. Nearby, a fleet of dugout canoes is pulled up on shore. Earlier we had encountered young men in these boats who showed us their catch of snared iguana and speared snook, both destined for the dinner table. The village is made up of the thatched-roof board houses we've seen often in rural Toledo District. At 2:30 we board the boat and leisurely return downstream, adding more species to the day list that eventually reaches 102.

Description: The mouth of the wide river opens to the Gulf of Honduras south of Punta Gorda and not far north of Belize's southern border with Guatemala. Redundantly, Moho River means "The Wet River." Traveling south from Punta Gorda, the boat follows the coastline for five miles to the mouth of Moho River. The broad river narrows as it passes through Red Mangrove littoral forest for almost seven miles. Secondary forest changes to disturbed forest when you reach Boom Creek Village, where you can stop for a break and stretch your legs at a good birding spot. Continuing upriver for another three or four miles, you will see bamboo lining the riversides and shortly thereafter come to Cotton Tree Lodge. Disembark here for toilets, refreshments, and birding around the resort grounds (see details, page 230). Another three miles upriver is the Maya village of Santa Anna. Toilets are available here, too, and birding is good along the riverfront and from the short trails leading into the wooded areas. Just beyond the village is a bridge, 20 miles since you left the Punta Gorda dock, beyond which the boat cannot travel. When you again reach the Bay of Honduras on the return trip, try to approach a small landing where gulls and terns gather, and check for rarities. The sea will be rougher as you head back to the dock in late afternoon, but easily manageable.

Gray-headed Kite   Bert Frenz

Birding strategy: Charter a boat in Punta Gorda, start at dawn (6 AM), and reach Santa Anna by 11 AM. Bird under and around the shade trees between the river and the village, including a short path into the jungle that starts to the left as you face the village from the river. Remember to show proper respect for the local people you meet; this excursion visits the native village where they live and work. If you brought lunch with you, along the cool river under the shade trees would be a pleasant picnic spot. Alternatively, return to Cotton Tree Lodge for lunch and more birding. The midday heat will limit birding possibilities, so you need to decide whether you want to take the boat back under bright and hot sunshine or wait until mid-afternoon before returning. With limited birding and casual boat driving along the river, the return trip to Punta Gorda takes about 2.5 hours.

K ey species of Moho River and riverside stops: [See also the list for Boom Creek Road, page 229]. Great Tinamou, **Muscovy Duck**, Crested Guan, Anhinga, White Ibis, Wood Stork, King Vulture, Osprey, Hook-billed and Swallow-tailed [S] Kites, **Plumbeous Kite** [S], Common Black-Hawk, Collared Forest-Falcon, Ruddy Crake, Gray-necked Wood-Rail, **Sungrebe**, Brown-hooded and Mealy Parrots, Northern Potoo, Scaly-breasted Hummingbird, Amazon Kingfisher, **American Pygmy Kingfisher**, White-necked Puffbird, **Great Antshrike**, **Western Slaty-Antshrike**, Plain Antvireo [R], Dot-winged Antwren, Dusky and Bare-crowned [R] Antbirds, Rufous-breasted Spinetail, Yellow-bellied Tyrannulet, Northern Beardless-Tyrannulet, **Paltry Tyrannulet**, Slate-headed Tody-Flycatcher, Stub-tailed Spadebill, Gray-crowned Yellowthroat, **Bananaquit**, Passerini's and Golden-hooded Tanagers, Grayish Saltator, Thick-billed Seed-Finch, Bronzed and Giant Cowbirds, White-vented Euphonia [R].

Ecoregion and habitats: Appendix A, Ecoregion 16, Toledo southern lowlands and foothills. Habitats include: riparian lowland broadleaf forest (BFL6), mostly pristine secondary forest of Red Mangrove and bamboo (LF4), eventually degrading to disturbed forest (BFL3).

Contacts: Roberto Echeverria, both boat operator and birding guide, of SFI Tours. Contact him by e-mail at seatoledobelize@gmail.com or kingkai4@hotmail.com; by phone at (011) 501-663-4559 or 702-0020. Roberto is the son-in-law of Larry and Carol Smith, who own Sea Front Inn. If you cannot reach Roberto by his e-mail, try the inn at office@seafrontinn.com, (011) 501-722-2300.

An alternative boat operator, although specializing mostly in fishing and snorkeling, is Dan Castellanos. He also conducts trips up the Moho River; Blue-Belize, 139 Front Stret, Punta Gorda (011) 501-722-2678; info@bluebelize.com; www.bluebelize.com.

Location: N 16° 3.35' W 88° 51.00' at river's mouth. The boat departs from the dock opposite Sea Front Inn, N 16° 6.34' W 88° 48.03', in Punta Gorda.

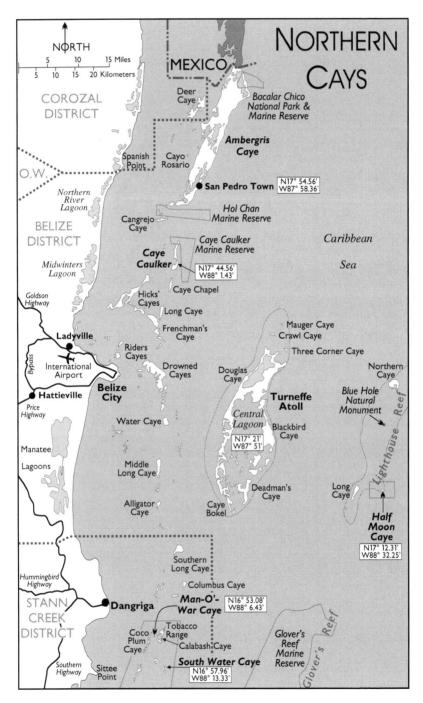

NORTH

5   10   15 Miles
5   10   15   20 Kilometers

COROZAL
DISTRICT

O.W.

Northern
River
Lagoon

BELIZE
DISTRICT

Midwinters
Lagoon

Goldson
Highway

Ladyville

Bypass

International
Airport

Hattieville

Price
Highway

Manatee

Lagoons

Belize
City

MEXICO

Deer
Caye

Spanish
Point

Cayo
Rosario

Bacalar Chico
National Park &
Marine Reserve

Ambergris
Caye

● **San Pedro Town** | N17° 54.56'
                         | W87° 58.36'

Cangrejo
Caye

Hol Chan
Marine Reserve

Caye Caulker
Marine Reserve

Caye
Caulker | N17° 44.56'
                  | W88° 1.43'

Caye Chapel

Hicks'
Cayes

Long Caye

Frenchman's
Caye

Riders
Cayes

Drowned
Cayes

Douglas
Caye

Water Caye

Middle
Long Caye

Alligator
Caye

Caye
Bokel

Mauger Caye
Crawl Caye

Three Corner Caye

Turneffe
Atoll

Central
Lagoon   Blackbird
            Caye

| N17° 21'
| W87° 51'

Deadman's
Caye

Caribbean

Sea

Northern
Caye

Blue Hole
Natural
Monument

Long
Caye

Half
Moon
Caye | N17° 12.31'
             | W88° 32.25'

Lighthouse Reef

Southern
Long Caye

Columbus Caye

Hummingbird
Highway

STANN
CREEK
DISTRICT

Southern
Highway

Sittee
Point

● **Dangriga**

Man-O'- | N16° 53.08'
War Caye | W88° 6.43'

Coco
Plum
Caye

Tobacco
Range

Calabash Caye

South Water Caye | N16° 57.96'
                         | W88° 13.33'

Glover's
Reef
Marine
Reserve

Glover's Reef

NORTHERN
CAYS

CHAPTER 6
THE CAYS

"C ayo" in Spanish-speaking countries, "cay" in the English-speaking Caribbean, "key" in Florida, but in Belize they spell specific islands "caye." A 180-mile reef stretches the entire length of Belize, from its northern border at Ambergris Caye to just beyond its southern border with Guatemala in the Bay of Honduras. This is North America's longest barrier reef and is second in the world only to Australia's Great Barrier Reef. Ambergris Caye is thought to have formed from coral fragments along with silt from the Río Hondo; the Barrier Reef lies 1,000 feet off its windward side. At its southern extremity, the reef is 25 miles from the mainland. Other cays are part of three coral atolls: Turneffe Atoll (the largest at 300 square miles), Glover's Reef, and Lighthouse Reef with its famous Blue Hole and, for birders, Half Moon Caye.

Many tourists visit Belize by ocean-going ship or flight to an island, missing the jewels of mainland jungles, rivers, and mountains. So also, many a birder has visited the mainland but missed the unique birds of the cays.

Concerns: While Ambergris Caye and Caye Caulker can be reached by boat or by plane, the other islands require travel by sea. Not everyone likes boat rides in open sea. If the seas are high, cancel your plans. Even though these waters are relatively calm, if you are prone to sea sickness you may want to forego this adventure. For the most comfortable ride, sit as far back in the boat as you can get. In Belize, boat operators and dive instructors must be licensed and must carry sufficient life preservers. Make sure your operator is licensed.

Getting to the cays

By air: Tourists typically arrive by air from one of the mainland airports, most often Belize City, with destinations to Ambergris Caye and Caye Caulker, a 20-minute flight.

Belize Coast, Caribbean Sea   Bert Frenz

Each of the two Belize airlines has hourly flights from about 7:30 AM to 5:30 PM. There are also direct flights from Corozal to Ambergris Caye and thence to Caye Caulker. See "Getting there" in Chapter 1 for details.

By sea: Water taxis connect to the mainland primarily through Belize City (hourly departures from 8 AM to 4:30 PM), but also through Corozal (twice daily). Ambergris Caye and Caye Caulker are the main stops. Travel time to Ambergris Caye is 75 minutes from Belize City and 2 hours from Corozal. In Belize City, the water taxis board at the Marine Terminal located next to the Swing Bridge, a 30-minute (US$20) land taxi ride from Philip Goldson International Airport. You can buy tickets at the dock.

Contacts: Caye Caulker Water Taxi Association: Daily water taxis between Belize City, Caye Caulker, Ambergris Caye, Long Caye, and Caye Chapel; special charters can be arranged to other reefs, atolls, and coral islands; prices are US$10 to $15 one-way; Caye Caulker Water Taxi, P.O. Box 60, Caye Caulker; (011) 501-223-5752 or 226-0992; ccwatertaxi@btl.net; www.cayecaulkerwatertaxi.com.

Thunderbolt: Departs from Corozal at 7 AM and 3 PM; leaves from Ambergris Caye 3 PM or next morning; the boat also stops at Sarteneja on the mainland; prices are US$45 one-way or $75 round trip; just show up at the pier near Corozal's Reunion Park for transport. Contact is Elisio Rivero, Corozal; (011) 501-422-0026; thunderbolttravels@yahoo.com.

Getting to the unpopulated or sparsely populated cays is more difficult, as boat operators to these destinations often do not stay in business long. (One operator with a web site is detailed in the Half Moon Caye section.) To charter a boat on your own, start by contacting Caye Caulker Water Taxi Association, or perhaps conduct a web search for other leads, particularly for companies catering to snorkeling and diving. One good source is www.guide tobelize.info/en/travel/belize-water-taxi-timetable-guide.shtml.

Alternatively, make your arrangements through a resort that offers boat trips to the cays. Often these resorts own property on one of the cays and have local boats to transport passengers. For example, Pelican Beach Resort in Dangriga has a companion resort 14 miles (45 minutes) out to sea on the private island of South Water Caye and you probably also can arrange to see Man-O'-War Caye on the way. In Punta Gorda, Cuxlin Ha owns a site in the Sapodilla Cayes and can arrange lodging and transport there.

AMBERGRIS CAYE

[26 February] Three 225-hp outboard motors push the torpedo-shaped boat across the smooth Caribbean, through Corozal Bay and directly toward the rising sun. I'm sitting at the stern. Forty passengers spill over the 28 seats and into the aisle and cargo area. Many in our group will be spending the night at resorts on the island. I scan the turquoise sea for wildlife, but see only a few Royal Terns and a cormorant. After two hours on the water, we turn into a lagoon of Ambergris Caye and dock at San Pedro. We rent a four-passenger golf cart with oversized tires and tour the island, first the resort end and then the more remote northern end, driving narrow dusty roads first and a rutted, bumpy trail second. If I were to remain overnight, I think I'd want to stay at lodging which has a small but thickly wooded bird sanctuary with a lookout tower. Most of the island is cleared of native vegetation so the prominent birds are grackles and White-winged Doves. But in these little woods we see many Black Catbirds and a small variety of other species. Then we do the tourist thing: shopping and eating lunch at a good restaurant. San Pedro ends at a river channel and we drive the golf cart up onto a ferry big enough for two carts and a few bicycles. A dark shirtless man strains on a rope to pull us across the narrow channel and then we lumber onto the other shore while he holds the raft steady. The ride northward at midday is stifling hot whenever we stop to look at birds or the seashore, but cooler when we are moving. I get a quick look at a Yellow-backed Oriole, but too short a view of an ani to tell whether it is Smooth-billed or Groove-billed. Many newly completed condos are for sale, as is vacant land. This island is quickly changing to a tropical resort spot and, undoubtedly, will be less of a wildlife habitat.

Description: Ambergris Caye (variously pronounced *Am-BUR-gris* or *Am-BUR-grease* Key by tourists, and *AM-bur-gris* Kay by Belizeans) is about 25 miles long and one mile wide. Geographically, the cay is more like a long

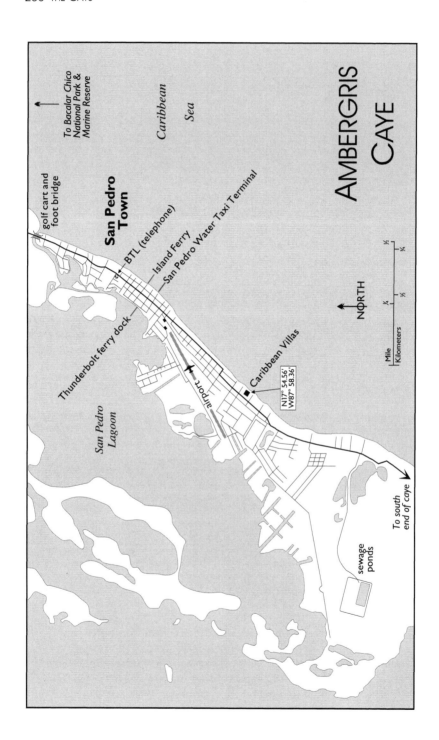

peninsula extending from Mexico that only became an island when pre-Columbian Maya dug a canal across its northern end. It is less isolated from the mainland than other cays and it has a different, more extensive, bird population, hence its treatment on a separate checklist from other cays. Over 275 species have been recorded here, although most are passage migrants, some occasional to accidental, and therefore not to be expected during a short winter visit. Early April to mid-May and September to early November are the best windows for transients.

There are dozens of places to stay on the cay—check the Internet—but one deserves special mention. The most accessible and most productive birding site is the 2.5-acre landscaped gardens and littoral forest within the grounds of Caribbean Villas Hotel. Within the bird sanctuary is a three-story observation tower, looking down on the tree canopy and with, as they say, "a 360-degree view of the Caribbean to the east, Hol Chan Marine Preserve to the south, San Pedro to the north, and west to the San Pedro Lagoon and the Chetumal Bay beyond." The bird sanctuary is in the cluster of hotels on the windward side of the cay, just south of the airport runway. In a week-long fall migration count, 81 of 108 species were identified at Caribbean Villa's bird sanctuary. A rare find on mainland Belize, a Great Horned Owl perched in the wooded sanctuary in February 2010. These owls can be heard most nights just about anywhere on the cay, even on the periphery of town.

Birding strategy: A day trip to the cay will get you a few species, but an overnight will be better. Alternatively, you could book a week-stay at a hotel and explore the island fully, as well as make an excursion to the mainland. For traveling information, refer to the beginning of this chapter.

You can get around San Pedro, the only town on the cay, on foot, but to see more of Ambergris Caye in a short time you will want to rent a bicycle, golf cart, or scooter. The golf carts rent by the hour, day (US$75), or week.

Many of the better sightings are at Bacalar Chico National Park, positioned farther north on Ambergris Caye, about 17 miles from San Pedro. To explore

---

Ecoregion checklist and habitats: Appendix A, Ecoregion 17, Ambergris Caye. Habitats include: lowland broadleaf forest (BFL2), mangrove and littoral forest (LF1), fresh and brackish water, beaches and commercial areas (PC).

Contacts: Caribbean Villas, P.O. Box 71, Seagrape Drive, San Pedro, Ambergris Caye; (011) 501-226-2715 or toll-free in US: 866-290-6341; fax (011) 501-226-2885; info@caribbeanvillashotel.com; www.caribbeanvillashotel.com.

Elbert Greer, General Delivery, Ambergris Caye; dive shop: (011) 501-226-2405; elbertgreer@fastmail.fm; http://ambergriscaye.com/birds.

Location: N 17° 54.56' W 87° 58.36' at base of observation tower in Caribbean Villas; N 18° 7.29' W 87° 49.68' at Bacalar Chico National Park; N 17° 53.80' W 87° 59.51' at sewage ponds.

the many channels, lagoons, and mangrove islands you will need a boat. Heavily promoted on the web and in the "Birds of Ambergris Caye" newspaper column he writes for the *San Pedro Sun*, Elbert Greer is available as a birding guide (and scuba instructor) and can arrange boat trips as well.

One other birding site not on the beaten path is the island's sewage ponds, located south of the airport. Here you can find Ruddy Crake, Clapper Rail, and Sora. Wilson's Phalarope was found here in spring 1999 and another nearby in fall 2011.

You will notice in the species mentioned below that the rarities list is considerably longer than for mainland sites. While your chance of seeing a particular one of these is slim, the long list demonstrates the high percentage of rarities found on Ambergris Caye and the islands. You may be fortunate enough to add species to this list.

Key species of Ambergris Caye and immediate offshore areas: [see the checklist at www.bafrenz.com for the 40+ transient migrant passerines that pass through, many of which are much harder to find on the mainland.] Magnificent Frigatebird, Brown Booby, **Reddish Egret**, Yellow-crowned Night-Heron, Roseate Spoonbill, Osprey, Common Black-Hawk, Broad-winged Hawk, Ruddy Crake, **Clapper Rail**, **Sora**, Black-bellied Plover, **Wilson's Plover**, Semipalmated Plover, Sanderling, Least and Black [T] Terns, **White-crowned Pigeon** [S], Common Ground-Dove, **Caribbean Dove**, Green-breasted Mango, **Cinnamon Hummingbird**, Yucatan Woodpecker, Common Tody-Flycatcher, **Yucatan Vireo**, Gray-crowned Yellowthroat, **Mangrove Yellow Warbler**, Palm Warbler, **Prairie Warbler**, **Bananaquit**, Yellow-backed Oriole, **Orange** and **Altamira Orioles**.

Rarities: Audubon's Shearwater, White-tailed Tropicbird, Masked and Red-footed Boobies, Least Bittern, Gray-headed, Hook-billed, and Double-toothed Kites, Sharp-shinned and Crane Hawks, Collared Plover, Upland Sandpiper [T], Red Knot, White-rumped [T] and Stilt Sandpipers, Wilson's Phalarope [T], Bonaparte's and Franklin's [T] Gulls, Brown Noddy, Sooty [S], Bridled [S], and Forster's Terns, Great Skua, Pomarine and Parasitic Jaegers, Mangrove and Black-billed [T] Cuckoos, Yucatan Nightjar, Eastern Whip-poor-will [T], Black-crested Coquette, Black-whiskered Vireo [T], Cave Swallow [T], Clay-colored [T] and Lark [T] Sparrows.

CAYE CAULKER

[31 January] From the air, we can see Corozal Bay and the narrow winding New River near the hand-drawn ferry. East of the spot where we visited Shipstern Nature Reserve, civilization ends: no roads, no buildings, no hint of people, just dark broadleaf forest sprinkled with lighter green palms and interspersed with

mudflats, watery marshes, and small pools. Near the coast, a few dime-sized islands dot half-dollar lagoons and one of them is speckled with white, undoubtedly an egret nesting colony. Now we are over coral reefs, transparently exposed through the crystal-clear turquoise Caribbean. The blue deepens to ultramarine before we reach Caye Caulker, an island diminutive from the air. We smoothly pull up to the small terminal building about 20 minutes after departure.

Many of us start birding immediately, and within minutes we find a Bananaquit (coboti subspecies), a pretty lemon-yellow and white bird, soft in texture, and spry in movement. We bird the loop trail through the CCBTIA Mini-Reserve and find a Yucatan Vireo. We are delighted to find a Prairie Warbler that rockets round-robin from bush to tree to bush. A better prize is our first good view of a Black Catbird, a resident of the cays, but infrequently found on the mainland. We head to the south end of the island, skirting the shore. Our walk along the palm-shaded shoreline yields Yellow-crowned Night-Herons, Whimbrel, Marbled Godwit, Ruddy Turnstones, and Sanderlings. Cinnamon Hummingbirds are common. We search in vain for Rufous-necked Wood-Rails at their known haunts, later to be told that our arrival is too late in the day.

Description: Caye Caulker may derive its name from caulking seams in wooden boats to make them watertight, as many shipwrights built boats on the island. Alternatively, "Cay Corker," the Old English spelling, suggests the story that sailors corked water bottles after replenishing their supply from the fresh water at La Aguada. Contrasting to Ambergris Caye, island life on Caye Caulker has a much different feel, being more laid back, more cultural, and less touristy. The limestone coral cay is only 5 miles long and less than a mile wide. About 21 miles northeast of Belize City, it can be reached by water taxi or hourly flights from the mainland, as described in Chapter 1. Water taxis also connect to Ambergris Caye, a 45-minute ride. If you are on the cay only for birding, an overnight or two will suffice. If you intend to visit other islands you will need to add a day or two.

Some 50 guesthouses, inns, and hotels are on the cay, although some may be more rustic than you would like. One of the best places is Seaside Cabanas, which boasts the only swimming pool on the island. It fronts the pier from which the water taxis come and go and is a block from Caye Caulker Golf Cart and Trailer Rentals, as well as a short walk from most restaurants and shops. Check the Internet for other choices.

Birding strategy: For migrants, the cays are the place to be, and Caye Caulker is about the best in terms of access, accommodations, and birdlife. Topping the list are three dozen warbler species, including regulars such as wintering Ovenbird, Worm-eating, Swainson's, Tennessee, and Kentucky Warblers, Northern Parula, Cape May, and Palm Warblers; regular transients such as Blue-winged, Bay-breasted, Mourning, and Blackburnian Warblers; and rarities such as Golden-winged, Nashville, Cerulean, Blackpoll, and Canada Warblers. Other transient migrants of note are: Yellow-billed and

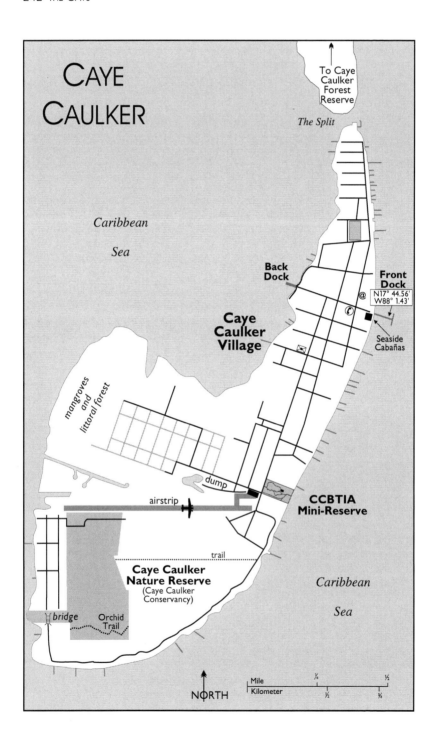

CAYE
CAULKER

To Caye
Caulker
Forest
Reserve

The Split

Caribbean

Sea

Back
Dock

Front
Dock

@ | N17° 44.56'
W88° 1.43'

ℂ

Caye
Caulker
Village

Seaside
Cabañas

mangroves
and
littoral forest

dump

airstrip

CCBTIA
Mini-Reserve

trail

Caye Caulker
Nature Reserve
(Caye Caulker
Conservancy)

Caribbean

Sea

bridge | Orchid
Trail

NORTH

| Mile | | ¼ | | ½ |
| Kilometer | | | ½ | | ¼ |

Black-billed Cuckoos, Olive-sided Flycatcher, Eastern Wood-Pewee, Acadian and Willow Flycatchers, Eastern Kingbird, Red-eyed Vireo, Bank, Cliff, and Barn Swallows, Veery, Gray-cheeked and Swainson's Thrushes, Scarlet Tanager, Painted Bunting, Dickcissel, and Bobolink.

Swainson's is one of the special warblers that is hard to find, not only in Belize but also in the US. It stays well hidden, low to the ground, in brushy habitat. Patiently scan the open areas under mangroves, ziricote, and buttonwood during the months August to April, but especially mid-September through October.

Over 225 species have been recorded on Caye Caulker. Among the most-sought after are Rufous-necked Wood-Rail, White-crowned Pigeon, Black Catbird, Yucatan Vireo, Bananaquit, and Mangrove Yellow Warbler. Caribbean Elaenia breeds here—the only place in Belize where it can be expected—some years but apparently is not resident, since it is absent other years. The southern part of the cay is small enough that you can walk to all birding sites, but if you are short on time you will find it easier to rent a bicycle or golf cart to reach the Caye Caulker Conservancy, where the Rufous-necked Wood-Rails reside. Because the rails are very difficult to find during the day, you should arrive at or before sunrise. Jim and Dorothy Beveridge feed the wood-rails twice a day, 6:15 AM and 2 PM. White-winged Doves and White-crowned Pigeons also participate in the feeding. On the south end, travel through the village along the shoreline and continue along the path amongst the mangrove and littoral forest. As the path turns north, you will need to park the golf cart and continue on foot over a bridge to begin your search for the wood-rails: a population of about two dozen is found from September to May among the roots of the Red Mangroves. White-crowned Pigeons can be found between late February and mid-October.

Another birding spot is the CCBTIA Mini-Reserve, a littoral forest just north of the airstrip on the east side of the island. CCBTIA is Caye Caulker Branch of the Belize Tourism Industry Association, the management entity. Although the reserve is only two acres, its natural flora attracts many of the island specialties such as Black Catbird, Yucatan Vireo, and Bananaquit. Also near the airport is the dump, a less tasteful birding spot that nonetheless attracts egrets, warblers (including Mangrove Yellow Warbler), and an odd assortment of other birds. Along the windward shore of the cay you can walk among mangroves, across beaches, and in residential areas, finding herons and shorebirds. Check out the piers, especially the long one where the water taxi docks, for terns, including an occasional Common and, at least once, Roseate.

About a third of the way northward on the cay, a breach prevents continued walking. To reach the 105-acre Caye Caulker Forest Reserve on the north tip of the island, you will need a boat. Inquire locally, or better yet,

Magnificent Frigatebird   Bert Frenz

hire a birding guide. Dorothy and Jim Beveridge live on the island and have contributed extensively to the knowledge of birdlife on Caye Caulker.

The cay has a long list of species seen only once or twice. Some in the Key Species list below are not seen even annually, though these and the Rarities show the possibilities, as well as demonstrating the potential for more unexpected species to show up.

Key species of Caye Caulker: Magnificent Frigatebird, **Brown Booby**, **Reddish Egret**, Roseate Spoonbill, Osprey, Common Black-Hawk, Peregrine Falcon, **Clapper Rail**, **Rufous-necked Wood-Rail**, Sora, Black-bellied Plover, **Wilson's Plover**, Semipalmated Plover, Black-necked Stilt, Willet, Whimbrel, **Marbled Godwit**, Sanderling, Western Sandpiper, Short-billed Dowitcher, Herring Gull, Least Tern, **Black Tern** [T], Sandwich Tern, **White-crowned Pigeon** [S], Mourning Dove [T], Green-breasted Mango, **Cinnamon Hummingbird**, Yucatan Woodpecker, Yellow-bellied Sapsucker, **Caribbean Elaenia**, Philadelphia Vireo [T], **Yucatan Vireo**, **Black Catbird**, **Mangrove Yellow Warbler**, **Bananaquit**, Hooded Oriole.

Rarities: Audubon's Shearwater, Red-footed Booby, Gray-headed Kite, Uniform Crake, Spotted Rail, Snowy Plover, American Avocet, Upland Sandpiper [T], Long-billed Curlew, Red Knot, White-rumped Sandpiper [T], Long-billed Dowitcher, Black-legged Kittiwake, Franklin's Gull [T], Black Noddy, Roseate Tern [S], Pomarine Jaeger, Caribbean Dove, Mangrove Cuckoo, Smooth-billed Ani, Short-tailed Nighthawk [T], Gray Kingbird, Cave Swallow [T], Virginia's Warbler [T], Lark [T], Savannah [T], Grasshopper [T], and Lincoln's Sparrows, Western Tanager [T], Orange Oriole, Tricolored Munia (non-native).

Ecoregion and habitats: *Appendix A, Ecoregion 18, Other cays. Habitats include: mangrove and strand forests (LF1), fresh and brackish water, beaches, and commercial areas (PC).*

Contacts: *Tropical Nature, Dorothy Beveridge, P.O. Box 10, Caye Caulker; (011) 501-220-4079; bzvisuals@yahoo.com.*

Seaside Cabanas, P. O. Box 39, Caye Caulker Village, Caye Caulker; (011) 501-226-0498; fax (011) 501-226-0125; info@seasidecabanas.com; www.seasidecabanas.com.

Location: *N 17° 44.56' W 88° 1.43' at water-taxi pier, about 21 miles northeast of Belize City.*

HALF MOON CAYE NATIONAL MONUMENT

[1 February] Boat captain Gilbert guides his 38-foot boat cautiously up to the Caye Caulker dock and we quickly board. While floating in calm water we eat a breakfast snack and then pass over the reef where the waves break, entering rougher seas. The turquoise water reaches to the horizon, devoid of other boats and all else but for a few flocks of Sandwich Terns, several flying fish, and a small pod of Bottlenose Dolphins. Choppy water, yet with few white caps, persists for a half-hour, but flattens on the leeward side of Turneffe Atoll where Gilbert throttles the twin outboards. Within the atoll we slow to a crawl and stand up to stretch. Onward toward Half Moon Caye, first rougher seas, then calmer, but a long two hours leaves us anxious to be on land again. The island is everyone's image of paradise: coconut palms swaying in a gentle breeze, frigatebirds smoothly soaring over acres of white sand, beckoning warm water tossing on coral reefs. We take to the hiking trail toward the booby colony, stopping to watch two Prairie Warblers and seeing many Hermit Crabs carrying their fist-sized shell homes on their backs. Close to the rookery we see our first Red-footed Booby perched above us in a tree. The highlight, though, comes upon our climbing the ladder up to the observation platform just at the edge of the rookery and eye level with the tree tops. Not eight feet from the railing sits a booby on her nest, unconcerned about our keen interest in her. Nesting Red-footed Boobies are everywhere, interspersed with Magnificent Frigatebirds, and above us soar dozens more frigatebirds and boobies.

Red-footed Booby   Bert Frenz

Description: Best known for its nesting population of Red-footed Boobies, Half Moon Caye is 50 miles offshore and southeast of Belize City. As Belize's first national protected area and managed by Belize Audubon Society, the 45-acre cay is part of the Lighthouse Reef, the most easterly of Belize's atolls.   The cay has a pier for docking, toilets, picnic tables, hiking trail with interpretative signs, and an observation tower.   Recently erected, a building houses Audubon staff, researchers, and other guests. Approximately 1,000 pairs of Red-footed Boobies inhabit the island, which they share with numerous Magnificent Frigatebirds and about 130 other bird species, of which almost all are migrants.

Ecoregion and habitats: Appendix A, Ecoregion 18, Other cays. Habitats include: coral reef, one-half covered by sand, Coconut Palm trees, and sparse vegetation, the other half covered with rich soil, fertilized by guano from thousands of seabirds, supporting Ziricote (Cordia dodecandra) thickets (LF1).

Fees and contact: In addition to the boat charter, there is an entrance fee of US$10 for non-residents, BZ$2.50 for residents, for visiting the cay.

For transport try Ecologic Divers. In Belize: Dive shop, (011) 501-226-4118 or toll-free in US: 800-244-7774; fax (011) 501-226-4117; charters@ecologicdivers.com or info@ecologicdivers.com; www.ecologicdivers.com.

Birding strategy: Plan your trip during the Red-footed Booby breeding season. The boobies sit on their nests most or all of the year, but beginning in mid-December they add to their nests. The young hatch around March. Chicks fledge a month later, but continue to be fed by both adults for another one to four months.

For spring migration, your best time would be about the last week of April. Migration boosts the checklist to 6 vireo species, 5 swallows, 4 thrushes, and 33 warblers. Other migrants that have occurred include Eastern Wood-Pewee, Eastern Kingbird, Scarlet Tanager, Dickcissel, Bobolink, and many more. The small cay also has hosted its own set of surprise appearances, including Collared Plover, Smooth-billed Ani, Yucatan Nightjar, Caribbean Elaenia, Black-whiskered Vireo, and Chipping, Grasshopper, White-throated, and White-crowned Sparrows. A sampling of other species occurring on the caye is: White-crowned Pigeon, Green-breasted Mango, Cinnamon Hummingbird, Yucatan Vireo, Black Catbird, and Mangrove Yellow Warbler.

The cay and surrounding cays are popular with divers, and it is via boats carrying divers that you most likely will find a way to get to the island. No regularly scheduled trips go to Half Moon Caye, so you will need to check with tour operators, hotels, and the Internet to secure transport. One such company is Ecologic Divers, which operates out of Ambergris Caye but will pick up passengers from Caye Caulker. See the beginning of this chapter for more information. The transport you charter can also provide equipment and a diving guide to accompany you for excellent snorkeling off Half Moon Caye. You would still have plenty of time for island birding and a picnic lunch.

Boat travel times depend on the condition of the sea beyond the Barrier Reef. If calm, the captain will go full throttle; if moderately choppy he will slow to avoid uncomfortable jostling and bumping. Under good to moderate conditions, plan on 40–50 minutes from Ambergris Caye to Caye Caulker, 50–60 minutes from Caye Caulker to Turneffe Atoll, 20–30 minutes slowly traveling through Turneffe Atoll—the water is calm, so it is up to you and the captain on how much time to spend here—and 95–110 minutes from Turneffe Atoll to Half Moon Caye. In 2006 the trip from Caye Caulker to Half Moon Caye took 185 minutes on the way out and 165 minutes on the way back.

TURNEFFE ATOLL

[1 February] Our return trip is over smoother seas and moves more quickly, with less bounce. We decelerate at Turneffe Atoll and coast slowly to watch a pair of Ospreys on a nest. Another high nest brings more intrigue. The nest holds a rare mated pair of a Great Blue Heron and a Great White Heron. On the way back to Caye Caulker and out of sight of the atoll, we see a line of four White Ibis winging just above the rolling waves in the direction of Turneffe. A half-hour later, Cindy spots a circling mass of distant birds, obviously feeding on a concentration of fish

near the surface. With bouncing binoculars I can make out the angular black bodies of frigatebirds and I surmise the smoother and smaller dark bodies are Brown Boobies, as I've often found this combination here in the intercoastal waters. By 5:15 we reach the Caye Caulker dock. We walk to a restaurant built over the water. Fried conch is my order, and delicious it is. After a long day at sea, sleep comes easily and early this night.

Description: Spanning 30 miles in length and 10 miles in width, Turneffe Atoll incorporates more than 200 mangrove islands. Known mostly to scuba divers for its vast marine life and coral formations, it is also recognized as a top Caribbean fishing destination for bonefish and tarpon. The sanctuary protects a substantial American Crocodile population, various bird nesting sites, and the endemic Belize Atoll Gecko. The Ospreys that nest on the cays are *Pandion haliaetus ridgwayi*, a Caribbean subspecies. The migratory *P. h. carolinensis* may also occur. Calabash Caye is a sandy cay on the eastern rim of the Turneffe Islands Atoll and is where three Yellow-naped Parrots were discovered shortly after Hurricane *Mitch* in 1998. Species that prefer cays such as these include: White-crowned Pigeon, Cinnamon Hummingbird, Yucatan Vireo, and Mangrove Yellow Warbler. Brown Noddy and Caribbean Elaenia have been reported.

Birding strategy: The atoll is a worthwhile area in which to slow down when traveling by boat between Caye Caulker and Half Moon Caye. Troll near the mangroves and savannas, scanning for nesting and feeding birds. Turneffe Atoll has more mangrove cays than anywhere else in Belize and, therefore, is a good place to find species such as Clapper Rail. Snorkeling enthusiasts can extend their stay by booking at Blackbird Caye Resort. They offer transport from Belize City, 32 miles distant, on a fast 50-foot boat.

Ecoregion and habitats: *Appendix A, Ecoregion 18, Other cays. Habitats include: shallow saline lagoon, mangroves, savanna, seagrass, and reef (LF1). Coconut Palms on Blackbird Caye.*

Contact: *Blackbird Caye Resort; in US: 13816 SW 142 Avenue, Suite 34, Miami, FL 33186; 866-909-7333 or 305-235-3514; fax 305-235-3574; info@blackbirdresort.com; www.blackbirdresort.com.*

MAN-O'-WAR CAYE AND
SOUTH WATER CAYE MARINE RESERVE

[5 March] Our afternoon itinerary is quite a change of venue, a jump from tropical jungles to tropical islands. Norlan's new boat transports us across the Inner Channel to the Barrier Reef. The calm, intensely turquoise water ripples smoothly below us, without bounce. In 45 minutes, we arrive at palm-studded South Water Caye. Even Chris, as hardcore a birder as you will ever find,

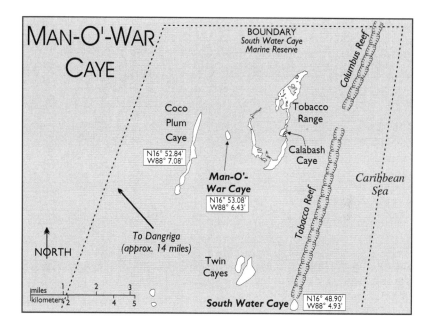

expresses enjoyment in the snorkeling experience as a diversion from birding. While all of us can identify hundreds of bird species, none of us seem to know the names of more than a couple of the colorful and fancy fish swimming at arm's length from our masks.

After plenty of exercise, we are back in the boat and headed to Man-O'-War Caye Bird Sanctuary, a small island famous for its nesting Magnificent Frigatebirds. Males with throats like bloated red balloons attempt to stimulate white-throated females, but most females seem indifferent to the overture. Hundreds more frigatebirds rest on every branch of the island trees. We hear them, smell them, and of course see them. . .Brown Boobies roost with the frigatebirds, and I count 62. Someone asks me how many frigatebirds I think are on the island; I guess 600. No sooner than I've made the statement, Tom announces he has counted 620. The northeast winds have picked up now at dusk and our ride back is bumpy, especially for me at the bow of the boat. Fortunately, those behind me at the stern have a smoother ride.

Description: The main birding attraction is the hundreds of Magnificent Frigatebirds that nest on **Man-O'-War Caye**, accompanied by dozens of Brown Boobies. A boat trip to the cay likely will be combined with visits to one or more nearby cays, either for snorkeling or for overnight lodging.

Within five miles are South Water Caye, Tobacco Caye, and Coco Plum Caye. South Water Caye is at the southern tip of Tobacco Reef and is one of the few islands that lie atop the Barrier Reef. The reef and the cay are at the northern part of a protected area called **South Water Caye Marine**

Reserve, and the island is variously labeled both Water and South Water, the southern 3.5 acres of which is Pelican Beach Resort. South Water Caye is about 14 miles from Dangriga, and between them lies Man-O'-War Caye. Small, sandy Coco Plum Caye features Coco Plum Island Resort. Most of the species listed in the above accounts of cays could also occur at Tobacco Reef. Rarities reported for South Water Caye include Brown Noddy, Short-tailed Nighthawk, and Gray Kingbird.

Tobacco Caye Marine Station began operation in January 2009, working in partnership with Gaviota Reef Resort and Monkey Bay Wildlife Sanctuary. It maintains a marine-programs base on five-acre Tobacco Caye and has facilities for up to 26 guests at Gaviota Resort, available for students and accommodating visiting birders as well.

Birding strategy: Man-O'-War Caye is an exciting birding spot that can be combined with snorkeling on the reef, all in a half-day trip. An alternative is to stay at resorts on South Water Caye, Tobacco Caye, or Coco Plum Caye and arrange boat trips to nearby Man-O'-War. Another transport is Captain Fermin, based on Tobacco Caye. He has a daily run to and from Dangriga and also makes the 15-minute trip between Tobacco Caye and Man-O'-War Caye. Contact him through Monkey Bay Wildlife Sanctuary or Tobacco Caye Marine Station.

Ecoregion and habitats: *Appendix A, Ecoregion 18, Other cays. Man-O'-War Caye is a small island densely covered with all three species of mangroves, but predominantly tall Red Mangrove, and lies in the middle of the Barrier Reef (LF1). South Water Caye is 15 acres of sand and palm trees above a coral lining with little native vegetation except for a windward fringe of Red Mangroves.*

Fees and contact: South Water Caye Marine Reserve charges a US$5 fee for one to three days, collected by the resort, boat operator, or tour operator.

Pelican Beach Resort, South Water Caye, P.O. Box 2, Dangriga. (011) 501-522-2044; fax (011) 501-522-2570; sales@pelicanbeachbelize.com; www.southwatercaye.com.

Coco Plum Island Resort, P.O. Box 239, Dangriga. Toll-free in US: 800-763-7360; contact@cocoplumcay.com; www.cocoplumcay.com.

Tobacco Caye Marine Station, Matthew Jasinski, Station Manager, mobile: (011) 501-620-9116; info@tcmsbelize.org; www.tcmsbelize.org.

Additional contacts for Captain Fermin, Gaviota Resort, and Tobacco Caye facilities through Monkey Bay Wildlife Sanctuary, P.O. Box 187, Belmopan. (011) 501-820-3032; fax (011) 501-822-3361; mbay@btl.net; www.monkeybaybelize.org.

Location: N 16° 53.08' W 88° 6.43' for Man-O'-War Caye. N 16° 48.90' W 88° 4.93' for South Water Caye. N 16° 52.84' W 88° 7.08' for Coco Plum Caye. All are offshore from Dangriga.

CHAPTER 7
ANNOTATED CHECKLIST OF THE BIRDS OF BELIZE

This is a comprehensive, annotated list of 591 Belize bird species, using AOU order up to date through 2011. Use this checklist in conjunction with the ecoregional checklists (see www.bafrenz.com) and the index of birding sites in Appendix D. Unless otherwise noted, species are year-round residents; consult the bar graphs in Chapter 8 for expected seasonal occurrence and abundance.

Several tables and other bird identification tips are included in this chapter for those species that newcomers to Belize often misidentify. Much of the identification information is not original. What is different is the table format. Sources for the information are Howell and Webb (1995), Jones and Vallely (2001), and Jones (2003), as referenced in Appendix C, References. Voice descriptions come from Jones (2003), who also refers to Moore (1992). Habitat descriptions, for the most part, are taken from the excellent descriptions given in Jones (2003).

Sites are listed from north to south in the same order they appear in the book chapters. Rarities are also listed from north to south, rather than chronologically. In most cases the listed sites are not meant to be comprehensive and are rather a sampling over the species' range. Site names are shortened, but they should be obvious from the index in Appendix D. For brevity, in this context Macal River refers to the access road and to the three resorts: Black Rock Lodge, Chaa Creek, and duPlooy's.

Great Tinamou (*Tinamus major*) – ground level in broadleaf forest, less commonly in pine forest. Found nearly throughout mainland, but scarce in Corozal District. Good sites: La Milpa, Chan Chich, TEC, Monkey Bay, Tikal, Blue Hole, Mayflower, Cockscomb, BFREE-Bladen, Wilson Landing, Boom Creek.

Little Tinamou (*Crypturellus soui*) – ground level within tall second-growth forest and scrub nearly throughout mainland, but scarce in Corozal District. Good sites: Big Falls Farm, Pook's Hill, Caracol, Blue Hole, Mayflower, Cockscomb, Red Bank, Monkey River, BFREE-Bladen, Nim Li Punit, Lubaantun, Blue Creek Cave, Aguacaliente, Boom Creek.

Thicket Tinamou (*Crypturellus cinnamomeus*) – ground level in broadleaf forest and scrub; occurs in north and west, especially Shipstern, Fireburn, La Milpa, Chan Chich. Other good sites: Lamanai, Altun Ha, Salt Creek, Community Baboon, Banana Bank, Macal River.

Slaty-breasted Tinamou (*Crypturellus boucardi*) – ground level within extensive tracts of broadleaf forest; concentrated in northwest and southwest. Good sites: La Milpa, Chan Chich, Las Cuevas, Caracol. Also Hidden Valley, Chaa Creek, Blue Hole, Cockscomb.

Black-bellied Whistling-Duck *(Dendrocygna autumnalis)* – lagoons and rice fields, especially Shipstern (mainly at Chacan Chac Mol), Blue Creek rice fields, Edenthal, New River, Crooked Tree, Banana Bank, Macal River, The Dump, Aguacaliente. An amazing 2,500 were in view at Crooked Tree 28 February 2003.

Fulvous Whistling-Duck *(Dendrocygna bicolor)* – large marsh-lined lagoons and estuaries; rice fields. Winter visitor, found only in a few places, most regularly at Crooked Tree. Infrequent at Blue Creek rice fields, New River, Old Northern Highway, Cox Lagoon. One record each for The Dump and Ambergris Caye.

Greater White-fronted Goose *(Anser albifrons)* – one specimen collected off Old Northern Highway, 22 miles northwest of Belize City, 15 January 1973.

Snow Goose *(Chen caerulescens)* – three records: Tres Leguas 29 January–12 February 1991, Big Falls Farm November 1975, and Fresh Catch December 2011–1 March 2012.

Canada Goose *(Branta canadensis)* – one record: Crooked Tree in lagoon beside Crooked Tree Lodge 25 October–late December 2007, the first record for Central America.

Muscovy Duck *(Cairina moschata)* – wooded lagoons and swamps, marshes, and margins of major river systems; widespread at lower elevations. Good sites: New River, Altun Ha, Crooked Tree, Monkey Bay, Aguacaliente, The Dump, Moho River.

Gadwall *(Anas strepera)* – two were found at Blue Creek rice fields 12 December 2011–14 February 2012.

American Wigeon *(Anas americana)* – marshes, estuaries, lagoons, rice fields, and farm ponds with shallow, standing water. Winter visitor; occurs in northern areas, especially Crooked Tree. Also Blue Creek rice fields, New River, one record Ambergris Caye.

Mallard *(Anas platyrhynchos)* – one record: Big Falls Farm 25 November 1976. Domesticated Mallards exist, e.g., a male in good plumage in rural Toledo District was subsequently found to be purchased (illegally) as a chick in Punta Gorda.

Blue-winged Teal *(Anas discors)* – rice fields, areas with shallow, standing or slow-moving water. Winter visitor; widespread, including cays.

Cinnamon Teal *(Anas cyanoptera)* – winter visitor, but few records: Blue Creek rice fields 1996–1998 and 2011, Nova Ladyville 1996 and 1999, Big Falls Farm 1986. Also Blue-winged X Cinnamon at Nova Ladyville.

Northern Shoveler *(Anas clypeata)* – marshes, lagoons, rice fields, farm ponds, and shrimp farms. Also Crooked Tree, Fresh Catch, Aguacaliente. Winter visitor.

Northern Pintail *(Anas acuta)* – occasional winter visitor at Shipstern, Blue Creek rice fields, and New River.

Green-winged Teal *(Anas crecca)* – few winter records: Shipstern, New River, Nova Ladyville, Big Falls Farm, All Pines; most recently at Blue Creek rice fields.

Redhead *(Aythya americana)* – first record at Blue Creek rice fields, up to five 11–13 December 2011, among flocks of nearly 20,000 coots, dowitchers, and ducks. Also Fresh Catch 20 January 2012 (photo).

Ring-necked Duck *(Aythya collaris)* – uncommon winter visitor, best found at Crooked Tree. Other sites: Corozal Bay, New River, Lago Petén Itzá, Fresh Catch, Golden Stream, Boden Creek, Ambergris Caye.

Lesser Scaup *(Aythya affinis)* – winter visitor, most likely in coastal bays, especially Corozal Bay and Shipstern Lagoon, where it has gathered in flocks as large as 300. Also lagoons and shrimp farms: New River, Crooked Tree, Fresh Catch, Manatee Lagoon, cays.

Hooded Merganser *(Lophodytes cucullatus)* – one undated record in 1990 or 1991 at Crooked Tree.

Red-breasted Merganser *(Mergus serrator)* – four December records 2000–2006: at sea two miles north of Belize City, offshore Belize City, Placencia Lagoon. Also 21 February 2007 at Placencia.

Masked Duck *(Nomonyx dominicus)* – three records: Crooked Tree 1 February 1997 and thereafter, Big Falls Farm 22 December 1985 (undocumented), and pond near Cristo Rey–San Antonio 18 March 1990.

Ruddy Duck *(Oxyura jamaicensis)* – one record: January–March 2012 at Fresh Catch; also Boden Creek Reserve March 2012.

Plain Chachalaca *(Ortalis vetula)* – forest floor to subcanopy within open woodland and scrub, forest edge. Common and widespread throughout mainland; also found on Ambergris Caye.

Crested Guan *(Penelope purpurascens)* – subcanopy of broadleaf and pine forest; less frequently on ground. Considered uncommon, but easily seen at La Milpa, Chan Chich, and Cockscomb. Scarce where hunted. Other sites: Hill Bank, Coastal Highway, Hidden Valley, Las Cuevas, Caracol, El Pilar, Macal River, Blue Hole, Red Bank, BFREE-Bladen.

Great Curassow *(Crax rubra)* – forest floor within primary broadleaf forest and, sometimes, secondary fragmented forest. Roosts in trees. Best found along Gallon Jug Road between La Milpa and Chan Chich, and at Caracol. Scarce where hunted. Also found at Shipstern, Fireburn, Hill Bank, Coastal Highway, Slate Creek, Hidden Valley, Las Cuevas, El Pilar, Blue Hole, Cockscomb, BFREE-Bladen.

Black-throated Bobwhite *(Colinus nigrogularis)* – savannas and meadows; also scrub bordering farmlands. Found in lowland areas from northwest Corozal District to Southern Highway at BFREE. Good sites: Gallon Jug Road near August Pine Ridge and beyond Tres Leguas, Honey Camp Lagoon, Shipyard Road, Crooked Tree, Community Baboon, Coastal Highway, Croc O'dile Isle.

Spotted Wood-Quail *(Odontophorus guttatus)* – ground level within primary broadleaf forest. Occurs mostly away from coast and is hard to find. However, during 286 days of field work around Chaa Creek, Figueroa et al. (2004) observed or heard quail 107 days. Often reported on the trails near Chan Chich Lodge. Other good sites: La Milpa, Cockscomb, Las Cuevas, Caracol. Also: Hill Bank, Sibun River near TEC, Slate Creek, Mountain Pine Ridge, Guacamallo Bridge, El Pilar, Macal River, BFREE-Bladen.

Singing Quail *(Dactylortyx thoracicus)* – ground level of semi-deciduous subtropical forest. Seldom reported, but most often at Chaa Creek and duPlooy's. Other sites: La Milpa, Doyle's Delight, Hydro Road, BFREE-Bladen, north Ambergris Caye.

Ocellated Turkey *(Meleagris ocellata)* – ground level of primary forest and clearings; roosts in trees. Cannot be missed at Tikal. Easily found at La Milpa, Chan Chich, the section of Gallon Jug Road connecting them, as well as Caracol. On the 31 December 2007 Gallon Jug CBC an amazing 277 were counted.

Least Grebe *(Tachybaptus dominicus)* – forest-lined rivers, streams, swamps, and lagoons; freshwater marshes and small ponds. Widespread on mainland, most easily seen at Crooked Tree. Good sites: Shipstern, Edenthal, La Milpa, Chan Chich, New River, Hill Bank, Old Northern Highway, Community Baboon, Fresh Catch, Guacamallo Bridge, Aguacate Lagoon, Macal River, Xunantunich, Tikal.

Pied-billed Grebe *(Podilymbus podiceps)* – wide range of water areas. Winter visitor, although some remain in summer. Widespread in mainland lowlands.

American Flamingo *(Phoenicopterus ruber)* – Few sightings, only one documented, that of two at Aguacaliente 28 March 2001. Other reports from Shipstern, New River, near Belize City.

Manx Shearwater *(Puffinus puffinus)* – one record: a beached carcass near Dangriga February 1990.

Audubon's Shearwater *(Puffinus lherminieri)* – three records: dying bird at Caye Caulker late July 2000, carcass at Hopkins Village 2 August 2000, and half-mile off Ambergris Caye 5 August 2005.

Wilson's Storm-Petrel *(Oceanites oceanicus)* – one record: flying beyond surf at Placencia 4 July 2007.

White-tailed Tropicbird *(Phaethon lepturus)* – three records: Drowned Cayes 21 April 1976 and two sightings south of Ambergris Caye in Hol Chan Nature Reserve 13 August 2005 and 21 April 2007.

Jabiru *(Jabiru mycteria)* – rice fields, estuaries, shrimp farms; nests in large trees in savannas such as the famous site on New River near Lamanai. Often seen soaring with vultures. Regularly found at Mennonite rice fields at Blue Creek and Edenthal, as well as the shallow lagoons of Crooked Tree and soaring along Price Highway from Belize Zoo eastward. Also found in large numbers, sometimes over 100, at shrimp and tilapia farms such as Fresh Catch.

Wood Stork *(Mycteria americana)* – lagoons, estuaries, marshes, shrimp farms, rice fields. Easily found at most lowland sites, especially: Shipstern Lagoon (nesting), Corozal farmlands, Blue Creek rice fields, New River, Crooked Tree, Sibun River (nesting), Aguacaliente (nesting), Moho River. In large numbers at same shrimp and tilapia farms as Jabiru is found. Progressively less common inland.

Magnificent Frigatebird *(Fregata magnificens)* – coastal areas and offshore waters, mangrove cays most notably at Half Moon Caye and Man-O'-War Caye, where they nest in large colonies. Easy to find along mainland coast. Occasional inland sightings. Has occurred at Lago Petén Itzá and over the airstrip at Tikal.

Masked Booby *(Sula dactylatra)* – only four records 1955–2000; one at beach of Ambergris Caye, others several miles offshore from Ambergris, Belize City, Glover's Reef.

Brown Booby *(Sula leucogaster)* – seen offshore and at smaller cays; reliably found at Man-O'-War Caye and on boat trips in Inner Channel. Also Caye Caulker. Sometimes seen from coast, e.g., Shipstern, Belize City, Manatee Lagoon, Dangriga. Does not nest in Belize.

Red-footed Booby *(Sula sula)* – nests on Half Moon Caye in large numbers. Rare at sea but might be seen at other cayes or from mainland during or following tropical storms. Reported at Caye Caulker.

Neotropic Cormorant *(Phalacrocorax brasilianus)* – lagoons, estuaries, shrimp farms, rice fields, coastline, and inner cays. Easily seen throughout much of Belize, most notably at Crooked Tree. At cays, mostly seen at Ambergris Caye.

Double-crested Cormorant *(Phalacrocorax auritus)* – mangroves, coastline, harbors, coastal beaches, occasionally shrimp farms. Found on cays and at coastal areas. Occasionally found inland at Crooked Tree and more often at New River. Much less common inland than Neotropic, and other inland sightings could be misidentified Neotropic Cormorants.

Anhinga *(Anhinga anhinga)* – Forest-lined lagoons, swamps, sluggish tree-lined rivers, mangrove forest; nests and often seen perched in trees. Widespread, most readily found at New River, Crooked Tree, Aguacaliente. Other good sites: Gallon Jug, Community Baboon, Aguacate Lagoon, Moho River. On mangrove cays between Punta Ycacos and Rio Grande in Toledo District and occasionally on other cays, including Caye Caulker.

American White Pelican *(Pelecanus erythrorhynchos)* – lagoons, estuaries, shrimp farms. Winter visitor. Not reliably reported in Belize until 1981; increasing reports. Good sites: Crooked Tree, Belize City.

Brown Pelican *(Pelecanus occidentalis)* – easily seen at cays and along coast. Rare inland away from Crooked Tree, yet reported at many inland sites and even over Doyle's Delight. Flyovers at Tikal and El Remate. Presumably, inland sightings are pelicans commuting from the coast to Chalillo Reservoir and Lago Petén Itzá.

Pinnated Bittern *(Botaurus pinnatus)* – tall grass and reeds in wet areas. Rarely seen; reported most often at Laguna Seca and Laguna Verde in Gallon Jug area; also at Blue Creek rice fields, New River, Community Baboon, Lago Petén Itzá, Hopkins Village. Only southern sighting is at The Dump.

American Bittern *(Botaurus lentiginosus)* – marshes and rice fields. Occasional winter visitor; few recent records, including at The Dump and Aguacaliente. Hill Bank marsh record dates to 1955.

Least Bittern *(Ixobrychus exilis)* – dense tall-grass marshes. Difficult to find; best chance is New River Lagoon at Dawson Creek or The Dump. Other sites: Shipstern, Blue Creek rice fields, Crooked Tree, coastal marshes from Belize City to Dangriga, Ambergris Caye. Multiple reports at Lago Petén Itzá.

Rufescent Tiger-Heron *(Tigrisoma lineatum)* – swampy lowland forest. One photodocumented record, 3 December 2010 at Laguna Seca.

Bare-throated Tiger-Heron *(Tigrisoma mexicanum)* – marshes, lagoon, riversides, swamp forest. Often in open areas and easily found throughout mainland at low elevations and occasionally at higher elevations and on Ambergris Caye. Most consistent sites: Laguna Seca, New River, Crooked Tree.

Great Blue Heron *(Ardea herodias)* – most unforested wet areas. Fairly common in lowlands throughout. Nests at cays and Shipstern. White morph (Great White Heron) uncommon on northern cays, including Turneffe Atoll.

Great Egret *(Ardea alba)* – readily found everywhere except higher elevations and Tikal. Impressive numbers found at Crooked Tree, Fresh Catch, and Aguacaliente. Nests locally on coast, including Shipstern.

Snowy Egret *(Egretta thula)* – common throughout at low elevations, including Tikal. Winter visitor, many remaining in summer, and a few may nest.

Little Blue Heron *(Egretta caerulea)* – common throughout at low elevations. Winter visitor, a few remaining into summer. Does not nest in Belize.

Tricolored Heron *(Egretta tricolor)* – mudflats, lagoons, estuaries, coastal shorelines, marshes. Found mostly in coastal areas and on cays. Winter visitor; also nests locally in north. Best sites: New River, Crooked Tree, Gra Gra Lagoon, Aguacaliente, Ambergris Caye, Caye Caulker.

Reddish Egret *(Egretta rufescens)* – mangrove islands, coastal mudflats and estuaries, shrimp farms. Found on cays west of Ambergris Caye and along coast. Best mainland site is Shipstern Lagoon where they nest; 20% are white morph. Also Aqua Mar Shrimp farm. Found once inland at Hill Bank and a few times at Crooked Tree.

Cattle Egret *(Bubulcus ibis)* – pastures, agricultural fields, newly planted rice fields, lawns, mangroves, small wooded cays. Readily found throughout Belize, including cays. Winter visitor, some remaining in summer. Breeding unconfirmed.

Green Heron *(Butorides virescens)* – forest-lined rivers, ponds, lagoons, mangroves, littoral forest. Common at low elevations throughout. Nests on cays and locally on mainland.

Agami Heron *(Agamia agami)* – dense vegetation along edges of swamps, rivers, and lagoons. Hard to find because of its reclusive nature; best timing is in dry season when shorelines are exposed. Good sites: Gallon Jug, New River, Crooked Tree, Chan Chich, Pook's Hill, Cockscomb, BFREE-Bladen. Other sites: Spanish Creek, Aguacate Lagoon, Manatee Lagoon, Sittee River, Monkey River. Nests locally; a former colony at Moho River supported 82 active nests in July 2002. Previously called Chestnut-bellied Heron.

Black-crowned Night-Heron *(Nycticorax nycticorax)* – marshes, lagoons, estuaries, mangroves; roosts communally in large trees. Winter visitor, some remaining through summer and may nest at Crooked Tree, the best site. Can be common, but easily missed. Good sites: New River, Aguacaliente. Other sites: Shipstern, Gra Gra Lagoon, Sittee River, The Dump. Recently found at higher elevations at Chalillo Reservoir.

Yellow-crowned Night-Heron *(Nyctanassa violacea)* – diverse wet habitats from lawns to mangroves. Readily found in lowland areas, especially near the coast and on the cays. Best sites: New River, Crooked Tree, Dangriga, Caye Caulker.

Boat-billed Heron *(Cochlearius cochlearius)* – daylight roosts well hidden in trees along banks of rivers and swamps; forages at night along shores. Easily overlooked. Best seen from slow boat trips on rivers. Good sites: Shipstern, New River, Crooked Tree, Cox Lagoon, Runaway Creek, Cockscomb, BFREE, Moho River. Has been found on many cays.

White Ibis *(Eudocimus albus)* – marshes, rice fields, shrimp farms, coastal lagoons, and littoral forest on larger cays. Good sites: Shipstern Lagoon (where it also nests), New River, Crooked Tree, Northern Lagoon (nesting on Bird Caye),

Gra Gra Lagoon, Sittee River. Harder to find at higher elevations, and less frequent in the south, e.g., Aguacaliente, Moho River.

Scarlet Ibis *(Eudocimus ruber)* – one record: Punta Ycacos, Toledo District, 17 March 1999. Thought to be hurricane assisted.

Glossy Ibis *(Plegadis falcinellus)* – flooded rice fields, marshes, wet meadows. Winter visitor. Relatively few records except for Crooked Tree, where as many as 300 have been counted in a single day. Other sites, often with only single records: New River, Dangriga shrimp farm, The Dump, VoA, Caye Caulker. Not all dark ibises are identified to species and White-faced Ibis is a potential vagrant.

Roseate Spoonbill *(Platalea ajaja)* – flooded rice fields, lagoons, shrimp farms, coastal bays. Reliably found at Crooked Tree. Other good sites: Corozal Bay, Cerros, Shipstern Lagoon (where it nests), Belize City, Dangriga, Aqua Mar. Also inland at: Blue Creek rice fields, Shipyard Road, New River, Fresh Catch, Aguacaliente. Sometimes found at Ambergris Caye and other cays, especially Chetumal Bay cays where it nests.

Black Vulture *(Coragyps atratus)* – easily seen everywhere on mainland; occasionally on Ambergris Caye.

Turkey Vulture *(Cathartes aura)* – easily seen everywhere on mainland and Ambergris Caye.

Lesser Yellow-headed Vulture *(Cathartes burrovianus)* – open country, especially savannas, rice fields. Primarily at shrimp and tilapia farms and in coastal areas near water: Corozal Beach, Shipstern, Blue Creek rice fields, New River, Honey Camp Lagoon, Crooked Tree, Belize City, Gra Gra Lagoon, The Dump, Ambergris Caye. Fewer reports far inland, but does occur at Lago Petén Itzá. Identification tips: flies low even when Turkey Vultures are soaring high overhead; wings from below display darker gray flight feathers than Turkey Vulture and wings from above display white primary quills rather than silvery gray patch on Black Vulture; wings narrower-based and tail squarer-tipped than Turkey Vulture; distinctive head color especially at close range.

King Vulture *(Sarcoramphus papa)* – above patchy and contiguous forests. Most readily seen in foothills and submontane open areas of Maya Mountains, especially King Vulture Falls at Hidden Valley, Thousand Foot Falls, Caracol, Blue Hole, Cockscomb, Red Bank. Also at Tikal, the Bravo Hills at La Milpa and Chan Chich. Widely found, but less frequently, at many inland riverine sites.

Osprey *(Pandion haliaetus)* – found throughout, especially near water. Less frequently seen inland and infrequently seen at higher elevations. Subspecies *ridgwayi* nests at cays and coastal lagoons; subspecies *carolinensis* is a winter visitor.

Gray-headed Kite *(Leptodon cayanensis)* – forested river edges, but also in and over heavily forested areas. Best looked for at: Blue Creek rice fields, La Milpa, Chan Chich, Honey Camp Road, Pook's Hill, Blue Hole, Cockscomb, Red Bank, Boom Creek.

Hook-billed Kite *(Chondrohierax uncinatus)* – primary and old secondary forest and soaring above. Few consistent sites except, perhaps, the Gallon Jug CBC, where it has been reported 13 of 21 years, but only 2 of last 9 years. Has been seen infrequently along forest edges at many sites: Sarteneja Road near New River ferry, La Milpa, Hill Bank, Crooked Tree, Aguacate Lagoon, El Pilar, Macal River, Pook's Hill, Mayflower, Sittee River, Cockscomb, BFREE-Bladen,

Aguacaliente, VoA, Moho River, Ambergris Caye. Resident, with some seasonal migration. Southbound migrating flocks totaling 96 kites were observed 21 October 2000 in Punta Gorda and 300 on 14 October 2007 near Belcampo Belize.

Swallow-tailed Kite *(Elanoides forficatus)* – open forest. Summer resident, most easily found at foothills and higher elevations: Thousand Foot Falls, Hidden Valley, Las Cuevas, Caracol, Blue Hole, Mayflower, Cockscomb, Red Bank. Also regular at Macal River, Tikal, BFREE-Bladen, Aguacaliente, Moho River. In migration, also seen along coast at Shipstern and over cays (e.g., 170 over Sarteneja 1 March 2008 and 69 at Snake Cayes 2 August 2002).

White-tailed Kite *(Elanus leucurus)* – grasslands, wet meadows, rice fields, and marshes; lowland open areas on mainland such as: August Pine Ridge, Blue Creek rice fields, Crooked Tree, Spanish Lookout, Macal River, The Dump, San Antonio Road. Several records for Ambergris Caye.

Snail Kite *(Rostrhamus sociabilis)* – lagoons and freshwater marshes, mostly in north and east; easiest at New River and Crooked Tree (especially common). Other sites: Blue Creek rice fields, Freshwater Creek, Belize City, Cox Lagoon, Sittee River. Only very rarely reaches as far south as Punta Gorda.

Double-toothed Kite *(Harpagus bidentatus)* – under forest canopy and sometimes soaring above especially in mid-morning, just as vultures start to soar. Prefers primary forest away from coast. Most reliable sites are La Milpa and Gallon Jug. Good sites: Douglas Da Silva, Chiquibul, Caracol, Blue Hole, Cockscomb, Red Bank, BFREE-Bladen.

Mississippi Kite *(Ictinia mississippiensis)* – scarce fall migrant along coast, most often reported at Cattle Landing and Punta Gorda. A 2006 record at La Milpa and fall 2011 records at Belize City and Spanish Lookout. At Tikal 25+ circled near the entrance 28 March 2003.

Plumbeous Kite *(Ictinia plumbea)* – open forest, savannas, milpas. Summer resident (beginning mid-February) on mainland, increasingly common to the south. Best sites: Gallon Jug, Monkey Bay, Mountain Pine Ridge, Chiquibul, Tikal, Cockscomb, Red Bank, BFREE-Bladen, Aguacaliente.

Black-collared Hawk *(Busarellus nigricollis)* – riparian sites on sluggish rivers, especially New River and Crooked Tree. Other good sites: Freshwater Creek, Laguna Seca, Community Baboon, Cox Lagoon.

Northern Harrier *(Circus cyaneus)* – rice fields, marshes, shrimp farms, estuaries, lagoons. Winter visitor. By far the most reliable site is the Mennonite farm area along Gallon Jug Road, particularly in the August Pine Ridge to Blue Creek village section. Less frequent in south; rare on cays.

Sharp-shinned Hawk *(Accipiter striatus)* – about two dozen records; transient along coast—especially Cattle Landing—and Ambergris Caye; most winter records are from Mountain Pine Ridge and its northern foothills.

Cooper's Hawk *(Accipiter cooperii)* – winter visitor with very few reports: New River, Mountain Pine Ridge, duPlooy's, Hummingbird Highway at Pomona, Maya Center near Cockscomb. Best chance would be Cattle Landing in migration mid-October to beginning of November.

Bicolored Hawk *(Accipiter bicolor)* – hard to find due to primary forest residence and silence away from nest. Look mid-story to subcanopy for perched solitary hawk. Rarely soars; will occasionally do Cooper's Hawk-like display flight above canopy. Highly vocal near nest during breeding season (April–June). Best chance at La Milpa, Chan Chich, Chiquibul, Caracol, Tikal. One seen on 8 of 13 visits along Salt Creek Estates Road. Other sites: New River, Aguacate Lagoon, Slate Creek, Blancaneaux Lodge, Hidden Valley, Las Cuevas, Cockscomb, BFREE-Bladen, Wilson Landing, Boom Creek.

Crane Hawk *(Geranospiza caerulescens)* – forested streamsides, forest edges, roadsides, savannas. Usually found in edge habitat in northern half of Belize. Good sites: Mennonite farming areas along Gallon Jug Road, La Milpa, Chan Chich, New River, Altun Ha, Crooked Tree, Caracol, Tikal, Gra Gra Lagoon.

White Hawk *(Leucopternis albicollis)* – old broadleaf forest and edge. Conspicuous in flight, most easily seen at La Milpa and Chan Chich and in foothills of Maya Mountains, especially the lower portions of Chiquibul Road, Pook's Hill, Green Hills, duPlooy's, Black Rock, Blue Hole, Mayflower, Cockscomb, Red Bank, BFREE-Bladen, Blue Creek Cave, Jimmy Cut. Other good sites: Mountain Pine Ridge, Rio Frio Caves, Caracol, Las Cuevas, Spanish Lookout primary forests.

Common Black-Hawk *(Buteogallus anthracinus)* – open wooded areas near water, mangrove forest, forest edge. Readily found on Ambergris Caye, Caye Caulker, and coastal areas: Shipstern, Gales Point, Dangriga, Gra Gra Lagoon, Placencia, Joe Taylor Creek, Wilson Landing, Punta Gorda, VoA, Moho River. In Belize, there are no well-documented reports away from coastal areas and all sightings farther inland are presumed to be misidentified Great Black-Hawks or other hawk species. Many inland local checklists are in error.

Great Black-Hawk *(Buteogallus urubitinga)* – compared to Common Black-Hawk, found in more densely wooded areas; also at rice fields and other open areas. The expected black-hawk at inland sites, especially upland sites; less common at coastal sites and perhaps some reports are misidentified Common Black-Hawks. Especially common at Crooked Tree. Good sites: La Milpa, Chan Chich, New River, Mountain Pine Ridge, Las Cuevas, Caracol, Crystal Paradise, Tikal, Cockscomb, Red Bank, BFREE-Bladen, Columbia River.

Solitary Eagle *(Buteogallus solitarius)* – extensive tracts of primary forest. Fewer than 1,000 of this near-threatened species exist. Although reported at multiple sites, most probably represent misidentified black-hawks. Photographs are essential to confirm its identity (Clark et al. 2006). One to two pairs are reliably found annually at Mountain Pine Ridge, especially Hidden Valley, where it is rare. Reported at sites above 1,200 feet elevation, including Sibun Gorge near Mountain Pine Ridge, Guacamallo, Chiquibul, Doyle's Delight, Bladen. In June 2011 an active nest was discovered, the first such nest found anywhere since 1959.

Roadside Hawk *(Buteo magnirostris)* – easily seen daily along roadsides and secondary forest edge throughout mainland. Uncommon on Ambergris Caye.

Broad-winged Hawk *(Buteo platypterus)* – migrant and rare winter visitor. Rarely reported and perhaps not recognized, most often at La Milpa and Chan Chich in the north, Mountain Pine Ridge in central, and Punta Gorda area in south. Fall migrant along coast. Most recent hawk migration studies indicate it is more regular, seen nearly every fall. Other sites: Shipstern, Altun Ha, Caracol, Cockscomb, Columbia River, Cattle Landing, Boom Creek, VoA.

Gray Hawk *(Buteo plagiatus)* – readily found in open areas and forest edge throughout mainland; occasionally on Ambergris Caye. Often found on utility wires along roads. Identity of immatures is sometimes confused with Roadside Hawks: note bold white cheek and supercilium, dark eye, and only vertical streaking pattern.

Short-tailed Hawk *(Buteo brachyurus)* – open habitats, more often seen in flight than perched. Fairly common at Corozal area, La Milpa, Chan Chich, New River, Coastal and Price Highways (east). Many other sites.

Swainson's Hawk *(Buteo swainsoni)* – although several reports, few are documented: two winters and one spring at Blue Creek rice fields, perhaps annual in small numbers in fall at Cattle Landing. Migrates through Central America on Pacific slope.

White-tailed Hawk *(Buteo albicaudatus)* – open savannas and pastures. Watch for them near grass fires. Not the easiest hawk to find, good sites are: Gallon Jug Road through the Mennonite farms, Edenthal, Gallon Jug (7 of 20 CBCs), open areas along New River such as Shipstern Road and Hill Bank, Monkey Bay and vicinity along Price Highway, northern part of Southern Highway. Rarely reaches southern Belize near Punta Gorda. Immature Short-tailed, White-tailed, and Red-tailed Hawks are frequently misidentified.

Zone-tailed Hawk *(Buteo albonotatus)* – pastures, savannas, rice fields, shrimp farms. Winter visitor; few records, but may be on increase. Reported sites: Gallon Jug, New River, Belize City, Fresh Catch, Runaway Creek, Mountain Pine Ridge, Spanish Lookout, near Sittee River, Monkey River, Punta Gorda.

Red-tailed Hawk *(Buteo jamaicensis)* – submontane pine and mixed pine/broadleaf forests of Mountain Pine Ridge and Chiquibul, including Hidden Valley and Caracol. Most recently reported at Booth's River through Blue Creek rice fields, Gallon Jug, Ladyville, Spanish Lookout, Cockscomb, Payne's Creek.

Crested Eagle *(Morphnus guianensis)* – undisturbed primary broadleaf forest; stays beneath canopy. Few records, occurring in remote areas of Chan Chich 19 March 1990, La Milpa 1990–2012 especially at the Maya site, and Pueblo Viejo 8 April 1995. An adult at Hickatee Cottages near Punta Gorda 16 December 2006 was a surprise. Recent (2010) sightings at Chiquibul. Compare identification with Harpy Eagle.

Harpy Eagle *(Harpia harpyja)* – rare resident of undisturbed rainforest. One shot near Aguacate Village (vicinity of Blue Creek, Toledo District) 1990; found in Southern Maya Mountains 1994; Las Cuevas 2001. More recently at Bladen Reserve 2005 and 2009, several reports Caracol 2000–2009, and Thousand Foot Falls 2010. At Bladen, a nest with a five-week-old chick discovered December 2010 is the first ever recorded in Belize. Scientists for Peregrine Fund have released and monitored several at La Milpa and Chiquibul. Identification can be confused with Crested Eagle.

Black Hawk-Eagle *(Spizaetus tyrannus)* – open forest, often flying high above canopy, where it is heard before seen. Widespread from Freshwater Creek, New River, and Altun Ha southward; easier to find in uplands and foothills: La Milpa, Chan Chich, Guanacaste, Pook's Hill, Las Cuevas, Caracol, El Pilar, Macal River, Hydro Road, Tikal, Blue Hole, Red Bank, BFREE-Bladen, Jalacte.

Ornate Hawk-Eagle *(Spizaetus ornatus)* – primary broadleaf forest and edge, occasionally pine forest; soars above canopy, heard before seen. Widespread, with better chances at: La Milpa, Chan Chich, Las Cuevas, Caracol, Macal River, Xunantunich, Tikal, BFREE-Bladen. Found nesting at Copper Bank Road near Cerros, at Gallon Jug Road between La Milpa and Chan Chich, a presumed pair at Irish Creek. Other sites: Chacan Chac Mol (Shipstern), Shipyard Road, Altun Ha, Coastal Highway, Guanacaste, Actun Tunichil Muknal, Pook's Hill, Slate Creek, Hidden Valley, Blue Hole, Cockscomb, Boom Creek.

Black-and-white Hawk-Eagle *(Spizaetus melanoleucus)* – primary and old secondary broadleaf forest, frequently seen flying above canopy; less vocal than other hawk-eagles. First time for Belize, a nest was found at Hidden Valley March 2008. Hardest hawk-eagle to find; best chance is southern Maya Mountains: Caracol, Chiquibul, BFREE-Bladen, Columbia River. Other reported sites: Shipstern, La Milpa, Gallon Jug, Spanish Creek, Aguacate Lagoon, Pook's Hill, Slate Creek, Green Hills, duPlooy's, Cockscomb.

Barred Forest-Falcon *(Micrastur ruficollis)* – primary broadleaf forest, hidden within canopy and subcanopy, perching quietly; can be heard calling before first light but not often seen; good sites: La Milpa, Chan Chich, Hill Bank, Pook's Hill, Las Cuevas, Caracol, Tikal, Blue Hole, Cockscomb, BFREE-Bladen, Columbia River. Other sites: Green Hills, Black Rock Lodge, Douglas Da Silva, Mayflower.

Collared Forest-Falcon *(Micrastur semitorquatus)* – more likely to be seen on edges of forested areas; found throughout forested mainland.

Crested Caracara *(Caracara cheriway)* – savannas, rice fields, pastures. Only recently documented in Belize. Repeated sightings 2007–2011 near Spanish Lookout at Running W Farm, mile 48.8 on Price Highway log and near Baking Pot ferry, where it has successfully nested. Other sightings since 2000: Blue Creek rice fields, near Clarissa Falls, Southern Highway near Golden Stream, The Dump, Cattle Landing.

Laughing Falcon *(Herpetotheres cachinnans)* – open woodland and savannas, often perched on exposed branches. Fairly common throughout mainland. Best sites: Gallon Jug Road, Honey Camp Road, Shipyard Road, Old Northern Highway, Goldson Highway beside Crooked Tree, Coastal Highway, Chiquibul Road near Caracol.

American Kestrel *(Falco sparverius)* – winter visitor, easiest to find along roadsides in Mennonite farmlands along Gallon Jug Road, Hill Bank Road, and Spanish Lookout. Also pine/palmetto savanna along Price Highway.

Merlin *(Falco columbarius)* – open habitats, forest edge, estuaries, lagoons, coastal beaches. Transient and winter visitor. Hard to find, but more often seen closer to the coast than inland; most likely on cays.

Aplomado Falcon *(Falco femoralis)* – pine savannas, rice fields, shrimp farms, agricultural fields. Found along Gallon Jug Road, Shipyard Road, and Hill Bank Road through Mennonite farmlands; along the pine/palmetto savannas of Coastal Highway and Price Highway, especially at Amigo's, and along northern part of Southern Highway. Rare away from savannas.

Bat Falcon *(Falco rufigularis)* – readily found throughout mainland; often perches on buildings, towers, and dead snags above forest.

Orange-breasted Falcon *(Falco deiroleucus)* – forests near cliffs where it nests; any area with karst faces or rock outcroppings is potential habitat. Belize hosts the largest known nesting population in Central America. Readily located near nesting sites at Thousand Foot Falls, King Vulture Falls in Hidden Valley, Black Rock, Tikal, and Caves Branch. Also nests at Roaring Creek near Actun Tunichil Muknal, Rio On, Santa Familia Sinkhole near Branchmouth Park, and remote parts of Chiquibul National Forest. Sometimes seen away from nesting sites or from unreported nest sites at: Pook's Hill, El Pilar, Chaa Creek, duPlooy's, Belmopan, Blue Hole. The most famous pair and its descendents have resided at the pyramid temples of Tikal since at least 1958.

Peregrine Falcon *(Falco peregrinus)* – open lowland areas, often near water; more common on cays. Transient and winter resident, most prominent in fall migration. Good sites: Sarteneja Road, Shipstern, Blue Creek rice fields, Edenthal, Gallon Jug, New River, Crooked Tree.

Ruddy Crake *(Laterallus ruber)* – grassy areas with shallow water. Can be heard at numerous lowland wet grassy sites, but infrequently seen without persistence. Consistently good sites: Sarteneja Road at Four Mile Lagoon and Pueblo Nuevo ferry, Crooked Tree by boat, Coastal Highway at Sibun River, Five Blues beside lake, Cockscomb at tubing starting point, The Dump, Cuxlin Ha entrance road, Joe Taylor Creek by kayak.

Gray-breasted Crake *(Laterallus exilis)* – seasonally flooded savannas. Consistently identified in Toledo District at The Dump and VoA, and north to Payne's Creek. Found 7 August 2007 at Georgetown off Southern Highway. Other (older) records: Gallon Jug, Monkey Bay, Hummingbird Highway at Middlesex.

Black Rail *(Laterallus jamaicensis)* – winter resident. The only locality where it has been reported on more than one occasion is The Dump. Heard in marshes on entrance road to Hopkins Village. Tape recorded at 7–9 PM at Monkey Bay 27–29 January 1992. Other historical records: New River, Hummingbird Highway at Middlesex, wet meadow at entrance road to BFREE.

Clapper Rail *(Rallus longirostris)* – mangrove forest, found most often on many cays and Punta Gorda area at Joe Taylor Creek, and in the north at Sarteneja and Shipstern. Other sites: Sittee River, Payne's Creek. Could possibly be found at other coastal sites in mangrove forest; Gra Gra Lagoon would be a good bet. Some seasonal movement.

Rufous-necked Wood-Rail *(Aramides axillaris)* – found in mangroves on cays, most notably the south side of Caye Caulker where as many as 20 have been in view at one time. Winter resident; perhaps an altitudinal migrant. Good coastal mainland sites: garbage dump at Bird's Isle in Belize City, Gra Gra Lagoon, Joe Taylor Creek. Also reported at Sarteneja, Bulkhead Lagoon, Mussel Creek quadrant of Belize City CBC, Manatee River (Coastal Highway near Gales Point), Mayflower, and Placencia.

Gray-necked Wood-Rail *(Aramides cajaneus)* – marshes, rice fields, wooded riversides, roadside wet ditches. Easily found nearly throughout mainland, more readily at wet areas at lower elevations. Best sites: New River, Crooked Tree, Macal River, Aguacaliente.

Uniform Crake *(Amaurolimnas concolor)* – only one record in north, on road to Hill Bank. All other records are in southern half of Belize: Manatee Lagoon,

Pook's Hill, Guacamallo Bridge, Caracol, Hydro Road, Cockscomb, Placencia area. Not reported annually, although reported thrice 2007–2008 at Cockscomb, including twice at the same location along Wari Loop trail 14 months apart and the other location less than a half-mile distant, connected by South Stann Creek.

Sora *(Porzana carolina)* – freshwater marshes at low elevations on mainland, especially Blue Creek rice fields, Edenthal, and The Dump. Occurs regularly on cays. Winter visitor.

Yellow-breasted Crake *(Porzana flaviventer)* – freshwater marshes, rice fields. Three sight records: Crooked Tree viewed and photographed December 1998–March 1999, near Belize City in June 1974, Big Falls Farm in May 1984. Other reports without details at New River and Monkey Bay.

Spotted Rail *(Pardirallus maculatus)* – freshwater marshes. Seldom seen but likely uncommon to northern half of Belize, including recent photo-documented records 1 January 2011 at Tres Leguas and 27 April 2011 at Hill Bank at New River Lagoon shoreline. Few records for southern half; try The Dump. One 2008 record at Caye Caulker.

Purple Gallinule *(Porphyrio martinicus)* – freshwater marshes, rice fields, lily pads along riversides. Found easily along New River and Crooked Tree lagoons. Other sites: Edenthal, Laguna Seca, Honey Camp Road, Freshwater Creek, Old Northern Highway, Altun Ha, Banana Bank, Macal River, The Dump.

Common Gallinule *(Gallinula galeata)* – best found in the freshwater lagoons of New River and Crooked Tree. Other good sites: Edenthal, Laguna Seca, Freshwater Creek, Old Northern Highway, Altun Ha, Banana Bank, Macal River. Not easily found in southern half. Winter visitor, although some may nest locally in north. Occasional migrant on cays.

American Coot *(Fulica americana)* – winter resident found at open water, lagoons, and lowland wet areas of northern half of Belize, especially: Corozal Bay, Shipstern, San Victor, Edenthal, Old Northern Highway, Crooked Tree (where also summers), Fresh Catch. Occasional at cays.

Sungrebe *(Heliornis fulica)* – swamp forest and forest-lined streams. Although secretive, it occurs throughout the mainland from Orange Walk south. Most easily seen from boats on New River, Irish Creek, Crooked Tree lagoons, Spanish Creek, Belize River, Cox Lagoon, Sibun River, Macal River, Sittee River, Monkey River, Rio Grande, Moho River. Other good sites: Laguna Seca, Chan Chich.

Limpkin *(Aramus guarauna)* – near water, preferably coastal lagoons or quiet rivers: Shipstern at Chacan Chac Mol, Laguna Seca, Honey Camp Road, New River, Crooked Tree, Community Baboon, Monkey Bay, Macal River, Gra Gra Lagoon, Sittee River, The Dump.

Southern Lapwing *(Vanellus chilensis)* – a single bird appeared at Crooked Tree April 2004 and remained to late May 2007. A second record was at Belize City shoreline 26 December 2006.

Black-bellied Plover *(Pluvialis squatarola)* – winter visitor, yet found every month. With few exceptions, found only along the coast and cays. Visit Sarteneja, Belize City, Gra Gra Lagoon, Hopkins.

American Golden-Plover *(Pluvialis dominica)* – newly planted rice fields, short-grass meadows, savannas. Spring migration only; unlikely to be found but best chance is Blue Creek rice fields. Other sites: Sarteneja, Crooked Tree, Payne's Creek.

Collared Plover *(Charadrius collaris)* – shrimp farm dikes, sandflats, mudflats. Very uncommon migrant and winter visitor; nested at Nova Ladyville in 1999 and suspected nesting elsewhere. Other sites: Gra Gra Lagoon, Aqua Mar, Nova Toledo, Ambergris Caye, Half Moon Caye, Calabash Caye.

Snowy Plover *(Charadrius nivosus)* – coastal sand beaches and drying ponds at shrimp farms. Three documented records: Corozal beach 3 March 2002, Nova Ladyville 19 October 1997, Caye Caulker 25 August 2001. One record for Tikal, near Visitor's Center 1 April 1991.

Wilson's Plover *(Charadrius wilsonia)* – sandflats, mud flats, and shrimp farm dikes along coast and on cays. Winter visitor and local resident. Best sites: Corozal beach, Shipstern, Ambergris Caye (nests), Caye Caulker. Good sites: Manatee Lagoon, Paradise Shrimp Farms, Gra Gra Lagoon, Aqua Mar.

Semipalmated Plover *(Charadrius semipalmatus)* – sandflats and mudflats, mostly coastal and cays; shrimp farms. Migrant and less common winter visitor. Occurs inland during migration at Blue Creek rice farms and Crooked Tree.

Killdeer *(Charadrius vociferus)* – open short-grass habitats. Fairly common winter visitor throughout mainland and Ambergris Caye; less common in foothills and Maya Mountains, where it lacks suitable habitat.

American Oystercatcher *(Haematopus palliatus)* – rare and local winter visitor; best opportunity is coastal sandy beaches of Dangriga and Gra Gra Lagoon, where seen annually. Other sites: Belize City, Monkey River, and cays.

Black-necked Stilt *(Himantopus mexicanus)* – winter visitor, a few staying to nest. Widespread in lowland wet areas, especially shrimp and tilapia farms: Fresh Catch, Spanish Lookout rice fields, Aqua Mar, Nova Toledo. New River and Crooked Tree (including nesting) are consistent sites. Also cays.

American Avocet *(Recurvirostra americana)* – estuaries, shrimp farms. Winter visitor, mostly to central coastal areas, with Nova Ladyville historically the most consistent. Other sites: Belize City, Crooked Tree, Fresh Catch, Lago Petén Itzá, Aqua Mar.

Northern Jacana *(Jacana spinosa)* – easily found on mainland at lowland wet sites: Blue Creek rice fields, Laguna Seca, New River, Honey Camp Road, Altun Ha, Crooked Tree, Aguacate Lagoon, Aguacaliente.

Spotted Sandpiper *(Actitis macularius)* – rice fields, farm ponds, lagoons, shrimp farms, mudflats, sandflats, beaches. Winter visitor easily found throughout, although less so at higher elevations.

Solitary Sandpiper *(Tringa solitaria)* – winter visitor fairly common in coastal wet areas, especially: New River, Crooked Tree, Gra Gra Lagoon, Aguacaliente.

Greater Yellowlegs *(Tringa melanoleuca)* – freshwater marshes, rice fields, shrimp farms, sandflats, mudflats. Winter visitor, occasionally staying through summer. Easily found at central and southern coastal areas: Dangriga, Gra Gra Lagoon, Nova Toledo, Aqua Mar. Less common on cays.

Willet *(Tringa semipalmata)* – beaches, shrimp farms. Winter visitor, although a few oversummer. Best chance is in central coastal areas: Dangriga, Gra

Gra Lagoon. Also on cays, especially Caye Caulker. Both Eastern (*semipalmata*) and Western (*inornata*) subspecies migrate, and Western also winters.

Lesser Yellowlegs *(Tringa flavipes)* – same habitats as Greater Yellowlegs. Winter visitor all months except June–mid-July. Found most easily in central and southern coastal areas: Belize City, Nova Toledo, Aqua Mar. Infrequently on cays.

Upland Sandpiper *(Bartramia longicauda)* – drying rice fields, agricultural fields. A transient mostly in spring; few records: between Blue Creek Village and La Milpa, Coastal Highway south of Gales Point, Hidden Valley, Dangriga, Toledo District just south of Red Bank, Ambergris Caye, Caye Caulker.

Whimbrel *(Numenius phaeopus)* – mudflats, sandflats, coastal shrimp farms. Winter visitor, occasionally summering. Best found at Dangriga, Gra Gra Lagoon, and Caye Caulker. Also reported at Belize City, Ambergris Caye, Caye Chapel, South Water Caye, and other cays.

Long-billed Curlew *(Numenius americanus)* – migrant and winter visitor. Over two dozen records; found at central coastal areas at Belize City, Dangriga, Gra Gra Lagoon, south to Placencia and Monkey River; on cays, particularly Caye Chapel and Caye Caulker (including 10 birds on 29 August 2001).

Hudsonian Godwit *(Limosa haemastica)* – two records: Crooked Tree 4 May 1986 and Aqua Mar 16 May 1999.

Marbled Godwit *(Limosa fedoa)* – rare winter visitor to central coast and cays. Best chance is Caye Caulker. Far fewer records for Nova Ladyville, Belize City, Aqua Mar, Ambergris Caye.

Ruddy Turnstone *(Arenaria interpres)* – shrimp farms, sandy beaches. Winter visitor, some occurring every month. Common on cays; readily found along central coast beaches with washed-up seaweed, especially: Belize City, Dangriga, Gra Gra Lagoon, Placencia, Nova Toledo, Aqua Mar. Sometimes found farther inland in migration.

Red Knot *(Calidris canutus)* – shrimp farms, beaches. Winter visitor not easy to find; try Belize City, Dangriga, Placencia, especially shrimp farms. Only a couple records for the cays.

Sanderling *(Calidris alba)* – sandy beaches, shrimp farms. Fairly common winter visitor on cays. Also found along central and southern coastal sites: Dangriga, Gra Gra Lagoon, Hopkins Village, Placencia, Monkey River.

Semipalmated Sandpiper *(Calidris pusilla)* – shrimp farms, rice fields, sandflats, mudflats. A fall and spring transient, with a few winter records. Best sites are shrimp farms. Infrequently at coastal sites: Sarteneja, Bird's Isle, Hopkins, Monkey River, Aguacaliente. More often at Ambergris, Caye Caulker, other cays. Occasionally inland at Crooked Tree.

Western Sandpiper *(Calidris mauri)* – shrimp farms, rice fields, sandflats, mudflats, occasionally beaches. Common in fall migration (sometimes thousands at shrimp farms), less common in spring migration, hard to find in winter except at shrimp farms. Alternative sites: Corozal beach, Belize City, Dangriga, Gra Gra Lagoon, and the cays.

Least Sandpiper *(Calidris minutilla)* – shrimp farms, rice fields, sandflats, mudflats, lagoons, estuaries, beaches. Common in migration and winter along coast and on cays.

White-rumped Sandpiper *(Calidris fuscicollis)* – late-spring migrant (one fall record) through lowland coastal areas and cays. Best sites: shrimp farms. Other sites: Shipstern, cays. Remarkably, 250 at Crooked Tree 15 May 1999.

Pectoral Sandpiper *(Calidris melanotos)* – spring and autumn migrant through wetlands. Best sites: Crooked Tree, Aguacaliente. Infrequently at: Shipstern, Blue Creek rice fields, Dangriga, cays.

Dunlin *(Calidris alpina)* – four records: Nova Ladyville 17 December 2000, Belize City CBC 29 December 1973, Gra Gra Lagoon 21–22 March 1990, Aqua Mar 6 January 1999.

Stilt Sandpiper *(Calidris himantopus)* – transient and sometimes winter visitor best found at shrimp farms. Sparingly found at: Crooked Tree, Belize City, Aguacaliente, Ambergris, and rice fields.

Buff-breasted Sandpiper *(Tryngites subruficollis)* – spring and fall transient, with very few records. Prefers wet fields of short grass. Reported at Aguacaliente and shrimp farms of Aqua Mar.

Short-billed Dowitcher *(Limnodromus griseus)* – seen in coastal areas and cays in migration; in winter most easily found at Ambergris Caye, Caye Caulker, Aqua Mar, but also found inland at Fresh Catch.

Long-billed Dowitcher *(Limnodromus scolopaceus)* – freshwater marshes, mudflats. Winter visitor; more likely dowitcher at inland sites. Flocks of up to 3,500 have been reported at Blue Creek rice fields, the best site. Other sites: Shipstern, Edenthal, Crooked Tree, shrimp farms, Caye Caulker.

Wilson's Snipe *(Gallinago delicata)* – winter visitor found in wetlands at low elevation. Most consistently at Sarteneja, Crooked Tree, Gra Gra Lagoon, The Dump, and at rice fields in Orange Walk District.

Wilson's Phalarope *(Phalaropus tricolor)* – five Belize records: Blue Creek rice fields 3 September 2006, Crooked Tree 30 April 1999, Nova Toledo 20 September 1997, Ambergris Caye 14 May 1999 and 30 September 2011. Also found 3 May 1988 on road to Uaxactún in Tikal.

Red-necked Phalarope *(Phalaropus lobatus)* – four records: Blue Creek rice fields 17 October 2007, Hidden Valley 8 September 2007, Cayo Rosario November 1993 and 4 January 1994, between Tom Owens Caye and Ranguana Caye 11 October 2009.

Black-legged Kittiwake *(Rissa tridactyla)* – one record: Caye Caulker 9 January 2000.

Bonaparte's Gull *(Chroicocephalus philadelphia)* – winter visitor with few records: Hill Bank in mid-1970s, Crooked Tree 4 March 1996, Belize City in mid-1980s, Ambergris Caye 26 February–23 March 2001.

Laughing Gull *(Leucophaeus atricilla)* – readily found in most coastal areas. Also seen at New River, Crooked Tree, Lago Petén Itzá.

Franklin's Gull *(Leucophaeus pipixcan)* – very rare transient, with about six records: Nova Ladyville, Belize City, Manatee Lagoon, Ambergris Caye, Caye Caulker, Harvest Caye.

Black-tailed Gull *(Larus crassirostris)* – one photographed at Dangriga 11 March 1988.

Ring-billed Gull *(Larus delawarensis)* – winter visitor with a few coastal records: Corozal Bay, Nova Ladyville, Belize City, Dangriga, Aqua Mar, Punta Gorda, Ambergris Caye. One inland record at Crooked Tree.

Herring Gull *(Larus argentatus)* – infrequently found winter visitor along coast: Corozal Bay, Belize City, Punta Gorda. Also Ambergris Caye, Caye Caulker. Once inland at Hill Bank.

Lesser Black-backed Gull *(Larus fuscus)* – one documented sight observation of a third-winter, mostly adult-like, gull at Belize City waterfront 28 March 2011.

Great Black-backed Gull *(Larus marinus)* – not confirmed. Reported in Howell et al. (1992) as observed and photographed at Belize City 11–12 January 1989, but Jones (2003) states, "reported twice but not confirmed." Jones suggests it as well as Kelp Gull (*L. dominicanus*) could turn up, most likely as immatures in first-basic plumage.

Brown Noddy *(Anous stolidus)* – open ocean near cays: Glover's Reef, Turneffe Atoll, South Water Caye. Ten adults on Tobacco Caye 26 July 2002 perhaps were nesting. Sometimes seen offshore well away from cays, including a sighting from Joe Taylor Creek in 1997 and one photographed at Corozal Bay 17 March 2011.

Black Noddy *(Anous minutus)* – extirpated in early 1900s. One sighting 31 October 1998 at Belize City, associated with Hurricane *Mitch*. Also single reports without details at Hol Chan Marine Reserve and Goff's Caye.

Sooty Tern *(Onychoprion fuscatus)* – seen offshore in summer at cays; nests on Middle Snake Caye in numbers estimated to be 1,000–2,000 birds. Rarely seen inland after major tropical storms.

Bridled Tern *(Onychoprion anaethetus)* – in summer offshore and at small cays; also Ambergris. Nests on cays off central and southern Belize; 12 adults at Tobacco Caye 26 July 2002.

Least Tern *(Sternula antillarum)* – found year-round but mostly in summer on some cays and along mainland coast, e.g., Shipstern, Belize City. Twenty+ with large chicks on Tobacco Caye 26 July 2002

Gull-billed Tern *(Gelochelidon nilotica)* – regularly seen at Crooked Tree early January to mid-March. Other good sites in migration and winter: Gales Point, Gra Gra Lagoon, Nova Toledo, Aqua Mar, mouth of Moho River.

Caspian Tern *(Hydroprogne caspia)* – winter visitor, yet reported all months except July. Most readily found at Crooked Tree and along central coast: Belize City, Dangriga, Gra Gra Lagoon, Hopkins Village. Less frequent south Belize coast and cays.

Black Tern *(Chlidonias niger)* – best found during fall migration at cays and along central coast: Belize City, Manatee Lagoon. Also Shipstern, Nova Toledo.

Roseate Tern *(Sterna dougallii)* – nesting colony on Tobacco Caye, including 200+ with chicks 26 July 2002. Most often seen offshore in summer; two records for Caye Caulker. Up to 60 seen from shore at Punta Gorda December 2007.

Common Tern *(Sterna hirundo)* – infrequently reported along coast, best in spring: Belize City, Dangriga, Gra Gra Lagoon, Punta Gorda, Caye Caulker. Very rarely found inland at New River Lagoon and Crooked Tree.

Forster's Tern *(Sterna forsteri)* – about a dozen records as transient and winter visitor. Documented off the northern coast at Rocky Point in Corozal District and as far south as Punta Gorda. Other sites: Sarteneja, Hill Bank, Crooked Tree, Nova Ladyville, Belize City, Ambergris Caye. Two records for Lago Petén Itzá.

Royal Tern *(Thalasseus maxima)* – year-round visitor, easily found on many cays and many coastal sites. Inland record at Fresh Catch. Breeding in Belize unconfirmed. Also fairly common at Lago Petén Itzá.

Sandwich Tern *(Thalasseus sandvicensis)* – resident, readily found along the coast and on many cays. Fifty+ with chicks and fledglings on Tobacco Caye 26 July 2002. Has been seen at Lago Petén Itzá.

Black Skimmer *(Rynchops niger)* – occasional visitor to central coast near Belize City and at Dangriga. Single records at Hill Bank and Crooked Tree.

Great Skua *(Stercorarius skua)* – specimen from Ambergris Caye 20 March 1971, and a skua species near Belize City mid-December 1976 to mid-January 1977.

Pomarine Jaeger *(Stercorarius pomarinus)* – occasional visitor to cays and offshore at Caye Caulker, Belize City, Dangriga, and Punta Gorda; 12 seen 30 March 2002 from boat between Punta Gorda and Livingston, Guatemala, and that area is probably the best chance for finding jaegers.

Parasitic Jaeger *(Stercorarius parasiticus)* – occasional transient and winter visitor, seen mostly around Belize City. Single records at Dangriga and Ambergris Caye. Jones (2003) states, "Less likely beyond reef than Pomarine."

Rock Pigeon *(Columba livia)* – present in all cities and even found in more isolated areas such as San Victor, Altun Ha, Spanish Lookout, Silk Grass Village, Red Bank, Pueblo Viejo, Barranco, Half Moon Caye.

Pale-vented Pigeon *(Patagioenas cayennensis)* – canopy of open and patchy forest, second-growth forest and edge, mangroves, littoral forest, villages. Found almost everywhere except Mountain Pine Ridge. Less readily found in the north, the cays, and densely forested areas.

Scaled Pigeon *(Patagioenas speciosa)* – forest canopy. Good sites: La Milpa, Hill Bank, Monkey Bay, Blue Hole, Hidden Valley, Mayflower, Cockscomb, Red Bank. Many other sites.

White-crowned Pigeon *(Patagioenas leucocephala)* – canopy within littoral forest. Summer resident, arriving late February and best found on many cays, especially Ambergris, Caulker, and Half Moon. Rarely found in mainland coastal areas: Shipstern, Gra Gra Lagoon, Sittee River, Placencia. Single records farther inland at Hill Bank and Cockscomb.

Red-billed Pigeon *(Patagioenas flavirostris)* – broadleaf forest and submontane pine forest. Easily found at many sites in the northern half of Belize; less so in the south, although rapidly expanding range. Good sites: Four Mile Lagoon, Honey Camp Road, Gallon Jug Road, New River, Las Cuevas, Macal River, Cockscomb, Red Bank. Also reported on Caye Caulker in 2001.

Short-billed Pigeon *(Patagioenas nigrirostris)* – subcanopy and canopy of broadleaf forest and edge, from Orange Walk south. Good sites: La Milpa, Chan Chich, Monkey Bay, Pook's Hill, Caracol, Blue Hole, Five Blues, Mayflower, Cockscomb, BFREE-Bladen, Lubaantun, Wilson Landing, Moho River.

Eurasian Collared-Dove *(Streptopelia decaocto)* – open areas near population centers. Three records at Ambergris Caye 1996–2010; apparently established thereafter. Multiple sightings on the south side of Belize City since December 2008, including nesting May 2009. Reported April 2009 in Belmopan, March 2010 in Spanish Lookout, November 2010 in Corozal, December 2010 in Placencia, and since December 2011 at Caye Caulker and Orange Walk Town. Good site: Best Western Belize Biltmore Plaza Hotel in Belize City.

White-winged Dove *(Zenaida asiatica)* – agricultural lands, scrub, villages. Most readily found in north, especially coastally in Corozal District and in Orange Walk Town; sporadic inland. In 2010 expanded westward, with sightings near Price Highway from Spanish Lookout to San Ignacio, and in 2011 expanded southward to Placencia. Coastal birds disperse in autumn. Common on Ambergris Caye, Caye Caulker.

Mourning Dove *(Zenaida macroura)* – pastures, cane fields, fallow fields, savannas, villages. Thinly widespread, mostly as fall migrant, and hard to find, especially in winter. Reported at Goldson Highway near San Victor, La Milpa, Gallon Jug, Hill Bank, Crooked Tree, TEC, Pook's Hill, Douglas Da Silva, Caracol, Chaa Creek, Placencia, The Dump, VoA, Ambergris Caye, Caye Caulker.

Inca Dove *(Columbina inca)* – one at Punta Gorda 9 August 1996; a subsequent record at Mayflower in May.

Common Ground-Dove *(Columbina passerina)* – low in pine and pine/oak/calabash savannas, roadsides, fields. Most readily found on Ambergris Caye and in northern Belize, becoming less likely toward Belize City. Good sites: Copper Bank Road, Shipstern, Freshwater Creek, Crooked Tree, Manatee Lagoon area. Marginally occurs—and is rare—in western Orange Walk District near August Pine Ridge. Best site in south is Placencia Peninsula. Identification of Common Ground-Dove is often confused with Plain-breasted Ground-Dove and female Ruddy Ground-Dove.

Plain-breasted Ground-Dove *(Columbina minuta)* – On mainland in northern half and and continuously in the coastal plain to Punta Gorda, usually associated with pine and pine/oak savannas, but also unforested areas of fallow fields and pastureland. Good sites: August Pine Ridge and Blue Creek areas of Gallon Jug Road, Spanish Lookout. Other sites: Honey Camp Road, New River, Old Northern Highway, Crooked Tree, Community Baboon, TEC, Belize Zoo, Monkey Bay, Banana Bank, Five Blues, Cattle Landing, The Dump, Boom Creek, VoA. More common in many areas than Common Ground-Dove, with which it is easily confused.

Ruddy Ground-Dove *(Columbina talpacoti)* – habitats similar to Common and Plain-breasted. Common throughout mainland Belize.

Blue Ground-Dove *(Claravis pretiosa)* – forested areas, primarily in central and southern lowlands and foothills. Feeds on ground, but usually observed perched in subcanopy, emitting easily recognized single call-note. Good sites: Coastal Highway, Monkey Bay, Pook's Hill, Las Cuevas, El Pilar, Blue Hole, Mayflower, Cockscomb, Red Bank, Nim Li Punit, Lubaantun, Aguacaliente.

Columba *dove calls*

Genus *Columba* +	# notes	Mnemonic	Description
Rock Pigeon	1+		Very deep, hollow *who-o-o* or *coo-o-o*
Pale-vented Pigeon (song)	1 + 3	"ooh, you cook good' or "you cook good" or "wooo, good for yooo"	1. *good for yOOOuu*, sometimes preceded by clear *oOOOooo* 2. unaccented weak *good for you* to emphatic *GOOD FOR YOOOU*
Red-billed Pigeon (song)	1 + ~3	"whooo, cooks fo-or you" or "cooks fo-or you" or "whoo, cooks it for you"	1. similar to that of Pale-vented but with middle note doubled *cooks fo-or you*, often preceded by a rich *whooooo*, rising, than falling in pitch. Second phrase repeated 2–5X. 2. a single swelling *whoo*, often repeated several times.
Scaled Pigeon (song)	1 (long) + 1 (short) + 1 (long)	"slow cook-slow cook-slow"	lower pitched than others. A deep, rhythmic, slightly gruff or moaning 1. *whooo-oo, hoo'ooo ...* 2. *hoo, oo'hoo ...* 3. *hooo hu'whooo ...* 2nd phrase repeated 2-3X. Gruffer than Red-billed or Pale-vented.
Short-billed Pigeon (song)	4 or more	"it feels so good"	different cadence and tonal quality than others; a clear, low-pitched, hollow, slightly tinny *it FEELS so good!* Repeated irregularly.
White-crowned Pigeon	1 + 4	"oh, you look so good"	*ooooo* followed by a pause, then *you look so goooood* (*look* is short and higher-pitched); sometimes without the introductory *ooooo*. Tone similar to White-winged Dove's, but less burry and with different pattern.
White-winged Dove	1 + 4	"who cooks for you"	tinny, burry *grrrr* plus *who cooks for youuu*, or *hoo-koo hoo kôôô*
Pale-vented Pigeon (call)			1. soft *wheoo* 2. burry *whhhooooo*
Red-billed Pigeon (call)			1. gruff growl with *ooo* at end 2. gruff *er-rrrr*
Short-billed Pigeon (call)			soft *gururrrrrr*
Scaled Pigeon (call)			short, low-pitched growl
White-crowned Pigeon (call)			low, strong purring, *puh'uhrr* and *purrr purr*, etc.
Eurasian Collared-Dove	3		slightly mournful, hollow *wha-whoo who* or *kuk-kooo-kook*
Mourning Dove			mournful *aah whOOoo who who who* with rising inflection on long second note (rarely, if ever, sings in Belize)

Ground-Dove calls

Genus *Columbina* +	# notes	Mnemonic	Description	Duration and repetition
Inca Dove	2	"no hope" or "too hot"	distinctive, burry *noah hope*	1–1½ second intervals 10 every 18–27 seconds
Blue Ground-Dove	1	Hope (optimist)	deep, hollow, clear *hope* or *'ope*	more clipped than Gray-headed 1–6X, usually 3–6X, 6 per 7–9 seconds
Ruddy Ground-Dove	2	No Hope (pessimist)	soft, hollow *no HOPE* or *per-woop*	1 note per sec 10 calls every 6–8 seconds
Common Ground-Dove	~1	NOO'ope	soft, hollow, slightly hoarse *oooup*	1 note per second 10 calls every 10–12 seconds
Plain-breasted Ground-Dove	1	Nope	soft, hollow *n'oup* or *wo'up*	faster: ≥1 note per second 10 calls per 6½–7½ seconds

White-tipped Dove (*Leptotila verreauxi*) – many forested habitats, also scrub and savannas. Easily heard throughout from Corozal to Cayo District; avoids humid tropical forest and is less common in southern Toledo District. Good sites: La Milpa, Monkey Bay, Blue Hole, Dangriga, Cockscomb.

Gray-headed Dove (*Leptotila plumbeiceps*) – forest dove on mainland most readily heard and sometimes seen at La Milpa, Chan Chich, Blue Hole, Mayflower, Cockscomb, BFREE-Bladen. Other sites: Fireburn, Lamanai, Altun Ha, Community Baboon, Monkey Bay, Caracol, duPlooy's, Lubaantun, Aguacaliente, Wilson Landing, Boom Creek. Formerly called Gray-fronted Dove (*L. rufaxilla*).

Caribbean Dove (*Leptotila jamaicensis*) – ground to mid-level of littoral forest and edge. Easiest found on Ambergris Caye and rarely at Caye Caulker. On northeast mainland, it is a common resident north of Shipstern Lagoon, most often heard mid-June to mid-August. Consistently found at Sarteneja, Fireburn, and Balam Jungle. Rarely seen in Belize City area.

Gray-chested Dove (*Leptotila cassini*) – primary and secondary humid broadleaf forest. Most easily found at central to southern sites: Blue Hole, Mayflower, Cockscomb, Red Bank, BFREE-Bladen, Lodge at Big Falls, Blue Creek Cave, Wilson Landing, Aguacaliente, Joe Taylor Creek, Boom Creek.

Ruddy Quail-Dove (*Geotrygon montana*) – same forest habitat as Gray-chested Dove; found reliably at La Milpa, Chan Chich, Blue Hole, Mayflower, Cockscomb, Red Bank, BFREE-Bladen. Other sites: Altun Ha, Community Baboon, Runaway Creek, Macal River, Croc O'dile Isle, Wilson Landing. Very hard to see, but often heard. Call is quite similar to Gray-chested Dove with which it often associates, and the two species can be heard in duets.

Forest dove calls

Genus Leptotila +	# notes	Mnemonic	Description	Duration and repetition
White-tipped Dove	2 or 3	"who are you?" like blowing over coke bottle	distinctly 2- or 3-parted; soft, low-pitched, lazy to mournful, hollow *whooo-youuuu?* to *who-ah-youuu?* Slaty-breasted Tinamou's vocalization somewhat similar but deeper, not mournful.	1 every 9–10 seconds
Caribbean Dove	4		lazy, mournful, low-pitched *who-whooo wh-whoo*, quite unlike other *Leptotila* vocalizations, but may suggest Mourning Dove.	1 every 7–9 seconds
Gray-headed Dove	1 (short)	whoo'	deep, hollow, soft *woe*; somewhat as in Blue Ground-Dove, but much softer and fades slightly. Call much shorter (<1 sec) than in other *Leptotila* species.	< 1 second 10 notes every 21–28 seconds
Gray-chested Dove	1 (long)	whooooo	drawn-out, low, mournful *ooooooo*. Much like that of Ruddy Quail-Dove, but each note distinctly longer, spaced farther apart, higher-pitched, and falling slightly in pitch and fading at the end. Much more drawn out than in Gray-headed, with which it is often heard, and not multi-syllabic as in White-tipped and Caribbean.	1½–1¾ second 10 notes every 48–65 seconds
Ruddy Quail-Dove	1	whooo	like Gray-chested Dove, but each note shorter, lower-pitched, and more monotone (does not fade or drop in pitch); less spacing between calls.	~1 second 10 notes every 25–98 seconds

Rose-ringed Parakeet *(Psittacula krameri)* – two escapees observed at Copper Bank January 2006.

Olive-throated Parakeet *(Aratinga nana)* – readily found almost everywhere in canopy of forest edge and scrub.

Scarlet Macaw *(Ara macao)* – canopy of primary broadleaf forest and sometimes interior of pine forest. Easiest site to find flocks is Red Bank from January to March. Core population resides in Chiquibul National Park and Forest Reserve near upper Macal and Raspaculo Rivers, viewable from Guacamallo Bridge (infrequently) and Las Cuevas (often), best seen in May and June. Much of its former nesting grounds now lie under the controversial Chalillo Dam reservoir. Subsequently they have been nesting upstream from the reservoir and away from any river. Their major threat is Guatemalans coming into Belize, shooting anything big enough to eat, including macaws. Macaws probably occur year-round at Cockscomb, but are not reported annually. Less reliably, traveling macaws are seen at Mountain Pine Ridge, Mayflower, and BFREE-Bladen, and have been reported at San Ignacio (once), El Pilar, and Tikal.

Brown-hooded Parrot *(Pyrilia haematotis)* – subcanopy and canopy of broadleaf forest and edge, southward of Orange Walk. Good sites: La Milpa, Chan Chich, Blue Hole, Blue Creek Cave, Moho River. Other sites: Lamanai, Guanacaste, Chiquibul, Macal River, Mayflower, Red Bank, BFREE-Bladen, Wilson Landing, Boom Creek. Often outnumbers White-crowned in south and west.

White-crowned Parrot *(Pionus senilis)* – subcanopy and canopy of forest and edge. Found nearly throughout, but more easily found at central sites: La Milpa, Chan Chich, Lamanai, Hill Bank, Caracol, Macal River, Mayflower. More common than Brown-hooded in north.

White-fronted Parrot *(Amazona albifrons)* – cultivated fields, open scrub, forest edge, savannas. Easily found throughout north and central sites from Corozal to Mayflower. Most likely parrot to be found in cultivated fields, especially corn and sorghum, and sometimes seen in flocks of up to 500–1,000. Sightings in southern Cayo and Stann Creek Districts and all of Toledo District are not recognized by Jones (2003); expected parrots in these southern areas are Brown-hooded, White-crowned, and Mealy.

Yellow-lored Parrot *(Amazona xantholora)* – Jones (2003) considers habitats of Yellow-lored to be same as White-fronted, yet Laesser (2007) found the two species well-segregated by habitat in northeast Belize, with White-fronteds occupying cultivated landscapes, whereas Yellow-lored located in forests. Best sites are Shipstern and other Corozal District sites. Other sites: New River, Altun Ha, Crooked Tree, Salt Creek, Big Falls Farm. Over 100 invaded Caye Caulker after Hurricane *Dean* in 2007. Easily confused with White-fronted Parrot and occupies same range, although less common in central Belize.

Red-lored Parrot *(Amazona autumnalis)* – subcanopy and canopy of forest, open pine savannas, and patchy forest. Common everywhere on mainland except Corozal District.

Mealy Parrot *(Amazona farinosa)* – a forest parrot usually in the canopy; good sites: La Milpa, Chan Chich, Pook's Hill, Mountain Pine Ridge, Caracol, Aguacate Lagoon, Blue Hole, Cockscomb, Wilson's Landing.

Yellow-headed Parrot *(Amazona oratrix)* – pine savannas, especially Hill Bank, Old Northern Highway, Crooked Tree, Coastal Highway, Runaway Creek, TEC, Monkey Bay, Amigo's. Also New River, Big Falls Farm, Stann Creek and Sittee River areas of Dangriga, Southern Highway as far south as BFREE-Bladen.

Yellow-naped Parrot *(Amazona auropalliata)* – three birds on Calabash Caye in Turneffe Atoll after 1998 Hurricane *Mitch;* one was shot and two remained until 2003, when the two remaining birds were last reported showing signs of courtship.

Squirrel Cuckoo *(Piaya cayana)* – forest and forest edge. Common throughout mainland; also on Ambergris Caye.

Yellow-billed Cuckoo *(Coccyzus americanus)* – uncommon migrant on mainland, fairly common at Sarteneja, more easily found on cays, e.g. Caye Caulker and Half Moon Caye. A high count of 20+ was on Lime Caye 29 April 2002.

Mangrove Cuckoo *(Coccyzus minor)* – littoral forest, mangroves, forested edge of rivers and lagoons, scrub. Few consistent sites on cays and along mainland coast. Formerly bred. Best chances: Shipstern, New River, Crooked Tree, creeks near Ladyville, Manatee Lagoon, Dangriga, Gra Gra Lagoon, Sittee River, Placencia, Ambergris Caye, Caye Caulker.

Black-billed Cuckoo *(Coccyzus erythropthalmus)* – annual migrant on the cays; rarely on mainland. Reports from: La Milpa, Altun Ha, Columbia River (high elevation), Punta Gorda, Ambergris Caye, Caye Caulker.

Striped Cuckoo *(Tapera naevia)* – low to mid-level in scrub, fallow fields. Difficult to see, but more common than expected once you learn its call. Good sites: San Victor, August Pine Ridge, Freshwater Creek, Crooked Tree, Community Baboon, Runaway Creek, Monkey Bay, Macal River, Lago Petén Itzá area, Southern Highway (north end), Cockscomb, The Dump, Blue Creek Cave, Aguacaliente, Cuxlin Ha, Boom Creek.

Pheasant Cuckoo *(Dromococcyx phasianellus)* – ground to subcanopy in broadleaf forest; dense second growth. Very difficult to see or even hear, although widespread in range and altitude. If present, loud tremulous call can be heard at dawn and dusk. Starts calling in Gallon Jug forests in mid-March, although sometimes as early as late February. Consistently reported at Black Rock and the old airport strip at Tikal. Other reports: Shipstern, La Milpa, Freshwater Creek, Lamanai, Irish Creek near Hill Bank, Runaway Creek, Pook's Hill, Mountain Pine Ridge, Xunantunich, Blue Hole, Cockscomb, Lodge at Big Falls, Columbia River.

Smooth-billed Ani *(Crotophaga ani)* – scrub edge, fallow fields, littoral forest edge. Occasional visitor to cays; reported on Caye Caulker, Half Moon Caye, and more often, Ambergris Caye, where it may remain to breed.

Groove-billed Ani *(Crotophaga sulcirostris)* – common in scrub habitat throughout mainland and Ambergris Caye.

Barn Owl *(Tyto alba)* – agricultural areas, quarries, population centers. Also found in coastal areas such as Gra Gra Lagoon where is flies over water. Most often reported at La Milpa and Chan Chich. Other sites: Corozal, Xol-Pol, Mennonite farms between Yo Creek and Blue Creek, Hill Bank, Big Falls Farm, Coastal Highway, TEC, Banana Bank, Pook's Hill, Slate Creek, Spanish Lookout, Clarissa Falls, Chaa Creek, duPlooy's, Blue Hole, Lodge at Big Falls, The Dump.

Vermiculated Screech-Owl *(Megascops guatemalae)* – nocturnal forest owl found over extensive range, with best chances at La Milpa and Chan Chich, Salt Creek, and duPlooy's. Two tent-campers heard the owls regularly in a one-week trip at Las Cuevas, Five Blues, and Cockscomb. Other sites: Shipstern, Crooked Tree, Runaway Creek, Monkey Bay, Banana Bank, Pook's Hill, Mountain Pine Ridge, Caracol, Macal River, Blue Hole, BFREE-Bladen, Aguacaliente, Wilson Landing, Boom Creek. Often found in same areas as Marine Toad (*Bufo marinus*), whose low-pitched trill is similar but longer and louder. The gray morph of the screech-owl is the expected form; however two red morphs have been photographed, one at Blancaneaux Lodge in Mountain Pine Ridge and one at La Milpa.

Crested Owl *(Lophostrix cristata)* – sparingly in mature broadleaf forest at mid-to-upper elevations of Maya Mountains: Rio Frio Caves, Vaca Plateau, Caracol, Five Blues, Billy Barquedier, Cockscomb, BFREE-Bladen.

Spectacled Owl *(Pulsatrix perspicillata)* – subcanopy within broadleaf forest, most reliably at Pook's Hill, Mayflower, Cockscomb. Other sites: La Milpa, Chan

Chich, Green Hills, Las Cuevas, Crystal Paradise, Chaa Creek, duPlooy's, Blue Hole, BFREE-Bladen, Columbia River. Several records for Tikal along airstrip.

Great Horned Owl *(Bubo virginianus)* – found on Ambergris Caye, where it has nested. Few other records: coastal lowlands from Shipstern to Belize City, once at Big Falls (Toledo District).

Central American Pygmy-Owl *(Glaucidium griseiceps)* – mid-level to subcanopy within broadleaf forest. Call similar to Ferruginous but somewhat faster and in shorter bursts (two–nine in series). Found at interior mainland sites, mostly in foothills and higher elevations: Chan Chich, Pook's Hill, Slate Creek, Mountain Pine Ridge, Las Cuevas, Chiquibul, Crystal Paradise Resort, Chaa Creek, duPlooy's, Mayflower, Cockscomb, BFREE-Bladen, Columbia River. Not found on the coastal plain.

Ferruginous Pygmy-Owl *(Glaucidium brasilianum)* – same habitat as Central American, plus submontane forest, urban areas. More likely to perch in open areas with scattered trees. Easily heard and often seen (in daylight), especially at northern sites, foothills, and Mountain Pine Ridge. Good sites: Corozal, Shipstern, San Victor, August Pine Ridge, Honey Camp Road, Pook's Hill, Hidden Valley, duPlooy's. Not found on coastal plain south of Sibun River at Coastal Highway.

Burrowing Owl *(Athene cunicularia)* – two records: beach at mouth of Manatee River in Belize District in 1901 (two specimens since lost), and quarry behind Belize Lodge & Excursions in Toledo District 8–9 April 1998.

Mottled Owl *(Ciccaba virgata)* – occurs throughout in forest and forest edges. Good sites: La Milpa, Chan Chich, New River, Lamanai, Hill Bank, Las Cuevas, Macal River, Tikal, BFREE-Bladen; many other sites.

Black-and-white Owl *(Ciccaba nigrolineata)* – present in subcanopy of broadleaf forest, yet often very hard to find. Most reliable sites: La Milpa, Chan Chich, Mayflower, Cockscomb, and at Lodge at Big Falls, where it has nested. Other sites: Pook's Hill, Mountain Pine Ridge, Chiquibul, Caracol, Crystal Paradise, Chaa Creek, duPlooy's, Blue Hole, BFREE-Bladen, Wilson Landing.

Stygian Owl *(Asio stygius)* – most reliable sites are in Mountain Pine Ridge, specifically at Hidden Valley, Gaïa Riverlodge, and Blancaneaux Lodge. Can be found in daylight roosting close to the trunk in the upper portions of tall pines, usually well hidden by branches and needles. Also atop pines shortly after dusk. Reported, including specimen, in pine savanna near Belize Zoo. Found in other pine belts such as at Hill Bank. An excellent video of a radio-tracking study by the Belize Raptor Research Institute that resulted in finding a nest and chick can be viewed at www.youtube.com/watch?v=i5DckfqTXmI. The juvenile fledged 15 April 2011.

Short-eared Owl *(Asio flammeus)* – single record, a mummified carcass found 4 March 1999 at Aqua Mar.

Striped Owl *(Pseudoscops clamator)* – rarely reported; occupies similar habitat to Short-eared Owl's—marshes, meadows, open disturbed areas, savannas with scattered trees—but is nocturnal and has steadier flight. Range extends coastally and in foothills from southern Belize District through Toledo District. Found on 8 of 10 Punta Gorda CBCs. Sites: Runaway Creek, Cockscomb, The Dump and rice fields near Blue Creek, Wilson Landing, VoA.

Short-tailed Nighthawk *(Lurocalis semitorquatus)* – riparian rivers and streams. Five records: Cockscomb 10 May 1998, Caye Caulker 25 January 2000 and 13 August 2002, South Water Caye 8 September 1998, Hidden Valley 15 May 2012.

Lesser Nighthawk *(Chordeiles acutipennis)* – study bar graphs and compare to Common Nighthawk. Best site is New River, where seen in flight at dawn and dusk and by day roosting lengthwise on branches overhanging the river. Other sites in winter: Shipstern, August Pine Ridge, Crooked Tree, Community Baboon, Big Falls Farm, Runaway Creek, TEC, Banana Bank, Mountain Pine Ridge, Caracol, Chaa Creek, Mayflower, The Dump, Ambergris Caye. Seen in summer in Corozal District, where it may nest.

Common Nighthawk *(Chordeiles minor)* – summer resident in Mountain Pine Ridge and a few coastal lowland sites: Hill Bank, Belize City, Payne's Creek. Widespread transient, peaking in autumn along coast and at cays.

Common Pauraque *(Nyctidromus albicollis)* – although common, typically found only predawn and in early evening in flight and calling, as it stays hidden at ground-roosting sites during daylight hours. Good sites: La Milpa, Chan Chich, New River, Hill Bank, Crooked Tree, Monkey Bay, entrance road to Mayflower, The Dump, Wilson's Landing, as well as many other sites with quiet, open roads.

Yucatan Poorwill *(Nyctiphrynus yucatanicus)* – broadleaf forest and edge, primarily in high trees. Sometimes observed on night cruises on New River. Difficult to find, and can be confused with Yucatan Nightjar. Both species vocalize at least February through June. Other sites: Shipstern, Freshwater Creek, Salt Creek, Cox Lagoon, Slate Creek, duPlooy's, Hydro Road. Fairly common at Tikal at airstrip, feeding at night with pauraques and observed in the daytime roosting along forest edge.

Chuck-will's-widow *(Antrostomus carolinensis)* – probably more common than the dozen or so records indicate; most are fall migrants. Heard vocalizing at Irish Creek near Lamanai (winter), Benque Viejo (spring), and Columbia River (spring); spotlighted at New River Lagoon; banded at Sarteneja; tower-killed at Cahal Pech; seen at Sapodilla Cayes. A rare winter sighting was 18–20 December 2008 at Tikal.

Yucatan Nightjar *(Antrostomus badius)* – found most winter evenings on cruises along New River. Usually perches in trees, not on ground. Other winter sites: Shipstern, La Milpa, Chan Chich, Freshwater Creek, Community Baboon, Belize City, TEC, duPlooy's, Ambergris Caye. Can be found in summer at Shipstern and New River; seasonal in south. Vocalizes March through June.

Eastern Whip-poor-will *(Antrostomus vociferus)* – confirmed records are tower kills and birds mist-netted in spring and fall; may be more frequent than few records indicate.

Great Potoo *(Nyctibius grandis)* – several reports but none confirmed until 29–30 September 2009 at Green Hills Butterfly Ranch in Cayo District. Much larger than Northern Potoo, fine barring across the undersides, and with a different voice. A low-resolution copy of the video/audio file is available at: www.biodiversity.bz/find/resource/profile.phtml?dcid=112859. A second was photographed 8 February 2011 at BFREE/Bladen, and a third followed quickly thereafter when several were found 23–25 February at Machaca Lodge (now Belcampo Belize) and again in March and April.

Northern Potoo *(Nyctibius jamaicensis)* – most easily found on New River in the daytime if the boat driver knows a roost or at nighttime with use of a searchlight looking for eyeshine. Night searches are also successful at La Milpa and Gallon Jug. Has hoarse and guttural call. Has nested at Shipstern, New River Lagoon, San Antonio (Cayo), and duPlooy's. Other sites: Hill Bank, Freshwater Creek, Old Northern Highway, Crooked Tree, Banana Bank, Pook's Hill, Slate Creek, Mountain Pine Ridge, Caracol, Chaa Creek, Mayflower, Five Blues, BFREE-Bladen, Columbia River, Payne's Creek, Moho River.

Black Swift *(Cypseloides niger)* – two sightings 14 August 2011, including photographs, were at Caracol and Chaillo Reservoir. Migration tracking has shown flight paths through Central America between Colorado and Brazil. See http://earbirding.com/blog/archives/3602.

White-chinned Swift *(Cypseloides cryptus)* – one or two records: Manatee Lagoon (9 August 1931, specimens) and probably Hidden Valley (19 March 1991). Perhaps occurs more often but goes undetected.

Chestnut-collared Swift *(Streptoprocne rutila)* – likely a rare and local seasonal resident at the cliff behind the upper falls of Tiger Fern Falls, N 16° 46.817' W 88° 26.457'. Although no nest has been found, swifts were seen flying into and from the falls at dawn and dusk, 2008–2011, and have been seen elsewhere at Cockscomb since 1993. Small flocks also observed at Monkey Bay, Pook's Hill, and Hidden Valley (1996–2011).

White-collared Swift *(Streptoprocne zonaris)* – more often seen in central and south in foothills and Maya Mountains. Found on all Belmopan and Punta Gorda CBCs. Good sites: Coastal Highway, Monkey Bay, Pook's Hill, Slate Creek, Thousand Foot Falls, Rio Frio Caves, Caracol, Macal River, Mayflower, Cockscomb, Red Bank, BFREE-Bladen, Lubaantun, Belcampo Belize, Moho River.

Chimney Swift *(Chaetura pelagica)* – fall migrant mostly along or near coast; probably uncommon spring migrant. Some reported sites: Shipstern, Hill Bank, Pook's Hill, Slate Creek, San Ignacio, Chaa Creek, Blue Hole, Aqua Mar, BFREE, VoA, Ambergris Caye, Caye Caulker.

Vaux's Swift *(Chaetura vauxi)* – widespread, most often seen at inland sites: Corozal, San Victor, Shipstern, La Milpa, Gallon Jug, Hill Bank, Guanacaste, Pook's Hill, Blue Hole, Mayflower, Cockscomb, Red Bank, Bladen.

Lesser Swallow-tailed Swift *(Panyptila cayennensis)* – similar range as Vaux's, but less common. Good sites: Shipstern, Fireburn, La Milpa, Chan Chich, Hill Bank, TEC, Monkey Bay, Slate Creek, Las Cuevas, Caracol, Tikal, Blue Hole, Five Blues, Sittee River, Cockscomb, Red Bank.

Band-tailed Barbthroat *(Threnetes ruckeri)* – difficult to find. Best in southwestern Toledo District, such as Blue Creek Village. Reported sites at edge of its range: Cockscomb, Columbia River, Wilson Landing, Boom Creek.

Long-billed Hermit *(Phaethornis longirostris)* – readily found from Bravo Hills to Punta Gorda in broadleaf forest edge and clearings. Found on all CBCs for Gallon Jug, Belmopan, and Punta Gorda, but only 7 of 33 Belize City CBCs. Many good sites, including: Caracol, Macal River, Tikal, Cockscomb, Wilson Landing. Renamed from Long-tailed Hermit after split with *P. superciliosus* of South America.

Stripe-throated Hermit *(Phaethornis striigularis)* – lower levels within broadleaf forest and edge, clearings, shrub. Found throughout although nearly absent north of New River, but has been found at Fireburn. Good sites: La Milpa, Chan Chich, Hill Bank, Belize Zoo, Pook's Hill, Caracol, Blue Hole, Five Blues, Mayflower, Cockscomb, Red Bank, Wilson Landing. Previously called Little Hermit; renamed after separation from *P. longuemareus* of northern South America.

Scaly-breasted Hummingbird *(Phaeochroa cuvierii)* – mid-level of broadleaf forest edge and clearings. Most easily found at Chan Chich, Mayflower, and Cockscomb. Other sites: La Milpa, Monkey Bay, Pook's Hill, Blue Hole, Red Bank, BFREE-Bladen, Blue Creek Cave, Boom Creek, Moho River.

Wedge-tailed Sabrewing *(Campylopterus curvipennis)* – low to mid-level in forest clearings and edge. Most easily found at La Milpa, Chan Chich, and Green Hills. Other good sites: Lamanai, Blue Hole, Cockscomb. Other sites: Hill Bank, TEC, Slate Creek, Las Cuevas, Crystal Paradise, Cahal Pech, Chaa Creek, duPlooy's, Xunantunich, BFREE-Bladen. Only recent sighting in far south is at Lodge at Big Falls.

Violet Sabrewing *(Campylopterus hemileucurus)* – low to mid-level in broadleaf forest, especially near streams. Mostly in foothills and Maya Mountains. Good sites: Green Hills, Hidden Valley, Chiquibul, Caracol, Blue Hole, Mayflower, Cockscomb, BFREE-Bladen, Columbia River. Other sites: Pook's Hill, duPlooy's, Lubaantun, Pueblo Viejo.

White-necked Jacobin *(Florisuga mellivora)* – mid-level to subcanopy of broadleaf forest edge, often over streams and ponds, from New River south to Punta Gorda. Good sites: La Milpa, Chan Chich, Hill Bank, Community Baboon, Monkey Bay, Pook's Hill, Green Hills, Caracol, Macal River, Blue Hole, Five Blues, Mayflower, Cockscomb, BFREE-Bladen, Lubaantun, Blue Creek Cave, Wilson Landing.

Brown Violetear *(Colibri delphinae)* – mid-level in tropical moist broadleaf forest. Uncommon but expected in Maya Mountains, e.g., Columbia River (fairly common at Little Quartz Ridge), but has also occurred in lowlands at Hill Bank, Manatee Lagoon, Cave's Branch, Cockscomb, Boom Creek.

Green-breasted Mango *(Anthracothorax prevostii)* – found almost throughout; good sites: Shipstern, San Victor, August Pine Ridge, La Milpa, Chan Chich, Hill Bank, Monkey Bay, Guanacaste, El Pilar, Macal River, Mayflower, Cockscomb, Lubaantun, Blue Creek Cave, Caye Caulker, Half Moon Caye.

Black-crested Coquette *(Lophornis helenae)* – found rarely at broadleaf forest edgings and clearings. Reported sites (often single occurrences): La Milpa, duPlooy's, Tikal, Placencia Peninsula, Lodge at Big Falls, Ambergris Caye. Most consistent sites may be higher elevations: Doyle's Delight, Columbia River at Little Quartz Ridge. A nesting pair was observed over a two-week period at Las Cuevas in February 1997.

Canivet's Emerald *(Chlorostilbon canivetii)* – low levels in deciduous and semi-deciduous forest edge, scrub, savannas, cultivated areas. Widespread, but better sites are in lowlands: Shipstern, La Milpa, Crooked Tree, TEC, Belize Zoo, Guanacaste, duPlooy's. Female can be confused with other species; look for white toward base of outermost rectrices.

Violet-crowned Woodnymph *(Thalurania colombica)* – tropical moist broadleaf forest. Rarely reported in foothills and Maya Mountains of Toledo District at BFREE-Bladen and Columbia River Forest Reserve, but also once downriver, northwest of San Pedro Columbia. Two records from Mountain Pine Ridge: Douglas Da Silva and Mt. Margaret.

Blue-throated Goldentail *(Hylocharis eliciae)* – three accepted records 1987–2007: in citrus orchard near Beaver Dam Creek on Price Highway, in *Heliconia* thicket near San Pedro Columbia, and at Lodge at Big Falls.

White-bellied Emerald *(Amazilia candida)* – broadleaf forest and edge. Found throughout the mainland at dozens of sites.

Azure-crowned Hummingbird *(Amazilia cyanocephala)* – mid-level to subcanopy in pine savanna, broadleaf forest and edge. With so many White-bellied Emeralds present, the similar-appearing Azure-crowned casually might be dismissed. Occupies the central parts of Belize, not the extremes. Most readily seen at Hidden Valley, Mountain Pine Ridge. Other good sites: savanna along New River lagoon, Hill Bank, Community Baboon, Runaway Creek, TEC, Belize Zoo, Monkey Bay, Guanacaste, Guacamallo Bridge, Caracol, Five Blues, BFREE-Bladen, Columbia River.

> See www.bafrenz.com for a comparison chart of hummingbirds, as well as other charts for tinamous, parrots, nightjars, woodcreepers, Myiarchus flycatchers, and ant-tanagers.

Rufous-tailed Hummingbird *(Amazilia tzacatl)* – most common hummingbird on mainland; seen at almost every site.

Buff-bellied Hummingbird *(Amazilia yucatanensis)* – low to mid-level in pinelands, arid scrub, and open second-growth. Mostly in the north, best found at: Copper Bank, Sarteneja, Shipstern, Fireburn. Less frequently at: La Milpa, Chan Chich, Lamanai, Crooked Tree.

Cinnamon Hummingbird *(Amazilia rutila)* – Prefers littoral forest, forest edge, mangroves, and cultivated areas. Readily found on many cays, including Ambergris, at most Corozal sites, Sarteneja, Shipstern, San Victor, farmlands near August Pine Ridge, Belize City. Other sites are coastal: Freshwater Creek, Altun Ha, Salt Creek, Runaway Creek, Gales Point, Gra Gra Lagoon, Sittee River loop, Placencia, Monkey River, Punta Gorda.

Stripe-tailed Hummingbird *(Eupherusa eximia)* – a higher-elevation hummingbird of broadleaf forest and forest edge of Maya Mountains; found at Chiquibul, Doyle's Delight, Cockscomb, Columbia River.

Purple-crowned Fairy *(Heliothryx barroti)* – broadleaf forest and edge. Best sites are in Bravo Hills, Maya Mountains and foothills.

Long-billed Starthroat *(Heliomaster longirostris)* – six Belize records 1999–2012: Coastal Highway at Runaway Creek, Beaver Dam Creek, Mt.Pleasant/Belmopan, Big Falls, San Pedro Columbia, Blue Creek Cave.

Sparkling-tailed Hummingbird *(Tilmatura dupontii)* – one sight record at Tres Leguas, off Gallon Jug Road 23 February 2002.

Ruby-throated Hummingbird *(Archilochus colubris)* – as a migrant, could appear almost anywhere. Consistent wintering sites are: La Milpa, Crooked Tree, Monkey Bay, Tikal, Blue Hole.

Slaty-tailed Trogon *(Trogon massena)* – found in primary forest and edge; good sites: La Milpa, Chan Chich, Lamanai, Hill Bank, Pook's Hill, Las Cuevas, Caracol, Aguacate Lagoon, Tikal, Blue Hole, Five Blues, Mayflower, Cockscomb, BFREE-Bladen, Lubaantun, Aguacaliente, Wilson Landing, Boom Creek.

Black-headed Trogon *(Trogon melanocephalus)* – easily found throughout mainland, resident on Ambergris Caye and visitor to Caye Caulker.

Gartered Trogon *(Trogon caligatus)* – readily found throughout mainland, but not cays. Split from Violaceous Trogon (*T. violaceus*) in 2010.

Collared Trogon *(Trogon collaris)* – primary broadleaf forest and edge. Good sites: Lamanai, Chan Chich, Las Cuevas, Caracol, Cockscomb. Other sites: La Milpa, Hill Bank, Pook's Hill, Barton Creek, Mountain Pine Ridge, Guacamallo Bridge, Macal River, Tikal, Blue Hole, Mayflower, BFREE-Bladen.

Tody Motmot *(Hylomanes momotula)* – a small, secretive motmot found in primary forest, often in cohune ridge: La Milpa, Chan Chich, Lamanai, Hill Bank, Pook's Hill, Las Cuevas, Caracol, El Pilar, Chaa Creek, Black Rock, Tikal, Blue Hole, Five Blues, Mayflower, BFREE-Bladen, Columbia River, Wilson Landing.

Blue-crowned Motmot *(Momotus momota)* – easily heard almost everywhere in forests, although not as easy to see; absent from Orange Walk farming areas, Crooked Tree, and the cays.

Keel-billed Motmot *(Electron carinatum)* – a rare and globally vulnerable species that survives in Belize in primary rainforest, preferring steep gullies and cliffs in dense, vine-covered hill forest. Best found when males are vocalizing on territory from January through March. Best site is Caracol, where a 1996 study reported 20–25 residing. A 1994 survey estimated 16–20 at Mullins River Basin, upper Manatee Forest Reserve. Other good sites: Doyle's Delight, Chiquibul, Mayflower, BFREE-Bladen, Columbia River. Other reported sites: Slate Creek, Hidden Valley, near El Pilar, Green Hills, Blue Hole, Billy Barquedier, Cockscomb's Victoria Peak Trail, Pueblo Viejo. A 1958 record for Tikal, but none reported subsequently in spite of intensive study.

Ringed Kingfisher *(Megaceryle torquata)* – throughout mainland and occasionally on Ambergris Caye.

Belted Kingfisher *(Megaceryle alcyon)* – winter visitor fairly common to common throughout, including cays, where it is the only kingfisher regularly seen. Occasional in summer.

Amazon Kingfisher *(Chloroceryle amazona)* – prefers forested rivers, streams, and lagoons. Good sites: Chan Chich, Guanacaste, Aguacate Lagoon, Macal River, Xunantunich, Cockscomb, Red Bank, BFREE-Bladen, Rio Grande at Lodge at Big Falls and Belcampo Belize, Aguacaliente, Moho River. Other sites: Community Baboon, Monkey Bay, Sittee River, Five Blues, The Dump, Blue Creek Cave, Pueblo Viejo. Amazon lacks white spots on wings which are prominent on Green.

Green Kingfisher *(Chloroceryle americana)* – found near water throughout mainland and occasionally on Ambergris Caye and Caye Caulker.

American Pygmy Kingfisher *(Chloroceryle aenea)* – quiet pools, backwaters, heavily vegetated lagoon margins; avoids faster-flowing rivers. Although fairly common in many places, often can be difficult to find because it perches quietly on low branches over water, which may be hidden from view depending on water levels. Good sites: Shipstern, New River, Irish Creek at Hill Bank, Crooked Tree, Tikal, Gra Gra Lagoon, The Dump, Blue Creek Cave, Aguacaliente, Joe Taylor Creek, Moho River. Other sites: New River, Cox Lagoon, Macal River, Sittee River, Cockscomb, BFREE-Bladen, Wilson Landing.

White-necked Puffbird *(Notharchus hyperrhynchos)* – sedentary nature allows puffbirds to be easily overlooked; perches mid-level to canopy at forest edges and semi-open country. Good sites: Shipstern, La Milpa, Chan Chich, Honey Camp Road, Hill Bank, Old Northern Highway, Community Baboon, Runaway Creek, Monkey Bay, Pook's Hill, Macal River, Blue Hole, Mayflower, Cockscomb, BFREE-Bladen, San Antonio Road, Belcampo Belize.

White-whiskered Puffbird *(Malacoptila panamensis)* – sits quietly at mid-levels of forest and forest edges away from coast. Good sites: Lamanai, Chan Chich, Pook's Hill, Caracol, Tikal, Blue Hole, Five Blues, BFREE-Bladen. Other sites: La Milpa, Hill Bank, Slate Creek, Rio Frio Caves, Las Cuevas, Macal River, Mayflower, Cockscomb, Pueblo Viejo, Belcampo Belize.

Rufous-tailed Jacamar *(Galbula ruficauda)* – more often detected by voice than seen; usually perches on bowed swinging vine in broadleaf forest. Good sites: La Milpa, Chan Chich, Lamanai, Hill Bank, Guanacaste, Pook's Hill, Caracol, Tikal, Croc O'dile Isle, Blue Hole, Mayflower, Cockscomb, BFREE-Bladen, Pueblo Viejo, Columbia River, Lubaantun.

Emerald Toucanet *(Aulacorhynchus prasinus)* – best found in submontane forest, preferably broadleaf; sites include: Hidden Valley, Rio Frio Caves, Guacamallo Bridge, Caracol, Blue Hole, Jaguar Creek, Mayflower, Cockscomb, BFREE-Bladen, Columbia River. Present at La Milpa, Chan Chich, and El Pilar in winter and in breeding season March to July; sometimes dispersing at end of rainy season to lower altitude, e.g., Lamanai. Fairly common year round at Tikal.

Collared Aracari *(Pteroglossus torquatus)* – found throughout mainland in broadleaf forest and edge.

Keel-billed Toucan *(Ramphastos sulfuratus)* – conspicuous throughout mainland. Wintered on Ambergris Caye after Hurricane *Dean* in 2007.

Acorn Woodpecker *(Melanerpes formicivorus)* – pine/oak forest. Good sites: Gallon Jug road through August Pine Ridge and San Felipe, Crooked Tree, Community Baboon, Coastal Highway, TEC, Belize Zoo, Monkey Bay, Hidden Valley, Thousand Foot Falls, Douglas Da Silva, Chiquibul, northeast Toledo District along Southern Highway.

Black-cheeked Woodpecker *(Melanerpes pucherani)* – broadleaf forest edges and clearings. Good sites: La Milpa, Chan Chich, Coastal Highway, Macal River, Pook's Hill, Las Cuevas, Caracol, Tikal, Blue Hole, Mayflower, Cockscomb, Red Bank, BFREE-Bladen, Lodge at Big Falls, Belcampo Belize.

Yucatan Woodpecker *(Melanerpes pygmaeus)* – open pine and broadleaf forests; also called Red-vented Woodpecker. Most readily found in Corozal District, fewer farther south to Belize City. Good sites: Sarteneja Road, Copper Bank Road to Cerros, Xo-Pol, Shipstern, New River, Crooked Tree. Other sites: August Pine Ridge, Altun Ha, Salt Creek, Community Baboon, Runaway Creek, Cox Lagoon, TEC, Monkey Bay, Ambergris Caye, Caye Caulker. Reports from farther south may be misidentified Golden-fronteds.

Golden-fronted Woodpecker *(Melanerpes aurifrons)* – found everywhere at forest edge and open areas with trees. Note, the subspecies *dubius* that is present in Belize has red nasal tufts, not golden.

Yellow-bellied Sapsucker *(Sphyrapicus varius)* – mid-level to subcanopy in forest and edge. More often seen in migration on cays than elsewhere. Uncommonly seen at many mainland sites in winter.

Ladder-backed Woodpecker *(Picoides scalaris)* – open pine forest on coastal plains. Good sites: Coastal Highway, Runaway Creek, Manatee Lagoon, Southern Highway, All Pines, Payne's Creek. Other sites: New River, Hill Bank, Crooked Tree, TEC, Monkey Bay, BFREE, Punta Ycacos.

Smoky-brown Woodpecker *(Veniliornis fumigatus)* – broadleaf forest interior and edge. Good sites: La Milpa, Chan Chich, Monkey Bay, Pook's Hill, Caracol, Tikal, Blue Hole, Five Blues, Cockscomb, BFREE-Bladen, Wilson Landing. Found at many other sites from Sarteneja to Punta Gorda.

Golden-olive Woodpecker *(Colaptes rubiginosus)* – found in pine and broadleaf forest and edge. Good sites: La Milpa, Monkey Bay, Guanacaste, Hidden Valley, Caracol, Tikal, Blue Hole, Five Blues, Mayflower, Red Bank, Lubaantun.

Chestnut-colored Woodpecker *(Celeus castaneus)* – prefers interior of broadleaf forest. Good sites: La Milpa, Chan Chich, Lamanai, Hill Bank, Caracol, Aguacate Lagoon, Tikal, Mayflower, Cockscomb, BFREE-Bladen.

Lineated Woodpecker *(Dryocopus lineatus)* – most wooded areas, including those with only scattered trees. Found at many sites throughout.

Pale-billed Woodpecker *(Campephilus guatemalensis)* – same habitats as Lineated's, but less frequent in pines and villages. Sites same as for Lineated. Readily identified by its double-tap while working wood.

Great Antshrike *(Taraba major)* – difficult to see in dense scrub and forest edge; found away from coast, more easily in south but extends as far north as Belize City. Good sites: Monkey Bay, Pook's Hill, Las Cuevas, Blue Hole, Cockscomb, BFREE-Bladen, Nim Li Punit, Lodge at Big Falls, The Dump, Blue Creek Cave, Aguacaliente, Santa Anna, Wilson Landing.

Barred Antshrike *(Thamnophilus doliatus)* – dense tangles, scrub, understory to mid-level of forest edge. Easy to hear throughout mainland, but can be difficult to see. Found twice on Ambergris Caye.

Western Slaty-Antshrike *(Thamnophilus atrinucha)* – found in Toledo District in understory to subcanopy of broadleaf forest and forest edge in the coastal plain. Numerous sites include: Monkey River, BFREE, Aguacaliente, Wilson Landing, Joe Taylor Creek, VoA, Boom Creek, Moho River.

Russet Antshrike *(Thamnistes anabatinus)* – tangles and vines of primary forest of Maya Mountains. For a low-elevation site, try Blue Creek Cave. Uncommon in foothills, fairly common at higher elevations. Good sites: Bladen, Columbia River, Little Quartz Ridge. Rare at Tikal.

Plain Antvireo *(Dysithamnus mentalis)* – understory to subcanopy of primary forest. Not documented at low elevation. Good sites: Chan Chich, Las Cuevas, Caracol, Tikal, BFREE-Bladen, Little Quartz Ridge, Columbia River. Other reported sites: Pook's Hill, Slate Creek, Chaa Creek, Cockscomb.

Slaty Antwren *(Myrmotherula schisticolor)* – primary broadleaf forest at high elevations of Maya Mountains. Good sites: Doyle's Delight, Bladen, Little Quartz Ridge, Columbia River.

Dot-winged Antwren *(Microrhopias quixensis)* – broadleaf forest interior and edge throughout most of interior mainland south of New River; fond of dead leaves in vine tangles. Good sites: Chan Chich, Hill Bank, Guanacaste, Pook's Hill, Caracol, Aguacate Lagoon, Tikal, Blue Hole, Five Blues, Cockscomb, BFREE-Bladen, Wilson Landing, many others.

Dusky Antbird *(Cercomacra tyrannina)* – dense tangles, scrub, and forest-edge understory. Often heard, but not easily seen. Easiest sites are Dusky Antbird Trail at Blue Hole and Cockscomb. Good sites: La Milpa, Chan Chich, Lamanai, Hill Bank, Monkey Bay, Pook's Hill, Caracol, Macal River, Hydro Road, Blue Hole, Five Blues, Mayflower, Red Bank, BFREE-Bladen, Aguacaliente, Wilson Landing.

Bare-crowned Antbird *(Gymnocichla nudiceps)* – rare in understory and edge of broadleaf forest at base of Maya Mountains. Reported sites (mostly single occurences): Blue Hole, Cockscomb, Lodge at Big Falls, San Pedro Columbia, Blue Creek Cave, Aguacaliente, Santa Anna.

Black-faced Antthrush *(Formicarius analis)* – often heard calling from ground and understory of broadleaf forest; infrequently seen walking slowly, sometimes following ant swarms. Widespread and at many good sites: Shipstern, La Milpa, Chan Chich, Lamanai, Coastal Highway, Monkey Bay, Guanacaste, Pook's Hill, Caracol, Tikal, Blue Hole, Mayflower, Cockscomb, BFREE-Bladen, Blue Creek Cave, Aguacaliente, Wilson Landing, Joe Taylor Creek, Boom Creek.

Tawny-throated Leaftosser *(Sclerurus mexicanus)* – found above 3,000 feet at Doyle's Delight in Chiquibul, Little Quartz Ridge in Columbia River, and Mt. Margaret in Maya Mountains across Hummingbird Highway from Five Blues.

Scaly-throated Leaftosser *(Sclerurus guatemalensis)* – stays well hidden on ground and in understory of broadleaf forest; more likely to be heard (singing or leaf-tossing) than seen. Good sites: La Milpa, Chan Chich, Las Cuevas, Caracol, Tikal, Blue Hole, Cockscomb, BFREE-Bladen, Columbia River.

Rufous-breasted Spinetail *(Synallaxis erythrothorax)* – well hidden in scrub close to rivers and creeks, often heard, infrequently seen. By far the easiest place to see them is Monkey Bay. Other good sites: Crooked Tree, Community Baboon, Pook's Hill, Macal River, Blue Hole, Cockscomb, Lodge at Big Falls, The Dump, Aguacaliente, Joe Taylor Creek, Moho River.

Scaly-throated Foliage-gleaner *(Anabacerthia variegaticeps)* – found only at Doyle's Delight and the upper reaches of Snake Creek in Chiquibul National Forest.

Buff-throated Foliage-gleaner *(Automolus ochrolaemus)* – forest understory; associates with mixed-species flocks and follows ant swarms. Good sites: Pook's Hill, Las Cuevas, Caracol, Blue Hole, Mayflower, Cockscomb.

Plain Xenops *(Xenops minutus)* – mid-to-upper canopy in broadleaf forest. Good sites: Fireburn, La Milpa, Chan Chich, Lamanai, Hill Bank, Guanacaste, Pook's Hill, Rio Frio Caves, Las Cuevas, Caracol, Aguacate Lagoon, Macal River, Xunantunich, Tikal, Blue Hole, Mayflower, Cockscomb, Wilson Landing.

Tawny-winged Woodcreeper *(Dendrocincla anabatina)* – follows ant swarms, occupies understory to subcanopy of broadleaf forest. Good sites: Shipstern, Chan Chich, Lamanai, Hill Bank, Caracol, Tikal, Blue Hole, Mayflower, Cockscomb, BFREE-Bladen, Wilson Landing, Boom Creek, many others.

Ruddy Woodcreeper *(Dendrocincla homochroa)* – habits, habitat, and good sites as in Tawny-winged.

Olivaceous Woodcreeper *(Sittasomus griseicapillus)* – mid-levels in broadleaf and pine forests. Good sites: La Milpa, Chan Chich, Lamanai, Hill Bank, Pook's Hill, Mountain Pine Ridge, Las Cuevas, Caracol, Aguacate Lagoon, El Pilar, Macal River, Xunantunich, Tikal, Blue Hole, Five Blues, BFREE-Bladen.

Wedge-billed Woodcreeper *(Glyphorynchus spirurus)* – mid-level to subcanopy in broadleaf forest; associates with mixed-species flocks. Good sites: Chan Chich, Guanacaste, Las Cuevas, Caracol, Macal River, Tikal, Blue Hole, Five Blues, Mayflower, Cockscomb, BFREE-Bladen, Nim Li Punit, Rio Blanco, Blue Creek Cave, Belcampo Belize.

Strong-billed Woodcreeper *(Xiphocolaptes promeropirhynchus)* – mid-level to subcanopy in broadleaf forest. Most consistent sites are Chan Chich and Tikal. Good sites: Laguna Seca, Chiquibul, Caracol, Columbia River. Not expected at lowland sites. Many reports extralimital to the range shown in Jones (2003) are incompletely documented and its similarity to Ivory-billed and Northern Barred-Woodcreepers leaves lingering doubt about identification.

Northern Barred-Woodcreeper *(Dendrocolaptes sanctithomae)* – pine and broadleaf forests. Good sites: Shipstern, Fireburn, La Milpa, Chan Chich, Salt Creek, Caracol, Tikal, Blue Hole, Cockscomb, BFREE-Bladen, Wilson Landing.

Ivory-billed Woodcreeper *(Xiphorhynchus flavigaster)* – most forested areas and edges; may accompany mixed-species flocks. The most common woodcreeper, it can be readily observed throughout the mainland.

Spotted Woodcreeper *(Xiphorhynchus erythropygius)* – Maya Mountains above 2,300 feet at Little Quartz Ridge in Columbia River and at Doyle's Delight in Chiquibul.

Streak-headed Woodcreeper *(Lepidocolaptes souleyetii)* – broadleaf and pine forest and edge. Good sites: Crooked Tree, TEC, Monkey Bay, Guanacaste, Las Cuevas, Caracol, Blue Hole, BFREE-Bladen.

Yellow-bellied Tyrannulet *(Ornithion semiflavum)* – subcanopy and canopy of broadleaf forest and edge. Good sites: La Milpa, Chan Chich, Guanacaste, Rio Frio Caves, Las Cuevas, Caracol, Aguacate Lagoon, Tikal, Blue Hole, Five Blues, Mayflower, Cockscomb, BFREE-Bladen, Aguacaliente, Boom Creek.

Northern Beardless-Tyrannulet *(Camptostoma imberbe)* – pine savanna, edges of broadleaf forest and scrub. When present, can be heard persistently, but hard to see in canopy. Good sites: Shipstern, La Milpa, Chan Chich, Freshwater Creek, New River, Hill Bank, Crooked Tree, Salt Creek, Community Baboon, Aqua Mar, Aguacaliente, Joe Taylor Creek, Boom Creek, Moho River.

Greenish Elaenia *(Myiopagis viridicata)* – throughout mainland in a variety of wooded habitats at mid-level to subcanopy. Occasional on Ambergris Caye.

Caribbean Elaenia *(Elaenia martinica)* – best found on Caye Caulker, where it has bred but probably is not resident; also occurs on Ambergris Caye and has been recorded a few times on other cays. Documented records for Altun Ha in 2006 and Nova Ladyville in 2001 and 2006, and undocumented records for Belize City area and other coastal areas. Quite similar to common Yellow-bellied Elaenia, so must be identified carefully.

Yellow-bellied Elaenia *(Elaenia flavogaster)* – mid-level to subcanopy at forest edge, mostly pines; open areas with scattered trees, villages. Common and widely distributed on mainland and Ambergris Caye; rare migrant on other cays.

Ochre-bellied Flycatcher *(Mionectes oleagineus)* – mid-level in broadleaf forest and clearings. Good sites: La Milpa, Chan Chich, Monkey Bay, Guanacaste, Hidden Valley, Aguacate Lagoon, Tikal, Blue Hole, Five Blues, Cockscomb, BFREE-Bladen, Nim Li Punit, Blue Creek Cave, Wilson Landing, many others.

Sepia-capped Flycatcher *(Leptopogon amaurocephalus)* – slow moving and easily overlooked in interior of broadleaf forest at mid-story; study its burry trill. Good sites: La Milpa, Chan Chich, Guanacaste, Caracol, Aguacate Lagoon, Tikal, Blue Hole, Five Blues, Mayflower, Cockscomb, BFREE-Bladen, Columbia River, Wilson Landing.

Paltry Tyrannulet *(Zimmerius vilissimus)* – occurs only in southern Toledo District broadleaf forest and edge. Reported sites: Bladen, Columbia River, Pueblo Viejo, Rio Blanco, Aguacaliente, Wilson Landing, VoA, Boom Creek, Cotton Tree. Rare at Tikal.

Northern Bentbill *(Oncostoma cinereigulare)* – common within broadleaf forest; infrequently seen, but easily identified by voice. Increasingly common farther south. Can be found at many sites, especially La Milpa, Chan Chich, Blue Hole, Mayflower, Commerce Bight, Cockscomb, BFREE, Nim Li Punit, Aguacaliente, Belcampo Belize, Joe Taylor Creek, Boom Creek.

Slate-headed Tody-Flycatcher *(Poecilotriccus sylvia)* – broadleaf forest edge in dense tangles, making it difficult to see. Consistent site is Aguacaliente. Good sites: Hill Bank at Irish Creek, Monkey Bay along road to Sibun River, Las Cuevas on access road, El Pilar along road at edge of ruins, Tikal along airstrip, Blue Hole just beyond Visitor Center on path to St. Herman's Cave, Cockscomb on open trails.

Common Tody-Flycatcher *(Todirostrum cinereum)* – open and disturbed areas. Good sites: San Victor, August Pine Ridge, Shipyard Road, Crooked Tree, Coastal Highway, Belize Zoo, Aguacate Lagoon, Five Blues, Gra Gra Lagoon, Red Bank, Blue Creek Cave, Jalacte, Boom Creek, Ambergris Caye.

Eye-ringed Flatbill *(Rhynchocyclus brevirostris)* – mid-level to subcanopy within broadleaf forest; its motionless behavior and infrequent, quiet song make it hard to detect. Good sites: La Milpa, Chan Chich, Lamanai, Caracol, Aguacate Lagoon, Black Rock, Xunantunich, Tikal, Blue Hole, Cockscomb, Columbia River.

Yellow-olive Flycatcher *(Tolmomyias sulphurescens)* – mid-level to canopy within broadleaf forest and edge, sometimes pine forest. Good sites: Shipstern, La Milpa, Chan Chich, Lamanai, Altun Ha, Monkey Bay, Caracol, Aguacate Lagoon, Macal River, Tikal, Blue Hole, Cockscomb, Red Bank, BFREE-Bladen, Belcampo Belize, many others.

Stub-tailed Spadebill *(Platyrinchus cancrominus)* – understory within broadleaf forest. Good sites: La Milpa, Chan Chich, Lamanai, Hill Bank, Guanacaste, Pook's Hill, Caracol, Black Rock, Xunantunich, Tikal, Blue Hole,

Mayflower, Commerce Bight, Cockscomb, BFREE-Bladen, Lodge at Big Falls, Columbia River, Wilson Landing.

Royal Flycatcher *(Onychorhynchus coronatus)* – broadleaf forest and edge; good sites: Chan Chich, Lamanai, Black Rock, Xunantunich, Tikal, Blue Hole, Cockscomb, Aguacaliente.

Ruddy-tailed Flycatcher *(Terenotriccus erythrurus)* – small size, weak call, quiet behavior and interior broadleaf forest habitat make it difficult to find even when present. Good sites: La Milpa, Chan Chich, Caracol, Tikal, BFREE-Bladen, Columbia River, hills outside Punta Gorda beyond Laguna Village.

Sulphur-rumped Flycatcher *(Myiobius sulphureipygius)* – interior broadleaf forest in understory to mid-level. Good sites: La Milpa, Chan Chich, Pook's Hill, Caracol, Aguacate Lagoon, Tikal, Blue Hole, Mayflower, Cockscomb, BFREE-Bladen, Columbia River, Boom Creek.

Olive-sided Flycatcher *(Contopus cooperi)* – bare upper branches on forest edge in migration; in winter mostly at higher elevations. A few consistently reported sites include La Milpa, Chan Chich, Coastal Highway at Plantation Creek, Cockscomb at Ben's Bluff, Little Quartz Ridge, Punta Gorda, Caye Caulker.

Greater Pewee *(Contopus pertinax)* – pine forest and edge. All accepted reports are at Mountain Pine Ridge, where it is resident.

Western Wood-Pewee *(Contopus sordidulus)* – Mountain Pine Ridge 25 October 1998. Eastern Wood-Pewee is the expected species.

Eastern Wood-Pewee *(Contopus virens)* – nearly all habitats with woody vegetation. Very common in migration; widespread on mainland and cays; does not winter although there are a few December reports.

Tropical Pewee *(Contopus cinereus)* – mid-level to subcanopy in open forest and edge. Found at many lowland and foothill sites.

Yellow-bellied Flycatcher *(Empidonax flaviventris)* – low to mid-level in forest interior and edge as winter visitor; more diverse habitat in migration. Almost all *Empidonax* sightings are this or Least Flycatcher. Readily found throughout.

Acadian Flycatcher *(Empidonax virescens)* – low to mid-level at forest edge and interior, especially mangroves. Transient throughout, especially Shipstern, but not every year at Blue Hole or Cockscomb; more common on cays.

Alder Flycatcher *(Empidonax alnorum)* – forest edge and scrub. Fall migrant; spring status is unclear. Owing to identification problems, abundance is unclear. Recent netting capture records at Shipstern show some fall migrants, no spring records. Probably uncommon in Toledo District and on cays. Uncommon fall migrant at Tikal.

Willow Flycatcher *(Empidonax traillii)* – similar habitat to Alder. Identification problems make status unclear, although thought to be a spring and fall migrant, as well as a winter resident in south Toledo District (about a half-dozen records). Recent netting capture records at Shipstern show it common in fall migration and absent in spring and winter. More numerous on cays. Consistent site is The Dump, where it has been heard singing in December. Has been identified by call 11 March 2009 at New River Lagoon from Hill Bank. Considered an uncommon fall migrant at Tikal from collected specimens.

White-throated Flycatcher *(Empidonax albigularis)* – edges of freshwater marshes. Winter visitor, though status poorly known, and an *Empidonax* easily misidentified. Species banded at Runaway Creek and Chaa Creek. Most recent reliable site is The Dump during the winter months. Accepted records from Chan Chich, Hill Bank, Columbia River.

Least Flycatcher *(Empidonax minimus)* – open scrubby habitats, forest edge. Most widespread *Empidonax* and found throughout mainland and cays all months except summer.

Black Phoebe *(Sayornis nigricans)* – along fast-flowing wooded steams. Good sites: Soldier (Plantation) Creek on Coastal Highway, Monkey Bay, Guanacaste, Guacamallo Bridge, San Ignacio Hotel, Bullet Tree Road, Macal River, Xunantunich, Five Blues, Cave's Branch, Red Bank, Rio Blanco, Blue Creek Cave.

Vermilion Flycatcher *(Pyrocephalus rubinus)* – agricultural lands, savannas, parks. Good sites: San Victor, Gallon Jug Road, Honey Camp Road, Shipyard road, New River, Hill Bank, Old Northern Highway, Crooked Tree, Baboon Sanctuary, TEC, Monkey Bay, Spanish Lookout, Macal River, Lago Petén Itzá, Five Blues, Cockscomb entrance road, Placencia. A few records on cays.

Bright-rumped Attila *(Attila spadiceus)* – mid-level to canopy in forest; widespread and common on mainland. Good sites: La Milpa, New River, Lamanai, Guanacaste, Hidden Valley, Chaa Creek, Tikal, Blue Hole, Mayflower, Croc O'dile Isle, Cockscomb, BFREE, Lodge at Big Falls, Blue Creek Cave, Aguacaliente, Joe Taylor Creek, Moho River.

Rufous Mourner *(Rhytipterna holerythra)* – interior of broadleaf forest at subcanopy to canopy; distinctive call but usually hard to see. Visually, can be confused with Rufous Piha. Good sites: Chan Chich, Las Cuevas, Caracol, Aguacate Lagoon, Tikal, Mayflower, Cockscomb, BFREE-Bladen, Belcampo Belize.

Yucatan Flycatcher *(Myiarchus yucatanensis)* – open woodlands and edge in northern half; easily misidentified. Follows army ants. Good sites: Corozal, Shipstern, Sarteneja, Fireburn, San Victor, La Milpa, Laguna Seca, Gallon Jug, Honey Camp Road, Freshwater Creek, New River, Big Falls Farm, Runaway Creek, Monkey Bay, Tikal, Ambergris Caye.

Dusky-capped Flycatcher *(Myiarchus tuberculifer)* – mid-level in forest and edge and second-growth scrub; most common *Myiarchus* during winter months.

Great Crested Flycatcher *(Myiarchus crinitus)* – subcanopy and canopy within broadleaf forest as winter visitor; more widespread in migration. Good sites: Shipstern, La Milpa, Chan Chich, Lamanai, Hill Bank, Altun Ha, Caracol, Macal River, Xunantunich, El Pilar, Tikal, Blue Hole, Cockscomb, BFREE-Bladen, Lubaantun, Wilson Landing, Moho River, Ambergris Caye, other cays.

Brown-crested Flycatcher *(Myiarchus tyrannulus)* – mid-level to subcanopy in forest and edge; common summer resident; uncommon in winter. Large influx occurs around first days of March. Gather identification details on any suspected Brown-cresteds seen between September and early March.

Great Kiskadee *(Pitangus sulphuratus)* – open habitats throughout mainland, Ambergris Caye, and Caye Caulker; rare on other cays.

Boat-billed Flycatcher *(Megarynchus pitangua)* – prefers more closed areas compared to Great Kiskadee. Many good sites.

Social Flycatcher *(Myiozetetes similis)* – adapts to many habitats and is very common throughout.

Streaked Flycatcher *(Myiodynastes maculatus)* – mid-level to canopy in broadleaf forest and edge. Summer resident, arriving in March. Appears similar to Sulphur-bellied but much less common, leaving undocumented sightings as suspect. Best site is duPlooy's. Other reported sites: La Milpa, Chan Chich, Chiquibul, Macal River, Tikal, Blue Hole, Cockscomb, BFREE-Bladen, Nim Li Punit.

Sulphur-bellied Flycatcher *(Myiodynastes luteiventris)* – mid-level to canopy in forest and edge; also open areas with trees. Summer resident, arriving in March. Good sites: Slate Creek, Las Cuevas, Caracol, Crystal Paradise, Macal River, Pook's Hill, Tikal, Blue Hole, Mayflower, Cockscomb, BFREE-Bladen, Lubaantun, Lodge at Big Falls, Columbia River, Boom Creek.

Piratic Flycatcher *(Legatus leucophaius)* – broadleaf forest and edge from subcanopy to canopy; distinctive call. Summer resident arriving late February. Good sites: La Milpa, Chan Chich, Lamanai, Hill Bank, Crystal Paradise, Macal River, Tikal, Blue Hole, Mayflower, Cockscomb, Red Bank, BFREE-Bladen, Lubaantun, Aguacaliente.

Tropical Kingbird *(Tyrannus melancholicus)* – mostly in open areas with bare ground (e.g., agricultural land, lawns). Found throughout, including cays; generally more common than Couch's.

Couch's Kingbird *(Tyrannus couchii)* – mostly in areas with brushy ground cover, small forest clearings; otherwise adopts same habitat as Tropical but more often in drier areas and in upland pine savanna. Jones (2003) estimates a Couch's to Tropical ratio of 1:5 to 1:10, except in some pine savanna where it can be 1:1.

Cassin's Kingbird *(Tyrannus vociferans)* – one confirmed record, Gallon Jug 22 December 1999–2 March 2000.

Western Kingbird *(Tyrannus verticalis)* – earlier undocumented records, but about six accepted records 2001–2009, including one wintering 2008–2010 at Radisson Fort George Hotel in Belize City. Other sites: La Milpa, duPlooy's, VoA.

Eastern Kingbird *(Tyrannus tyrannus)* – wooded areas and edge; also on exposed perches in more open areas. Migrates diurnally along or near coast and through cays. Good coastal sites include: Shipstern, Bird's Isle at Belize City, Gra Gra Lagoon, All Pines, Placencia. Daily reports of 1,000–3,500 passing Punta Gorda in first two hours after daylight during the last two weeks of September.

Gray Kingbird *(Tyrannus dominicensis)* – areas with exposed perches. About two dozen records mid-March to mid-October, mostly of migrants, through northern cays and along mainland coast, including Belize City, Southern Highway (north), Ambergris Caye, Caye Caulker, South Water Caye, other cays. Very rarely recorded farther inland: La Milpa, Beaver Dam Creek, Belmopan, San Ignacio, Middlesex.

Scissor-tailed Flycatcher *(Tyrannus forficatus)* – open fields and pastures; winter visitor. Good sites: Sarteneja Road, San Victor, Gallon Jug Road, Belize

City, Spanish Lookout, Sittee River, The Dump, VoA. Can be found in migration in large numbers, topped by 67 through Punta Gorda 27 October 2007.

Fork-tailed Flycatcher *(Tyrannus savana)* – pastures and pine savannas. Good sites: Corozal beach, San Victor, Gallon Jug Road, Edenthal, Shipyard Road, Old Northern Highway, Crooked Tree, Coastal Highway, Monkey Bay, Spanish Lookout, Clarissa Falls, Macal River, Tikal, Five Blues, Southern Highway, Croc O'dile Isle, Hopkins.

Northern Schiffornis *(Schiffornis veraepacis)* – secluded within dark broadleaf forest at low to mid-level; difficult to see but easily heard. Good sites: Shipstern, La Milpa, Chan Chich, Lamanai, Hill Bank, Hidden Valley, Caracol, Macal River, Tikal, Blue Hole, Mayflower, Croc O'dile Isle, Cockscomb, Red Bank, BFREE-Bladen, Blue Creek Cave, Wilson Landing, Moho River.

Speckled Mourner *(Laniocera rufescens)* – mid-level to subcanopy within primary broadleaf forest; could be confused with Rufous Mourner and Rufous Piha. Scarcity and habits make it difficult to find. Best chances: La Milpa, Chan Chich, Columbia River.

Masked Tityra *(Tityra semifasciata)* – mostly in open areas with scattered trees. Easily seen throughout mainland.

Black-crowned Tityra *(Tityra inquisitor)* – similar habitats to those of Masked Tityra. Good sites: Corozal, Four Mile Lagoon, La Milpa, Gallon Jug, Hill Bank, Coastal Highway, Monkey Bay, Caracol, Clarissa Falls, Macal River, Guanacaste, Cockscomb, Nim Li Punit, Lubaantun, Boom Creek.

Cinnamon Becard *(Pachyramphus cinnamomeus)* – mid-level to canopy in forest and edge. Good sites: Chan Chich, Monkey Bay, Pook's Hill, Caracol, Blue Hole, Mayflower, Cockscomb, BFREE-Bladen, Lodge at Big Falls, Blue Creek Cave, Columbia River, Jalacte.

White-winged Becard *(Pachyramphus polychopterus)* – mid-level of broadleaf forest, edge or scrub with scattered trees. Similar to and easily confused with Gray-collared Becard. Mostly in southern half of Belize, steadily moving north, recently reaching Mexico. Good sites: Coastal Highway, Monkey Bay, Pook's Hill, Macal River, Blue Hole, Mayflower, Cockscomb, Lodge at Big Falls, Lubaantun, Boom Creek.

Gray-collared Becard *(Pachyramphus major)* – mid-level within forest and edge. Similar to White-winged Becard; female similar to Rose-throated. Scarce, but best chances are: Crooked Tree, La Milpa, Chan Chich, Lamanai, Hill Bank, Runaway Creek, duPlooy's, Tikal, Mayflower, BFREE-Bladen, Lubaantun.

Rose-throated Becard *(Pachyramphus aglaiae)* – mid-level to subcanopy in or near broadleaf forest and scrub; more common in north. Found throughout mainland.

Lovely Cotinga *(Cotinga amabilis)* – the male cotinga is a much-sought bird, but is rarely found. Can be missed when it silently occupies mid-level to canopy of broadleaf forest, but early mornings it perches atop the canopy, so a viewpoint—such as atop a Maya temple or the Bird Tower at Las Cuevas—is best. Sometimes perches mid-level in open areas on large exposed trees. Eleven of 21 Gallon Jug CBCs recorded it at Chan Chich. Good (recent) sites: Hidden Valley, Caracol, Blue Hole, Five Blues. Other reported sites: La Milpa, Lamanai,

Community Baboon, Slate Creek, Las Cuevas, Crystal Paradise, duPlooy's, Tikal, Cockscomb, Columbia River.

Rufous Piha (*Lipaugus unirufus*) – mid-level to subcanopy within broadleaf forest in same habitat as similar-appearing smaller Rufous Mourner, but has different call. Sedentary and easy to miss when not calling. Good sites: La Milpa, Chan Chich, Las Cuevas, Caracol, Aguacate Lagoon, Cockscomb, Bladen.

White-collared Manakin (*Manacus candei*) – understory and mid-level of broadleaf forest; its wing-popping (like an electric insect zapper) and weird noises are readily heard, although the bird often can be difficult to see at its lek in the dense undergrowth. Best sites: La Milpa, Chan Chich, Lamanai, Hill Bank, Guanacaste, Pook's Hill, Tikal, Blue Hole, Five Blues, Cockscomb, BFREE-Bladen, Aguacaliente, Boom Creek, many others.

Red-capped Manakin (*Pipra mentalis*) – mid-level to canopy in mature broadleaf forest, sometimes at edge. Good sites: Shipstern, La Milpa, Chan Chich, Lamanai, Hill Bank, Belize Zoo, Monkey Bay, Guanacaste, Hidden Valley, Aguacate Lagoon, Tikal, Blue Hole, Five Blues, Mayflower, Cockscomb, Boom Creek.

White-eyed Vireo (*Vireo griseus*) – scrub, tangles, forest edge, mangroves. Winter visitor, found throughout mainland and cays.

Mangrove Vireo (*Vireo pallens*) – in spite of its name, Mangrove Vireo is more often found in scrub, tangles, and forest edge, on cays, mainland coast, and well inland. Found throughout, except scarce at higher elevations.

Yellow-throated Vireo (*Vireo flavifrons*) – mid-level to upper strata in mature and old secondary forests and edge; winter visitor. Good sites: La Milpa, Chan Chich, Hill Bank, TEC, Guanacaste, Caracol, Macal River, Xunantunich, Tikal, Mayflower, Cockscomb, BFREE-Bladen, Lubaantun, Belcampo Belize, Joe Taylor Creek, Boom Creek, Ambergris Caye; transient through other cays.

Plumbeous Vireo (*Vireo plumbeus*) – subcanopy to canopy in mature pine forest and edge; also broadleaf and pine/oak forests. Readily found at Thousand Foot Falls, Hidden Valley, and other parts of Mountain Pine Ridge. Uncommon at Las Cuevas. Note: Blue-headed also has been identified in Mountain Pine Ridge.

Blue-headed Vireo (*Vireo solitarius*) – several records, three documented, for Mountain Pine Ridge, most recently January 2011. Also documented records for Belmopan December 2000 and 18 February–22 April 2007. More often seen at Tikal. Earlier records of "Solitary Vireo" usually were not differentiated, so the status of migrant and wintering Blue-headed and resident Plumbeous (in Belize) is not fully resolved. See additional notes in Jones (2003).

Warbling Vireo (*Vireo gilvus*) – Jones and Vallely (2001) accepted two records: Crooked Tree 21 March 1999 and Little Quartz Ridge 4 April 1992. Other reports lack adequate details.

Philadelphia Vireo (*Vireo philadelphicus*) – scrub, orchards, broadleaf forest edge. Fairly common transient, but irregular winter visitor; widespread throughout, found at cays and many mainland sites.

Red-eyed Vireo (*Vireo olivaceus*) – mid-level to upper strata of second growth and forest edge; migrant only, including early December records in Punta Gorda.

Yellow-green Vireo *(Vireo flavoviridis)* – summer resident, arriving early March, in varied habitats of forest and open woodland. Good sites: La Milpa, Chan Chich, Hill Bank, Altun Ha, Crooked Tree, Community Baboon, Runaway Creek, Manatee Lagoon, TEC, Monkey Bay, Pook's Hill, Caracol, Slate Creek, Crystal Paradise, Macal River, Tikal, Blue Hole, Mayflower, Cockscomb, BFREE-Bladen, Lubaantun, Lodge at Big Falls, Aguacaliente, Wilson Landing, Boom Creek.

Black-whiskered Vireo *(Vireo altiloquus)* – Six accepted records, all in spring: Bullet Tree Road in 2012, Ambergris Caye in 2002 and 2003, Half Moon Caye in 1926, Northeast Caye in Glover's Reef in 2005 and 2007.

Yucatan Vireo *(Vireo magister)* – mangroves and littoral forest. Most readily found on the cays: Ambergris, Caye Caulker, Turneffe Atoll, Glover's Reef, and many other cays south to Snake (Sapodillas) Cayes. Mainland sites are near the coast: Sarteneja, Shipstern, Freshwater Creek, Salt Creek, Manatee Lagoon, Dangriga, Gra Gra Lagoon, Monkey River.

Tawny-crowned Greenlet *(Hylophilus ochraceiceps)* – understory and mid-levels in mature broadleaf forest. Hard to see and can be overlooked, but for its distinctive thin whistle. Good sites: Shipstern, Fireburn, La Milpa, Chan Chich, Lamanai, Hill Bank, Runaway Creek, TEC, Monkey Bay, Pook's Hill, Hidden Valley, Caracol, Aguacate Lagoon, Chaa Creek, Tikal, Blue Hole, Mayflower, Cockscomb, BFREE-Bladen, Wilson Landing, Joe Taylor Creek, Boom Creek.

Lesser Greenlet *(Hylophilus decurtatus)* – high in canopy and subcanopy of second growth to mature broadleaf forest; often heard, but usually too hidden in foliage to identify easily by sight. Found throughout mainland.

Green Shrike-Vireo *(Vireolanius pulchellus)* – canopy and subcanopy in interior of primary broadleaf forest; stays so high in dense leaves and its green color blends so well that it is extremely difficult to see, but its distinctive and oft-repeated song announces its presence. Best chance to see, as well as to hear, is at recent selective-logging sites in primary forests with openings to the canopy, such as the forests beyond Aguacate Lagoon. Other good sites: La Milpa, Chan Chich, Las Cuevas, Caracol, Blue Hole, Mayflower, Cockscomb, BFREE-Bladen, Columbia River, Boom Creek.

Rufous-browed Peppershrike *(Cyclarhis gujanensis)* – varied habitats in open country. More common in north. Good sites: Corozal, Progresso Lagoon, Shipstern, San Victor, August Pine Ridge, Honey Camp Road, Freshwater Creek, New River, Old Northern Highway, Crooked Tree, Salt Creek, Community Baboon, Gales Point, Belize Zoo, Monkey Bay. Uncommon on Ambergris Caye.

Brown Jay *(Psilorhinus morio)* – one of the most common—or at least one of the most noticeable—birds. Seen daily almost everywhere on mainland except dense forest interior. A few records for Ambergris Caye.

Green Jay *(Cyanocorax yncas)* – mid-level within forest interior and edge. Easily found at Hidden Valley and other Mountain Pine Ridge sites. Other sites: Shipstern, La Milpa, Chan Chich, New River, Pook's Hill, Las Cuevas, Guacamallo Bridge, Caracol, Macal River, Xunantunich, Blue Hole, Mayflower, Moho River.

Yucatan Jay *(Cyanocorax yucatanicus)* – mid-level within and at edge of forests; common in north and progressively less common southward. Most often reported at Crooked Tree. Good sites: Rio Hondo, Corozal, Sarteneja Road, Four Mile Lagoon, Shipstern, Sarteneja, Fireburn, Freshwater Creek, New River,

Hill Bank, Salt Creek, Manatee Lagoon, Gales Point, Sittee River. Southernmost site is Placencia (once). Resident on north Ambergris Caye.

Purple Martin (*Progne subis*) – aerial over open areas in migration throughout lowlands, particularly over coastal savannas. Most common martin on cays. Arrives mid-January in spring and mid-June in autumn.

Caribbean Martin or **Sinaloa Martin** (*Progne dominicensis* or *P. sinaloae*) – Several flying out to sea from Belize City in August 1962 could be identified to the super-species "Snowy-bellied Martin," but not to species.

Gray-breasted Martin (*Progne chalybea*) – aerial over open country throughout mainland; occasional on cays. Summer resident arriving as early as mid-December; no confirmed records after September. Less common than Purple Martin on cays in migration.

Tree Swallow (*Tachycineta bicolor*) – aerial over open areas, especially over wetlands. Winter visitor, more easily found at coastal sites; less so at inland sites. Good sites: Corozal, Four Mile Lagoon, Progresso Lagoon, Shipstern, Blue Creek rice fields, Honey Camp Lagoon, Fresh Catch, Manatee Lagoon.

Mangrove Swallow (*Tachycineta albilinea*) – found near water throughout mainland, Ambergris Caye, and Caye Caulker.

Northern Rough-winged Swallow (*Stelgidopteryx serripennis*) – migrants found in most open areas; winter visitors and residents found in forest clearings throughout, although status is not fully understood. Appearance very similar to Ridgway's Rough-winged.

Ridgway's Rough-winged Swallow (*Stelgidopteryx ridgwayi*) – resident species treated by AOU as form of Northern Rough-winged Swallow. Found in forest clearings and wooded streams in karst limestone areas; nests in caves. Good sites: La Milpa, Mountain Pine Ridge, Rio Frio Caves, Las Cuevas, Guacamallo Bridge, Caracol, duPlooy's, Tikal, Blue Hole.

Bank Swallow (*Riparia riparia*) – open areas mostly along coast; some migrate along interior ridgelines, including Mountain Pine Ridge. Occasionally in winter.

Cliff Swallow (*Petrochelidon pyrrhonota*) – migrant found in open areas, especially along coast where numbers can be impressive, e.g., 1,038 in one hour at Cattle Landing on 1 October. Some migrate along ridgelines. At Mountain Pine Ridge in 2008, 5,000+ were observed daily 21 September–2 October.

Cave Swallow (*Petrochelidon fulva*) – about a dozen records during fall migration, mostly along coast, but also records for Blue Creek rice fields 30 March 1999 and Mountain Pine Ridge 2 October 2008. Very few people have searched systematically for Cave Swallows so actual numbers and sites are not well known. Speculating on known or potential sites to watch fall migration of swallows, the list could include Shipstern Lagoon, the heli-pad on Cooma Cairn just before Baldy Beacon Road in Mountain Pine Ridge, coastal shrimp farms, The Dump, Cattle Landing, and VoA. Consult Bar Graphs (Chapter 8) for migration times.

Barn Swallow (*Hirundo rustica*) – widespread and common migrant and winter visitor.

Band-backed Wren *(Campylorhynchus zonatus)* – forages in bromeliads in broadleaf forest and edge. Good sites: Monkey Bay, Banana Bank, Pook's Hill, Slate Creek, Las Cuevas, Caracol, Crystal Paradise, Macal River, Blue Hole.

Spot-breasted Wren *(Pheugopedius maculipectus)* – forest interior and edge, tangles, scrub. Found throughout mainland.

Carolina Wren *(Thryothorus ludovicianus)* – thickets within deciduous forest and edge; locally in streamside trees and brush within savannas. Some authorities separate this resident subspecies—"White-browed Wren," *T. l. albinucha*—from the well-known form that occurs north of the Yucatán. Only known sites: La Milpa, Chan Chich, near Lamanai, Macal River, Hydro Road. Fairly common at Tikal.

Plain Wren *(Cantorchilus modestus)* – understory within submontane pine forest; locally in broadleaf forest. Found at Hidden Valley and other Mountain Pine Ridge sites. Thrice has been reported elsewhere: three miles south of El Pilar, at BFREE, and extreme southwest Belize at Dolores Village.

House Wren *(Troglodytes aedon)* – open country, including villages. Common on mainland, except Maya Mountains.

Sedge Wren *(Cistothorus platensis)* – seasonally flooded coastal lowlands; also well-drained hillside meadows. Good sites: Gra Gra Lagoon, Croc O'dile Isle, Mountain Pine Ridge (especially Bald Hills), entrance to Bladen Reserve, Monkey River. Subspecies *russelli* is endemic to Belize.

White-bellied Wren *(Uropsila leucogastra)* – scrub and broadleaf forest understory and edge. Best sites: Sarteneja and Shipstern, north of the lagoon, where it is one of the most abundant species. Good sites: Cerros, Fireburn, La Milpa, Chan Chich, Honey Camp Lagoon, Freshwater Creek, Hill Bank, Old Northern Highway, Salt Creek, Big Falls Farm, TEC, Monkey Bay, Guanacaste, Aguacate Lagoon, Crystal Paradise, Macal River, El Pilar, Tikal, Five Blues.

White-breasted Wood-Wren *(Henicorhina leucosticta)* – understory of broadleaf forest and edge; more likely than Spot-breasted Wren in forest interior and less likely in second-growth scrub. Found throughout mainland, except Corozal area.

Gray-breasted Wood-Wren *(Henicorhina leucophrys)* – understory of pine/oak forest at high elevation. Photographed 1 September 2005 at top of Outlier in Cockscomb Basin.

Nightingale Wren *(Microcerculus philomela)* – understory within foothill and montane broadleaf forest. Consistent at St. Herman's Cave in Blue Hole. Other sites: Las Cuevas, Bladen, Blue Creek Cave, Columbia River, Pueblo Viejo.

Long-billed Gnatwren *(Ramphocaenus melanurus)* – vines and tangles at forest edge. Good sites: Shipstern, La Milpa, Lamanai, Monkey Bay, Caracol, Tikal, Blue Hole, Cockscomb, BFREE-Bladen, Boom Creek, many others.

Blue-gray Gnatcatcher *(Polioptila caerulea)* – includes both residents in pine and pine/oak woodlands and savanna and migrants found in most any wooded habitat throughout Belize.

Tropical Gnatcatcher *(Polioptila plumbea)* – mid-level to canopy in broadleaf forest and edge. More frequent in south. Good sites: Shipstern, Sarteneja Tree Sanctuary, La Milpa, Chan Chich, Caracol, El Pilar, Tikal,

Mayflower, Cockscomb, BFREE-Bladen, Columbia River, Cuxlin Ha, Boom Creek.

Eastern Bluebird *(Sialia sialis)* – submontane pine forest openings and edge in Mountain Pine Ridge. Thought extirpated from the area, with last sightings in 1997 (4 birds) and 2007 (1 bird); 2 juveniles rediscovered 11 August 2012. Some reported sites: Hidden Valley, Baldy Beacon, Gaïa Riverlodge, Douglas Da Silva.

Slate-colored Solitaire *(Myadestes unicolor)* – mid-level to canopy within montane broadleaf forest. Occasional in foothills, but not expected below 2,000 feet elevation. Good sites: Las Cuevas, Chiquibul, Columbia River, and can be heard way down in some deep valleys at, e.g., Thousand Foot Falls, Bald Hills. Occurs at Cockscomb, but not at an altitude most birders visit.

Veery *(Catharus fuscescens)* – migrant; seen mostly on cays. Mainland sightings at coastal sites from Shipstern to Punta Gorda, and inland to foothills at Cockscomb and Blue Hole.

Gray-cheeked Thrush *(Catharus minimus)* – migrant, most frequent on cays. Mainland migrants spread across Belize, but more often reported in Vaca Plateau, e.g., Las Cuevas.

Hermit Thrush *(Catharus guttatus)* – one photographed 12 December 2010 and seen again on the 18th on Cooma Cairn in Mountain Pine Ridge.

Swainson's Thrush *(Catharus ustulatus)* – ground and understory of broadleaf forest. Seen mostly as a transient, but some in winter, primarily in the south. Most frequent as migrant on cays. Mainland sightings at Shipstern, La Milpa, Chan Chich, Slate Creek, Las Cuevas, San Ignacio, Macal River, Mayflower, Cockscomb, BFREE-Bladen, Aguacaliente, Wilson Landing, Boom Creek.

Wood Thrush *(Hylocichla mustelina)* – ground and understory of broadleaf forest. Winter visitor, found at widespread sites.

Clay-colored Thrush *(Turdus grayi)* – near broadleaf trees in more open areas than other thrushes. Common throughout mainland and occasionally on Ambergris Caye and Caye Caulker.

White-throated Thrush *(Turdus assimilis)* – mid-level to subcanopy in montane and foothill broadleaf forest and edge in Maya Mountains. Some altitudinal migration to lower elevations such as Bravo Hills, Monkey Bay and Cockscomb. Good sites: La Milpa, Chan Chich, Hidden Valley, Rio Frio Caves, Las Cuevas, Caracol, Little Quartz Ridge, Columbia River.

American Robin *(Turdus migratorius)* – two records: Hill Bank 5 January 1981 and Crooked Tree 23 March 2002.

Gray Catbird *(Dumetella carolinensis)* – forest edge and secondary shrub. Winter visitor, found throughout, although less common in mountains.

Black Catbird *(Melanoptila glabrirostris)* – ground to mid-level in littoral forest of cays and semi-deciduous to deciduous forest of mainland, primarily along coast from Corozal to Belize City, including Copper Bank, Progresso Lagoon, Shipstern, Sarteneja, Fireburn, Freshwater Creek, Runaway Creek. Inland sites include: New River at Dawson Creek, Crooked Tree.

Tropical Mockingbird *(Mimus gilvus)* – open country with scattered shrubs and trees. Easily found at all Corozal District sites. Other good sites: Gallon Jug Road, Honey Camp Road, Shipyard Road, Old Northern Highway, Crooked Tree,

Coastal Highway, Belize Zoo, Macal River, Dangriga, Sittee River, Mayflower, Cockscomb, Placencia, VoA, Ambergris Caye, Caye Caulker.

American Pipit *(Anthus rubescens)* – open areas. Three records: Gallon Jug 23–25 October 2007, near Punta Gorda 5 November 2001, VoA 3 November 1999.

Cedar Waxwing *(Bombycilla cedrorum)* – at or near canopy of wooded areas. Irruptive, being relatively common and/or widespread during some years but absent in others.

Ovenbird *(Seiurus aurocapilla)* – ground level inside broadleaf forest. Winter visitor; widespread sites. Migration on the cays can be impressive: 49 birds on Sapodillas, including 30 on one small cay, 29 September 2000.

Worm-eating Warbler *(Helmitheros vermivorum)* – low levels to subcanopy in broadleaf forest and edge. Winter visitor found at many sites.

Louisiana Waterthrush *(Parkesia motacilla)* – habitat similar to Northern, but in winter more restricted to wooded areas along moving streams that are in interior Belize; not as common as Northern, but outnumbers Northern at higher elevations. Good sites: Shipstern, Chan Chich, Lamanai, Cox Lagoon, Monkey Bay, Guanacaste, Guacamallo Bridge, Caracol, Macal River, Five Blues, Sittee River, Cockscomb, Red Bank, Blue Creek Cave, Pueblo Viejo, Moho River.

Northern Waterthrush *(Parkesia noveboracensis)* – ground level in mangroves and other wooded wet areas. Winter visitor; widespread good sites.

Golden-winged Warbler *(Vermivora chrysoptera)* – mid-level to subcanopy in forest and edge. Winter visitor. Good sites: La Milpa, Chan Chich, Lamanai, Hill Bank, TEC, Monkey Bay, Pook's Hill, Las Cuevas, Tikal, Blue Hole, Mayflower, Cockscomb, BFREE, Lodge at Big Falls, Lubaantun, Columbia River, Wilson Landing. Also transient on cays, but less frequent.

Blue-winged Warbler *(Vermivora cyanoptera)* – mid-level at forest edge and scrub. Winter visitor, found at many mainland sites. Less frequent on cays.

Golden-winged X Blue-winged Warbler *(Vermivora chrysoptera X Vermivora cyanoptera)* – hybrid Brewster's are seen occasionally in migration, most recently 29 January 2011 near Lamanai. Lawrence's has been reported at Lamanai Outpost Lodge winter 1998–1999, Monkey Bay March 1995, Cahal Pech October 1992, Rio Frio Cave 2012, and Wilson Landing December 1992.

Black-and-white Warbler *(Mniotilta varia)* – tree trunks and limbs; common winter visitor throughout.

Prothonotary Warbler *(Protonotaria citrea)* – winter visitor, found low on branches extending over water; most readily seen from a boat. A mist-netting study found Magnolia, Prothonotary, and Yellow to account for more than a third of all Nearctic passerine captures in fall migration through citrus groves along the Sibun River. Good sites: Shipstern, New River, Crooked Tree, Belize City, Runaway Creek, Las Cuevas, Chaa Creek, Gra Gra Lagoon, Mayflower, Cockscomb, BFREE-Bladen, Wilson Landing, Moho River, Ambergris Caye, Caye Caulker.

Swainson's Warbler *(Limnothlypis swainsonii)* – ground and understory of broadleaf forest, especially swamp and littoral forests; difficult to locate in dense undergrowth and does not sing in Belize. Best found in migration on cays, particularly Caye Caulker, but also Ambergris, Chapel, and as far south as

Sapodillas. Local resident Jim Beveridge has identified Swainson's on 27 occasions on Caye Caulker between 1999–2005, but none in the succeeding three years. Scarce at mainland sites, yet one–five birds seen on four dates 12 March–9 April 2002 at San Pedro Columbia. Other sites: La Milpa, Gallon Jug, Lamanai, Hill Bank, Altun Ha, Crooked Tree, Community Baboon, Runaway Creek, Manatee Lagoon, TEC, Monkey Bay, Banana Bank, Guanacaste, Pook's Hill, Blue Hole, Cockscomb, Bladen, Columbia River. Well documented at Tikal in 1978, 1989, 2001, and 2009, and is probably more common than few records indicate.

Tennessee Warbler *(Oreothlypis peregrina)* – forest edge and scrub. Migrant and winter visitor. Many good sites, including cays.

Orange-crowned Warbler *(Oreothlypis celata)* – forest edge and scrub. Reported almost annually without supporting documentation and can easily be confused with Tennessee Warbler and immature female Mangrove Yellow Warbler. Two documented records: one mist-netted at Runaway Creek, five miles west of Gracie Bank 16 December 2001; and a second at a remote part of Mountain Pine Ridge, east of Douglas de Silva 6 March 2011, this one described as the nominate *celata*.

Nashville Warbler *(Oreothlypis ruficapilla)* – winter visitor with a bit over a dozen records, including Gallon Jug, Baboon Sanctuary, Banana Bank, Black Rock, Chaa Creek, Tikal, BFREE, Caye Caulker, Sapodilla Cays, and other cays. Reported more often, but without documentation; can be confused with winter-plumaged Magnolia Warbler.

Virginia's Warbler *(Oreothlypis virginiae)* – one convincing record is a male at Caye Caulker 6 May 1995. One at Lago Petén Itzá 23 February 1977. While adult males are distinctive, females and immatures closely resemble immature female Mangrove Yellow Warblers, and thus coastal and cay birds must be carefully documented or photographed to be convincing.

Gray-crowned Yellowthroat *(Geothlypis poliocephala)* – pine/oak savanna, open pine forest, wooded edge of marshes. Good sites: Four Mile Lagoon, Shipstern, San Victor, Gallon Jug Road, Hill Bank, Old Northern Highway, Coastal Highway, TEC, Banana Bank, Mountain Pine Ridge, Spanish Lookout, Macal River Road, Five Blues, Gra Gra Lagoon, Southern Highway, The Dump.

Mourning Warbler *(Geothlypis philadelphia)* – understory of shrub, forest edge. Mostly reported as transient on cays. Few records for mainland. Connecticut Warbler *(Oporornis agilis)* is insufficiently documented for acceptance on Belize list, although it may have occurred on Half Moon Caye 7 May 1958.

Kentucky Warbler *(Geothlypis formosa)* – ground and understory of broadleaf forest. Winter visitor. Many good sites.

Common Yellowthroat *(Geothlypis trichas)* – understory in many scrubby and wet areas. Winter resident with widespread good sites.

Hooded Warbler *(Setophaga citrina)* – understory of broadleaf forest; winter visitor, common within wooded areas throughout.

American Redstart *(Setophaga ruticilla)* – multiple habitats; widespread and common winter visitor.

Cape May Warbler *(Setophaga tigrina)* – littoral forest and edge. Uncommon on cays: Ambergris, Caulker, Glover's Reef, Half Moon. Few mainland records outside of migration: La Milpa, Chan Chich, Lamanai, Belize City, Cox Lagoon, Punta Gorda. One wintered 2000–2001 in Belmopan.

Cerulean Warbler *(Setophaga cerulea)* – subcanopy and canopy inside broadleaf forest; occasionally in scrub. Migrates through higher elevations at least in spring, e.g. Columbia River (common at Union Camp and Gloria Camp), Mountain Pine Ridge, Chiquibul, Che Chem Ha. Scarce migrant in lowlands and foothills: Hill Bank, Blue Hole, Cockscomb, Monkey River. Identified 21 times on Caye Caulker from 2001–2005 in fall migration, but none in spring.

Northern Parula *(Setophaga americana)* – mid-level to canopy in forest interior and edge and tall scrub. Migrant, mostly in north; most frequent on cays.

Tropical Parula *(Setophaga pitiayumi)* – subcanopy and canopy of broadleaf forest and edge at mid-to-high elevations of Maya Mountains: Mountain Pine Ridge (once only), Caracol, Chiquibul, Little Quartz Ridge, Columbia River (Union Camp, Gloria Camp). Four sight records for Tikal.

Magnolia Warbler *(Setophaga magnolia)* – found throughout; the most common wintering warbler in Belize.

Bay-breasted Warbler *(Setophaga castanea)* – migrant found in subcanopy and canopy of broadleaf forest and edge. Most likely to be seen on cays, but also along the mainland coast, especially at Shipstern.

Blackburnian Warbler *(Setophaga fusca)* – subcanopy and canopy of broadleaf forest and edge. Migrant; reported also in winter but not convincingly documented. Migrates mostly through cays and along coastal plain from Shipstern to Punta Gorda, and less frequently in foothills and mountains, e.g., Mountain Pine Ridge, Chaa Creek, Blue Hole, Cockscomb, Bladen.

Yellow Warbler *(Setophaga petechia)* – diverse open habitats with woody vegetation; found throughout mainland and cays. Winter visitor present all months except June and part of July.

Mangrove Yellow Warbler *(Setophaga petechia bryanti)* – mangroves on cays and close to coastal mainland. Good sites: Ambergris Caye, Caye Caulker, Turneffe Atoll, and many other cays. Mainland sites from Shipstern to central Toledo District, including: Sarteneja, Shipstern, Belize City, Dangriga, Gra Gra Lagoon, Sittee River loop, and Placencia.

Chestnut-sided Warbler *(Setophaga pensylvanica)* – mid-level at forest edge and scrub. Winter visitor. Widespread on mainland and cays, with many good sites.

Blackpoll Warbler *(Setophaga striata)* – subcanopy and canopy of broadleaf and littoral forest and edge. Spring migrant, not expected in autumn. Rare migrant, but reported on cays at least once during most springs; only two accepted fall records. Accepted record sites: Hill Bank, Caye Caulker, Glover's Reef, Sapodilla Cayes, other cays.

Black-throated Blue Warbler *(Setophaga caerulescens)* – littoral forest and scrub; winter visitor found on north cays and rarely on the mainland, including a recent 14 January 2011 record at Maya Mountain Lodge.

Palm Warbler *(Setophaga palmarum)* – near and on ground in disturbed areas, fallow fields, pine savanna. Winter visitor, readily found on cays. Some mainland sites: Belize City, Macal River Road, Dangriga, Gra Gra Lagoon, Cattle

Landing, Boom Creek, VoA. Expected subspecies is "Western" Palm (*palmarum*), but "Yellow" Palm (*hypochrysea*) has been identified twice on south Ambergris Caye, photographed 26 February 1996 and 8 December 2000.

Yellow-rumped (Myrtle) Warbler *(Setophaga coronata)* – pine forest, pine/oak savanna, fallow fields, scrub. Winter residents' abundance varies year to year, so some sites have none one year and dozens another year. Good sites: San Victor, August Pine Ridge, La Milpa, Gallon Jug, Honey Camp Lagoon, Hill Bank, Crooked Tree, Coastal Highway, Gales Point, TEC, Guanacaste, Hidden Valley, Macal River, Dangriga, Aguacaliente, Ambergris Caye, many cays.

Yellow-rumped (Audubon's) Warbler *(Setophaga coronata)* – Three records: Gallon Jug 21 January 1958, May Pen on Belize River 17 December 1999, Lubaantun 30 November 2006. One Tikal record 17–18 April 1972.

Yellow-throated Warbler *(Setophaga dominica)* – winter visitor, found in variety of open habitats, but especially coconut palms, pines, and around eaves of houses. Curiously, it is one of first birds seen when entering Belize by road, as it may be seen near the ceiling inside customs buildings. Many good sites.

Prairie Warbler *(Setophaga discolor)* – low in disturbed areas and scrub. Winter visitor, primarily found on Ambergris Caye, Caye Caulker, Glover's Reef, Half Moon Caye, other cays. Few mainland sightings, but best chance would be Belize City and Dangriga (specifically at Pelican Beach).

Grace's Warbler *(Setophaga graciae)* – pine forest and pine savanna. Most easily found along Coastal and Southern Highways and at Mountain Pine Ridge, including Thousand Foot Falls, Hidden Valley, Gaïa Riverlodge, Douglas Da Silva. Other good sites: New River, Crooked Tree, TEC, Belize Zoo, Monkey Bay, Chiquibul, Cockscomb at Ben's Bluff.

Black-throated Gray Warbler *(Setophaga nigrescens)* – one record: a male on south Ambergris Caye, 1 April 1990.

Townsend's Warbler *(Setophaga townsendi)* – one record: hills behind San Felipe, Toledo District 19–21 December 2001.

Hermit Warbler *(Setophaga occidentalis)* – four records: Monkey Bay 28 January 2012, Bermudian Landing 28 December 1991, Thousand Foot Falls 13–23 March 2000 and 20 February 2001.

Golden-cheeked Warbler *(Setophaga chrysoparia)* – several reports, but only three documented records: an adult male at Jaguar Creek 6 November 2001, a male on Caye Chapel 1–3 October 2008, and a male at Mountain Pine Ridge 9 and 16 January 2011.

Black-throated Green Warbler *(Setophaga virens)* – common winter visitor in subcanopy and canopy of forest interior and edge. Many sites.

Rufous-capped Warbler *(Basileuterus rufifrons)* – pine forest interior and edge, broadleaf forest edge, scrub. Resident of Maya Mountains and select foothills. Good sites: Slate Creek, Black Rock, Hidden Valley, Thousand Foot Falls, Baldy Beacon, Douglas Da Silva and other Mountain Pine Ridge sites, Las Cuevas, Guacamallo Bridge, Caracol, Cockscomb at Ben's Bluff.

Golden-crowned Warbler *(Basileuterus culicivorus)* – interior understory to subcanopy of mature broadleaf forest. Good sites: La Milpa, Chan Chich,

Pook's Hill, Slate Creek, Caracol, Aguacate Lagoon, Chaa Creek, Tikal, Blue Hole, Columbia River, Blue Creek Cave.

Canada Warbler *(Cardellina canadensis)* – understory of broadleaf forest and edge. Seen most years once or more on cays during spring migration: Ambergris Caye, Caye Caulker, Half Moon Caye. Only two records in fall, both at Hunting Caye. Few mainland records. Tikal has at least five records.

Wilson's Warbler *(Cardellina pusilla)* – mid-level to subcanopy in forest interior and edge; also shrub. Winter visitor, increasingly common to the south, especially in foothill and submontane sites. Good sites: Monkey Bay, Caracol, Black Rock Lodge, Hydro Road, Tikal, Blue Hole, Mayflower, Cockscomb, Red Bank, BFREE-Bladen, Columbia River, Rio Blanco, Wilson Landing.

Yellow-breasted Chat *(Icteria virens)* – understory and forest edge; scrub. Widespread winter visitor on mainland and cays.

Bananaquit *(Coereba flaveola)* – mid-level to canopy of broadleaf forest and edge; associates with honeycreepers. *Caboti* subspecies on Ambergris Caye and Caye Caulker; *mexicana* subspecies on mainland, where best site is Cockscomb. Other reported sites: New River at Tower Bridge, Macal River, Banana Bank, Pook's Hill, Las Cuevas, Caracol, Mayflower, Lodge at Big Falls, Blue Creek Cave, Columbia River, Boom Creek, Cotton Tree Lodge.

Gray-headed Tanager *(Eucometis penicillata)* – understory of broadleaf forest; usually following ant swarms; also found at organic garbage dumps secluded in forest, such as at La Milpa. Good sites: Shipstern, La Milpa, Chan Chich, Lamanai, Hill Bank, Old Northern Highway, Community Baboon, Pook's Hill, Las Cuevas, Macal River, Tikal, Blue Hole, Mayflower, Cockscomb, BFREE, Wilson Landing, Boom Creek.

Black-throated Shrike-Tanager *(Lanio aurantius)* – subcanopy and canopy in interior of mature broadleaf forest; easy to hear, difficult to see in foliage. Acts as sentinel for mixed-species flocks, so is a strong indicator for finding other desired birds. Good sites: La Milpa, Chan Chich, Lamanai, Las Cuevas, Caracol, Tikal, Blue Hole, Mayflower, Cockscomb, BFREE-Bladen, Columbia River.

Crimson-collared Tanager *(Ramphocelus sanguinolentus)* – second-growth thickets and scrub, mostly in southern half of country. Good sites: Monkey Bay, Pook's Hill, Caracol, Crystal Paradise, Macal River, Blue Hole, Five Blues, Mayflower, Cockscomb, Red Bank, Lubaantun, Jalacte, Cuxlin Ha, Boom Creek.

Passerini's Tanager *(Ramphocelus passerinii)* – second-growth scrub, brush, and tangles. Good sites: Coastal Highway, Monkey Bay, Slate Creek, Macal River, Blue Hole, Five Blues, Mayflower, Sittee River, Cockscomb, Red Bank, Lodge at Big Falls, Santa Anna.

Blue-gray Tanager *(Thraupis episcopus)* – mid-level to canopy in open areas with scattered trees, especially fruiting trees. Common throughout mainland, except scarce in Shipstern area and hard to find in Maya Mountains.

Yellow-winged Tanager *(Thraupis abbas)* – Often found in same trees as Blue-gray Tanagers, although somewhat higher. Distribution is somewhat different, but still present or even more common in the same areas.

Golden-hooded Tanager *(Tangara larvata)* – subcanopy and canopy of forest and edge, mostly in foothills and Maya Mountains. Good sites: Chan Chich,

Monkey Bay, Thousand Foot Falls, Hidden Valley, Mountain Pine Ridge, Guacamallo Bridge, Caracol, Tikal, Blue Hole, Mayflower, Cockscomb, Red Bank, BFREE-Bladen, Columbia River, Belcampo Belize, Boom Creek, Moho River.

Green Honeycreeper (*Chlorophanes spiza*) – subcanopy and canopy of broadleaf forest. Female Red-legged Honeycreepers frequently misidentified as Green Honeycreepers. Good sites: La Milpa, Las Cuevas, Caracol, Chan Chich, El Pilar, Blue Hole, Mayflower, Cockscomb, BFREE-Bladen, Blue Creek Cave, Columbia River, Pueblo Viejo.

Shining Honeycreeper (*Cyanerpes lucidus*) – subcanopy and canopy of broadleaf forest, particularly flowering trees at interior and edge. Found mostly in Maya Mountains at higher elevations along a narrow strip at Cayo/Toledo district border; occasionally in eastern foothills. Good sites: Chiquibul including Doyle's Delight, Columbia River including Little Quartz Ridge. A few lowland records at Mayflower, Cockscomb, BFREE, Moho River.

Red-legged Honeycreeper (*Cyanerpes cyaneus*) – same habitats as other honeycreepers, but will also be in pine forest and more open areas with scattered trees, especially flowering ones. Contrary to earlier references, also occurs in winter in Corozal District, e.g., Corozal, San Victor. Many other good sites farther south to Toledo District.

Grayish Saltator (*Saltator coerulescens*) – mid-level in open habitat with scattered brush and trees. Found at many sites throughout mainland.

Buff-throated Saltator (*Saltator maximus*) – mid-level to canopy at broadleaf forest edge in southern half of Belize. Good sites: Coastal Highway, Monkey Bay, Guanacaste, Pook's Hill, Aguacate Lagoon, Macal River, Blue Hole, Five Blues, Mayflower, Cockscomb, Red Bank, Lubaantun, Boom Creek.

Black-headed Saltator (*Saltator atriceps*) – mid-level to canopy at edge of broadleaf forest and second-growth scrub; fruiting trees. Common throughout mainland and Ambergris Caye.

Blue-black Grassquit (*Volatinia jacarina*) – rice fields, fallow fields, roadside brush. Widespread good sites.

Slate-colored Seedeater (*Sporophila schistacea*) – subcanopy and canopy of broadleaf forest edge and in spiny bamboo. Has been reported in three isolated areas since its discovery in 1989, including multiple observations of territorial pairs, suggesting local breeding. At least in the case of the Monkey Bay site, Slate-colored adopts the same spiny bamboo patch where similar seedeaters are regular, including White-collared, Blue, and Thick-billed—with Variable nearby—making female identification tricky. Known sites: Hill Bank at Irish Creek, Gallon Jug, far southern part of Spanish Creek in Belize River drainage east of Big Falls Farm, Monkey Bay about a quarter-mile from Sibun River, Sibun River 0.6 mile downstream from confluence with Caves Branch at Hellgate (the Sibun River sites are about three miles apart), Boom Creek near Moho River. See Blue Seedeater for more suggestions.

Variable Seedeater (*Sporophila americana*) – fallow fields, scrub, roadside brush, orchards, forest edge. Many sites from Belize City south to Punta Gorda.

White-collared Seedeater (*Sporophila torqueola*) – fallow fields, scrub, roadside brush, orchards, forest edge. Found throughout mainland and on Ambergris Caye. Also occurs on Caye Caulker. Easily the most common seedeater and, in fact, the author's most often identified species during nine winter seasons of birding throughout Belize.

Thick-billed Seed-Finch *(Oryzoborus funereus)* – mostly in pine savanna, also broadleaf forest edge, scrub, and roadside brush. Good sites: Crooked Tree, Community Baboon, Coastal Highway, Belize Zoo, Monkey Bay, Mountain Pine Ridge, Guacamallo Bridge, Macal River, Blue Hole, Croc O'dile Isle, Cockscomb, Red Bank, Aguacaliente Swamp, Joe Taylor Creek, Boom Creek.

Yellow-faced Grassquit *(Tiaris olivaceus)* – roadside brush, scrub, orchards. Rapidly spreading northward across Belize since first recorded in late 1970s. Widespread good sites south and west of Belize City.

Grassland Yellow-Finch *(Sicalis luteola)* – fallow fields, grassland, and pine savannas, including areas that flood seasonally. Discovered in Belize in 1971 and disjunct sites subsequently found. Nomadic. Reported sites: farmlands between August Pine Ridge and two miles west of San Felipe; Mussel Creek drainage (which includes Big Falls Farm) at Double Run Road (at about mile 75 on Goldson Highway log), northern end of Coastal Highway (N17° 21', W88° 22'), TEC, Southern Highway near Hopkins Village and Silk Grass, Placencia, Aqua Mar. Has been reported 2006–2008 at The Dump.

Orange-billed Sparrow *(Arremon aurantiirostris)* – ground and understory well within broadleaf forest. Much more common than suspected by casual observers, but because of its secretive behavior in dense understory it can be overlooked; learn to recognize its chip call. Good sites: Rio Frio Caves, Caracol, Macal River, Blue Hole, Mayflower, Cockscomb, Red Bank, BFREE-Bladen, Lubaantun, Blue Creek Cave, Aguacaliente, Boom Creek.

Olive Sparrow *(Arremonops rufivirgatus)* – arid and semiarid forest edge and scrub. Identification easily confused with Green-backed Sparrow. Good sites: Shipstern, Freshwater Creek, Lamanai, Salt Creek, Community Baboon, Coastal Highway, TEC, Belize Zoo.

Green-backed Sparrow *(Arremonops chloronotus)* – wetter habitats than Olive Sparrow, more in broadleaf second-growth woodlands, thickets, and forest edge, less in open pine woodland and second growth. Both species can be found together. Quite similar to Olive Sparrow but has brighter, greener upperparts and brighter, yellower undertail coverts. Found at dozens of sites.

Rusty Sparrow *(Aimophila rufescens)* – understory of open pine forest and edge; less often in open broadleaf forest edge. Easily found at many Mountain Pine Ridge sites. Also along Chiquibul Road through Chiquibul National Forest and at Guacamallo Bridge. Disjunct population at Payne's Creek to Puente Ycacos Lagoon, Stann Creek/Toledo district border. An isolated sighting in 2001 was at Jalacte on the Belize/Guatemala border, some 28 miles from pine forests.

Botteri's Sparrow *(Peucaea botterii)* – open pine and pine/oak/calabash savannas. Best site is savanna surrounding Dawson Creek, across New River Lagoon from Lamanai. Also has been seen along Shipyard Road and at Runaway Creek. The range map in Jones (2003) extends to northwest Belize District, which includes Old Northern Highway and Altun Ha. His map also includes pine ridge along Gallon Jug Road. Historic record (1963) of two collected 17 miles northwest of Monkey River, but population now probably extirpated. Records near Tikal are from grassy fields, brush, and open savanna south of Lago Petén Itzá.

Chipping Sparrow *(Spizella passerina)* – ground to subcanopy in pine forest and pine savanna. Good sites: Coastal Highway, Hidden Valley, Baldy Beacon, Douglas Da Silva, Chiquibul Road. Other sites: August Pine Ridge, Crooked Tree, Belize City outskirts, Community Baboon, TEC, Monkey Bay, Sittee River, Southern Highway to northeast Toledo District.

Clay-colored Sparrow *(Spizella pallida)* – ground to low level in open areas with woody vegetation. Five records, 1996–2007: Sarteneja, Payne's Creek, Punta Gorda, Ambergris Caye; all during fall migration. One photographed at Tikal 28 October 2008 is the first record for the Atlantic slope of Guatemala.

Vesper Sparrow *(Pooecetes gramineus)* – grasslands, fallow fields, brush. One documented record: Cattle Landing 26 August 2001, an exceptionally early date. Perhaps another 16 January 2001 at Crooked Tree.

Lark Sparrow *(Chondestes grammacus)* – open areas usually with scattered trees. A rare migrant that could turn up most anywhere; two winter records. Eight records (1986–2001, none thereafter): Crooked Tree, Belize City, Payne's Creek, Blue Creek Cave, Punta Gorda, Ambergris Caye, Caye Caulker.

Savannah Sparrow *(Passerculus sandwichensis)* – grasslands, fallow fields. Migrant; few sightings at scattered locations, most recently at VoA 30 October 2001, Ambergris Caye 2 January 2003, and Frank's Caye 31 October 2000. Tikal's first record was 13 December 2010.

Grasshopper Sparrow *(Ammodramus savannarum)* – local residents *(A. s. cracens)* on ground and low-level perches in pine savanna; wintering migrants from North America (rare, mid October to late April) in any open weedy area. Good sites: Coastal and Southern Highways from Belize City to northeast Toledo District, including Manatee Forest Reserve, All Pines, entrance to Bladen Reserve, Payne's Creek, Punta Ycacos, Aqua Mar. Migrants on cays at: Caye Caulker, Frank's Caye, Half Moon Caye. First record for Tikal 28 January 2008.

Lincoln's Sparrow *(Melospiza lincolnii)* – open areas of fallow fields and brush. Winter visitor, though few records. Most often at Hidden Valley (November 2002–April 2003, and again in 2010 and 2011). Other recent records: Seal Caye October 2000, Northeast Caye in Glover's Reef October–November 2004.

White-throated Sparrow *(Zonotrichia albicollis)* – one record: Half Moon Caye 18 May 2005.

White-crowned Sparrow *(Zonotrichia leucophrys)* – two records: Ambergris Caye 28 October 1988 and Half Moon Caye 14 November 2006.

Common Bush-Tanager *(Chlorospingus flavopectus)* – mid-level to canopy in submontane broadleaf forest and edge; very common above 2,300 feet in Maya Mountains; one of most common species at Doyle's Delight; 15–40 seen daily at summit of Little Quartz Ridge. Other sites: Las Cuevas (rare), Chiquibul, Cockscomb (high elevations), Columbia River.

Rose-throated Tanager *(Piranga roseogularis)* – subcanopy to canopy in deciduous and semi-deciduous bajo (swamp) forest interiors. Good sites: Shipstern, Fireburn, La Milpa, Chan Chich, Freshwater Creek, Salt Creek, Community Baboon, Runaway Creek, Tikal.

Hepatic Tanager *(Piranga flava)* – subcanopy and canopy of pine forest. Good sites: Coastal Highway, TEC, Belize Zoo, Monkey Bay, Thousand Foot Falls, Hidden Valley, Douglas Da Silva and other Mountain Pine Ridge sites, Chiquibul, Cockscomb at Ben's Bluff, BFREE-Bladen, Southern Highway.

Summer Tanager *(Piranga rubra)* – mid-level to canopy of broadleaf and pine forests and edge; open country with scattered trees, especially fruiting trees. Common winter visitor throughout, including on cays.

Scarlet Tanager *(Piranga olivacea)* – subcanopy and canopy of broadleaf forest and edge. Fairly widespread in migration, but most commonly at coastal sites (Shipstern, Belize City, Cattle Landing), eastern foothills (Cockscomb, Bladen), and the cays.

Western Tanager *(Piranga ludoviciana)* – few accepted (recent) records: Crooked Tree mid-March 1998, Belize City 6–10 January 2010, Burrell Boom 16 December 2007, Caye Caulker 2 May 2004 and 2 October 2005.

Flame-colored Tanager *(Piranga bidentata)* – small disjunct population atop 3,084-foot Mt. Margaret. Discovered in 1994, four pairs were found in 1997 but only one seen in 2006.

White-winged Tanager *(Piranga leucoptera)* – mid-level at montane and foothill broadleaf forest edge. Good sites: Mountain Pine Ridge, Chiquibul, Cockscomb, Columbia River.

Red-crowned Ant-Tanager *(Habia rubica)* – understory to canopy of broadleaf forest and edge. More common at higher elevations, e.g., both species seen every day at Las Cuevas, where during banding studies 29 Red-crowned and 41 Red-throated captured. Good sites: La Milpa, Chan Chich, Lamanai, Hill Bank, Hidden Valley, Rio Frio Caves, Caracol, Crystal Paradise, Macal River, Tikal, Blue Hole, Mayflower, Cockscomb, Bladen, Blue Creek Cave, Columbia River.

Red-throated Ant-Tanager *(Habia fuscicauda)* – understory and mid-level of broadleaf forest and edge. Found throughout mainland and, especially in lowland forest, where it almost always outnumbers the Red-crowned by a sizeable margin.

Black-faced Grosbeak *(Caryothraustes poliogaster)* – mid-level to canopy of forest interior and edge. Good sites are west and south: La Milpa, Chan Chich, Lamanai, Hill Bank, Hidden Valley, Caracol, Macal River, Hydro Road, Blue Hole, Five Blues, Cockscomb, BFREE-Bladen, Blue Creek Cave, Boom Creek.

Northern Cardinal *(Cardinalis cardinalis)* – understory to mid-level at forest edge and scrub of lowlands in northern third of Belize. Good sites: Shipstern, Gallon Jug Road through Mennonite farms, Honey Camp Road, Old Northern Highway, Crooked Tree, Salt Creek, Belize City, Coastal Highway.

Rose-breasted Grosbeak *(Pheucticus ludovicianus)* – mid-level to canopy at edge of broadleaf forest; open areas with scattered trees. Winter visitor found at many sites.

Black-headed Grosbeak *(Pheucticus melanocephalus)* – One record from Pook's Hill 23 January 2003.

Gray-throated Chat *(Granatellus sallaei)* – low- to mid-level of deciduous and semi-deciduous forest and edge, particularly bajo (swamp) forest. Restricted to specific habitat and not found in surrounding area. Good sites: Shipstern,

Fireburn, August Pine Ridge, La Milpa, Chan Chich, Honey Camp Road, Freshwater Creek, Hill Bank, Old Northern Highway, Monkey Bay, Las Cuevas, Caracol, Macal River, Tikal, Five Blues, Cockscomb, Aguacaliente.

Blue Seedeater *(Amaurospiza concolor)* – spiny bamboo *(Guadua longifolia)* near rivers. Not found in Belize until 1991. Consistent site is Monkey Bay about a quarter-mile from Sibun River, where it is found along with similar-appearing seedeater species. Also occurs beside Belize River at Community Baboon, near Bermudian Landing. Other sites: Hill Bank, Runaway Creek at Sibun River. Canoe trips on Belize River and Sibun River, seeking bamboo stands, may well produce additional sites for Blue Seedeater, and perhaps Slate-colored Seedeater. Also, bamboo stands at other river and creek crossings along Coastal Highway would be worth searching.

Blue-black Grosbeak *(Cyanocompsa cyanoides)* – understory of broadleaf forest and edge as well as second-growth scrub. Good sites: La Milpa, Chan Chich, Lamanai, Coastal Highway, Mountain Pine Ridge, Hydro Road, Blue Hole, Five Blues, Red Bank, BFREE-Bladen, Blue Creek Cave, Moho River, many others.

Blue Bunting *(Cyanocompsa parellina)* – understory to mid-level of deciduous and semi-deciduous forest edge. Good sites: Shipstern, La Milpa, Chan Chich, Lamanai, Hill Bank, Guanacaste, Crystal Paradise, Macal River, Tikal.

Blue Grosbeak *(Passerina caerulea)* – fallow fields, roadside brush, rice fields. Winter visitor, found at dozens of sites, including cays.

Indigo Bunting *(Passerina cyanea)* – winter visitor; same habitats and sites as Blue Grosbeak, plus scrub and forest edge.

Painted Bunting *(Passerina ciris)* – fallow fields, roadside scrub, broadleaf forest edge. Winter visitor. Widespread sites include: Sarteneja Road, La Milpa, Coastal Highway, Las Cuevas, Caracol, Spanish Lookout, Bullet Tree Road, Macal River, Stann Creek at ITVET, Nim Li Punit, Lubaantun, Aguacaliente.

Dickcissel *(Spiza americana)* – rice fields, fallow fields, scrub. Good migration sites: Shipstern, New River Lagoon at Dawson Creek, The Dump, Punta Gorda. Other reported sites: Gallon Jug, Altun Ha, Runaway Creek, Baldy Beacon, Douglas Da Silva, Blue Hole, Cockscomb, Ambergris Caye, Caye Caulker, Half Moon Caye, other cays.

Bobolink *(Dolichonyx oryzivorus)* – fallow fields, weedy areas. One of scarcest migrants; best chance is on cays. Rare on mainland; single reports at Gallon Jug, Hill Bank, Aqua Mar.

Red-winged Blackbird *(Agelaius phoeniceus)* – fallow fields, pastures, freshwater marshes. Good sites: Sarteneja Road, Shipstern, San Victor, Gallon Jug Road, Edenthal, Honey Camp Road, New River, Crooked Tree, Goldson Highway, Belize City outskirts, Belize Bypass, Dangriga outskirts. Far south of its normal range, the species occurred 22 March 2004 at The Dump.

Eastern Meadowlark *(Sturnella magna)* – fallow fields, farmlands, mowed fields, savannas. Good sites: Corozal beach, San Victor, Gallon Jug Road, Shipyard Road, New River, Old Northern Highway, Community Baboon, Amigo's, Spanish Lookout, Bullet Tree Road, Clarissa Falls, Hopkins, Aqua Mar. Recently (2005) expanded its range to Punta Gorda, with sightings at The Dump and VoA.

Yellow-headed Blackbird *(Xanthocephalus xanthocephalus)* – one accepted record at Caye Caulker 23 September–1 October 2001; two early records on cays may have been captives.

Melodious Blackbird *(Dives dives)* – ground to canopy in most open areas with scattered trees, forest edge or clearings. Common throughout mainland; may be resident on north Ambergris Caye.

Great-tailed Grackle *(Quiscalus mexicanus)* – nearly all open areas. Very common throughout mainland and cays.

Shiny Cowbird *(Molothrus bonariensis)* – three documented records: Orange Walk 10 October 2010, Douglas Da Silva 20–24 June 2009, Cattle Landing near Punta Gorda 23 October 2007.

Bronzed Cowbird *(Molothrus aeneus)* – fallow and agricultural fields, brush, open areas with scattered trees. Good sites: Copper Bank, Shipstern, San Victor, Gallon Jug Road, Edenthal, Honey Camp Road, Altun Ha (first nesting record, 1968), Spanish Lookout, Lago Petén Itzá, The Dump, Cuxlin Ha, many others.

Brown-headed Cowbird *(Molothrus ater)* – three records: Progresso Lagoon 26 May 2010, Gallon Jug 1 March 2000, and TEC 8 November 2007.

Giant Cowbird *(Molothrus oryzivorus)* – nests in and raids oropendola colonies in open areas with isolated large trees; forages in plowed fields and other sparsely vegetated fields. Good sites: La Milpa, Laguna Seca, Chan Chich, New River, TEC, Crystal Paradise, Macal River, Tikal, Nim Li Punit, The Dump, Belcampo Belize, Boom Creek, Moho River.

Black-cowled Oriole *(Icterus prosthemelas)* – mid-level to canopy in forest and edge, open areas with scattered trees, especially Coconut Palms. Common throughout mainland and Ambergris Caye, although much less so in Maya Mountains.

Orchard Oriole *(Icterus spurius)* – low level to canopy of forest edge, scrub, fallow fields, open areas with scattered trees, especially flowering and fruiting trees and vines. Winter visitor, common throughout mainland and Ambergris Caye, although much less so in Maya Mountains.

Hooded Oriole *(Icterus cucullatus)* – open areas with scattered trees, especially palms, flowering and fruiting trees. Common in the north and along the coast, less so to Placencia. Common at Ambergris, Caye Caulker, other cays.

Yellow-backed Oriole *(Icterus chrysater)* – mid-level to canopy, mostly in pines, but also in open broadleaf forest and edge. Good sites: Hidden Valley and other Mountain Pine Ridge sites where it occurs with Yellow-tailed Oriole; also Ambergris Caye. Other sites: Shipstern, Freshwater Creek, New River, Pook's Hill, Slate Creek, Crystal Paradise, Macal River, Gra Gra Lagoon, Sittee River. Extends along coastal plain to Monkey River and Aqua Mar, but range does not include Vaca Plateau and higher elevations of Maya Mountains.

Yellow-tailed Oriole *(Icterus mesomelas)* – mid-level to canopy of broadleaf forest edge, often along streams; sometimes in open areas with scattered trees around villages. Has an easily recognized beautifully complicated song, often sung as a duet. Good sites: Santa Rita, Four Mile Lagoon, Gallon Jug Road, Honey Camp Road, New River, Crooked Tree, Community Baboon, Belize Zoo, Monkey Bay, Mountain Pine Ridge, Macal River, Sittee River, Moho River, many others.

Orange Oriole *(Icterus auratus)* – mid-level to subcanopy in deciduous and semi-deciduous forest edge and open areas with scattered trees. Good sites: Copper Bank, Shipstern, Ambergris Caye. Hooded Oriole occurs in same range and is more common.

Spot-breasted Oriole *(Icterus pectoralis)* – two early records at Hopkins-Sittee River 13 March 2005 and Cattle Landing 22 October 2007 through 2 March 2008, and then more or less consistently at Punta Gorda since 22 February 2011.

Altamira Oriole *(Icterus gularis)* – mid-level to canopy in broadleaf forest edge and open areas with scattered trees. Expected in northern Belize, but recently (2010) found at Hopkins Village and a pair February 2011 to at least March 2012 at Punta Gorda. Good sites: Four Mile Lagoon, Corozal, Shipstern, San Victor, Gallon Jug Road, Honey Camp Lagoon, Freshwater Creek, Shipyard Road, Old Northern Highway, Ambergris Caye.

Baltimore Oriole *(Icterus galbula)* – subcanopy to canopy of broadleaf forest and edge; open areas with scattered trees, especially flowering and fruiting trees. Common winter visitor throughout.

Yellow-billed Cacique *(Amblycercus holosericeus)* – understory of forest interior and edge; scrub. Remains well hidden, giving the illusion of scarcity, but its variety of calls reveal it is common. Dozens of good sites, although infrequent at Mountain Pine Ridge and Tikal.

Yellow-winged Cacique *(Cacicus melanicterus)* – one record at turnoff toward Gales Point from Coastal Highway 6 October 2003.

Chestnut-headed Oropendola *(Psarocolius wagleri)* – canopy of broadleaf forest interior. For colonial nesting, uses large trees in broadleaf forest clearings and open areas near forest. Does not occur in the north. Good sites: Las Cuevas, Caracol, Black Rock, Hydro Road, Cockscomb, BFREE-Bladen, southern part of Southern Highway.

Montezuma Oropendola *(Psarocolius montezuma)* – similar habitats as Chestnut-headed, particularly fruiting trees. Typically chooses *Ceiba pentandra* for colonial nesting. Good sites: La Milpa, Chan Chich, Hill Bank, Coastal Highway, Monkey Bay, Las Cuevas, Caracol, Aguacate Lagoon, Xunantunich, Tikal, Blue Hole, Cockscomb, Red Bank, BFREE-Bladen, Nim Li Punit, Aguacaliente, Belcampo Belize, Moho River, many others. Has nested on Ambergris Caye.

Scrub Euphonia *(Euphonia affinis)* – subcanopy and canopy of forest edge, pine/oak savanna, scrub. Good sites: Shipstern, Gallon Jug, Freshwater Creek, Crooked Tree, Monkey Bay, Pook's Hill, Crystal Paradise, Xunantunich, Blue Hole, Lodge at Big Falls, Aguacaliente, Boom Creek, many others.

Yellow-throated Euphonia *(Euphonia hirundinacea)* – mid-level to canopy of broadleaf forest edge; open areas with scattered trees, including villages; visits flowering and fruiting trees, bromeliads. Dozens of sites throughout mainland.

Elegant Euphonia *(Euphonia elegantissima)* – subcanopy and canopy of submontane and foothill broadleaf forest and edge. Few sightings; historically restricted to Maya Mountains sites: Caracol, Chiquibul including Doyle's Delight, Columbia River including Little Quartz Ridge. Documented at Chan Chich January 2002–February 2003 and 20 March 2011; also Lamanai Outpost Lodge 18 March 2011.

Olive-backed Euphonia *(Euphonia gouldi)* – subcanopy and canopy of broadleaf forest and edge, especially at bromeliads. Many good sites, including: La Milpa, Lamanai, Guanacaste, Rio Frio Caves, Caracol, Macal River, Tikal, Mayflower, Boom Creek.

White-vented Euphonia *(Euphonia minuta)* – subcanopy and canopy of broadleaf forest and edge. Best chance is at higher elevations of Cockscomb, Columbia River, and Little Quartz Ridge. It could also be found at a more accessible location, Pueblo Viejo, with effort. More by chance, it has been seen in the Punta Gorda area at Boom Creek and Cotton Tree Lodge. Two specimens were collected near Belize City (1931) and a more recent 2006 sighting was at Monkey Bay.

Red Crossbill *(Loxia curvirostra)* – ground to canopy in pine forest. Rare resident of Mountain Pine Ridge, reported at Hidden Valley, Thousand Foot Falls, Baldy Beacon, Douglas Da Silva and other higher-elevation areas where plenty of Mountain Pine *(Pinus oocarpa)* still grows. Nomadic. Isolated records at Hill Bank and near Belize Zoo.

Black-headed Siskin *(Spinus notata)* – subcanopy and canopy of pine forest and edge. Common in Mountain Pine Ridge and to the edge of Chiquibul Forest at Guacamallo Bridge. Unexpectedly, at Monkey Bay 28 February 2001.

Lesser Goldfinch *(Spinus psaltria)* – open areas, including fallow fields, scrub, and villages. First reported in 1998. Good sites: first part of Sarteneja Road near Four Mile Lagoon, San Victor, Gallon Jug Road from Trinidad to August Pine Ridge, New River at Tower Hill Bridge and savannas at Dawson Creek.

House Sparrow *(Passer domesticus)* – urban areas. Small populations at Dangriga, Punta Gorda since mid-1980s, and along Hummingbird Highway from Alta Vista (mile 39.5) to ITVET (mile 46.4). Has been reported occasionally at Belize City, San Ignacio, Belmopan, Placencia and, surprisingly, at Half Moon Caye 14–15 April 2003.

Tricolored Munia *(Lonchura malacca)* – an import from Southeast Asia to the West Indies and then spreading to Central America, these have turned up at four disjunct sites since 2003: Sarteneja, San Narciso on San Victor loop, Booth's River near Blue Creek Village, and Caye Caulker. Guatemala's first record was 29 September 2009 when it was photographed at Lago Petén Itzá.

See www.bafrenz.com for a comparison chart of hummingbirds, as well as other charts for tinamous, parrots, nightjars, woodcreepers, Myiarchus flycatchers, and ant-tanagers.

CHAPTER 8
SEASONAL ABUNDANCE
OF THE BIRDS OF BELIZE –
BAR GRAPHS

by H. Lee Jones

The following bar graphs, contributed by H. Lee Jones, provide previously unpublished data about the seasonal abundance of the birds of Belize (records throughMarch 2012). Abbreviated comments about habitat, area, or scarcity are also included. In some cases, a species abundance is subdivided by geographic area, e.g., Short-billed Dowitcher has a different abundance when on the coast or cays than at inland sites. The bar graphs are designed to show the actual abundance and seasonal occurrence of a species, as much as the probability of seeing the bird. In 2001 The American Birding Association implemented the standardized abundance definitions shown on the next page.

The key to finding your target birds is simply to be in the right place at the right time. In other words, arrange to be in proper habitat in appropriate season. On your first trip, you may think that some of the birds are harder to find than is indicated. However, if you are in the right area and the right habitat at the proper season, you should find the Common birds on nearly every trip afield, the Fairly Common on over 50% of the trips, the Uncommon on about 25%, and the Rare on 10% or fewer. The Casual or Accidental species cannot be expected, but there are always surprises on any birding trip. Just because your target birds have not been reported lately or local birders cannot direct you to them, don't give up.

If you locate a bird which you feel is noteworthy due to its rarity, or seasonal rarity, take careful notes and/or photographs and report your observation to the regional editor for the Central America region of ABA's *North American Birds* (www.aba.org/nab).

In this book, tabulated lists of Belize birds are presented using three different approaches and serve different purposes. This chapter contains the bar graphs, Chapter 7 is the Annotated Checklist, and, in a separate publication (see www.bafrenz.com) are the ecoregion checklists. These are designed for the following uses:

1. Use the bar graphs for seasonal abundance, particularly useful for noting the comings and goings of seasonal migrants, but also for the overall abundance of resident species.

2. Use the ecoregional checklists for locating the geographic regions where species occur and for the chance of finding them there.

3. Use the annotated checklist (page 251) for learning details about habitat preferences and best sites to find specific species.

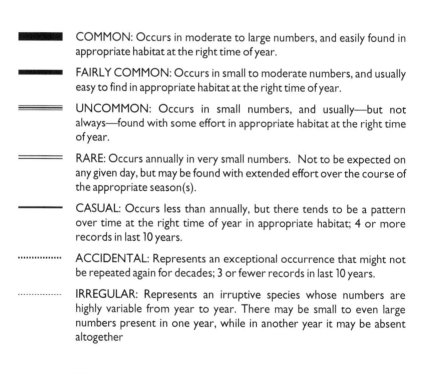

COMMON: Occurs in moderate to large numbers, and easily found in appropriate habitat at the right time of year.

FAIRLY COMMON: Occurs in small to moderate numbers, and usually easy to find in appropriate habitat at the right time of year.

UNCOMMON: Occurs in small numbers, and usually—but not always—found with some effort in appropriate habitat at the right time of year.

RARE: Occurs annually in very small numbers. Not to be expected on any given day, but may be found with extended effort over the course of the appropriate season(s).

CASUAL: Occurs less than annually, but there tends to be a pattern over time at the right time of year in appropriate habitat; 4 or more records in last 10 years.

ACCIDENTAL: Represents an exceptional occurrence that might not be repeated again for decades; 3 or fewer records in last 10 years.

IRREGULAR: Represents an irruptive species whose numbers are highly variable from year to year. There may be small to even large numbers present in one year, while in another year it may be absent altogether

The use of < > across a date range indicates a species record (or records) for which exact dates are not available.

		January	February	March	April	May	June	July	August	September	October	November	December
Great Tinamou	mainland												
Little Tinamou	mainland												
Thicket Tinamou	N & W												
Slaty-breasted Tinamou	inland												
Black-bellied Whistling-Duck	lowlands (local)												
Fulvous Whistling-Duck occasionally elsewhere in N	primarily Crooked Tree												
Greater White-fronted Goose	accidental												
Snow Goose	accidental												
Canada Goose one record; extended stay	accidental												
Muscovy Duck	lowlands												
Gadwall	accidental												
American Wigeon	N lowlands												
Mallard	accidental												
Blue-winged Teal	throughout												
Cinnamon Teal	lowlands												
Northern Shoveler	lowlands												
Northern Pintail	N lowlands												
Green-winged Teal	lowlands												
Redhead	accidental												
Ring-necked Duck	lowlands												
Lesser Scaup primarily Shipstern Lagoon	N lowlands												
Lesser Scaup	S lowlands & cays												
Hooded Merganser undated photograph 1990 or 1991	accidental												
Red-breasted Merganser	coast												
Masked Duck	accidental												
Ruddy Duck	accidental												
Plain Chachalaca	mainland/Ambergris												
Crested Guan scarce where hunted	mainland												

		January	February	March	April	May	June	July	August	September	October	November	December
Great Curassow scarce where hunted	mainland												
Black-throated Bobwhite	N & C												
Spotted Wood-Quail	mainland												
Singing Quail also N Ambergris	N & W (local)												
Ocellated Turkey	N & W (local)												
Least Grebe	lowlands (local)												
Pied-billed Grebe	lowlands												
American (Greater) Flamingo	accidental		<···>	••••						••			
Manx Shearwater carcass	accidental		••										
Audubon's Shearwater	offshore								••••				
Wilson's Storm-Petrel	accidental						••						
White-tailed Tropicbird	accidental				••				••				
Jabiru	lowlands												
Jabiru	NE & W												
Wood Stork nests locally; progressively less common inland	lowlands												
Wood Stork	W												
Magnificent Frigatebird nests locally on cays; rare inland	coast & cays												
Magnificent Frigatebird	inland												
Masked Booby	accidental		••			••		••					••
Brown Booby does not nest in Belize	offshore												
Red-footed Booby seldom seen away from breeding colony	Half Moon Caye												
Neotropic Cormorant	mainland/Ambergris												
Double-crested Cormorant nests locally in N	coast & cays												
Anhinga	lowlands												
American White Pelican	lowlands												
Brown Pelican rare inland away from Crooked Tree	coast & cays												

		January	February	March	April	May	June	July	August	September	October	November	December
Pinnated Bittern seldom seen in S	lowlands												
American Bittern few recent records	lowlands												
Least Bittern	lowlands (local)												
Rufescent Tiger-Heron	accidental												
Bare-throated Tiger-Heron occasional on Ambergris	lowlands												
Great Blue Heron nests locally in N	throughout												
'Great White' Heron	cays												
Great Egret nests locally on coast	throughout												
Snowy Egret not confirmed breeding in Belize since 1862	throughout												
Little Blue Heron not known to nest in Belize	throughout												
Tricolored Heron nests locally in N	lowlands & cays												
Tricolored Heron	W												
Reddish Egret nests locally in N; 20% are white morph	N coast & cays												
Cattle Egret breeding in Belize unconfirmed	throughout												
Green Heron	throughout												
Agami Heron nests locally	mainland												
Black-crowned Night-Heron most common at Crooked Tree	lowlands (local)												
Yellow-crowned Night-Heron	throughout												
Boat-billed Heron	lowlands/Ambergris												
White Ibis nests locally	coast & cays												
White Ibis	inland (local)												
Scarlet Ibis	accidental												
Glossy Ibis fairly common at Crooked Tree	N & C lowlands												

		January	February	March	April	May	June	July	August	September	October	November	December
Roseate Spoonbill nests locally in N	N & C lowlands/cays												
Roseate Spoonbill	S lowlands												
Black Vulture	mainland												
Turkey Vulture	mainland/Ambergris												
Lesser Yellow-headed Vulture	lowlands												
King Vulture	mainland												
Osprey less common inland	coast & cays												
Gray-headed Kite casual on cays	mainland												
Hook-billed Kite occasional in NE and on Ambergris	S coast												
Hook-billed Kite	S & W inland												
Swallow-tailed Kite	S mainland												
Swallow-tailed Kite	N mainland												
White-tailed Kite	lowlands												
Snail Kite especially common at Crooked Tree	N lowlands												
Snail Kite	S lowlands												
Double-toothed Kite casual on Ambergris	mainland												
Mississippi Kite	S coast												
Plumbeous Kite	mainland												
Black-collared Hawk	N lowlands												
Northern Harrier less frequent in S, rare on cays	N lowlands												
Sharp-shinned Hawk	mainland/Ambergris												
Cooper's Hawk	mainland												
Bicolored Hawk	mainland												
Crane Hawk scarce in S	lowlands												
White Hawk	S & C mainland												
Common Black-Hawk	coast & cays												

		January	February	March	April	May	June	July	August	September	October	November	December
Great Black-Hawk	mainland only												
Solitary Eagle nesting recently confirmed	mountains												
Roadside Hawk uncommon on Ambergris	mainland												
Broad-winged Hawk fall migrants on coast	mainland												
Gray Hawk	mainland												
Short-tailed Hawk	mainland												
Swainson's Hawk	lowlands												
White-tailed Hawk	lowlands												
Zone-tailed Hawk	mainland												
Red-tailed Hawk	pine ridge												
Red-tailed Hawk	N & S												
Crested Eagle	mainland												
Harpy Eagle	S mainland												
Black Hawk-Eagle	mainland												
Ornate Hawk-Eagle	mainland												
Black-and-white Hawk-Eagle	inland												
Barred Forest-Falcon	inland												
Collared Forest-Falcon	mainland												
Crested Caracara increasing	lowlands												
Laughing Falcon uncommon on Ambergris	mainland												
American Kestrel	throughout												
Merlin	lowlands & cays												
Aplomado Falcon rare away from savannas	lowlands												
Bat Falcon occasional on N cays	mainland												
Orange-breasted Falcon seldom seen elsewhere	Cayo District												
Peregrine Falcon	cays												

		January	February	March	April	May	June	July	August	September	October	November	December
Peregrine Falcon	mainland												
Ruddy Crake	S lowlands												
Ruddy Crake	N lowlands/ Ambergris												
Gray-breasted Crake rare N of Toledo	S lowlands (local)												
Black Rail	local												
Clapper Rail some seasonal movement	coast/Ambergris												
Rufous-necked Wood-Rail	cays												
Rufous-necked Wood-Rail	coast												
Gray-necked Wood-Rail	mainland												
Uniform Crake	S & C mainland												
Sora	lowlands												
Yellow-breasted Crake	local												
Spotted Rail scarce in S	lowlands (local)												
Purple Gallinule occasional at cays	lowlands												
Common Gallinule occasional at cays	lowlands												
American Coot occasional at cays	lowlands												
Sungrebe	lowlands												
Limpkin	lowlands/ N Ambergris												
Southern Lapwing 2 records	Crooked Tree												
Black-bellied Plover	coast & cays												
American Golden-Plover	lowlands (local)												
Collared Plover	N coast/Ambergris												
Snowy Plover	coast & cays												
Wilson's Plover	coast & cays												
Semipalmated Plover	coast & cays												
Semipalmated Plover	inland (local)												

Species	Habitat	January	February	March	April	May	June	July	August	September	October	November	December
Killdeer	throughout												
American Oystercatcher	coast & cays (local)												
Black-necked Stilt	lowlands & cays												
American Avocet	lowlands												
Northern Jacana	lowlands (local)												
Spotted Sandpiper	throughout												
Solitary Sandpiper	throughout												
Greater Yellowlegs	lowlands												
Willet	coast & cays												
Lesser Yellowlegs	lowlands												
Upland Sandpiper	throughout												
Whimbrel	coast & cays												
Long-billed Curlew	lowlands & cays												
Hudsonian Godwit	accidental												
Marbled Godwit	coast & cays												
Ruddy Turnstone (rare inland in migration)	coast & cays												
Red Knot	C coast												
Sanderling	coast & cays												
Semipalmated Sandpiper	coast & cays												
Western Sandpiper (uncommon inland)	lowlands & cays												
Least Sandpiper	lowlands & cays												
White-rumped Sandpiper	lowlands & cays												
Pectoral Sandpiper	lowlands (local)												
Dunlin	coast												
Stilt Sandpiper	lowlands												
Buff-breasted Sandpiper	lowlands												
Short-billed Dowitcher	coast & cays												
Short-billed Dowitcher	inland												
Long-billed Dowitcher (primarily inland in winter)	lowlands (local)												

		January	February	March	April	May	June	July	August	September	October	November	December
Wilson's Snipe	lowlands & cays												
Wilson's Phalarope	accidental												
Red-necked Phalarope 4 records	accidental												
Black-legged Kittiwake	accidental												
Bonaparte's Gull	scattered records												
Laughing Gull	coast & cays												
Laughing Gull	Crooked Tree												
Franklin's Gull	lowlands & cays												
Black-tailed Gull	accidental												
Ring-billed Gull	coast & cays												
Herring Gull	coast & cays												
Lesser Black-backed Gull	accidental												
Brown Noddy nests locally; formerly more common	offshore												
Black Noddy extirpated in early 1900s	accidental												
Sooty Tern nesting colony on Middle Snake Caye	S offshore (local)												
Bridled Tern	offshore												
Least Tern	coast & cays												
Gull-billed Tern	coast												
Gull-billed Tern	Crooked Tree												
Caspian Tern	coast & Crooked Tree												
Black Tern	lowlands, offshore, cays												
Roseate Tern nests locally on cays	offshore												
Common Tern seasonality complex and poorly known	coast, offshore, cays												
Forster's Tern	coast												
Royal Tern rare inland	coast & cays												

		January	February	March	April	May	June	July	August	September	October	November	December
Sandwich Tern nests locally on cays	coast	██	██	██	██	██	██	██	██	██	██	██	██
Sandwich Tern	cays	═	═	═			███	███	███			═	═
Black Skimmer casual on inland lagoons	C coast	─	─	─									─ ═
Great Skua carcass on beach	accidental			••									
Pomarine Jaeger seasonal distribution poorly understood	offshore				─						▬		
Parasitic Jaeger seasonal distribution poorly understood	offshore				─								
Rock Pigeon	urban	██	██	██	██	██	██	██	██	██	██	██	██
Pale-vented Pigeon occasional on cays	mainland	██	██	██	██	██	██	██	██	██	██	██	██
Scaled Pigeon	N mainland	═	═	═	═	═	═	═	═	═	═	═	═
Scaled Pigeon	S mainland	═	═	═	═	═	═	═	═	═	═	═	═
White-crowned Pigeon	cays	═	═	███	███	███	███	███	███	═	═	═	═
White-crowned Pigeon	lowlands	─	─	─	─								─
Red-billed Pigeon	N & W mainland	██	██	██	██	██	██	██	██	██	██	██	██
Red-billed Pigeon	S mainland	═	═	═	═	═	═	═	═	═	═	═	═
Short-billed Pigeon	mainland (absent NE)	═	═	═	═	═	═	═	═	═	═	═	═
Eurasian Collared-Dove increasing	recent colonist	═	═	═	═	═	═	═	═	═	═	═	═
White-winged Dove sporadic inland	N & cays	██	██	██	██	██	██	██	██	██	██	██	██
White-winged Dove	C & S coast	•	─	═ ══	══						─ ══ ██ ══ ─	•••	
Mourning Dove	throughout	─	─	─							═══	─	
Inca Dove	accidental					••			••				
Common Ground-Dove	N lowlands/ Ambergris	██	██	██	██	██	██	██	██	██	██	██	██
Common Ground-Dove	W & S lowlands	═	═	═							═	═	═
Plain-breasted Ground-Dove	lowlands	██	██	██	██	██	██	██	██	██	██	██	██
Ruddy Ground-Dove	lowlands	██	██	██	██	██	██	██	██	██	██	██	██
Blue Ground-Dove	S mainland	██	██	██	██	██	██	██	██	██	██	██	██

	January	February	March	April	May	June	July	August	September	October	November	December
Blue Ground-Dove absent in NE — N mainland												
White-tipped Dove — N & C mainland												
White-tipped Dove — S mainland												
Gray-headed Dove — S mainland												
Gray-headed Dove — N mainland												
Caribbean Dove — NE lowlands/Ambergris												
Gray-chested Dove — S & C mainland												
Ruddy Quail-Dove — mainland												
Olive-throated Parakeet — mainland/Ambergris												
Olive-throated Parakeet — Caye Caulker												
Scarlet Macaw — W foothills												
Scarlet Macaw — E foothills (local)												
Brown-hooded Parrot — S & W mainland												
Brown-hooded Parrot — C mainland												
White-crowned Parrot — mainland												
White-fronted Parrot — N & C mainland												
Yellow-lored Parrot briefly invaded cays after Hurricane Dean — NE mainland												
Red-lored Parrot — mainland												
Mealy Parrot more common inland — mainland												
Yellow-headed Parrot — savanna												
Yellow-naped Parrot 3 on Turneffe Atoll after Hurricane Mitch — accidental												
Squirrel Cuckoo — mainland/Ambergris												
Yellow-billed Cuckoo — cays												
Yellow-billed Cuckoo — mainland												
Mangrove Cuckoo formerly bred — lowlands & cays												
Black-billed Cuckoo — cays												
Black-billed Cuckoo — mainland												

		January	February	March	April	May	June	July	August	September	October	November	December
Striped Cuckoo	lowlands												
Pheasant Cuckoo	mainland												
Smooth-billed Ani	N cays												
Groove-billed Ani	mainland/Ambergris												
Groove-billed Ani	cays												
Barn Owl	mainland												
Vermiculated Screech-Owl	mainland												
Crested Owl	mountains & foothills												
Spectacled Owl	S & W inland												
Great Horned Owl	Ambergris												
Great Horned Owl	N coast												
Central American Pygmy-Owl	inland												
Ferruginous Pygmy-Owl	N mainland & mountains												
Burrowing Owl	accidental												
Mottled Owl	mainland												
Black-and-white Owl	mainland												
Stygian Owl	pines, lowlands												
Stygian Owl	Mtn Pine Ridge												
Short-eared Owl mummified carcass	accidental												
Striped Owl	S & C lowlands												
Short-tailed Nighthawk	accidental												
Lesser Nighthawk	N												
Lesser Nighthawk	S												
Common Nighthawk	pine ridge												
Common Nighthawk	elsewhere												
Common Pauraque	mainland/Ambergris												
Yucatan Poorwill	N mainland												
Chuck-will's-widow most records from cays	throughout												

		January	February	March	April	May	June	July	August	September	October	November	December
Yucatan Nightjar rare, seasonal in S	N mainland												
Eastern Whip-poor-will	mainland												
Great Potoo	mainland												
Northern Potoo	mainland/Ambergris												
Black Swift	accidental												
White-chinned Swift	accidental			?									
Chestnut-collared Swift	scattered records												
White-collared Swift	S & C mainland												
Chimney Swift	coast												
Chimney Swift	cays & inland												
Vaux's Swift	mainland												
Lesser Swallow-tailed Swift	S & C mainland												
Lesser Swallow-tailed Swift	NE mainland												
Band-tailed Barbthroat	S mainland												
Long-billed Hermit	S & C mainland												
Stripe-throated Hermit	S & C mainland												
Stripe-throated Hermit	N mainland												
Scaly-breasted Hummingbird	inland												
Wedge-tailed Sabrewing	NE mainland, hills, mountains												
Violet Sabrewing	mountains												
Violet Sabrewing	foothills												
White-necked Jacobin	mainland												
Brown Violetear casual in lowlands	mountains												
Green-breasted Mango	cays												
Green-breasted Mango	mainland												
Black-crested Coquette accidental elsewhere	S mainland												
Canivet's Emerald	N, C, & Ambergris												
Canivet's Emerald	S lowlands												

		January	February	March	April	May	June	July	August	September	October	November	December
Violet-crowned Woodnymph	S inland (local)												
Blue-throated Goldentail	accidental				·· ··	··							
White-bellied Emerald	mainland												
Azure-crowned Hummingbird	C mainland												
Rufous-tailed Hummingbird	lowlands/foothills												
Rufous-tailed Hummingbird	mountains												
Rufous-tailed Hummingbird	N cays												
Buff-bellied Hummingbird	NE mainland												
Buff-bellied Hummingbird	N & C mainland												
Cinnamon Hummingbird	coast & cays												
Stripe-tailed Hummingbird	mountains												
Stripe-tailed Hummingbird	foothills												
Purple-crowned Fairy few records from central part	S & N inland												
Long-billed Starthroat	accidental					··		·· ··		··			
Ruby-throated Hummingbird	throughout												
Slaty-tailed Trogon	S & W mainland												
Black-headed Trogon	mainland												
Black-headed Trogon	Ambergris												
Black-headed Trogon	Caye Caulker												
Gartered (Violaceous) Trogon	mainland												
Collared Trogon	foothills/mountains												
Tody Motmot	mainland												
Blue-crowned Motmot	mainland												
Keel-billed Motmot	mountains/foothills												
Ringed Kingfisher	mainland												
Belted Kingfisher	throughout												
Amazon Kingfisher	S mainland												
Amazon Kingfisher	N mainland												
Green Kingfisher	mainland												
American Pygmy Kingfisher	mainland												

		January	February	March	April	May	June	July	August	September	October	November	December
☐ White-necked Puffbird	mainland												
☐ White-whiskered Puffbird	mainland												
☐ Rufous-tailed Jacamar	inland												
☐ Emerald Toucanet	mountains												
Emerald Toucanet	foothills												
☐ Collared Aracari	mainland												
☐ Keel-billed Toucan	mainland												
☐ Acorn Woodpecker	pines												
☐ Black-cheeked Woodpecker	S & W mainland												
☐ Yucatan Woodpecker	N mainland & cays												
☐ Golden-fronted Woodpecker	mainland & cays												
☐ Yellow-bellied Sapsucker	throughout												
☐ Ladder-backed Woodpecker	savanna												
☐ Smoky-brown Woodpecker	mainland												
☐ Golden-olive Woodpecker	mainland												
☐ Chestnut-colored Woodpecker	mainland												
☐ Lineated Woodpecker	mainland												
☐ Pale-billed Woodpecker	mainland												
☐ Great Antshrike	S & C lowlands												
☐ Barred Antshrike	mainland												
☐ Western Slaty-Antshrike	SE lowlands												
☐ Russet Antshrike	mountains												
Russet Antshrike	S foothills												
☐ Plain Antvireo	mountains & W												
☐ Slaty Antwren	mountains												
☐ Dot-winged Antwren	S & inland												
Dot-winged Antwren	N (absent NE)												
☐ Dusky Antbird	S & C mainland												
Dusky Antbird	N mainland (absent NE)												
☐ Bare-crowned Antbird	S lowlands												

		January	February	March	April	May	June	July	August	September	October	November	December
Black-faced Antthrush	mainland												
Tawny-throated Leaftosser	mountains												
Scaly-throated Leaftosser	inland												
Rufous-breasted Spinetail	mainland												
Scaly-throated Foliage-gleaner	Doyle's Delight												
Buff-throated Foliage-gleaner	inland												
Plain Xenops	mainland												
Tawny-winged Woodcreeper	mainland												
Ruddy Woodcreeper	mainland												
Olivaceous Woodcreeper	mainland												
Wedge-billed Woodcreeper	S & W mainland												
Strong-billed Woodcreeper	W & mountains												
Northern Barred-Woodcreeper	mainland												
Ivory-billed Woodcreeper	mainland												
Spotted Woodcreeper	mountains												
Streak-headed Woodcreeper	S & C mainland												
Yellow-bellied Tyrannulet	mainland (absent NE)												
Northern Beardless-Tyrannulet	N & C lowlands												
Northern Beardless-Tyrannulet	S lowlands												
Greenish Elaenia occasional on Ambergris	mainland												
Caribbean Elaenia has bred; only 2 reports since 2007	Caye Caulker						???						
Caribbean Elaenia	other cays												
Yellow-bellied Elaenia rare stray on true cays	mainland/Ambergris												
Ochre-bellied Flycatcher	mainland												
Sepia-capped Flycatcher	mainland												
Paltry Tyrannulet	S mainland												
Northern Bentbill	mainland												
Slate-headed Tody-Flycatcher	mainland												

Species	Region	January	February	March	April	May	June	July	August	September	October	November	December
Common Tody-Flycatcher	mainland/Ambergris												
Eye-ringed Flatbill	inland												
Yellow-olive Flycatcher	mainland												
Stub-tailed Spadebill	mainland												
Royal Flycatcher	mainland												
Ruddy-tailed Flycatcher	inland												
Sulphur-rumped Flycatcher	inland (absent NE)												
Olive-sided Flycatcher	mountains												
Olive-sided Flycatcher	lowlands												
Greater Pewee	mountains (local)												
Western Wood-Pewee	accidental												
Eastern Wood-Pewee	throughout												
Tropical Pewee	mainland												
Yellow-bellied Flycatcher	throughout												
Acadian Flycatcher	throughout												
Alder Flycatcher status in spring unknown	throughout												
Willow Flycatcher	throughout												
White-throated Flycatcher	local												
Least Flycatcher	throughout												
Black Phoebe	inland (rivers)												
Vermilion Flycatcher	lowlands (except S)												
Bright-rumped Attila	mainland												
Rufous Mourner	inland												
Yucatan Flycatcher	N mainland												
Dusky-capped Flycatcher	mainland/Ambergris												
Great Crested Flycatcher	throughout												
Brown-crested Flycatcher	mainland/Ambergris												
Great Kiskadee	mainland												
Great Kiskadee	Ambergris												
Great Kiskadee	Caye Caulker												

		January	February	March	April	May	June	July	August	September	October	November	December
Boat-billed Flycatcher	mainland												
Social Flycatcher	mainland/Ambergris												
Streaked Flycatcher	inland												
Sulphur-bellied Flycatcher (one wintered 1994-1995)	mainland												
Sulphur-bellied Flycatcher	cays												
Piratic Flycatcher	mainland												
Tropical Kingbird	throughout												
Couch's Kingbird	throughout												
Cassin's Kingbird (one record)	accidental												
Western Kingbird	scattered records												
Eastern Kingbird	coast & cays												
Eastern Kingbird	inland												
Gray Kingbird	coast & cays												
Scissor-tailed Flycatcher	coast (local)												
Scissor-tailed Flycatcher	cays & inland												
Fork-tailed Flycatcher	NC & savanna												
Northern Schiffornis	mainland												
Speckled Mourner	mountains/foothills												
Masked Tityra	mainland												
Masked Tityra	Ambergris												
Black-crowned Tityra	mainland												
Cinnamon Becard	inland												
White-winged Becard	S & C lowlands												
Gray-collared Becard	mainland												
Rose-throated Becard	N mainland												
Rose-throated Becard	S mainland												
Lovely Cotinga	inland												
Rufous Piha	inland												
White-collared Manakin	S & C mainland												

		January	February	March	April	May	June	July	August	September	October	November	December
White-collared Manakin	N mainland												
Red-capped Manakin	mainland												
White-eyed Vireo	throughout												
Mangrove Vireo	lowlands/Ambergris												
Yellow-throated Vireo	throughout												
Plumbeous Vireo	mountains												
Plumbeous Vireo	C lowlands (local)												
Blue-headed Vireo	scattered records												
Warbling Vireo	accidental												
Philadelphia Vireo	throughout												
Red-eyed Vireo	throughout												
Yellow-green Vireo	mainland/Ambergris												
Yellow-green Vireo	cays												
Black-whiskered Vireo	cays												
Yucatan Vireo	coast & cays												
Tawny-crowned Greenlet	S & C mainland												
Tawny-crowned Greenlet	N mainland												
Lesser Greenlet	mainland												
Green Shrike-Vireo resident but hard to find when not singing	inland												
Rufous-browed Peppershrike uncommon on Ambergris	N & C lowlands												
Brown Jay	mainland/ N Ambergris												
Green Jay	pine ridge												
Green Jay	elsewhere inland												
Yucatan Jay	N mainland/ N Ambergris												
Purple Martin	throughout												
'Snowy-bellied' Martin either Caribbean Martin or Sinaloa Martin	accidental												
Gray-breasted Martin occasional on cays	mainland												

		January	February	March	April	May	June	July	August	September	October	November	December
☐ Tree Swallow	*throughout*												
☐ Mangrove Swallow	*lowlands/Ambergris*												
☐ Northern Rough-winged Swallow northern populations	*throughout*												
Northern Rough-winged Swallow resident populations, including *ridgwayi*	*inland (local)*												
☐ Bank Swallow much less common inland	*coast & cays*												
☐ Cliff Swallow less common inland	*coast & cays*												
☐ Cave Swallow	*lowlands & cays*												
☐ Barn Swallow local in winter	*throughout*												
☐ Band-backed Wren	*inland (local)*												
☐ Spot-breasted Wren	*mainland*												
☐ Carolina Wren	*N & W (local)*												
☐ Plain Wren	*pine ridge primarily*												
☐ House Wren	*mainland*												
☐ Sedge Wren	*S savanna/pine ridge*												
☐ White-bellied Wren	*N & W mainland*												
☐ White-breasted Wood-Wren	*S & C mainland*												
White-breasted Wood-Wren	*N mainland*												
☐ Gray-breasted Wood-Wren one record, adult with fledglings	*near Victoria Peak*												
☐ Nightingale Wren	*S inland (local)*												
☐ Long-billed Gnatwren	*mainland*												
☐ Blue-gray Gnatcatcher	*pines & NE*												
Blue-gray Gnatcatcher	*elsewhere*												
☐ Tropical Gnatcatcher	*S mainland*												
Tropical Gnatcatcher	*N mainland*												
☐ Eastern Bluebird	*pine ridge*												
☐ Slate-colored Solitaire occasional in foothills	*mountains*												

		January	February	March	April	May	June	July	August	September	October	November	December
Veery — most frequent on cays	throughout												
Gray-cheeked Thrush — most frequent on cays	throughout												
Swainson's Thrush — most frequent on cays	throughout												
Hermit Thrush	accidental												
Wood Thrush	throughout												
Clay-colored Thrush	mainland (absent mountains)												
White-throated Thrush	mountains												
White-throated Thrush	foothills												
American Robin	accidental												
Gray Catbird — much less common in mountains	throughout												
Black Catbird	N cays												
Black Catbird	N lowlands (local)												
Tropical Mockingbird	NE & N cays												
Tropical Mockingbird	W & S												
American Pipit	accidental												
Cedar Waxwing	throughout												
Ovenbird	throughout												
Worm-eating Warbler	throughout												
Louisiana Waterthrush	mountains												
Louisiana Waterthrush	lowlands												
Louisiana Waterthrush	cays												
Northern Waterthrush	lowlands & cays												
Northern Waterthrush	mountains												
Golden-winged Warbler	N mainland												
Golden-winged Warbler — less frequent on cays	S mainland												
Blue-winged Warbler — less frequent on cays	mainland												
Golden-w. X Blue-w. Warbler	mainland												

		January	February	March	April	May	June	July	August	September	October	November	December
Black-and-white Warbler	throughout												
Prothonotary Warbler	throughout												
Swainson's Warbler	N lowlands & cays												
Tennessee Warbler	throughout												
Orange-crowned Warbler	accidental												
Nashville Warbler	throughout												
Virginia's Warbler	accidental												
Gray-crowned Yellowthroat	N & C lowlands												
Gray-crowned Yellowthroat	S lowlands/ Ambergris												
Mourning Warbler most frequent on cays	lowlands & cays												
Kentucky Warbler less frequent on cays	throughout												
Common Yellowthroat	throughout												
Hooded Warbler	throughout												
American Redstart	throughout												
Cape May Warbler	cays												
Cape May Warbler	mainland												
Cerulean Warbler fall migration in mountains unknown	mountains							???????????					
Cerulean Warbler	lowlands & cays												
Northern Parula most frequent on cays	lowlands & cays												
Tropical Parula	mountains												
Magnolia Warbler	throughout												
Bay-breasted Warbler	throughout												
Blackburnian Warbler	throughout												
Yellow Warbler	throughout												
Mangrove Yellow Warbler	coast & cays												
Chestnut-sided Warbler	S mainland												
Chestnut-sided Warbler	N mainland & cays												
Blackpoll Warbler	cays												

		January	February	March	April	May	June	July	August	September	October	November	December
Black-throated Blue Warbler	cays												
Black-throated Blue Warbler	mainland												
Palm Warbler	cays												
Palm Warbler	N mainland												
Palm Warbler	S mainland												
Yellow-rumped (Myrtle) Warbler	N mainland & cays												
Yellow-rumped (Myrtle) Warbler	S mainland												
Yellow-rumped (Audubon's) Warbler	accidental												
Yellow-throated Warbler	throughout												
Prairie Warbler	cays												
Prairie Warbler	mainland												
Grace's Warbler	pines												
Black-throated Gray Warbler	accidental												
Townsend's Warbler	accidental												
Hermit Warbler	accidental												
Golden-cheeked Warbler	accidental												
Black-throated Green Warbler	throughout												
Rufous-capped Warbler	pine ridge												
Rufous-capped Warbler	foothills (local)												
Golden-crowned Warbler	mountains/foothills												
Canada Warbler	lowlands & cays												
Wilson's Warbler	throughout												
Yellow-breasted Chat	throughout												
Bananaquit (Mexican)	mountains												
Bananaquit (Mexican)	S lowlands												
Bananaquit (Cabot's)	Caye Caulker												
Bananaquit (Cabot's)	N & C Ambergris												
Gray-headed Tanager	mainland												
Black-throated Shrike-Tanager	S & W inland												

Species	Region	January	February	March	April	May	June	July	August	September	October	November	December
Crimson-collared Tanager	S & C mainland	■	■	■	■	■	■	■	■	■	■	■	■
Passerini's Tanager	S mainland	■	■	■	■	■	■	■	■	■	■	■	■
Passerini's Tanager	C mainland	■	■	■	■	■	■	■	■	■	■	■	■
Blue-gray Tanager (occasional on Ambergris)	S & C mainland	■	■	■	■	■	■	■	■	■	■	■	■
Blue-gray Tanager	N mainland	■	■	■	■	■	■	■	■	■	■	■	■
Yellow-winged Tanager	mainland (absent NE)	■	■	■	■	■	■	■	■	■	■	■	■
Golden-hooded Tanager	S & C lowlands	■	■	■	■	■	■	■	■	■	■	■	■
Green Honeycreeper	S & W mainland	■	■	■	■	■	■	■	■	■	■	■	■
Shining Honeycreeper (casual in lowlands)	mountains	■	■	■	■	■	■	■	■	■	■	■	■
Red-legged Honeycreeper	mainland (absent NE)					■	■	■	■	■			
Red-legged Honeycreeper	NE			■	■	■	■	■	■	■	■		
Grayish Saltator (rare on Ambergris)	mainland	■	■	■	■	■	■	■	■	■	■	■	■
Buff-throated Saltator	S & C mainland	■	■	■	■	■	■	■	■	■	■	■	■
Black-headed Saltator	mainland/Ambergris	■	■	■	■	■	■	■	■	■	■	■	■
Blue-black Grassquit	mainland	■	■	■	■	■	■	■	■	■	■	■	■
Slate-colored Seedeater	mainland	⋯	⋯	⋯	⋯	⋯	⋯	⋯	⋯	⋯	⋯	⋯	⋯
Variable Seedeater	S & C mainland	■	■	■	■	■	■	■	■	■	■	■	■
White-collared Seedeater	mainland/Ambergris	■	■	■	■	■	■	■	■	■	■	■	■
Thick-billed Seed-Finch	mainland (absent NE)	■	■	■	■	■	■	■	■	■	■	■	■
Yellow-faced Grassquit	S & C interior lowlands	■	■	■	■	■	■	■	■	■	■	■	■
Grassland Yellow-Finch	local & nomadic	⋯	⋯	⋯	⋯	⋯	⋯	⋯	⋯	⋯	⋯	⋯	⋯
Orange-billed Sparrow	S & C mainland	■	■	■	■	■	■	■	■	■	■	■	■
Olive Sparrow	N mainland	■	■	■	■	■	■	■	■	■	■	■	■
Green-backed Sparrow	mainland	■	■	■	■	■	■	■	■	■	■	■	■
Rusty Sparrow	pine ridge/S savanna	■	■	■	■	■	■	■	■	■	■	■	■
Botteri's Sparrow	N savanna	■	■	■	■	■	■	■	■	■	■	■	■
Chipping Sparrow	pines	■	■	■	■	■	■	■	■	■	■	■	■

		January	February	March	April	May	June	July	August	September	October	November	December
Clay-colored Sparrow	throughout												
Vesper Sparrow (exceptionally early date)	accidental								••				
Lark Sparrow	throughout	••		••									
Savannah Sparrow	throughout												
Grasshopper Sparrow	savanna												
Grasshopper Sparrow	pine ridge (local)												
Grasshopper Sparrow	elsewhere												
Lincoln's Sparrow	throughout												
White-throated Sparrow	accidental						••						
White-crowned Sparrow	accidental											••	••
Common Bush-Tanager	mountains												
Rose-throated Tanager	N mainland												
Hepatic Tanager	pines												
Summer Tanager	throughout												
Scarlet Tanager	throughout												
Western Tanager	scattered records												
Flame-colored Tanager (small disjunct population)	Mt. Margaret												
White-winged Tanager (occasional in foothills)	mountains												
Red-crowned Ant-Tanager	mountains												
Red-crowned Ant-Tanager	lowlands												
Red-throated Ant-Tanager	lowlands												
Red-throated Ant-Tanager	mountains												
Black-faced Grosbeak	inland												
Northern Cardinal	N mainland												
Rose-breasted Grosbeak	throughout												
Black-headed Grosbeak	accidental	••											
Gray-throated Chat	N mainland												
Gray-throated Chat	S mainland (local)												
Blue Seedeater	local												

		January	February	March	April	May	June	July	August	September	October	November	December
☐ Blue-black Grosbeak	mainland (absent NE)												
☐ Blue Bunting	N & W mainland												
☐ Blue Grosbeak	throughout												
☐ Indigo Bunting	throughout												
☐ Painted Bunting	throughout												
☐ Dickcissel	throughout												
☐ Bobolink	coast & cays												
☐ Red-winged Blackbird	N lowlands												
☐ Eastern Meadowlark	lowlands (absent NE)												
☐ Yellow-headed Blackbird one acceptable record	accidental												
☐ Melodious Blackbird may be resident on N Ambergris	mainland												
☐ Great-tailed Grackle	throughout												
☐ Shiny Cowbird	accidental												
☐ Bronzed Cowbird	N mainland/ Ambergris												
Bronzed Cowbird	C & S inland												
☐ Brown-headed Cowbird	accidental												
☐ Giant Cowbird	S & C mainland												
Giant Cowbird	N mainland												
☐ Black-cowled Oriole	mainland/ N Ambergris												
☐ Orchard Oriole less frequent on cays	throughout												
☐ Hooded Oriole	N lowlands & cays												
☐ Yellow-backed Oriole	pines, N lowlands, Ambergris												
☐ Yellow-tailed Oriole	mainland (rivers)												
☐ Orange Oriole	NE												
Orange Oriole	Ambergris & Caye Caulker												
☐ Spot-breasted Oriole	Punta Gorda												

		January	February	March	April	May	June	July	August	September	October	November	December
☐ Altamira Oriole	N mainland												
Altamira Oriole	Ambergris												
☐ Baltimore Oriole	throughout												
☐ Yellow-billed Cacique	mainland/Ambergris												
☐ Yellow-winged Cacique	accidental												
☐ Chestnut-headed Oropendola	S lowland (local)												
☐ Montezuma Oropendola	S & C mainland												
Montezuma Oropendola	NE mainland												
☐ Scrub Euphonia	N & C mainland												
Scrub Euphonia	S mainland/Ambergris												
☐ Yellow-throated Euphonia	mainland												
☐ Elegant Euphonia	mountains & W foothills												
☐ Olive-backed Euphonia	mainland (absent NE)												
☐ White-vented Euphonia	S mountains/foothills												
White-vented Euphonia	S lowlands												
☐ Red Crossbill	pine ridge												
☐ Black-headed Siskin	pine ridge												
☐ Lesser Goldfinch	NE mainland (local)												
☐ House Sparrow	urban (local) non-native												
☐ Tricolored Munia	non-native												

APPENDIX A
ECOREGIONS

The following habitat breakdown derives in part from that used by Jones and Vallely (2000), but it includes subsets within the main types in a manner similar to those used by Beletsky (2005). These categories are used in the book to characterize birding sites and ecoregions.

AGRICULTURAL LAND

Large portions of the northern districts as well as the coastal plain and inland lowlands of central Belize are devoted to agriculture. These land-uses are broken down into four types of agriculture and aquaculture.

AG1. Northern Coastal Plain Cane Fields. Corozal and Orange Walk Districts are devoted to agriculture, most notably sugarcane. Scrubby field edges, roadsides, and fallow and abandoned fields provide forage and protective cover for buntings, seedeaters, and finches.

AG2. Orange Walk Rice Fields. The Mennonite farms, primarily in the Blue Creek Village area along Gallon Jug Road, are low, wet flatlands used for growing rice. The fields attract long-legged waders, rails, shorebirds, and, rarely, thousands of ducks. Surrounding the fields are dikes, creeks, woodland strips, scrub, and abandoned grassy fields.

AG3. Northern and Central Agricultural Fields. These are principally comprised of sorghum and legume crops grown in moist soils in the Mennonite areas of August Pine Ridge, Little Belize, and Spanish Lookout. The sorghum heads attract Red-billed Pigeons and White-fronted Parrots.

AG4. Central Belize Citrus Groves. In Stann Creek District, orange groves gobble up much of the lower foothills and lowlands adjacent to Hummingbird and Southern Highways. Other small orchards are near Corozal, along the Coastal Highway, and along the road to Black Rock Lodge near Macal River. Bananas and other citrus are also grown. The blossoms and fruit attract insects, parrots, hummingbirds, toucans, and insect eaters, and the semi-open areas with grassy and shrub edges attract seedeaters.

AG5. Central and Southern Belize Shrimp and Tilapia Farms. Just as the rice-field wetlands attract birds, so do the shrimp and fish farms. The latter, however, are closer to the coast and brackish, therefore attracting more shorebirds such as sandpipers and, rarely, oystercatchers and avocets. Some farms attract numbers of Jabirus.

BROADLEAF FOREST LOWLANDS

The most common descriptor of the birding areas of northern and western Belize and extending through the Petén region of Guatemala is lowland broadleaf forest. These are closed-canopy broadleaved hardwood forests, often referred to as tropical rainforests. Altun Ha, Lamanai, Chan Chich, Tikal, and many others fall into this category of habitat. Guanacaste National Park, named after the

Guanacaste trees *(Enterolobium cyclocarpum)* growing there, has only one mature tree remaining of these giants that can reach 130 feet and a diameter of over 6 feet. At the Community Baboon Sanctuary in Bermudian Landing, the Yucatan Black Howler's main food source is the leaves of Hogplum *(Spondias mobin)* and Sapodilla *(Manilkara zapota)*. Broadleaf trees in riparian areas include Bri-bri *(Inga edulis)*, Bullet Tree *(Bucida buceras)*, Cabbage Palm *(Euterpe macrospadix)*, and fig *(Ficus* spp.).

Within the broad classification of lowland broadleaf forest are several specialty types that vary with rainfall, water table, and soil.

BFL1. Riparian Forest. Also called **riverine** or **gallery** forests, trees growing along rivers are often the same species as elsewhere, but may be more abundant along rivers where they can tolerate seasonal flooding. The presence of creeks and rivers provides habitat for species such as kingfishers and swallows that would not be expected in dense broadleaf forests in absence of water.

BFL2. Northern Swamp Forest. A type of northern broadleaf forest is swamp forest or **bajo**. Examples are found along the Bajo Trails at Chan Chich near Gallon Jug and at La Milpa in the Rio Bravo Conservation Area of northwestern Belize, excellent places to find Rose-throated Tanager and Gray-throated Chat. Other examples are along the waterways of Crooked Tree Wildlife Sanctuary and along the New River near Orange Walk Town. These swamp forests are very dense, impenetrable thickets of Spiny Bamboo *(Guadua spinosa)*, Wild Grape *(Coccoloba belizensis)*, Give-and-Take Palm *(Chrysophila argentea)*, and other palms. Conspicuous on New River boat trips are the exquisite blooms of the Provision Tree *(Pachira aquatica)*, which last only a day. Within the realm of swamp forests are the logwood thickets famously found at Crooked Tree. Extracted in the 17th Century by the British, the Logwood Tree *(Haematoxylon campechianum)* played an important role in European history as a source for wool dye, which when mixed with additives could produce colors from yellow to black.

BFL3. Broken Ridge. This transitional broadleaf forest is characterized by light-demanding, fast-growing, shorter trees, less than 50 feet tall. The oft-present and easily recognized Trumpet Tree *(Cecropia peltata* and *C. palmate)* is a good example. These trees are often found where the vegetative cover has been removed and the forest is in the process of regaining the land. Scrubland and low second-growth is another way to describe this forest type. Broken ridge is scattered throughout the northern half of Belize, including along portions of Price Highway, which traverses five forest types between Belize City and Belmopan.

BFL4. Cohune Ridge. Cohune ridge is found in many of the birding areas. Dominated by Cohune Palm *(Orbigyna cohune)*, these groves are often interspersed within other forest types and include many of the same trees as those listed under lowland broadleaf forest. There is cohune ridge habitat in the Maya ruins at La Milpa and those at Lamanai, as well as in many other densely forested birding areas. The Cohune Palm is a remarkable tree with fronds up to 30 feet long, based on the ground or from trunks and forming a cathedral canopy. Other trees of the cohune ridge include Quamwood *(Schizolobium parahybum)*, whose canopy yellow flowers attract birds, and Gumbo Limbo *(Bursera simaruba)*, which the tour guides enthusiastically call "tourist tree" because its red peeling bark resembles sunburn.

BFL5. High Ridge. La Milpa and Chan Chich are in the Bravo Hills section of northwestern Belize, reached after ascending the Rio Bravo escarpment. Annual rainfall is 50–80 inches. Called High Ridge, the semi-deciduous broadleaf forests are 450–500 feet above the coastal plain and are less likely to endure seasonal flooding. Historically, these areas were logged for precious Mahogany *(Swietenia macrophylla)*, Santa Maria *(Calophyllum antillanum)*, and cedar *(Cedrela mexicana* or *C. odorata)*. The Sapodilla trees were tapped for chicle, the chewing gum sap.

BFL6. Toledo Broadleaf Forest Lowland and Flood Plains. Here at the southern end of the country, the highest rainfall is in the Toledo District lowlands, variously reported as 160 to 200 inches annually. This region comes the closest in Belize to supporting tropical wet forests. Extensive flood plains, notably Aguacaliente Swamp and Moho River, support Rosewood *(Dalbergia stevensonii)*, Santa Maria/Guanandi *(Calopphyllum brasiliense)*, Ceiba *(Ceiba pentandra)*, Banak *(Virola koschnyi)*, and many others. Stands of tall Red Mangrove *(Rhizophora mangle)* line Moho River near its mouth to the Bay of Honduras.

BROADLEAF FOREST FOOTHILLS

Driving along Price Highway near the birding areas of the Belize Zoo and the Tropical Education Center, one is struck by the strange karst landscape of limestone hills erupting from flatlands, the separation between the coastal plain and the Maya Mountains. The birding sites within the foothill belt around Maya Mountains are at 200–600 feet elevation. Most of the foothills are densely forested, but for the openings for resorts along the rivers and a succession of small villages along the major highways. Trees in the foothills often differ from other areas because of the limestone soils and drainage. Typical trees include Sapodilla, Wild Mammee *(Alseis yucatanensis)*, Turtlebone *(Inga stevensonii)*, and Black Poisonwood *(Metopium brownii)*. The following breakdown is based on geography.

BFF1. Cayo Broadleaf Forest Foothills. The central foothills of the Cayo District receive 80–100 inches of annual rainfall. Many of the vacation resorts are within the vegetated foothills, particularly in the San Ignacio area, and are excellent birding sites. Daytime temperatures are cooler, with less humidity, than toward the coast. Flowing through the foothills are the Mopan and Macal Rivers which converge to form the Belize River at San Ignacio. Farther toward the coast the Sibun River passes through foothills between Blue Hole National Park and Five Blues Lake National Park to Monkey Bay Wildlife Sanctuary, before it crosses under the Coastal Highway. All provide good riparian habitat for birding.

BFF2. Stann Creek Broadleaf Forest Foothills. The eastern coastal foothills include the lush rainforests of Mayflower Bocawina National Park and Cockscomb Basin Wildlife Sanctuary.

BFF3. Toledo Broadleaf Forest Foothills. Characteristic trees of the high rainfall foothills include Rosewood, Santa Maria, and Monkey Apple *(Licania platypus)*.

SUBMONTANE BROADLEAF FOREST

The Maya Mountains dominate the southern half of Belize. Rainfall is 60–80 inches and elevations are 600–2300 feet. The semi-deciduous broadleaf forest is interspersed with isolated stands of pine shrubland. Characteristic broadleaf trees are Sapodilla, Ramón *(Brosimum alicastrum),* and Ironwood *(Dialium guianese).* The following breakdown is based on geography.

BFM1. Central Belize Submontane Broadleaf Forest. The down-slope northern peripheral of Mountain Pine Ridge plateau is submontane broadleaf forest and includes Tapir Mountain Nature Reserve. Tree species in this area closely parallel those at lower elevations. Pook's Hill, an excellent birding site, lies at the western edge of the reserve.

BFM2. Western Upland Submontane Broadleaf Forest. Submontane broadleaf forest also describes the western uplands of the Maya Mountains along the Guatemala border, an area known as the Vaca Plateau that includes Rio Frio Caves and the Caracol Archaeological Reserve, as well as Chiquibul National Park.

BFM3. Maya Mountain Cloud Forest. South of Caracol is Doyle's Delight along the Maya Mountain divide and the highest point in Belize at 3,688 feet (1,124 m), just barely edging out 3,675-foot (1,120 m) Victoria Peak above Cockscomb Basin. Owing to its remote and relatively inaccessible location, Doyle's Delight is a cloud-forest habitat-island that has been explored only by scientific expeditions. Scaly-throated Foliage-gleaner and Tawny-throated Leaftosser have been discovered on Doyle's Delight, the only known Belize location for these species. The cloud-covered peaks foster mosses and ferns; the tallest trees are only 20 feet at Victoria Peak and 30 feet at Doyle's Delight, earning the names dwarf forest and elfin woodland.

LITTORAL FOREST

Also referred to as **coastal forest**. Along the coast and edges of inland rivers are **strand forests**, characterized by Coconut Palm *(Cocos nucifera),* built on beach sands, as well as **mangrove forests,** which are in saltwater areas. The strand forests are most noticeable on the cays, whereas the mangrove forests are both on the cays and along the coastline, becoming more common southward. Mangrove forests include a variety of tree types including Red Mangrove, White Mangrove *(Laguncularia racemosa),* and Black Mangrove *(Avicennia germinans).* The category is subdivided by region:

LF1. Cays Littoral Forest. Virtually all of the cays include strand and/or mangrove forests. Those most often visited by birders are Ambergris Caye, Caye Caulker, and Half Moon Caye. When snorkeling and diving, birders visit many other cays as well. Coconut Palm has been introduced to the resort areas.

LF2. Northern Coastal Littoral Forest. Strand forests are along Corozal Bay and Shipstern Nature Reserve, as are mangrove forests. Inland areas are characterized by coastal savanna.

LF3. Central Coastal Littoral Forest. Central Belize is a coastal plain transitioning to inland foothills and then western uplands. Belize City, the Coastal

Highway, and its peninsular offshoot at Gales Point lie in the flat coastal areas, characterized by mangrove and littoral forests, saline marshes, and large calm-water lagoons at the coast, and by pine savanna along the Coastal Highway and northern end of the Southern Highway, with some broadleaf forest along the interspersed rivers and creeks. The area receives more rainfall than farther north. Near Dangriga, Stann Creek drains from Cockscomb Basin to the sea. Remnant mangrove forests are north of the city and at the more accessible Gra Gra Lagoon National Park to the south of the city.

LF4. Southern Coastal Littoral Forest. Mangrove forests include Joe Taylor Creek, Moho River, Rio Grande, and other rivers that drain from the southern foothills.

PINE FOREST

PFL. Lowland Pine Forest. The northern coastal plain extends over the three Districts of Corozal, Orange Walk, and Belize. The most often seen forest type is **pine ridge** consisting of **savannas** variously covered with pine, oak, and palmetto. Most pines are Honduran or Caribbean Pine *(Pinus caribaea* var. *hondurensis)*, the oaks are various *Quercus* species, and the Palmetto Palm is *Acoelorrhaphe wrightii* which can be densely distributed. Birding areas in these habitats include Crooked Tree Wildlife Sanctuary, August Pine Ridge, Tropical Education Center, and Monkey Bay Wildlife Sanctuary. The coastal plain of Stann Creek and Toledo districts stretches from Dangriga to Punta Gorda and resembles the northern coastal plain but with a much wider band of lowland pine savanna extending inland up to the foothills of the Maya Mountains. Caribbean Pine dominates.

PFM. Submontane Pine Forest. A dramatic contrast to other habitats is the submontane pine forest of Mountain Pine Ridge at an elevation of 1740–2950 feet in the Maya Mountains. Mountain Pine Ridge was once a dense forest of Mountain Pine *(Pinus oocarpa)*, but timber extraction and Southern Pine Beetles *(Dendroctonus frontalis)* have decimated all but a few small sections. Remnant trees still support Acorn Woodpeckers and Black-headed Siskins, as well as specialists such as Rusty Sparrow not readily found elsewhere in Belize. Unusual plants found, particularly at Hidden Valley, are tree ferns *(Cyathea mysuroides* and *Hemitelia multiflora)*.

POPULATION CENTERS

PC. Population Centers. These include the largest cities—Belize City, Orange Walk, San Ignacio, Belmopan, Dangriga, Corozal, and San Pedro—as well as smaller towns, villages, and resorts. Generally, the habitat in these areas is broken ridge (BFL3) supplemented by ornamental plantings which may attract certain birds, particularly hummingbirds.

ECOREGIONS

Data used in these accounts were collected through October 2012. For this book over 175,000 records were used and these included sightings, literature references, and printed checklists. Ecoregions are geographic regions characterized by dominant habitat types. Detailed bird checklists for the 18 ecoregions, including abundance codes, are available as a separate publication entitled *Birds of Belize: An Ecoregional Checklist.* **See www.bafrenz.com for further information.**

NORTHERN BELIZE

1. Corozal coastal savannas

Habitats: Predominantly agricultural (AG1); littoral forests (LF2) and broadleaf forests (BFL3); also orange groves (AG4) and small villages (PC), including Corozal Town.

Elevation: 0–55 feet.

District: Corozal.

Sites: The Santa Elena area (Four Mile Lagoon North, Rio Hondo, Santa Elena), Consejo, the Corozal Town area (Campo Amor Aquarium Eco Camp, Caribbean Village Campground and RV Park, Corozal airport, Santa Rita Maya site), the road to Cerros (Cerros Maya site, Copper Bank, Corozal abandoned beach property, Four Mile Lagoon South, New River road, Pueblo Nuevo ferry), and the San Victor loop.

Species: 254, probably underreported.

Resources: This ecoregion has relatively little data and therefore is likely to be missing many species actually present in the coastal savannas.

2. Shipstern and Freshwater Creek lowlands and wetlands

Habitats: Predominantly littoral (LF2) and broadleaf (BFL2, BFL3) forests; also agricultural (AG1, AG3) and small villages (PC).

Elevation: 0–40 feet.

District: Corozal.

Sites: The road connecting Progresso Lagoon village to Sarteneja, including Progresso Lagoon, Shipstern Nature Reserve, Cowpen, Robin's Land, Xo-Pol, Warree Bight, Sarteneja National Tree Park, Sarteneja, Fireburn Village, Balam Jungle, and Rocky Point. Also Freshwater Creek Forest Reserve.

Species: 358.

3. Orange Walk agricultural lowlands

Habitats: Predominantly agricultural (AG2, AG3) and pine savanna (PFL); broadleaf forests (BFL1, BFL3); remnant forested uplands near Tres Leguas (BFL5); also cane fields (AG1) and small villages (PC).

Elevation: mostly 10–100 feet, but beyond escarpment to 500 feet.

District: Orange Walk.

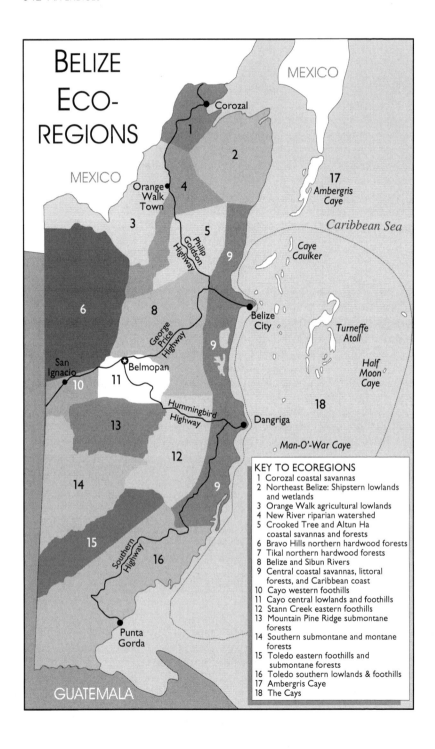

BELIZE
ECO-
REGIONS

MEXICO

MEXICO

Caribbean Sea

Corozal

1

2

17
Ambergris
Caye

Orange
Walk
Town

4

3

5

Caye
Caulker

9

Philip
Goldson
Highway

6

8

Belize
City

Turneffe
Atoll

George
Price
Highway

9

Half
Moon
Caye

San
Ignacio

10

Belmopan

11

18

13

Hummingbird
Highway

Dangriga

12

Man-O'-War Caye

14

9

15

Southern
Highway

16

Punta
Gorda

GUATEMALA

KEY TO ECOREGIONS
1 Corozal coastal savannas
2 Northeast Belize: Shipstern lowlands
    and wetlands
3 Orange Walk agricultural lowlands
4 New River riparian watershed
5 Crooked Tree and Altun Ha
    coastal savannas and forests
6 Bravo Hills northern hardwood forests
7 Tikal northern hardwood forests
8 Belize and Sibun Rivers
9 Central coastal savannas, littoral
    forests, and Caribbean coast
10 Cayo western foothills
11 Cayo central lowlands and foothills
12 Stann Creek eastern foothills
13 Mountain Pine Ridge submontane
    forests
14 Southern submontane and montane
    forests
15 Toledo eastern foothills and
    submontane forests
16 Toledo southern lowlands & foothills
17 Ambergris Caye
18 The Cays

Sites: The Mennonite farmlands and rice fields along Gallon Jug Road, including Yo Creek, Trinidad, Gold Button Ranch, August Pine Ridge, San Felipe, Blue Creek Village, Tres Leguas, Edenthal-Neustadt. Also farmlands along Shipyard Road, including Guinea Grass and Shipyard.
Species: 287.

4. New River riparian watershed

Habitats: Predominantly lowland broadleaf forests (BFL1, BFL2, BFL3, BFL4); pine savannas (PFL); also agricultural (AG1, AG3), and a few villages (PC).
Elevation: 30–90 feet.
District: Orange Walk.
Sites: San Estevan, Honey Camp Road, Victor's Inn and Foodery, Honey Camp Lagoon, Goldson Highway and Old Northern Highway within Orange Walk District, New River, Lamanai, New River Lagoon, Dawson Creek, Rio Bravo Conservation Area near Hill Bank Field Station, Irish Creek.
Species: 415.

5. Crooked Tree and Altun Ha coastal savannas and forests

Habitats: Predominantly lowland pine and palmetto savannas (PFL), lagoons and creeks (LF2, BFL1, BFL2); also other broadleaf forest patches (BFL3), agricultural (AG1), and a few small villages (PC).
Elevation: 30–95 feet.
District: Belize.
Sites: Goldson Highway and Old Northern Highway within Belize District, Altun Ha, Crooked Tree Wildlife Sanctuary.
Species: 364.

6. Bravo Hills northern hardwood forests

Habitats: Predominantly High Ridge broadleaf forests (BFL5) including other broadleaf forest types (BFL1, BFL2, BFL3, BFL4); also agriculture at Gallon Jug and Spanish Lookout (AG3), two lodges/resorts, a groomed Maya site at El Pilar, and the sprawling town of Spanish Lookout (PC).
Elevation: Primarily 375–1,040 feet, but also including the lower portions of the Rio Bravo Conservation Area and Spanish Lookout down to 110 feet.
Districts: Orange Walk and a portion of northwestern Cayo.
Sites: Rio Bravo Conservation Area near La Milpa, Laguna Seca, Gallon Jug, Chan Chich, Aguas Turbias National Park, El Pilar Maya site, Aguacate Lagoon, primary forests near Spanish Lookout, Yalbac Hills.
Species: 387.

7. Tikal northern hardwood forests

Habitats: Predominantly lowland broadleaf forests (BFL2, BFL3, BFL5); also a hotel and tourist area (PC). Large lake outside park boundary at El Remate.
Elevation: 800 feet.
District: Petén, Guatemala.

Sites: Tikal National Park, El Remate on shore of Lago Petén Itzá.
Species: 386.

CENTRAL BELIZE

8. Belize and Sibun Rivers riparian forests and coastal savannas

Habitats: Mixed lowland habitats including broadleaf forests (BFL1, BFL2, BFL3, BFL4) and pine/palmetto savannas (PFL); also agricultural (AG3, AG4, AG5) and villages and commercial areas (PC).
Elevation: 10–150 feet.
District: Belize.
Sites: Bermudian Landing, Double Head Cabbage, Community Baboon Sanctuary, Spanish Creek (Orange Walk District), Flowers Bank, Mussel Creek drainage, Belize River, Hattieville, Price Highway savanna and lowland sites, Big Falls Farm, Cox Lagoon, Coastal Highway (in part), Fresh Catch Belize Ltd. tilapia farm, Belize Zoo River Camp, Runaway Creek Nature Preserve (in part), Belize Zoo, Sibun River, Tropical Education Center, Monkey Bay Wildlife Sanctuary, Amigo's Restaurant, citrus groves, and Banana Bank Lodge.
Species: 415.

9. Central coastal savannas, littoral forests, and Caribbean coast

Habitats: Predominantly littoral forests (LF3) and lowland broadleaf forests (BFL1, BFL2, BFL3); extensive developed lands, scrub lands, and population centers at Belize City and Dangriga, as well as smaller villages and resorts (PC); also agriculture (AG4, AG5).
Elevation: 0–60 feet in northern parts, 0–150 feet in southern parts.
Districts: Belize and Stann Creek.
Sites: Goldson Highway within Belize District, Salt Creek Estates Road, Double Run, Belize City Bypass, Burrell Boom, Nova Ladyville, Captain Hook's Restaurant and Shrimp Farm, Ladyville, Philip Goldson International Airport, Belize City, Bird's Isle, Freetown, Coastal Highway (in part), Fresh Catch Belize Ltd. tilapia farm, Runaway Creek Nature Preserve (in part), Manatee Lagoons, Manatee Forest Reserve, Gales Point, Manatee Lodge, Paradise Shrimp Farms, Melinda, Pomona, ITVET, Marie Sharp lands, Stann Creek, Pelican Beach Resort, Dangriga, Dangriga airport and abandoned shrimp farms, Gra Gra Lagoon National Park, Old England, Hopkins Village, Kendal Bridge, Sittee River, Sittee River loop, Silk Grass Village, Croc O'dile Isle, Commerce Bight Forest Reserve (remnant portion), All Pines, All Pines shrimp ponds, Southern Highway (north portion), Maya Center, Mango Creek, Placencia Peninsula, Placencia.
Species: 467.

10. Cayo western foothills

Habitats: Predominantly broadleaf forests (BFF1) in the foothills of Maya Mountains; ornamental plantings at resorts and at twin cities of San Ignacio and Santa Elena (PC); also agricultural (AG3, AG4).

Elevation: 250–1,130 feet.

District: Cayo.

Sites: Caesar's Place, Barton Creek, Barton Creek Archaeological Site, portion of Belize River, Aguada Hotel, Maya Mountain Lodge, Cristo Rey, Crystal Paradise Resort, San Antonio, Maya Ranch, Green Hills Butterfly Farm, Mountain Equestrian Trails Lodge, Slate Creek Preserve, Elijo Panti National Park, San Ignacio, Santa Elena, San Ignacio Resort Hotel, Branchmouth Park, Cahal Pech Maya site, Bullet Tree Road, Log Cab-Inn Resort, Windy Hill Resort, Inglewood Camping Ground, Clarissa Falls resort, Macal River, Macal River Resorts Road, Black Rock Lodge, Ek' Tun, The Lodge at Chaa Creek, duPlooy's Jungle Lodge, Belize Botanic Gardens, Xunantunich Maya site, Mopan River Resort, Arenal Road, Hydro Road, Benque Viejo.

Species: 374.

11. Cayo central lowlands and foothills

Habitats: Predominantly broadleaf forest (BFL1, BFL2, BFL3, BFF1); extensive agricultural areas (AG4), residential areas (particularly Belmopan), and ornamental plantings at resorts (PC).

Elevation: 140–1,100 feet.

District: Cayo.

Sites: Beaver Dam Creek, Belmopan, CBC Belmopan, Guanacaste National Park, Roaring River, Teakettle Village, Actun Tunichil Muknal, Pook's Hill Lodge, Blue Hole National Park, Jaguar Creek, Caves Branch, Hummingbird Highway (west portion, Cayo District), Jaguar Paw, Five Blues Lake National Park.

Species: 373.

12. Stann Creek eastern foothills

Habitats: Predominantly broadleaf forests (BFL1, BFL3, BFF2); also submontane and cloud forest at Victoria Peak (PFM, BFM3), agricultural along road (AG4) and in foothills (AG3), and small villages (PC).

Elevation: primarily 250–700 feet, but also includes Victoria Peak at 3,675 feet.

District: Stann Creek.

Sites: Hummingbird Highway (Stann Creek foothill portion), Manatee Forest Reserve (upper portion), Middlesex, Billy Barquedier National Park, Davis Falls, ANRI (school), Southern Highway (north portion, Stann Creek District), Mayflower Bocawina National Park, Mama Noots Eco Resort, Cockscomb Basin Wildlife Sanctuary (including high elevations), Georgetown Road, Red Bank.

Species: 347.

13. Mountain Pine Ridge submontane forests

Habitats: Predominantly submontane pine forests and shrubland (PFM); also submontane broadleaf forests (BFM1) and ornamental plantings at resorts (PC).

Elevation: 1,050–3,346 feet.

District: Cayo.

Sites: Mountain Pine Ridge roads, particularly Chiquibul and Cooma Cairn roads, Mountain Pine Ridge Forestry Gate, Slate Creek Lookout Trail, Hidden Valley, Thousand Foot Falls, Bald Hills, 3,346-foot Baldy Beacon, Blancaneaux Lodge, Gaïa Riverlodge, Rio On, Rio Frio Caves, Douglas Da Silva. Also, 3,084-foot Mt. Margaret, accessed by hiking from Hummingbird Highway.

Species: 354.

SOUTHERN BELIZE

14. Southern submontane and montane forests

Habitats: Predominantly submontane broadleaf forests (BFM2); important patches of submontane pine forests (PFM) and a broadleaf riparian zone along the Macal River. Higher elevations are montane broadleaf forest and cloud forest (BFM3). The 1995 completion of Chalillo Dam and the 2,500-acre reservoir have introduced many aquatic-loving species such as pelicans, herons, and gulls, normally found in coastal areas.

Elevation: 1,400–2,200 feet for BFM2, but up to 3,688 feet for BFM3.

District: Cayo and border of Toledo.

Sites: Chiquibul Road (southern portion), Vaca Plateau, Guacamallo Bridge, Macal River (upper), Chalillo Reservoir, Caracol, Chiquibul National Forest, Chiquibul National Park, Mountain Cow, Natural Arch. Las Cuevas Research Station, Doyle's Delight.

Species: 358.

15. Toledo eastern foothills and submontane forests

Habitats: Accessible portions are mostly lowland broadleaf (BFL1, BFL2, BFL6) and pine (PFL) forests; restricted portions are foothill (BFF3) and submontane broadleaf forests (BFM); also a research camp (PC).

Elevation: 100–3,412 feet.

District: Toledo.

Sites: BFREE Protected Area, Bladen River Nature Reserve, Columbia River Forest Reserve including Little Quartz Ridge, at approximately 2,950 feet.

Species: 338.

16. Toledo southern lowlands and foothills

Habitats: In coastal areas, predominantly littoral forest (LF4) and lowland broadleaf forests (BFL1, BFL2, BFL3); population centers including Punta Gorda and small villages as well as ornamental plantings at resorts (PC); also limited agricultural (AG2, AG4). In foothills, predominantly broadleaf forest (BFL1, BFL3, BFL6, BFF3); also small villages (PC) and some agricultural (AG3).

Elevation: 0–1,050 feet.

District: Toledo.

Sites: Lowland sites include: Southern Highway (south portion, Toledo District), Las Sierritas, Nova-Toledo, Aqua Mar Shrimp Farm, Monkey River, Payne's Creek National Park, Golden Stream Corridor, Medina Bank, Boden

Creek Reserve, Ycacos Lagoon, Big Falls, The Lodge at Big Falls, San Antonio Road lowlands, The Dump, Mafredi, Aguacaliente Wildlife Sanctuary, Jacinto Creek, Rio Grande, Toledo Settlement, Cuxlin Ha resort, Belcampo Belize, Wilson Road, Wilson Landing, Cattle Landing, Joe Taylor Creek, Punta Gorda, CBC Punta Gorda, Punta Gorda (Orange Point) marina, Falcon Forest, VoA Station, Boom Creek Road, Hickatee Cottages, Boom Creek Village, Santa Anna, Cotton Tree Lodge, Moho River, Barranco Road, Temash and Sarstoon Delta Wildlife Sanctuary. Foothill sites include: Nim Li Punit Maya site, Lubaantun Maya site, San Pedro Columbia, Belize Agroforestry Research Center, Blue Creek Cave and Village, Blue Creek River, San Antonio, Santa Cruz, Rio Blanco National Park, Pueblo Viejo, Pueblo Viejo Falls, San Jose Village, Jalacte.

Species: 482, the highest count among the ecoregions.

THE CAYS

17. Ambergris Caye

Habitats: Mostly a population and resort community (PC); littoral forests (LF1). More like a long peninsula than an island, its bird population is different and more extensive than those on other cays.

Elevation: 0–8 feet.

District: Belize.

Site: Ambergris Caye, Bacalar Chico National Park, Hol Chan Nature Reserve.

Species: 274.

18. Other cays

Habitats: Predominantly littoral forests (LF1); major resort community on Caye Caulker (PC).

Elevation: 0–12 feet.

District: Belize, Stann Creek, and Toledo.

Sites: Shipstern Caye, Caye Caulker, Caye Chapel, Wee Wee Caye, Glover's Reef, Turneffe Atoll, Half Moon Caye, Northern Two Cayes, Tobacco Cayes, Man-O'-War Caye, Coco Plum Caye, South Water Caye, Calabash Caye, Silk Cayes, Laughing Bird Caye, Hunting Caye, Lime Caye, Frank's Caye, Sapodilla Cayes, the Inner Channel and other barrier reef cays and waterways.

Species: 255.

APPENDIX B
MAMMALS, REPTILES, AND AMPHIBIANS OF BELIZE

MAMMALS

Opossums Didelphidae
Common Opossum *Didelphis marsupialis*
Virginia Opossum *Didelphis virginiana*
Gray Four-eyed Opossum *Philander opossum*
Water Opossum *Chironectes minimus*
Mexican Mouse Opossum *Marmosa mexicana*
Robinson's Mouse Opossum *Marmosa robinsoni*
Alston's Mouse Opossum *Micoureus alstoni*
Central American Woolly Opossum
 Caluromys derbianus
American Anteaters
 Myrmecophagidae
Giant Anteater *Myrmecophaga tridactyla*
Northern Tamandua *Tamandua mexicana*
Silky Anteater *Cyclopes didactylus*
Armadillos Dasypodidae
Northern Naked-tailed Armadillo
 Cabassous centralis
Nine-banded Armadillo *Dasypus novemcinctus*
Shrews Soricidae
Least Shrew *Cryptotis parva*
Maya Small-eared Shrew *Cryptotis mayensis*
Sac-winged Bats Emballonuridae
Proboscis Bat *Rhynchonycteris naso*
Greater White-lined Bat *Saccopteryx bilineata*
Lesser White-lined Bat *Saccopteryx leptura*
Shaggy Bat *Centronycteris maximiliani*
Lesser Doglike Bat *Peropteryx macrotis*
Greater Doglike Bat *Peropteryx kappleri*
Lesser Sac-winged Bat *Balantiopteryx io*
Northern Ghost Bat *Diclidurus albus*
Fishing or Bulldog Bats Noctilionidae
Greater Fishing Bat *Noctilio leporinus*
Leaf-chinned Bats Mormoopidae
Ghost-faced Bat *Mormoops megalophylla*
Common Mustached Bat *Pteronotus parnellii*
Lesser Mustached Bat *Pteronotus personatus*
Davy's Naked-backed Bat *Pteronotus davyi*
Big Naked-backed Bat *Pteronotus gymnonotus*
Leaf-nosed Bats Phyllostomidae
Common Big-eared Bat *Micronycteris microtis*
Schmidts's Big-eared Bat
 Micronycteris schmidtorum
Orange-throated Bat *Lampronycteris brachyotis*
Niceforo's Bat *Trinycteris nicefori*
Common Sword-nosed Bat *Lonchorhina aurita*
Long-legged Bat *Macrophyllum macrophyllum*
Stripe-headed Round-eared Bat
 Tonatia saurophila
Pygmy Round-eared Bat *Lophostoma brasiliense*

Davis's Round-eared Bat *Lophostoma evotis*
Golden Bat *Mimon bennettii*
Striped Hairy-nosed Bat *Mimon crenulatum*
Pale Spear-nosed Bat *Phyllostomus discolor*
Greater Spear-nosed Bat *Phyllostomus hastatus*
Pale-faced Bat *Phylloderma stenops*
Fringe-lipped Bat *Trachops cirrhosus*
Woolly False Vampire Bat *Chrotopterus auritus*
Great False Vampire Bat *Vampyrum spectrum*
Common Long-tongued Bat
 Glossophaga soricina
Brown Long-tongued Bat
 Glossophaga commissarisi
Dark Long-tongued Bat *Lichonycteris obscura*
Underwood's Long-tongued Bat
 Hylonycteris underwoodi
Silky Short-tailed Bat *Carollia sowelli*
Seba's Short-tailed Bat. *Carollia perspicillata*
Little Yellow-shouldered Bat *Sturnira lilium*
Great Fruit-eating Bat *Artibeus lituratus*
Intermediate Fruit-eating Bat
 Artibeus intermedius
Jamaican Fruit-eating Bat *Artibeus jamaicensis*
Toltec Fruit-eating Bat *Artibeus toltecus*
Pygmy Fruit-eating Bat *Artibeus phaeotis*
Thomas's Fruit-eating Bat *Artibeus watsoni*
Common Tent-making Bat *Uroderma bilobatum*
Heller's Broad-nosed Bat *Platyrrhinus helleri*
Great Stripe-faced Bat *Vampyrodes caraccioli*
Hairy Big-eyed Bat *Chiroderma villosum*
Little Yellow-eared Bat *Vampyressa pusilla*
Wrinkle-faced Bat *Centurio senex*
Common Vampire Bat *Desmodus rotundus*
Hairy-legged Vampire Bat *Diphylla ecaudata*
Funnel-eared Bats Natalidae
Mexican Funnel-eared Bat *Natalus stramineus*
Disk-winged Bats Thyropteridae
Spix's Disk-winged Bat *Thyroptera tricolor*
Plain-nosed Bats Vespertilionidae
Elegant Myotis *Myotis elegans*
Hairy-legged Myotis *Myotis keaysi*
Argentine Brown Bat *Eptesicus furinalis*
Central American Yellow Bat *Rhodeessa tumida*
Van Gelder's Bat *Bauerus dubiaquercus*
Western Red Bat *Lasiurus blossevillii*
Northern Yellow Bat *Lasiurus intermedius*
Southern Yellow Bat *Lasiurus ega*
Free-tailed Bats Molossidae
Broad-eared Bat *Nyctinomops laticaudatus*
Black Bonneted Bat *Eumops auripendulus*
Underwood's Bonneted Bat
 Eumops underwoodi

Wagner's Bonneted Bat *Eumops glaucinus*
Dwarf Bonneted Bat *Eumops bonariensis*
Black Mastiff Bat *Molossus ater*
Sinaloan Mastiff Bat *Molossus sinaloae*
Little Mastiff Bat *Molossus molossus*
Monkeys Cebidae
Yucatan Black Howler *Alouatta pigra*
Central American Spider Monkey
    Ateles geoffroyi
Squirrels Sciuridae
Yucatan Squirrel *Sciurus yucatanensis*
Deppe's Squirrel *Sciurus deppei*
Gophers Geomyidae
Hispid Pocket Gopher *Orthogeomys hispidus*
Pocket Mice Heteromyidae
Gaumer's Spiny Pocket Mouse
    Heteromys gaumeri
Forest Spiny Pocket Mouse
    Heteromys desmarestianus
Rats and Mice Muridae
Coues' Rice Rat *Oryzomys couesi*
Rusty Rice Rat *Oryzomys rostratus*
Alfaro's Rice Rat *Oryzomys alfaroi*
Northern Pygmy Rice Rat *Oligoryzomys fulvescens*
Hispid Cotton Rat *Sigmodon hispidus*
Northern Climbing Rat *Tylomys nudicaudus*
Big-eared Climbing Rat *Ototylomys phyllotis*
Vesper Rat *Nyctomys sumichrasti*
Yucatan Vesper Rat *Otonyctomys hatti*
Slender Harvest Mouse *Reithrodontomys gracilis*
Mexican Deer Mouse *Peromyscus mexicanus*
Porcupines Erethizontidae
Mexican Porcupine *Sphiggurus mexicanus*
Agoutis Dasyproctidae
Central American Agouti *Dasyprocta punctata*
Pacas Agoutidae
Paca *Agouti paca*
Rabbits and Hares Leporidae
Forest Rabbit *Sylvilagus brasiliensis*
Dogs and Foxes Canidae
Gray Fox *Urocyon cinereoargenteus*
Raccoons Procyonidae
Cacomistle *Bassariscus sumichrasti*
Northern Raccoon *Procyon lotor*
White-nosed Coati *Nasua narica*
Kinkajou *Potos flavus*
Weasels, Skunks, and Allies Mustelidae
Long-tailed Weasel *Mustela frenata*
Greater Grison *Galictis vittata*
Tayra *Eira barbara*
Spotted Skunk *Spilogale putorius*
Striped Hog-nosed Skunk *Conepatus semistriatus*
Neotropical River Otter *Lutra longicaudis*
Cats Felidae
Ocelot *Leopardus pardalis*
Margay *Leopardus wiedii*

Jaguarundi *Puma yaguarondi*
Puma *Puma concolor*
Jaguar *Panthera onca*
Manatees Trichechidae
West Indian Manatee *Trichechus manatus*
Tapirs Tapiridae
Baird's Tapir *Tapirus bairdii*
Peccaries Tayassuidae
Collared Peccary *Tayassu tajacu*
White-lipped Peccary *Tayassu pecari*
Deer Cervidae
White-tailed deer *Odocoileus virginianus*
Red Brocket *Mazama americana*
Ocean Dolphins Delphinidae
Atlantic Spotted Dolphin *Stenella frontalis*
Bottle-nosed Dolphin *Tursiops truncatus*
Sperm Whales Physteridae
Great Sperm Whale *Physeter catodon*
Beaked Whales Ziphidae
Blainville's Beaked Whale
    Mesoplodon densirostris

REPTILES

Crocodiles Crocodylidae
American Crocodile *Crocodylus acutus*
Morelet's Crocodile *Crocodylus moreletii*
Alligator Lizards Anguidae
Rozella's Lesser Galliwasp *Celestus rozellae*
Boas and Pythons Boidae
Boa Constrictor *Boa constrictor*
Typical Snakes Colubridae
Middle American Earth Snake
    Adelphicos quadrivirgatus
Rustyhead Snake *Amastridium veliferum*
Mussurana *Clelia clelia*
Mexican Snake Eater *Clelia scytalina*
Racer *Coluber constrictor*
Two-spotted Snake *Coniophanes bipunctatus*
White-lipped Spotbelly Snake
    Coniophanes fissidens
Black-striped Snake *Coniophanes imperialis*
Schmidt's Black-striped Snake
    Coniophanes schmidti
Road Guarder *Conophis lineatus*
Black-naped Forest Racer
    Dendrophidion nuchale
Barred Forest Racer *Dendrophidion vinitor*
Snail-eating Thirst Snake *Dipsas brevifacies*
Lizard Eater *Dryadophis melanolomus*
Indigo Snake *Drymarchon corais*
Speckled Racer *Drymobius margaritiferus*
Tropical Rat Snake *Elaphe flavifura*
Blotched Hooknose Snake *Ficimia publia*
Blunthead Tree Snake *Imantodes cenchoa*
Milk Snake *Lampropeltis triangulum*
Rain Forest Cat-eyed Snake *Leptodeira frenata*

Central American Cat-eyed Snake
  Leptodeira septentrionalis
Parrot Snake *Leptophis ahaetulla*
Mexican Parrot Snake *Leptophis mexicanus*
Turneffe Parrot Snake
  Leptophis mexicanus hoeversi
Neotropical Whipsnake
  Masticophis mentovarius
Ringneck Coffee Snake *Ninia diademata*
Redback Coffee Snake *Ninia sebae*
Mexican Vine Snake *Oxybelis aeneus*
Green Vine Snake *Oxybelis fulgidus*
Calico False Coral Snake *Oxyrhopus petola*
Puffing Snake *Pseustes poecilinotus*
none *Rhadinaea anachoreta*
Adorned Graceful Brown Snake
  Rhadinaea decorata
Guatemalan Neckband Snake
  Scaphiodontophis annulatus
Peninsular Rat Snake *Senticolis triaspis*
Slender Snail Sucker *Sibon dimidiatus*
Cloudy Snail Sucker *Sibon nebulata*
Pygmy Snail Sucker *Sibon sanniolus*
Terrestrial Snail Sucker *Sibon sartorii*
Tiger Tree Snake *Spilotes pullatus*
Degenhardt's Scorpion-eating Snake
  Stenorrhina degenhardtii
Freminville's Scorpion-eating Snake
  Stenorrhina freminvillii
Yucatan White-lipped Snake *Symphimus mayae*
Yucatan Centipede Snake *Tantilla cuniculator*
Red Earth Centipede Snake *Tantilla schistosa*
Yucatan Dwarf Short-tailed Snake
  Tantillita canula
Linton's Dwarf Short-tailed Snake
  Tantillita lintoni
Checkered Garter Snake
  Thamnophis marcianus
Western Ribbon Snake *Thamnophis proximus*
Orangebelly Swamp Snake
  Tretanorhinus nigroluteus
False Coral Snake *Urotheca elapoides*
False Terciopelo *Xenodon rabdocephalus*
Casque-headed Lizards Corytophanidae
Striped or Brown Basilisk *Basiliscus vittatus*
Smoothhead Helmeted Basilisk
  Corytophanes cristatus
Hernandez's Helmeted Basilisk
  Corytophanes hernandezii
Eastern Casquehead Iguana
  Laemanctus longipes
Serrated Casquehead Iguana
  Laemanctus serratus
Coral Snakes Elaphidae
Variable Coral Snake *Micrurus diastema*
Maya Coral Snake *Micrurus hippocrepis*
Central American Coral Snake
  Micrurus nigrocinctus

Banded Geckos Eublepharidae
Yucatan Banded Gecko *Coleonyx elegans*
Geckos Gekkonidae
Saint George Island Gecko
  Aristelliger georgeensis
Gecko *Gekko gecko*
Yellowhead Gecko *Gonatodes albogularis*
House Gecko *Hemidactylus frenatus*
Island Leaf-toed Gecko *Phyllodactylus insularis*
Tuberculate Leaf-toed Gecko
  Phyllodactylus tuberculosus
Dwarf Gecko *Sphaerodactylus glaucus*
Spotted Gecko
  Sphaerodactylus millepunctuatus
Turnip Tail *Thecadactylus rapicauda*
Spectacled Lizards Gymnophthalmidae
Golden Spectacled Lizard
  Gymnophthalmus speciosus
Iguanas Iguanidae
Black Iguana *Ctenosaura similis*
Green Iguana *Iguana iguana*
Thread Snakes Leptotyphlopidaee
Black Blind Snake *Leptotyphlops goudoti*
Spiny Lizards Phrynosomatidae
Yucatan Spiny Lizard *Sceloporus chrysostictus*
Lundell's Spiny Lizard *Sceloporus lundelli*
Blue-spotted Spiny Lizard *Sceloporus serrifer*
Rosebelly Lizard *Sceloporus variabilis*
Anoles Polychrotidae
Allison's Anole *Anolis allisoni*
Green Anole *Anolis carolinensis*
Neotropical Green Anole *Norops biporcatus*
Bighead Anole *Norops capito*
Ghost Anole *Norops lemurinus*
Lichen Anole *Norops pentaprion*
Smooth Anole *Norops rodriguezii*
Brown Anole *Norops sagrei*
Silky Anole *Norops sericeus*
Greater Scaly Anole *Norops tropidonotus*
Lesser Scaly Anole *Norops uniformis*
Skinks Scincidae
Schwartze's Skink *Eumeces schwartzei*
Sumicrast's Skink *Eumeces sumichrasti*
Central American Mabuya *Mabuya unimarginata*
Brown Forest Skink
  Sphenomorphus cherriei
Whip-tailed Lizards Teiidae
Middle American Ameiva *Ameiva festiva*
Rainbow Ameiva *Ameiva undulata*
Yucatan Whiptail *Aspidoscelis angusticeps*
Maslin's Whiptail *Aspidoscelis maslini*
Striped Racerunner *Cnemidophorus lemniscatus*
Blind Snakes Typhlopidae
Brahminy blind snake *Ramphotyphlops braminus*
Yucatecan Blind Snake *Typhlops microstomus*

Pit Vipers and Rattlesnakes Viperidae
Cantil *Agkistrodon bilineatus*
Jumping Pitviper *Atropoides nummifer*
Eyelash Palm-Pitviper *Bothriechis schlegelii*
Fer-de-Lance *Bothrops asper*
Neotropical Rattlesnake *Crotalus durissus*
Rainforest Hognose Pitviper *Porthidium nasutum*
Night Lizards Xantusidae
Yellow-spotted Night Lizard
  Lepidophyma flavimaculatum
Maya Night Lizard *Lepidophyma mayae*
Hard-shelled Sea Turtles Cheloniidae
Loggerhead *Caretta caretta*
Green Turtle *Chelonia mydas*
Hawksbill *Eretmochelys imbricata*
Snapping Turtles Chelydridae
Snapping Turtle *Chelydra serpentina*
Central American River Turtles
Dermatemydidae
Central American River Turtle
  Dermatemys mawii
Leatherback Sea Turtle Dermochelyidae
Leatherback *Dermochelys coriacea*
Wood Turtles and Sliders Emydidae
Furrowed Wood Turtle *Rhinoclemmys areolata*
Meso-American Slider
  Trachemys venusta venusta
Mud and Musk Turtles Kinosteridae
Narrowbridge Musk Turtle *Claudius angustatus*
Tabasco Mud Turtle *Kinosternon acutum*
White-lipped Mud Turtle
  Kinosternon leucostomum
Scorpion Mud Turtle *Kinosternon scorpioides*
Mexican Giant Musk Turtle
  Staurotypus triporcatus

AMPHIBIANS

Craugastoridae
none *Craugastor rostralis*
Toads Bufonidae
Campbell's Rainforest Toad *Incilius campbelli*
Gulf Coast Toad *Incilius valliceps*
Cane Toad *Rhinella marinus*
Glass Frogs Centrolenidae
Fleischmann's Glass Frog
  Hyalinobatrachium fleischmanni
Tree Frogs Hylidae
Red-eyed Treefrog *Agalychnis callidryas*
Morelet's Treefrog *Agalychnis moreletii*
Bromeliad Treefrog *Bromeliohyla bromeliacia*
Yellow Treefrog *Dendropsophus microcephala*
Fringe-limbed Treefrog *Ecnomiohyla minera*

Hourglass Treefrog *Hyla ebraccata*
Stauffer's Treefrog *Scinax staufferi*
Common Mexican Treefrog *Smilisca baudini*
Blue-spotted Mexican Treefrog
  Smilisca cyanosticta
Mahogany (Loquacious) Treefrog
  Tlalocohyla loquax
Painted Treefrog *Tlalocohyla picta*
Veined Treefrog *Trachycephalus venulosus*
Yucatecan Casquehead Treefrog
  Triprion petasatus
Rain Frogs Leptodactylidae
Alfred's Rain Frog *Craugastor alfredi*
Chac's Rainfrog *Craugastor chac*
Broadhead Rainfrog *Craugastor laticeps*
Limestone Rainfrog *Craugastor psephosypharus*
Polymorphic Robber Frog *Craugastor rhodopsis*
none *Craugastor sabrinus*
Sanderson's Rainfrog *Craugastor sandersoni*
Leprus Chirping Frog *Eleutherodactylus leprus*
Tungara Frog *Engystomops pustulosus*
White-lipped Frog *Leptodactylus fragilis*
Sabinal Frog *Leptodactylus melanonotus*
Sheep Frogs Microhylidae
Elegant Narrowmouth Toad
  Gastrophryne elegans
Sheep Frog *Hypopachus variolosus*
True Frogs Ranidae
Rio Grande Leopard Frog *Lithobates berlandieri*
Maya Mountain Frog *Lithobates juliani*
Vaillant's Frog *Lithobates vaillanti*
Burrowing Toads Rhinophrynidae
Burrowing Toad *Rhinophrynus dorsalis*
Lungless Salamanders Plethodontidae
Doflein's Mushroomtongue Salamander *Bolitoglossa dofleini*
Mexican Mushroomtongue Salamander *Bolitoglossa mexicana*
Southern Banana Salamander
  Bolitoglossa occidentalis
O'Donnell's Salamander *Bolitoglossa odonnelli*
Northern Banana Salamander
  Bolitoglossa rufescens
Yucatan Mushroomtongue Salamander
  Bolitoglossa yucatana
Central American Worm Salamander
  Oedipina elongata
Caecilians Caecilidae
Mountain Caecilian *Gymnopis syntrema*

Sources:
– Beletsky (2005) for mammals
– www.biodiversity.bz for reptiles and amphibians

APPENDIX C
REFERENCES

Anonymous. *Chaa Creek Nature Reserve Bird List.*
www.chaacreek.com/tours-activities/onsite/bird-watching/new-page/.

Anonymous. *Cockscomb Basin Wildlife Sanctuary Checklist.* Belize Audubon Society. Unpublished report.

Anonymous. *St. Herman's Blue Hole National Park Checklist.* Belize Audubon Society. Unpublished report.

Anonymous. *Windy Hill Resort Bird Checklist.* Unpublished report.

Anonymous. 2000. *Hidden Valley Inn Checklist of the Birds of Belize.* Unpublished report.

Anonymous. 2006. *Pook's Hill Checklist for the Birds of Belize.*
www.pookshilllodge.com/birding.html.

Anonymous. 2006. *The Lodge at Big Falls Birding.*
www.thelodgeatbigfalls.com/birding.php

Anonymous. 2011. *Lamanai Outpost Lodge Bird List.*
www.lamanai.com/PDF/lol-bird-checklist.pdf

Barcott, B. 2008. *The Last Flight of the Scarlet Macaw – One Woman's Fight to Save the World's Most Beautiful Bird.* Random House, New York.

Barlow, J.C, J.A. Dick, and E. Pendergast. 1970. Additional records of birds from British Honduras (Belize). *Condor,* 72(3):371–372.

Bayly, N., and C. Gomez. 2008. *Evaluating a Stepping Stone for Neotropical Migratory Birds – the Belizean North-east Biological Corridor.* The Rufford Small Grants Foundation. www.ruffordsmallgrants.org/rsg/projects/nicholas_bayly

Beavers, R.A. 1992. *The Birds of Tikal.* Texas A&M University Press, College Station.

Beletsky, L. 2005. *Belize & Northern Guatemala (Travellers' Wildlife Guides).* Interlink Books, Northampton.

Beveridge, D., J. Beveridge, K.J. Johnson, J. Lumb, A. Perez, and N. White. 1999. *A Guide to The Birds of Caye Caulker.* Published for the Caye Caulker Branch, Belize Tourism Industry Association, by Producciones de la Hamaca, Caye Caulker.

Carr, C. 2009. *Banana Bank Bird Checklist.*
www.wix.com/bananabank/birding

Clark, W.S, H.L. Jones, C.D. Benesh, and N.J. Schmitt. 2006. Field identification of the Solitary Eagle. *Birding* 38:66–74.

Crawford, G., D. Francisco, J. Hammond, E. Pop, E. Saqui, and J. Saqui. *Birds of Cockscomb Basin Wildlife Sanctuary.* Unpublished report.

duPlooy, K., S.N.G. Howell, and P. Mai. *duPlooy's Bird Checklist, within 5 Miles.* Unpublished report.

eBird. 2012. eBird: An online database of bird distribution and abundance [web application]. Version 3. eBird, Ithaca. www.ebird.org.

Eisermann, K., and C. Avendaño. 2007. *Annotated Checklist of the Birds of Guatemala.* Lynx Edicions, Barcelona.

England, M.C. 2000. The landbird monitoring programme at Lamanai, Belize: a preliminary assessment. *Cotinga* 13:32–43.

Figueroa, O.A., W. Martinez, M. Teul, G. Albanese, and V. Piaskowski. 2004. Additional notes on eight bird species from Belize. *Cotinga* 21:31–33.

Garel, T., and S. Matola. 1995. *A Field Guide to the Snakes of Belize.* The Belize Zoo and Tropical Education Center, Belize City.

Gentle, L. 2005. *Birds of the Vaca Area.* Tunich-Nah Consultants, Belize. Unpublished report.

Howell, S.N.G., B.A. Dowell, D.A. James, R.A. Behrstock, and C. S. Robbins. 1992. New and noteworthy bird records from Belize. *Bull. B.O.C.* 112(4):235–244.

Howell, S.N.G. and S. Webb. 1995. *A Guide to the Birds of Mexico and Northern Central America.* Oxford University Press, New York.

Johnson, R.R., and L.T. Haight. 2011. Biology and status of the Black Catbird (*Melanoptila glabrirostris*) in Belize. *The Wilson Journal of Ornithology* 123(2):229–232.

Jones, H.L. 1999. *Paradise Shrimp Farm Bird List 1998–1999.* Personal communication.

Jones, H.L. 2001. *Nova Toledo Shrimp Farm Bird List 1999–2001.* Personal communication.

Jones, H.L. 2003. *Birds of Belize.* University of Texas Press, Austin.

Jones, H.L. 2005. *Birds of Blue Hole and Caves Branch 1997–2005.* Personal communication.

Jones, H.L. 2006. *Birds of Boom Creek Road.* Personal communication.

Jones, H.L. 2006. *Nova Ladyville Shrimp Farm Bird List 1996–2006.* Personal communication.

Jones, H.L. 2006. *Salt Creek Estates Road Bird List 1996–2006.* Personal communication.

Jones, H.L. 2006. *Birds of Voice of America Property 1996–2006.* Personal communication.

Jones, H.L. 2007. *Aqua Mar Shrimp Farm Bird List 1997–2007.* Personal communication.

Jones, H.L. 2007. *Birds of Aguacaliente Swamp 1996–2007.* Personal communication.

Jones, H.L. 2007. *Birds of Wilson Landing/Machaca Hill 1992–2007.* Personal communication.

Jones, H.L. 2007. *Birds of Mayflower Bocawina National Park 1998–2007.* Personal communication.

Jones, H.L. 2007. *Birds of The Dump 1992-2007.* Personal communication.

Jones, H.L. 2007. *Crooked Tree Wildlife Sanctuary Bird List 1996–2007.* Personal communication.

Jones, H.L. 2007. *Cockscomb Basin Wildlife Sanctuary Bird List 1997–2007.* Personal communication.

Jones, H.L. 2007. *Birds of Fireburn 2007.* Personal communication.

Jones, H.L. 2001–2011. The regional reports, Central America. *North American Birds* Volumes 55–65.

Jones, H.L., P. Balderamos, J. and A. Caulfield, G. Crawford, T.M. Donegan, E. McRae, M. Meadows, M. Muschamp, P. Saqui, V. van der Spek, J. Urbina, and B. Zimmer. 2002. Fourteen new bird species for Belize. *Cotinga* 17:33–42.

Jones, H.L., E. McRae, M. Meadows, and S.N.G. Howell. 2000. Status updates for selected bird species in Belize, including several previously undocumented from the country. *Cotinga* 13:17–31.

Jones, H.L., and A.C. Vallely. 2001. *Annotated Checklist of The Birds of Belize.* Lynx Edicions, Barcelona.

Jones, I.L., T. Fitzgerald, and P. Taylor. 2008. *Annotated Checklist of Birds of the Vicinity of Las Cuevas Research Station, Chiquibul Forest Reserve, Belize.* Unpublished report.

Jones, L., and D. Gardner. 1997. Bird species recorded in the vicinity of Little Quartz Ridge, 10–24 February 1997, pp. 71–77 in: J.C. Meerman and S. Matola, eds. *The Columbia River Forest Reserve – Little Quartz Ridge Expedition – A Biological Assessment.*
www.biological-diversity.info/Downloads/CUP0060%20LQR%20Report%20v8_s.pdf

Laesser, J. 2007. *Birds of Shipstern Nature Reserve and the Sartenejan region, Census 2002–2003.*
www.shipstern.org/CMS/default.asp?ID=152&Language=EN

McRae, E.M. 1995. Bird survey, pp. 73–85. In: *Monkey River Special Development Area, Biodiversity Study.* J.C. Meerman, ed. Belize Tropical Forest Studies Publication #5.
www.biodiversity.bz/find/resource/profile.phtml?dcid=41541

Matola, S. 1991. Bird species recorded from the Columbia River Forest Reserve, pp. 35–37. In: *The Columbia River Forest Reserve Expedition 9–16 December 1990.*
www.biodiversity.bz/find/resource/profile.phtml?dcid=112844

Meerman, J.C. 1993. Checklist of the birds of the Shipstern Nature Reserve. *Occasional Papers of The Belize Natural History Society* 2:70–82.
www.shipstern.org/documents/showFile.asp?ID=1849

Meerman, J.C. 1995. Western Long Caye, Glover's Atoll, Terrestrial biological survey. *Belize Tropical Forest Studies Publication #4.*
www.biodiversity.bz/find/resource/profile.phtml?dcid=102540

Meerman, J.C. 1996. *Checklist – Birds of Slate Creek Preserve.* Personal communication.

Meerman, J.C. 1998. Bird species list, pp. 36–40. In: *Rapid Ecological Assessment – El Pilar Archaeological Reserve.*
www.biodiversity.bz/find/resource/profile.phtml?dcid=54344

Meerman, J.C. 1999. Bird species list, pp. 27–31. In: *Rapid Ecological Assessment – Runaway Creek Belize.*
www.biodiversity.bz/downloads/Runaway_Creek_REA.pdf

Meerman, J.C., B. Holland, A. Howe, H.L. Jones, and B.W. Miller. 2003. Birdlist of Mayflower Bocawina National Park pp. 2–30. In: *Rapid ecological assessment – Mayflower Bocawina National Park*, Volume II.
www.biodiversity.bz/find/resource/profile.phtml?dcid=267

Meerman, J.C., P. Herrera, and A. Howe. 2003. Birdlist, pp. 44–55. In: *Rapid Ecological Assessment – Sarstoon-Temash National Park, Toledo District, Belize, Volume II.* www.biodiversity.bz/find/resource/profile.phtml?dcid=273

Meerman, J.C., A. Howe, S. Choco, A. Act, E. Choc, S. Kok, and A. Muku. 2006. Species lists, pp. 78–85. In: *Rapid Ecological Assessment – Aguacaliente Wildlife Sanctuary.* www.biodiversity.bz/find/resource/profile.phtml?dcid=54916

Meerman, J.C., and S. Matola. 2007. *The August 2004, Expedition to Doyle's Delight.* Draft report June 2007. www.biodiversity.bz/find/resource/profile.phtml?dcid=91784

Meerman, J.C., and R. Wilson. 2006. Appendix 9. Species list, pp. 104-109. In: *Gra Gra Lagoon National Park Management Plan 2006.* http://biological-diversity.info/Downloads/GraGra_ManagementPlan_2006s.pdf

Miller, B.W. 1966. New information on the status and distribution of Keel-billed Motmot in Belize, Central America. *Cotinga* 6:61–63.

Miller, B.W., and C.M. Miller. 1994. *Avian Studies in the Upper Mullins River Basin, Feb. and May.* Appendix I. Species List – Birds. Report to Forest Department. Unpublished report.

Miller, B.W., and C.M. Miller. 1995. *Avian Surveys: Half Moon Caye Natural Monument.* Belize Audubon Society. Unpublished report.

Miller, B.W., and C.M. Miller. 2006. *A Waterbird Assessment for Belize.* Wildlife Conservation Society Technical Report. www.biodiversity.bz/find/resource/profile.phtml?dcid=54402

Miller, B.W., and C.M. Miller. 2006. *Exploring the Tropical Forest at Chan Chich Lodge Belize.* Producciones de la Hamaca, Caye Caulker, Belize.

Miller, B.W., and C.M. Miller. 2009. *A Checklist of Birds of the Gallon Jug Estate.* wwww.chanchich.com/activities-excursions/checklist.html.

Mills, E.D., and D.T. Rodgers Jr. 1990. Nearctic passerine fall migration in central Belize. *The Wilson Bulletin* 102(1):146–150.

Mills, E.D., and D.T. Rodgers Jr. 1992. Ratios of neotropical migrant and neotropical resident birds in winter in a citrus plantation in central Belize. *Journal of Field Ornithology., 63(2):109–116.*

Morgenthaler, A. 2003. *Ecology of the Black Catbird,* Melanoptila glabriirostris, *at Shipstern Nature Reserve (Belize), and Distribution in Yucatan.* www.shipstern.org/CMS/default.asp?ID=152&Language=EN

Morris, D. 1883. *The Colony of British Honduras.* Edward Stanford, London.

National Audubon Society. Bird Count (CBC) data for Gallon Jug, Belize City, Belmopan, and Punta Gorda. www.audubon.org/bird/CBC.

Paradise Expeditions tour guides and guests. 2007. *Crystal Paradise Bird Species Checklist.* www.crystalparadise.com/html/birdlist.pdf.

Parker III, T.A. 1993. Birds of the Columbia River Forest Reserve, pp. 21–23 and 71–79. In: Parker, T.A. III, B.K. Holst, L.H. Emmons, and J.R. Meyer. *A Biological Assessment of the Columbia River Forest Reserve, Toledo District, Belize.* www.conservation.org/Documents/RAP_Reports/RAP03_Toledo_Belize _Apr-1993.pdf

Piaskowski, V.D., M. Teul, R.N. Cal, K.M. Williams, and D. Tzul. 2006. *The Birds Without Borders – Aves Sin Fronteras, Recommendations for Landowners: How to Manage Your Land to Help Birds* (Belize and Mesoamerica edition). Foundation for Wildlife Conservation, Inc., and Zoological Society of Milwauke.
www.zoosociety.org/pdf/BWBPubs/BelizeLandownerManual.pdf

Piaskowski, V., O. Figueroa, M. Teul, M. Choco, W. Martinez, J. Ramos, M. Velasquez, and R. Manzanero. *A report for landowners on the bird species using the Chaa Creek and Tropical Education Center study sites from Nov. 1, 1997 – Feb. 13, 1998.* Foundation for Wildlife Conservation, Inc., and Zoological Society of Milwaukee.

Rabinowitz, A. 2000. *Jaguar: One Man's Struggle to Establish the World's First Jaguar Preserve.* Island Press, Washington, D.C.

Reid, F.A. 2009. *A Field Guide to the Mammals of Central America and Southeast Mexico.* Second edition. Oxford University Press, New York.

Rotenberg, J.A., J. Marlin, S. Meacham, and S. Tolfree. 2008. An integrated community-based Harpy Eagle and avian conservation program for the Maya Mountains massif, Belize, pp. 493–507. In: Rich, T.D., C. Arizmendi, D.W. Demarest, and C. Thompson, eds., *Tundra to Tropics: Connecting People to Habitats; Proceedings of the 4th International Partners in Flight Conference, 13–16 February 2008, McAllen, TX.* Partners in Flight.

Russell, S.M. 1964. A distributional study of the birds of British Honduras. American Ornithologists' Union, *Ornithological Monographs*, No. 1. American Ornithologists' Union, Washington, DC.

Russell, S.M. 1966. Status of the Black Rail and the Gray-breasted Crake in British Honduras. *Cotinga*, 69(1):105–107.

Schulz, J.H., and T. Chase. 2002. *Birding in Belize: The San Ignacio area.*
www.swarthmore.edu/go/isc/birds.doc

Smithe, F.B. 1966. *The Birds of Tikal.* The Natural History Press. Garden City, NY.

Smith, N., S.A. Mori, A. Henderson, D.W. Stevenson, and S.V. Heald, eds. 2003. *Flowering Plants of the Neotropics.* Princeton University Press, Princeton.

Smith, S.M. 2011. *Checklist of the Birds of the Gallon Jug Area and Chan Chich Lodge, Belize.*
http://dl.dropbox.com/u/3686717/Gallon_Jug_Birds_Checklist_2011.pdf

Vallely, A.C., and A.A. Whitman. 1997. The birds of Hill Bank, northern Belize. *Cotinga*, 8:39–49.

Walker, Z. 2010. Birds of north-east Belize. Personal communication.

Walker, Z. 2010. Half Moon Caye checklist. Personal communication.

Walker, Z., and P. Walker. 2006. Birds of Bladen Nature Reserve. In: *Bladen Nature Reserve Management Plan.* Bladen Management Consortium. Unpublished report.

INDEX OF BIRDING SITES

KEY: Page = page number
Gazetteer = site number on inside back-cover map
Ecoregion = numbered ecoregion (see pages 341–347)
Latitude and Longitude = GPS coordinates measured at or near site
OW = Orange Walk District; TO = Toledo District

Birding Sites	Page	Gazet- teer	Eco- region	Access	Latitude (N)	Longi- tude (W)
Actun Tunichil Muknal	109	48	11	Price Hwy.	17.22567	-88.85283
Aqua Mar Shrimp Farm	178	84	16	Southern Hwy.	16.49804	-88.43934
Aguacaliente Wildlife Sanctuary	216	98	16	Southern Hwy.	16.17452	-88.96720
Aguacate Lagoon	127	38	6	Price Hwy.	17.32278	-89.07412
All Pines shrimp ponds	178	72	9	Southern Hwy.	16.76800	-88.33898
Altun Ha Maya site	87	22	5	Goldson Hwy.	17.76670	-88.34630
Ambergris Caye	237	16	17	Barrier Reef & Cays	17.90933	-87.97262
Amigo's Restaurant	91	40	8	Price Hwy.	17.31888	-88.57055
Arenal Road	144	56	10	Hydro Rd.	17.03587	-89.12505
August Pine Ridge	51	15	3	Gallon Jug Rd.	17.97838	-88.72717
Bacalar Chico National Park	239	16	17	Barrier Reef & Cays	18.12118	-87.82795
Baldy Beacon	120	62	13	Cooma Cairn Rd.	17.00412	-88.79083
Banana Bank Lodge	108	41	11	Price Hwy.	17.28879	-88.77771
Barton Creek	92	46	10	Price Hwy.	17.20333	-88.95355
Barton Creek Archaeological Reserve	113	54	10	Chiquibul Rd.	17.13397	-88.96007
Beaver Dam Creek bridge	92	41	11	Price Hwy.	17.27705	-88.66652
Belcampo Belize	220	99	60	Southern Hwy.	16.16610	-88.81160
Belize Botanic Gardens	141	55	10	Macal River Resorts Rd	17.09582	-89.06938
Belize City	38	34	9	Goldson Hwy.	17.50512	-88.20242
Belize Lodge & Excursions CLOSED	206	86	16	Southern Hwy.	16.31695	-88.82392
Belize Zoo	95	37	8	Price Hwy.	17.35117	-88.55233
Belize Zoo River Camp	93	37	8	Coastal Hwy.	17.33918	-88.51527
BFREE Protected Area	201	82	15	Southern Hwy.	16.55525	-88.70627
Big Falls Farm	92	33	8	Price Hwy.	17.49217	-88.58950
Big Falls, TO	207	92	16	Southern Hwy.	16.26295	-88.88198
Billy Barquedier National Park	159	64	12	Hummingbird Hwy.	17.00027	-88.43151
Black Rock Lodge	139	60	10	Macal River Resorts Rd	17.04705	-89.06098
Bladen River Nature Reserve	201	80	15	Southern Hwy.	16.59920	-88.77932
Blancaneau Lodge	116	58	13	Chiquibul Rd.	17.03905	-88.95422
Blue Creek Cave & Village, TO	213	96	16	San Antonio Rd.	16.20077	-89.04578
Blue Creek rice fields, OW	51	18	3	Gallon Jug Rd.	17.89577	-88.90207
Blue Hole National Park, St. Herman's	160	50	11	Hummingbird Hwy.	17.14862	-88.69480
Boden Creek Reserve	206	86	16	Southern Hwy.	16.31695	-88.82392
Boom Creek Road	228	102	16	Southern Hwy.	16.09410	-88.81120
Boom Creek Village	228	102	16	Southern Hwy.	16.07519	-88.91158
Branchmouth Park	133	49	10	Price Hwy.	17.17692	-89.08015
Bullet Tree Road	134	49–44	10	Price Hwy.	17.15693	-89.07388
Caesar's Place	92	46	10	Price Hwy.	17.20333	-88.95355
Cahal Pech Maya site	131	49	10	Price Hwy.	17.14762	-89.07450
Capt. Hook's Restaurant/Shrimp Farm	103	29	9	Goldson Hwy.	17.56687	-88.29984
Caracol Archaeological Reserve	125	77	14	Chiquibul Rd.	16.76245	-89.11525
Caribbean Village RV	40	2	1	Goldson Hwy.	18.38322	-88.39602
Cattle Landing	222	101	16	Southern Hwy.	16.11537	-88.79820
Caves Branch Jungle Lodge	165	50	11	Hummingbird Hwy.	17.16485	-88.68358
Caye Caulker	240	24	18	Barrier Reef & Cays	17.74258	-88.02377
Caye Chapel	236	25	18	Barrier Reef & Cays	17.69680	-88.04210
Cerros Maya site	45	3	1	Barrier Reef & Cays	18.35430	-88.35433
Chaa Creek & Butterfly Preserve	140	55	10	Macal River Resorts Rd	17.10740	-89.07398
Chan Chich & Gallon Jug	62	32	6	Gallon Jug Rd.	17.53893	-89.11193
Chiquibul National Park	123	78	14	Chiquibul Rd.	16.73315	-88.98605
Chiquibul Road	112	46–81	13,14	Price Hwy.	17.19237	-88.98223
Clarissa Falls Resort	136	53	10	Price Hwy.	17.11108	-89.12700
Coastal Hwy. (N)	100	37	8	Price Hwy.	17.34245	-88.55457
Coastal Hwy. (S)	100	63	8	Hummingbird Hwy.	16.99765	-88.31473
Cockscomb Basin Wildlife Sanctuary	190	75	12	Southern Hwy.	16.78033	-88.45902
Coco Plum Caye	250	69	18	Barrier Reef & Cays	16.88072	-88.11805
Columbia River Forest Reserve	209	85	15	see San Jose Village	16.39639	-89.14194

Birding Sites	Page	Gazet-teer	Eco-region	Access	Latitude (N)	Longi-tude (W)
Commerce Bight Forest Reserve	177	70	9	Southern Hwy.	16.87090	-88.31138
Community Baboon Sanctuary	38	30	8	Belize City bypass	17.55567	-88.53470
Cooma Cairn Road	113	58–66	13	Chiquibul Rd.	17.05088	-88.94728
Copper Bank	45	6	1	Sarteneja Rd.	18.32153	-88.35542
Corozal beach property	42	2	1	Sarteneja Rd.	18.36250	-88.40008
Cotton Tree Lodge	230	102	16	Southern Hwy.	16.09937	-88.92865
Cox Lagoon	92	35	8	Price Hwy.	17.45282	-88.54250
Croc O'dile Isle	177	70	9	Southern Hwy.	16.87090	-88.31138
Crooked Tree Wildlife Sanctuary	81	21	5	Goldson Hwy.	17.77597	-88.53113
Crystal Paradise Resort	112	51	10	Price Hwy.	17.12687	-89.05861
Cuxlin Ha Resort	219	99	16	Southern Hwy.	16.16612	-88.84320
Dangriga	170	67	9	Hummingbird Hwy.	16.96593	-88.22218
Davis Falls	159	64	12	Hummingbird Hwy.	16.99033	-88.40287
Douglas Da Silva	120	66	13	Chiquibul Rd.	16.97038	-88.99190
Doyle's Delight	124	83	14	see Chiquibul N.P.	16.50000	-89.05000
duPlooy's Jungle Lodge	141	55	10	Macal River Resorts Rd	17.09582	-89.06938
Edenthal-Neustadt marshes	55	17	3	Gallon Jug Rd.	17.90152	-88.97513
El Pilar Maya site.	133	44	6	Price Hwy.	17.25062	-89.14367
El Remate, Guatemala	150	none	7	Tikal Hwy.	16.98555	-89.69205
Fireburn Nature Reserve	43	10	2	Sarteneja Rd.	18.20878	-88.19940
Five Blues Lake National Park	166	52	11	Hummingbird Hwy.	17.13248	-88.59787
Four Mile Lagoon, New River	42	2	1	Sarteneja Rd.	18.36578	-88.40150
Four Mile Lagoon, Rio Hondo	40	1	1	Goldson Hwy.	18.47118	-88.39898
Fresh Catch Belize, Ltd.	104	37	8	Coastal Hwy.	17.32442	-88.53719
Freshwater Creek Forest Reserve	68	11	2	Honey Camp Rd.	18.11667	-88.38333
Gaïa Riverlodge	116	58	13	Chiquibul Rd.	17.03857	-88.98425
Gales Point	105	47	9	Coastal Hwy.	17.17850	-88.33208
Gallon Jug Road	51	12–32	3,6	Goldson Hwy.	18.08148	-88.54848
Glover's Reef	235	76	18	Barrier Reef & Cays	16.76389	-87.82500
Gra Gra Lagoon National Park	173	67	9	Hummingbird Hwy.	16.94777	-88.22405
Green Hills Butterfly Ranch	113	54	10	Chiquibul Rd.	17.09867	-88.97165
Guacamallo Bridge	123	71	14	Chiquibul Rd.	16.86545	-89.03850
Guanacaste National Park	106	42	11	Price Hwy.	17.26150	-88.78723
Half Moon Caye	245	45	18	Barrier Reef & Cays	17.20518	-87.53753
Hickatee Cottages	228	102	16	Southern Hwy.	16.09000	-88.83443
Hidden Valley Inn	117	59	13	Cooma Cairn Rd.	17.04930	-88.90002
Hill Bank Field Station	78	28	4	Goldson Hwy.	17.60142	-88.70075
Honey Camp Lagoon	67	13	4	Honey Camp Rd.	18.04947	-88.43207
Honey Camp Road	67	12–13	4	Goldson Hwy.	18.08150	-88.54850
Hopkins Village	187	72	9	Southern Hwy.	16.86337	-88.28458
Hydro Road	144	56–65	10	Price Hwy.	17.07092	-89.13893
Irish Creek	79	28	4	see Hill Bank	17.60002	-88.72433
ITVET at Stann Creek	159	63	9	Hummingbird Hwy.	16.99695	-88.31650
Jacinto Creek	219	99	16	Southern Highway	16.16528	-88.80805
Jaguar Creek Ministries	164	50	11	Hummingbird Hwy.	17.16142	-88.68003
Jalacte forest	208	97	16	San Antonio Rd.	16.18820	-89.17832
Jimmy Cut	208	88	16	San Antonio Rd.	16.29162	-89.04697
Joe Taylor Creek	223	101	16	Southern Hwy.	16.10987	-88.79898
Kendal Bridge over Sittee River	178	72	9	Southern Hwy.	16.81513	-88.37823
La Milpa Ecolodge & Research Center	58	20	6	Gallon Jug Rd.	17.84120	-89.01902
Lago Petén Itzá, Guatemala	150	none	7	Tikal Hwy.	16.98555	-89.69205
Laguna Seca	67	27	6	Gallon Jug Rd.	17.63595	-89.03560
Lamanai Maya site	73	23	4	Goldson Hwy.	17.76162	-88.65377
Las Cuevas Research Station	123	78	14	Chiquibul Rd.	16.73315	-88.98605
Laughing Falcon Reserve	220	99	16	Southern Hwy.	16.16610	-88.81160
Little Quartz Ridge	176	85	15	see San Jose Village	16.40533	-89.10286
Lodge at Big Falls, The	207	92	16	Southern Hwy.	16.26058	-88.89072
Log Cab-Inn Resort	136	53	10	Price Hwy.	17.13900	-89.08483
Lubaantun Maya site	211	89	16	San Antonio Rd.	16.28225	-88.95740
Macal River resorts	138	55	10	Macal River Resorts Rd		
Macal River Resorts Road	138	53	10	Price Hwy.	17.10592	-89.11655
Machaca Hill (now Belcampo Belize)	220	99	16	Southern Hwy.	16.16610	-88.81160
Mama Noots Eco Resort	186	68	12	Southern Hwy.	16.93000	-88.38722
Manatee Lodge	105	47	9	Coastal Hwy.	17.20007	-88.33448
Man-O'-War Caye	248	69	18	Barrier Reef &Cays	16.88460	-88.10720
Mayflower Bocawina National Park	183	68	12	Southern Hwy.	16.93222	-88.38333

Birding Sites	Page	Gazet-teer	Eco-region	Access	Latitude (N)	Longi-tude (W)
Moho River	231	104	16	Southern Hwy.	16.05930	-88.85135
Monkey Bay Wildlife Sanctuary	97	40	8	Price Hwy.	17.29992	-88.55427
Monkey River	180	84	16	Southern Hwy.	16.43620	-88.46241
Mountain Pine Ridge (at "T")	115	58	13	Chiquibul Rd.	17.05088	-88.94728
Mt. Margaret	158	61	13	Hummingbird Hwy.	17.04266	-88.59572
New River at Tower Hill Bridge	68	14	4	Goldson Hwy.	18.02750	-88.55600
Nim Li Punit Maya site	205	86	16	Southern Hwy.	16.32140	-88.82375
Nova Ladyville	38	29	9	Goldson Hwy.	17.57302	-88.33568
Nova Toledo	178	84	16	Southern Hwy.	16.42502	-88.47348
Old Northern Hwy. (N)	87	14	4	Goldson Hwy.	18.02030	-88.54383
Old Northern Hwy. (S)	87	26	5	Goldson Hwy.	17.64630	-88.37370
Payne's Creek National Park	176	87	16	boat from Punta Gorda	16.30000	-88.58333
Pelican Beach Resort	170	67	9	Hummingbird Hwy.	16.98165	-88.22633
Philip Goldson International Airport	38	31	9	Goldson Hwy.	17.54220	-88.30037
Placencia	178	81	9	Southern Hwy.	16.56667	-88.36667
Pook's Hill Lodge	109	48	11	Price Hwy.	17.15430	-88.85245
Progresso Lagoon	43	9	2	Sarteneja Rd.	18.22832	-88.40307
Pueblo Nuevo Ferry	42	5	1	Sarteneja Rd.	18.33152	-88.40987
Pueblo Viejo Falls	215	95	16	San Antonio Rd.	16.20222	-89.13980
Punta Gorda	225	101	16	Southern Hwy.	16.10528	-88.80042
Punta Gorda Marina	228	101	16	Southern Hwy.	16.08605	-88.81108
Punta Ycacos & Ycacos Lagoon	374	91	16	boat from Punta Gorda	16.26667	-88.60000
Red Bank	198	79	12	Southern Hwy.	16.62235	-88.56007
Rio Blanco National Park	215	94	16	San Antonio Rd.	16.22903	-89.09395
Rio Frio Caves	120	66	13	Chiquibul Rd.	16.97910	-89.00567
Runaway Creek Nature Preserve	102	39	8	Coastal Hwy.	17.30143	-88.45887
Salt Creek Estates Road	38	26	5	Goldson Hwy.	17.63807	-88.36970
San Antonio Road	208	93–97	16	Southern Hwy.	16.22835	-88.93902
San Estevan Road	44	9–12	4	Goldson Hwy.	18.08448	-88.54463
San Felipe	53	19	3	Gallon Jug Rd.	17.87250	-88.77250
San Ignacio Resort Hotel	131	49	10	Price Hwy.	17.15297	-89.06803
San Jose Village	208	90	16	San Antonio Rd.	16.26710	-89.09590
San Pedro Columbia	212	89	16	San Antonio Rd.	16.27024	-88.95336
San Victor loop (N)	50	8	1	Goldson Highway	18.31013	-88.51112
San Victor loop (S)	50	8	1	Goldson Highway	18.25148	-88.52000
Santa Anna	230	102	16	Southern Highway	16.10360	-88.95250
Santa Rita Maya site.	40	2	1	Santa Elena	18.40160	-88.39497
Sapodilla Cayes	237	100	18	Barrier Reef & Cays	16.10825	-88.27230
Sarteneja	43	4	2	Sarteneja Rd.	18.35198	-88.14877
Sarteneja National Tree Park	46	4	2	Sarteneja Rd.	18.34105	-88.16043
Sarteneja Road	41	2–9–4	1	Goldson Hwy.	18.38168	-88.40227
Sea Front Inn	225	101	16	Southern Hwy.	16.10570	-88.80045
Shipstern Nature Reserve	46	7	2	Sarteneja Rd.	18.31812	-88.18320
Shipyard Road	71	14	3	Goldson Hwy.	18.03263	-88.56138
Sittee River (marina)	187	72	9	Southern Hwy.	16.82208	-88.26828
Slate Creek Preserve	113	54	10	Chiquibul Rd.	17.09318	-88.97654
Smuggler's Run Plantation	38	26	5	Goldson Hwy.	17.63807	-88.36970
South Water Caye	248	73	18	Barrier Reef & Cays	16.81505	-88.08210
Spanish Lookout	127	43	6	Price Hwy.	17.25592	-89.00252
The Dump	208	93	16	San Antonio Rd.	16.22998	-88.94822
Thousand Foot Falls	119	57	13	Cooma Cairn Rd.	17.05995	-88.84832
Tikal Hwy., Guatemala	152	none		Price Hwy.	17.05758	-89.14865
Tikal National Park, Guatemala	146	none	7	Tikal Hwy.	17.22445	-89.61202
Tower Hill Bridge (New River)	69	14	4	Goldson Hwy.	18.02750	-88.55600
Tres Leguas	55	18	3	Gallon Jug Rd.	17.88788	-88.95745
Tropical Education Center (TEC)	93	37	8	Price Hwy.	17.35415	-88.55122
Turneffe Atoll	247	36	18	Barrier Reef & Cays	17.35453	-87.86057
Vaca Plateau (at Macal River)	123	71	14	Chiquibul Rd.	16.86545	-89.03850
Victoria Peak	191	74	12	Southern Hwy.	16.81310	-88.61942
Victor's Inn & Foodery	67	12	4	Honey Camp Rd.	18.08350	-88.54083
VoA	228	101	16	Southern Hwy.	16.08473	-88.81802
Vuelta Grande, Guatemala	154	none		Tikal Hwy.	17.00600	-89.32233
Wilson Road & Wilson Landing	220	99	16	Southern Hwy.	16.16528	-88.80805
Windy Hill Resort	136	53	10	Price Hwy.	17.14162	-89.08742
Xunantunich Maya site	143	59	10	Price Hwy.	17.08932	-89.13908

AMERICAN BIRDING ASSOCIATION

PRINCIPLES OF BIRDING ETHICS

Everyone who enjoys birds and birding must always respect wild-life, its environment, and the rights of others. In any conflict of interest between birds and birders, the welfare of the birds and their environment comes first.

CODE OF BIRDING ETHICS

1. Promote the welfare of birds and their environment.

1(a) Support the protection of important bird habitat.

1(b) To avoid stressing birds or exposing them to danger, exercise restraint and caution during observation, photography, sound recording, or filming.

Limit the use of recordings and other methods of attracting birds, and never use such methods in heavily birded areas or for attracting any species that is Threatened, Endangered, or of Special Concern, or is rare in your local area.

Keep well back from nests and nesting colonies, roosts, display areas, and important feeding sites. In such sensitive areas, if there is a need for extended observation, photography, filming, or recording, try to use a blind or hide, and take advantage of natural cover.

Use artificial light sparingly for filming or photography, especially for close-ups.

1(c) Before advertising the presence of a rare bird, evaluate the potential for disturbance to the bird, its surroundings, and other people in the area, and proceed only if access can be controlled, disturbance can be minimized, and permission has been obtained from private land-owners. The sites of rare nesting birds should be divulged only to the proper conservation authorities.

1(d) Stay on roads, trails, and paths where they exist; otherwise keep habitat disturbance to a minimum.

2. Respect the law and the rights of others.

2(a) Do not enter private property without the owner's explicit permission.

2(b) Follow all laws, rules, and regulations governing use of roads and public areas, both at home and abroad.

2(c) Practice common courtesy in contacts with other people. Your exemplary behavior will generate goodwill with birders and non-birders alike.

3. Ensure that feeders, nest structures, and other artificial bird environ-ments are safe.

3(a) Keep dispensers, water, and food clean and free of decay or disease. It is impor-tant to feed birds continually during harsh weather.

3(b) Maintain and clean nest structures regularly.

3(c) If you are attracting birds to an area, ensure the birds are not exposed to predation from cats and other domestic animals, or dangers posed by artificial hazards.

4. Group birding, whether organized or impromptu, requires special care.

Each individual in the group, in addition to the obligations spelled out in Items #1 and #2, has responsibilities as a Group Member.

4(a) Respect the interests, rights, and skills of fellow birders, as well as those of peo-ple participating in other legitimate outdoor activities. Freely share your knowl-edge and experience, except where code 1(c) applies. Be especially helpful to beginning birders.

4(b) If you witness unethical birding behavior, assess the situation and intervene if you think it prudent. When interceding, inform the person(s) of the inappropri-ate action and attempt, within reason, to have it stopped. If the behavior contin-ues, document it and notify appropriate individuals or organizations.

Group Leader Responsibilities [amateur and professional trips and tours].

4(c) Be an exemplary ethical role model for the group. Teach through word and ex-ample.

4(d) Keep groups to a size that limits impact on the environment and does not interfere with others using the same area.

4(e) Ensure everyone in the group knows of and practices this code.

4(f) Learn and inform the group of any special circumstances applicable to the areas being visited (e.g., no tape recorders allowed).

4(g) Acknowledge that professional tour companies bear a special responsibility to place the welfare of birds and the benefits of public knowledge ahead of the company's commercial interests. Ideally, leaders should keep track of tour sightings, document unusual occurrences, and submit records to appropriate or-ganizations.

PLEASE FOLLOW THIS CODE— DISTRIBUTE IT AND TEACH IT TO OTHERS.

Additional copies of the Code of Birding Ethics can be obtained from: ABA, PO Box 6599, Colorado Springs, CO 80934-6599. Phone 800/850-2473 or 719/578-1614; fax 800/247-3329 or 719/578-1480; e-mail: member@aba.org

This ABA Code of Birding Ethics may be reprinted, reproduced, and distributed without restriction. Please acknowledge the role of ABA in developing and promoting this code.

7/1/96

Join Today!

American Birding
A S S O C I A T I O N

Name _____

Address _____

_____

City _____ State _____ Zip _____

Country _____ Phone _____

Email _____

Each level entitles members to certain benefits.
Visit <https://www2.aba.org/join> or call 800-850-2473 to find out more.

O Individual . . . . US $45

O Joint . . . . US $52

O Student . . . . US $25

O International / Canada Individual . . . US $55

O International / Canada Joint . . . . . . US $63

O International / Canada Student . . . . US $35

Send this form to:

ABA Membership
1618 W. Colorado Ave.
Colorado Springs, CO
80904

You may also join by phone or web:
Phone 800-850-2473
www.aba.org/join

Membership: $ _____
Additional Contribution: $ _____ for: O Unrestricted O Conservation O Education
Total: $ _____
US dollars; check or money order payable to American Birding Association, or charge to:

O *VISA*   O *Mastercard*   O *Discover*

Card # _____ Exp Date _____

Signature _____

INDEX

A

Accommodations 19
Actun Tunichil Muknal 109
Agouti, Central American 61, 107, 147
Aguacaliente Wildlife Sanctuary 8, 181, 216-218
Aguacate Lagoon 127, 130
Aguada Tikal 150
Airport
    Ambergris Caye 239
    Belize Municipal 14, 235
    Caye Caulker 243
    Dangriga 159, 171-172
    Flores (Guatemala) 152
    Philip Goldson International 14, 19, 38, 85, 94,
        111, 118, 131, 135, 172, 236
    Punta Gorda 225
Alta Vista Village 159
Altun Ha Jungle Resort 88
Altun Ha Maya Site 2, 37, 87-89
Ambergris Caye 4, 8, 40, 78, 235-240, 247
Ameiva, Festive 12
Amigo's 91, 99, 344
Anhinga 67, 106, 115, 233, 255, 311
Ani
    Groove-billed 139, 237, 274, 320
    Smooth-billed 237, 245, 247, 274, 320
Ant swarm 7, 10, 60, 74, 76, 86, 193, 195, 283, 299
Ant-Tanager
    Red-crowned 10, 74, 117, 121, 146, 185, 195, 303,
        333
    Red-throated 10, 117, 121, 162, 195, 303, 333
Antbird
    Bare-crowned 207, 212, 214, 219, 233, 283, 323
    Dusky 10-11, 77, 81, 100, 109, 111, 124, 126, 135,
        146, 160, 163-164, 169, 186, 193, 195, 198, 201,
        205, 207, 212, 219, 222, 229, 233, 283, 323
Anteater, Northern Tamandua 7, 12, 147, 196
Antelope Falls 184
Antshrike
    Barred 10, 98, 141, 193, 195, 282, 323
    Great 98, 100, 103, 111, 124, 164, 193, 198, 201,
        206-207, 211, 214, 219, 221, 229, 233, 282,
        323
    Russet 126, 155, 205, 214, 282, 323
Antthrush, Black-faced 62, 74, 77, 81, 99-100, 103,
    109, 111, 126, 135, 146, 155, 162, 164, 184, 186, 198,
    205, 214, 216-217, 219, 222-223, 229, 283, 324
Antvireo, Plain 11, 62, 111, 124, 126, 155, 159, 198,
    205, 233, 282, 323
Antwren
    Dot-winged 10-11, 108-109, 121, 124, 129, 146,
        160, 164, 169, 185-186, 233, 283, 323
    Slaty 124, 205, 282, 323
Aracari, Collared 40, 58, 64, 85, 109, 131, 144, 189,
    281, 323
Arenal (Hydro) Road 123, 144-145
Armadillo, Nine-banded 50, 196
Armenia 21, 157
Attila, Bright-rumped 10-11, 59, 68, 78, 109, 150, 186,
    204, 207, 211-212, 215, 223, 229, 231, 287, 325
August Pine Ridge 7-8, 51, 53-55, 58
Avocet, American 104-105, 245, 264, 316

B

BFREE (Belize Foundation for Research and
    Environmental Education) 21, 180, 201-205
Bacalar Chico National Park 239
Baird's Tapir 95
Baldy Beacon 115
Banana Bank Lodge 20
Bananaquit 110, 126, 190, 207, 229, 233, 240-241,
    243-244, 299, 331
Barbthroat, Band-tailed 197, 216, 229, 277, 321

Barranco 179, 181, 230
Barred-Woodcreeper, Northern 62, 111, 126, 155,
    164, 195, 204-205, 222, 284, 324
Barrier Reef 235, 248
Barton Creek Archaeological Reserve 113
Basilisk, Brown (Striped) 12-13, 187
Bat
    Greater Fishing 69, 202
    Proboscis 69, 231
Bay
    Chetumal 40, 46, 239
    Corozal 42, 237, 240
    Honduras 225, 235
    Tiger Sandy 102
Beardless-Tyrannulet, Northern 49, 73, 86, 97, 103,
    135, 219, 223, 233, 284, 324
Becard
    Cinnamon 62, 100, 126, 160, 163-164, 184, 186,
        198, 205, 215-216, 289, 326
    Gray-collared 81, 109, 154-155, 184, 186, 289,
        326
    Rose-throated 139, 141, 172, 184, 289, 326
    White-winged 97, 100, 103, 109-111, 164, 184,
        186, 198, 207, 215-216, 229, 289, 326
Becol Hydro Electric Power Generation Plant 144
Belcampo Belize 21, 181, 220-221
Belize Audubon Society 32, 81, 85, 109, 163, 194,
    246
Belize Botanic Gardens 8, 141-143
Belize City 2-4, 6-7, 14-15, 20, 25, 27, 36, 38, 87, 91,
    112, 152, 157, 225, 235-236, 241, 246, 248
Belize Jungle Gardens 87
Belize Zoo, Jungle Lodge, & River Camp 20, 91,
    93-96, 102
Bella Vista Village 180
Belmopan 3, 6, 91, 107, 109, 157
Benque Viejo del Carmen 145
Bentbill, Northern 77-78, 85, 163, 186, 198, 202,
    206, 217, 219-220, 222-223, 229, 285, 324
Best Western Belize Biltmore Hotel 20, 38
Big Falls, The Lodge at 21, 181, 207
Billy Barquedier National Park 159
Birding tours 18
Bird's Eye View Lodge 20, 85
Bittern
    American 54, 58, 211, 217, 255, 312
    Least 54, 58, 73, 86-87, 154, 211, 240, 255, 312
    Pinnated 54, 58, 61, 65, 67, 130, 187, 189, 211,
        255, 312
Black Rock Lodge 21, 139
Black-Hawk
    Common 49, 68, 70, 97, 103-104, 106, 171, 174,
        189, 200, 207, 214, 223, 231, 233, 240, 244,
        259, 313
    Great 70, 73, 86, 97, 103, 106, 121, 124, 189, 195,
        200, 214, 259, 314
Blackbird
    Melodious 10, 95, 172, 305, 334
    Red-winged 58, 154, 304, 334
    Yellow-headed 305, 334
Bladen River Nature Reserve 180, 201-205
Blancaneaux Lodge 21-22, 113, 116
Blue Creek Cave 213-214
Blue Creek Hillside B&B 20, 56
Blue Creek Village (Orange Walk District) 36, 51,
    55
Blue Creek Village (Toledo District) 208-209,
    213-214
Blue Creek rice fields 8, 52, 54, 56, 58
Blue Hole (Lighthouse Reef) 235
Blue Hole (St. Herman's) National Park 7, 158,
    160-164

Bluebird, Eastern 294, 328
Bobolink 243, 304, 334
Bobwhite, Black-throated 56, 58, 68, 73, 86-87, 99,
   102-103, 181, 204, 253, 311
Bocawina Falls 185
Boden Creek Reserve 180, 206
Bols Cave 113
Booby
   Brown 106, 240, 244, 248-249, 254, 311
   Masked 240, 254, 311
   Red-footed 240, 245-247, 255, 311
Boom Creek Road 226, 229
Boom Creek Village 231
Botfly 26
Branchmouth Park 131, 133
Bufo marinus 13, 146, 202
Bullet Tree Road 134
Bunting
   Blue 48, 56, 62, 65, 78, 109, 124, 138, 155, 304,
      334
   Indigo 43, 47, 304, 334
   Painted 47, 128, 206, 212, 219, 243, 304, 334
Bush-Tanager, Common 198, 302, 333

C

CCBTIA Mini-Reserve 241, 243
Cacique
   Yellow-billed 9, 97, 100, 140-141, 154, 219, 306,
      335
   Yellow-winged 103, 306, 335
Caesar's Place Guesthouse 20
Cahal Pech Maya Site 131-132
Cahal Pech Village Resort 21, 132
Calabash Caye 248
Captain Hook's Restaurant & Shrimp Farm 38, 103
Caracara, Crested 55, 58, 128-130, 136, 150, 219,
   222, 259, 261, 314
Caracol Archaeological Reserve 7, 10, 27, 112-113,
   115, 123, 125-126
Cardinal, Northern 41, 49, 85-86, 103, 303, 333
Caribbean Villas Hotel 20, 239
Catbird
   Black 40-42, 45, 47, 49, 73, 237, 241, 243-244,
      247, 294, 329
   Gray 95, 294, 329
Cattle Landing 181, 222
Caves Branch Adventure Co. & Jungle Lodge 20,
   165-166
Caye Caulker 4, 7-8, 235-236, 240-244, 247-248
Caye Caulker Conservancy 243
Caye Chapel 236
Cays, The 4, 235-250
Cerros Maya Site 35, 43, 45
Chaa Creek, The Lodge at 21, 140
Chachalaca, Plain 131, 139, 220, 253, 310
Chalillo Dam 113, 115, 199, 346
Chan Chich Lodge 6-7, 20, 26, 36-37, 61-67
Chan Chich Maya Site 62
Charlton Inn 225
Chat
   Gray-throated 49, 53, 61-62, 65, 68, 81, 86, 88,
      146, 149, 155, 169, 303, 333
   Yellow-breasted 47, 97, 100, 103, 219, 299, 331
Chechem Ha Cave 145
Cheers Restaurant and Cabanas 20, 91, 99
Chiquibul Forest Reserve 115, 123
Chiquibul National Park 115, 123-124, 126
Chiquibul Road 112-113, 122, 124
Christmas Bird Counts 6, 38, 62, 208, 228
Chuck-will's-widow 47, 73, 131, 150, 155, 276, 320
Clapper Rail 248
Clarissa Falls Resort 21, 136
Coastal Highway 100-103
Coati, White-nosed 12, 50, 61, 76, 147, 196
Cockscomb Basin Wildlife Sanctuary 8, 10, 21, 26,
   170, 178, 190-197

Coco Plum Caye 249
Coco Plum Island Resort 21, 250
Collared-Dove, Eurasian 38, 40, 130, 269, 318
Commerce Bight Forest Reserve 177
Community Baboon Sanctuary 38
Cooma Cairn Road 113, 120
Coot, American 40, 82, 86, 104, 154, 206, 263, 315
Copper Bank 8, 35, 43, 45
Coquette, Black-crested 138, 155, 179, 207, 216,
   240, 278, 321
Coral House Inn 225
Cormorant
   Double-crested 40, 84, 106, 255, 311
   Neotropic 82, 84, 104, 106, 144, 217, 255, 311
Corozal Town 8, 35, 38-40, 50, 236
Cosmos Camping and Cabanas 131-132
Cotinga, Lovely 62, 65, 67, 117, 119, 124, 126,
   168-169, 195, 198, 222, 289, 326
Cotton Tree Lodge 21, 181, 230-232
Cowbird
   Bronzed 51, 128, 130, 207, 219-220, 233, 305,
      334
   Brown-headed 305, 334
   Giant 62, 64, 67, 155, 206, 219, 222, 229, 233,
      305, 334
   Shiny 121, 222, 305, 334
Crake
   Gray-breasted 99, 159, 179, 208, 211, 213-214,
      228, 259, 262, 315
   Ruddy 38, 40, 42, 54, 58, 65, 67, 81, 99, 102, 106,
      154, 166, 169, 173, 189, 207-208, 211, 219,
      221, 223, 233, 240, 259, 262, 315
   Uniform 80-81, 110, 123, 144-146, 193, 197, 245,
      262, 315
   Yellow-breasted 82, 263, 315
Creek
   Barton 112
   Beaver Dam 92
   Big 180
   Black 81-82
   Blue 213
   Calla 136
   Chan Chich 64
   Dawson 71, 73
   Dry 168
   Freshwater 178
   Irish 79-80
   Jacinto 219
   Jaguar 164-166
   Joe Taylor 7, 181, 223
   Little Vaqueros 116
   North Stann 159
   Plantation 101-102
   Privassion 22
   Roaring 107, 109-110
   Silk Grass 184
   Soldier 100-102
   South Stann 178
   Spanish 81-82
Cristo Rey 112, 116
Crocodile
   American 12, 50, 248
   Morelet's 12, 41, 50, 67, 82, 150, 193
Crooked Tree Lodge 20, 85
Crooked Tree Wildlife Sanctuary 7-8, 21, 37, 81-86
Crossbill, Red 117, 307, 335
Crystal Paradise Resort 21, 112, 116
Cuckoo
   Black-billed 240, 243, 274, 319
   Mangrove 49, 73, 81, 86, 106, 170, 174, 179, 187,
      189, 240, 245, 273, 319
   Pheasant 74, 77, 79, 81, 110-111, 138, 140, 144,
      146, 149, 155, 164, 274, 320
   Squirrel 68, 273, 319

Striped 51, 53, 86, 103, 138, 154, 177, 181, 211, 217, 219, 274, 320
Yellow-billed 5, 47, 241, 273, 319
Curassow, Great 43, 55-56, 60-62, 81, 124, 126, 135, 146, 154, 159, 195, 253, 311
Curlew, Long-billed 104, 174, 245, 265, 316
Cuxlin Ha Resort 21, 181, 219-220, 237

D

Dangriga 3, 6, 8, 170-174, 177, 179-180, 225
Davis Falls 159
Deep River Forest Reserve 180
Deer, White-tailed 7, 147, 197
Dickcissel 6, 47, 49, 73, 103, 117, 208, 211, 222, 243, 304, 334
Dolphin, Atlantic Bottlenose 174, 245
Double Run Road 38
Douglas Da Silva 113, 120-121
Dove
    Caribbean 41, 49, 240, 245, 271, 319
    Gray-chested 10, 99, 103, 111, 126, 162, 164, 186, 194-195, 197, 200-202, 205, 207, 212, 214, 217, 219, 221, 223, 229, 271, 319
    Gray-headed 61, 64, 99, 103, 110-111, 141, 155, 162, 186, 194, 197, 205, 219, 221, 229, 271, 319
    Inca 269, 318
    Mourning 211, 228, 244, 269, 318
    Plain-breasted 211
    White-tipped 98, 131, 162, 271, 319
    White-winged 40, 49, 58, 154, 189, 207, 237, 243, 269, 318
Dowitcher
    Long-billed 49, 55, 58, 82, 104, 266, 316
    Short-billed 49, 104-105, 174, 244, 266, 316
Doyle's Delight 4, 124
duPlooy's Jungle Lodge 21, 141-143
Duck
    Masked 253, 310
    Muscovy 37, 43, 48, 50, 70, 73, 86, 211, 214, 217, 221, 233, 252, 310
    Ring-necked 40, 86, 104, 154, 206, 253, 310
    Ruddy 253
Dump, The (San Antonio Road) 8, 208, 211
Dunlin 266, 316

E

Eagle
    Crested 155, 216, 259-260, 314
    Harpy 126, 204-205, 259-260, 314
    Solitary 117, 119, 121, 126, 205, 259, 314
Eden Conservancy 165
Edenthal-Neustadt marshes 8, 52, 55, 58
Egret
    Cattle 256, 312
    Great 50, 82, 104, 217, 256, 312
    Reddish 42, 48, 50, 104, 240, 244, 256, 312
    Snowy 104, 108, 181, 256, 312
El Pilar Maya Site 2, 27, 133-135
El Remate, Guatemala 151
Elaenia
    Caribbean 87, 243-244, 247-248, 284, 324
    Greenish 108, 284, 324
    Yellow-bellied 172, 219, 285, 324
Emerald
    Canivet's 49, 86, 97, 109, 130, 135, 138, 144, 146, 155, 278, 321
    White-bellied 60, 279, 322
Euphonia
    Elegant 62, 306, 335
    Olive-backed 11, 75, 100, 307, 335
    Scrub 64, 75, 97, 100, 135, 139, 144, 164, 229, 306, 335
    White-vented 198, 216, 229, 233, 307, 335
    Yellow-throated 75, 87, 121, 150, 306, 335

F

Fairy, Purple-crowned 61, 77, 110-111, 117, 120, 126, 130, 155, 162, 205, 279, 322
Falcon
    Aplomado 51, 58, 86, 99, 102-103, 178, 181, 187, 189, 222, 259, 261, 314
    Bat 98, 138-139, 141, 171, 259, 261, 314
    Laughing 37, 69, 103, 181, 221, 259, 261, 314
    Orange-breasted 109, 113, 117-119, 123, 131, 135, 138-140, 146, 149, 155, 164-165, 222, 259, 262, 314
    Peregrine 40, 58, 104, 178, 181, 244, 259, 262, 314-315
Fer-de-lance 26, 185, 202
Fernando's Seaside Guesthouse 20, 49
Five Sisters Lodge, now Gaïa Riverlodge 21, 113, 116
Fireburn Nature Reserve 43
Fireburn Village 20, 49
Fish & Shrimp Farms
    All Pines 178
    Aqua Mar 178
    Dept. of Agriculture 103
    Fresh Catch Belize, Ltd. 91, 101, 103-105
    Nova 8
    Nova Toledo 178
    Paradise 103
Five Blues Lake National Park 8, 22, 158, 166-170
Flamingo, American 217, 254, 311
Flatbill, Eye-ringed 10-11, 62, 77, 111, 121, 126-127, 130, 140, 146, 155, 160, 163-164, 169, 285, 325
Flycatcher
    Acadian 47, 174, 243, 286, 325
    Alder 47, 49, 155, 286, 325
    Boat-billed 172, 205, 287, 326
    Brown-crested 206, 287, 325
    Dusky-capped 134, 172, 211, 287, 325
    Fork-tailed 41-42, 51, 53, 56, 58, 67, 84, 86, 97, 102-104, 130, 139, 169, 178, 181, 187, 189, 289, 326
    Great Crested 47, 211, 219, 287, 325
    Least 47, 287, 325
    Ochre-bellied 59, 64, 78, 81, 97, 108, 124, 130, 135, 206, 211, 285, 324
    Olive-sided 102-103, 121, 196, 243, 286, 325
    Piratic 5, 87, 155, 164, 186, 190-191, 201, 205, 288, 326
    Royal 64, 78, 81, 111, 121, 144, 155, 163-164, 169, 198, 215, 219, 222, 229, 286, 325
    Ruddy-tailed 62, 110-111, 155, 205, 286, 325
    Scissor-tailed 41, 58, 130, 174, 211, 228, 288, 326
    Sepia-capped 11, 62, 108-109, 111, 124, 126-127, 130, 138, 155, 169, 185, 198, 205, 229, 285, 324
    Social 288, 326
    Streaked 5, 123, 138, 155, 198, 205-206, 288, 326
    Stub-tailed 81
    Sulphur-bellied 5, 135, 138, 164, 186, 198, 205, 207, 212, 288, 326
    Sulphur-rumped 11, 59, 110-111, 121, 127, 155, 186-187, 286, 325
    Vermilion 58, 67, 86, 139, 154, 195, 287, 325
    White-throated 65, 81, 103, 138, 208, 211, 287, 325
    Willow 47, 49, 155, 164, 208, 211, 243, 286, 325
    Yellow-bellied 10, 64, 184, 286, 325
    Yellow-olive 68, 97, 108, 121, 141, 220, 285, 325
    Yucatan 41, 47, 49, 62, 67-68, 73, 86, 100, 155, 287, 325
Foliage-gleaner
    Buff-throated 10-11, 62, 100, 111, 121, 126, 135, 149, 155, 164, 186, 195, 198, 205, 283, 324
    Scaly-throated 283, 324
Forest-Falcon
    Barred 61, 64, 81, 121, 124, 126, 145-146, 155, 164, 186, 190, 195-197, 205, 259, 261, 314

Collared 68-69, 73, 75, 77, 103, 124, 138-139, 169, 186, 201, 207, 233, 259, 261, 314
Foundation for Wildlife Conservation, Inc. 102
Four Mile Lagoon 8, 35, 40-42, 45
Fox, Gray 7, 51, 147, 197
Fresh Catch Belize, Ltd. 91, 101, 104-105
Freshwater Creek Forest Reserve 68
Friends for Conservation & Development, Chiquibul 115
Frigatebird, Magnificent 40, 43, 106, 115, 173-174, 240, 244-246, 249, 254, 311
Frog, Rainforest 13

G

Gadwall 252
Gaïa Riverlodge 21, 113, 116
Gales Point 21, 103, 105-106
Gallinule
 Common 58, 86, 104, 138, 211, 263, 315
 Purple 58, 67-68, 70, 73, 86, 130, 154, 211, 263, 315
Gallon Jug Road 36, 51, 53-62
Gaviota Reef Resort 250
Gecko, Belize Atoll 248
Glover's Reef 235
Gnatcatcher
 Blue-gray 293, 328
 Tropical 134, 186, 215, 220, 293, 328
Gnatwren, Long-billed 76, 78, 109, 216, 223, 293, 328
Godwit
 Hudsonian 104, 265, 316
 Marbled 104, 241, 244, 265, 316
Golden Stream Corridor Preserve 180
Golden-Plover, American 58, 82, 263, 315
Goldentail, Blue-throated 92, 207, 279, 322
Goldfinch, Lesser 41-42, 50-51, 58, 73, 307, 335
Goldson (Northern) Highway 35
Goose
 Canada 86, 252, 310
 Greater White-fronted 252, 310
 Snow 252, 310
Gra Gra Lagoon National Park 7, 170, 173-174
Grackle, Great-tailed 237, 305, 334
Grassquit
 Blue-black 43, 98, 138, 154, 172, 220, 300, 332
 Yellow-faced 100, 103, 117, 119, 130, 134-135, 138, 193, 216, 220, 301, 332
Grebe
 Least 67, 70, 73, 86, 138, 141, 144, 154, 254, 311
 Pied-billed 73, 115, 254, 311
Green Hills Butterfly Ranch 112-113
Green Iguana Park 131
Greenlet
 Lesser 10, 127, 131, 141, 204, 291, 327
 Tawny-crowned 76, 78, 100, 111, 127, 135, 155, 160, 164, 186, 198, 219, 222-223, 229, 291, 327
Grosbeak
 Black-faced 78, 111, 145-146, 164, 185, 194, 198, 205, 215-216, 219, 303, 333
 Black-headed 110, 303, 333
 Blue 41, 43, 58, 304, 334
 Blue-black 78, 121, 146, 160, 164, 169, 184-185, 198, 201, 212, 216, 219, 304, 334
 Rose-breasted 47, 172, 303, 333
Ground-Dove
 Blue 10, 98-99, 103, 109, 130, 162, 169, 186, 193, 206, 269, 318
 Common 40, 45, 49, 53, 128, 189, 240, 269, 318
 Plain-breasted 42, 51, 53, 58, 103, 128, 130, 181, 219, 269, 318
 Ruddy 53, 98, 127-128, 131, 162, 269, 318
Guacamallo Bridge 115, 123
Guan, Crested 8, 59-61, 97, 117, 135, 154, 186, 193, 197, 201, 205, 233, 253, 310
Guanacaste National Park 91, 106-109

Gull
 Black-tailed 266, 317
 Bonaparte's 240, 266, 317
 Franklin's 240, 245, 266, 317
 Great Black-backed 267, 317
 Herring 40, 106, 174, 244, 267, 317
 Laughing 104, 115, 150, 266, 317
 Lesser Black-backed 267, 317
 Ring-billed 104, 267, 317

H

Half Moon Caye 235, 237, 245-248
Harrier, Northern 58, 166, 211, 258, 313
Hawk
 Bicolored 38, 61, 64, 126, 129, 186, 197, 229, 258, 313
 Black-collared 37-38, 67, 70, 73, 81, 86, 258, 313
 Broad-winged 47, 49, 117, 119, 222, 228, 240, 259, 314
 Cooper's 117, 222, 258, 313
 Crane 58, 61, 87, 173, 240, 259, 313
 Gray 121, 131, 139, 259-260, 314
 Red-tailed 54, 58, 117, 120, 125, 128, 130, 259-260, 314
 Roadside 97, 139, 217, 259, 314
 Sharp-shinned 117, 123, 222, 240, 258, 313
 Short-tailed 65, 73, 97, 99, 103, 121, 189, 214, 259-260, 314
 Swainson's 58, 207, 222, 228, 259-260, 314
 White 60-61, 65, 110, 117, 121, 126, 130, 135, 138-139, 155, 158, 160, 163-164, 169, 185-186, 197, 200-201, 208, 213-214, 259, 313
 White-tailed 55-56, 58, 97, 99, 103, 130, 178, 181, 189, 211, 259-260, 314
 Zone-tailed 103, 127, 219, 222, 259-260, 314
Hawk-Eagle
 Black 60-61, 64-65, 89, 98, 108-110, 124, 134-135, 138-139, 144-145, 160, 164, 169, 197, 200-201, 205, 207, 214, 219, 259-260, 314
 Black-and-white 61, 65, 117, 119, 126, 155, 159, 205, 259, 261, 314
 Ornate 40, 45-46, 56, 60-61, 64, 67, 81, 89, 109, 124-126, 144, 155, 207, 259, 261, 314
Hermit
 Long-billed 8, 109-110, 184, 186, 190, 193, 201, 204, 212, 277, 321
 Stripe-throated 64, 97, 109, 135, 164, 169, 184, 186, 190, 193, 201, 223, 277, 321
Heron
 Agami 61, 65, 67-68, 70, 73, 81-82, 110, 129-130, 193, 196-197, 201, 204-205, 256, 312
 Boat-billed 43, 69, 73, 78, 81, 86, 95, 106, 134, 193, 197, 201, 204-205, 207, 231, 256, 312
 Great Blue 82, 104, 247, 255, 312
 "Great White" 247, 255, 312
 Green 64, 70, 82, 108, 256, 312
 Little Blue 42, 82, 108, 256, 312
 Tricolored 82, 154, 256, 312
Hickatee Cottages B&B 21, 226, 229
Hidden Valley Inn 7, 21, 113, 117-119
Hill Bank Field Station 20, 37, 72, 78-81
Hol Chan Marine Preserve 239
Homestay program 21
Honey Camp Road & Lagoon 37, 66-68
Honeycreeper
 Green 62, 64, 121, 126, 134, 164, 184, 186, 198, 205, 215-216, 300, 332
 Red-legged 58, 134, 144, 184, 219, 300, 332
 Shining 184, 186, 198, 205, 300, 332
Hopkins Village 170, 178, 187-189
Hummingbird
 Azure-crowned 81, 97, 99-100, 117, 279, 322
 Buff-bellied 42-43, 45, 47, 49, 65, 77, 86, 149, 155, 279, 322
 Cinnamon 40-42, 45, 49, 51, 68, 97, 106, 174, 189, 240-241, 244, 247-248, 279, 322

Ruby-throated 144, 206, 279, 322
Rufous-tailed 45, 60, 279, 322
Scaly-breasted 60-61, 64, 111, 155, 186, 194, 197, 201, 205, 207, 212, 214, 229, 233, 278, 321
Sparkling-tailed 279
Stripe-tailed 197, 216, 279, 322
Stripe-throated 183
Hydro (Arenal) Road 123, 144-145

I

ITVET (Institute for Technical, Vocational, & Educational Training) 159
Ibis
Glossy 81, 86, 104, 171, 228, 257, 312
Scarlet 257, 312
White 50, 70, 82, 86, 106, 217, 233, 247, 256, 312
Iguana
Brown 13, 82, 187
Green 12, 81-82, 187
In the Bush Resort 112
Insect bites 26

J

Jabiru 37, 54-55, 58, 70, 73, 79, 81-82, 86, 95, 97, 104-106, 217, 254, 311
Jacamar, Rufous-tailed 75, 77, 81, 108, 111, 124, 130, 162, 164, 169, 190, 193, 197, 204, 281, 323
Jacana, Northern 70, 81-82, 138, 150, 155, 171, 264, 316
Jacobin, White-necked 58, 61, 97, 103, 110-111, 155, 164, 169, 186, 197, 205, 207, 212, 214, 221, 229, 278, 321
Jaeger
Parasitic 240, 268, 318
Pomarine 174, 226, 240, 245, 268, 318
Jaguar 12, 50, 79-80, 95, 190, 195-196, 200, 215
Jaguar Creek Lodge 20, 166
Jaguar Reef Lodge 21, 189
Jaguarundi 50, 196
Jalacte 208, 211
Jay
Brown 146, 183, 291, 327
Green 117, 124, 126, 135, 143-144, 164, 291, 327
Yucatan 38, 41-43, 49, 85-86, 291, 327
Jimmy Cut 208-209

K

Kendal 178, 189
Kestrel, American 58, 130, 174, 178, 259, 261, 314
Killdeer 104, 138, 154, 173, 217, 219, 264, 316
King Vulture Falls 117
Kingbird
Cassin's 288, 326
Couch's 97, 288, 326
Eastern 6, 47, 222, 243, 247, 288, 326
Gray 245, 250, 288, 326
Tropical 97, 288, 326
Western 288, 326
Kingfisher
Amazon 56, 62, 64, 70, 100, 108-109, 134, 144, 169, 189, 201, 207, 214, 216, 219, 233, 280, 322
American Pygmy 43, 53, 65, 67-68, 70, 73, 79, 81, 86, 100, 138, 144, 150, 155, 173-174, 189, 195, 211, 214, 216, 219, 221, 223, 233, 280, 322
Belted 70, 79, 81, 104, 108, 280, 322
Green 70, 79, 81, 87, 104, 108, 195, 280, 322
Ringed 70, 79, 81, 104, 280, 322
Kinkajou 7, 9, 12, 60, 78, 143
Kiskadee, Great 287, 325
Kite
Double-toothed 60-61, 65, 117, 119, 121, 126, 155, 186, 195, 197, 201, 205, 214, 240, 258, 313

Gray-headed 68, 98, 138, 149, 155, 186, 196-197, 207, 212, 229, 240, 245, 257, 313
Hook-billed 40, 81, 109-110, 121, 130, 135, 144, 165, 189, 207, 221-222, 228, 231, 233, 240, 257, 313
Mississippi 155, 222, 228, 258, 313
Plumbeous 5, 67, 98-99, 103, 117, 121, 124-126, 138-139, 155, 173, 186, 189-190, 195, 197, 201, 204-207, 212, 216-217, 228, 231, 233, 258, 313
Snail 48, 58, 68, 70, 73, 82, 84, 86, 154, 258, 313
Swallow-tailed 5, 47, 68, 89, 106, 117, 119-121, 123-124, 126, 155, 164, 185-186, 189, 195, 197, 201, 206, 220, 228, 231, 233, 258, 313
White-tailed 58, 67-68, 123, 130, 136, 138-139, 145, 154, 171, 178, 189, 211, 220, 258, 313
Kittiwake, Black-legged 266, 317
Knot, Red 104, 170, 174, 240, 245, 265, 316

L

La Democracia 21, 103, 105
La Milpa Ecolodge and Research Center 6-8, 20, 37, 56-61
La Milpa Maya Site 2, 58-59
Ladyville 38
Lago Petén Itzá, Guatemala 150, 154
Laguna 181, 217
Laguna Seca 8, 67
Lamanai Maya Site 2, 36-37, 72-78
Lamanai Outpost Lodge 20, 73, 77
Lapwing, Southern 84, 263, 315
Las Cuevas Research Station 7, 21, 115, 123-124
Las Flores 157
Leaftosser
Scaly-throated 62, 64, 81, 123-124, 126, 155, 164, 205, 283, 324
Tawny-throated 158, 283, 324
Lighthouse Reef 235
Limpkin 43, 67-69, 73, 79, 81-82, 86, 103-104, 106, 130, 150, 155, 174, 189, 263, 315
Lizard, Jesus Christ 13
Lodging 19
Log Cab-Inn Resort 21, 136
Long Caye 236
Lubaantun Maya Site 2, 8, 180, 208-212

M

Macaw Bank 112
Macaw, Scarlet 113, 117, 124, 126, 179, 193, 197-201, 205, 272, 319
Mafredi 208-209
Mallard 252, 310
Mama Noots Eco Resort 183-184, 186
Man-O'-War Caye 8, 22, 249-250
Manakin
Red-capped 48, 64, 76, 78, 95, 97, 100, 109, 164, 166, 216, 290, 327
White-collared 10, 64, 78, 110, 160, 163-164, 166, 190, 193, 219, 290, 326
Manatee Lagoons 103, 105-106
Manatee Lodge 20, 100, 105-106
Manatee, West Indian 50, 105, 173
Mango Walk Inn 21, 112, 116
Mango, Green-breasted 40, 50, 53, 58, 60, 68, 106, 109, 183, 240, 244, 247, 278, 321
Margay 50, 215
Marie Sharp Factory 160
Martin
Caribbean 292, 327
Gray-breasted 42, 104, 292, 327
Purple 5, 47, 73, 222, 292, 327
Martz Farm 145
Maruba Resort Jungle Spa 20, 88-89
Matola, Sharon (Belize Zoo) 95, 199
Maya Mountain Forest Reserve 215
Maya Mountain Lodge 112

Maya Mountains 92, 111-122, 180
Maya Site
 Altun Ha 2, 37, 87-89
 Cahal Pech 131-132
 Caracol 2, 10, 27, 112-113, 115, 123, 125-126
 Cerros 2, 35, 43, 45
 Chan Chich 62
 El Pilar 2, 27, 133-135
 La Milpa 2, 58-59
 Lamanai 2, 36-37, 72-78
 Lubaantun 2, 8, 180, 208-212
 Nim Li Punit 2, 180, 202, 205-206
 Santa Rita 2, 35, 40
 Xunantunich 2, 143-144
Mayflower Bocawina National Park 7, 170, 177, 182-186
Meadowlark, Eastern 41, 51, 58, 67, 130, 181, 187, 304, 334
Mennonite communities 3, 37, 41, 43, 51, 54, 71, 78, 127
Merganser
 Hooded 253, 310
 Red-breasted 179, 253, 310
Merlin 117, 121, 259, 261, 314
Middlesex 158
Millionario Road 115, 122, 124
Mixed-species flocks 10, 76, 127, 195, 283-284, 299
Mockingbird, Tropical 179, 294, 329
Mollejon Dam Road 144-145
Monkey
 Central American Spider 65, 147
 Yucatan Black Howler 73, 76, 82, 98, 147, 196, 231
Monkey Bay Wildlife Sanctuary 20, 91, 94, 97-100, 250
Motmot
 Blue-crowned 1, 74, 99, 109, 131, 135, 141, 201, 204, 280, 322
 Keel-billed 117, 119, 126, 134, 159, 185-186, 197, 205, 216, 280, 322
 Tody 61, 64, 67, 77, 111, 117, 123-124, 126, 135, 138, 140, 146, 155, 159, 163-164, 169, 186, 196-197, 204-205, 221, 280, 322
Mountain Pine Ridge 6-7, 22, 92, 111-122
Mourner
 Rufous 62, 64, 111, 126, 130, 146, 155, 164, 185-186, 195, 198, 205, 215, 220, 222, 287, 325
 Speckled 62, 159, 289, 326
Mo'H Group, Red Bank Village 200
Mt. Margaret 158
Munia, Tricolored 41, 50, 58, 154, 245, 307, 335
Mystic River Resort 112

N

National Park
 Bacalar Chico 239
 Billy Barquedier 159
 Blue Hole (St. Herman's) 7, 158, 160-164
 Chiquibul 115, 123-124, 126
 Five Blues Lake 8, 22, 158, 166-170
 Gra Gra Lagoon 7, 170, 173-174
 Guanacaste 91, 106-109
 Mayflower Bocawina 7, 170, 177, 182-186
 Payne's Creek 176
 Rio Blanco 208-209, 215
 Sarstoon-Temash 181, 214, 230
 St. Herman's Blue Hole 7, 158, 160-164
 Tikal 146-155, 344
Neotropical River Otter 231
New River Lagoon 6, 70
Night-Heron
 Black-crowned 73, 86, 104, 106, 174, 207, 211, 217, 256, 312
 Yellow-crowned 69, 223, 240-241, 256, 312

Nighthawk
 Common 47, 49, 81, 97, 99, 117, 276, 320
 Lesser 49, 69-70, 73, 86, 97, 117, 276, 320
 Short-tailed 245, 250, 275, 320
Nightjar, Yucatan 47, 49, 60-61, 69, 73, 81, 240, 247, 276, 321
Nim Li Punit Maya Site 2, 180, 202, 205-206
Noddy
 Black 245, 267, 317
 Brown 40, 240, 248, 250, 267, 317
Northern Lagoon (Coastal Highway) 105
Northern (Goldson) Highway 35

O

Ocelot 50, 95, 215
Old Mai Gate Village 113
Old Northern Highway 7-8, 37
Orange Walk Town 3, 36, 50, 54
Oriole
 Altamira 41-42, 49, 58, 68, 240, 306, 335
 Baltimore 47, 219, 306, 335
 Black-cowled 55, 150, 305, 334
 Hooded 41, 172, 244, 305, 334
 Orange 41, 45, 48-49, 240, 245, 306, 334
 Orchard 139, 305, 334
 Spot-breasted 222, 306, 334
 Yellow-backed 97, 111, 117, 126, 181, 189, 201, 237, 240, 305, 334
 Yellow-tailed 42, 68, 97-98, 100, 117, 146, 150, 194, 231, 305, 334
Oropendola
 Chestnut-headed 124, 126, 146, 159, 190, 195, 198, 205, 306, 335
 Montezuma 56, 64, 150, 306, 335
Osprey 103-104, 106, 154, 171, 174, 189, 231, 233, 240, 244, 248, 257, 313
Otter, Neotropical River 193, 197, 215
Outlier Peak 196
Ovenbird 5, 47, 74, 108, 230, 241, 295, 329
Owl
 Barn 40, 67, 138, 143, 174, 207, 274, 320
 Black-and-white 61, 126, 138, 143, 155, 159, 164, 183, 186, 195, 197, 205, 207, 221, 275, 320
 Burrowing 206, 275, 320
 Crested 120, 126, 159, 166, 169, 205, 274, 320
 Great Horned 49, 239, 275, 320
 Mottled 49, 59-61, 73, 77-79, 81, 143, 146, 150, 166, 169, 202, 205, 207, 221, 229, 275, 320
 Short-eared 275, 320
 Spectacled 103, 110-111, 126, 138, 140, 163-164, 183, 186, 193, 197, 205, 221, 274, 320
 Striped 103, 197, 208, 221, 228, 275, 320
 Stygian 81, 97, 116-117, 119, 275, 320
Oystercatcher, American 170, 173-174, 264, 316

P

Paca 7, 50-51, 95
Paradise Shrimp Farms 103
Parakeet
 Olive-throated 9, 131, 134, 138, 272, 319
 Rose-ringed 272
Parrot
 Brown-hooded 61, 155, 164, 169, 186, 197, 201, 205, 207, 214, 219, 221, 229, 233, 272, 319
 Mealy 61, 111, 126, 130, 135, 146, 155, 157, 164, 221, 233, 273, 319
 Red-lored 1, 58, 62, 98, 102, 187, 273, 319
 White-crowned 77, 185, 273, 319
 White-fronted 1, 51, 54, 98, 131, 139, 143, 273, 319
 Yellow-headed 37, 73, 78, 81, 86, 88, 99-100, 102-103, 181, 189, 273, 319
 Yellow-lored 40, 42-43, 45, 49, 68, 73, 86, 93, 273, 319
 Yellow-naped 248, 273, 319

Parula
  Northern 47, 172, 241, 297, 330
  Tropical 297, 330
Pauraque, Common 69, 159, 183, 220, 276, 320
Peccary
  Collared 76
  White-lipped 27
Pelican
  American White 86, 104, 106, 255, 311
  Brown 115, 150, 255, 311
Pelican Beach Resort (Dangriga) 8, 21, 170-171, 237
Pelican Beach Resort (S. Water Caye) 21, 250
Pelican Beach Resort (S. Water Caye)) 237
Peppershrike, Rufous-browed 41, 49, 68, 86, 97, 100, 291, 327
Petén Itzá, Lago 150, 154
Pewee
  Greater 117, 121, 286, 325
  Tropical 56, 97, 150, 286, 325
Phalarope
  Red-necked 266, 317
  Wilson's 86, 104, 240, 266, 317
Phoebe, Black 100, 103, 109, 111, 123, 126, 131, 138, 144, 158, 166, 169, 201, 215, 287, 325
Piedra Lagoon 181
Pigeon
  Pale-vented 41-42, 106, 162, 190, 268, 318
  Red-billed 41-42, 53, 58, 139, 144, 162, 268, 318
  Rock 268, 318
  Scaled 61, 81, 98-99, 110, 117, 155, 162, 186, 193, 197, 201, 207, 268, 318
  Short-billed 10, 98-99, 162, 164, 169, 186, 190, 201, 221, 268, 318
  White-crowned 49, 174, 179, 187, 189, 240, 243-244, 247-248, 268, 318
Piha, Rufous 62, 64, 126, 129-130, 195, 198, 205, 215, 290, 326
Pine Ridge Lodge 21, 113, 116
Pintail, Northern 86, 104, 252, 310
Pipit, American 295, 329
Placencia 178, 225
Plover
  Black-bellied 43, 49, 82, 104-105, 170, 173-174, 187, 189, 240, 244, 263, 315
  Collared 104, 173-174, 240, 247, 264, 315
  Semipalmated 86, 104, 106, 170, 174, 240, 244, 264, 315
  Snowy 104, 245, 264, 315
  Wilson's 40, 42, 49, 104, 106, 173-174, 244, 264, 315
Pook's Hill Lodge 20, 109-110
Poorwill, Yucatan 38, 47, 60, 69, 73, 81, 138, 146, 150, 155, 276, 320
Potoo
  Great 205, 220-221, 276, 321
  Northern 47, 60-61, 69-70, 73, 81, 87, 136, 138, 143, 146, 166, 169, 233, 276, 321
Price (Western) Highway 91
Programme for Belize 56, 59, 61, 79-80
Progresso Lagoon 35, 41, 43
Pueblo Nuevo Ferry 35, 42, 45
Pueblo Viejo & Pueblo Viejo Falls 208, 211, 215-216
Puffbird
  White-necked 48, 68, 81, 97, 135, 205, 208, 212, 233, 281, 323
  White-whiskered 11, 61, 64, 74, 77, 110-111, 126, 135, 138, 155, 162, 164, 169, 184, 186, 204-205, 216, 281, 323
Puma 50
Punta Gorda 6, 177, 181, 209, 224-228
Punta Gorda (Orange Point) Marina 228
Pygmy-Owl
  Central American 60, 111, 124, 183, 186, 205, 275, 320

Ferruginous 40, 50, 58, 68, 102, 117, 136, 143, 275, 320

Q
Quail, Singing 138, 145, 253, 311
Quail-Dove, Ruddy 48, 59, 61, 65, 126, 149, 155, 162, 164, 186, 194, 197, 200-202, 205, 219, 271, 319

R
Rabinowitz, Alan 190
Rail
  Black 159, 187, 189, 208, 211, 262, 315
  Clapper 49, 104, 189, 211, 223, 240, 244, 248, 262, 315
  Spotted 56, 58, 208, 213, 245, 263, 315
Red Bank 7, 170, 179, 193, 198-202
Redhead 252
Redstart, American 47, 296, 330
Reef
  Glover's 235
  Lighthouse 235, 246
  Tobacco 249
Richardson Peak 180
Rio Blanco National Park 208-209, 215
Rio Bravo Conservation and Management Area 20, 37, 59, 78-79
Rio Frio Caves 113, 115, 120
Rio Hondo 40
Rio On Pool 113
River
  Belize 38, 92, 107-108, 127, 130, 143
  Bladen 180, 201-202, 204
  Booth's 54
  Caves Branch 99, 157, 164-165
  Hondo 3
  Macal 92, 112, 115-116, 123, 131, 133, 138-143, 145, 199
  Manatee 102, 105
  Moho 8, 214, 228, 230-233
  Monkey 180
  Mopan 92, 131, 133, 135-136, 143-144
  New 7-8, 37, 41, 43, 68-74, 76, 78-79, 240
  Privassion 116
  Raspacula 199
  Rio Grande 181, 207, 220-221
  Sarstoon 3
  Sibun 91, 93-94, 97-100, 102
  Sittee 8, 170, 178, 187-189
  Swasey 180, 199-200
River Otter, Neotropical 82
Robin, American 294, 329
Runaway Creek Nature Preserve 102-103

S
Sabrewing
  Violet 8, 126, 164, 183-184, 186, 197, 216, 278, 321
  Wedge-tailed 48, 61, 64, 111, 123, 126, 131, 135, 138, 144, 146, 155, 164, 205, 207, 278, 321
Sac Tunich 112
Salt Creek Estates Road 38
Saltator
  Black-headed 211, 220, 300, 332
  Buff-throated 100, 103, 109, 164, 189-190, 201, 207, 212, 219, 222, 229, 300, 332
  Grayish 50, 86, 100, 103, 169, 172, 211, 233, 300, 332
San Antonio 112, 209
San Antonio Road 112, 208-214
San Estevan 43-44, 67
San Felipe 54, 58, 79
San Ignacio 3, 6, 8, 26, 91-92, 107, 109, 112, 127-135, 152
San Ignacio Resort Hotel 20, 131-132
San Jose 208-209
San Jose Succotz 143

San Narciso 50
San Pedro (Ambergris Caye) 3-4, 237, 239-240
San Pedro Columbia 209, 212
San Pedro Lagoon 239
San Victor Loop 8, 36, 40, 50-51
Sanderling 104, 170, 173-174, 187, 189, 240-241, 244, 265, 316
Sandpiper
  Buff-breasted 219, 266, 316
  Least 40, 47, 55, 104, 154, 170, 219, 265, 316
  Pectoral 58, 82, 86, 104, 174, 189, 219, 266, 316
  Semipalmated 104, 219, 265, 316
  Solitary 70, 86, 93, 104, 138, 154, 173, 189, 219, 264, 316
  Spotted 70, 104, 115, 170, 173, 264, 316
  Stilt 82, 86, 104, 219, 240, 266, 316
  Upland 240, 245, 265, 316
  Western 40, 47, 104, 170, 174, 219, 244, 265, 316
  White-rumped 58, 86, 104, 240, 266, 316
Santa Anna 181, 214, 230-232
Santa Cruz 179, 209
Santa Cruz, Guatemala 211
Santa Elena (Cayo District) 91, 131
Santa Elena (Corozal District) 341
Santa Elena (Toledo District) 211, 215
Santa Rita Maya Site 2, 35, 40
Sapodilla Cayes 237
Sapsucker, Yellow-bellied 97, 117, 186, 195, 244, 282, 323
Sarstoon-Temash National Park 181, 230
Sarteneja Road 35, 40-50
Sarteneja Tree Park 35, 43
Scaup, Lesser 40, 49, 86, 104, 106, 253, 310
Schiffornis, Northern 59, 61-62, 64, 77, 130, 146, 164, 186, 195, 215, 222-223, 229, 289, 326
Screech-Owl, Vermiculated 38, 49, 61, 111, 117, 126, 134, 138, 143, 166, 169, 174, 189, 197, 202, 204-205, 221, 274, 320
Sea Front Inn 21, 225
Sea Turtle, Hawksbill 105
Seaside Cabanas 20, 241
Seed-Finch, Thick-billed 97-98, 100, 102-103, 172, 194, 207, 223, 233, 301, 332
Seedeater
  Blue 9, 81, 93, 98, 100, 102-103, 304, 333
  Slate-colored 9, 79, 81, 97, 99-100, 229, 300, 332
  Variable 98, 172, 189, 220, 300, 332
  White-collared 43, 98, 138, 300, 332
Shearwater
  Audubon's 240, 245, 254, 311
  Manx 170, 254, 311
Shipstern Nature Reserve 35, 41, 43-44, 46-50, 240
Shoveler, Northern 104, 217, 252, 310
Shrike-Tanager, Black-throated 10, 59, 62, 64, 76, 78, 126, 155, 169, 186, 196, 205, 215, 299, 331
Shrike-Vireo, Green 62, 121, 124, 129-130, 164, 185-186, 198, 205, 216, 291, 327
Shrimp & Fish Farms 255-256, 262-263, 267
  All Pines 178
  Aqua Mar 178
  Captain Hook's Restaurant & Shrimp Farm 38
  Dept. of Agriculture 103
  Fresh Catch Belize, Ltd. 91, 101, 103-105
  Nova 8
  Nova Toledo 178
  Paradise 103
Sibun Forest Reserve 165
Silk Grass Village 177
Silver Fox Guest House 20, 88-89
Siskin, Black-headed 117, 119, 121, 123, 307, 335
Skimmer, Black 174, 268, 318
Skua, Great 240, 268, 318
Slate Creek Preserve 113

Slaty-Antshrike, Western 217, 219-220, 222-223, 225, 228-229, 233, 282, 323
Snakes 26, 349
Snipe, Wilson's 49, 58, 64, 106, 138, 173, 211, 219, 266, 317
Solitaire, Slate-colored 117, 119, 124, 126, 198, 294, 328
Sora 56, 58, 73, 104, 154, 171, 174, 208, 211, 223, 240, 244, 263, 315
South Water Caye 237, 248-249
Spadebill, Stub-tailed 53, 58, 74, 78, 100, 109-111, 140, 164, 186, 198, 207, 216, 219, 233, 285, 325
Spanish Lookout 8, 92, 127-130
Sparrow
  Botteri's 73, 103, 301, 332
  Chipping 85-86, 97, 102-103, 117, 121, 181, 247, 301, 332
  Clay-colored 240, 302, 333
  Grasshopper 73, 97, 102-103, 117, 180-181, 204, 245, 247, 302, 333
  Green-backed 41, 48-49, 51, 55, 61, 77, 86, 97-98, 124, 138, 144, 169, 207, 211, 216, 229, 301, 332
  House 159, 170, 174, 225, 307, 335
  Lark 240, 245, 302, 333
  Lincoln's 117, 245, 302, 333
  Olive 41, 48-49, 86, 97, 102-103, 301, 332
  Orange-billed 121, 126, 162-164, 169, 184, 186, 195, 198, 201, 204-205, 215, 217, 219, 222, 229, 301, 332
  Rusty 117, 119-120, 123, 126, 181, 301, 332
  Savannah 103, 245, 302, 333
  Vesper 302, 333
  White-crowned 247, 302, 333
  White-throated 247, 302, 333
Spinetail, Rufous-breasted 10, 86, 97-98, 100, 102-103, 146, 187, 189, 193, 198, 201, 207, 211, 219, 223, 233, 283, 323
Spoonbill, Roseate 42, 48, 50, 58, 73, 82, 86, 104, 106, 181, 217, 240, 244, 257, 313
Squirrel
  Deppe's 125, 197
  Yucatan 12, 107, 147, 197, 355
St. Charles Inn 225
St. Herman's Blue Hole National Park 7, 158, 160-164
St. Margaret's Village 21, 158, 166, 169
Starthroat, Long-billed 92, 279, 322
Stilt, Black-necked 49, 58, 70, 73, 82, 86, 104, 174, 219, 244, 264, 316
Stork, Wood 46, 48, 50, 58, 68, 82, 84, 86, 95, 104-106, 216-217, 220, 233, 254, 311
Storm-Petrel, Wilson's 179, 254, 311
Sungrebe 43, 65, 67-68, 70, 73, 79, 86, 99, 109, 123, 131, 138, 174, 189, 207, 219, 221, 230, 233, 263, 315
Swallow
  Bank 41, 47, 86, 104, 211, 222, 243, 292, 328
  Barn 47, 73, 222, 243, 292, 328
  Cave 117, 222, 228, 240, 245, 292, 328
  Cliff 47, 86, 117, 211, 222, 243, 292, 328
  Mangrove 42, 67-68, 81, 86, 104, 108, 144, 231, 292, 328
  Northern Rough-winged 47, 73, 104, 155, 292, 328
  Ridgway's Northern Rough-winged 117, 120, 126, 143, 155, 163-164, 292, 328
  Tree 47, 73, 86, 104, 211, 222, 292, 327
Swift
  Chestnut-collared 110-111, 117, 196-197, 277, 321
  Chimney 47, 49, 228, 277, 321
  Lesser Swallow-tailed 61, 77, 99, 111, 117, 120, 155, 169, 186-187, 197, 207, 229, 277, 321
  Vaux's 49, 110-111, 277, 321
  White-chinned 277, 321

White-collared 99, 103, 111, 117, 119, 164, 186, 197, 214, 229, 277, 321

T

Tanager
Blue-gray 150, 172, 211, 299, 332
Crimson-collared 100, 111, 126, 138, 141, 146, 160, 164, 169, 186, 189, 201, 207, 212, 215-216, 222, 229, 299, 332
Flame-colored 158, 303, 333
Golden-hooded 100, 102, 117, 119, 126, 164, 186, 190, 193, 198, 201, 205, 215, 222, 229, 233, 299, 332
Gray-headed 10, 48, 61-62, 74, 78, 86, 100, 110, 155, 164, 194, 222, 229, 299, 331
Hepatic 95, 97, 100, 103, 117, 119-121, 123, 181, 196, 205, 302, 333
Passerini's 95, 100, 103, 164, 169, 187, 189-190, 198, 201, 205, 207, 212, 215, 222, 229, 233, 299, 332
Rose-throated 42, 47, 49, 61-62, 65, 68, 92, 139, 146, 149, 155, 302, 333
Scarlet 47, 165, 205, 243, 247, 303, 333
Summer 47, 95, 219, 303, 333
Western 245, 303, 333
White-winged 117, 126, 198, 303, 333
Yellow-winged 150, 219, 299, 332
Tapir Mountain Nature Reserve 109
Tapir, Baird's 12, 50, 78, 95, 200
Teal
Blue-winged 40, 58, 81-82, 104, 115, 154, 174, 217, 252, 310
Cinnamon 58, 104, 252, 310
Green-winged 104, 252, 310
Tern
Black 47, 104, 106, 240, 244, 267, 317
Bridled 240, 267, 317
Caspian 82, 84, 86, 104, 170, 174, 189, 267, 317
Common 174, 243, 267, 317
Forster's 49, 86, 104, 154, 240, 268, 317
Gull-billed 86, 104, 106, 267, 317
Least 104, 240, 244, 267, 317
Roseate 225, 243, 245, 267, 317
Royal 43, 104, 150, 154, 170, 174, 237, 268, 317
Sandwich 40, 104, 106, 150, 154, 170, 174, 189, 244, 268, 318
Sooty 240, 267, 317
Thousand Foot Falls National Monument 7, 112-113, 115, 117, 119-120
Thrush
Clay-colored 204, 294, 329
Gray-cheeked 47, 126, 243, 294, 329
Hermit 294, 329
Swainson's 5, 47, 126, 243, 294, 329
White-throated 62, 117, 121, 124, 126, 198, 294, 329
Wood 62, 74, 108, 131, 294, 329
Tiger-Heron
Bare-throated 67, 70, 81, 86, 95, 104, 109, 130, 171, 189, 201, 207, 211, 217, 220-221, 231, 255, 312
Rufescent 255, 312
Tikal National Park 146-155, 344
Tinamou
Great 43, 61, 64, 81, 87, 97, 99, 110, 117, 126, 130, 154, 186, 197, 201, 205, 221, 229, 233, 251, 310
Little 97, 99, 110, 117, 124, 126, 135, 162, 164, 184-186, 197, 201, 205-207, 212, 214, 216-217, 229, 251, 310
Slaty-breasted 61, 110, 117, 126, 196-197, 251, 310
Thicket 38, 42, 49, 61, 81, 87, 130, 145, 154, 251, 310
Tityra
Black-crowned 58, 68, 81, 109, 130, 155, 206, 212, 289, 326

Masked 131, 139, 172, 206, 289, 326
Toad
Cane 13
Marine 13
Tobacco Caye 22, 249
Tody-Flycatcher
Common 51, 58, 84, 97, 102, 150, 240, 285, 325
Slate-headed 81, 86, 100, 111, 124, 134-135, 155, 160, 163-164, 195, 216, 219, 233, 285, 324
Toledo Settlement 219
Tony's Inn & Beach Resort 20, 40
Toucan Alley B&B 87
Toucan, Keel-billed 1, 40, 58, 75, 98, 143, 146, 149-150, 187, 190, 195, 220, 225, 281, 323
Toucanet, Emerald 62, 65, 111, 123, 126, 138, 146, 155, 160, 164-165, 184, 186, 197, 205, 221, 281, 323
Tranquility Lodge 230
Travel tips 23-28
Tres Leguas 55
Trogon
Black-headed 87, 95, 99, 141, 280, 322
Collared 77, 81, 117, 126, 155, 186, 197, 205, 280, 322
Gartered 1, 87, 99, 141, 280, 322
Slaty-tailed 1, 75, 77, 130, 164, 169, 184, 186, 197, 229, 279, 322
Tropical Education Center 8, 93
Tropicbird, White-tailed 240, 254, 311
Turkey, Ocellated 56, 59, 61-62, 92, 117, 123, 125-126, 154, 254, 311
Turneffe Atoll 235, 245, 247-248
Turnstone, Ruddy 104, 170, 174, 241, 265, 316
Turtle, Central American River 13
Tyrannulet
Paltry 124, 205, 215-216, 229, 233, 285, 324
Yellow-bellied 62, 81, 100, 109, 111, 126, 129-130, 155, 158, 164, 169, 198, 204-205, 219-220, 222-223, 229, 233, 284, 324

U

Upper Tiger Fern Falls 196

V

Vaca Falls 123, 139-140, 145
Vaca Plateau 112-113, 115, 123-126, 139-140
Veery 47, 49, 243, 294, 328
Victoria Peak 4, 196
Victor's Inn and Foodery 67
Violetear, Brown 165-166, 197, 229, 278, 321
Vireo
Black-whiskered 240, 247, 291, 327
Blue-headed 117, 290, 327
Mangrove 68, 81, 84, 104, 149, 220, 290, 327
Philadelphia 50, 100, 206, 212, 222, 244, 290, 327
Plumbeous 117, 119, 198, 290, 327
Red-eyed 47, 97, 243, 290, 327
Warbling 155, 290, 326
White-eyed 47, 290, 327
Yellow-green 5, 97, 100, 131, 134, 290, 327
Yellow-throated 47, 139, 144, 290, 327
Yucatan 49-50, 68, 104, 106, 174, 240-241, 243-244, 247-248, 291, 327
VoA (Punta Gorda) 228
Vuelta Grande marsh 150
Vulture
Black 87, 257, 313
King 60-61, 65, 87, 95, 99, 110, 117, 119, 123, 126, 135, 138-139, 154, 163-164, 169, 189, 197, 201, 205, 208, 212-214, 216, 229, 233, 257, 313
Lesser Yellow-headed 42, 49, 58, 65, 68, 73, 86-87, 99, 103-104, 154, 174, 189, 211, 214, 217, 257, 313
Turkey 87, 257, 313

W

Warbler
  Bay-breasted 5, 47, 241, 297, 330
  Black-and-white 10, 47, 127, 295, 330
  Black-throated Blue 297, 331
  Black-throated Gray 298, 331
  Black-throated Green 47, 298, 331
  Blackburnian 47, 241, 297, 330
  Blackpoll 241, 297, 330
  Blue-winged 241, 295, 329
  Canada 47, 241, 299, 331
  Cape May 241, 296, 330
  Cerulean 47, 241, 297, 330
  Chestnut-sided 11, 47, 193, 297, 330
  Golden-cheeked 165, 298, 331
  Golden-crowned 10, 62, 67, 117, 126-127, 135, 143, 155, 298, 331
  Golden-winged 47, 241, 295, 329
  Golden-winged X Blue-winged 295, 329
  Grace's 85-86, 97, 100, 102-103, 119, 123, 181, 196, 298, 331
  Hermit 119, 298, 331
  Hooded 10-11, 47, 77, 230, 296, 330
  Kentucky 47, 61, 74, 77, 230, 241, 296, 330
  Magnolia 11, 297, 330
  Mangrove Yellow 47, 49, 106, 173-174, 189, 240, 243-244, 247-248, 297, 330
  Mourning 47, 165, 241, 296, 330
  Nashville 241, 296, 330
  Orange-crowned 102, 296, 330
  Palm 174, 189, 240-241, 297, 331
  Prairie 170, 174, 240-241, 245, 298, 331
  Prothonotary 47, 82, 124, 174, 184, 194, 219, 222, 295, 330
  Rufous-capped 117, 119-121, 123, 126, 138-140, 196, 198, 298, 331
  Swainson's 47, 62, 103, 109, 155, 212, 241, 243, 295, 330
  Tennessee 47, 241, 296, 330
  Townsend's 298, 331
  Virginia's 245, 296, 330
  Wilson's 47, 299, 331
  Worm-eating 10, 47, 77, 241, 295, 329
  Yellow 47, 144, 297, 330
  Yellow-rumped 47
  Yellow-rumped (Audubon's) 298, 331
  Yellow-rumped (Myrtle) 298, 331
  Yellow-throated 47, 102, 298, 331
Water Taxis 236-237, 241
Waterthrush
  Louisiana 47, 93, 144, 295, 329
  Northern 47, 217, 295, 329
Waxwing, Cedar 97, 295, 329
Western Lagoon 105
Western (Price) Highway 91
Whimbrel 104, 170, 174, 241, 244, 265, 316
Whip-poor-will, Eastern 240, 276, 321
Whistling-Duck
  Black-bellied 43, 49, 58, 70, 73, 82, 86, 104, 130, 171, 207, 211, 217, 252, 310
  Fulvous 82, 86, 88, 252, 310
Wigeon, American 86, 104, 217, 252, 310
Willet 104, 106, 170, 174, 244, 264, 316
Wilson Landing 220-221
Windy Hill Resort 21, 136
Wood-Pewee
  Eastern 47, 86, 164, 243, 247, 286, 325
  Western 286, 325
Wood-Quail, Spotted 61, 64, 123-124, 126, 138, 197, 253, 311
Wood-Rail
  Gray-necked 37, 65, 70, 73, 81, 86, 93, 97, 131, 134, 138, 150, 211, 219, 233, 262, 315
  Rufous-necked 106, 173-174, 179, 223, 241, 243-244, 262, 315

Wood-Wren
  Gray-breasted 196, 198, 293, 328
  White-breasted 11, 108, 160, 204, 293, 328
Woodcreeper
  Ivory-billed 10, 74, 86, 131, 223, 284, 324
  Olivaceous 10, 77, 81, 111, 130, 135, 138, 144, 155, 164, 169, 205, 284, 324
  Ruddy 10, 74, 86, 108-109, 121, 126, 155, 169, 195, 204-205, 222, 229, 284, 324
  Spotted 284, 324
  Streak-headed 77, 97, 100, 103, 108-109, 126, 164, 284, 324
  Strong-billed 62, 64, 67, 126, 155, 284, 324
  Tawny-winged 10, 61, 74, 86, 109, 111, 126, 195, 205, 222-223, 229, 283, 324
  Wedge-billed 11, 108-109, 126, 155, 164, 169, 186, 205-207, 214-215, 219, 222, 229, 284, 324
Woodnymph, Violet-crowned 121, 158, 205, 278, 322
Woodpecker
  Acorn 58, 85-86, 93, 97, 100, 102-103, 117, 120, 181, 281, 323
  Black-cheeked 164, 186, 201, 212, 281, 323
  Chestnut-colored 62, 64, 75, 77, 126, 130, 155, 198, 205, 216, 282, 323
  Golden-fronted 46-47, 281, 323
  Golden-olive 77, 109, 282, 323
  Ladder-backed 85-86, 103, 181, 282, 323
  Lineated 68, 131, 282, 323
  Pale-billed 282, 323
  Smoky-brown 10, 55, 77, 109, 169, 190, 282, 323
  Yucatan 41-42, 45, 47, 49, 58, 86, 240, 244, 281, 323
World Heritage Site, Belize Barrier Reef Reserve System 235, 248
Wren
  Band-backed 100, 111, 124, 126, 135, 138, 141, 164-165, 215, 292, 328
  Carolina 65, 73, 138, 142, 146, 155, 293, 328
  House 150, 293, 328
  Nightingale 124, 160, 164, 196, 213, 216, 293, 328
  Plain 117, 119, 121, 134-135, 293, 328
  Sedge 117, 121, 173, 180-181, 204, 293, 328
  Spot-breasted 10, 141, 172, 293, 328
  White-bellied 49, 81, 97, 100, 109, 126, 155, 293, 328

X

Xenops, Plain 11, 74, 76-77, 81, 109, 111, 127, 135, 160, 169, 198, 283, 324
Xo-Pol (Shipstern Nature Reserve) 48
Xunantunich Maya Site 2, 143-144

Y

Yalbac Hills 92, 127, 130
Ya'axché Conservation Trust 203
Yellow-Finch, Grassland 38, 55, 58, 103, 179, 208, 211, 301, 332
Yellowlegs
  Greater 58, 68, 82, 104, 170, 173-174, 219, 264, 316
  Lesser 58, 68, 82, 104, 219, 265, 316
Yellowthroat
  Common 5, 47, 296, 330
  Gray-crowned 41, 51, 58, 88, 97, 103, 117, 130, 139, 154, 169, 181, 187, 189, 196, 211, 233, 240, 296, 330
Yo Creek Village 53, 79

ABOUT THE AUTHOR

Bert Frenz, a birder since childhood, developed his birding skills when he moved to Texas as a post-doctoral student in crystallography and began organizing and/or leading hundreds of trips for the Audubon Society and Texas Ornithological Society. After retiring from the computer arena, he and his wife Shari sold their home and began traveling across North America in a motor-home, eventually accumulating over 290,000 RV miles in 16 years of full-time travels. In 2000 the two began leading RV birding caravans to Mexico and expanded the next year to include Belize. When they arrived in 2001 they found a country long on beauty and short on the infrastructure that makes touring easy. Much was improved as they went back year after year, extending the length of each stay. In the process, Bert accumulated a lot of useful knowledge on good birding spots and the logistics needed to get to them.

In addition to birding Belize, Bert has led RV birding tours to the Canadian Maritimes, Newfoundland, Manitoba, British Columbia, Yukon Territory, Northwest Territories, Alaska, Australia, New Zealand, and throughout Central America and Mexico. For a decade Bert was on the Board of Directors for the Texas Ornithological Society. He continues as subregional editor for East Texas for *North American Birds* and as eBird reviewer for Belize and Tikal, and is a regular contributor to the Belize birders forum.

Bert Frenz maintains an extensive web site, ***www.bafrenz.com,*** which includes birding information about Texas and Belize, as well as travel journals.

GAZETTEER

(key to map on back cover)

1 Four Mile Lagoon, Rio Hondo
2 Corozal
3 Cerros Maya site
4 Sarteneja
5 Pueblo Nuevo Ferry
6 Copper Bank
7 Shipstern Nature Reserve
8 San Victor
9 Progresso Lagoon
10 Fireburn Nature Reserve
11 Freshwater Creek Forest Reserve
12 Orange Walk Town
13 Honey Camp Lagoon
14 New River at Tower Hill Bridge
15 August Pine Ridge
16 Ambergris Caye
17 Edenthal-Neustadt marshes
18 Blue Creek rice fields, Orange Walk
19 San Felipe
20 La Milpa Ecolodge and Research Center
21 Crooked Tree Wildlife Sanctuary
22 Altun Ha Maya site
23 Lamanai Maya site
24 Caye Caulker
25 Caye Chapel
26 Salt Creek Estates Road
27 Laguna Seca
28 Hill Bank Field Station
29 Capt. Hook's Restaurant & Shrimp Farm
30 Community Baboon Sanctuary
31 Philip Goldson International Airport
32 Chan Chich and Gallon Jug
33 Big Falls Farm
34 Belize City
35 Cox Lagoon
36 Turneffe Atoll
37 Belize Zoo
38 Aguacate Lagoon
39 Runaway Creek Nature Preserve
40 Monkey Bay Wildlife Sanctuary
41 Beaver Dam Creek
42 Guanacaste National Park (Belmopan)
43 Spanish Lookout
44 El Pilar Maya site
45 Half Moon Caye
46 Caesar's Place
47 Gales Point
48 Pook's Hill Lodge
49 San Ignacio
50 Blue Hole National Park
51 Crystal Paradise Resort
52 Five Blues Lake National Park
53 George Price Highway (resort area)
54 Chiquibul Road
55 duPlooy's Jungle Lodge
56 Xunantunich Maya site
57 Thousand Foot Falls
58 Mountain Pine Ridge
59 Hidden Valley
60 Black Rock Lodge
61 Mt. Margaret
62 Baldy Beacon
63 Stann Creek at ITVET
64 Davis Falls
65 Becol Dam (entrance)
66 Rio Frio Caves
67 Dangriga
68 Mayflower Bocawina National Park
69 Man-O'-War Caye
70 Commerce Bight Forest Reserve
71 Guacamallo Bridge
72 Sittee River (marina)
73 South Water Caye
74 Victoria Peak
75 Cockscomb Basin Wildlife Sanctuary
76 Glover's Reef
77 Caracol Archaeological Reserve
78 Las Cuevas Research Station
79 Red Bank
80 Bladen River Nature Reserve
81 Placencia
82 BFREE Protected Area
83 Doyle's Delight
84 Monkey River
85 Columbia River Forest Reserve
86 Nim Li Punit Maya site
87 Payne's Creek National Park
88 Jimmy Cut
89 Lubaantun Maya site
90 San Jose Village
91 Punta Ycacos and Ycacos Lagoon
92 The Lodge at Big Falls
93 The Dump
94 Rio Blanco National Park
95 Pueblo Viejo Falls
96 Blue Creek Cave and Village, Toledo
97 Jalacte forest
98 Aguacaliente Wildlife Sanctuary
99 Belcampo Belize, Wilson Landing
100 Sapodilla Cayes
101 Punta Gorda
102 Boom Creek and Santa Anna
103 Moho River

~~Caract Ruins~~
✓ Avoid Coastal Highway.
✓ pg 18 for Hot spots
✓ U$ exc 2:1
✓ 10% Tip
   Clothes pg 24
   Permethrin spray
✓ No Visa
   ~~Bird Book pg 30~~ ✓
✓ Cash Colmb Pg 190
✓ 4×4 A MUST!

23
20

Lamani log

Locations

Jaguar ~~Hill Bank Field Station~~ } 75

① Pg 182   Mayflower ½ day (Early)
② Pg 190   Cockscolmb 3 days (2½)   3 days 5 7/8/9
③ Pg 114   Hilda Valley / 1000ft Falls   stay at Lodge 21
   Pg 81   Crooked Tree
④

Printed in Great Britain
by Amazon